African American Literature

African American Literature

A Guide to Reading Interests

Edited by Alma Dawson
and Connie Van Fleet

Genreflecting Advisory Series

Diana T. Herald, Series Editor

A Member of the Greenwood Publishing Group

Westport, Connecticut • London

Library of Congress Cataloging-in-Publication Data

African American literature : a guide to reading interests / edited by Alma Dawson and
  Connie Van Fleet.
    p. cm. – (Genreflecting Advisory Series)
    Includes indexes.
    ISBN 1-56308-931-9 (alk. paper)
    1. American literature—African American authors—History and criticism—Handbooks,
manuals, etc. 2. African Americans—Intellectual life—Handbooks, manuals, etc. 3.
American literature—African American authors—Bibliography. 4.African Americans in
Literature—Handbooks, manuals, etc. 5. African Americans—Intellectual life—Bibliography.
6. African Americans in literature—Bibliography. I. Dawson, Alma. II. Van Fleet, Connie
Jean, 1950- III. Series.
PS153.N5A3364 2004
810.9'896073—dc22   2004048928

British Library Cataloguing in Publication Data is available.

Library of Congress Catalog Card Number: 2004048928
ISBN: 1-56308-931-9

First published in 2004

Libraries Unlimited, 88 Post Road West, Westport, CT 06881
A Member of the Greenwood Publishing Group, Inc.
www.lu.com

Printed in the United States of America

♾™

The paper used in this book complies with the
Permanent Paper Standard issued by the National
Information Standards Organization (Z39.48–1984).

10   9   8   7   6   5   4   3   2   1

Contents

Part I
African American Literature in a Multicultural Society

Part II
African American Literature

Chapter 6—Historical Fiction 115
Ola Carter Riley

Chapter 7—Inspirational Literature......................................151
Melanie Sims

Acknowledgments

This volume has been a dream come true. Special thanks to the contributors who allowed themselves to be persuaded to join us in this venture. Special thanks to Dean Paskoff and the School of Library and Information Science for their support of the project and to graduate assistants Jennifer Schultz and Blinn Sheffield for their hard work. A special thanks to the Educational Resources staff of the LSU Libraries and Ida Brown of the East Baton Rouge Parish Library for assistance and support.

—Alma Dawson

Thank you to all of my African American students, past and present, who have been willing to share their experiences with me and have shaped my commitment and perceptions. I am grateful for the generous moral and material support of the University of Oklahoma School of Library and Information Studies and all of my colleagues there. I particularly want to express my appreciation to my wonderful graduate assistants, Karen Antell, JoAnn Palmeri, and Linda Temple, for all their hard work on this project and to the staff of the Interlibrary Loan Department of the OU Bizzell Library for their extraordinary efforts on my behalf. Finally, I am extremely grateful to Barbara Ittner for her excellent guidance, patience, and never-failing sense of humor.

—Connie Van Fleet

Introduction

Connie Van Fleet

If it encourages black people to read, it also serves the goal of achieving black freedom.—Charles Johnson in *Sacred Fire: The QBR 100 Essential Black Books* (1999, xix)

Something exciting is happening. Many talented African American authors have found their voices—and their voices are being heard, loud and clear. Major publishing houses are creating new African American imprints, books by black authors are receiving attention in standard and specialized review sources, bookstores are stocking black interest books as a matter of course, and African American authors such as Toni Morrison and Walter Mosley are appearing on best-seller lists.

Today's African American authors are making unique contributions to every facet of American literature. As in the past, there are serious allegorical stories and political statements, but now there are also African American books for people who read solely for pleasure, for the sheer joy of being "lost in a book." African American readers now can enjoy the same variety that the majority of recreational readers have long taken for granted.

The validity of popular literature has only recently and grudgingly been accepted by a society whose values and criteria were set by a tradition that valued a white upper-class, predominantly male, aesthetic. Social, cultural, and economic changes of the past half-century have increased not just the numbers of African American readers but also the depth and diversity of literature published by African American writers. Just as genre literature followed in the wake of more literary mainstream fiction for other audiences, popular and accessible work is being published now that literary work has established the credibility (and profitability) of African American authors. As popular writer Walter Mosley (2003) observed, "Black writers being published have always been some of the best. You had to be. It's like white people saying 'I wouldn't mind living next door to somebody black—Martin Luther King would be fine.' . . . I can't be a bricklayer? But we're going through a period that is wonderful because black writers, from great to mediocre are getting published" (2003, 7).

This diversity leads to a somewhat academic argument. Does work by African American authors comprise a genre? The answer is "yes" and "no". In literary terms, a genre is typically defined as a group of works or authors that have some common characteristics that generally appeal to a distinct group of readers. Using this broad definition, it can certainly be argued that works by African American authors loosely constitute a genre. They reflect a shared perspective unique to this group and thus appeal to readers who share a worldview born of minority status within the dominant white culture. Themes of oppression and liberation, family and community are common within this body of literature. It could even be said that African American literature often shares literary features, such as use of everyday language conventions, including vernacular and street language.

But just as not every writer born south of the Mason-Dixon line belongs to the Southern School of writers typified by Faulkner, it is difficult to construct a definition of African American literature that applies universally to works written by African Americans. Indeed, the corpus of work by African Americans is celebrated for its diversity.

In readers' advisory circles, genre fiction has come to mean popular fiction written to a formula or pattern. These are books we classify by such terms as romance, or mystery, or Western. In this book, we have defined African American literature as any work written by an African American author and then organized those works into chapters by type of story pattern.

Although some advisory and critical sources offer guidance in selecting "worthwhile" literature about the black experience, fewer give equal attention to the growing availability and popularity of African American genre literature. Today, although the canon is still firmly in place, readers and publishers seek a diversity that was once excluded. *African American Literature: A Guide to Reading Interests* is designed to provide a more comprehensive picture of the work of African American authors and to help readers find the books they enjoy reading.

As library educators, we've taught classes on collection development, public librarianship, readers' advisory services, and services to multicultural populations. We've watched our new librarians as they go to work in the field, and we've talked to them about what they do and the people they serve. We've watched publishing trends and we've observed library practice. We've watched as wonderful genre and literary guides were published and used. And although we espoused the theories of multiculturalism, tools to meet the needs of minority readers were few and far between. It seemed to us that somebody had to write *African American Literature: A Guide to Reading Interests*. We wanted to do it.

Purpose

This handbook is intended for anyone interested in African American literature. It is not a critical guide, a list of "best" authors and titles, or a recommended reading list, although certainly readers' advisors are encouraged to acquaint themselves with titles and authors in each of the genres. Nor is it meant as a history of African American literature. Instead, it has been created as a professional tool for librarians, as a guide for readers, and as a resource for popular culture and literary scholars. It is meant to meet the specific needs of African American readers, but it will appeal to anyone interested in African American literature. Although it is written primarily for librarians, we expect average readers will find it accessible and useful.

We wrote this book:

- to celebrate African American lives and culture;
- to recognize the diverse work of African American authors;
- to connect African American readers with their literary heritage and future;
- to link all readers with books about the African American experience;
- to help people who read for fun find books they'll enjoy;
- to assist librarians in providing readers' advisory services;
- to use as a collection development tool for librarians; and
- to shed a new light on this body of literature for teachers, students, and scholars.

Audience

African American Literature is intended for use by and with adult readers, although many of the works will also be of interest to young adults. Young adults enjoy speculative fiction, and most of it is accessible to them, even if it is not created specifically for them. The inspirational fiction chapter includes a series of Christian fiction novels written expressly for young adults. In addition, many of the biographies are by or about personalities who appeal to the younger audience.

The books covered in this guide will appeal to readers of all ethnic and cultural backgrounds. African Americans may especially enjoy books written by African American authors, but so will other readers. Mystery readers who are fans of Sue Grafton's Kinsey Milhone will be pleased to meet Wesley's Tamara Hayle; music lovers will be engaged by Quincy Jones's autobiography. While offering a variety of perspectives, many African American authors touch a common chord.

Scope and Criteria for Selection

Authors

The first criterion that we used in selecting titles for inclusion was authorship. Only works by African American authors are included. African American authors are those who have spent their formative years in the United States. Growing up black in America is a unique experience; the voices of those who have lived it offer distinct perspectives grounded in individual experiences.

Work by writers of the African Diaspora from countries other than the United States is excluded. Agymah Kamau, author of *Flickering Shadows* and *Pictures of a Dying Man,* was born in Barbados and moved to the United States to attend school in New York City. He comments on the impact of a different environment: "As someone who was born and lived for several years outside the United States, my view of world affairs differs significantly from those who are United States natives" (Potts 2003, E1).

Publication Dates

Emphasis is on works published between 1990 and 2003. Most of these titles are still in print and available for purchase. These dates also reflect the recent explosion in interest, creation, and publication of genre literature by African American authors. Some classic or benchmark older works have been included to provide perspective, with preference given to those that have been reissued in the last decade. Some earlier titles are included without annotation to provide a complete list of works in a series.

Formats

Novels are the focus of this book, but short story collections are included when they are significant to the genre. Three types of nonfiction have been included because they reflect areas of particular importance or growing popularity. An entire chapter is devoted to life stories, which have a place of central importance in the African American community and share elements of appeal with fiction. Inspirational nonfiction by black authors, which *Ebony* writer Kelly Starling has called "the hottest ticket in literature" (1998, 96), has been incorporated into the inspirational literature chapter in recognition of this trend, and because it is popular with readers who enjoy inspirational fiction. Chapter 11 includes factual works about African Americans on the frontier along with Western fiction, again, because the books share thematic characteristics and appeal to the same audiences.

Media productions based on print materials may be noted in annotations of the print titles but are not examined independently.

Method

Contributors

African American Literature represents the efforts of many people. Librarians who enjoyed particular genres or who were interested in African American authors were invited to contribute chapters based on a template that outlined the major components. Above all, we recruited people with a readers' advisory background, rather than literary critics. As primary authors and editors, we tried to preserve the individual voices of each of the contributors while providing consistency throughout the guide. In addition, we developed overview chapters and, with the help of outstanding graduate assistants, compiled the appendixes.

Selection

For some categories of titles, inclusion is the result of a deeper selective process. Titles in the mainstream or literary fiction chapter were chosen on the basis of appearance in selective bibliographies such as *Sacred Fire,* edited by Max Rodriguez of *Quarterly Black Review*; standard sources such as *Contemporary African American Novelists*; syllabi for college classes in African American literature; and award lists. In an attempt to provide a list of the most important and influential of the mainstream novels, a number of older (and thus technically out of scope) novels are included.

The approach for most of the genre chapters, however, is inclusive rather than selective. Because there are fewer titles and only a handful of African American authors who are well known in any genre, the primary goal of these chapters is identifying appropriate titles and categorizing them to facilitate access. A number of strategies were used to find suitable titles.

Award lists for each of the genres, as well as more generalized lists that recognize outstanding work by African Americans, were consulted. For instance, both the Edgar Award list and the Black Caucus of the American Library Association (BCALA) Literary Award list were consulted to find the best of African American crime and detective fiction.

General, genre-specific, and multicultural readers' advisory sources were used as a starting point for selection. *What Do I Read Next? Multicultural Literature* is organized by ethnicity of the author; subject and genre indexes facilitate compiling preliminary lists. *NoveList*'s keyword searching and subject-specific articles are useful, although all authors were checked because indexing in *NoveList* (as in most sources and catalogs) is based on characters and themes of the works, not author. Some genre-specific bibliographies, such as

Mort's *Christian Fiction,* have sections on work by African American authors or index African American authors or characters. Publishing houses produce catalogs for genre-specific or audience-specific imprints, and these are excellent sources for identifying recent releases.

A search of periodical databases led to useful articles and reviews; especially relevant are those in *Publishers Weekly, Ebony, Quarterly Black Review*, and *Black Issues Book Review*. Standard tools such as *Book Review Digest* reflect the general trend that recognizes only a few better-known African American genre authors. Internet searching is useful for finding bibliographies of African American titles, lists of awards presented by organizations, and information on lesser-known authors and their work.

All of the sources we consulted are listed in the "Resources" chapter (Chapter 12) of this book.

Keywords

Although it was tempting to use a standard classification system, we wanted this guide to be as easy to use as possible for readers as well as librarians. We found that most of the subject headings lists and thesauri were either too formal or too general for our purposes. After exploring several thesauri and indexes, we chose to let the thesaurus develop naturally from a list of keywords assigned by the authors. After examining the keywords applied by our various contributors, we developed a thesaurus and standardized the keywords applied to each title.

Organization

African American Literature is divided into two parts: "African American Literature in a Multicultural Society" and "African American Literature".

Part I: African American Literature in a Multicultural Society

Part I provides an overview of the field that addresses issues and processes basic to providing library service to the African American community. Intended for librarians, it includes essays on the development of African American literature from colonial days to the present, publishing trends, collection development, and readers' advisory services.

Chapter 1, "Readers' Advisory Services," provides a foundation for service. It delineates general readers' advisory approaches and adapts them for African American patrons and readers who may (whether they know it or not) be interested in literature by black authors. Chapter 2 traces publishing trends and identifies key publishers for librarians who want to add African American authors to their collections or develop specialized collections. Chapter 3 suggests basic principles and strategies for collecting African American literature. It offers general guidelines and considerations, outlines selection criteria and policy, and discusses some core selection resources.

Together, these introductory chapters and Chapter 12 provide strategies and resources for effective readers' advisory service and a conceptual framework for approaching the genre-specific chapters in Part II. In addition, the "References" section consists of sources cited in all of the chapters.

Part II: African American Literature

Part II explores genres and provides annotated bibliographies for each. It is typical of most titles in the <u>Genreflecting</u> series in that each chapter is devoted to a different genre and works are categorized within each genre by subgenre and theme, although the definition of some of the genres has been broadened as noted previously. Each chapter in Part II comprises two parts: a narrative overview and a list of annotations.

Chapter Narratives

A narrative composed of the following elements introduces each chapter:

- A *definition* that outlines the characteristics of the genre

- An explanation of the *appeal* of a particular genre

- A brief account of the *evolution* of the genre in terms of African American contributions and impact

- A discussion of *themes and trends* in current African American genre literature

- An explanation of s*election criteria* and *scope* specific to the chapter

- An overview of the *organization* of each chapter and how it facilitates *advising the reader,* including a description of categories. Although the organization of most chapters relies heavily on widely used classification systems (for example, as in *Genreflecting: A Guide to Reading Interests in Genre Fiction,* 5th ed., Libraries Unlimited, 2000) to facilitate use by librarians and readers, some categories have been modified to better reflect current practice, the nature of African American contributions, and selection criteria used by African American genre readers.

Annotations

Annotations for specific titles are grouped by category. Annotations provide bibliographic details for identifying and purchasing titles. They also describe books and offer other information to assist in selecting and recommending titles. Annotations are provided for individual titles, each series as a whole, and individual titles within a series.

- **Organization.** Titles in chapters are divided into major categories. Within each of the categories, entries are arranged alphabetically by the author's last name. Series books are grouped under the name of the series. Titles in series are arranged chronologically in order of original publication date.

- **Bibliographic entry.** Bibliographic information is given for each title. The information is applicable to the edition read by the reviewer.

   - The author's name is provided in inverted order. Coauthor's names follow in normal order.

   - The full title is given as it appears on the title page, including subtitles. In some cases, the subtitle is the series title. Alternative titles are provided in parentheses.

   - Place of publication.

- The publisher's name is given as it appears on the title page. When a division or imprint is given, the information appears as division/publisher or imprint/publisher.

- The publication date of the copy examined is provided. If the edition is a reissue, original publication information is given in parentheses.

- The ISBN is given, followed by the designation "pa." if the copy examined is a paperback. If no designation is given, the copy is a hardcover edition.

- The number of pages follows. This information is useful in readers' advisory for patrons who prefer books of a certain length.

- **Notes.** Notes about pseudonyms or the author's work in a different chapter are provided in parentheses after the bibliographic citation.

- **Award designation.** Award-winning titles are identified by ♟ placed before the title in the entry. The name of the award and date are given at the end of the annotation. A list of awards and their descriptions is included in Chapter 12.

- **Keywords.** At the end of the entries are keywords that provide information about the subject matter of the book. The annotations and keywords can be scanned to assist the reader in selecting topics of interest and avoiding topics that may be problematic. If a book might as easily have been put in another category or chapter, the alternative placement is listed as a keyword. As an example, some suspense thrillers could as easily be described as romantic suspense, so the keywords might include "romantic suspense".

  Keywords are used as entries in the subject index to group together works that are about the same subject, regardless of author or genre.

- **Plot summary.** A description of the series or title includes a brief plot summary. Style features (such as graphic language, dialogue, or first person) may also influence the reader's enjoyment of a particular title; these are addressed as well.

- **Quotations.** Representative quotations are provided for each series or individual work to give a sense of the author's style.

Chapter 12 includes additional information that will support readers' advisory services. Awards are described, and lists of titles of award winners are included. The resources section offers an annotated list of general and genre-specific resources that provide further information and guidance.

Using This Book

For Individual Study

Librarians may want to learn more about African American authors and serving diverse audiences. Although they may be aware of changing audiences and the ever-growing demand for popular literature, they may not have access to educational activities or resources that they can use to quickly and conveniently enhance their knowledge of a specialized area. These librarians will find this book useful as an independent study guide to help them in expanding service and exploring a new area of literature.

For Continuing Education with Peers

The information in this book can form the basis for training in readers' advisory for new librarians and staff. Experienced librarians can use this book as a way of organizing continuing education activities. Selecting one genre chapter per month and sharing readings from it is a good—and pleasurable—way to keep up with a genre and learn about African American authors as well. In addition, discussing the titles and approaches in this book can serve as a focus for interaction between selectors and public service personnel.

For Advising Readers

The popularity of anthologies such as Sheree Thomas's *Dark Matter: A Century of Speculative Fiction from the African Diaspora* (New York: Warner Books, 2000) and Paula Woods's *Spooks, Spies and Private Eyes: Black Mystery, Crime, and Suspense Fiction of the 20th Century* (New York: Doubleday, 1995) indicates that readers are interested in the development of various genres and the contributions that have been made by African American authors. Some readers will want to use this book independently to learn about African American literature.

Examining the annotations with readers allows librarians to learn quickly about the reader's preferences and dislikes. As such, it can serve as a valuable introductory readers' advisory tool.

For Public Awareness

This book will also serve as an excellent resource for developing bookmarks, displays, and other public awareness and marketing materials. Lists of works by African American authors, with African American characters, and addressing African American themes are virtually ready made. The organization makes it a simple matter to find titles by African American authors that can be included in more general lists. For example, a librarian who is creating a list of inspirational romances for young adults can easily include the Skky series. It is a simple matter to find a mystery that features a lesbian, African American amateur detective.

For Motivation and a Beginning

This book is intended as an introduction to African American literature and its importance to African Americans and the entire community of readers. More, we hope it will excite others about the diversity of theme, style, character, and perspective presented by African American authors. We hope you will be inspired to start here and read more, not just as a duty to the readers we serve, but because you've enjoyed these authors as much as we have.

Part I

African American Literature in a Multicultural Society

Chapter 1

Readers' Advisory Services

Connie Van Fleet

An Object Lesson

I had her pegged. She walked into the library: warm cocoa skin, graying hair pulled into a neat bun underneath her straw hat, white cotton gloves, and a purse carried by the strap in the crook of her elbow. I knew what she wanted before she opened her mouth, and a list of gentle reads and the location of Bible study books began to form themselves in my mind. I was thrown completely off balance when she asked for books about the Sacco and Vanzetti case.

The moral: You can't always judge a book by its cover, and you can't judge a reader by her appearance. This is the first and most important rule of readers' advisory service: *Look at people as individuals*. Don't expect that all African Americans will want to read the same book or confine their reading to books by African American authors. Recognize that people who are not African American may very much enjoy literature by black authors.

Linking Readers and Books

The primary goal of readers' advisory service is to link readers and books. To accomplish this, readers' advisors must bring together knowledge and skill in four areas:

- **Understanding readers**. Generally, why do people read? What difference does reading make in their lives?

- **Analyzing appeal**. What books are available to the reader based on the advisor's reading experience? How will a particular text affect different readers?

- **Using readers' advisory sources**. How can we expand the choices available to the reader beyond the advisor's firsthand knowledge of the literature?

- **Interviewing individuals**. What does this particular reader want today?

Understanding Readers

A readers' advisor who understands the attraction and effects of pleasure reading will respect and appreciate individual choice. Building a conceptual framework prepares the advisor to be an effective advocate and service provider. Knowing that pleasure reading is a complex and vital activity, advisors will adopt Rosenberg's Rule: *Never apologize for your reading tastes* (Rosenberg 1982, flyleaf) and Connie's Corollary: *or anyone else's.*

Researchers find that pleasure reading induces a physical and psychological change in people, producing a trancelike state (Nell 1988; Sturm 2001). Victor Nell's fascinating research indicates that the stress-reducing power of reading may be a matter of physical process as well as emotional well-being: "Among the mysteries of reading, the greatest is certainly its power to absorb the reader completely and effortlessly and, on occasion, to change his or her state of consciousness through entrancement" (1988, 73). Physiological changes occur when people read for pleasure, and although we may perceive of this activity as soothing and relaxing, physiological responses indicate a state of arousal. Interestingly, Nell (1988) also found that people who were reading difficult or complex materials were more easily distracted than those who were reading "light" novels. The reader enters an "altered state of consciousness," becoming so involved with the text as to become unaware of his or her surroundings (Sturm 2001, 97).

The active role the reader plays in creating a uniquely individual reading experience is another attraction of pleasure reading. Reading theorists speculate that it is the process of reader/text interaction that draws readers (Wiegand 1997). Light reading allows the reader to have control, inviting him or her to fill in the blanks, ascribe motivations to the characters, or validate personal perceptions by having them echo from a self-constructed text. "As readers, we invest the cold signs on the pages of *Native Son* with our *own* emotions, *our* understanding of poverty, oppression, and fear . . . returning our subjective feelings to us transformed, refined, and alchemized by language into a new vision with the capacity to change our lives forever" (Johnson 1999, xx).

Readers talk about reading as a core part of their identities and an indispensable aspect of life (Ross 1991, 2001). Amazingly, Hathaway cites over 1,600 motives for reading (McClellan 1997). McClellan (1977, 43–44) offers useful broad categories of motivations, divided into conscious and unconscious:

- Conscious: purposive
    - information
    - plan testing
    - compensation (for an otherwise boring life)
    - social status and prestige
    - appreciative and aesthetic satisfactions in reading for its own sake
- Conscious: diversionary or spectator
    - catalytic: solving problems and engaging in creative thought (catalyst) through apparently irrelevant reading
    - remedial: relaxing and forgetting temporarily

- pseudoactivity: avoiding other activities

- narcotic: achieving continuing divorce from reality

- Unconscious:

  - search for meaning: orienting oneself in relation to life and other people

  - strategy for coping: allowing the conscious mind to maintain an undisturbed rhythm, thus permitting the unconscious mind to deal with problems and frustrations

  - confirmation: realizing that someone thinks and feels as we do

  - sense of belonging: linking minorities unknown to each other, reinforcing both differentiation and individualization

  - cathartic discharge: releasing feelings normally suppressed

  - extension of vocabulary: broadening the range of concepts and experience

  - empathy: putting oneself into another's situation.

Those motivations that McClellan classifies as unconscious—search for meaning, strategy for coping, confirmation, a sense of belonging, and the cathartic release of feelings—are well-served by African American literature and may account for its growing popularity with diverse audiences. Woodruff's observation that "books reflect the truth of our experience better than any other medium at this point" is shared by many readers (Jacques 1995).

In *Sacred Fire: The QBR 100 Essential Black Books*, Rodriguez et al. (1999) include books spanning three centuries, reflecting that African Americans have always valued reading. Johnson expands on the necessity of reading and underscores the importance of the thought, analysis, and critical interpretation inherent in interacting with the printed word. "In the midst of formulaic entertainment, in a popular culture where 'dumbing down' is the rule, *reading* becomes the most radical of all enterprises" (Johnson 1999, xix).

Analyzing Appeal

In the collection development process, a selector uses standard criteria to evaluate materials with the purpose of deciding whether to add an item to the library's collection. Chapter 3, "Collection Development." discusses considerations in collecting fiction and provides guidelines and standardized criteria for selecting and evaluating multicultural fiction.

Reading for readers' advisory purposes is a different process. It focuses on the text solely in relation to the individual reader. Saricks and Brown (1997) call this "reading for appeal." The purpose of reading for appeal is to identify and describe the aspects of a book in light of how they will affect the individual reader's reaction to it. Primarily, the questions are, "What does this author do best?" "What are the most outstanding features of this book?" and "What characteristics of this book might appeal to a reader?" Because readers will often ask for another book "like" one they've read, advisors should think about books or authors with common appeal factors

The ethnicity of the author is one appeal factor to consider in talking about readers' advisory and multicultural literature. For some, but not all, readers, it is the most important element. It is a rare reader, however, who will be satisfied with author ethnicity as the sole criterion. Any attention to the appeal factors listed below demonstrates that the body of African American literature is too diverse for all of its works to please a reader. Advisors must learn to discriminate if they are to serve their readers well.

The following appeal factors are based on those identified by Saricks and Brown (1997). They are explained here with particular attention to their interpretation and aspects in regard to multicultural literature, both fiction and nonfiction.

Subject

What is this book about? Does this book deal with topics and issues that are of particular importance to the black community, or does it focus on more universal themes? Some people want to read about the black experience, with stories centering on slavery, Jim Crow laws, or the Civil Rights Movement. Some people will want a murder mystery set in Colorado, while others will select a contemporary crime book that focuses on a description of ghetto lifestyles. An autobiography may give a personal view, focusing on the subject as a unique individual, or it may use an individual's life story as an example of the impact of social and political contexts.

Pacing

How quickly does the book move? Is it a page-turner, pulling the reader through the story with short sentences and chapters, lots of action, and crisp dialogue, or is it a book to be savored and lingered over, with elaborate descriptions? Is the reader immediately plunged into the action, or does the story build slowly and deliberately? Are the characters likely to take action, or do they wait for something to happen to them?

Characterization

Do we know and recognize the characters instantaneously because they are character types, or does it take time for us to get to know them? Are they multifaceted and complex, or straightforward? Do the characters change and grow, or do they remain fairly constant? Is the focus on a single character or many? Are the relationships among the characters the central thrust of the story, or are they the means by which the action is carried out?

The degree to which the characters are developed in terms of race is of particular importance to some African American readers. In some stories, it would be a simple matter to substitute a white protagonist for a black one; the ethnicity of the characters is found only in the most straightforward physical description. At the other end of the spectrum are books that are about being black in America. The characters' racial identities drive the story and are the most important elements of the book. In between are the stories in which being black is an important background consideration. Heritage and experience shape the character and his or her perspective and problems, but the focus is on the storyline.

Another aspect of characterization in African American literature is the treatment of white characters. Are they stereotypical or complex? Do they play a role in the story, or are they background?

Interracial relationships may be peripheral or central to the theme of a book. Even when an interracial relationship is treated with about the same level of attention, the nature of the relationship may influence readers' reactions. Both Bland and Smith-Levin write mystery series featuring black women detectives and their white male partners. Some readers may enjoy the professional relationship between Bland's Marti MacAlister and Vik Jessenovik but balk at Smith-Levin's <u>Starletta Duvall</u> series. Starletta dates a white coroner, and Dominic, her white partner, becomes involved with Vee, Starletta's black roommate. Other readers will relate to Starletta and Vee's girlfriend talks about interracial relationships. Still others will concentrate on story line and find this aspect of the books unremarkable.

Story Line

Is the story moved forward through action, character revelation or growth, or changing situations? Is the emphasis on what is happening or on what the characters are thinking or feeling? Is there a single, linear plot line, or are there multiple interwoven stories? Are there flashbacks, memories, time travel? Does the book switch back and forth between different points of view?

Many African American authors explore the impact of the past on the present and future. Acutely aware of the forces that shape individual lives and decisions, some have an almost fatalistic tone. Flashbacks and references to earlier times through chronicles, reminiscences, ghosts, or actual time travel are common devices that black authors use in exploring these themes.

Story line will also vary among life stories. Some autobiographies are a straightforward, chronological recounting of the author's life, following a straight line from birth to the present. Others place more emphasis on reflection and emotion or on description of context and events. The authors of these accounts might emphasize one period and give no attention to others. Beginning with the present and then reflecting back to the past, or intertwining the two throughout, is a structure often used by authors who want to explore the impact of the past. Authors who want to examine events from different perspectives will sometimes develop parallel story lines or shift voices.

Some readers will enjoy shifting between chains of events, time periods, or perspectives, reveling in the complexity and richly textured picture multiple story lines produce. Other readers will find such shifts annoying or distracting.

Setting

Is the setting instantly recognizable as a specific place or time? Are there only broad brushstrokes, or is the setting richly described? Does the description give a visual image, or is it evocative, calling to mind sensations or emotions?

Providing rich descriptions of setting, whether of time or place, from the viewpoint of African Americans is a way of revising or reclaiming history. An author's primary goal may be to give a picture of a time meaningful to the black community, perhaps the antebellum period or the Harlem Renaissance or the 1950s. Perhaps describing a place is important—a neighborhood, a housing project, a small town, or Montgomery, Alabama.

In many African American books, descriptions of place define not only a physical setting but also an emotional outlook. Neighborhoods and neighborhood places provide a sense of community. Ghettos create a sense of danger and entrapment.

Style

How is this book written? How does the author use language? Is the author's prose spare and straightforward or elegant and flowery? Is it reflective or action oriented? Is the story written in the first person, giving a sense of intimacy, or in the third person, providing the reader with a broader view of the action?

African American literature runs the gamut from cozy to noir. Some readers want to feel safe and secure, to escape to a warm and gentle place through their reading. Others prefer facing and examining the darker side and will want books that convey a brooding, menacing mood. Some readers will prefer an appeal to the intellect, while others look for an emotional or visceral reaction.

Attention to appeal factors is a key part of professional reading for readers' advisory service. Reading widely and consciously is the best way to learn about the literature. It doesn't take very long for a readers' advisor to start thinking, "Oh, this reminds me of *Title X* or author A" or "This is just the book for patron P."

Using Readers' Advisory Resources

No one can read everything. Although personal reading is essential, advisors should be familiar with basic readers' advisory sources (see Chapter 12). For many readers, the most obvious elements in selection are genre and subject. It is in this area that readers' advisory sources are most useful. Beyond subject, however, advisors should be able to relate books to one another on the basis of appeal factors. To address this issue, many guides provide annotations, reviews, or links to reviews that discuss appeal factors.

An exception to the subject- or genre-based approach is the <u>Now Read This</u> series (Pearl 1999, 2002), which organizes mainstream titles into chapters by primary elements of appeal: characterization, setting, story, characters, and language. Saricks's guide (2001) explains primary appeal factors of various genres and subgenres and offers cross-genre recommendations based on similarity of appeal factors.

Although black authors are represented in most readers' advisory sources, that representation is naturally limited in more general works. Reading and understanding the manner in which guides define and represent African American literature is important to readers' advisors. Guides typically index by the content of the book, so African American literature may be defined as featuring black characters, not necessarily written by black authors.

Advisors should take care when using readers' advisory sources to make recommendations about African American literature. It is unfortunate that some guides to multicultural literature will simply lump together all black authors who write in a particular genre. For example, one source suggests that readers who enjoy Gar Anthony Haywood's *Bad*

News Travels Fast might also like *In the Game* by Nikki Baker (Castro et al. 1997, 86). Both authors are African American, and both books are murder mysteries featuring amateur detectives. Both books are properly assigned an additional subject heading of family relationships. But whereas Haywood's lighthearted series features a humorous, happily married retired couple and outrageous plots, Baker's series is very dark and features an alienated black lesbian and depressingly plausible story lines. They are entirely different in feel and impact.

Although readers' advisory resources are excellent tools, they cannot take the place of a well-read readers' advisor, nor is that the intention of their publishers and authors. *NoveList's Readers' Advisory 101* (2001), for instance, doesn't simply teach subscribers to use the database but provides extensive training in readers' advisory skills.

Interviewing Individuals

In my readers' advisory class, I have students try to match lists of five favorite books with the faculty member who submitted them. We always have fun, but students inevitably find this a challenging exercise. In spite of having a group of people with very similar demographics, few books are repeated across the faculty lists. The object of the exercise, of course, is to demonstrate that people's reading tastes are individualized, even when they have much in common.

The readers' advisory interview is the opportunity to take generalized knowledge about readers and reading and put it to work for the individual. A good interview will help the advisor determine what this particular reader wants at this particular time in his or her life. Asking a reader for a description and using standard reference interview techniques (see RUSA Guidelines 1996) are the foundation of an effective readers' advisory interview. Following are some basic tips:

- **Show your approachability**. Many readers are reluctant to approach the desk with a request as amorphous and insignificant as, "Can you help me find a good book to read?" Signs on the desk ("Have you read a good book lately?") signal that the service is available.

- **Ask for description, not analysis**. "Can you tell me about a good book you've read lately?" Many readers have difficulty with analysis; they may not be able to tell the advisor what kind of book they want, other than a broad category such as mystery, or even what it is about a book that appeals to them (Smith 1993). Asking a reader to describe a book rather than to enumerate the aspects that he or she is looking for is typically more effective.

- **Be positive**. You may not particularly like romances, but your patron might. Never presume to make value judgments about someone else's reading preferences.

- **Use language that is descriptive rather than evaluative**. This is not the time for literary criticism. "This book has a lot of description and a deliberate pace" is better than, "This book is terrible. It's such a slow read." "The characters in this book use realistic street language" is better than, "This is a dirty book full of nasty language."

- **Be a good listener**. Follow the patron's lead. Pick up on the elements that the patron has emphasized in the description and ask open-ended questions that invite more description. "It sounds as though you enjoy murder mysteries with women detectives. Is there anything else you particularly liked about the Starletta Duval stories?"

- **Check the reader's mood**. "Do you think you'd like something else like that, or are you in the mood for something different?"

- **Confirm and verify**. "We are going to look for murder mysteries with black women protagonists, but you don't care if they are amateur detectives or police detectives. Is that correct?" It might be useful to confirm understanding by making comparisons to books that are known by the reader and the advisor.

- **Ask about appeal factors, both positive and negative**. "This book has very complex and fully described characters, but they use realistic and fairly graphic street language. Is that okay?" "Is there anything you really didn't like about this book?"

- **Engage the reader in the process**. Share your thought process and the criteria you've developed. If you use a readers' advisory source, explain what it is and how you're using it.

- **Expect to continue learning about the literature**. Appreciate your patron's expertise rather than feeling threatened by it.

- **If possible, watch how the reader examines books and makes a decision once you've suggested a few titles**. Some readers won't check out a book if the cover is too gory or if there is no picture of the author.

- **Remember that you're offering suggestions and guidance**. There is no one perfect, correct answer. Tolerate the ambiguity.

- **Invite the reader back**. "Let me know whether you liked those." "I'd like to hear your opinion of this book when you've finished." Understand that your ability to match a particular patron and a book will grow over repeated interactions.

- **Enjoy yourself**. Enthusiasm is contagious.

Conclusion

The essence of readers' advisory service is the fulfillment of Ranganathan's first two laws: every reader his book and every book its reader. Pleasure reading plays an important role in the lives of individuals and helps develop a sense of history and community. Knowing readers and knowing books is the only way in which a readers' advisor can fulfill the goal of bringing them together.

Chapter 2

Trends in African American Publishing

Alma Dawson

Introduction

The African American community is one of the fastest growing segments of the book buying market (Brown 1995, 108). Industry watchers use such terms as "publishing boom," "black book bounty," and "new renaissance" to describe the excitement of a continuously flourishing market of titles aimed at "African American readers who are hungry to see their lives and interests reflected in the pages of mass-produced romance, mystery, science fiction, and self-help books" (Phillip 1996, 22). The recent surge of interest in titles by and about African Americans is reminiscent of the literary scene during the Harlem Renaissance of the 1920s and the Civil Rights Movement of the 1960s (Brown 1995). Surveys conducted by *Publishers Weekly* from 1997 to 2003 indicate continued growth in the black market for a diversity of genres and subjects (Fleming 2001; Jackson 2000; Jacques 1997, 1998; Labbé 1999, 2000b; Rosen 2002b; Talkin' about black books 2003; Taylor 1999). African American authors appear regularly on best-seller lists and receive literary awards for their works. According to all reports, African American books have grown beyond niche status to become part of mainstream publishing. African American writers "are asserting their voices into a national, and indeed international conversation" (Phillip 1996, 22). Publishers (large and small, specialty and general) have produced inspirational materials, including religion and spirituality books for a growing niche market. (A selected list of African American publishers and distributors is included in this chapter.)

Vandella Brown captures the state of genre fiction categories: "Since the 1970s, African American novels have slammed, slid, infiltrated, and blended into the mainstream of shelves of libraries. Once submerged in general fiction, these novels now have an authorship and readership to match other genres" (1997, 48). As Mary-Christine Phillip points out in her review of the literature of the 1990s, "what distinguishes today's crop of Black writers from earlier writers is their middle-brow appeal" (1996, 21). They write in more than one genre and both fiction and nonfiction. The five African American authors recently profiled by Bernadette Davis (2004) illustrate the diversity of genres.

Zane, whose works include *Addicted* (Atria Books, 2001), *Nervous* (Atria Books, 2003), *Shame on It All* (Atria Books, 2003), *Skyscraper* (Atria Books, 2003), and *Heat Seekers* (Atria Books, 2002), is described as dominating the erotica fiction category (see Chapter 10, "Romance") . Carl Weber, author of *Baby Momma Drama* (Kensington, 2003), is placed at the forefront of the urban fiction (hip-hop) writers (as covered in Chapter 4). Weber also writes in the romance category (see Chapter 10). A bookstore owner in New York, Weber started his own company in 2003 to publish urban "heavy drama" books, in which readers are taken out of their own problems and into the characters' drama (Davis 2004, 40). "Shannon Holmes is claiming the niche once owned by Donald Goines and Iceberg Slim" [who wrote street life fiction] (Davis 2004, 41). Holmes's works include *B-More Careful* (Meow Meow Productions, 2001) (see Chapter 4, "Crime and Detective Stories"). Leslie Esdaile Banks, a prominent author of romance fiction, now writes vampire/horror stories (*Minion: A Vampire Huntress Legend*, St. Martin, 2003) and has a crime series planned. Leslie Esdaile Banks also writes under the name Leslie Esdaile (see Chapter 10). Finally, award-winning author Paula Woods (*Inner City Blues*, Norton, 2001) represents the mystery/crime noir fiction writers (see Chapter 4). Many African American authors are reaping the rewards of commercial popularity, and their books have crossed over into the mainstream, drawing readers from all walks of life.

Market Demands

Authors attribute the interest of mainstream publishers in black interest titles to the increased buying power of African Americans. Target Market News conducts surveys of spending preferences and purchases of black consumers for the Book Industry Group. According to their study released in 2001, African Americans spent approximately $356 million on consumer books during 2000, with approximately $297 million through retail outlets. Books that reflected the African American perspective were the most popular types of books, with 67 percent of respondents replying that they enjoy reading anything by black authors, and 53 percent saying that they like reading anything that deals with black issues (Target Market News 2001). Figures released in 2003 show a slight decline in book expenditures, yet African Americans spent $303 million on books in 2002 (Target Market News 2003). The growth and range of the titles aimed at African American readers, including the launching of imprints at major New York publishing houses, reflect change in the industry.

Within the last four years, major New York publishing houses have responded to the demand for black interest titles by launching imprints devoted to publishing African American literature. These include Amistad, which was recently acquired by HarperCollins and is the oldest of the mainstream black publishing imprints. Amistad has published works by and about people of African descent since 1986 on subjects and themes that have significant influence on the intellectual, cultural, and historical perspectives of a world audience.

Random House has three imprints devoted to African American literature: Strivers Row, Harlem Moon, and One World Books. A fourth imprint is under development. Strivers Row is a sub-imprint of Villard, which specializes in publishing current and contemporary fiction by African American authors. Named for the street dubbed "Strivers Row"—West 138th and 139th Streets between Adam Clayton Powell and Frederick Douglass Boulevards—which was largely inhabited by first-generation African American professionals during the time of the Harlem Renaissance, this imprint has as its mission the publication of quality African American literature that captures the same spirit of hope, creativity, and promise as its namesake (Random House Adult Trade Group n.d.). Strivers Row released its first books during 2001. Initially, Strivers Row published fiction and nonfiction, but according to the publisher, it will now focus on fiction. Successful fiction titles published by Strivers Row include Gloria Mallette's *Shades of Jade* (Villard, 2001) and Parry A. Brown's *Sittin' in the Front Pew* (Villard, 2002), an *Essence* #1 Bestseller.

Harlem Moon made its debut September 2002. Its goal is to publish both quality trade paperbacks of original works and out-of-print classics. Harlem Moon is the brainchild of Executive Editor Janet Hill, who created the imprint to support and promote new literary talents and to "make end roads into the avid reading group market with fiction titles, and provide nonfiction titles that are suitable for course adoption" (Doubleday-Broadway Publishing Group n.d.).

The last Random House imprint is One World. This imprint was launched in 1992 and is the multicultural imprint of Ballantine Books. One World's list includes books written by and focused on African Americans, Native Americans, Asian Americans, and Latino Americans (One World n.d.).

Dafina is an imprint of Kensington Publishing Company. Kensington has become known for its emphasis on commercial fiction and continues to distribute the Arabesque Romance imprint for BET Books. Recently, Kensington added a topical nonfiction line and will serve as distributor for Urban Books, the new publishing enterprise of Carl Weber's "urban heavy" drama (Davis 2004, 40). (See also Urban Books at www.urbanbooks.net.) Once known as "books from the black experience," urban fiction is currently called ghetto fiction, hip-hop novels, "street life" novels, "blaxploitation" novels, and urban pulp fiction (Patrick 2003, 31).

In 2000, Warner Publishing entered into a partnership with Denise Stinson, a successful literacy agent and former journalist, launching the Christian fiction imprint Walk Worthy Press. Walk Worthy Press has a ministry dedicated to showing, through books, how the Word of God in the Bible can be applied to every area of our daily lives (Reid 2000, 22).

Jump at the Sun, paraphrased from a Zora Neale Hurston, is a special imprint of Hyperion, a division of Disney. The imprint is designed for children and young adult readers, offering both picture books and chapter books. Though they are not solely African American imprints, Simon & Schuster has both Atria Books and Pocket Books, which publish significant numbers of African American titles each year. Other major publishers, such as Wiley, St. Martin's, and Crown, have published significant numbers of African American authors and black-oriented titles. Imprints continue to be added to major publishers. (A list of African American imprints of major publishing houses is included in this chapter.)

In addition to imprints, mainstream publishers have established marketing tools targeted on African American authors and titles. For example, AOL Time Warner Book Group features the HALALA Web site (www.twbookmark/features/halala/about.html), dedicated to the promotion of books written by or pertaining to African Americans from the Arcade, Black Bay, Bullfinch, Little, Brown, Mysterious Press, Time Warner AudioBooks, Aspect, Warner, and Warner Business imprints. It is also possible to subscribe to publisher industry newsletters such as

BlackbooksCentral (www.simonsays.com/content/index.cfm?sid=292) from Simon & Schuster or *Black Ink* (www.randomhouse.com/broadway/blackink/) from Doubleday/ Random House.

African American Publishers, Distributors, and Retailers

African American publishers have had a unique role in the cultural history of African Americans. Donald Franklin Joyce (1983, 1991, 1997) describes the relationship of black-owned book publishers to the American book publishing industry and contends that by publishing a diversified range of titles, African American publishers have contributed to the development of many areas of African American literature. He identified several types of American publishers: self-published authors, religious publishers, other organizational publishers, magazines and newspapers, university presses, and trade books:

> *Historically, African American book publishers have produced annually only a small number of titles of the total titles output of the American book publishing industry. These titles, representative of various African American areas of African American literature from sociopolitical treatises to belles lettres, have largely been purposive. . . . Historically, several genres have dominated the market: sociopolitical commentaries and treatises; autobiographies and biographies; religious treaties, songbooks and handbooks, histories; sociological and political studies; cookbooks; children books; reference books; race-conscious novels; and poetry.* (Joyce 1997, 610)

Joyce (1997) contends that self-published African American authors have absorbed the cost of making books unique to the African American experience available to the public. These books have contributed to the growth and development of African American literature. For example, *Walker's Appeal, in Four Articles: Together With a Preamble, to the Coloured Citizens of the World* (Boston: D. Walker, 1829) was self-published. A sociopolitical text embracing black nationalism, *Walker's Appeal* was one of the most widely circulated books written by an African American in the United States prior to the Civil War, and is now considered a classic sociopolitical commentary in African American literature (Joyce 1997). A second type of self-published book still popular is the slave narrative, a specialized form of the autobiography. *Our Nig, or Sketches from the Life of a Free Black, in a Two-Story White House, North. Showing That Slavery's Shadows Fall Even There* (1859) is believed to be the first novel written by a female African American. *Our Nig* was published under a pseudonym and later republished by the author, Harriet E. Wilson.

Religious publishers have been a force in African American publishing since the African American Methodist Episcopal Church created the A.M.E. Book Concern in 1817. Other religious publishers that have been influential in African American publishing are the A.M.E. Zion Publishing House of the African American Episcopal Zion Church in Charlotte, North Carolina; the CME Publishing House of the Christian Methodist Episcopal Church in Memphis, Tennessee; and the National Baptist Publishing Board in Nashville, Tennessee. African American religious publishers, which also publish secular material, are the largest producers and distributors of African American religious literature.

Nonreligious organizations—such as the American Negro Academy (ANA) from 1987 to 1928; the NAACP, formed in 1910; the National Urban League, founded in 1911; and the Association for the Study of Negro Life and History (ASALH), founded in 1915—have also been a force in African American publishing.

Several African American newspaper and magazine publishers have published books. For example, the Dabney Publishing Company, which published the *Union* from 1907 to 1952, published books written by the owner, Wendell P. Dabney. Thomas Hamilton Sr.'s firm, which published the *Anglo-American Magazine* from 1859 to 1865, was the first African American magazine publisher to publish books.

African American university presses have been publishing books since the late 1890s. Atlanta University published the earliest urban sociological studies from 1896 to 1916. Howard University became the first official African American university press when it began publishing in 1972.

Trade publishers have always been the largest group in African American publishing. Carter G. Woodson created the Associated Publishers in 1921 and published titles in a variety of genres. Broadside Press, founded by Dudley Randall in1965, was created to publish African American poetry. Just Us Books, founded by Wade Hudson and Cheryl Hudson in 1988, is the most prolific African American children's literature publisher.

In addition to the publishers, African American distributors and retailers have had a major impact on the availability of books, especially hard-to-find black titles. Rosen (2002a) profiles three distributors including the sister presses Africa World Press and Red Sea Press Distributions (www.africanworld.com) for their publishing and distribution of black books on African, African American, Caribbean, and Latin American issues. Red Sea Press Distributions represents other African American publishers in the marketplace, including the Black Classic Press (www.africanworld.com). A&B Distributions & Publishers, another Rosen example, also publishes and distributes out-of-print African American titles. Despite the gains on the publishing side, independent African American publishers and retailers still face challenges in the marketplace from mega chains such as Barnes and Noble. Therefore, marketing and partnering directly to users through book clubs has become an important strategy in attracting new readers of African American literature.

African American Book Clubs and Bookstores

The African American book clubs serve as a means to connect readers and books. Membership in black book clubs, both on and off the Internet, has increased dramatically within the last five years, demonstrating that African Americans are interested in a wide range of subjects and genres. According to Zlatica Hoke (2001), the American publishing industry has reacted to the proliferation of black book clubs by publishing more works for African American readers. Industry insiders give credit to the rise of the African American Book Club for connecting readers to authors, thus affecting sales. Diane Patrick (2001, 21–22) reported several interviews with black booksellers and Carol Mackey of Black Expressions

Book Club, who said, "We do a lot of author interviews, giving them added value and enabling them to make informed choices." Black Expressions Book Club now has a membership of over 500,000 members (Patrick 2001, 12).

Founded in 1997, the African American Literature Book Club (aalbc.com), a clearinghouse for black books and reading groups, seeks to increase everyone's knowledge of the diversity of African American literature, facilitate the exchange of opinions, satisfy online book buying needs of customers, and serve as a resource and vehicle of expression for aspiring and professional writers. The Web site features not only books by authors, but also resources for writers, reviews, discussion forums, and chat. The founder and director, Troy Johnson, operates the book club as a Web site. His purpose is to distribute information about books and authors, advertise new authors, and link to Web sites of some African American authors. The site is also an affiliate of barnesandnoble.com and publishes a list of the site's 10 top-selling titles. Similarly, mosaicbooks.com, an affiliate of Amazon.com, features black literature, maintains a nationwide database of black book clubs, and publishes a newsletter, among other features.

African American bookstores serve as a connection point or a place to bring together an African American audience for a book that did not have one before. According to Patrick, "each retailer stresses the importance of handselling, knowing their customers, and using creative ways to promote books—through newsletters, events, staff recommendations, and eye catching displays" (Patrick 2001, 22).

The African American book clubs and African American bookstores support self-publishing by African American authors. Industry observers call it a burgeoning publishing subculture in which self-published authors promote their books through book clubs and independent African American bookstores. These efforts help promote authors to mainstream publishers (Jacques 1998; Fleming 2001; and Talkin' about black books 2003).

The Self-Publishing Trend

The current explosion of self-published works and small presses by African Americans is reported widely in the literature. So successful have these author-entrepreneurs been in selling their own works that they have secured book contracts with mainstream publishers (Jacques 1998; Fleming 2001; Patrick 2003; Talkin' about black books 2003). According to Jacques (1998), best-selling author E. Lynn Harris self-published and self-promoted *Invisible Life* (1992) before it was picked up and reissued by Doubleday. Similarly, Patrick (2003) reports that Teri Woods sold more than 200,000 copies of *True to the Game* from the trunk of her car in 1998. Two years later, Woods published Shannon Holmes's *B—More Careful* under her own imprint, Meow Meow Productions. Shannon Holmes was then able to strike a deal with Atria for his next two books. The *Publishers Weekly* panel (Talkin' about black books 2003) observed that some self-published authors such as Zane (erotic fiction) are more than writers; they are entrepreneurs developing themselves as a brand. Pocket Books at Simon & Schuster signed Zane to a lucrative multibook contract after her success as a self-published author of three books. Fleming (1999, 2001) warns that although self-published African American authors continue to show up in new editions on the lists of mainstream publishers, their quality can vary considerably.

To assist self-published authors, *Black Issues Book Review* regularly reviews self-published authors and includes a special column to answer questions on the subject by Dr. Rosie Milligan, who owns her own successful publishing company, Milligan Books. *Black Issues Book Review* also featured Omar Tyree, a self-publishing success, as a cover subject in its July–August 2002 issue. To further encourage self-published authors and their independent presses, the Sistah Circle Book Club, an African American Women's Book Club, will award its fifth annual "Self-Published African American Award" in 2004 (www.thesistahcircle.com).

Current Trends in the African American Genres

Over the past 10 years, not only has there been a boom in black-oriented titles, there also has been steady growth in the range and number of titles aimed at African-American readers (Fleming 2001). Carol Taylor (1999) expressed the view of many black publishers, booksellers, and editors who have seen these trends before and have wondered about what happened to writers of previous periods. However, it is agreed in the industry that the publication of Terry McMillan's *Waiting to Exhale* (1992) sparked the movement of the African American contemporary novel to mainstream publishing. Tracy Sherrod, senior editor at Simon & Schuster books, says, "Readers want fiction that reflects the complexity of their lives and also offers an element of escape" (Labbé 2000b, 37).

General trends can be observed from a review of the market and the published reports in the literature. The most popular categories among African American readers appear to be contemporary literature, romance, inspirational literature, biographies, slave narratives, and mysteries.

According to Judith Rosen (2002b, 40), African American commercial and romance fiction continued to rack up the largest sales, followed by illustrated books, art and historical events, and celebrity nonfiction titles. She also stated that black books ran the gamut from self-help to commercial fiction, to literary nonfiction, to art, to cooking. The most important element apparent in the sales was diversity of subject and genre available to African American readers.

Several developments within the genres are significant. The romance and inspirational literature genres had interesting growth patterns. According to Osborne, "romance is a billion-dollar industry which accounts for more than half the mass-market paperbacks sold—more than westerns, science fiction, and mysteries combined. African Americans comprise the fastest growing segment of that market" (2003, 11). BET Books acquired the Arabesque imprint, the first line of original African American romance novels, from a major publishing house, Kensington Publishing, and launched Sepia, a new imprint that features both established and new authors. Romance Slam Jam was established in March 1995 by Dallas booksellers Emma Rogers, Ashira Tosihwe, and author Francis Ray as an annual event to bring romance writers together. Since that time, Romance Slam Jam has become the largest African American genre-specific event for published and aspiring authors and readers (Osborne 2003). In 2001, the Emma Awards were established in honor of Emma Rogers to recognize excellent writing in the romance genre by African Americans.

Inspirational fiction has also seen many developments, resulting in a wealth of new authors and subjects for readers. Sharita Hunt sets the context for this growth within the mainstream industry.

> *Historically, the "traditional" mainstream Christian publishing industry in the U.S. ignored the African American issues of faith, so black denominational publishers like the National Baptist Convention and nondenominational ones like Urban Ministries, Inc. filled the void. . . . But now with the incredible success of authors like T.D. Jakes, the publishing industry—secular, small and large, black and white–has embraced the African American community in religious/inspirational genre.* (2001, 50)

The latest development in black Christian publishing is in the area of fiction. More men are now writing in a field previously dominated by women. According to Christopher Murray (2002), spiritually inspired fiction and nonfiction for the African American reader is increasing in popularity. *Black Issues Book Review* inaugurated its "Faith Reviews" column in 2001 to identify and assess current publications.

In the crime and suspense genres, it is interesting to note that publishers have recently released many new thrillers aimed at black readership. Although established authors like Valerie Wilson Wesley have crossed over to write contemporary African American fiction, many new voices were added. According to Robert Fleming (1999), African American men blazed a trail in mystery writing with works such as the 1937 *Conjure Man* by Rudolph Fisher.

Individual contributors in this guide provide overviews of the specific themes and trends in their chapters (crime and detective fiction, historical fiction, inspirational literature, general and mainstream fiction, speculative fiction, frontier literature, romances, and life stories). A few examples are discussed below.

In her review of the crime and fiction genre, Van Fleet (Chapter 4) found an explosion in the number of African American mystery authors in general, beginning with the decade of the 1990s, with a marked interest in mystery fiction among black women writers. These African American women writers often used the mystery genre as a vehicle for social observation and political comment.

Sims (Chapter 7) discovered that Christian fiction and inspirational literature in general has become one of the fastest growing genres in the publishing industry and that since 1990, there has been a surge of African Americans into the Christian fiction genre.

Watson (Chapter 10) concentrated on the publishing aspects of African American romance and encountered dedicated imprints, dedicated houses, and separate lines for African American romance fiction at major publishing houses.

Moore (Chapter 11) found that although black authors have only recently entered into the horror genre, their numbers are growing as middle class black audiences are creating larger markets for all types of fiction. Themes such as family and community, immortality, and morality are often explored in speculative fiction, and these were echoed in forms used by African American authors.

Finally, although African Americans were explorers, fur traders, cowboys, miners, founders of early settlements, cooks, mule drivers, blacksmiths and otherwise engaged in the occupations that helped to build a new nation, Jones (Chapter 5) observed that more than 100 years passed before African American Western writers appeared in print. Blacks began to achieve prominence in frontier fiction during the mid-1960s. Black cowboys and museums and bookstores continue to celebrate this aspect of African American culture as black writers contribute to the frontier genre.

The African American community is one of the fastest growing segments of the book buying market. Not only have publishers responded to heretofore untapped segments of the market, they have also created diverse subjects and genres, new imprints, and new lines at the major publishing houses. Established and new African American writers are sharing their stories in more than one genre, in fiction and nonfiction. It is an exciting, diverse group of authors and subjects. We invite you to enjoy.

Selected African American Publishers and Distributors

In this volume, African American authors were published by approximately 225 publishers, including African American publishers, mainstream publishers, university presses, small presses, and one self-published author. This annotated list represents selected key African American publishers and distributors. It includes unique African American imprints at major publishing houses.

A&B Books Publishers Group

146 Lawrence St.
Brooklyn, NY 11201

> Founded in 1986, A&B publishes many neglected, out-of-print books in addition to current authors under the Upstream Publications imprint.

Africa World Press & The Red Sea Press, Inc.

541 West Ingham Dr., Suite B
Trenton, NJ 08638
awprsp@africanworld.com

> Africa World Press and The Red Sea Press publish and distribute books about people of African descent and from Third World countries.

All the While Reconcile

P.O. Box 631
Bowie, MD 20718
www.allthewhilereconcile.com

> Founded by Jamellah Ellis and Malik Ellis, the publisher focuses on Christian literature.

Amber Communications Group

1334 E. Chandler Blvd., Suite 5-D67
Phoenix, AZ 85048
www.amberbooks.com

Amber Communications Group, consisting of five imprints, was awarded the Blackboard African-American Publisher of the Year Award in 2003. Amber Books publishes self-help and career guidebooks. Busta Books publishes celebrity biographies. Colossus Books features titles about famous personalities and history-making topics. Ambrosia Books publishes nonfiction and fiction, novels, and docudramas.

Ananse Press

P. O. Box 22565
Seattle, WA 98112
home.usaa.n_Hlt63573296eBM_1_t/~gumbomedia/an_Hlt63573254aBM_2_nse/index.htm

The focus of Ananse Press is on African American history in the Pacific Northwest.

BET Books/Arabesque/Sepia/New Spirit

1900 W. P., NE
Washington, DC 20018
www.bet.com/books/betbooks

BET Books was formed in 1998 with the purchase of the Arabesque romance line and now includes Sepia and New Spirit. Kensington Publishing Corporation distributes BET Books. Best-selling and first-time authors are published.

Black Classic Press

P.O. Box 13414
Baltimore, MD 21203
www.blackclassic.com

In 1978 Black Classic Press was founded to publish obscure and important works by authors of African heritage. It specializes in republishing works that are out of print.

Blackwords, Inc.

P.O. Box 21
Alexandria, VA 22313
www.blackwordsonline.com

Blackwords, Inc. focuses on black poetry, but the company also publishes works of fiction. Blackwords aims to provide publishing opportunities for new writers and sponsors the Blackwords Publishing Program to produce quality, original, and innovative books for the African American community.

Broadside Press

P.O. Box 04257
Detroit, MI 48204
313-963-8526

Started in 1965 by Dudley Randall, Broadside Press specializes in black poetry.

Genesis Press, Inc.

315 Third Ave., N.
Columbus, MS 39701
www.genesis-press.com

Started in 1993 by African American attorneys Wilbur Colom and Dorothy Colom, Genesis Press specializes in African American, Hispanic, Asian, and interracial fiction. The company is also a pioneer in African American romance titles with its Indigo Imprint, started in 1995.

Holloway House Publishing Co

8060 Melrose Ave.
Los Angeles, CA 90046
www.hollowayhousebooks.com

Holloway House is the largest publisher of "black experience paperbacks." These include biographies, histories, Westerns, mysteries, crime, romance, and other fields.

Howard University Press

2225 Georgia Ave., Suite 218
Washington, DC 20001
www.founders.howard.edu/HUPRESS
howardupress@howard.edu

Howard University Press publishes new nonfiction scholarly titles that are concerned with the contributions, concerns, and conditions of people of African descent.

John H. Johnson Publishing Company

820 S. Michigan Ave.
Chicago, IL 60605

The largest black-owned publishing company in the United States, Johnson publishes *Ebony* and *Jet* magazines and operates a book division.

Milligan Books

1425 W. Manchester Ave, Suite C
Los Angeles, CA 90047
www.milliganbooks.com/

Founded in 1990, its founder was a self-published author, and the company continues to offer a variety of literary services to authors, whether they are interested in self-publishing or mainstream publishing. Milligan books publishes in autobiography and biography, business and finance, children's books, nonfiction, fiction, poetry, religion and spirituality, relationships, psychology, and self help.

National Baptist Publishing Board

6712 Centennial Blvd.
Nashville, TN 37209
www.nbpb.org

Produces religious literature for the African American market and specializes in the development of contemporary Christian education materials for churches and families. The R.H. Boyd Company is its parent company.

ReGeJe Press
7515 Bruno Way
Sacramento, CA 95828
www.angelfire.com/mi/regejepress/
> Founded by Jacqueline Turner Banks, ReGeJe Press publishes mystery, romance, thriller, and other fiction titles.

Rinard Publishing
P.O. Box 821248
Houston, TX 77282
www.rinardcommunications.citymax.com/page/page/522604.htm
> Publishes historical fiction written by Anita Buckley.

Third World Press
7822 S. Dobson
Chicago, IL 60619
www.thirdworldpressinc.com/
> Founded in 1967 by Haki Madhunbuti, Third World Press provides quality literature that primarily focuses on issues, themes, and critique related to an African American public.

Triple Crown Publications
2959 Stelzer Rd., Suite C
Columbus, OH 43219
www.triplecrownpublications.com/about.php
> Specializing in urban fiction, Triple Crown Publications was founded in 2001 by self-published author Vickie Stringer. Red Sea Press serves as distributor.

Write the Vision
P.O. Box 12926
Wilmington, DE 19850
www.writethevision.net
> Publishes manuscripts by Christian writers.

African American Imprints at Major Publishing Houses

HarperCollins Publishers
10 East 53rd St.
New York, NY 10022
www.harpercollins.com/hc/aboutus/imprints/amistad.asp
Amistad Press
> Founded in 1986, Amistad Press continues to publish works by and about people of African descent on subjects and themes that have significant influence on the intellectual, cultural, and historical perspectives of a world audience.

Kensingston Publishing Corporation

850 Third Ave.
New York, NY 10022
www.kensingstonbooks.com

Dafina Books

Launched in 2000, Dafina Books publishes fiction and nonfiction books for an African American audience in mass market format and including romance titles.

Urban Books

www.urbanbooks.net
Started by owner/publisher Carl Weber in 2003, this is a new publishing enterprise for hip-hop fiction. Kensington Publishing Corporation serves as distributor.

W. W. Norton and Company

500 Fifth Avenue
New York, NY 10110
www.wwnorton.com/osb

Old School Books

Makes available the "Old School Books" of detective and crime fiction.

Random House/Ballantine Books

201 E. 50th St.
New York, NY 10022
www.randomhouse.com/BB/category/african_american/

One World

Created in 1991, the One World imprint focuses on subjects of African American, Asian, Latin, and Native American interest across all categories and formats.

Random House/ Doubleday

1540 Broadway
New York, NY 10036
www.randomhouse.com/doubleday/

Harlem Moon

Launched in 2002, Harlem Moon focuses on original and reprint books, fiction, and nonfiction by African American authors.

Random House/Villard

299 Park Ave.
New York, NY 10171
www.randomhouse.com/randomhouse/about/index.html#sr

Strivers Row

Launched in 2001, Strivers Row focuses on contemporary fiction by African American authors.

Warner Books

33290 West Fourteen Mile Rd. #482
West Bloomfield, MI 48322
www.walkworthypress.net/

Walk Worthy Press

Created in 2000, Walk Worthy Press publishes titles that reflect Christian themes.

Chapter 3

Collection Development

Alma Dawson

Introduction

In 1997, Vandella Brown acknowledged the debate among librarians about whether to create a separate African American fiction collection in public libraries. After considering the arguments and the combined efforts it took for authors, booksellers, publishers, and librarians working together to establish the African American novel, she considered the 27-year path enough to declare the African American novel, "a slamming genre," given its authorship and readership.

Graham (1997) contends that the African American novel emerged in the middle of the nineteenth century during the highly charged debates over slavery and freedom and became a fully recognized literary form during the 1920s. "By the 1970s, the African American novel had become a complex discursive field where inventive language, innovative structure, and historical meaning came together in texts with varying degrees of literacy and literalness for a wide range of readers" (544). According to Suzanne Dietzel, "Black-owned publishing companies, during both the nineteenth and twentieth centuries, rarely produced 'cheap' and easily available literature whose primary function was to entertain" (1997, 610). In addition, she indicates that until recently "African Americans have been more the subjects and readers of pulp fiction [formulaic literature] than its writers and publishers" (1997, 610).

More recently, *Publishers Weekly* reported: "Over the last ten years, African-American publishing has seen its longest sustained growth ever. Independent presses and many corporate divisions, including six imprints—Amistad, Dafina, Harlem Moon, One World/Strivers Row, Walk Worthy, and the children's imprint Jump at the Moon, are publishing black authors across the spectrum, in every adult fiction and nonfiction genre as well as in the children's market" ("Talkin' about black books" 2003, 24). Kensington Publishing Company added the Urban Books imprint in 2003 to cover urban heavy drama novels. This proliferation of African American authors and readers suggests readers' advisory librarians can use help building their collections of African American genre fiction.

Defining African American Genre Literature

A topic of some debate is whether African American literature should be described as a genre. In *the Readers' Advisory Guide to Genre Fiction*, Saricks (2001) rejects the idea of an African American genre. She defines a genre as "any sizeable group of fiction authors and/or specific titles that have similar characteristics and appeal; these are books written to a particular, specific pattern" (6). Saricks's definition embodies two perspectives in defining genre and suggests the source of the disagreement. The first clause reflects the traditional definition of *genre* accepted in literary circles; the second embodies the meaning of "genre fiction" used on a daily basis by readers' advisors.

This book incorporates the duality of the definition. African American authors share history and experience that, although it may manifest itself in different ways, nevertheless justifies considering their body of work as a genre in the broader literary sense. Brown (1997) contends that African American novels constitute a genre even though not all of them include structured narratives with rules governing plots, specific styles, and acceptable scenarios. They consistently speak about black diversity and culture and have an authorship and a readership that holds its own with other genres. It is for this reason that the scope of this book has been defined in terms of the culture, nationality, and ethnicity of the author.

The categorization of work within this book reflects Saricks's argument and the more utilitarian definition of "genre fiction" as "books that are written to a pattern" (2001, 6). She notes that multicultural authors write across genres, arguing that African American mysteries have more in common with mysteries by whites and Hispanics than with African American romances or African American inspirational fiction. Saricks also asserts that just because authors are African American "does not mean that they write a unique type of book. It is not possible to group their writing and identify characteristics shared by Multicultural authors; their writing does not constitute an individual, separate genre" (2001, 9).

Antell (see Chapter 9, "Mainstream Fiction") discusses the relationship among mainstream fiction, literary fiction, and genre fiction. Van Fleet describes mainstream fiction as "works intended for a popular audience and the emphasis is on characterization, plot development, thematic relevance, narrative style and to some extent, originality" (2003, 6). Mainstream fiction is often judged and reviewed according to standards set by the academic and literary establishments. Although mainstream fiction includes literary fiction, not all mainstream fiction is literary. Literary fiction is mainstream fiction that is held to a higher standard and is distinguished by unique style, social impact, and lasting significance. Literary fiction writers are acknowledged as the "group of authors that writes complex, literate, multilayered, novels that wrestle with universal dilemmas" (Saricks 1997, 27).

Genre fiction, on the other hand, is formulaic or patterned literature written for a popular audience. It is easily accessible to a wide variety of readers. African Americans write across traditional genres, including crime and detective stories, historical fiction, inspirational literature, romance novels, speculative fiction, and frontier literature. In addition, the black experience novel of the 1970s, now resurfacing as urban fiction, includes hip-hop fiction (Osborne 2001; Patrick 2003; Holt 2003), a genre form unique to African American authors.

All of these forms, including contemporary mainstream fiction titles, are included in this work and merit the attention of readers' advisory librarians. Librarians are used to dealing with mainstream fiction and nonfiction and have well-developed criteria for evaluating and selecting in those areas. Genre literature requires special attention in the collection development process, as it should be evaluated on its own terms. "Because popular literature serves a unique purpose and is valuable for its effect on the reader, it is judged by different criteria than literary work" (Van Fleet 2003, 64). Even in nonfiction areas where libraries may have well-developed criteria, attention to multicultural concerns adds another dimension (Van Fleet and Dawson, in press). Before collection development activities can begin, there is a critical need for librarians to understand and support services and collections for diverse populations.

Diverse Populations and Readers' Advisory Services

Early in the multicultural movement of the 1990s, California's librarians worked to establish services and to develop collections for a diverse and changing population (Kravitz, Lines, and Sykes 1991; Scarborough 1991). Proponents of readers' advisory services for diverse populations support development of collections and marketing to ethnic communities (Abdullahi 1993; Dawson and Van Fleet 2001; Johnson-Cooper 1994; Marquis 2003; Roy 1993; Van Fleet 2003). Abdullahi (1993) identifies the (multicultural) readers' advisor as a link between the individuals in need and the services provided by the library. He also asserts that readers' advisory service "is oriented toward the cultural enrichment of all cultural groups through the preservation of exchange of literature" (Abdulla 1993, 85). Glendora Johnson-Cooper (1994) offers specific suggestions that involve identification of resources for building Afrocentric collections. Dudley Randall, African American poet, publisher, editor, and librarian, reflects on the interests and value of reading to African Americans:

> *The new readers have a heightened black consciousness. They read books about people and characters they can relate to; they seek their identity, a meaning to their lives, direction for their questions, solutions to their problems, control over their lives and surroundings, and practical knowledge to enable them to survive and advance in their everyday living.* (1976, 97)

Authors emphasize the need for an understanding of popular culture and popular fiction, including the intrinsic value of reading for pleasure (McCook de la Peña 1993; Van Fleet 2003; Wagers 1981). In a recent overview of research on popular collections and their treatment in academic and public libraries, Van Fleet (2003) provides both theoretical and practical suggestions that can be applied to selection and evaluation of African American genre collections.

Building an African American Collection

"In order to make appropriate selection and collection and management decisions, a librarian should develop and maintain an understanding of three aspects: the literature, the patron, the library" (Van Fleet 2003, 73). Ideally, African American authors and works should be an integral part of the collection development plan of any library. If this is not currently the case, an immediate review is required. Resources should be acquired according to a collection development plan and in keeping with the library's mission statement. Services should be provided to all readers interested in the literature and in formats the library collects. There are several challenges facing readers' advisory librarians who may wish to collect the genre literature of African American authors.

Because African American genre fiction began flourishing during the 1970s, there are now many new authors writing in the different genres. Furthermore, although mainstream publishers are adding new imprints and publisher lines geared to readers of African American literature, small presses are still vital to the selection and acquisitions process. African American distributors are also key to locating titles, as they will carry hard-to-find titles not always available at larger distributors. Many of the new African American authors are self-published; therefore, it is important for selection or readers' advisor librarians to become knowledgeable about all avenues of information. In this book, 225 publishers are represented, approximately 24 percent of which produce titles in two or more genres. Further, publisher types range from self-published author to small press to mainstream press.

Standard review sources regularly feature reviews of African American works, but the numbers are small given the number of works being written each year by African Americans. Traditional readers' advisory sources, with the exception of *NoveList* and *What Do I Read Next?: Multicultural Literature*, feature only a small selection of titles within any given issue. It is often difficult to identify books by African American authors, books written about African Americans, or books that feature African American characters. For many readers, especially ethnic groups, it is important to know who wrote the work for purposes of cultural identification. In addition, Ford warns that the librarian's role in providing equal access to information is quite critical and requires a tolerance in providing materials on competing points of view; that librarians "must resist the urge to censor voices that we may not personally agree with" (2000, 286) regarding sensitive subjects that may be explored in African American novels. Given these challenges, what are the guiding principles in selection of African American genre fiction that will enable the readers' advisory librarian to know the literature, the patron, and the library?

Guiding Principles

The mission of the library should clearly link to the information and cultural needs of a diverse clientele.

To retain their viability as institutions, libraries must develop library polices and action plans that identify the needs of the diverse populations within their service communities. These plans should provide for needs-based services and reader-centered activities designed by readers' advisory librarians. Librarians can begin by examining services to ethnic groups in general and to the African American population in particular in terms of information and cultural needs. It is also important to understand the diversity within the group so that services can be planned and the appropriate materials acquired for readers. The general purpose of needs analysis is to learn more about a user population (Evans 1992). Readers' advisory librarians must also assist readers in finding books they will enjoy in many areas of interest. Therefore, to successfully develop a fiction collection, readers' advisory librarians must not only understand the needs of diverse groups within a community but also know the literature and the readers.

> *African American genre fiction should be included in the selection policies of the library for effective development of a collection.*

It is commonplace for libraries to include contemporary fiction in public library collections. Public libraries have long collected mainstream fiction and have set established criteria and evaluation procedures in their library collection policies, but genre fiction has been given less formal attention. Many authors point out the collection development challenges of handling genre fiction: perceptions of popular culture as trivial, popular fiction as irrelevant to the library's mission, lack of diversity in library staffs, the ephemeral nature of popular fiction, paperback format and its attendant preservation and maintenance issues, access and delivery systems, and education and training (Van Fleet 2003). For example, Ramsdell notes the difficulty of building a romance collection: "Romances tend to be haphazardly acquired (often through gifts) minimally catalogued and processed (if at all), randomly tossed onto revolving paperback racks, and weeded without thought to replacement when they fall apart" (1999, 33). Nevertheless, to service a growing and diverse African American population, genre fiction should be included among the selection policies of the library for effective development of a collection.

> *Selectors of African American genre fiction must be aware of sources of current literature.*

Standard review journals such as *Booklist, Library Journal,* and *Publishers Weekly,* including those within particular genres, are important sources of information on African American authors. Of particular value are specialized journals such as *Black Issues Book Review, QBR Black Quarterly Book Review, Essence Magazine,* and *Multicultural Review* for their depth of coverage of African American authors. Libraries can also form direct links to the African American community through book clubs and other organizations. Book club members can aid in identification of local African American authors, resources, and contacts that can be useful to the library in establishing services to the African American community. They can assist in identifying new and best-selling authors and in providing links to readers. In addition, African American bookstores and retailers not only offer readers opportunity to order books at discount, but also now feature author profiles, book reviews, best sellers, book clubs, featured books, and other information that the selector can use to stay current (see Chapter 12). Selectors of African American genre fiction should also be aware of African American publishers that produce a wide range of popular fiction, nonfiction, and African American biography. Readers' advisory librarians should also stay apprised of the growing numbers of imprints of mainstream publishers and publishers that feature African American lines. In addition, it is important for librarians to know the different strengths of publishers that specialize in specific genres. For example, several mainstream publishers were found to produce significant numbers of African American genre fiction titles included in this volume. Among them are Alfred A. Knopf, Atria Books, Bantam Books, Dell Publishing Group, Dial, Doubleday, Dutton, GK Hall, Henry Holt, Houghton Mifflin, Little, Brown, Morrow, Penguin Press, G.P. Putnam, St. Martin's Press, Scribner's Pocket Books, Simon & Schuster, Time-Warner Books, and

John Wiley & Sons. Although these publishers provide no unique imprint, they have adopted marketing strategies that bring attention to African American authors and their works. For a review of the trends, a selected, annotated list of African American publishers, and mainstream publishers with specific imprints identified, see "Trends in Publishing" in Chapter 2). *Publishers Weekly* frequently includes articles on African American interest titles arranged by publisher. For a more detailed discussion of publishers in specific genres, see Sims and Watson's reviews of publishers for inspirational literature (Chapter 7) and romance (Chapter 10), respectively. After the collection development specialist understands these general principles and strategies, specific steps for the collection development process, including selection and evaluation procedures, are provided.

Procedures for Building African American Collections

As indicated previously, the first step in formulating a plan for building an African American genre collection is to review or develop a collection development plan for the library. Developing that review and collection development plan entails conducting a demographic survey and a needs assessment to link the mission of the library to the needs of African American patrons. During the collection development review and development process, an evaluation of current holdings of African American genre literature should be conducted, and the plan should be revised or developed as necessary.

Step 1: Needs Assessment and the Collection Development Plan

Olson (1997) urges libraries to be as thoughtful about their fiction collections as they are about their nonfiction collections when designing a collection development plan. He suggests that the process is cyclic in nature, from mission statement and long-range plan to collection development plan, from budget for materials to selection and acquisition of materials. These steps should lead to collection assessment and a study of use, which will develop into a community analysis. The process is a continuous review or cyclic in nature for purposes of revision and review and establishment of new services. Kravitz, Lines, and Sykes write of collection development plans and ethnic groups: "The plan requires a process that is complete with needs assessment, staff support, and community involvement. Such a process enables library managers to make informed decisions, reach a consensus among staff, and prepare the funding bodies for community and change" (1991, 186). Johnson-Cooper (1994, 158) advises libraries to examine the inclusiveness of their collection development policies and assess the staff's knowledge of diverse peoples and cultures. Further, she advises librarians to know the racial makeup of the user population and to allocate collection funds so that they reflect the institution's commitment to diversity.

Within the collection development and selection plan, libraries normally establish policies that include levels of collection intensity indicators to guide selection activity and collection evaluation. The collection plan should address the level at which African American genre literature will be collected. In Anderson's *Guide for Written Policy Statements* (ALA 1995, 15), the "Fiction Collection Intensity Indications," originally created for the Lincoln Trail and Corn Belt Library Systems in Illinois, allow libraries to choose the appropriate levels for their collections depending on clientele served (Baker and Boze 1992). The five levels are 1, Minimal; 2, Basic; 3, Basic Resource; 4, Research; and 5, Comprehensive. In public libraries, levels 1 and 2 represent collections trying to meet local needs; levels 4 and 5 represent collections of national importance. Futas (1993, 41–42) suggests that the levels of collection intensity indicators could be adapted to genre fiction in ways that could be understood by the reading public. For example, she suggests that the levels that make the most sense for genre literature are the recreational level, or the best current titles on the market; the general information level, including large numbers of current titles and limited selection of retrospective titles; and the instructional level, including a selection of current titles and a good selection of retrospective titles. Popular fiction at the reference level might include current titles and a wide assortment of retrospective titles. After the collection development plan is in place with the level of collecting intensity indicators for African American fiction, it is important to acquire and use the appropriate selection tools and resources.

Step 2: Acquire and Become Familiar with Appropriate Resources for Building African American Collections

Numerous resources exist to aid the librarian in building a knowledge base of African American literature. Many tools exist specifically for building African American genre collections, including basic background works; specialized readers advisory sources, some in the particular genre; unique African American review journals; best-seller lists that appear in print and online in magazines and on publisher Web sites; online sources; and literary events and awards. (See Chapter 12.)

Basic works such as the *Oxford Companion to African American Literature* (Oxford University Press, 1997) and the *Norton Anthology of African American Literature* (Norton, 1997) can provide background information on the literature and a variety of topics. Aside from *What Do I Read Next?: Multicultural Literature* (Gale, 1997), readers' advisory librarians and patrons might find special works such as the *Best Literature by and about Blacks* (Gale, 2000) helpful. Biographical information on authors and their works is crucial for libraries. Librarians and patrons can gain knowledge of African American authors and their works from biographical sources. However, finding information on newer voices can be particularly challenging. No single source exists for comprehensive access to current profiles. Information on African American authors may appear in online databases; in biographical dictionaries or directories (both African American and non-African American); in specialized volumes produced by individual writers; on covers or book jackets; and on personal, publisher, book club, or African American booksellers' Web sites. In some instances, no published information is available. A review of the 286 authors in this book found that approximately 30 percent had information available only on personal, publisher, or book club Web sites, or on book jackets or covers and other informal sources. However, approximately 50.2 percent have biographical information available in the *Contemporary Authors* online database through the Biography Resource Center (The Gale Group). Four percent of the authors have book jacket information only, and 2 percent have no available biographical information published. The latter category includes newer voices with just one publication. For those authors, verification of titles was done through

WorldCat. Both formal sources and informal channels must be pursued to locate information on the lives and works of African American authors. We offer some suggestions below for researching African American authors.

Researching African American Authors

African American biographical information can be located through both formal sources and informal channels. Formal sources are defined as standard biographical reference sources and include databases, indexes, dictionaries, and directories. Informal channels are defined as those sources found on the Internet to promote and advertise authors. These include Web sites of individual authors, publishers, retailers and bookstores, book clubs, and authors on tour promotions. It should be noted that African American booksellers and retailers often link author Web pages and resources for writers and potential customers. To be noted also is the impact of African American book clubs that promote reading and authors in local communities.

Search Strategies

Because biographical sources may provide brief factual notes or include extensive essays on an author, how much and what kind of information the reader requires determines the source(s) used. One should start by using a biographical database such as the Biography Resource Center (The Gale Group), *Biography and Genealogy Master Index* (The Gale Group) or Wilson Biography Plus (H. W. Wilson Company). These databases offer readers a series of search options through unique packaging and indexing of both print and online products. A single search of Biography Resource Center or Wilson Biography Plus can yield extensive essays in full text, photographs, and other information such as primary and secondary sources for further study. These databases index many of the print biographical sources. The *Biography and Genealogy Master Index* can also be a starting point for both primary and secondary source information on African American authors. If the library has only print sources, works such as *Contemporary Black Biography* (Gale Group, 1992–present) can be manually searched through the author, subject, or occupations indexes. Between 1992 and 2004, approximately 525 African American writers were listed in the cumulative occupations index. Approximately 70 authors in this volume were profiled. For quick background information on well-known individuals, the *Who's Who Among African Americans* can be consulted. General online indexes such as EBSCO's Academic Search Premier or InfoTrac can be used to find articles by or about an author. Some authors may also appear in subject-specific volumes produced by individual experts. However, searching the Internet may prove to be one of the best ways to find information on newer African American authors because many are not well known. African American authors with available personal, publisher, or book club Web sites and announcements of authors on tour or other popular sources would be retrieved. To find information on the Internet, one can execute a simple name search using one of the search engines such as Google, Yahoo, or Lycos.

To facilitate research, we have created a list of sources for select African American authors. This list directs users to both print sources and Web sites where valuable author information can be found. The list can be accessed through the Libraries Unlimited Web site under the "book companions" link, or directly at www.lu.com/africanamericanlit.

Informal Channels

Because Web resources are volatile, these have been included in the category of informal channels of communication. Many of the author Web pages provide scant biographical information and were less reliable as permanent sources of information. However, these Web pages provided the only link to some authors. Where authors were listed on African American booksellers' and bookstores' Web sites, author biographies, book reviews, best-selling authors, excerpts of publications, and resources for writers were often included. Reliable Web resources do exist for additional information on African American authors. (See Chapter 12.)

Formal Sources

Formal sources are defined as biographical reference sources: databases, indexes, directories, and biographical dictionaries. Increasingly commercial databases are providing profiles of African Americans, as evidenced by the approximately 50 percent coverage of the African American authors in this volume in the Biography Resources Center (Gale Group) database. It should be noted that the Biography Center includes the print version of *Contemporary Black Biography, Notable Black Men* (Gale, 1998), *Notable Black Women* (1992, 1996, 2002), *St James Guide to Black Artists* (1997), and *Who's Who Among African Americans* (Gale, 1998–2003). Although no formal study was conducted, several authors were searched in the H. W. Wilson indexes with approximately the same results. The Wilson Plus database begins with important people at 800 BC and includes over 100 print sources in their coverage. Familiar products are *Biography Index* and *Current Biography*. African American writers are included within the database. The *Biography and Genealogy Master Index* (Gale Group) provides coverage of current and retrospective biographical dictionaries as well as *Who's Who*s.

Subject-focused biographical dictionaries provide in-depth coverage of selected authors and include both primary and secondary sources. Examples of specialized African American biographical dictionaries are Emanuel Nelson's *Contemporary African American Novelists: A Bibliographical Critical Source Book* (Westport, CT: Greenwood Press, 1999) and Valarie Smith's *African American Writers,* 2nd ed. (New York: Scribner's, 2001). Many African American biographies and directories are not devoted exclusively to writers, but authors are included. For example, Jessie Carney Smith's *Notable Black Women* and her *Notable Black Men* include African American authors. Rachel Kranz and Philip J. Koslow's *Biographical Dictionary of African Americans* (Facts on File, 1999) also includes writers. For this review, profiles of African American authors appeared most often in *Contemporary Authors* online (Gale Group), followed by *Contemporary Black Biography*, and Smith's *Notable Black Women* and *Notable Black Men.* Given the time frame for the selection of works (those published primarily between 1990 and 2004) and the number of new authors, *African American Novelists* (1999) and *African American Writers* (2001) were less useful for this specific project.

Black Issues Book Review and *QBR: The Black Book Review,* two inexpensive magazines that combine coverage of trends in African American culture along with reviews of established authors, new authors, and self-published authors, as well as other features, can be valuable additions to a library's list of selection tools. Collection developers and readers' advisory librarians should also become familiar with online resources that promote African American authors in many of the genres. African American publishers and retailers can have on hand hard-to-find African American works.

African American organizations, such as the Black Caucus of the American Library Association (BCALA), sponsor special events that feature black authors and present special awards to selected authors each year to recognize excellence in scholarship. Checking these annual awards of literary organizations is an excellent way to assess the quality of the current collection and to add titles and authors to the African American genre collection. For example, the BCALA Literary Awards are presented to African American authors annually to recognize outstanding works of fiction and nonfiction. The Emma Awards and Romance in Color Awards recognize outstanding work in African American romance fiction. The Go On Girl! Book Club Author Awards recognize authors and publishers who have made significant contributions in the writing and publication of quality books. The Gold Pen Awards, the Hurston-Wright Legacy Awards, and the NAACP Image Awards all recognize African American authors for excellence in different categories. *Sacred Fire: The QBR 100 Essential Black Books* (1999) can serve as a beginning core checklist for libraries wishing to expand their African American literature collections. Chapter 12 provides a description of awards and list of award recipients included in this book, but readers should go to the sources to get a complete and current list of other titles. Selection and evaluation are the next steps in the process.

Step 3: Selection and Evaluation

In this guide, each chapter offers specific selection criteria for the relevant genre: crime and detective stories, historical fiction, life stories, mainstream fiction, the romance genre, speculative fiction, and frontier literature. Although the volume focuses on works from 1990 onward, older works are included where appropriate. The literature is replete with references on the status and treatment of popular literature or fiction in public libraries. Futas (1993, 41) highlights important criteria for selection of genre fiction, including plausible plots, effective characterization, imaginative writing, accurate era descriptions, and ability to sustain readers' interest. Katz (1980) focuses on the individual novel, which he feels should be distinguished by its ability to provide pleasurable reading. He provides the following criteria:

- Is it true to life? Sensational? Exaggerated? Distorted?
- Has it vitality and consistency in character depiction? Valid psychology? Insight into human nature?
- Is the plot original? Hackneyed? Probable? Simple? Involved?
- Is dramatic interest sustained?
- Does it stimulate? Provoke thought? Satisfy? Inspire? Amuse? (1980, 100)

Many libraries contend with the quality versus demand debate in fiction selection. Do we provide patrons with materials that they demand, or should we examine potential purchases in terms of lasting value to the collection? This debate is especially relevant for African American genre collection building. Ford advises, "Eagerness to cash in on the recent wave of African American literary success and/or ignorance of the African American market has resulted in the publication of some titles that are of questionable merit and value" (2000, 287). Librarians should consult the specialized review sources such as *Black Issues Book Review* and *QBR: Quarterly Review of Black Books* or the Web resources of African American bookstores and booksellers for guidance when needed. (See Chapter 12.) Baker (1994) provides both philosophical and practical methods for fiction collection evaluation. She argues that public libraries should consider both quality and demand. She follows this with recommendations for evaluation of the fiction collection:

- **Quality and Demand**

  - Examine the size and growth rate of the general fiction and genre collections, looking at both diversity (examining the total number of authors and titles owned) and duplication levels (comparing the number of titles and volumes owned);

  - determine from these figures the level of collection intensity in given areas (e.g., minimal level or comprehensive level); and

  - check library holdings against three specially compiled lists of recent award-winning titles of classic fiction titles and of ALA's notable titles. Checking of the specialized African American awards lists can be substituted for the ALA Notable Books and other awards. African American authors also garner national and regional awards across the literary spectrum for the quality of their works. (See Chapter 12 for a list of awards and award winning titles.) Baker (1994) also provides criteria for evaluation of fiction collections, which can be adapted to African American fiction evaluation:

- **Evaluation of Fiction Collections**

  - Scrutinize reserve lists to identify heavily used fiction;

  - examine aggregate circulation records to determine the extent to which patrons can find desired fiction titles when they are initially sought; and

  - check library holdings against a specially compiled list of recent best-selling fiction and identify items that are desired but are not in the collection, through examination of interlibrary loan records, systematic solicitation of patron purchase suggestions, and focus group discussions.

For libraries that need a method to collect data about African authors and genres, Davis's (1994) fiction assessment worksheet offers a methodology. In Nebraska, Davis built on the work of Sharon Baker and the Lincoln Trail and Corn Belt Library Systems, which used the WLN Conspectus database for data collection and analysis. Davis's project developed fiction assessment worksheets that combined collection-oriented data with user-oriented data by genre (1994, 74–77). The goal was to provide librarians at the local level with a simple way to evaluate their fiction collections.

African American authors are writing in every medium, and this gives libraries the opportunity to offer readers a rich variety of African American literature. The steps outlined above ensure that African American genre fiction will be included in the collection development plan of the library, that budgets are appropriately developed, that selection criteria are appropriately expansive so as to allow for selection of African American authors and titles based on an analysis of the library's fiction collection and in response to user needs and requests, and that selection indicators to guide selection activity have been chosen to allow for continuous review and evaluation. Just as important, those fiction selection indicators allow the selector to continuously add to the collection books that appeal to genre readers.

Part II

African American Literature

Chapter 4

Detective and Crime Fiction

Connie Van Fleet

The mystery story is the literature of crime—of robbery, chicanery, murder, and worse. And it is a continuous celebration of the best of what it means to be human.—William L. DeAndrea in *Encyclopedia Mysteriosa*

Definition

Detective and crime novels use the vehicle of crime stories to explore thematic conflicts between good and evil, order and chaos, truth and deception. The expected and appropriate outcome—that is, the triumph of good, order, and truth—is the result of individual intelligence and personal integrity. Even in crime novels in which the criminal is never brought to justice in a formal sense, he or she pays the price of a self-indulgent existence in a chaotic and lawless underworld.

Readers often use the term "mystery" inclusively to describe any of several subgenres of crime fiction, so it is valuable for readers' advisors to distinguish among these forms. Although criminal activity is central to each, emphasis varies, from detection to description to sensation, and readers may have distinct preferences.

The *detective story* (also known as a *whodunit*) focuses on the puzzle and its solution. In the detective story, the protagonist attempts to solve the puzzle by assembling facts and using reason to build a case. A crime is discovered, the detective is called in, clues are identified and analyzed, a pattern is revealed, the solution is determined, and the criminal is brought to justice. In the detective story, the character of the detective is usually the primary appeal of the book. Hence, many detective novels are written in series based on a particular detective and his or her experiences.

In the *crime novel*, there is little true mystery. The author's emphasis is on description rather than detection, and the perspective is that of the perpetrator rather than the detective. It offers readers a glimpse into the life and mind of the criminal, and the tone is often dark, sometimes psychological. This category may include a wide range of patterns, but in African American crime fiction, noir stories about underworld life are the most common. This emphasis is reflected in the alternative terms often used for these novels, which are sometimes called *black experience novels, black urban crime novels, street literature,* or *ghetto literature*. These stories describe a society caught in despair—one of drug addiction, prostitution, and violence. Whereas the purpose of earlier crime novels was often simply "to stare the real world in the face" (Jones 2003), contemporary examples are usually overt in their moral lessons.

Finally, the mystery genre includes *mystery-suspense or psychological-suspense.* The real focus in these novels is on emotion, psychology, and personal and private relationships that lead up to the crime. This subgenre's most overt impact is the sensation of unease and tension that it evokes. Psychological suspense may delve into the criminal mind, often a psychopath or sociopath. The most common theme in African American fiction, however, explores the psyches of normal people pushed to the edge of rational behavior, typically seeking vengeance for themselves or for a loved one. Although readers may disagree with a protagonist's actions—even find them repugnant—the behavior is at least understandable. The reader may feel a certain sense of empathy, recognizing that each person may be pushed beyond the limit of "normal" behavior by physical or emotional pain.

Appeal

People read mysteries and crime fiction because they like to believe in a rational process leading to a predictable outcome and within a moral and rational universe. The detective story follows a predictable pattern, offers an intellectual puzzle, and affords the reader the comfort of a rational process. The crime novel or urban black experience novel, with its emphasis on description in the mode of social realism, gives "clues about how society works, or doesn't work" (Jones 2003), but still affirms that, in the end, the nature of one's life is the result of personal judgment and choice. And finally, although the psychological suspense story's most obvious attraction may be visceral, the ultimate appeal is often to the intellect. If one can unlock the secrets of the human mind and discover the causes of violent and aberrant behavior, one can understand and thus impose order (at least in one's own mind).

In times of rapid change, unpredictability, and social unrest, the seemingly light entertainment of the mystery novel serves an important function by providing a measure of security and satisfaction—an escape into a world where we know that justice, or at least order, will prevail. For African American readers, there is undoubtedly appeal in the strength and independence of the characters and their ability to work both inside and parallel to the system that has offered justice unevenly and unequally.

Evolution

As Paula Woods (1995) noted in *Spooks, Spies, and Private Eyes*, it is sometimes difficult to find evidence of widespread involvement of black authors in popular or genre fiction production prior to the 1970s. Yet one can reach back over 100 years to see the beginnings of themes and patterns that influence today's mystery authors. In some cases, these earlier works have been reissued as African American genre fiction has gained a wider (and more lucrative) audience.

The first mystery story authored by an African American appears to have been *Hagar's Daughter* by Pauline E. Hopkins. Hopkins's work, appearing as a serial (1901–1902), showed the influence of the sensational nineteenth-century dime novels, a format created almost exclusively by whites for a white audience (Dietzel 1997). Hopkins, as so many of her white contemporaries, used the locked room mystery pattern popularized by Edgar Allan Poe. In *Hagar's Daughter*, she created a novel about "passing," a practice that is still being explored in mystery novels today. Her Venus Johnson, a black female amateur detective, relies on both her ethnic identity and her position as a domestic to solve a case (Soitos 1997). Another element developed by Hopkins is a close, positive relationship between Venus and her mother and daughter, a theme frequently recurring in today's mysteries.

Between 1908 and 1909, John E. Bruce created in *Black Sleuth* an African-born detective as a way of demonstrating black intelligence, ability, and pride (Soitos 1997). A conscious and assertive black perspective was introduced to the mystery genre, and the use of such a perspective for sociopolitical ends and cultural validation persists.

Most scholars of African American detective fiction date the true beginning of the genre to 1932, the year Rudolph Fisher published *The Conjure Man Dies*. Set in Harlem, it was the first detective novel with all black characters (Woods 1995; Soitos 1997). Fisher forecast the modern police procedural and adhered to the structure of the classic detective story with his use of forensic medicine but expanded the genre with the novel's grounding in black urban culture and Harlem Renaissance themes.

It was during the 1930s that African American mystery writers began to question and expand the purpose and meaning of their work. Some openly wondered whether the exploration of a culture unfamiliar to white audiences was equally, if not more, important than complex characters and well-drawn plots. In corresponding with his editors regarding his play, *The Trial of Dr. Beck* (1937), Hughes Allison asked, "Could tough, hard-boiled Sam Spade or suave, gentlemanly Ellery Queen enter that dark, costly museum room [of Negro culture] and single out the culprits? While it's possible they could, it's improbable they really would. For neither . . . is equipped to think with his skin. Moreover, merely apprehending the room's culprits is not the most important factor involved" (Woods in Macdonald and Macdonald 1999, 70).

Chester Himes continued and expanded on this theme. Arguably the most prolific and influential of early black writers in crime and mystery fiction, Himes began writing in prison. He broadened the black urban context offered by Fisher, setting his novel among the Harlem underclass. His work is peopled with con men, killers, and victims; it is replete with forlorn hope, unfulfilled dreams, and desperation. His Digger Jones and Coffin Ed Johnson, although policemen, are formed in the hard-boiled detective mold, dispensing justice according to an internal set of rigid personal ethics.

This "social realism" presented from the black experience is an important element that has formed a thread throughout African American contributions to the crime fiction genre, reappearing in the 1960s and 1970s in black experience novels and serving as the framework for current writers such as Mosley, Phillips, and Woods.

Novels grounded in the black urban experience took a brutal, and some might say realistic, turn between 1958 and 1975, as a small group of black men drew on their own experiences as drug addicts, criminals, or prisoners to write novels that described the violent and hopeless society that created them. Gerald and Blumenfeld (1996) define these works as "Old School." Holloway House Publishers calls them "black experience novels." Others use the term "social realism." Hard-boiled and brutal in their depiction of life, the titles of these works give a sense of their themes: *The Scene* (Clarence Cooper), *Portrait of a Young Man Drowning* (Charles Perry), and *The Angry Ones* (John A. Williams). Robert Beck, a.k.a. "Iceberg Slim," was among the first in the "ghetto realism" school. His *Trick Baby* popularized the hard-boiled gangster novel, in which a talented and ambitious young man succeeds in the only way open to him—as a hustler and eventual criminal leader—only to die a sudden, violent, and early death (Dietzel 1997). Donald Goines, a career criminal, wrote his first two novels in prison. A prolific writer, he went on to publish 17 crime novels with Holloway House Publishers. Although the gritty "black experience novels" did not capture much critical attention at the time of publication, by selling more than five million copies they established the profitability of the African American genre market (Dietzel 1997).

The 1980s saw an increased growth in the number of African American mystery authors, and that trend has continued and exploded in the past decade. Woods calls this period the "Third Renaissance of black thought and writing" (1995, xvii). Much of this phenomenon can be credited to a reawakening of interest in mystery fiction among black women writers, who often use the genre as a vehicle for social observation and political comment. African American women authors must deal with—but frequently rejoice in—several classes of minority status. They face problems because they're black; they face problems because they're women. Some, like Woods's Charlotte Justice, deal with institutionalized racism and sexism; others, like Grimes's Theresa Galloway, are mothers who cope with universal problems of juggling professional jobs, husbands, children, and demanding mothers. Nikki Baker, with her lesbian amateur detective Ginny Kelly, introduces a third element of minority status that invites a multilayered and complex approach.

DeAndrea (1994) credits Walter Mosley and his <u>Easy Rawlins</u> series with returning popular attention to male detectives after the female-dominated 1980s. Gary Phillips, Walter Mosley, and Gar Anthony Haywood all incorporate political themes, a sense of history, and the grittiness of inner-city life. They offer a new complexity in their hard-boiled private eyes, however, by giving them a sense of community and family.

Urban fiction, sometimes called ghetto fiction, street life, or hip-hop, is the new millennium's version of the black experience or urban crime novels of the sixties and seventies. These novels are enjoying enormous popularity, with brisk sales (Patrick 2003) and booming circulation (BCALA 2003). Teri Woods, who sold photocopied and hand-bound copies of her first novel from the trunk of her car, is credited with popularizing the street writing originally self-published and now legitimized by major publishing houses. This new wave of ghetto lit is characterized by updated slang and an unprecedented woman's perspective. The similarities in tone and plot are distressingly similar to the earlier black experience novels, as ghetto life with its waste of life and spirit seems virtually unchanged. Most of these novels are rather one dimensional, appealing to young urban readers more interested in fast pacing and a linear story line than grammar or punctuation (Patrick 2003). However, a few authors, most notably Sister Souljah, demonstrate a powerful command of language and style. In *The Coldest Winter Ever*, she presents a compelling and realistic picture of the ghetto, peopling it with multidimensional and surprisingly sympathetic characters.

Themes and Trends

Today's African American authors rely on the traditional patterns that appeal to the reader's sense of order and security. The styles and approaches among these authors are widely varied, however. There is a rich mixture of character, style, and theme. For African American authors (and audiences), there is no single voice.

Character

The wonderful individuality of African American sleuths is evidence of the diversity of approach among their creators. African American authors provide some readers with characters they recognize, philosophies and language they understand, and a perspective on society that is unique to their experience. For other audiences, African American detectives may act as cultural guides or political interpreters, offering the opportunity to experience or understand the unfamiliar.

In the basic detective story, it is essential that the reader be able to relate in some way to the detective—to appreciate his or her sense of justice or cleverness or shrewdness, or to recognize kindred human frailty. Mystery series usually revolve around the protagonist, and readers will generally select on the basis of author, then featured detective. Among black detectives, there is someone for everyone. Detectives may be amateurs or professionals; male or female; Southern or Northern; straight or lesbian; scraping by, middle class, or incredibly wealthy; single or married.

Black authors also approach racial relations in various ways: from superficial to multifaceted, from confrontational to slyly manipulative, from simplistic to complex and exploratory. They invite the reader to "explore cultural differences— in perception, in way of life, in visions of the world—and act as links between cultures, interpreting each to each, mainstream to minority and minority to mainstream" (Macdonald and Macdonald 1999, 60).

People who live outside the law are the focus of crime novels. In African American crime novels, these characters are generally portrayed as individuals who are the products of a world of poverty and crime, evoking the reader's understanding or sympathy. These novels are meant to serve as cautionary tales, political commentaries, or ethnographic studies. Many of the old school crime novels were written by men who had experienced this world, made poor choices, and suffered the consequences. Underworld crime novels today often contrast two protagonists.

One has managed to escape violence and poverty and another is trapped in a life of hopelessness and crime. Through this contrast, the novels explore black identity, intraracial relations, class bias, and the nature of fate and personal responsibility.

African American Identity and Issues

Not all black authors place race at the center of their work. While some use black culture as an important dimension of the character's personality and outlook, others provide it as background. A few authors provide almost no allusion to race other than in the descriptions of physical appearance. "Because race is almost never the main event in their stories, these [modern crime] writers don't look at racial issues as problems to resolve. They look at them as clues about how society works, or doesn't work" (Jones 2002). Other authors will tell stories in which the exploration of African American identity and issues drive the plot.

African American authors provide an important and sometimes unfamiliar viewpoint in a way that affirms personal and cultural identity for some of us and raises awareness for others. Crime novels deliver social commentary with brutal aggression; detective stories more often use empathy or humor. Although some authors ignore race and others are openly confrontational in advancing a political agenda, most use stories to make a culture and perspective understandable, relevant, and valid.

Although some white authors have attempted to include honest and sympathetic portrayals of African American detectives, it is often difficult for those who have not experienced firsthand what it means to be black to strike the right note or to gain credibility with readers. For African American authors, a worldview is inherent, not learned. Typically, either subtly through the use of "blackground" (Soitos 1997) or overtly through the actions of their characters, African American mystery authors remind us that the fight for civil rights—for blacks, for women, for the poor, for homosexuals—is not yet won.

Family and Friends

African American authors often focus on the importance of family and friendship. Personal relationships play an important role for black detectives, as does a sense of community and belonging. Understanding that such relationships are often stormy and frequently irritating does not lessen the value of love and loyalty. Mothers especially have a greater presence in these novels than in typical mysteries, and strong-willed and capable heroines frequently confer with them, even if from a distance (Décuré 1999). Children—whether biological, adopted, or someone else's—are recognized as valuable and vulnerable, central to the identity and future of African Americans. Because the support of family and friends is so integral to the culture, it is particularly poignant when a hero or heroine feels isolated not only from society at large but also from his or her black community, family, or identity.

Style

African American mystery novels run the gamut of style, from cozy to noir. Many of the amateur detective novels reflect an essentially benign world, one in which criminal activity is clearly an aberration—an isolated case to be solved so we can all get back to our safe and secure world. In these stories, African American authors bring us a joy of living, an appreciation of the physical world with which we've been blessed. Even when their characters are down, there is a certain gusto. Good friends and good food abound. An infectious enthusiasm for living in the moment pervades. There is an earthy and common-sensical appreciation of the attractiveness of sex. Wit is enjoyed, a clever turn of phrase relished, and plays on words bring a wry grin. The dialogue is realistic, occasionally coarse, but the descriptive passages are often musical and sometimes lyrical.

The crime novel, set in a dark world of hopelessness and despair in which violence and death are commonplace, lies at the other end of the spectrum. Love, friendship, and hope are replaced by sex as commodity, gang loyalty, and fatalism. In these noir stories, the descriptive passages are grim but often compelling. Dialogue is graphic, derogatory, and brutal.

Universality

African American mysteries succeed because they speak to universal themes grounded in a specific context. They provide examples of loyalty and betrayal, of the importance of community and family, of cherishing life while enduring hardship, and of the difficulty and necessity of individual affirmation and integrity. They allow us to address serious issues, often unconsciously and painlessly, while providing escape and entertainment.

And, of course, this is the final and most important element of appeal. Reading mysteries is fun. We like to solve the puzzle, to put the pieces together, to use our intellects and our experience to create the picture. We can experience vicariously the thrill of the hunt or participate in rightful vengeance, or just enjoy the characters who put things right while we relax and observe.

Selection Criteria and Scope

This chapter presents a wide selection of mystery and crime novels by African American authors published since 1990. Older works in series have been included, as have old school crime novels that were published earlier but have been reissued since 1990. Some standard lists, as well as reviews appearing in current journals, were used to provide as comprehensive and representative a selection of contemporary authors in the field as possible.

Advising the Reader

Detective fiction, crime novels, urban fiction, and suspense stories all delve into the world of crime, but from different perspectives. Because these perspectives are often the first decision point of readers, the annotations in this chapter have been organized into those three major categories. Arrangement within categories is based on the key elements used by readers in making selection decisions:

- **Crime novels**. Crime novels tell the story of a crime or intended crime from the perspective of a criminal, very often a minor player who gets caught up in another smarter, more powerful criminal's affairs. These are sometimes called crime capers.

- **Detective stories**. Although the detective story subgenre includes stories related to different types of crimes, all of the stories in this book are murder mysteries. Readers of detective stories are often attracted to a particular type of detective—amateur, police, or private detective—so the detective story section is divided along those lines. Within each of those categories, the entries are grouped by gender of the detective, another factor important to many readers.

- **Psychological suspense**. African American authors have produced only a limited number of psychological suspense novels. Because only a small number of representative novels have been published, this section is not further subdivided. Although the genre of psychological suspense may include many different perspectives, all of the novels in this section deal with an ordinary person pushed to the limit.

- **Urban fiction**. These novels describe street life in the ghetto or "hood." The two major categories in this section are old school (also known as "black experience" or "urban crime" novels, originally published between 1958 and 1975) and street life (or hip-hop novels or urban pulp fiction, published since 1990). Both are characterized by violence, brutality, graphic descriptions, and adult language. They represent the "ghetto realism" style and frequently depict a protagonist who is molded by society and trapped within a dysfunctional community, one who can make only limited choices and whose destiny is to a large degree preordained.

Crime Novels

Hardwick, Gary.

The Detroit Series.

Gary Hardwick provides a harsh, realistic view of black urban life in Detroit. But although he relentlessly reveals the hard, negative side, he is not without hope. The contrast of those who have escaped ghetto life with those who are trapped in it offers a compelling array of perspectives. Hardwick's characters and themes are complex; his dialogue is brutal, but his narrative is at times sensitive and evocative. He offers no easy solutions.

> *He smiled a little. He loved his city. He loved it even though it was a place as much affected by the actions of his own people as it was by anyone else's racism. He loved it because it was the only place that could ever be home to him. He saw in the city his own humanity and evolution.* (Cold Medina, p. 344)

Keywords: inner city life and culture • murder mysteries • politics and politicians • racial identity

Cold Medina. New York: Penguin Books, 1996. ISBN 0-525-93919-9. 344p.

Tony Hill, head of Detroit's Special Crimes Unit, and T-Bone, head of the city's drug dealing Union, are both men near the top of their careers. A psychopathic killer who kills and maims drug dealers and an insidious new illegal drug draw both men into increasingly violent and uncharted territory.

Keywords: drug dealers and dealing • gangs and gangsters • police corruption • serial killers

Double Dead. New York: Dutton/Penguin Books, 1997. ISBN 0525939202. 357p.

The beloved black mayor of Detroit is murdered, his mistress wrongly accused, and a seamless black briefcase disappears. Jesse King, a brilliant and ambitious district attorney, initiates his own investigation and finds himself back in the ghetto, threatened by a corrupt political machine, hunted by the law, and embroiled in a battle of the sexes gang war. This suspenseful, carefully plotted novel combines a sensitive and likeable hero with strong, realistic dialogue and harsh description.

Keywords: drug addiction • drug dealers and dealing • gangs and gangsters • political corruption

Phillips, Gary.

The Martha Chainey Series.

Phillips brings his gritty, noir style to Las Vegas with this crime caper featuring Chainey (whom no one calls Martha), a statuesque former showgirl who retains her impressive figure and in-your-face attitude. In this harsh world, none of the characters is truly sympathetic. Violence, sexuality, and ruthlessness are depicted, but not in explicit or brutal detail; dialogue is realistic, with some profanity.

> So here it was; there was no choice, really. She'd have to hunt down the shooters. To turn it over to Baker, or worse, to ask his help, would be a sign that she couldn't cut it. When it came down to the nitty-gritty, she had to have a man bail her out. Fuck that. (High Hand, p. 110)

Notes: Gary Phillips is also listed in the "Private Eyes—Male" section of this chapter.

Keywords: crime capers • money laundering • organized crime

High Hand. New York: Kensington Books, 2000. ISBN 1-57566-616-2. 242p.

Robbed of $7 million of off-the-books money she is transporting in her job as courier for a mobster, Chainey has to use all of her street smarts and confidence to recover the package before her 72- hour deadline runs out.

Notes: Gold Pen Best Award Best Mystery/Thriller Nominee 2001

Keywords: con artists and con games • double-crosses • robbery

Shooter's Point: A Martha Chainey Mystery. New York: Kensington Publishing, 2002. ISBN 1575667452. 304p.

When boxing champ Tyler Jeffries is shot during his title bout, riots ensue and martial law is declared in Las Vegas. When the side-bets that were kept in a locked safe disappear, Chainey is called in to track down the money. With the help of reporter pal Rena Solomon, Chainey follows the trail among street-level hookers, the entourage of rapper King Diamond, and the Black Jihad.

Keywords: Black Jihad • boxers and boxing • gambling and gamblers • rap music and musicians

Phillips, Gary.

The Perpetrators. Los Angeles: UglyTown, 2002. ISBN 0-9663473-7-4pa. 173p.

Marley, who fancies himself a slick expediter, accepts a job that looks to be a walk in the park: pick up Lena Guzman, heiress to a drug fortune in Tijuana, and deliver her within 24 hours to Sacramento. He should have realized something was up when he was offered $2 million for the delivery. Marley and Guzman use an arsenal of weapons and a bevy of vehicles to escape their attackers, including a ruthless band of Furies in the pay of a dishonest lawman. Marley is a modern-day James Bond with an attitude—handsome, resourceful, undeterrable, and supported by modern gadgetry and an expensive wardrobe. Fast action and faster dialogue abound, as do raw sex and language. Readers will want to look for insider references to earlier crime writers.

> *The hombre with the knife stepped in close, waving his pig sticker back and forth. The steely tip whisked past Marley's Armani shirt, slicing a button off as he twisted aside. A tight smile creased his rugged face. "That's your ass, amigo, you don't fuck with my gear."* (p. 16)

Keywords: crime capers • drug dealers and dealing • police corruption

Ridley, John.

Stray Dogs. New York: Ballantine Books, 1997. ISBN 0-345-41345-8. 168p.

A broken radiator hose strands John Stewart in Sierra, a barren, dusty flyspeck of a town. He needs to get to Las Vegas to settle a debt. A loner, drifter, gambler, and loser, he is easy prey for Grace, the archetypical seductress who'll betray a man as quickly as sleep with him. When Grace offers John money (and sex) to kill her husband, it's no surprise. When her husband Jake offers to split the insurance money with the man who'll kill his wife, things start getting interesting.

> *For a moment John felt himself drowning in her. He felt as if there was no point in fighting, and for a moment he didn't want to. There was a bliss and a nirvana that came just beyond letting go . . . He knew it was the feeling that came when death was present, and the only thing left was to give in. But a thought came to him: Whose death was it?* (p. 89)

Notes: John Ridley is also listed in the "Psionic Powers" section of Chapter 11.

Keywords: adultery • betrayal • drifters • ghost towns • police corruption

Love Is a Racket. New York: Alfred A. Knopf, 1998. ISBN 0-375-40142-3. 295p.

Ridley's crime noir story of small-time con man Jeffty Kittridge is deftly told with a darkly humorous edge. The inside workings of various scams, the vivid descriptions, and the fast-moving plot will appeal to fans of crime capers. Hapless, teetering on the edge of alcoholism, in hock to a loan shark who has just broken two of his fingers, Jeffty thinks he's found the perfect con in the person of his beautiful angel Mona—only to discover once again that he's a born loser.

> *I sat there, me in nothing but a towel on a hot day in a third-rate apartment, drinking in front of the tube. I would've felt lonely and near terminally de-pressed, but I was so used to my life all I felt was content.* (p. 24)

Notes: John Ridley is also listed in the "Psionic Powers" section of Chapter 11.

Keywords: con artists and con games • crime capers • loan sharks

Everybody Smokes in Hell. **New York: Alfred A. Knopf, 1999. ISBN 0-375-40143-1. 235p.**

Fortune smiles on Paris Scott, a failure at everything (including being a convenience store clerk), when a fortune in drug money and the last tape of a dead rock star fall into his lap. But will Paris lose his soul as he navigates his way through the treacherous, violent, and seamy Hollywood and Las Vegas undergrounds? Ridley paints a graphic, sad, sick, and hopeless picture, tinged with irony and dark humor.

> *Yet, with its nickel slots and twenty-five cent roulette chips, the Plaza held on. The army of living dead who populated it now gambled with something besides cash. They gambled with their lives and with their last chances. But, same as if they were gambling with money, the House had the odds.* (p. 191)

Notes: John Ridley is also listed in the "Psionic Powers" section of Chapter 11.

Keywords: crime capers • drug dealers and dealing • music business • professional assassins • sadism • sexual deviance

The Drift. **New York: Alfred A. Knopf, 2002. ISBN 0375411828. 269p.**

Charles Harmon, once a successful tax attorney, devoted husband, and wealthy suburbanite, spirals down through drink, drugs, and dementia to find a hard freedom riding the rails as Brain Nigger Charlie. When Chocolate Walt, his tramp mentor, asks him to find his teenaged niece who has taken to the life, Brain Nigger finds himself up against police, white supremacist drug smugglers, and a serial murderer. Charles's descent, the hard life of the rail rider, and the sometimes brutal character of the hobo are portrayed realistically in a story told with sadness, humor, and unflinching honesty.

> *What was done to men on the rails was sickening. I knew. I had front-row seats for those parties. Sometimes been the specially invited guest. What*

> *was done to women, a person who owned any humanity*
> *did not care to think about.* (p. 36)

Notes: John Ridley is also listed in the "Psionic Powers" section of Chapter 11.

Keywords: drug dealers and dealing • hobos • people with mental illness • rail riders • runaways • white supremacy

Tramble, Nichelle D.

The Dying Ground: A Hip-Hop Noir Novel. **New York: Strivers Row, 2001pa. ISBN 0-375-75653-1. 323p.**

Marco Redfield, protagonist of this coming-of-age story cum mystery, finds himself caught up in the violence of the Oakland drug culture when he returns from college to find best friend and successful drug dealer Billy dead and Billy's girlfriend—Marco's secret love—on the run. The powerful writing and realistic dialogue contribute to this novel's focus on systemic racism and the hopelessness of poverty.

> *Billy: dead. Felicia: missing. None of the words made*
> *sense together, but the doom I'd expected announced it-*
> *self. I felt iron in my mouth, like I'd gargled with pennies, a*
> *taste like blood, a bitter taste that always followed bad*
> *news.* (p. 28)

Notes: This edition includes an interview with the author and a reading group guide.

Keywords: coming of age • drug dealers and dealing • family relationships • friendships • gangs and gangsters • love

Detective Stories

Amateur Detectives—Men

Arnold, N. Xavier.

The Genocide Files. **Marlow Heights, Md.: Tana Lake Publishing, 1997. ISBN 0-9651007-0-7. 332p.**

Xavier uses first-person narrative to create a sense of growing awareness and immediacy in this story of Matthew Peterson, a privileged black professional who has little sense of cultural identity. Peterson, a wealthy executive and self-proclaimed "successful and respected arbitrageur," has it all—an office in Chicago's Woolworth Tower, a chauffeur, a beautiful blonde lover, and a complacent assurance that his own abilities and intelligence have helped him succeed where other blacks have failed. His determination to rescue the firm's latest acquisition, the venerable but failing *Chicago News*, puts him first on a murder scene and involves him in an investigation that will threaten not only his life but his entire worldview. The author is adept at selecting quotes from a variety of sources to begin each chapter, providing context and a sense of connection that contrasts with the more closed first person used to tell the story. Arnold is also a poet and includes an original poem in this novel, which concludes with "to be continued."

> *Being so close to death, I glimpsed the vanity of the life I had lived up to that time. I had few commitments, fewer friends, and even less passion. That stay in the hospital showed me how much more there was. I wanted it; I needed it. What had started as a simple search for a headline, was now a search for a lifeline.* (p. 73)

Keywords: genocide plots • intraracial relations • murder mysteries • political radicals • racial identity • white supremacy

Carter, Stephen L.

 The Emperor of Ocean Park. **New York: A Borzoi Book/Alfred A. Knopf, 2002. ISBN 0-375-41363-4. 657p.**

Carter tells a story of ambition, vengeance, and political intrigue at the highest levels. Couched in terms of a chess "puzzle," the narrative unfolds interweaving personal relationships and political repercussions in a setting of contemporary America with its equally complex racial paradoxes. Talcott Garland has always had to live in the shadow of his famous father, Oliver Garden, the Emperor of Ocean Park, "the judge," even to his children. A conservative black jurist whose nomination to the Supreme Court was scuttled by his loyalty to an unsavory old friend and the envy of members of the paler nation, the judge was at once hailed as brilliant and vilified as a traitor to his people. Tal, an introspective, handsome, dedicated law professor, refuses to believe his father's death was due to anything but natural causes until he receives a posthumous message from "the Emperor." Tal's career, marriage, and sanity begin to crumble as he attempts to unlock the secrets of his father's past, decipher "the arrangements," and keep himself and his family alive. Carter includes a three- page "Author's Note."

> *Depression is seductive; it offends and teases, frightens you and draws you in, tempting you with its promise of sweet oblivion, then overwhelming you with a nearly sexual power, squirming past your defenses, dissolving your will, invading the tired spirit so utterly that it becomes difficult to recall that you ever lived without it . . . or to imagine that you might live that way again.* (p. 153)

Notes: BCALA First Novelist Award 2003; Black Issues Book Review Best Book 2002; A Book-of-the-Month Club Main Selection 2002; *Essence* Bestseller List 2002; *New York Times* Notable Book 2002

Keywords: attorneys • family relationships • husbands and wives • intraracial relations • judges • murder mysteries • politics and politicians

Gibson, John.

Dummy. Rochester, N.Y.: Greenfield, 1997. ISBN 0-9658586-7-7pa. 288p.

Julien Campbell ushers Coby Taylor, the hospital's black deaf mute maintenance man, to a surprise birthday party. They arrive on the bloody scene to find all of their friends brutally murdered and must flee before they join the macabre guest list. Who was the real target—and why?

> *Staring at the rug, Julien gravitated toward the door. When he got there, he pushed it. Harder. And when he had gotten the door opened enough to get his head and shoulders through, when the enormity of the scene that met his glance melted through to reality, at that moment Julien knew that the world he had known was not and would never again, be the same.* (p. 54).

Keywords: arms dealers • murder mysteries • professional assassins

Greer, Robert O.

The CJ Floyd Series.

CJ Floyd is a forty-something Vietnam vet, self-proclaimed loner, collector of vintage license plates, small-time bail bondsman, and sometime bounty hunter. Greer adroitly develops his protagonist through description of his possessions, interactions, and actions. Although keenly aware of his own blackness and its impact on his life and society, Floyd is by nature suspicious of everyone, regardless of color—an attribute that has saved his life and money on many occasions. Greer's description of the African American community in Denver provides a unique setting, and his explanations of the colloquialisms used in his titles add intriguing sidelights.

> *He also wondered if he hadn't just stepped into the kind of manure pile his uncle used to like to call "home-grown corn-bread Negro shit." Like most black people, CJ had spent a good part of his life looking in the rearview mirror, making certain that his ass wasn't hanging out unprotected in a white man's world.* (The Devil's Hatband, p. 62)

Keywords: bail bondsmen • bounty hunters • murder mysteries

The Devil's Hatband. New York: Mysterious Press/Warner Books, 1996. ISBN 0-89296-634-3. 336p.

CJ is offered the biggest payday of his career by two "Oreos": bring back the radical environmentalist daughter of a prominent black judge and the documents in her possession. He arrives on the scene only minutes after the local sheriff to find his quarry strangled with barbed wire and himself enmeshed in a case even more treacherous than he had originally suspected.

Keywords: corporate intrigue • environmentalists • political radicals

The Devil's Red Nickel. New York: Mysterious Press/Warner Books, 1997. ISBN 0-89296-652-1. 350p.

Clothilde Polk's certainty that her father, Daddy Doo Wop, did not die a natural death, leads CJ to the Chicago mob, a 50-year-old payola scandal, and into present danger while he copes with more mundane matters such as collecting on bad debts.

Keywords: counterfeit money • disc jockeys • gangs and gangsters • music business

The Devil's Backbone. New York: Mysterious Press/Warner Books, 1998. ISBN 0-89296-653-X. 352p.

Hell hath no fury, and Bobby Two-Shirts's sister is out to get the man who put her brother in jail. CJ can little afford the distraction as he tracks down the killer of retired black rodeo star Hambone Dolbey through a trail of greed and deception.

Keywords: cowboys • rodeos • vengeance

Limited Time. New York: Mysterious Press/Warner Books, 2000. ISBN 0-89296-684-X. 338p.

At the request of Henry Bales, research scientist and Vietnam war buddy, CJ enters a world in which medical research, athletic ambition, and greed overlap. Can he find the ruthless mastermind behind the drug scheme before more people die?

Keywords: bioengineering • Cuba • medical research

Mosley, Walter.

The Fearless Jones Series.

Paris Minton, bookstore owner, thinker, and self-avowed coward, narrates the exploits he shares with friend and foil Fearless Jones, World War II army veteran, defender and avenger of the weak, who is good in a fight, true to his word, and emotionally perceptive. Living in Los Angeles in the 1950s at a time when black citizens were sometimes hard pressed to tell whether they had more to fear from the police or the criminals, Fearless and Paris often work outside the law to ensure a rough justice. This series contains many of the elements of the traditional hard-boiled private eye story, with corrupt officials, a dark mood, femmes fatales, and a rough but honest protagonist committed to his own moral code.

Fearless was tall and dark, thin and handsome, but mostly he was powerful . . . Fearless wasn't a smart man. A twelve-year-old might have been a better reader, but if he ever looked into your eyes he would know more about your character than any psychiatrist, detective, or priest. (Fear Itself, p. 4)

Notes: Walter Mosley is also listed in the "Private Investigators—Men" section of this chapter and is listed in the "Horror—Supernatural" and "Short Fiction" sections of Chapter 11.

Keywords: bibliophiles • murder mysteries • 1950s

🏵 *Fearless Jones: A Novel.* Boston: Little, Brown, 2001. ISBN0-316-59238-2. 312p.

Meeting Elena Love was the beginning of a very bad day for Paris. In short order, he's seduced, robbed, and loses his bookstore to arson. Homeless and no longer in business, he uses the last of his money to bail Fearless out of jail to track down the woman, cash in on her scam, and find retribution. The case becomes a mission when Fearless gives his word to protect an elderly Jewish woman, the bodies start stacking up, and large-scale fraud is uncovered.

Notes: *Essence* Bestseller List 2001

Keywords: fraud • Nazi collaborators

Fear Itself. Boston: Little, Brown, 2003. ISBN 0-316-59112-2. 316p.

Fearless's soft heart once again embroils Paris in a dangerous caper. A young woman with a child in tow approaches Fearless for help in finding her husband, a mysterious stranger shows up at Paris's door looking for Fearless, and bail bonds-man Milo Street sends the duo on a missing person's case. Weaving all of the threads together to reveal the pattern is a dangerous task that calls for Paris's intelligence and Fearless's strength, perceptiveness, and unwavering commitment to doing the right thing.

Keywords: family history • family relationships • missing persons • private investigators

Walker, Persia.

Harlem Redux. New York: Simon & Schuster, 2002 (2000). ISBN 0-7432-2497-3. 311p.

David McKay, civil rights attorney, is summoned home after the apparent suicide of his genteel older sister Lilian. Attractive, successful, well dressed, David had moved away from Harlem to escape a past that now seems destined to reclaim him. His exploration into Lilian's death uncovers tangled family relationships, unfaithfulness, vengeance, and murder, but in confronting the past he has so successfully denied, he also discovers the true meaning of home and family.

> *The night before, he had dreamed that by returning home, he would be walking into a trap, that his family, Striver's Row, Harlem—they were all bundled together—would swallow him, smother him. He had seen mocking phantoms, knowing smiles, and pointing fingers. . . .He had known that he couldn't run forever. Known he would be summoned back. Someday. Somehow. (pp. 13–14)*

Keywords: brothers and sisters • class relations • family relationships • Harlem Renaissance • illegitimate children • passing • Striver's Row

Amateur Detectives—Teams

Bates, Karen Grigsby.

 Plain Brown Wrapper. **New York: Avon Books/HarperCollins, 2001. ISBN 0-38080-8-900pa. 321p.**

Alex Powell, savvy and sassy columnist for the *Los Angeles Standard*, teams up with *Washington Post* correspondent Paul Butler to uncover the murderer of the editor of *Diaspora*, a leading African American journal. Professional and personal motives abound as man-about-town Ev Carson's secret past and professional machinations are revealed. Many readers will enjoy the rich descriptions of food, clothing, and hotels, but depending on their own status, they may be either amused or insulted by the insider slang.

> *"Why on earth would I eat before going to a cocktail party?" "Because that party will probably be critically Caucasian, and you know what peeples say about white parties. White folks' hospitality is usually limited to"—"a mayonnaise sandwich and a glass of ice water!"* (p. 120)

Notes: BCALA Literary Award Honor Book 2002

Keywords: journalism and journalists • Los Angeles, California • Martha's Vineyard • New York City • Washington, D.C.

Carter, Charlotte.

Jackson Park: A Cook County Mystery. **New York: One World Books/ Random House Ballantine Books, 2003. ISBN 0-345-44782-4pa. 213p.**

Eight days after the assassination of Reverend Martin Luther King Jr., Cassandra, a smart, chip-on-her-shoulder, 20-year-old reluctant virgin, becomes embroiled in the search for a missing young woman. The search reveals the strength of her elegant Aunt Ivy, the unexpectedly violent and streetwise side of her beloved Uncle Woody, and the ugly secrets of the campus revolutionary movement.

> *I became the worst kind of kissass teacher's pet. I was showered with gold stars, spelling medals, and A's—and regular beatings from classmates who hated my goody-goody, library-loving, gimpy left footed ass from day one.* (p. 2)

Notes: Charlotte Carter is also listed in the "Amateur Detectives— Women" section of this chapter.

Keywords: Chicago, Illinois • 1960s • police corruption • political radicals

DeLoach, Nora.

The Mama Series.

This lighthearted series follows Simone Covington, a paralegal with an Atlanta firm, and Grace Covington, her small-town social worker mother, who is known as Candi ("because of her complexion. It's like candied sweet potatoes."). Thanks to Mama's gracious nature and sweet potato pie, Sheriff Abe is a willing ally. Drawn into one mystery after another, Simone, who narrates, is often swept up by circumstance (and Mama) but can always count on family for love and support. Mama is calm, in charge, caring—and always has fresh brewed coffee and baked goods as well as a plan. Recurring characters, family values, and community spirit lend this series a cozy feel.

> *My family said nothing. They sat, studying me, their mental gears ready to go to work.* (p. 140). *Mama took the photo from his hand. "I've got a plan that will net Kline, the girl and whoever else is in this mess with them!"* (Mama Saves a Victim, p. 144)

Keywords: family relationships • Otis, South Carolina • small-town life and culture

Mama Solves a Murder. Los Angeles: Holloway House, 1994. ISBN 0-87067-741-1. 192p.

Simone chronicles two overlapping cases. Mama believes that the arson deaths of her Aunt Aggie and Aggie's daughter Rita are the result of a child molestation report, and Simone must find evidence to defend her college roommate, who shot a man in front of five witnesses.

Keywords: child molestation • courtroom defense • psychopathic killers • repressed memory

Mama Traps a Killer. Los Angeles: Holloway House, 1995. ISBN 0-87067-747-0. 191p.

Mama and Simone's trust is put to the test when Danny Jones, a young man recently and uncharacteristically befriended by James Covington, is found murdered —and all evidence points to their loving husband and father.

Keywords: alcohol abuse and alcoholics • fathers and sons • husbands and wives • mothers and sons

Mama Stalks the Past. New York: Bantam, 1997. ISBN 0-553-57721-2. 244p.

Mama receives an unexpected and unwanted bequest of land that makes her the target of local gossips and an angry heir. When it is revealed that her benefactress was murdered, Mama must save her reputation by bringing the murderer to justice.

Keywords: family land • family relationships • heirs

Mama Stands Accused. Los Angeles: Holloway House, 1997. ISBN 0-87067-873-6. 157p.

Mama is accused of stealing food stamps but is diverted from her own problems by the murder of her quarrelsome and mendacious half-sister Agnes. Uncle Ben, Agnes's husband, is the prime suspect, but Mama is convinced of his innocence as her investigation reveals twisted relationships, unrequited love, and fraud.

Keywords: family land • family relationships • fraud • heirs

Mama Saves a Victim. Los Angeles: Holloway House, 1997. ISBN 0-87067-874-4. 156p.

Mama phones Simone to ask her to drive with her to retrieve a silver music box taken by Fingers, the kleptomaniac child of her second cousin Hester. Returning home, Simone hits a young woman who runs into the path of her car, setting in motion a chain of events, the outcome of which is as important to Simone as it is to the mysterious woman.

Keywords: absentee parents • con artists and con games • fraud • kleptomania • mixed-race children • race relations

Mama Pursues Murderous Shadows. New York: Bantam, 2000. ISBN 0-553-57722-0. 179p.

Simone is worrying about planning a party for Mama's thirty-fifth wedding anniversary. Sarah, one of three town gossips, is worrying about paying her taxes. Mama is worrying about proving that Ruby's apparent suicide was really murder, and everyone's worried about a rapist loose in Otis.

Notes: Gold Pen Best Award Best Mystery/Thriller Nominee 2001

Keywords: blackmail • brothers and sisters • family celebrations • infidelity

Mama Cracks a Mask of Innocence. New York: Bantam, 2001. ISBN 0-553-57724-7. 196p.

Brenda Long, a holier-than-thou high school student with a penchant for interfering in other people's lives, is found dead in a shallow grave. Mama and Simone uncover old and new secrets in not-so-sleepy small-town Georgia on their way to finding the murderer.

Keywords: drug dealers and dealing • intergenerational love affairs • religious hypocrisy

Haywood, Gar Anthony.

The Loudermilk Series.

Two happy beneficiaries of early retirement, Joe "Big Joe" Loudermilk (from the El Segundo, California, police force) and wife Dottie (from the faculty of Loyola Marymount University) have purchased an Airstream and keep on the road and away from their five adult children. Dottie narrates their adventures in crime solving and child-rearing with light irony, a mother's fierce protectiveness, and the zest of an amateur detective. Readers will find it easy to relate to the appealing characters in this lighthearted series.

> *If I haven't made this abundantly clear, all our other chil-*
> *dren are pains in the derriere, for a vast assortment of de-*
> *pressing reasons, and when Joe and I left California, we*
> *didn't exactly leave them behind by accident.* (Going No-
> where Fast, p. 25)

Notes: Gar Anthony Haywood is also listed in the "Private Eyes—Men" section of this chapter.

Keywords: Airstream owners • husbands and wives • murder mysteries • parents and children • retired people

Going Nowhere Fast. New York: Putnam, 1994. ISBN 0-399-13917-6.192p.

The only thing worse than having their Grand Canyon visit interrupted by finding a corpse on the toilet of Lucille, the beloved Airstream, is finding their youngest son Mad Dog (neè Theodore) hiding in the closet. Is Mad Dog the conned or the con man?

Keywords: football players • gangs and gangsters • witness protection program

Bad News Travels Fast. New York: Putnam, 1995. ISBN 0-399-14017-4. 244p.

Eddie, their charming and handsome political activist son, is accused of murder, and Dottie and Joe must find a way to clear him. As they follow the trail of a mysterious book that appears to be at the center of the mystery, no one seems trustworthy. Everyone is confessing to everything except the murder that Eddie is accused of committing.

Keywords: blackmail • political activism and activists • Washington, D.C.

Amateur Detectives—Women

Bailey, Frankie Y.

The Lizzie Stuart Series.

Professor Lizzie Stuart is a complex and often contradictory woman, at once intellectual and emotional, independent and vulnerable. A criminologist and a professor of criminal justice, she is not excited to be involved in solving crimes firsthand. Her analysis of the crimes with which she is personally involved is colored by superstition and personal demons. Bailey contrasts Lizzie's ordered, safe, rational professional persona with the disruption that results from murder. She uses classic plot devices to good effect. Her use of language and juxtaposition of normalcy with a sense of foreboding subtly build suspense in the tradition of the best classic mystery writers.

> *The old oak tree in the backyard had been struck by light-*
> *ning. Blasted to its roots. Hester Rose, my grandmother,*
> *would have said it was an omen. A "sign." But a sign is only*
> *useful if you know how to read it. At any rate, it was a mo-*
> *ment of transition. Not dying was amazingly therapeutic.*
> (Death's Favorite Child, p. 3)

Keywords: men and women • murder mysteries • romantic suspense

Death's Favorite Child. [Johnson City, Tenn.]: Silver Dagger Mysteries, Overmountain Press, 2000. ISBN 1-57072-146-7pa. 218p.

After her elderly grandmother's death, Lizzie's vacations in Cornwall, England, where she witnesses the departure of another soul. But the comely and feisty Dee's death was due to anaphylactic shock, not old age. Lizzie meets a vacationing fellow American, Philadelphia detective John Quinn, who becomes involved in the case—and in Lizzie's life.

Keywords: adultery • police detectives—men

A Dead Man's Honor. Johnson City, Tenn.: Silver Dagger Mysteries, 2001. ISBN 1-57072-171-8. 218p.

Lizzie's academic life as a visiting professor and researcher is disturbed by her reflection on her grandmother's secretive nature, ghosts from the past, and John Quinn's romantic pursuit. When an arrogant colleague is murdered, Lizzie finds herself in danger as the case unravels.

Keywords: academic mysteries • lynching • police corruption

Baker, Nikki.

The Virginia Kelly Series.

Virginia Kelly, a securities analyst at the investment firm of Whytebread and Greese, is a reluctant amateur detective. Strong and outspoken, she is also a political iconoclast; a black lesbian who seems to prefer blondes; and one of the few African American mystery heroines who is isolated from family, friends, and community. Ginny is at odds with her parents, who do not understand her sexual preference and liberal politics, and is hurt by their preference for her conservative sister and ultraconservative brother-in-law. Baker's fast-paced yet sensitive work explores complex relationships, and Ginny is not always treated gently by herself or by her creator.

> *He [Ginny's father] stopped breaking the ice into the trays long enough to squeeze my collarbone the way you'd scratch around a puppy's neck. His hands were cold. What he meant was: we love you but we wish you could be someone else. We wish you could be Sandra in there with that nice black man.* (Long Goodbyes, p. 34)

Keywords: cultural identity • homophobia • lesbian relationships • murder mysteries

The Lavender House Murder. Tallahassee, Fla.: Naiad Press, 1993 (1992). ISBN 1-56280-012-4pa. 202p.

Lots of people had reason to kill Joan De Maio, a lesbian journalist who specializes in promiscuous sex and outing people who would prefer that their sexual preferences remain private. When she's found shot to death, what started as a Cape Cod vacation for Ginny and friend Naomi becomes a murder investigation.

Keywords: blackmail • journalism and journalists • promiscuity • resort town life and culture

Long Goodbyes. Tallahassee, Fla.: Naiad Press, 1993. ISBN 1-56280-042-6pa. 235p.

Virginia Kelly, prompted by a mysterious call from her high school crush, returns home for the Christmas holidays and high school reunion. Here she faces strained family relationships and mixed signals from her first love as she untangles relationships and uncovers this small town's hidden scandal.

Keywords: high school reunions • infidelity • lesbian relationships • sibling rivalry

In the Game. Tallahassee, Fla.: Naiad Press, 1994. ISBN 1-56280-004-3. 171p.

"Which would you choose—order and peace, or passion and craziness?" (p. 20) Ginny explores the question as she tries to prove her friend Bev innocent of murder and extricate herself from an obsessed lover.

Keywords: embezzlers • infidelity • love affairs • stalkers

The Ultimate Exit Strategy. Tallahassee, Fla.: Naiad Press, 1996. ISBN 1-56280-080-9pa. 240p. Reissued Ferndale, Mich.: Bella Books, 2001. ISBN 1-93151-303-1pa. 229p.

Tensions were high enough at Whytebread and Greese when the buyout was announced, and the suspicious death of their CEO didn't help. Virginia Kelly's life is not made any easier when bitter former girlfriend Cassandra Hope is put in charge of the investigation. Already vulnerable and contemplative, Ginny is unable to resist Cassandra or her demands.

Keywords: corporate intrigue • former lovers • police detectives—women

Banks, Jacqueline Turner.

Maid in the Shade. Sacramento: ReGeJe Press, 1998. ISBN 0-96391-473-1pa. 159p.

Ruby Gordon, maid from Petit, Tennessee, revels in her blackness, largeness, and womanness. Strong and independent, she is straightforward in her cooking, her observations, and her loyalties. About the only things that worry her on a regular basis are her sister Emerald (who lives with her) and her language (which is "too black"). The dialect and humor contribute to the lighthearted style. When Ruby receives a desperate note, she flies to Oakland and takes on a San Francisco gang to find out who's been trying to kill friend Jan Chaney and her son Rasan.

> *I was feeling a bit generous so I made a toast for the many that don't look like me too, but only if they're the kind that don't mind when I get too relaxed on the cross-town bus, that's the ninety-eight, and my left leg gets heavy and flops over to the side and touches theirs just a bit. . . . I don't worry none about what they be saying when I overhear them talking to each other, 'cause a whole lot of us Americans been raised by fools. (Maid in the Shade, p. 7).*

Keywords: domestic workers • family relationships • gangs and gangsters • inner-city life and culture • intraracial relations • sisters

Carter, Charlotte.

The Nanette Series.

Grace Jones look-alike Nanette Hayes is a saxophone player, street musician, and former child prodigy with a degree in French and a minor in music from Wellesley. Occasionally prone to rage, she depends on friend Aubrey, an exotic dancer with business acumen and down-home good sense, to keep her grounded. With its allusions to jazz greats and its gritty depiction of the city, this series immerses the reader in music, urban life, and the dark side of human nature.

> *Please God, if you can't let me forget him or forgive him, then let it feel good when I blow his damn knee-caps off tomorrow. Please God, if I don't find somebody to talk to—be with—tonight, I'm going to pass away from loneliness.* (Rhode Island Red, p. 155)

Notes: Charlotte Carter is also listed in the "Amateur Detectives—Teams" section of this chapter.

Keywords: jazz music and musicians • murder mysteries • New York City • street musicians • women's friendships

Rhode Island Red. New York: Serpent's Tail, 1997. ISBN 1-85242-564-4. 170p.

Nan lets a down-on-his luck street musician crash at her place, but he doesn't survive the night. Finding him in her kitchen the next morning with an ice pick in his throat is only the beginning of a mystery that results in a trail of violence, betrayal, and greed.

Keywords: Charlie "Bird" Parker • police brutality • undercover police

Coq au Vin. New York: Serpent's Tail, 1999. ISBN 1-85242-631-4. 200p.

Nan sets off to Paris to bail free spirit Aunt Viv out of whatever difficulty she's in, but first she has to find her. On the way to tracing Aunt Viv and her one-time lover, Little Rube Haskins, Nan enjoys a torrid but ill-fated love affair and the chance to discover Paris and the jazz scene.

Keywords: blues music and musicians • love affairs • Paris underground

Drumsticks. New York: Mysterious Press, 2000. ISBN 0-89296-679-3. 213p.

A yearbook and voodoo dolls appear to link the shooting of Nan's new-found friend and the deaths of seven young men involved in the rap wars. Voodoo, sweet jazz, badass rap, and murder are a potent quartet that takes Nan's investigation into a prominent family and another doomed love affair.

Keywords: con artists and con games • people with mental illness • rap music and musicians • rap wars • upper class • vengeance

Coleman, Evelyn.

What a Woman's Gotta Do. New York: Simon & Schuster, 1998. ISBN 0-684-83175-9. 319p.

When newspaper reporter Patricia Conely overcomes a lifetime of mistrust and isolation to marry Kenneth Lawson and then is left standing at the altar, her world falls apart. But a visit from the police inquiring about her abandoned and bloody car and a call from the "other" woman pique her curiosity and journalist's instinct. The need for an explanation starts her on a journey that leads her to danger, conspiracy, and salvation.

> There's an old saying that if you love a man, let him go, and if he loves you, he'll come back to you. I say hunt him down and kill him. One thing was sure, I was going to find his trifling ass in order to know exactly why he had picked today of all days to jerk me off. Hell, I'm not that bad. (p. 35)

Keywords: conspiracies • eugenics • journalism and journalists • mad scientists • twins

Edwards, Grace.

The Mali Anderson Series.

Vibrant and independent, Mali Anderson is an ex-cop and graduate student who lives on Striver's Row in Harlem with her musician father and orphaned nephew. When crime strikes close to home, Mali's lack of trust in the police leads her to undertake her own investigations. The vivid portrayals of contemporary Harlem culture—music, fashion, sex, food, even hairstyles—lend an earthy sense of pleasure to this fast-paced series.

> Some folks think beauticians should earn more than a therapist or a guidance counselor. . . . My hair is less than two inches long, and one medium egg in a little shampoo under a hot shower would be sufficient to condition it. And a lot cheaper. But there's something to be said for the timeless ritual that hairdressers have perfected: the laying on of hands. (If I Should Die, p. 85).

Keywords: jazz music and musicians • murder mysteries • Striver's Row • urban life and culture

If I Should Die. New York: Doubleday, 1997. ISBN 0-385-48523-9. 257p.

Erskin Harding, Mali's friend and the tour director of the Harlem-based Uptown Children's Chorus, is murdered while saving a child from attempted kidnapping. Not trusting the police to solve the case, Mali lifts some of Erskin's personal papers from his office and begins her own investigation with the help of the one cop she still trusts. But the closer she gets to the truth, the more danger stalks her and everyone she cares about.

Keywords: drug dealers and dealing • police corruption • racism • sexual harassment

A Toast Before Dying. New York: Bantam Books, 1999. ISBN 0-55357-953-3pa. (reprint edition). 293p.

In the alley of the Half-Moon Bar, popular bartender and former beauty queen Thea Morris' thirty-third birthday ends with a bang—from a murderer's gun. When her friend Kendrick Owen is arrested and a wealthy white woman hires her to investigate, Mali reveals motives and suspects overlooked by disinterested cops.

Notes: BCALA Literary Award Fiction Honor Book 1999

Keywords: bartenders • gossip • police apathy • politics and politicians

No Time to Die. New York: Bantam Books, 2000. ISBN 0-55357-956-8pa. 225p.

Mali helps her friend Claudine celebrate her long overdue divorce from her womanizing, abusive husband. When Claudine is brutally murdered, it seems obvious that her ex-husband is responsible. But another murder puts Mali on the trail of a serial killer and into danger.

Keywords: domestic violence • men and women • serial killers

Do or Die. New York: Doubleday, 2000. ISBN 0-385-49248-0. 256p.

Ozzie plays a mean piano to accompany Dad's bass, but the music goes out of his life when he finds his beloved daughter Star with her throat slashed. Mali has to deal with jealousy and pride to find the murderer and to restore order to her own life.

Notes: Gold Pen Best Award Best Mystery/Thriller Nominee 2001

Keywords: drug dealers and dealing • fathers and daughters • men and women • pimps • prostitutes and prostitution

Edwards, Louis.

N: A Romantic Mystery. New York: A Dutton Book/Penguin Books, 1997. ISBN 0-52594-182-7. 228p.

Aimee Dubois is editor of *New Orleans Weekly*, the local black newspaper. Intrigued by the murder of a young black man, she decides to investigate firsthand. During the course of the investigation, she finds and loses love and follows the trail to a surprising conclusion that strikes perilously close to home. Aimee has the feeling that she is observing herself in a movie, and the novel juxtaposes the removed, artificial third person with the emotional, intimate first person to good effect. Edwards's use of a tortured anagram theme is less successful.

> I just remembered the feeling of magic that would overtake me—that had always overtaken me—when in the presence of coincidence, overwhelmed by the sensation that fate, having distilled certain elements of one's life using both the torch of time and the filter of propinquity, could bring two or even three or four things together perfectly, like

*a bullet and a bull's eye, like the lines of a triangle, like lips
in a kiss, in the process making the four, the three, the two,
one.* (p. 21)

Keywords: black on black crime • drug dealers and dealing • housing projects • journalism and journalists • love affairs • men and women • murder mysteries • suicide • teen pregnancy

Garland, Ardella.

The Georgia Barnett Series.

Chicago-based Georgia Barnett is a dedicated, ambitious, and no-holds-barred broadcast journalist with a blues-singing twin sister, demanding mother, comrade-in-arms cameraman, and sensual policeman lover. Journalistic jargon, broadcast scripts, newsroom politics, workplace realities, and the constant awareness of deadlines and competition combine to create a fast-paced read that addresses important current issues. First-person narrative, heavy on dialect, lends intimacy and immediacy and enhances the contrast between Georgia's private and professional personas. This series is sympathetic in its treatment of the underclass and positive in its approach to overcoming racial discrimination.

*A lead story is hard to lock down. This is especially true for
a black woman reporter. Very often we are underestimated, forced to work the fluffy stories, pimped. I'm not
having it. For me, it's a simple case of pride and prejudice—
to show some pride, you work around the journalistic prejudice.* (Details at Ten, p. 13)

Notes: Ardella Garland is also listed (as Yolanda Joe) in the "Psychological Suspense" section of this chapter, the "Contemporary Life" section of Chapter 9, and the "Sensual" section of Chapter 10.

Keywords: broadcast journalism and journalists

Details at Ten. New York: Simon & Schuster, 2000. ISBN 0-684-87375-3. 207p.

Butter, an appealing six-year-old, witnesses a drive-by shooting and turns up missing after she appears on television. Georgia stays on the story, risking her career, her heart, and her life to rescue the child.

Keywords: anti-police sentiment • family relationships • gangs and gangsters • kidnapping • missing children

Hit Time. New York: Simon & Schuster, 2002. ISBN 0-684-87376-1. 222p.

When the body of wealthy but unscrupulous record producer Fab Weaver is unexpectedly pulled from Lake Michigan during Georgia's coverage of a charity polar bear swim, an easy-pleasy story turns into a major exclusive. Georgia's murder investigation uncovers old scandals and the rich history of Chicago's faded Record Row.

Keywords: murder mysteries • music business

Grimes, Terris McMahan.

Theresa Galloway Series.

Galloway is a strong, competent personnel officer for the California State Department of Environmental Quality in Sacramento. A demanding and feisty mother, who ignores the demands of Theresa's husband, children, and workplace, pulls her into one dangerous situation after another. Grimes adds a dose of reality to the amateur detective story by showing the impact of sleuthing on work and family life.

> *Mother, listen. Four days ago I was held hostage by a man intent on killing someone, who had very few qualms about taking me as well. . . . My husband tells me his business is failing. . . . I have dinner to make, a house to clean, homework to check. Mother, I feel guilty if I sneak twenty minutes for myself. That is the state of my life . . . Then I hung up the phone and threw up in my wastebasket.* (Blood Will Tell, p. 19).

Keywords: family relationships • mothers and daughters • murder mysteries • personnel officers • working mothers

Somebody Else's Child. New York: An Onyx Book/Penguin Books: 1996. ISBN 0-451-18672-9. 262p.

When her mother's neighbor is murdered, Theresa looks for clues among the seemingly harmless geriatric set and the very threatening street thugs. To protect three children and appease her mother, she risks her job and husband to unwrap the mystery of Sister Turner's murder.

Keywords: blackmail • drive-by shootings • drug addiction • husbands and wives • race relations • vengeance

Blood Will Tell. New York: Penguin Books, 1997. ISBN 0-451-40696-6pa. 262p.

Theresa is suspicious of the man who moves in with her mother—especially his claim to be Theresa's long lost (and previously unknown) half-brother. Her relief at his disappearance turns to guilt, then fear, after he is found brutally murdered and her mother seems to be the next target.

Keywords: con artists and con games • workplace politics

Mickelbury, Penny.

The Carole Ann Gibson Series.

Carol Ann (C.A. to friends) Gibson is a brilliant defense attorney and beautiful woman. Tall, slim, and elegant, she has a flair for the dramatic in her professional life and a generous heart in her private moments. Wealthy and newly bereaved, she leaves a highly lucrative but emotionally sterile job with a prestigious law firm to find work to which she can devote her life and considerable talents. Sometimes guilt-ridden by her success and wealth, she often feels alienated from the black community and her own identity. Complex interpersonal relationships and personal growth distinguish this sensitive, emotional series.

> *She felt the familiar stirrings of restlessness and competitiveness. And anger. . . She felt the widow's veil slip away, revealing the lawyer who was one of the best in the business. Today was June 1 and Carole Ann had something worth living for.* (One Must Wait, p. 102)

Notes: Penny Mickelbury is also listed in the "Police Detectives—Women" section of this chapter.

Keywords: attorneys • cultural identity • family relationships • friendships • murder mysteries • racial identity • widows

One Must Wait. New York: Simon & Schuster, 1998. ISBN 0-68483741-2. 252p.

When being successful attorneys means caring more about billable hours and winning cases than justice, criminal attorney Carole Ann and her corporate attorney and soul mate husband Alain decide to resign from their respective firms. After Alain is found dead on a D.C. sidewalk, Carole Ann overcomes her grief and combines legal know-how, persistence, and courage to discover not only his killers, but also herself.

Keywords: environmental pollution • grief • passing • Louisiana • Washington, D.C. • white collar crime

Where to Choose. New York: St. Martin's Paperbacks, 1999. ISBN 0-312-97708-5pa. 239p.

Carol Ann is still grieving for her husband when she returns to Los Angeles to defend her mother and her feisty geriatric friends from the recent wave of violence visited on idyllic Jacaranda Estates, a long-term, previously successful experiment in ethnically mixed neighborhoods. She discovers the long-buried secrets that have led to modern crime and in so doing discovers the healing powers and true meaning of home.

Keywords: martial arts • race relations • smuggling • undocumented workers • utopian communities

The Step Between. New York: Simon & Schuster, 2000. ISBN 0-684-85990-4. 236p.

A missing daughter, wealthy father, interlocking corporations, and greed lead to a series of baffling events, including murder and a kidnapping. Carole Ann and Jake must overcome their individual fears to solve the equation, in which Gibson Graham International appears to be the only common denominator.

Notes: Gold Pen Best Award Best Mystery/Thriller Nominee 2000

Keywords: absentee parents • corporate intrigue • cybercrime • kidnapping • missing persons

Paradise Interrupted. New York: Simon & Schuster, 2001. ISBN 0-684-85991-2. 286p.

Gibson Graham International, the newly formed "investigative services" firm co-owned by C.A. and crusty ex-policeman Jake Graham, has taken on the challenging but exciting prospect of guiding the development of the entire infrastructure—governmental, physical, and technical—of Caribbean Isle de Paix. But Philippe Collette, the new president who staged the coup that overthrew the communist government, is not being completely forthcoming, and C.A. must discover why.

Keywords: Caribbean nations • developing nations • drug dealers and dealing • drug enforcement agencies • politics and politicians • undercover police

Neely, Barbara.

The Blanche White Series.

Blanche White, domestic, cook, and amateur sleuth, shares her wry observations and no-nonsense outlook on life. She has little patience for African Americans who emulate whites instead of taking pride in themselves and their heritage, and she is contemptuous of the wealthy, selfish, hurtful, and careless, regardless of their color. Blanche is an ancestor worshipper, and the importance of family and community permeates these novels. Blanche is drawn into a series of murder investigations and must use her innate shrewdness and natural nosiness to bring evil-doers to justice while coping with rearing two children (her widowed sisters'), maintaining a loving (but sometimes irritating) relationship with her mother, and trying to make ends meet. Through it all, she maintains her sense of self and her zest for life. As Blanche observes: "Life might not be fair, but it sure as hell could be satisfying." This satisfying series is fast-paced and, at times, humorous.

> *She realized how small a part her complexion played in what it meant to her to be black.* (Blanche Among the Talented Tenth, p. 20)

Keywords: class relations • domestic workers • employers and employees • murder mysteries • race relations • working poor

 Blanche on the Lam. New York: St. Martin's Press, 1992. ISBN 0-312-06908-1. 180p.

Blanche hires on with a wealthy white Southern family to escape a jail sentence and ends up solving a murder to avenge a friend. She finds it difficult to keep her emotional distance from a mentally challenged but sensitive and insightful young employer.

Notes: Agatha Award Best First Novel 1993; Anthony Award Best First Novel 1993; Macavity Award Best First Mystery Novel 1993

Keywords: people with disabilities • rural North Carolina • small-town life and culture

🏵 ***Blanche Among the Talented Tenth***. New York: Penguin Books, 1995. ISBN 014-025036-0pa. 232p.

Blanche goes to Amber Cove, an exclusive all-black resort in Maine, to spend time with her children, and finds herself face to face with "light-bright" snobbery, old money, color bias—and treachery.

Notes: Blackboard Bestseller List 1996

Keywords: intraracial relations • racial identity • resort-town life and culture • skin color • upper class

🏵 ***Blanche Cleans Up***. New York: Penguin Books, 1998. ISBN 0-140-27747-1. 306p.

At the behest of Cousin Charlotte, Blanche substitutes for Ms. Inez as cook and housekeeper for a wealthy gubernatorial candidate with an unhappy family and a lot to hide.

Notes: Blackboard Bestseller List 1998

Keywords: church men • environmental pollution • intraracial relations • political corruption • sexual deviance • teen pregnancy

Blanche Passes Go. New York: Viking, 2000. ISBN 0-67089-165-7pa. 275p.

Blanche's vendetta against the leading family of her hometown is justified. David Palmer, who went unpunished when Blanche failed to report his raping her years before, may be implicated in the death of an abused woman. David's unscrupulous sister is engaged to Mumfield, a wealthy, sensitive, and mentally challenged young man for whom Blanche has a deep affection. But is Blanche's desire for vengeance blinding her to the truth?

Keywords: men and women • rape • sexism • small-town life and culture • vengeance

Police Detectives—Men

Holton, Hugh.

The Larry Cole Series.

Chief of detectives for the Chicago Police Department, Larry Cole is a smart, thoughtful, honest cop in a world filled with criminals, self-serving politicians, and victims. Criminals tend to be drawn larger than life, supernatural elements are included, and the battles between good and evil sometimes take on epic proportions in Holton's novels. The impact of crime and the nature of evil are drawn effectively but without use of graphic violence or language. Loyal friends and dedicated officers Lieutenant Blackie Silvestri and Sergeant Judy Daniels (a.k.a. The Mistress of Disguise) and love interest journalist Kate Ford are recurring characters who bring out the human and vulnerable side of Cole.

> *With the frozen snow crunching beneath its tires, the hearse pulled to a stop at the curb directly in front of Larry Cole. No movement was visible inside, nor were the windows lowered or any of the doors opened. Finally, Cole*

stepped forward and opened the door. As if he were descending into Hell, he got into the hearse. (Time of the Assassins, p. 358)

Keywords: murder mysteries • politics and politicians

Windy City. New York: A Forge Book/A Tom Doherty Associates Book, 1995. ISBN 0-812-56714-5pa. 310p.

Margo and Neil DeWitt are just two fun-loving, super-rich people whose hobby is murdering women and children using methods learned from mystery novels. Cole sees the pattern while investigating the death of another officer.

Keywords: copycat killings • serial killers • undercover police

Chicago Blues. New York: A Forge Book/A Tom Doherty Associates Book, 1995. ISBN 0-812-54464-1. 373p.

Mob boss Tony DeLisa "was many things: gambler, father, and successful businessman" and he was ruthless and abusive in each of those roles. But his contract on a crusading politician and his brutal parenting style are about to catch up with him.

Keywords: child abuse • fathers and daughters • gangs and gangsters

Violent Crimes. New York: A Forge Book/A Tom Doherty Associates Book, 1997. ISBN 0312862814. 383p.

Martin Zykus, the confessed multiple murderer who 15 years earlier was apprehended by Commander Larry Cole and Sergeant Blackie Silvestri on numerous occasions but always released, is now millionaire Steven Zalkin. Still a psychopath, he is determined to wreak vengeance on all those who failed to offer him the proper respect years earlier, but this time he has far greater resources and an arsenal at his disposal.

Keywords: political corruption • serial killers • vengeance

Red Lightning. New York: A Forge Book/A Tom Doherty Associates Book, 1998. ISBN 0-312-86687-9. 319p.

Mysticism and a classic battle between good and evil permeate this case of murder, political corruption, and evil genius.

Keywords: mad scientists • Native American mythology • political corruption • supernatural

The Left Hand of God. New York: A Forge Book/A Tom Doherty Associates Book, 1999. ISBN 0-312-86763-8. 384p.

The final scenes in a local political fixer's scheme, the mob's play for power, a mysterious Institute's plan to control the world, and beautiful Orga Syriac's secret quest all come together in Chicago, with Cole and Kate playing pivotal roles.

Keywords: Abo-Yorba • conspiracies • gangs and gangsters • political corruption • shapeshifting • she-devils • supernatural

Time of the Assassins. New York: A Forge Book/A Tom Doherty Associates Book, 2000. ISBN 0-312-87333-6. 383p.

Cole, in the wrong place at the wrong time, has twice inadvertently foiled the well-laid plans of hit man Baron von Rianocek; consequently he becomes the next target. But is Rianocek really in the employ of powerful drug lords, or could the CIA actually be funding crack distribution in U.S. ghettos?

Keywords: CIA conspiracy • drug dealers and dealing • international intrigue • professional assassins • undercover police

The Devil's Shadow. New York: A Forge Book/A Tom Doherty Associates Book, 2001. ISBN 0-312-87784-6. 382p.

Beautiful Julianna Saint, L'Ombre du Diable (The Devil's Shadow), is a daring, clever professional thief for hire. Cole is in danger of losing his professional distance as he duels with the provocative Juliana, who is under contract to steal a film for a Mafia boss and blood for a bishop.

Keywords: bank robberies • mystery writers • professional thieves • voodoo

Criminal Element. New York: St Martin's Press, 2002. ISBN 0312877870. 511p.

A mishap in which alderman Skip Murphy kills his sexual partner turns him to a life of crime and a partnership with Joe Donegan, a corrupt detective in the violent crimes unit. Cole and Silvestri are hard-pressed to apprehend the two, who embark on a series of crimes including arson, murder, and political assassination.

Keywords: police corruption • political assassins • political corruption • sexual deviance

Olden, Marc.

The Manny Decker Series.

Marc Olden, Vietnam veteran and NYPD detective sergeant, employs martial arts and philosophy in a series of cases that pit him against international criminals. Fighting criminals of cunning, brutality, and sadism, Manny Decker is a modern-day knight grounded in the ancient arts. Fast-moving action, a personal code of ethics, and graphic descriptions of sex and violence are the hallmarks of Olden's work.

> *Dazed and breathless, Decker moved his arms a bit. Then his legs and hips. Everything was still attached. He felt his balls rub against the floor, meaning he hadn't lost his dick, which was the first thing you thought about in firefights and explosions. (Kisaeng, p.77)*

Notes: Marc Olden is also listed in the "Horror—Supernatural" section of Chapter 11.

Keywords: international intrigue • martial arts • oriental philosophy and religion • Vietnam War impact

Giri. New York: Jove Books/Berkley Publishing, 1982. ISBN 0-515-10048-Xpa. 338p.

Giri, the principle of obligation, loyalty, and duty, is woven through the multiple plots of organized crime, brutal rape murders, and personal vengeance. International intrigue is played out against a backdrop of martial arts and oriental philosophy.

Keywords: organized crime • psychopathic killers • serial killers • vengeance

Kisaeng. New York: Zebra Books/Kensington Publishing, 1991. ISBN 0-8217-3897-6. 415p.

Gail DaSilva, a former lover, wants Detective Sergeant Manny Decker to find her only child, a beautiful teenager who has gone missing. The case brings an old enemy and an old love back into his life, as Manny finds himself caught up in a complex case that involves forgery, money laundering, political intrigue, and depravity.

Keywords: child prostitution • counterfeit money • drug dealers and dealing • kidnapping • political intrigue • sexual deviance • slave trade

Olden, Marc.

Fear's Justice. New York: Villard Books/Random House, 1996. ISBN 0679448381. 317p.

Fear Meagher, Queens police detective, will tell anyone he doesn't like minorities, women, or gays. But Fear has taken on crooked white cops on behalf of a black woman, and the love of his life is Jewish detective Lynda Schiafino. Carlyle Taylor, an African American woman journalist, has sworn to get Fear dismissed as a racist. But when the woman Fear loves is murdered, these two join forces to uncover the murderer and both learn to see below the surface.

> Black women are a problem for cops. They're not shy about mouthing off, and they know their rights. An angry black woman can leave a cop feeling like a horse's ass. She can abuse you to her heart's content and you can't do a thing about it. Not unless you want to look like a trigger happy bigot whose only delight is beating the shit out of innocent citizens like herself. (p. 38)

Keywords: conspiracies • fathers and sons • journalism and journalists • police corruption • race relations

Police Detectives—Teams

Bland, Eleanor Taylor.

The Marti MacAlister (and Vik Jessenovik) Series.

Competent and confident, Marti Macalister is a homicide detective with the Lincoln Prairie, Illinois, police department, a welcome change from her former stint with the Chicago PD. Marti lives in a fully integrated world, in which she is a professional and solidly middle class. People respect her, and she respects them. Although aware of racism and its effects, she deals with it calmly and optimistically. A widowed mother of two, she receives support and advice from her roommate as her children work through conflicts of black cultural identity. Vik Jessenovik, a grouchy white sexist male who nevertheless likes and respects Marti, is a three-dimensional character who has difficulty coping with his beloved wife's multiple sclerosis. Together, Marti and Vik solve crimes that take them into contact with all races and classes. This fast-paced police procedural series is well-plotted, and the characters change and grow throughout the series.

> *Gladys gave Marti a stern look as if reprimanding her for being sassy, or maybe just reminding her that they were both black and had both been raised to be deferential to older folk. Marti shrugged off the emotional response that suggested that Gladys was right.* (Gone Quiet, p. 39)

Keywords: childrearing • cultural identity • friendships • murder mysteries • single parents • widows

Dead Time. New York: St. Martin's Press, 1992. ISBN 0-312-97719-0pa. 211p.

Solving the seemingly motiveless murder of a mentally ill woman in a rundown residence hotel falls to Marti and Vik, whose commitment to solving the case is deepened when it becomes clear that the murderer is determined to eliminate the two young boys who witnessed the crime. With unreliable witnesses and a motive buried deep in the past, Marti and Vik have their work cut out for them.

Keywords: Chicago, Illinois • inner-city life and culture • poor people

Slow Burn. New York: St. Martin's Press/Signet/NAL, 1994. ISBN 0451179447pa. 320p.

The discovery of an unidentified young black girl's body in a burned-out inner-city clinic starts Marti Macalister on an investigation that brings her into contact with all segments of society, from pimps and prostitutes to wealthy doctors, where she uncovers violence, exploitation, and fraud.

Keywords: anti-abortionists • arson • child abuse • child prostitution • inner-city life and culture

Gone Quiet. New York: St. Martin's Press, 1994. ISBN 0-312-11018-9. 214p.

The investigation into Henry Hamilton's death reveals that the upright church deacon was a domestic tyrant—and worse. Marti and Vik work to bring a murderer to justice, even though their sympathies lie more with the suspects than with the victim.

Keywords: child abuse • church life • church men • domestic violence • pedophilia • psychological abuse • spirituality and spiritual life

Done Wrong. New York: St. Martin's Press, 1995. ISBN 0-312-95794-7pa. 216p.

Two widows, two dead undercover narcotics agents, two official suicide verdicts. The death of another undercover policeman under circumstances similar to that of her husband Johnny three years earlier prompts Marti to return to Chicago to find out the truth.

Keywords: police corruption • racism • suicide • undercover police

Keep Still. New York: St. Martin's Press, 1996. ISBN 0-312-14318-4. 216p.

An elderly widow falls down her basement steps; a teacher's aide drowns. Marti and Vic find an unexpected link: a young schoolgirl returned to her abusive family and her disappearance eight years earlier. Who is next on the killer's list?

Keywords: child abuse • dysfunctional families • serial killers

See No Evil. New York: St. Martin's Press, 1998. ISBN 0-312-16910-8. 274p.

Marti and Vic have a full blotter this Halloween week: a young woman from Chicago drowns, a street corner snitch's friend disappears, a young man is intent on becoming a gang member, and the pumpkin suit flasher is on the prowl again. Things at home are tough too: a teacher is attempting to separate her son from his best friend, her daughter is learning to cope with her sexuality, and her roommate is once again embroiled in a disastrous love affair. Marti is so distracted that she doesn't realize that her family is the target of a deranged stalker.

Notes: BCALA Literary Award Fiction Honor Book 1999

Keywords: flashers • homeless people • men and women • stalkers

Tell No Tales. New York: St. Martin's Press, 1999. ISBN 0312200676. 264p.

The murder of the estranged, mentally ill son of a wealthy Chicago family cuts short Marti's honeymoon and calls Vic away from caring for his wife, who has multiple sclerosis. A mummy is discovered in a long defunct and boarded-up theater. Marti and Vic's working relationship and friendship are strained by the demanding effort of solving the two cases while dealing with personal adjustments at home.

Keywords: blended families • caregivers • politics and politicians • prejudice

Scream in Silence. New York: St. Martin's Minotaur, 2000. ISBN 0-312-20378-0. 290p.

Arson, two bombings, and the death of Vik's one-time and much disliked classmate bring big-city crime to idyllic Lincoln Prairie. Marti, who'd rather be honeymooning with new husband Ben, and Vik, who'd rather be home with his beloved and ailing wife, are under pressure to clear up the case—or cases.

Notes: Gold Pen Best Award Best Mystery/Thriller Nominee 2001

Keywords: arson • bombings • domestic violence

Whispers in the Dark. New York: St. Martin's Minotaur, 2001. ISBN 0-312-20379-9. 244p.

A severed hand protruding from the ground starts Marti and Vic on a trail of murder that spans 20 years and leads them to trouble in the elitist and secretive artist's community. At the same time, Marti's concern that her roommate Sharon is neglecting her daughter becomes secondary when their lives are endangered.

Notes: Gold Pen Best Mystery/Thriller Award 2002

Keywords: artist communities • Bahamas • Chicago, Illinois • mothers and daughters • psychological abuse • urban life and culture

Windy City Dying. New York: St. Martin's Minotaur, 2002. ISBN 0-312-30098-0. 324p.

Marti's past becomes her present when a mysterious stranger arrives looking for her deceased husband Johnny and she revisits a group of troubled children for whom she had previously served as counselor. Marti senses a connection between the two events, and her sense of foreboding compels her to act to ensure a more promising future for the children—and herself.

Keywords: at-risk children

Fatal Remains. New York: St. Martin's Minotaur, 2003. ISBN 0-312-30097-2. 272p.

The skeleton of an unidentified young Native American man is uncovered. A young archaeology student, hired to look for artifacts on private land, suffers a fatal accident, followed in quick succession by the family handyman and the family patriarch. Is it all just part of the wealthy family's history of bad luck and fatal accidents, is it a plot to ensure that a lucrative deal is made, or have spirits from the past found their revenge? Especially interesting are the historical and supernatural elements.

Keywords: genealogy • Native American history • real estate developers • slave trade

Hardwick, Gary.

The Justice (Danny Cavanaugh and Marshall Jackson) Series.

Hardwick ponders the meaning of being "black" or "white" in his Justice series, featuring Marshall Jackson and Danny Cavanaugh. Marshall and Danny are "the Swirl," black and white best friends and closer than brothers. Danny was the only white kid raised in a tough urban neighborhood and in many ways identifies with the black community. His language, attitude, and police partner/girlfriend Vinny are all African American inner city. His checkered past includes charges of using excessive force, and his inability to control his anger means he may never follow in his father's footsteps to become a police detective. Marshall Jackson is the good half of a set of fraternal twins, the young man who escaped the perils of inner-city life to become a federal assistant attorney general noted for his astute handling of cases and sense of justice. "In a world dominated by stereotypes, they were a paradox: the white man was black, and the black man was white" (*Supreme Justice*, p. 58). These are thoughtful explorations and fast-paced stories. The dialogue is casually profane, and descriptions of violence are detailed.

> *Danny didn't think a guy like Gordon could understand how black people took their pain and pushed it into a deep place where it stayed just behind every thought, perception, hope, and fear . . . And there in the bosom of your deepest humanity, it became a fire, a power that propelled you over the obstacles of life and allowed you to find peace and joy even as you suffered.* (Color of Justice, p. 31)

Keywords: class relations • intraracial relations • men and women • race relations • workplace politics

Color of Justice: A Novel of Suspense. New York: Morrow, 2002. ISBN 0-688-16514-1 (acid-free paper). 289p.

Someone is brutally torturing and murdering the black elite of Detroit. Cavanaugh is assigned to the case, but the racial overtones and sheer barbarity may prove too much for him to handle. As he continues his investigation, he makes enemies and uncovers secrets that may destroy him both professionally and personally.

Notes: Gold Pen Award Best Mystery/Thriller Nominee 2002

Keywords: hate crimes • serial killers

Supreme Justice: A Novel of Suspense. New York: Morrow, 1999. ISBN 0-688-16513-3. 356p.

Associate justice of the United States Supreme Court, Farrel Douglas is almost universally hated in the black community as a turncoat for his conservative political philosophy and decisions that undermine previous gains in the civil rights arena. When he is assassinated, Marshall Jackson is given the plum assignment that can mean rapid career advancement— or his own death.

Keywords: husbands and wives • judges • police brutality • political corruption • professional assassins

Smith-Levin, Judith.

The Starletta Duvall (and Dominic Parisi) Series.

Starletta Duvall is a tough, black, beautiful woman and a police lieutenant. She is independent and strong, yet cherishes the support and friendship of best friend Vee (Verenita Gloria Spencer-Martin) and hunky partner Dominic Parisi. An obviously successful professional, her personal life is less settled, and she is forced to examine her motives, career, and life choices. Attractive (white) Chief Medical Examiner Grant Mitchell only adds to her confusion. Starletta's complexity and vulnerability are revealed as she and Vee exchange confidences and opinions on everything from food to children, from the problems with black men and white women to interracial dating. The clever banter among the wise guy cops is entertaining. Sexual encounters are described fairly explicitly; descriptions of bodies and crime scenes are detailed and graphic.

> *The women walked in her dreams, calling her, beckoning her . . . The closer she moved, the farther away they floated, until she suddenly found herself surrounded by the three of them. They moved closer, and she could smell death. As they became clear in her vision, she started screaming. All three of them had her face.* (Do Not Go Gently, p. 127)

Keywords: friendships • interracial relationships • Los Angeles, California • murder mysteries • police procedurals • sexual harassment • widows

Do Not Go Gently. New York: Harper Paperbacks/HarperCollins Publishers, 1996. ISBN 0-06-101109-6pa. 285p.

Starletta is pushed to the edge when she becomes personally involved in a series of brutal rape homicides. The victims are all beautiful, successful black women—and Starletta fits the profile.

Keywords: hate crimes • rape • serial killers • vengeance

The Hoodoo Man. New York: Ballantine Books, 1998. ISBN 0345420659pa. 276p.

Contrary to popular opinion, voodoo priest Desmond St. John wasn't immortal. It's up to Starletta to find out who proved it by using six bullet holes to make a perfect cross in his body.

Keywords: voodoo • workplace politics

Green Money. New York: Fawcett/Ballantine Publishing, 2000. ISBN 0-345-42084-5pa. 278p.

Is a popular and bloody fantasy game a blueprint for rich young sociopaths? Star and Parisi must interpret the clues from three bizarre murders to find the true killers before the game escalates.

Keywords: fantasy games • homeless people • juvenile offenders • parents and children • prep schools

Police Detectives—Women

Darden, Christopher, and Dick Lochte.
The Nikki Hill Series.

Nicolette Hill is beautiful, black, and on the verge of burnout as a result of her work as an assistant district attorney in Los Angeles's dysfunctional justice system. Although Nikki is sometimes emotionally vulnerable, her personal weaknesses only serve to underscore her independence and commitment to justice in the face of all odds. Darden, a member of the O.J. Simpson prosecuting team, and Lochte depict the legal system with knowledge (and cynicism) based on experience, portraying people on both sides of the law with balance and accuracy. They know the politics, the bureaucracy, and the principles. They know how the system should work, how it sometimes fails, and how it often succeeds in spite of itself.

> She hadn't quite finished her coffee or the paper when Virgil arrived, in desperate need of a woman's touch after a weary and depressing night on duty. There went her schedule. There went her good intentions. There went her violet robe. (L.A. Justice, p. 27)

Keywords: criminal justice system • district attorneys • Los Angeles, California • murder mysteries • workplace politics

The Trials of Nikki Hill. New York: Warner Books, 1999 ISBN 0446523267. 434p.

When the victim of a murder is a white television talk show host with a penchant for blackmail and all of the suspects in the case are African American, Nikki Hill is the perfect addition to the prosecution team—black, female, and beautiful. She and her support team, including detective Ed Goodman, must contend with highly visible and well-placed suspects, street hoodlums, the inevitable highly paid team of sleazy defense lawyers, and police corruption.

Keywords: blackmail • entertainment industry • music business • police corruption • race relations • television talk shows

L.A. Justice. New York: Warner Books, 2000. ISBN 0-446-52327-5. 434p.

Detectives Virgil Sykes and Dan McNeil are called out to investigate a murder in one of Los Angeles's old money suburbs, where they find a staged suicide and a precocious 10-year-old witness who points directly to the victim's wealthy and influential fiancée. Do a hooker's oral diary, corrupt police officials, and high-level criminals play a part? When deputy district attorney Nikki Hill is assigned to the case, she and Sykes find time for enjoying their love life, uncovering the truth, coping with office politics, and caring for old colleagues.

Keywords: organized crime • police corruption • prostitutes and prostitution

Mickelbury, Penny.

The Gianna Maglione and Mimi Patterson Series.

Lieutenant Gianna Maglione is beautiful, Italian, and head of the Washington, D.C., Hate Crimes Unit. Strong and competent, she is nevertheless sensitive to the needs of people who are victimized because of their culture or beliefs and never becomes hardened to the constant evidence of people's inhumanity to each other. Complex sociological questions of justice, intellectual freedom, and the relationship of the police and the press in a democratic society are explored through Gianna's personal relationship with Montgomery (Mimi) Patterson, a beautiful black journalist. This is an emotional and sensitively written series that is explicit in its description of the lesbian relationship of the main characters.

> *The moon hung high and luminous in the inky sky. Gun-shots vibrated, dogs howled, sirens split the air. Life and death, love and hate, beauty and evil—all danced to the songs of the night as another April night in the Nation's cap-ital ticked its way into memory.* (Night Songs, p. 6)

Notes: Penny Mickelbury is also listed in the "Amateur Detectives—Female" section of this chapter.

Keywords: hate crimes • journalism and journalists • lesbian relationships • murder mysteries • ritual killings

Keeping Secrets. Tallahassee, Fla.: The Naiad Press, 1994. ISBN 1-56280-052-3.189p.

Gianna and Mimi meet and become involved, starting a rocky relationship that suffers as each covers the same event from her own professional perspective. Four wealthy professional, in-the-closet gay people have been murdered—all in the same heinous way. Gianna must preserve the integrity of the investigation by guarding the nature of the victims and the murder method, while Mimi is driven by the public's right to know.

Keywords: gay men • serial killers • vengeance

Night Songs. Tallahassee, Fla.: The Naiad Press, 1995. ISBN 1-56280-097-3pa. 217p.

Four hookers have been found murdered—all by a thrown hunting knife. Gianna struggles not only to find a brutal murderer but to force her administration to recognize that crimes against women should be recognized as hate crimes. The perpetrator(s) turn out to be more cold-hearted than even Gianna expected.

Keywords: hate crimes • serial killers • sociopaths

Love Notes: A Mimi Patterson/Gianna Maglione Mystery. Los Angeles: migibooks, 2001. ISBN 0971422206. 193p.

Beating the local drug dealers to a cache of illegal weapons may be the only way Gianna can save her Special Crimes Unit from being disbanded. More subtle and closer to home is the Jane Doe case Mimi stumbles across and which Gianna discovers is only one case in a larger pattern. Older lesbian women are being lured to D.C. by a chatroom lover, only to be murdered and warehoused in the morgue as Jane Does. Mimi tries to understand why beautiful, talented, mature women respond to the bait, but Gianna has only one goal: to catch the killer before another woman responds to the e-mail love notes.

Keywords: cybercrime • dating • drug dealers and dealing

Olden, Mark.

The Ghost. **New York: Simon & Schuster, 1999 (1998). ISBN 0-684-83467-7. 313p.**

Rosalind "Ross" Magellan is a smart and beautiful undercover cop addicted to the adrenalin rush of bringing down the bad guys. Burnout veteran sergeant Harry Earless, who is assigned as her "ghost"—the backup who is there in case anything goes sour—is secretly and obsessively in love with her. A five-person team, with Ross in a sensitive and dangerous role, is working on a case to bring a crooked judge to justice when someone declares open season on undercover lady cops. Even the good guys have secrets to hide, and in the end it may be hard to tell which side is which. Olden tells a brutal, dark story with energy, ironic overtones, and realistic use of police jargon.

> *Ross smiled at the fireflies outside the window. Muscle meant nothing in undercover work, whereas the ability to talk, particularly the ability to talk your way out of trouble, meant everything. Undercover work was about being an actress, about playing with a perp's head and manipulating people. She loved it.* (p. 20)

Notes: BCALA Literary Award Fiction Honor Book 2000

Keywords: child abuse • drug dealers and dealing • murder mysteries • political corruption • stalkers • undercover police • vengeance

Woods, Paula L.

The Charlotte Justice Series.

A strong yet vulnerable woman, Charlotte Justice joined the Los Angeles Police Department after the drive-by shooting of her husband and infant daughter. Years later, a homicide detective and the first woman in the LAPD's elite Robbery and Homicide Division, she still faces sexual harassment, racial bias, and family resistance as she solves murders and works for justice. Woods provides a realistic, gritty picture, but one not without hope. Charlotte's sometimes annoying but always loving, supportive, and vocal family, provides relief from the violent and corrupt world in which she lives her professional life.

> *My Grandmama Cile says I'm just like every other black woman she knows—trying to keep the solar system in order by juggling the planets herself.* (Inner City Blues, p. 38).

Keywords: family relationships • hostile work environment • murder mysteries • sexism • sexual harassment • widows • workplace politics

Inner City Blues. New York: W. W. Norton, 1999. ISBN 0-393-04680-X. 316p.

In the midst of widespread rioting, Charlotte protects a black doctor from overzealous police, only later to find him implicated in the murder of the drug dealer who destroyed her family. When Dr. Mitchell turns up dead, the plot becomes even more complex.

Notes: Anthony Award Best First Mystery Novel Nominee 2000; BCALA Literary Award First Novelist 2000; Gold Pen Best Award Best Mystery/Thriller Nominee 2000; Macavity Award Best First Mystery Novel 2000

Keywords: gangs and gangsters • inner-city life and culture • police brutality • racism • race riots

Stormy Weather. New York: W. W. Norton, 2001. ISBN 0-393-02021-5. 299p.

When the pioneering filmmaker's cause of death changes from cancer to murder, Charlotte has her own reasons for finding out the truth about Maynard Duncan's death. She uncovers professional and personal secrets, a "killer angel," chinks in an already solved case, and police corruption.

Keywords: euthanasia • films and filmmakers • police corruption

Dirty Laundry. New York: Ballantine Books, 2003. ISBN 0-345-45700-5. 264p.

On her first case back after an extended suspension, Charlotte is given a political hot potato. A young Korean woman, political consultant to an Hispanic mayoral candidate, is found brutally murdered. Charlotte, distracted by romantic and family tensions, must step carefully as classes and cultures clash and her investigation uncovers dirty tricks and corruption.

Keywords: political campaigns • race relations

Private Investigators—Men

Haywood, Gar Anthony.

The Aaron Gunner Series.

Reflective and introspective, Aaron Gunner is the classic reluctant hard-boiled private eye. Always on the verge of losing his private investigator's license, rarely financially secure enough to turn down unpleasant jobs, he wrestles with his career decision and questions his ability to do the job well. In true PI fashion, Gunner shows us the seamier side of the city and of ourselves. Haywood's work is dark, teetering on the edge of hopelessness and despair, but lifted by the very personal moral code of his character. The strong sense of place and community are drawn through descriptions of Mickey Moore's Trueblood Barbershop, where Gunner keeps his office, the Acey-Deuce Bar, and neighborhood institutions he frequents and shares with other regulars. The stories are well plotted, often with an unexpected twist, and the endings are surprising yet inevitable.

> *Sleep was what he needed most, but sleep was where her memory found him most vulnerable. . . . He heard her laugh a thousand times, and felt her body rocking beneath him over and over again. All he had to do was close his eyes, and she was there. But she wasn't real. She was dead, and there was nothing he could do about it.* (It's Not a Pretty Sight, p. 38)

Notes: Gar Anthony Haywood is also listed in the "Amateur Detectives—Teams" section of this chapter.

Keywords: Acey-Deuce Bar • hard-boiled private eyes • Los Angeles, California • murder mysteries • Trueblood Barbershop

Fear of the Dark. New York: St. Martin's Press, 1988. ISBN 0-312-01796-0. 185p.

Were Buddy Dorris, a guiding light in the black revolutionary Brothers of Volition, and J.T., the Acey Deucy's owner, random victims of a white supremacist's violent bid for attention, or were they the intentional targets of a carefully planned murder for hire? Gunner is forced at gunpoint to take the case by Buddy's sister, "a spiteful little girl with serpent's eyes and an angel's face"—and a body to match.

Notes: Shamus Award Best First Private-Eye Novel 1987; St. Martin's Press/PWA Best First Private-Eye Novel 1987

Keywords: blackmail • gangs and gangsters • illegal weapons • political radicals • politics and politicians • race relations

Not Long for This World. New York: St. Martin's Press, 1990. ISBN 0-312-04398-8. 260p.

Darryl Lovejoy, quixotic founder of a group to combat ghetto violence, is killed in a drive-by shooting, and Gunner reluctantly undertakes an investigation to clear the obvious—perhaps too obvious?—suspect, gangbanger Toby Mills.

Keywords: church men • evangelical churches • gangs and gangsters • political activism and activists • urban violence

You Can Die Trying. New York: St. Martin's Press, 1993; New York: Penguin Books, 1994. ISBN 0-312-09425-6pa. 216p.

No one seems very upset when Jack McGovern, former L.A. cop, blows his brains out—until a previously silent witness hires Gunner to look into the case that got the bigoted, abusive McGovern fired. Why would an upstanding black citizen pay his own money to clear McGovern's name?

Keywords: internal affairs investigations • police corruption • police relations • political activism and activists

It's Not a Pretty Sight. New York: Putnam, 1996. ISBN 0-399-14132-4. 230p.

The pervasiveness and complexity of wife abuse in the African American community creates the somber backdrop for Gunner's investigation of the murder of Nina Pearson, the woman he should have married. After he critically wounds Nina's abusive and unfaithful husband, Gunner recognizes that he may have put the wrong man in the hospital.

Keywords: domestic violence • men and women • women's shelters

When Last Seen Alive. New York: Putnam, 1998. ISBN 0-399-14303-3. 223p.

Months after Elroy Covington fails to return from the Million Man March, Gunner reluctantly picks up the cold trail, only to be caught in a tug-of-war between Covington's beautiful sister, the radical Defenders of the Bloodline, and the FBI.

Keywords: journalism and journalists • political radicals

All the Lucky Ones Are Dead. New York: Putnam, 1999. ISBN 0-399-14540-0pa. 232p.

Did millionaire gangsta rapper C.E. Digga Jones commit suicide, or was he murdered? Who's threatening ultraconservative talk show host Sparkle Johnson? Are the two cases linked? Aaron Gunner untangles the threads to their unexpected and chilling conclusion.

Keywords: cultural identity • family relationships • music business • personal identity • rap music and musicians • suicide

Meadows, Lee E.

The Lincoln Keller Series.

Lee Meadows introduces a soft-boiled private eye in the modern tradition. Introspective and literate, his Lincoln Keller is an ex-Raider, former Oakland cop with strong ties to his brothers and their families and ongoing woman problems with the love of his life, Detroit homicide detective Candy Malone. The son of a mother with a penchant for presidents (his brothers are Jefferson, Roosevelt, and Truman), Linc is sometimes wise-cracker ("Hi, Mr. Keller. How goes the dick business?" "Mostly up and down."), sometimes tough guy, but always protector of the innocent and defender of justice.

> *Endless hours staking out a motel, pictures of rendezvous, illegally recorded conversations, and peeping through keyholes for that one conclusive fact. I don't complain. Most of what I do sends me down the darker, seduced side of the human experience. But, hell—it's all billable.* (Silent Conspiracy, p. 1)

Keywords: brothers • football players

Silent Conspiracy. Ann Arbor, Mich.: Proctor Publications of Ann Arbor, 1996. ISBN 1-882792-38-6. 273p.

Acting on her husband's behalf, but without his knowledge, the beautiful and bewitching Erotica Tremaine hires Linc to find The Sentiments, a group of five musicians who vanished without a trace 40 years earlier. The search brings Linc into contact with musical nostalgia and a cast of intriguing characters, but he must sort through various motives—jealous passion, virulent McCarthyism, and institutionalized racial prejudice—to find the real reason for the group's disappearance.

Keywords: McCarthyism • music business • OSI (Office of Strategic Intelligence) • racism

Silent Suspicion: A Lincoln Keller Mystery. Ann Arbor, Mich.: Proctor Publications, LLC, 2000. ISBN 1-882792-93-9. 417p.

Linc is persuaded by Judge "War" Zone to look into the unsolved and seemingly random street killing of his sister-in-law Deborah Norris, a dedicated journalist with "eyes that would draw a confession from the Pope." Death threats, political intrigue, upper-class scandal, and police resistance to private citizens taking on unresolved homicides all make Linc more determined to find the true reason for the murder that wasn't random at all.

Keywords: journalism and journalists • politics and politicians • power brokers • unresolved murders

Mosley, Walter.

The Easy Rawlins Series.

Mosley's Easy Rawlins novels are each set in a particular time and place, and the descriptions of prevailing black culture and race relations in Los Angeles clearly reflect these. In many ways, Rawlins is the quintessential private eye, moving from amateur to professional status, engaged only reluctantly, at odds with the justice system, but not with justice. He is unique, however, in that he is extraordinarily sensitive to the weak and helpless and has two adopted children to care for. The recurring figure of Mouse, Easy's longtime, ruthless, and violently unpredictable best friend, serves as a foil, representing the darker side of Easy's own personality and his community. The evolution of Rawlins and the society he reflects is masterfully handled, and Mosley's descriptions are evocative, his approach to history is reflective, and his stories are well-plotted.

> Southeast L.A. was palm trees and poverty; neat little lawns tended by the descendents of ex-slaves and massacred Indians. It was beautiful and wild; a place that was almost a nation, populated by lost peoples that were never talked about in the newspapers or seen on the TV. (Little Yellow Dog, p. 32)

Keywords: hard-boiled private eyes • murder mysteries • race relations

🏵 *Devil in a Blue Dress*. New York: W. W. Norton, 1990. ISBN 0-39302-854-2.
🏵 219p.

1948: Unemployed and in danger of losing his home and middle class status, young veteran Easy Rawlins reluctantly accepts a missing persons job from a white man. The search for the beautiful and mysterious Frenchwoman takes Easy through a gritty Los Angeles underworld of despair, intrigue, and corruption.

Notes: Blackboard Bestseller List 1994, 1995; Edgar Award Nominee Best First Novel 1991; John Creasey Award 1991; Shamus Best First Novel 1991
Film by the same name, directed by Carl Franklin and starring Denzel Washington and Jennifer Beals (1995).

Keywords: criminal underclass • gangs and gangsters • movie novels • 1940s • racism • World War II veterans

A Red Death. New York: W. W. Norton, 1991. ISBN 0393029980. 284p.

1953: Enter an IRS agent with evidence of Easy's unreported earnings on his rental property and an FBI agent who wants Easy to spy on a Communist union organizer. Add the hanging of one of Easy's tenants who has long since stopped paying rent, the shooting of a preacher and his mistress caught in the act, and finally the death of the union organizer himself, and Easy is caught up in a case so convoluted that he doesn't know who to trust—if anyone.

Keywords: African migration movement • Communism • labor union organizers • 1950s • Red Scare

White Butterfly. New York: W. W. Norton, 1992. ISBN 039303366X. 272p.

1956: Nobody much cares about the sex killer's activities as long as he confines himself to black women. But the police are goaded into action with the death of a not-so-innocent UCLA coed who earns her tuition as stripper Cyndi Starr, the White Butterfly. Easy takes the case under duress, and he and his gangster friend Mouse soon find that his reluctance was well-justified.

Keywords: men and women • 1950s • San Francisco, California • serial killers • strippers

🏵 *Black Betty*. New York: W. W. Norton, 1994. ISBN 0-39303-644-8. 255p.

1961: Hired by a white private eye to find Betty Eady, a black housekeeper for a rich Beverly Hills family and a woman from his own past, Easy must also face the job of caring for his two children, a real estate deal gone bad, and the release from prison of his dangerous and unpredictable friend, Mouse. Easy encounters murder, deceit, revenge, and the mounting tensions of racism in Los Angeles in 1961.

Notes: Blackboard Bestseller List 1994, 1995, 1996; *Publishers Weekly* Best Books of 1994; *Sacred Fire: The QBR 100 Essential Black Books*

Keywords: black on black crime • men's friendships • 1960s • racism

A Little Yellow Dog. New York: W. W. Norton, 1996. ISBN 0-393-03924-2. 300p.

1963: Easy's impulsive affair with school teacher Idabell Turner leaves him with a yapping little yellow dog and the suspicion of murder hanging over his head. Meanwhile, petty workplace rivalries nip at his heels.

Keywords: drug dealers and dealing • 1960s • racism • school custodians • workplace politics

*★ **Bad Boy Brawly Brown.*** New York: Little, Brown, 2002. ISBN 0316073016. 311p.

1964: Easy finally has a secure middle-class life, with a home of his own, a steady job, and two adopted children, but his peace is disturbed by a rebellious son, guilt over his friend Mouse's death, and the troubles of old friends. When Alva Torres calls on him to intercede with her son before he gets into trouble running with a gang of black revolutionaries, Easy finds himself embroiled in a dangerous case replete with multiple murders, suspicious police, a secret weapons arsenal, and the corruption and betrayal of the young.

Notes: Black Issues Book Review Best Book 2002

Keywords: childrearing • Civil Rights Movement • family relationships • mourning • 1960s • political radicals

Phillips, Gary.

The Ivan Monk Series.

Phillips's Ivan Monk has many characteristics of the quintessential hard-boiled private eye—he's a tough-guy idealist with an individual and unshakeable personal code of honor in a world of dark despair, corruption, and cynicism. But he's a step above with his plush office, classic '64 Galaxy in mint condition, designer clothes, a second business—and Judge Jill Kodama as his significant other. The Los Angeles settings are realistically drawn, actual political events are used to good effect to set the stage, and the stories are well-plotted. The Abyssinia Barber Shop and Shine Parlor, Monk's base of operations, is peopled with characters who provide a light but authentic touch. Phillips creates authentic voices through dialogue, which is used effectively in contrast to his literate narration. Mystery fans will enjoy references to fictional detectives. Social commentary permeates Phillips's work, but as an integral part of the lives of the characters rather than as distinct and overt opinion of the author.

> *Monk crouched down to a lower drawer under the yellow-and-white tile counter. A throb lanced his lower leg, and he winced, sinking to a knee. It had been nine months since he'd been shot. . . . There was only so much resiliency to the flesh, the doctor had warned Monk. The older you got, the more knocks you took, it added up. And there were the psychological ramifications, too.* (Only the Wicked, p. 27)

Notes: Gary Phillips is also listed in the "Crime Novels" section of this chapter.

Keywords: Abyssinia Barber Shop and Shine Parlor • hard-boiled private eyes • murder mysteries • race relations • urban life and culture

Violent Spring. New York: Berkley Prime Crime Books, 1994. ISBN 0-425-15625-7pa. 257p.

A groundbreaking ceremony in South Central, site of the 1992 riots in the aftermath of acquittal of the policemen accused in the Rodney King beating, turns from a celebration of rebuilding to another political hotspot when the body of a Korean shopkeeper is unearthed. Monk is alternatively hired by the Korean Merchant's Group and the local African American group in this story that reveals corruption and greed at every turn and in every culture.

Keywords: political activism and activists • race relations • real estate developers

Perdition, USA. Salem, Ore.: John Brown Books, 1996. ISBN 0-9639050-6-6pa. 255p.

A young, single mother is unable to convince Monk to find the murderer of her baby's father until three young black men are killed. Driven by self-anger at dismissing the case as just another ghetto killing and impressed by the girl's spirit, Monk tries to determine whether the killings are related and who is behind them.

Keywords: hate groups • race relations • serial killers • small-town life and culture

Bad Night Is Falling. New York: Berkley Prime Crime Books, 1998. ISBN 0425163024. 312p.

Enfran Cruzado, former Mexican politico, his mother, and his seven-year-old daughter are killed when someone throws a Molotov cocktail through their window at the Rancho Tajuata housing project. When tensions mount and spread throughout the city, Monk is called in to get to the root of the problem. As he investigates, he finds that he must dig deeper and deeper into the past.

Keywords: arson • gangs and gangsters • political corruption • public housing • race relations

Only the Wicked. Aurora, Colo.: Write Way Publishing, 2000. ISBN 1-885173-64-4. 335p.

"Old Man Spears," a player in the defunct Negro Baseball League, suddenly drops dead in the Abyssinia Barber Shop. Monk realizes that he knew little about the man whom he'd seen regularly for years. When Kinnesaw Riles, Monk's long-absent cousin, shows up at the funeral, old secrets are uncovered, Riles's funeral quickly follows, and Monk's mother is accused. But was the motive political revenge or something more profitable?

Keywords: Negro Baseball League • older adults • political activism and activists • white supremacy

Private Investigators—Women

Coner, Kenyetta.

The Mockingbirds: A Maxine Michaels Mystery. **Washington, D.C.: 52 Weeks Publishing, 1998. ISBN 0-9665005-0-4. 242p.**

Maxine Michaels, tall, beautiful, and shrewd, is proprietor of Eye to Eye Private Investigations in New Orleans. Although she's tough enough for the job, she is feminine to the core. She enjoys wearing sophisticated clothes, takes pains with her appearance and her friends, and never leaves town without having Charlie, her godfather, promise to look after Clyde and Dominique, her plants. She may have her admirers among the men in blue, but she often runs into the animosity that policemen have for private investigators. In this first novel, Maxine's best friend is murdered, but not before leaving a desperate and cryptic message on Maxine's answering machine. The investigation uncovers links between New Orleans and D.C., jewel thieves, and highly placed and influential people operating on the wrong side of the law. On the bright side, Maxine meets Detective Nick Cameron of the D.C. police.

> *Nick's eyes slowly moved from her eyes to her shoes. He immediately sized her up for a model. Tall. Exquisite. She was undeniably beautiful. . . . But what intrigued him most were her eyes, which were the most inquisitive eyes he had ever seen, eyes that kept jumping around, catching all the action in the room. She had the eyes of a veteran cop when he first stumbles on a crime scene. He wondered where she had picked that up.* (The Mockingbirds, p. 21)

Keywords: jewel thieves • murder mysteries

Wesley, Valerie Wilson.

The Tamara Hayle Series.

Tamara Hayle is an ex-cop turned private eye struggling to raise her teenaged son, Jamal, and keep her 15-year-old Jetta running. If anyone is up to the challenge, she is. Tough and hardworking, Tamara has a strong sense of self that keeps her centered even when provoked. Her occasional vulnerability, her struggle to deal with the memories of an abusive mother, and her on-again, off-again love life make her character appealingly real. The minor characters are also well drawn, and the plots are fast-paced but memorable. Who else would begin almost every case by checking out the gossip with Wyvetta at Jan's Beauty Biscuit?

> *There are three things in this life I cherish: my independence, my son Jamal, and my peace of mind. . . . I used to be a cop. Some might say I couldn't handle the shit I was supposed to put up with— being black, being a woman—and I guess that's*

about right. I knew who I was and I wouldn't let them change it. (When Death Comes Stealing, p. 6)

Keywords: childrearing • Jan's Beauty Biscuit • murder mysteries • Newark, New Jersey • single parents

When Death Comes Stealing. New York: Avon, 1994. ISBN 0-380-72491-X. 302p.

The police have ruled that her ex-husband's older son died of an accidental overdose, but Tamara knows better. She must uncover the murderer before her own son is the next victim of the vengeful homicidal maniac.

Notes: Blackboard Bestseller List 1995, 1996; Shamus Award Nominee Best First Private-Eye Novel 1995

Keywords: absentee parents • family relationships • former husbands • husbands and wives • stepchildren • vengeance

Devil's Gonna Get Him. New York: Avon, 1995. ISBN 0-380-72492-8. 276p.

Lincoln Storey, the richest and most ruthless black man in Newark, hires Tamara to investigate his stepdaughter's lover. She needs his business but doesn't count on her client being murdered, her friend being one of the suspects, and her name being next on the killer's list.

Notes: Blackboard Bestseller List 1995, 1996

Keywords: family relationships • husbands and wives • infidelity • intraracial relations • stepchildren • upper class

Where Evil Sleeps. New York: Putnam, 1996. ISBN 0-399-14145-6. 208p.

A night out in Jamaica goes terribly wrong. Tamara survives a shootout in a bar but is left penniless, without identification, and fearful for both her life and freedom. Is Basil Dupre, the sexy islander she's never quite trusted, her salvation or downfall?

Notes: Blackboard Bestseller List 1997

Keywords: con artists and con games • drug dealers and dealing

No Hiding Place. New York: Putnam, 1997. ISBN 0-399-14318-1. 207p.

No one much cares about, and Tamara is only reluctantly persuaded to look into, the murder of Shawn Raymond, a young, handsome, charming, philandering, selfish hoodlum. In the course of investigating, Tamara unravels family relationships and finds that even Shawn's betters are not free from their own ugly secrets.

Notes: Blackboard Bestseller List 1998, 1999

Keywords: men and women • psychological abuse

Easier to Kill. New York: Putnam, 1998. ISBN 0-399-14445-5. 193p.

When the threats to Mandy Magic, popular radio talk show host, move from anonymous notes to systematic execution of those closest to her, Tamara digs into the past to discover who could want the beloved and philanthropic celebrity dead.

Notes: Blackboard Bestseller List 1999; Gold Pen Best Award Best Mystery/ Thriller Nominee 2000

Keywords: celebrities • restitution

The Devil Riding. New York: Putnam, 2000. ISBN 0-399-14617-2. 189 p.

Finding Darnella Desmond, who has run away from her wealthy stepfather and mother, leads Tamara through a trail of murdered young women, unscrupulous pimps and johns, drug dealers, and sexual perversion.

Notes: Blackboard Bestseller List 2000

Keywords: Atlantic City, New Jersey • child abuse • drug dealers and dealing • prostitutes and prostitution • runaways • sexual abuse • unwed mothers

West, Chassie.

The Leigh Ann Warren Series.

Leigh Ann Warren, a Washington, D.C., policewoman on disability, revels in her love of her foster mother, Italian shoes, and good food, but is less confident about her relationship with Duk (Dillon Upshur Kennedy). Because Leigh Ann often finds herself outside of her jurisdiction, this series tends to read as though she is an amateur detective. As one mystery after another pulls Leigh Ann out of the city, West provides vivid and affectionate descriptions of small-town life and characters.

> *It was one of those days when nothing had gone right. Not your garden variety nothing, like when you're dressed to kill, looking good and know it, and the sky opens up in a mini-monsoon, your umbrella's at home and you aren't. . . .I'm talking about the kind of rotten luck that, by the end of the day, had me giving serious consideration to popping in on Madam Selena to stock up on as many talismans, charms, and chicken feet as I could afford.* (Killing Kin, p. 1)

Notes: Chassie West also writes under the pseudonyms Tracy West, Joyce McGill, and Carolyn Keene.

Keywords: family relationships • murder mysteries • small-town life and culture

Sunrise. New York: Harper Monogram, 1994. ISBN 0-06-108110-8pa. 324p.

Leigh Ann, home in Sunrise for a class reunion, finds that the sleepy town is being torn apart by plans to build a mall that will provide a much-needed economic boost. The anger over the proposed location on the site of the black cemetery is overshadowed as Leigh Ann unearths an old scandal—with fatal results.

Notes: Edgar Nominee Best Original Paperback 1995

Keywords: class relations • high school reunions • moral codes • noblesse oblige

Killing Kin. New York: Avon, 2000. ISBN 0-06-104389-3pa. 329p.

Leigh Ann's former fiancé, Duk, is so far undercover, he's missing. Finding his will impels her to action. Are the molding body in her kitchen, missing evidence, and mysterious piggy bank related? And does Duk need rescuing or redemption?

Notes: Anthony Nominee Best Paperback Original 2000; Edgar Best Original Paperback Nominee 2000; Gold Pen Best Award Best Mystery/Thriller Nominee 2001

Keywords: absentee parents • artist communities • drug dealers and dealing • undercover police

Killer Riches. New York: Avon, 2001. ISBN 0-061-04391-5. 294p.

Nunna and Walter are kidnapped while honeymooning in their new Airstream, but Leigh can't convince anyone that they're really missing. To rescue her beloved foster mother, she puts together a genealogical puzzle to retrieve the family heirloom required for the ransom and to reveal a family she's never known.

Keywords: family feuds • family relationships • heritage • kidnapping • Ourland, Maryland • vengeance

West, Chassie.

***Loss of Innocence*. New York: Harper Paperbacks, 1997. ISBN 0061081116. 283p.**

Troy Burdette, justly proud coordinator of an adult education center, is 31 and has four gray hairs, skin the color of cinnamon toast, a figure that hasn't yet lost its fight with gravity, and a big, mean cat who goes everywhere with her because he can't be left with anyone else. A generous and loving woman, she divorced her beloved Wade because she was unable to have children. Her view of herself as "damaged goods" and her continued love for her ex-husband are poignant. When her ex-husband's elderly great aunt confesses to a 50-year-old murder, Troy's much-needed vacation is ruined. Eighty-year-old Aunt Julia is demanding to be jailed, but she can only get her way if Troy proves that the murder actually took place.

> *She'd clearly meant to be arrested in style. She wore a
> navy suit I would normally be drooling over, her favorite pin,
> a simple gold circle, and low-healed navy pumps. Snow
> white hair was captured by a mother-of-pearl barrette atop*

her head. . . . And in her left hand, the biggest, ugliest revolver on the East Coast. (p. 22)

Keywords: church men • family relationships • illegitimate children • murder mysteries • small-town life and culture

Psychological Suspense Stories

Gause-Jackson, Arlene.

Howling Against the Wind. **Nashville: James C. Winston Publishing, 1999. ISBN 1-55523-862-9pa. 345p.**

Lenore Hanson has lived in pain since unscrupulous Dr. Samuel Gleeson inserted an untested mandibular implant. As her bones deteriorate, so do her mental state and her marriage. If anyone deserves to die, it's abusive, money hungry, and arrogant Dr. Gleeson. Will Lenore cross the line from stalking to murder? A page from Lenore's diary precedes each chapter and gives an intimate look into her mind and heart.

> *Her anger started as smoldering embers which quickly proceeded to ignite sparks. If she'd been standing near a huge pile of leaves, her anger being combustible could have started a bonfire. And, like a hot stoker, Lenore felt ready to obliterate Dr. Gleeson's memory off the face of the earth. "Mercy me," thought Lenore, "I'm convinced that I'm losing my mind."* (p. 87)

Keywords: domestic violence • husbands and wives • medical malpractice • stalkers • vengeance

Joe, Yolanda.

Falling Leaves of Ivy. **Stamford, Conn.: Longmeadow Press, 1992. ISBN 0-681-41396-4. 319p.**

The lives of four recent Yale graduates are torn apart by the demands of new careers and the secret they share. Can jealousy and guilt have driven one of them to murder? Told alternately from four different points of view, this story is well crafted, and its plot twists are believable.

> *At the edge of a small platform where small boats would dock, the body hit the water with a tremendous force. The river accepted the gift of chaos and in return sent a cold, oily splash over the four numbed friends standing on the edge.* (p. 25)

Notes: Yolanda Joe is also listed in the "Contemporary Life" section of Chapter 9, the "Sensual" section of Chapter 10, and (as Ardella Garland) in the "Amateur Detectives—Women" section of this chapter.

Keywords: broadcast journalism and journalists • drug addiction • family relationships • homeless people • interracial relationships • investment firms • parents and children • race relations

Wright, William.

Justice Denied: A Novel of Ultimate Revenge. **Princeton, N.J.: Xlibris Corporation, 1998. ISBN 0-7388-0071-6. 252p.**

Virginia Tole, surgeon, cherishes her relationship with Kate Thomas, the niece she has raised as her own daughter. When Kate is gang-raped, tortured, and murdered, Virginia can barely function. But when an arrogant district attorney botches the trial and the murderer walks on a technicality, Ginny vows revenge and proceeds to exact it. To do so, she enters the world of the gangbangers and exposes herself to danger, depravity, and the disintegration of her own personal and professional ethic. The descriptions are very realistic—graphic and brutal.

> *Ginny swam up to consciousness. Her first thought was relief at awakening from a horrible dream. She bolted from bed to run to Kate's room only to crack her shin against an unfamiliar chair. . . .Grief punched her back on the bed, eyes refusing to open to a new reality.* (p. 27)

Keywords: gangs and gangsters • murder • rape • torture • vengeance

Urban Fiction

Old School

Cooper, Clarence, Jr.

The Scene. **New York: Old School Books/W. W. Norton, 1996. ISBN 0-393-31463-4pa. 288p.**

Cooper tells a gritty, realistic story of drug addiction in the inner city and the criminal cottage industries—drug dealing, theft, prostitution, and assault—that go with it. Although the story centers on the contrast between Rudy Black, addict, small-time pusher, and pimp, and Virgil Peterson, clean-cut family man and new detective, we see into many lives destroyed by drugs and despair. This noir tale is effectively told but uses surprisingly little profanity, graphic violence, and sex.

> *He tied the belt around the upper part of his left arm quickly, making the veins puff up blackly under the well-worn crusts . . . When he shot the drug in, it felt as though something smashed him sharply in the stomach . . . The drugs were good. If he played with them he might pass out. He might die. No better way to leave this world.* (p. 63)

Keywords: drug addiction • drug dealers and dealing • police detectives—men • urban life and culture

Goines, Donald.

Daddy Cool. Los Angeles: Holloway House, 1974. ISBN 0-87067-964-3pa. 223p.

Goines writes in a violent, gritty noir style, describing crime, criminal mentality, and life in general among the underclass. The violent and self-destructive style of life is a morass, pulling in and destroying each succeeding generation. Some readers will resent the reinforcement of stereotypes; others will read these graphic works as cautionary tales. Goines's crime novels are fast-paced, realistic, and very explicit with regard to sex, violence, and language. Some readers will enjoy the 1970s slang. In this novel, which is representative of Goines's ghetto realism style, Daddy Cool, knife-throwing professional assassin and family man, takes on an assignment that strikes too close to home. Distracted by concern for his daughter Janet, the only person whom he truly loves, he begins to lose the edge that makes him "one of the deadliest killers the earth had ever spawned."

> *Before it's over, them two niggers are going to wish like hell they had awakened me this morning. I don't give a fuck what you say, Shirley, I know where I'm coming from.* (Daddy Cool, p. 36).

Notes: Goines is the author of 16 novels published by Holloway House.

Keywords: criminal underclass • inner-city life and culture • professional assassins • prostitutes and prostitution • rape • vengeance

Himes, Chester.

The Grave Digger Jones and Coffin Ed Johnson Series.

This grim, realistic series describes the violence and bleakness of underclass life in a gritty but honest way. Goines' descriptions are vivid and the rhythm of his language is seductive, even as the scenes depicted are repulsive. Grave Digger and Coffin Ed, two black police detectives in Harlem, have their own sense of justice. The sometimes slapstick nature of the action makes sudden violence unexpected and shocking.

> *Below the surface, in the murky waters of fetid tenements, a city of black people who are convulsed in desperate living, like the voracious churning of millions of hungry cannibal fish. Blind mouths eating their own guts. Stick in a hand and draw back a nub. That is Harlem.* (A Rage in Harlem, p. 93)

Keywords: crime capers • underclass

A Rage in Harlem. First Vintage Books Edition 1989. New York: Vintage Crime/Random House, 1957, 1985. ISBN 0679720405. 159p. (Originally published in Great Britain by Alison and Busby, 1985. Originally published as *For the Love of Imabelle*.)

Jackson, an innocent "square," is victim of one con scheme after another, all the result of his larcenous, yet innocent, heart and his desire to impress (and keep) his woman, Imabelle. When he turns to his brother Goldy, a shrewd drug addict, con artist, and incidental police informant, Grave Digger and Coffin enter the picture, and one misadventure follows another.

Notes: Grand Prix for Best Detective Novel of the Year 1958

Keywords: con artists and con games • drug dealers and dealing • men and women

Other Grave Digger Jones and Coffin Ed Johnson novels:

The Real Cool Killers. New York: Avon, 1959; reissued New York: Vintage/Random House, 1988. ISBN 0679720391. 159p.

The Crazy Kill. New York: Avon, 1959; reissued Chatham, N.J.: Chatham Booksellers, 1973. ISBN 0-911860-32-0; New York: Vintage/Random House, 1989. ISBN 0679725725. 160p.

All Shot Up. 1960. New York: Thunder's Mouth Press, 1996. ISBN 1-56025-103-4pa. 160p.

The Big Gold Dream. Chatham, N.J.: Chatham Booksellers, 1973 (1960). ISBN 911860-30-4. New York: Thunder's Mouth Press, 1996. ISBN 1560251042pa. 156p.

The Heat's On. New York: Putnam, 1966; reissued Chatham, N.J.: Chatham Bookseller by arrangement with Putnam, 1975. ISBN 0-911860-57-6. New York: Vintage/Random House, 1988. ISBN 0394759974. 174p. Film *Come Back Charleston Blue*, directed by Mark Warren, starring Raymond St. Jacques, Godfrey Cambridge and Jonelle Allen (1972).

Blind Man with a Pistol. New York: Morrow, 1969; New York: Vintage/Random House, 1989. ISBN 0394759982pa. 191p.

Other titles by Chester Himes:

A Case of Rape. Washington, D.C.: Howard University Press, 1984. ISBN 0-88258-143-0; New York: Carroll & Graf, 1994. 140p.

Cotton Comes to Harlem. London: Allen & Busby, 1964, 1965. ISBN 0-85031-589-1. ISBN 0-85931-594-8pa. New York: Dell, 1965; New York: Random House, 1988. 159p. Film *Cotton Comes to Harlem*, directed by Ossie Davis, starring Godfrey Cambridge and Raymond St. Jacques (1970).

Plan B. Jackson: University Press of Mississippi, 1993. ISBN 0-87805-645-9. 203p.

The End of a Primitive. New York: Old School Books, 1997. ISBN 0-393-31540-1pa. 207p.

Pharr, Robert Dean.

***Giveadamn Brown*. New York: Old School Books, W. W. Norton, 1997 (1978). ISBN 0-393-31539-8. 236p.**

Violent, unpredictable ghetto life is revealed through the exploits of Harry Brown and young Giveadamn Brown, a Southern boy who travels to Harlem and becomes a success in the only way a young black man can. Giveadamn builds an elaborate scheme to use his uncle Harry's secret weapon—the Golden Fleece, a machine that defies the laws of chemistry and physics to produce heroin.

> *Dope is a dream of wealth, and sometimes the only dream for the black ghetto youth. To set up a great dope empire is a dream, the very same kind of dream that Wall Street and the exploits of Robert Vesco offer to slum (and upper-class, too) white boys. . . . But people are fighting and dying for dreams every day all over Harlem, all the time.* (p. 21)

Keywords: drug dealers and dealing • fugitives • intraracial relationships • men and women

Simmons, Herbert.

Corner Boy. **New York: Old School Books, W. W. Norton, 1996 (1957). ISBN 0-393-31465-0. 250p.**

Jake Adams, 18, is on his way up in the organization. A small-time dope pusher, he assumes an arrogant front, complete with custom-made clothes, a fancy car, and a reputation as a ladies' man. Ultimately, he is undone by his genuine love for two people and the expectations thrust on him as the smartest, toughest man in the hood. Simmons paints a picture of a complex young man, intelligent enough to see the dangers of his life but too immersed in its values and insecurities to break free.

> *It was what happened to a guy when he was poor and looked around and found out the whole world wasn't like that. It made you want things. You wanted a lot of clothes, a big shiny car, money, and plenty of babes, unless you were a square. You had to prove you were somebody, didn't you?* (p. 49)

Notes: Houghton Mifflin Literary Fellowship 1957

Keywords: drug addiction • drug dealers and dealing • gangs and gangsters • inner-city life and culture • men and women

Street Life

Holmes, Shannon.

B-More Careful. **New York: Meow Meow Productions/Entertainment Investment, 2003. ISBN 0-9672249-1-8pa. 280p.**

Netta and Mimi, founding members of the notorious Pussy Pound, are friends until envy, drugs, and greed pull them apart. Each thinks she is on top of "the game"—surviving and thriving in the violent and dangerous neighborhood. In reality, each suffers brutality, loss, and degradation and is ultimately used to cause the other's destruction. This is a typically fatalistic ghetto novel. The descriptions of rape and abuse are very graphic.

Includes an epilogue and a poem, "Now Give It to 'Em Raw!" by Teri Woods.

> *As a group, they would go on to make the Pussy Pound fa-*
> *mous. Before Netta took over they were running around*
> *fucking corner hustlers. Cats that had champagne tastes*
> *and beer money. Netta taught them how to get paid.*
> (p.102)

Notes: *Essence* Bestseller List 2002, 2003

Keywords: Baltimore, Maryland • criminals • drug dealers and dealing • HIV/AIDS • inner-city life and culture • prostitutes and prostitution

Sister Souljah.

The Coldest Winter Ever. **New York: Washington Square Press/Pocket Books. 1999. ISBN 0-7434-2681-9pa. 308p.**

Born of drug aristocracy, loved, spoiled, and always expensively dressed, Winter rebels against the constraints imposed by her protective father. Her world is turned upside down when her father is sent to prison and all of the family's assets are confiscated under the RICO Act. Willful, ruthless, and focused on all the wrong things, she uses every bit of her street smarts, experience, and sexual abilities to keep things together. But sometimes being beautiful and greedy isn't enough. Sister Souljah, a character in her own novel, represents the voice of reason, responsibility, and hope.

> *Brooklyn-born I don't have no sob stories for you about rats*
> *and roaches and pissy-pew hallways. I came busting out of*
> *my momma's big coochie on January 28, 1977, during one*
> *of New York's worst snowstorms. . . . The same night I got*
> *home my pops gave me a diamond ring set in 24-karat*
> *gold.* (p.1)

Keywords: coming of age • drug dealers and dealing • family relationships • inner-city life and culture

Woods, Teri.

True to the Game: A Teri Woods Fable. **New York: Meow Meow Productions/Entertainment Investment, 1994. ISBN 0-9672249-0-Xpa. 257p.**

Young Gena hits the streets looking for a good time and against all odds, meets the love of her life, Quadir, a millionaire drug dealer. The two come to realize that their love for one another is more important than flash cars and jewelry, but too late to escape the tragic consequences of a life committed to "the game."

> *"It seems like you just don't be getting too far out here in life,*
> *Quadir. You do what you got to do to survive out here, you*
> *try your damndest to see that there's some food on the table*
> *and clothes for the kids, but it don't get you nowhere. Bad*
> *ass motherfuckers around here now don't listen."* (p. 27)

Keywords: childrearing • coming of age • drug dealers and dealing • men and women • parents and children

Chapter 5

Frontier Literature

Jacqueline L. Jones

They numbered in the thousands, among them many of the best riders, ropers and wranglers. They hunted wild horses and wolves, and a few of them hunted men. Some were villains, some were heroes, some were called offensive names, and others were given almost equally offensive compliments. But even when one of them was praised as "the whitest man I've ever known," he was not white. For they were the Negro Cowboys.—Philip Durham and Everett Jones (1965, 1)

"Invisible men" best describes literary accounts of African American frontiersmen in the American Western novel genre. A phrase borrowed from novelist Ralph Ellison's 1952 novel, *Invisible Man*, offers a realistic image of this group's participation in the narrative treatment of early American history. The black cowboy rode through the real West but found no place in the West of fiction. He vanished.

Although large numbers of African American men lived in the emerging west before the nineteenth century, very little has been written about them (Durham and Jones 1965, 2). They were explorers, fur traders, cowboys, miners, founders of early settlements, cooks, mule drivers, and blacksmiths and took part in every courageous and aggressive endeavor necessary to build a new nation. Historian Lawrence B. DeGraaf (1975) contends that at least one-fifth of the cowboys in America's history were black. Today, their written stories are emerging and reaching audiences of interested readers eager for adventure and curious about African American tales of the Old West. The experiences of the black cowboys also included elements of romance, myths, legends, anecdotes, and reminiscences.

Definition

Wellman (1996) defines Western fiction as stories set on a North American frontier about characters transcending perilous circumstances. The protagonist, plot, setting, and other elements alter with each story as writers forever seek new wrinkles and twists. However, at the core, most Westerns focus on character. Westerns include many of the same elements that readers of historical fiction find appealing, particularly those who enjoy frontier settings (Herald 2000). One of the distinguishing elements that piques the appetite of Western readers is the element of adventure.

Like traditional Western fiction, African American frontier literature tells a story of adventure. The setting, North America, is thoroughly canvassed within an early frontier. Issues of race and ethnicity, along with the social conditions confronted by the black cowboy, distinguish these stories. Add to this a black protagonist, armed with tenacity to survive harsh and often brutal conditions of the untamed wild while simultaneously confronting racial indifference, and the story becomes more compelling. African American readers find these stories especially interesting and meaningful, for they are stories of the day-to-day social struggles of heroic characters with whom they can identify. Thus, it is race or ethnicity of the character that must be made obvious when defining African American frontier literature for African American audiences. Endurance and stalwartness of a group of American pioneers who have been virtually excluded from the frontier and exploratory period of America's history add to the adventure and colorfulness of this American early folklore literature, the African American Western.

Appeal

The basic themes of frontier literature are those that resonate with African American readers. In the real and mythical West, a man defines himself. Interwoven themes recur in Westerns: freedom of action and from artificial and often corrupt societies, a return to nature and a rejection of the artificial, an appreciation for essence rather than superficialities, the dignity of labor and a hard but meaningful existence, and the regenerative quality of the combination of all of these. These themes are important to the consciousness and history of a people confronting a heritage of slavery.

The most distinguishing element of these novels is the western frontier, a symbolic landscape that provides a setting and influences the character and actions of the hero. The symbolic landscape of the Western is the place where opposing forces come into conflict: "civilization and wilderness, East and West, settled society and lawless openness . . . Historically, the western represents a moment when the forces of civilization and wilderness life are in balance, the epic moment at which the old life and the new confront each other and individual actions may tip the balance one way or another, thus shaping the future history of the whole settlement" (Cawelti 1976, 193). It is then, "a psychological and spiritual place known by definite physical markers . . . [that serves as] a symbol of freedom, and of the opportunity for conquest . . . an escape from the conditions of life in modern industrial society" (Tompkins 1992, 4). Frontier literature speaks to the need for self-transformation, to leave the artificial existence of modern society and to somehow, through adversity, freedom, and the forces of nature, become something purer, more intense, more real.

African Americans relish strong characters with whom they can identify. The character of the protagonist, a heroic individual whether buffalo soldier, cowboy, or pioneer woman, is central to this genre's appeal. Western fiction enthusiasts can now enjoy characters and situations with which they can identify and feel a sense of connection. The level of cultural discovery will be rewarding. Who were these men? What brought them to the West? How did these black cowboys become heroes? How did they deal with the untamed wilderness and cultural exclusion simultaneously? The answers to these and other questions await those fond of Western literature.

African American frontier literature, like traditional fiction, is reading for entertainment, but to some black readers these Western titles may mean more. They give African Americans the opportunity to visit an exciting and previously overlooked time period and afford them the opportunity to see their history as free individuals who shaped a nation.

Though Western fiction's primary purpose is to entertain, work by and about African Americans in the West sheds light on a previously overlooked portion of our nation's history. Exploring and understanding this new perspective is important to all segments of America's multicultural society. As Wellman observes, "To study westerns, is to study ourselves, for they are in fact, a form of our cultural expression" (1996, 155).

Evolution

The cattle kingdom was centered in Texas, a former slave state with a large black population. Many former slaves and blacks born after emancipation worked for Texas cattle companies. According to Hardaway (2001, 28), many African American cowboys participated in the frontier and cattle industry. Just how many is unknown. It is estimated that they numbered in the thousands. Unfortunately for the black cowboy, his fictitious character would not be among printed novels until much later in another century, and he would rely on non-African American authors to tell his story.

African American authors wrote few Westerns before 1975. African American Thomas Detter (1826–?) freeman, short story writer, and essayist, is recorded among the innovators of African American Western fiction (Foster 1997, 212). In 1864, Detter became known as one of the "Old Wheelhorses" of the western Civil Rights Movement. Living in the isolated frontier settlement of Elko, Nevada, he wrote about the status and prospects of gold or silver mines and descriptions of towns and westward expansion. His published work, *Nellie Brown, or the Jealous Wife, with other Sketches* (1871) includes fiction and other essays set in the antebellum South. Although *Nellie Brown* contains elements prescriptive to the Western genre, this work is not officially classified as a Western. Almost 100 would pass before African Americans writers would look to the West with any frequency.

Historians, drawing on written histories and memoirs, began to focus on the literature of the early West, and a different western story began to surface. Scores of Negro profiles with names and personal accounts began to appear. Estevanico and

James Beckwourth are two figures whose stories were finally told. In 1965, Olive Burt published a biography of Estevanico, a black Spanish slave who discovered the American West. Undoubtedly his story is one of adventure and filled with danger, courage, intelligence, and most assuredly, good luck. James Beckwourth, whose biography appeared in 1969, was a black mountain man who served as leader for General William Ashley's fur troops and the black buffalo soldiers (Clark 1976).

African American Western fiction writers gained visibility in the twentieth century with J. Jason Grant, Charles R. Goodman, and Hiram King, among others. *Coal*, written by J. Jason Grant and published in 1978, can be considered among the first adult Western fiction titles by an African American writer. *Coal* is the story of a teenaged cowboy who, influenced by his infamous gunsmith slavemaster, went from slave to "El Diablo Negrito" (The Black Devil). This black hero was unprecedented, to say the least. All elements of traditional Western fiction are included in this Western: chivalry, boldness, love, romance, savagery, and so forth. Viewed by some as a very good Western novel, *Coal* unfortunately appears to be Grant's only contribution to the genre.

Other African American writers of Western fiction followed, but not until almost a decade later. Acclaimed writer Charles R. Goodman gives the buffalo soldiers their just due in *The Outskirts of Hell* (1986), *Buffalo Soldier* (1992), *Black Cheyenne* (1993), and *Bound by Blood* (1993). Spur Award winner Hiram King continues the portrayal of African Americans in Western fiction with two novels about buffalo soldiers, *Dark Trails* (1998) and *Broken Ranks* (2001). Although the numbers are small, African American Westerns seem to have made their way into mainstream Western fiction.

Drew (1993, 13) notes that there were almost no African Americans to be found in Western series before 1990. Today, African American writers have made themselves known in this Western arena as well. In 1991, Poston introduced his Western series with *A Man Called Trouble*, which features a black ex-outlaw cowboy by the name of Jason (Jay) Peares. Jason's troubles seem to follow him in the next three installments in the series: *The Peacekeeper* (1997), *Gallagher* (2000), and *Courage on Trial* (2002).

Once black writers had completed their works, locating a publisher was yet another hurdle. Outlets available to black writers before the early twentieth century were limited, and they often had great difficulty getting their works published. Holloway House Publishing Company in Los Angeles was among the first to offer publishing opportunities to black writers, especially those in the Western fiction area. Even today, Holloway House remains one of the leading publishers of African American fiction. Holloway House has published such Western authors as Jason Grant, Jeffery Poston, Charles R. Goodman, and Rina Keaton. Today, mainstream publishers are accepting—even demanding—work by African American authors.

The innovations of technology and the Internet have broadened the field for African Americans interested in electronic publishing. Currently, self-published authors who write about blacks on the early American frontier maintain public Web sites that feature their work. Representative examples of the plethora of Internet sites on black participation in the Old West are listed in Chapter 12.

Themes and Trends

Familiar Faces, Tried and True Themes

Traditional Western themes and characters have been faithfully preserved by African American writers. The traditional heroic cowboy is still popular with many readers. Known for his skill in riding horses, herding cattle, and performing other strenuous jobs requiring strength and agility, the cowboy is respected for his bravery and his innate ability to survive surrounded by uncertainty and danger. Other traditional characters are apparent in works by African American fiction writers as well. The gunfighter protagonist featured in Poston's *Peacekeepers* is an example of the similarities between works by whites and blacks.

Traditional plots, which call on the hero to survive against nature, civilize an untamed West, move cattle, protect the innocent, and defend life and honor, resonate in African American frontier literature. True to traditional Western literature, African American frontier literature also may also contain multiple themes. Such is the case in Goodman's *The Outskirts of Hell*, a story that involves romance, Native Americans, and slavery. For the most part, the essential themes remain the same, but the cast of characters is more inclusive and, perhaps, more accurate.

Buffalo Soldiers

A major character that has captured the imagination of Western readers is the buffalo soldier, the name given by Native Americans to black soldiers. A popular character type in recent African American Western fiction, the buffalo soldier is either a former slave who has turned to the military or simply a soldier involved with the same military issues as any other soldier. There are various accounts of where the name actually came from, , but some historians have written that the Cheyenne dubbed the 10th Cavalry "Buffalo Soldiers" in 1867, following an incredible two-day battle near Leavenworth, Kansas. A mere 90 of these soldiers held off 800 Cheyenne attackers, losing only three men in the process. Others report that the name was give by the Comanche. Awed by the black soldiers' fierceness, Indian warriors also highly valued their scalps, for they bore a resemblance to the dark, woolly hide of the revered buffalo. The buffalo soldiers' evolution and purpose introduced a new and vital force to the Western frontier genre.

Individuality

The African American frontier novel moves away from a monolithic, stereotypical black everyman to represent characters with individual aspirations, morals, and personalities. Conflict within buffalo soldier regiments, as depicted in Goodman's *Buffalo Soldier*, reinforces the concept of African Americans as individuals. The men are described in variety; there is no single individual who represents "the" buffalo soldier. Interior conflict and uncertainty, family disagreements and reconciliation, and interaction with other African Americans with different perspectives are thematic devices that help us recognize and appreciate characters as individuals rather than representative types.

African American Issues

African American writers often express views on issues that have affected them personally and historically. The Western lends itself to an ironic depiction of the African American on the frontier, inviting an examination of professed and actual social mores. In many stories, the protagonist is bound by slavery or limited by racial prejudice in the symbolic western landscape, a place that is supposed to be physically open and morally free of society's corruption and artifices.

Black Westerns also explore the meaning of freedom, its relative value, and its challenges. In many, a newly freed slave is searching for displaced family members. Some authors use this simply as a plot device for the hero to embark on a quest. Others, however, explore thematic issues of family, loyalty, and responsibility.

Interactions with other races are major components of many African American frontier novels. In some, black and white soldiers join forces to defeat the Indians. In others, Native Americans and African Americans recognize whites as the common enemy. In still others, African Americans stand alone and function independently of other groups, preferring to settle in black territories or establish black towns. Although these interactions are often described in terms of military conflict or individual fights, a number simply describe everyday life in multicultural communities. Fewer describe interracial romance and marriage, though mixed-race individuals appear in many African American Westerns.

Trends have certainly come and gone since the inception of the Western genre in the early nineteenth century. Twentieth-century writers began to depict the West as it really was, and it was in that spirit that African American experiences were acknowledged and African American voices began to be heard. The appearance of African Americans in Western fiction may have been a small but significant factor in maintaining the longevity of the genre. Though Western fiction may not be as popular as it once was, frontier history still manages to capture the imagination of many readers today. Perhaps introducing a new generation of readers to a new generation of writers will prompt new interest in frontier literature.

Selection Scope and Criteria

This chapter presents Westerns and stories of the West written by African Americans. It includes both fiction and nonfiction. The approach is inclusive, as there are few Western titles published by African Americans, and because true stories of the West share many features and themes with Western genre fiction (e.g., heroic characters, adventure) and will likely appeal to the same readers. Standard readers' advisory sources were consulted for titles written by African Americans. Because it is often difficult to determine the ethnicity of authors, several biographical sources were consulted. The author made a personal visit to the Black American West Museum and Heritage Center Bookstore (Denver, Colorado) and interviewed cowboy and 2000 World Champion Calf Roper Fred Whitfield as he participated in the 2002 Pro-rodeo Hall of Fame Competition. The author also interviewed Curator Chuck Ambers of the African American Pioneers (San Diego) and California Museum & Bookstore, Casa Del Moro Museum during 2001. These individuals provided additional information.

This chapter includes a few titles geared to young adult readers. Those who make suggestions to younger readers will want to familiarize themselves with the individual titles to make appropriate recommendations. For example, although Walter Dean Myers's *The*

Righteous Revenge of Artemis Bonner involves a coming-of-age theme that will be relevant to young adults and it does not contain explicit sex, there is violence, and this title may be more appropriate for a mature young adult reader.

Advising the Reader

Stories of America's West encompass adventures encountered by individuals exploring and discovering ways to manage day-to-day life in a new and untamed wilderness. The Western story is a narrative of adventure with the focus on a main character and his ability to survive in a frontier setting.

All titles selected for annotation in this chapter were placed into two broad categories, fiction and nonfiction. The categories were further subdivided by major themes. Fiction is categorized by emphasis on character; nonfiction is categorized by form: autobiography, general history, and young adult.

- **Western Fiction**

    - **Buffalo Soldiers.** The unique character and experiences of African American soldiers are the primary features of these books.

    - **Cowboys.** These are the stories of black cowhands and involve experiences that have been the mainstay of traditional Westerns.

    - **Women of the West.** These stories feature women protagonists, who are generally regarded as the primary force in civilizing the frontier.

    - **Western Romance.** These love stories focus on the relationship between a man and a woman.

- **Western Nonfiction**

    - **Biography.** This section includes autobiographies, biographies, and memoirs of the lives and experiences of African Americans in the West.

    - **Frontier History.** African American historians offer factual accounts of African Americans and the roles they played in the West.

    - **Young Adult.** These titles are written with younger audiences in mind.

Readers who specifically seek out "true Westerns" should be directed to the titles under "Cowboys" in the "Western Fiction" section.

Karen Antell (see Chapter 9) wrote some of the annotations in this chapter. Her annotations are followed by (KA).

Fiction

Buffalo Soldiers

Ballard, Allen B.

Where I'm Bound. **New York: Simon & Schuster, 2000. ISBN 0-64-87031-2. 316p.**

Joe Duckett finds one way to escape the bondage of slavery. Leaving his family behind, he joins the Northern army and earns the rank of cavalry scout. Within this newfound role as a fighting solider, he must endure the agonizing effects of war, learning to kill another man and experience the cruelty and moral corruption that occurs in war. Duckett becomes more than just a free man, he becomes a hero, but his greatest challenge is to return to the plantation from which he escaped and unite with his family.

> *As the Rebs hustled across the road and down the riverbank, Joe and Zack cut off into the swamps. Over fifty miles to go—they needed to get them some horses. The colonel had promised them twenty-four-hours' leave if they made it.* (p. 60)

Keywords: army scouts • cavalry • Civil War • escaped slaves

Goodman, Charles R.

Black Cheyenne. **Los Angeles: Holloway House, 1993. ISBN 0-87067-854-X. 223p.**

With the Civil War over, Will Wiley is a free man who now has a choice in his destiny. He soon realizes that life in the U.S. Army is not for him. Having lived among several tribes of Indians, he rejects the army's practice of capturing and slaughtering these native people. Now a deserter, he eludes capture, using his experience as a trained scout to live in the wilderness. In this untamed world, living among the Indians, he meets Blue Bird, a Comanche woman outcast from her tribe. Living among the Cheyenne, Will is transformed and discovers his destiny, but not without cost.

> *Tomorrow you ride with Eagle Claw. He will lead the raid on the white man's camp you saw when we returned to our village. You prove yourself on this raid you will be a Cheyenne.* (p. 221)

Keywords: army scouts • Cheyenne Indians • deserters • slavery

Bound By Blood. **Los Angeles: Holloway House, 1993. ISBN 0870673963. 277p.**

Goodman combines a story within a story. What could John Eric Williams, a retired black marine Corps Lieutenant Colonel, possibly have in common with Isaac Turner, a former slave and buffalo soldier; Maria Turner, a Mexican wife; and Jeff Sanders, a descendent of slave owners? Lured to the barn of his newly acquired ranch in southern Georgia by a ghostly stranger, Williams finds a journal and discovers that he is part of an unlikely foursome. He learns that they are BOUND BY BLOOD.

*It was some time in summer, 1861, before Isaac
knew anything in about a war between the states.
He knew it had to do with his freedom, but did not
understand how that could be. He knew he belonged to Lucas Willard. He was property.* (p. 75)

Keywords: family history • journals and diaries • supernatural

Buffalo Soldier. **Los Angeles: Holloway House, 1992. ISBN 0-87067-
373-4. 246p.**

After a slave kills a drunken white overseer who is on a killing rampage,
the slaves, who are left with three white bodies and are fearful of unjust
retribution, flee the plantation under Luke's leadership. Luke eventually
joins the cavalry, only to find himself a fugitive once again after he is
forced to shoot his vicious commanding officer. Befriended by the Comanche Indians, he becomes war chief and leads attacks on the buffalo
soldiers.

> *As Luke spoke he slipped his sidearm from its hol-
> ster. He fired from the hip. The bullet struck Lang-
> ford's neck. A surprised look came across his face,
> then he fell over, Luke grabbed Langford's horse
> by the reins and swung into the saddle. With a gun
> in each hand, he rode through camp toward the
> corralled horses. Each time he fired, a trooper fell
> from the saddle.* (p. 156)

Notes: Golden Spur Nominee 1997

Keywords: cavalry • Comanche Indians • deserters • escaped slaves

The Outskirts of Hell. **Los Angeles: Holloway Publishing, 1986. ISBN
0-87067-831-0. 285p.**

Josh was an honorable army scout and buffalo soldier until racial hatred
and bigotry made him an outlaw. Drummed out of the army on
trumped-up charges, Josh found work doing everything from branding
cattle to working in a general store. He befriends Ben, an elderly man
who holds claim to land in California that harbors gold. Josh discovers
the treasure but loses it to a couple of old army comrades who cheat him.
They sell Josh into slavery aboard a ship bound for China, where he encounters new forms of prejudice. His destiny changes when he meets and
marries racially mixed Mei Ling.

> *"He's a spoiled nigger sir," Grossman said. "First
> Overton spoiled him, then Col. Merritt spoiled him,
> then the United States Congress spoiled him by
> giving him the Medal of Honor. He is unfit to wear
> that high honor."* (p. 138)

Keywords: army scouts • prejudice • slavery • vengeance

King, Hiram.

Broken Ranks. New York: Leisure Books, 2001. ISBN 0843948728. 393p.

As the Civil War ended, a new battle began. This fight would be one of survival for many of the newly displaced black men, both young and old. Hope for a large group of them rested in the decision to become U.S. Army volunteers. The new recruits had survived slavery and the Civil War. Their immediate challenge now was to get to their training camp, just on the other side of Fort Leavenworth, where six ex-rebels were scheming to "redeem" their country.

> *Close to five hundred black enlisted men that Lieutenant Badger had recruited had come in from every direction of the compass and by every mode of transportation. And still coming in. Ragged, bedraggled, and bewildered.* (p. 64)

Keywords: Civil War • freed slaves • Reconstruction

Dark Trail. New York: Leisure Books/Dorchester, 1998. ISBN 0843944188. 374p.

The end of the War Between the States promised a new life for some, but not for the family of Bodie Johnson. He returns home to find no home and no family. All that he'd loved and left behind was gone. He learns that his family has been moved and sold back into slavery. With only this fragment of information, Bodie sets out to find his family. He's determined to face head-on the harshness of the vast untamed West and its equally untamed human inhabitants. This Spur Award-winning story is the saga of a newly freed ex-slave's determination to reclaim what is his.

> *Josh looked admiringly across his shoulder at Bodie. He had never heard of a black man handling a gun until lately. "Where'd you learn that?" "Army, Bodie said. "Fifth Massa-chusetts Volunteers."* (p. 38)

Notes: Spur Award for Original Western Paperback 1999

Keywords: betrayal • freed slaves • survival

Cowboys

Durham, David Anthony.

Gabriel's Story. New York: Doubleday, 2001. ISBN 0-385-49814-4. 291 p.

Gabriel, at age 15, is transplanted from Baltimore to Kansas, where his mother and new stepfather are attempting to establish a homestead claim shortly after the Civil War. Gabriel already resents his stepfather, is angry about leaving Baltimore where he'd hoped to become a doctor, and hates the hard work of farming. Joining a band of cowboys headed for Texas seems like Gabriel's ticket away from the homestead, but the journey descends into nightmare as the brutal cowboy leader, Marshall Hogg, commits murder and leads the others on a spree of thievery, rape, and more bloodshed. Although he wants to flee, Gabriel is terrorized by Hogg's threats. When he finally makes it back to his family, he is changed: a man now, he understands the value of everything he left. (KA)

> *The rapists toasted their deeds and talked of penetration and blood and the joy of total power as if there were no such thing as remorse . . . . Gabriel watched them all, especially the girl, who sat cross-legged, bound, and still. She neither moved nor stretched nor slept, but just stared. She didn't return his gaze. (p. 181)*

Notes: Alex Award 2002; BCALA Literary Award for First Novelist 2001; Zora Neale Hurston/Richard Wright Fiction Award 1992

Keywords: coming of age • 1800s • homesteading • kidnapping • murder • prodigal son stories • rape

Everett, Percival L.

God's Country: A Novel. Boston: Faber & Faber, 1994. ISBN 0571198325. 219p.

Curt Mader, an immoral bigot, coward, and cheat, loses all of his worldly possessions to some of the West's worst hooligans. He is forced to solicit the help of "Bubba," a renowned trapper who just happens to be black. They face the gang of white men dressed as Indians who kidnapped his wife and killed his dog. Together, this odd couple encounter a bank robbery, have a run in with General Custer, and use their wits to survive other hilarious episodes in God's Country during 1871.

> *"What's your business?" he asked. He tossed a glance at the boy beside me. "How do you know this ain't a social call?" "Your color and mine." "Christ, man, it's 1871, ain't you people ever gonna forget about that slavery stuff?" (p. 24)*

Keywords: 1800s • kidnapping • race relations • racism • vengeance

Grant, J. Jason.

Coal. Los Angeles: Holloway House, 1978. ISBN 0870677187. 256p.

From age six, young Coal learned the meaning of anger, hate, and how to kill his infamous gunfighter master, Solomon Pinkney. After Pinkney sells Coal's mother and young sister, Coal turns his fast-draw skills on the very one who taught him and earns a reputation as the fastest, as well as the most savage and brutal, gunslinger between Texas and Mexico.

> *Coal's right hand found his six gun and fired twice—sounding more like once—sending one bullet into each of Bad Frank Stitch's eyes. Blood gushed from those vacant holes. Pausing over Stitch, Coal nosily spat into the two empty sockets. (pp. 54–55)*

Keywords: 1800s • freed slaves • gunfighters • vengeance

King, Hiram.

High Prairie. **New York: Leisure Books/Dorchester, 1997. ISBN 0843943246. 215p.**

Distinguished only by his sense of honor, Cole Granger was just one of the many black men who pushed out on the Western frontier. Having promised to deliver a group of prized horses to a nearby rancher, Cole would be damned if he'd let horse thieves or a band of vigilantes threaten his ranch, his horses, or his word. This fast-paced story is certain to please any fan fond of Westerns.

> *Cole moved his feet apart, his right hand carelessly at his holster. Jim Seely stepped out of the bunkhouse door where the loud talking had gotten his attention. Seely stopped, paralyzed by the sight before him. He knew right away what was happening.* (p. 214)

Keywords: American West • 1800s • horse traders

Myers, Walter Dean.

The Righteous Revenge of Artemis Bonner. **New York: HarperCollins, 1992. ISBN 0060208449. 140p.**

Only 15 years old but the oldest male in the family, young Artemis is faced with the manly task of avenging the death of his uncle, "Ugly Ned." He must track down the murderous Grimes and find the map leading to his uncle's buried treasures. Artemis and his Cherokee friend Frolic travel the untamed West with only determination on their side.

> *I have saved four hundred dollars in cash money, and half of it will be yours Artemis Bonner, if you will avenge your uncle's cruel death.* (p. 38)

Keywords: American West • buried treasure • vengeance

Poston, Jeffrey A.

A Man Called Trouble Series.

Jason "Trouble" Peares, a half-black, half-Indian gunfighter and ex-outlaw, has been tried for murder and acquitted but can't seem to shake his reputation for getting into trouble. The character develops throughout the series, and the events that lead to his many bouts with trouble validate his infamous name.

Keywords: American West • gunfighters

A Man Called Trouble. Los Angeles: Holloway House, 1991. ISBN 0870673696. 191p.

Jason (Jay) Peares is a quiet man who never looked for a fight, but the fights always came looking for him. His only relief from defending himself in countless duels is in the arms of his sweet Chocolate Joanne. This story of revenge keeps Jay looking over his shoulder to see who his next victim will be.

> *Jay looked back on all the gunfights and all the confrontations he'd had during his outlaw years. Only a few were really close and only a couple of those had been challenging. He'd never really felt fear, never really fought someone better than himself.* (p. 96)

Keywords: vengeance

Peacekeeper. New York: Walker, 1997. ISBN 0-80274-160-6. 162p.

Jay is hired as a peacekeeper for a powerful rancher named Pritchett and is relishing an opportunity to settle down. The rancher is having trouble from squatters attempting to encroach on his land and claims to want this problem solved without bloodshed. However, when Jay finds out that Pritchett is taking the law into his own hands and is ready to kill anyone who gets in his way, he switches allegiance and takes the side of the homesteaders.

> *This ain't about color. There's more than twenty farmers around the county, black, white, and Mexican. We all got the same problem with Pritchett. He's payin' gunfighters to take what don't belong to him.* (p. 44)

Keywords: betrayal • homesteading

Women of the West

Keaton, Rina.

Revenge of June Daley. **Los Angeles: Holloway House, 1996. ISBN 087069708. 191p.**

June Daily escapes from Devonfield plantation with another slave, Harlin Mason. Once they are free, cowardly Mason sells June back into slavery. Seizing another chance for freedom, June heads West and seeks revenge. She becomes a bounty hunter as a way to get the job done.

> *"Can I have one word with you before the stage leaves, Miss June?" Charlie asked. He steered June away from the coach. "I reckon I have no cause to speak like this, but if I were you, I'd keep an eye on your friend. I like you a lot and I'd hate to see anything happen to you."* (p. 45)

Keywords: betrayal • bounty hunters • escaped slaves • vengeance

Western Romance

Yerby, Frank.

Western: A Saga of the Great Plains. **New York: Dial Press, 1982. ISBN 038527230-8. 444p.**

In a tale of passionate love, revenge, and counter-revenge, Yerby's protagonist, Ethan Lovejoy, is married to a spunky former actress. However, his heart belongs to Nora, a young Kansas schoolgirl. The novel details pioneer life in Kansas immediately after the Civil War. With an insane wife and a jealous mistress, Ethan finds material success but not happiness. The characters are as vivid as they are varied. They include farmers, card sharks, blacksmiths, saloonkeepers, and women who helped tame the West.

> If I am killed, please notify Mr. Philip Harris at his farm three miles east of Abilene on the Smokey Hill River, and Mr. Ned Tyler, President of the Abilene Citizens State Bank, who is my attorney. Last of all, having informed these two, please advise of my passing Miss Nora Curtiss, at her restaurant, corner of Quincy and Holliday Streets in Topeka. I thank you. Ethan Lovejoy. (p. 390)

Keywords: Great Plains • vengeance

Nonfiction

Biography

Beckwourth, James P.

The Life and Adventures of James P. Beckwourth. **New York: Arno Press and The New York Times, 1969. 537p.**

The unique story of one African American is told in his own words. James Beckwourth, noted mountain man, trapper, and all-around frontiersman, tells the story of his life during America's developing years. Beckwourth offers insight into real-life encounters with the wilderness as a frontiersman and a black man. .

> We spent the summer months at our leisure, trading with Indians, hunting, sporting, and preparing for the fall harvest of beaver. We made acquaintance with several of the Black Feet, who came to the post to trade. (p. 113)

Keywords: frontiersmen • life stories • mountain men • trappers

Burton, Arthur T.

Black, Red, and Deadly: Black and Indian Gunfighters of the Indian Territory, 1870–1907. **Austin, Tex.: Eakin Press, 1991. ISBN 0-89015-798-7. 304p.**

Arthur T. Burton describes the extraordinary contributions and participation of African American and Native American men, both famous and infamous, in the Old West. Historical characters include Bass Reeves, the invincible black marshal; Indian lawman Sam SixKiller; Ned Christie, the most feared Indian outlaw of his time; Grant Johnson, the freedman marshal; and Cherokee Bill, one of the meanest of the mean. Includes a comprehensive bibliography.

> *Grant Johnson has been a deputy United States marshal in these parts for fourteen years and has arrested more bad men than any officer in the Indian Territory. He never before killed a man and has been forced to wound but one or two others.*
> (p. 230)

Keywords: Native American history

Flipper, Henry Ossian.

Black Frontiersman: The Memoirs of Henry O. Flipper, First Black Graduate of West Point. **Compiled and edited by Theodore D. Harris. Fort Worth: Texas Christian University Press, 1997. ISBN 0-87565-171-2. 190p.**

This collection of memoirs by the first African American cadet at West Point gives a firsthand glimpse into the military life of a buffalo soldier. Readers will have an opportunity to view the early history of the nation's most noted institution of formal military training.

> *"BRAINS BACK OF VILLA. A NEGRO GRADUATE OF WEST POINT SAID TO BE THE RIGHT-HAND MAN OF THE CONSTITUTIONALIST LEADER."* The United States War Department believed that Flipper had become Villa's principal military advisor and that *"whatever successes Villa has had in a military way are declared to be due to Flipper."*
> (p. 95)

Keywords: buffalo soldiers • memoirs • military life • racial discrimination • West Point

Love, Nat.

The Life and Adventures of Nat Love. **Baltimore, Md.: Black Classic Press, 1988. ISBN 0933121172. 162p.**

One of the most famous cowboys of the American West, Nat Love shares the true story of his life from his humble beginnings on a small farm in Tennessee to his working days at the Duval Ranch in Texas and later Gillinger Ranch in Arizona. He recounts the event that led to his name change and his friendships with Wild Bill and Calamity Jane. His story is a gift for those seeking factual accounts of social conditions in the real West and the life of a real black cowboy in the days following Civil War.

> The world is before me. I join the Texas cowboys. Red River Dick. My first outfit. My first Indian fight. I learn to use my gun. (p. 40)

Keywords: cattle roping • cowboys • life stories

Purdue, Fray Marcos, and Paul W. Stewart.

Westward Soul! Denver, Colo.: Black American West Foundation, 1976. Historical centennial-bicentennial edition. 1976. Unpaged. LCCN 76-27812

Purdue and Stewart, who is the African American founder and owner of the Black American West Museum and Heritage Center, have produced a unique compilation of biographical profiles that are important in the development of Colorado's early history.

Keywords: American West • biography collections

Frontier History

Burton, Arthur T.

Black, Buckskin, and Blue: African American Soldiers on the Western Frontier. Austin, Tex.: Eakin Press, 1999. ISBN 1571682953. 286p.

Burton takes an in-depth look at the lives of the many African Americans who served as scouts and soldiers in early American history. He explores their individual lives as well as events and racial hostilities endured during the Western frontier era. This is a well-researched compilation of facts concerning African Americans in the nineteenth and twentieth centuries.

> By the 1890's there were still some black veterans in the infantry who had served in the Civil War or had been members of the 38th or 41st Infantry Regiments at the close of the war. Another important task for the black infantry was escort duty for survey parties, stagecoaches, contract trains, supply trains and wagon trains. (p. 141)

Keywords: army scouts • 1800s • military life • 1900s • soldiers

Clark, Arthur A.

Black Pioneers in Colorado: A History 1528–1921. Baton Rouge, La.: Arthur A. Clark, 2001 (c. 1976). 125p.

In this well-documented history of black participation in Colorado's history, Clark includes significant information on people only briefly mentioned in compilations of early black pioneers. Documentation authenticates this group's pivotal role in America's development during the frontier years.

> Aunt Clara Brown . . . boarded a wagon as a cook and was caught in the Pikes Peak gold rush, having made her capital by opening the first laundry in the Central City area. She

brought not only her husband and children to Colorado, but thirty-four nephews, nieces, uncles, aunts, and in-laws, as well. (p. 42)

Keywords: American West • pioneers

Cox, Clinton.

The Forgotten Heroes: The Story of the Buffalo Soldiers. New York: Scholastic, 1993. ISBN 0590451210. 180p.

Their job was to protect new settlers on the Western frontier. The buffalo soldiers of the 9th and 10th Cavalry did just that even if it meant chasing outlaws or Indians. Meticulously written and researched, Cox's book also tells the tragic story of how the buffalo soldiers and Native Americans were often pitted against each other in their efforts to survive.

The Buffalo Soldiers spent more time fighting in the West than any other cavalry regiments in the United States Army, and their courage and sacrifices helped create the United States that we now know. (p. 159)

Keywords: American West • buffalo soldiers • cavalry • frontier life

 5

DeGraaf, Lawrence B., Kevin Mulroy, and Quintard Taylor.

Seeking El Dorado: African Americans in California. Seattle: Autry Museum of Western Heritage, University of Seattle Press, 2001. ISBN 0295980826. 537p.

Though not a contemporary and exhaustive resource on the history of African Americans, portions of this book cover black expansion during the frontier era. There are informative facts about African Americans that reflect their cultural activity during the developmental stages of California's history.

I have been working for myself for the past two months . . . and have cleared three hundred dollars. California is the best country in the world to make money. It is also the best place for black folks on the globe. All a man has to do, is to work, and he will make money. (pp. 8–9)

Keywords: American West

Taylor, Quintard.

In Search of the Racial Frontier: African Americans in the American West, 1528–1990. New York: W. W. Norton, 1998. ISBN 0-393-04105-0. 415p.

Noted as one of the foremost historians on the black West, Taylor makes available this well-researched, comprehensive survey of conclusive evidence on the important role African Americans played in creating and developing the "Old and New West." He describes black western women and men in varying relationships with other westerners. Spanning 400 years, this is a major contribution to the study of African American history.

> *Two other African Americans, Edward Rose and James Beckwourth, committed their lives to the region. Rose, the son of a white trader and a black-Cherokee woman, grew up near Louisville, Kentucky. Unlike other "Mountain Men" who married Native American women but remained white, Rose joined two aboriginal societies.* (p. 49)

Keywords: American West • black towns

Young Adult

Miller, Robert Henry.

Reflections of a Black Cowboy Series.

Morristown, N.J.: Silver Burdett Press, 1991. Illustrated by Richard Leonard.

Because Miller wants young African American youth to understand that even during a time of slavery in this country, black people were not all picking cotton or singing hymns but were cowboys, pioneers, ranchers, and builders in every sense of the word, he examines the contributions black cowboys made to this country and shares the legacy of unsung black heroes of the old West.

Keywords: American West • frontier life • life stories • pioneers

Reflections of a Black Cowboy (Book One): Cowboys. Morristown, N.J.: Silver Burdett Press, 1991. ISBN 0-382-24079-0. 4p.

After the Civil War African Americans were eager to take their place as American citizens. In the untamed West, they found themselves in the right place with the skills to accommodate their environment. Slavery, despite its wickedness, had produced a new breed of cowboys who seemed to match the needs of Texas ranchers. Biographical content includes Nat Love, "Deadwood Dick," Mary Fields, Cherokee Bill, Black Marshal, Willie Kennard, and Bill Pickett, "The Dusty Demon."

Keywords: cowboys

Reflections of a Black Cowboy (Book 2): The Buffalo Soldiers. Morristown, N.J.: Silver Burdett Press, 1991–1992. ISBN 0-382-24080-4. 4p.

Focusing on the unsung heroes, the buffalo soldiers, this volume includes profiles of Emanuel Stance; Victorio, the "Apache Wolf"; and Lieutenant Henry O. Flipper. Events include the Boomer Rebellion and the Battle of San Juan Hill.

Keywords: Battle of San Juan Hill • Boomer Rebellion • buffalo soldiers

Reflections of a Black Cowboy (Book 3): Pioneers. Morristown, N.J.: Silver Burdett Press, 1991. ISBN 0-382-24081-2. 4p.

African Americans broke new ground and paved new paths for others to follow. In this volume, Miller illuminates the adventurous careers of York, the Black frontiersman with the Lewis and Clark Expedition; Ed "Cut Nose" Rose, fur trapper; Alvin Coffey and the California Gold Rush; George Monroe; Biddy Mason, woman pioneer; and the riders of the Pony Express.

Keywords: California Gold Rush • Lewis and Clark Expedition • pioneers • Pony Express riders • trappers

Reflections of a Black Cowboy (Book 4): Mountain Men. Morristown, N.J.: Silver Burdett Press, 1991. ISBN 0-382-24082-0. 4p.

Miller focuses on four men who made significant contributions to the development of America. These mountain men span time and events that eventually became legendary in our country's history. Young readers will become acquainted with Esteban, a Moroccan slave, who is recognized as the first African to enter the land that is now known as New Mexico and Arizona; Jean Baptiste Pointe Du Sable, founder of Chicago; Jim Beckwourth, mountain man and Indian chief; and George McJunkin, scholar and cowboy.

Keywords: cowboys • mountain men • Seven Cities of Gold

Chapter 6

Historical Fiction

Ola Carter Riley

> *Historians must necessarily speak in generalities and must examine recorded sources . . . They habitually leave out life lived by everyday people. History for them is what great men have done. But artists don't have any such limitation, and as the truest of historians they are obligated not to. I was scared that the world would fall away before somebody put together a thing that got close to the way we [blacks] really were.*—Toni Morrison (1974, 88)

It is on the truth that underlies this quote that African American historical fiction takes its stand. Historians have recorded the works of great people in many forms, but the common person's story frequently remains untold. Not until recently have historians begun writing in any depth about famous African Americans, and even then the historiography provides little information about their backgrounds in broader social and political contexts. Intentionally or not, early recordings of North America's history have in many cases omitted African American contributions and even an acknowledgment of their existence as individuals.

Only since the 1970s have African Americans written their own histories with any frequency. The omission of the African American in works of fiction is therefore perhaps not so surprising. From writer Toni Morrison's perspective, "black people signified little or nothing in the imagination of white American writers. Other than as the objects of an occasional bout of jungle fever, other than to provide local colour or to lend some touch to verisimilitude or to supply a needed moral gesture, humour, or bit of pathos, blacks made no appearance at all" (Morrison 1992, 34).

Through historical fiction, today's black writers seek to reclaim their lost or stolen histories. Many writers and readers concur that only through these stories can history be made whole. The growing body of literature that tells the stories of African Americans throughout history is both significant and laudable.

Definition

For the purposes of this guide, historical fiction encompasses those fictional stories that take place in the past, prior to the mid-twentieth century, in which historical background plays a prominent role. Several characteristics are considered universal to historical fiction:

- It brings the past to life for its readers;
- it is about the lives of real (usually famous) or fictional characters and events; and
- it is the result of research that reconstructs the customs, culture, beliefs, and society of the past.

All these elements hold true for African American historical fiction as well, but in African American contributions to this genre there is a greater emphasis on the personal lives of ordinary people and the impact of the African American's unique status on the founding and evolution of American society. African American historical fiction differs from other types of historical fiction in its attention to the circumstances by which blacks arrived in North America and their subsequent treatment and living conditions. These experiences and circumstances continue to serve as the bedrock and background for plots, character development, and narration of African American historical novels.

Just as the act of bringing African American history to life in novel form has required a reworking of the historical fiction model, so that the story does not necessarily focus on historical figures and events in the traditional sense, neither does African American historical fiction rely solely on European Americans' methods of recordkeeping and evaluation. Traditional historical recorded documents have omitted much about African American experiences and contributions, so African American writers have turned to other sources.

Because there is a lack of recorded information about early African American culture, customs, and beliefs, writers have had to turn to nontraditional sources to re-create and reclaim the past. Many novels reflect research based on "unofficial sources such as oral traditions of song, recipes, and storytelling" (Sale 1997, 358). Black novelists write historical fiction from their experiences and include characters known only to the writer. Such a technique is often not comfortable. As James Baldwin notes: "One writes out of one thing only—one's own experience. . . . The difficulty then, for me, of being a Negro writer was the fact that I was, in effect, prohibited from examining my own experience too closely by the tremendous demands and very real dangers of my social situations" (Christian 2000, 412).

Defining African American historical fiction presents challenges because it does not fall into standard, universally accepted guidelines. African American historical fiction writers have the overriding task of actually re-creating history. "History has been a contested terrain in which European Americans have had more authority to define what is worthy of recognition, what may be considered of historical significance, and what version or aspect of the past were important to keep alive in the present as a way of understanding who and what we are today" (Sale 1997, 358). In essence, content as well as technique have been prescribed from a perspective that is often at odds with the experience and perspective of the African American author.

Thus, the act of writing about people who have until recent times been excluded from the canons of historical records often becomes something other than an intellectual exercise. Consider, for example, the furor surrounding fictionalized accounts based on historical research about President Thomas Jefferson's relationship with the enslaved African American Sally Hemings. Yet where does truth lie? African American historical fiction touches hearts as well as informing minds, and the response is often emotional as much as intellectual.

Another inherent problem with defining African American historical fiction (as well as historical fiction in general) is the fact that time is not static. Many seminal works of African American historical fiction were written during the lifetimes of the authors and are thus not "historical" as defined in the larger genre of historical fiction. At what point does an era transcend contemporary status and become historical?

African American historical fiction is defined, for this chapter, as the works of African American authors who write about the culture, beliefs, contributions, and diversity of famous, enslaved, and African American people in the past as they interacted with other cultures and ethnic groups.

African American historical fiction is both the official and unofficial history of African American life in America. The novels that are included reflect on such historic events in American history as slavery, the Civil War, the Civil Rights Movement, and the Vietnam conflict. History, in these novels, does not simply provide a backdrop for a story; history *is* the story. African Americans have lived with "centuries of being defined by others, of intended and unintended misrepresentations and misinterpretations of African American life" (Mitchell 1998, 49). For many African American novelists, it is time for African Americans to write their own story.

Appeal to Readers

"The reading public wants historical fiction, and they want it when and where they want it" (Hawking 1999, 1394). Because historical fiction often combines with other popular genres, it appeals to a wide variety of readers. All readers look for meaningful, stimulating, and imaginative stories; therefore, African American historical fiction will appeal to readers of many ethnicities. This appeal is evident in the popularity of such authors as Anita Bunkley and Connie Briscoe, whose works have made best-seller lists and sold million of copies. At another level, all readers want to be able to identify with characters in their books, and black readers will be attracted by recognizable and realistic images that reflect their lives and themselves (Taylor 1999, 37).

Perhaps most important of all to African Americans is the chance to reclaim history, to read about events and society from the perspective of people with whom they identify and whose voices they can trust. It is a chance to discover where we came from and reflect on how and where we have arrived. It is an opportunity to learn about the power and independence of ancestors and to recognize that we have a strong and vibrant legacy to support individual efforts and visions for a meaningful and self-determined future.

Evolution of the Genre

Much African American fiction deals with issues of political, social, and cultural concerns, but these works have typically been defined as mainstream, not historical fiction. Frederick Douglass's *The Heroic Slave* (1853) and the biography of Madison Washington, a rebel slave leader are among early works that "challenged official versions of history" (Sale 1997, 358).

For the most part, however, African American authors' forays into historical fiction are rare before 1970. Even after the Harlem Renaissance, with its emphasis on creativity, innovation, and progress, mid-century America saw few works of historical fiction by black authors, other than Arna Bontemps's meticulously researched *Black Thunder* (1936) and Frank Yerby's *Foxes of Harrow* (1946), which was the first of a number of historical novels by the latter author.

Many scholars attribute the dearth of historical fiction by black authors during the 1950s to uneasiness with the impact of a slave legacy on the new generation. They suggest that, "a generation of Afro-Americans of the post-World War II era who had seen the new possibilities that a period seemed to promise for their children and who thought that knowledge of their history—one of enslavement, disfranchisement, and racism—might deter the younger generations' hopes for the future . . . X'd out the southern grandfather who had been a sharecropper and tried to forget the brutality of the African-American past" (Christian 1990, 326).

This antipathy continued through the 1960s, with two notable exceptions. Frank Yerby continued his work in the historical fiction genre into the 1960s, and Margaret Walker combined conventional and nontraditional sources to produce her classic *Jubilee* in 1966.

It was not until after 1970 that the African American historical novel became truly recognized as a mature genre. The 1972 publication of John Blassingame's *The Slave Community* is generally considered to be the major turning point (Sale 1997, 358). Blassingame's work is considered to be the first major work about African American slaves from the slave's perspective, and it had significant influence on the black literary community, resulting in the publication of several novels, including historical fiction, by African American authors. The subsequent publication and television production of Arthur Haley's enormously popular *Roots* secured a place of importance for historical fiction among publishers and readers. According to Sale, "The two decades after 1970 witnessed the publication of more than ten major historical novels" (1997, 358). Many of these novels were about civil rights, Black Power, the antebellum South, and the twentieth century.

Since the 1970s, the popularity of black historical fiction has increased. Black writers, according to Whitaker, have become more productive in all genres, and their readership has grown. "People think it's just relationship books that are selling, but you have all these Black writers producing everything . . . [including] historical fiction. And their readers are eating it up" (Whitaker 2000, 35). The improved economic status of African Americans, especially women, has resulted in more middle-class blacks and a considerable growth in readership over the last decade.

Historical fiction in particular appears to be the current choice of many African American readers. As of 2000, three of Connie Briscoe's novels, including historical fiction, had sold a combined 1.3 million copies. The author comments, "Black people were always reading and buying books . . . by us [African American authors]" (Whitaker 2000, 36). Perhaps more tellingly, Janet Hill, the director of Harlem Moon, says she "would like to acquire more African—American historical fiction, a genre that can fill the yawn between commercial and literary tastes. 'There's a huge opportunity for books of that nature. Readers are looking for different kinds of fiction' " (Labbé 2000, 38).

Current Themes and Trends

Intimate Perspectives

African American women play a prominent role in writing historical fiction, and recently they have turned to exploring individual psyches of their protagonists, making their perspectives as complex, individuated, and heterogeneous as possible (Sale 1997). Female authors' works tend to concentrate on families, relationships, and love. Anita Richmond Bunkley's *Black Gold* (1994) and J. California Cooper's *Family* (1991) describe families and family life, although they are set in two different eras. Although the themes of family and family relationships seem dominant in female writings, some male authors, such as John Edgar Wideman (*Cattle Killing,* 1996), incorporate the same themes.

Traditional Historical Themes

Traditional historical themes have continued throughout the most recent decade. Authors today may focus on the broader sociopolitical contexts of war and politics or on the uniquely African American experience of individual survival amid the danger and adversity of war or everyday life in a hostile society. James McEachin, in *Farewell to the Mockingbirds* (1997), explores the irony of African American soldiers compelled to fight battles at home; while James McBride's World War II story, *Miracle at St. Anna* (2002), leads to reflection on our common humanity.

New Novelists

Another major trend in African American historical fiction is the number of authors new to the genre. More than a decade ago, only the African American literary giants, such as Toni Morrison and Barbara Chase-Riboud, wrote historical fiction. These are productive authors whose newer works find eager audiences and whose older works are classics that are still in demand. Today, many beginning writers are publishing in the area of historical fiction, and other established writers are venturing into the genre.

Genreblending

"What is most striking in surveying historical fiction in the 20th century is its multiplicity of forms. Historical fiction can be found in almost every section of the modern bookstore [and library]: shelved alongside the classics or serious contemporary fiction or in the romance, mystery, fantasy, and biographical sections" (Burt 1997, xiv). This diversity in both general and in African American historical fiction attracts readers to the genre. "Now is an exciting time to be writing historicals, because so many authors are pushing the boundaries" (Donahue and Rosen 2001, 24).

Selection Criteria and Scope

Selection for this chapter was based on the ethnicity of the author (African Americans) and on the definition of the genre, historical fiction. Novels are included regardless of the author's source material, whether these are conventional documentary sources or oral reports, folktales or other nontraditional forms. Only work published between 1990 and 2003 is included. Stories in this chapter take place between 1619 and the present, although few are set later than the mid-1970s. The focus is on the African American experience, including such significant events as slavery, the Civil War, and the Civil Rights Movement. Although many of these novels could easily fall into several genres, they are included here if the primary appeal factor is setting and the overriding theme is historical in nature. In the event that it was difficult to definitively assign a work to the genre, the descriptor "historical fiction" in either WorldCat or *NoveList* was used as the deciding factor in placing the title in this chapter.

The approach of this chapter is inclusive. Although several of the authors' works have won awards, no author whose novels met the basic criteria was excluded. Awards in this section range from the BCALA (Black Caucus of the American Library Association) to the Pulitzer Prize. Authors who rank among the literary icons and have thousands of books in libraries across the United States are included, as well as Ernest Hill, whose *Satisfied With Nothin'* is, according to WorldCat's statistics, held in only 399 libraries.

A number of strategies and tools were used to select titles. Some authors were selected because of their known expertise as historical fiction authors. Other authors were selected through book review sources such as *Black Issues Book Review, Publishers Weekly*, and *Booklist*. In addition, basic readers' advisory sources such as *NoveList* were used to identify titles. Web resources such as the African American Literature Club were monitored. There were many such Web sites that provided information on African American historical fiction authors. Award lists were examined. Online tools such as OCLC's WorldCat were used to verify information about titles and authors.

Advising the Reader

Readers' choices in historical fiction are diverse. Historical fiction includes other genres and thereby makes the pool much larger than other genres. Having this knowledge makes directing the reader more challenging. To assist readers in the location of African American historical fiction, this chapter is divided into eras defined by events that had profound effects on the lives of African Americans in particular and North America in general.

- **Slavery: 1619–1860**. This era begins with the introduction of Africans into North America and follows through the years during which slavery was an accepted institution in the United States, to the beginning of the conflict that was to result in the Great Emancipation.

- **Civil War and Reconstruction: 1861–1900**. This era includes the time period from the beginning of the Civil War until the turn of the century. In addition to works that cover the Civil War and Reconstruction are those that include the abolitionists and the Underground Railroad.

- **World War I and World War II: 1901–1949**. Titles in this section cover the Great Depression, the Roaring 20s, the Harlem Renaissance, and the race riots that occurred during this period.

- **Civil Rights and Political Unrest: 1950–Present**. The stories selected for this section describe a major turning point in the lives of many African Americans. The works cover unrest on college campuses, civil rights, and desegregation. Other major issues of this period are the Vietnam War and the assassinations of President John F. Kennedy, Martin Luther King Jr., and Senator Robert "Bobby" Kennedy.

Karen Elaine Clay provided significant background information on historical fiction and contributed substantially to the development of this chapter. Karen Antell (see Chapter 9) wrote some of the annotations in this chapter. The note (KA) appears at the end of the annotations for which she is responsible.

Slavery: 1619–1860

Bontemps, Arna.

Black Thunder. Boston: Beacon Press, 1963 (1936). ISBN 0-8070-6429-7. 224p.

Based loosely on an actual planned slave revolt in 1800 that failed to come to fruition, this novel tells the story of Gabriel, a slave in Virginia who yearns for freedom and who gradually realizes that an organized revolt is the only way to achieve it. A carriage driver for his owner, Gabriel frequently visits Richmond, where he has the opportunity to eavesdrop on some French men's conversations about freedom and equality. He also listens to Bible readings and uses them as evidence for slaves' right to freedom. A leader among the slaves on his plantation, Gabriel is able to organize more than a thousand of them in his planned attack on Richmond. However, when a heavy thunderstorm delays the rebellion, many of the insurgents back down, and Gabriel faces betrayal by even his closest supporters. (KA)

> *"I tell you. I been studying about freedom a heap, me. I heard a plenty folks talk and I listened a heap. And everything I heard made me feel like I wanted to be free. It was on my mind hard, and it's right there the same way yet. On'erstand? That's all."*
> (p. 210)

Keywords: 1800s • Gabriel, a slave • plantation life • slave revolts

Briscoe, Connie.

A Long Way from Home. **New York: HarperCollins, 1999. ISBN 0060172789. 348p.**

James and Dolley Madison's house slaves experience joy and pain while serving them, and they share love for one another. House slave Susie, her daughter Clara, and her granddaughter Susan live a life markedly different from the field hands. Although Susie is comfortable at the Madison's home, believing she and her family will never be sold and will always be appreciated, Clara wants to go North to find freedom. It is not until Mass Jimmy's death that things change dramatically on the plantation in Montpelier.

> At first, Clara thought a spider was crawling on her cheek. . . .
> But just as she reached up to smack it away, the smell of li-
> quor hit her nose, and she knew this was a two-legged
> creature on her. . . . When she turned onto her back and
> opened her eyes, the face she saw was white. Mass Todd.
> (p. 68)

Notes: NAACP Image Award Nominee 2000

Keywords: plantation life • slaves and owners

Cary, Lorene.

The Price of a Child. **New York: Alfred A. Knopf, 1995. ISBN 0-679-42106-8. 317p.**

Ginnie Pryor is a slave in Virginia shortly before the Civil War. As her master's concubine, Ginnie accompanies him on a trip North, along with two of her children. But to prevent her from escaping to freedom while in the free states, the master insists that Ginnie leave her youngest child behind in Virginia. When an abolitionist group in Philadelphia gives Ginnie and her two older children the chance to walk away from slavery, the thought of the baby almost makes her falter. But Ginnie chooses freedom, changes her name to Mercer Gray, and becomes involved in the abolitionist movement herself, all the while working to get her baby back. (KA)

> Mercer stood on pulpits and stages and risers, talking her
> talks, and she never forgot that as she spoke, two of her
> children lay warm and healthy between clean sheets and
> underneath striped blankets and one lay next to Suzy's pal-
> let in Virginia. (p. 260)

Keywords: abolition and abolitionists • escaped slaves • slaves and owners

Chase-Riboud, Barbara.

The President's Daughter. **New York: Crown, 1994. ISBN 0517598612. 467p.**

This novel chronicles the life of President Thomas Jefferson's daughter by his slave mistress, Sally Hemings. Harriet Hemings's light complexion gives her the option of passing for white, and she does so. However, Harriet lives with the fear that one day her identity may be revealed, which would create havoc for her family.

> *I thought the North would be different! I thought I would find freedom! Equality! Instead, I've found how white people really feel about the Negro!* (p. 112)

Keywords: antebellum North • illegitimate children • mixed-race children • passing

Sally Hemings. **New York: Griffin, 2000, 1979. ISBN 0-312-24704-4. 348p.**

Based on historical research, but combined with the novelist's art for storytelling, *Sally Hemings* delves into the complex dynamics of slave–owner relationships at the turn of the nineteenth century and creates a plausible account of a long-lasting love affair. The power of this love causes Jefferson not to remarry after he is widowed and even leads Sally to choose slavery over freedom. (KA)

> *"On French soil you are free and you shall stay free. But return to him. Give him the chance to express his instincts as a father and a lover. You may be surprised. He loves you." "I don't want to be loved. I want to be free." "Do you really, my child? You love him as well, and there is no freedom in that."* (p. 143)

Notes: Janet Heidinger Kafka Prize 1979; *Sacred Fire: The QBR 100 Essential Black Books*

Keywords: 1800s • love affairs • mixed-race children • Paris • slaves and owners

Cooper, J. California.

Family: A Novel. **New York: Doubleday, 1991. ISBN 0385411715. 231p.**

From the other side of the grave, Clora narrates the lives of her children—Always, Sun, Peach, and Plum. Clora, the granddaughter of a slave and the slave master, planned to kill herself and her children to escape slavery, but she is the only one who dies. Although Clora's spirit hovers over all of her children and she tells about each one's life, her focus is her dark-skinned daughter Always, who risks death by learning to read and manages to ensure freedom for her son through a masterful and selfless deception.

> *My first baby was a very light baby, almost white. . . . It was a girl. Lord how I cried for this girl-child. . . . I would look at her through tears and love cause I knew SOMEBODY had already decided what her life was to be.* (p. 17)

Notes: J. California Cooper is also listed in the "Civil War and Reconstruction: 1861–1900" section of this chapter.

Keywords: family chronicles • slaves and owners • spirits • war stories

Davis, Kathleen Legeia.

Serpentina. **Miami, Fla.: Barnhardt & Ashe Publishing, 2002. ISBN 0971540217. 323p.**

Born on a Louisiana plantation and named for her shameful birthmark, Serpentina moves from being a lonely and sad girl to a young woman in love. She attempts to escape from slavery, rapists, and murderers to find freedom in Canada and finds love and a new life.

> *Each and every night of her life, Serpentina had slept upon the bed that her father had made, with her mother. She hadn't been aware of her mother's departure from her side until she was roused by the strange voice of a man and the anxious voice of her mother, pleading . . . . The sound of a resounding slap and a gasp from her mother shocked her fully awake.* (p.10)

Keywords: coming of age • escaped slaves • love affairs • plantation life • race relations • Underground Railroad

Davis, Mary Kemp.

Nat Turner before the Bar of Judgment: Fictional Treatments of the Southampton Slave Insurrection. **Baton Rouge: Louisiana State University Press, 1999. ISBN 0807122491. 298p.**

Drawing from accounts by reporters, novelists, historians, and politicians, the author writes this fictional account of the trial of those involved in the Southampton (Virginia) slave insurrection. The research was derived from four novels in the nineteenth century and two of the twentieth century, along with other documents including the governor's speech after Nat Turner's uprising. The novel is divided into three sections: "Seizing the Word," "Rendering a Verdict," and "Restless Peace."

> *By 1831, Southampton County in particular has a sizable black population sharply outnumbering the white. Specifically, there were 9,500 blacks to 6,500 whites. Of the former group 1,745 were free. Also, at one time the county had two famous antislavery ministers. The first was the Baptist minister. . . . After twenty-four years of preaching . . . [he] emigrated . . . to Kentucky . . . because he did not want to be dependent on slave labor.* (p. 36)

Keywords: court cases • slave revolts

Durham, David Anthony.

 Walk through Darkness. **New York: Doubleday, 2002. ISBN 0385499256. 291p.**

William's life for 21 years was that of a typical slave; that is, he was hired out to fields, tavern kitchens, and boats. At 22 years of age, his mother dies and everything changes. He meets Dover, and life for him will never to be the same. When a pregnant Dover is spirited away by her owner to distant Philadelphia and William escapes to follow her, he is tracked by a clever and ruthless hunter. This is a richly textured and vivid story peopled with complex characters and unexpected turnings.

> *He stopped swimming and bobbed. His arms floated around him with numb buoyancy. . . . He feared they couldn't possibly push him beyond that, across the miles of land ahead . . . his legs couldn't carry him beyond that. . . . He was in pursuit of a single being in the entire universe.* (p. 10)

Notes: Black Issues Book Review Best Book 2002; New York Times Notable Book 2002

Keywords: Annapolis, Maryland • escaped slaves • husbands and wives • love affairs

Gaines, Ernest J.

***The Autobiography of Miss Jane Pittman.* New York: Dial Press, 1971. 245p. ISBN: None.**

This well-written fictional "biography" tells the story of centenarian Miss Jane Pittman, whose life spanned the years from the Civil War to the Civil Rights Movement. Jane's story begins when she was about eight or nine years old and named Ticey. A Yankee corporal renamed her Jane Brown after his daughter in Ohio. In four major sections, Jane's story covers the war years, Reconstruction, the plantation years, and the quarters. Within each section Miss Jane also tells the story of others who made many sacrifices to improve the life of blacks. From the war years, there are the stories of freedom and massacres. During Reconstruction, Jane provides portrayals of the Ku Klux Klan, the Freedman's Bureau, and her adopted son Ned, who was assassinated when he tried to open a school. In the section on the plantation, the author describes religious experiences, sharecropping, and other events. In the last section, Miss Jane talks about life in the quarters and the search for "the One," a community leader to save them, and a hope that the leader would be Jimmy Aaron. In the end, Jimmy is assassinated and Miss Jane leads the protest about it. In spite of all obstacles, Miss Jane's human spirit and dignity survive.

 6

> *I had been trying to get Miss Jane Pittman to tell me the story of her life for several years now. . . . I told her she was over a hundred years old, she had been a slave in this country, so there had to be a story. When school closed in the summer in 1962 I went back to the plantation where she lived and I told her I wanted her story before school opened in September, and I would not take no for an answer . . . . "Then I reckoned I better say something," she said.* (p. vii)

Notes: Ernest J. Gaines is also listed in the "Racial and Political Issues" section of Chapter 9.

Keywords: autobiographies • centenarians • Civil Rights Movement

Gates, Henry Louis.

***The Bondwoman's Narrative*. New York: Warner Books, 2002. ISBN 0446530085. 338p.**

The everyday life of a slave is related by Hannah Craft. Hannah, a slave, tells of her life from childhood through adulthood, from neglect to waiting on mistress after mistress. Scriptural references at the beginning of each chapter provide the introduction for Hannah.

> *I was not brought up by any body in particular that I know of. I had no training, no cultivation. . . . No one seemed to care for me till I was able to work, and then it was Hannah do . . . .* (p. 6)

Keywords: escaped slaves • North Carolina • passing • plantation life • slaves and owners • Virginia

Gurley-Highgate, Hilda.

🎗 ***Sapphire's Grave*. New York: Doubleday, 2003. ISBN 0385503237. 248p.**

Sapphire is the progeny of a "blue-black woman" from Sierra Leone, West Africa, who was brought to North Carolina as a slave. Sapphire mirrored her mother in physical features, spirit, tenaciousness, and willingness to destroy or be destroyed, and to protect her daughters from slave masters even unto death. Sapphire's spirit was passed to her daughters, Ndeuv, Eshe, and Zoe. "Collectively, their name was Life" (p. 45), and they live today in modern America.

> *One generation passeth away, and another generation cometh." Ecclesiastes 1:4.* (p. 9)

Notes: *Essence* Bestseller List 2004

Keywords: domestic workers • family chronicles

Haley, Alex.

🎗 ***Roots*. Garden City, N.Y.: Doubleday, 1976. ISBN 0-385-03787-2. 688p.**

Based on painstaking genealogical research, *Roots* traces seven generations of Alex Haley's family history, starting with Kunte Kinte, known in Haley's family's lore as "the African," who was captured in West Africa in 1767 and taken to Virginia as a slave. Kinte's stories of Africa were passed down through seven generations. The stories of the intervening generations—part fact, part fiction—tell of slavery, emancipation, Reconstruction, the Ku Klux Klan, and above all, human ambition and perseverance. (KA)

> *One pushed the trunk under Kunta's right foot as the other tied the foot to the trunk so tightly that all of Kunta's raging couldn't free it. . . . Kunta was screaming and thrashing as the ax flashed up, then down so fast—severing skin, tendons,*

*muscles, bone—that Kunta heard the ax thud into
the trunk as the shock of it sent the agony deep into
his brain.* (p. 244)

Notes: National Book Award 1977; Pulitzer Prize 1977; *Sacred Fire: The QBR
100 Essential Black Books*

Keywords: Civil War • emancipation • family chronicles • family life • genealogy • Ku Klux Klan • Reconstruction • slave trade

Jackson-Opoku, Sandra.

The River Where Blood Is Born. New York: Ballantine, 1997. ISBN
0-345-39514-X. 401p.

Ananse, the mythical storytelling spider, weaves a web of tales about
nine generations of descendants of two West African women sold into
slavery in the eighteenth century. Using the structure and elements of
folklore, the novel expresses the yearning for roots felt by the children of
the Diaspora and, ultimately, the healing that can be found only in a return to Mother Africa. (KA)

> *Of course we were all kings and queens before we
> got ourselves kidnapped, never mind the fact that
> the kings and queens were the ones organizing the
> slave raids. And the ignorance cuts both ways.
> Some Ugandan chap in grad school write a long,
> convoluted paper trying to convince himself that
> Africans signed up for slavery on a voluntary basis.
> Oh, the things we believe trying to make ourselves
> whole again.* (p. 363)

Notes: BCALA Literary Award for Fiction 1998

Keywords: African Diaspora • cultural identity • family chronicles • folklore •
racial identity • storytelling

Johnson, Charles Richard.

Charles Richard Johnson is a 1998 MacArthur Fellow.

Middle Passage. New York: Plume, 1991. ISBN 0-452-26638-6. 209p.

This novel, set in 1830, is written in the style of a journal whose narrator,
Rutherford Calhoun, stows away aboard a slave ship to escape his credi-
tors and his fiancée in New Orleans. An educated freed slave, Rutherford
is not prepared for the horrors he witnesses when the ship picks up its human cargo. The "middle passage" is marked by slave revolt, mutiny, and
shipwreck, and ironically it transforms Rutherford into the kind of person he stowed away to avoid becoming: someone ready to settle down
and accept responsibility. (KA)

> *Once the Allmuseri saw the great ship and the
> squalid pit that would house them sardined
> belly-to-buttocks in the orlop, with its dead air and*

> *razor-teethed bilge rats . . . the Africans panicked . . . this*
> *sudden flurry of resistance brought out the worst in Falcon,*
> *if you can imagine that. He beat them until blood came. . . .*
> *[H]ow in God's name could I go on after this?* (pp. 65–67)

Notes: Charles Johnson is also listed in the "Civil Rights and Political Unrest: 1950–Present" section of this chapter.
National Book Award 1990

Keywords: freed slaves • journalism and journalists • New Orleans • seafaring life • slave revolts • slave trade

Jones, Edward P.

Edward P. Jones is a 2004 MacArthur Fellow.

The Known World. New York: Amistad, 2003. ISBN 0060557540. 388p.

Covering a period of over 100 years, this novel describes bits of history about fictional Manchester County, Virginia. Henry Townsend, a former slave, is now slave owner. His former master, William Robbins, has taught Henry lessons in owning slaves and the relationship that is to exist between the slave and his master. Henry's sudden death from unknown causes brings about many changes in the lives of his slaves and his widow, Caldonia.

> *Sleeping in a cabin beside Henry the first two weeks after*
> *the sale, Moses had thought that it was already a strange*
> *world that made him a slave to a white man, but God had in-*
> *deed set it twirling and twisting every which way when he*
> *put black people to owning their own kind.* (pp. 8–9)

Notes: ALA Notable Book 2004; BCALA First Novelist Award 2004; *Essence* Bestseller List 2004; National Book Award Finalist 2003; National Books Critics Circle Award for Fiction 2004; Pulitzer Prize for Fiction 2004

Keywords: black slaveholders • plantation life • slaves and owners

Lewis, Ora Martin.

Seeds in the Wind: A Historical Novel, Louisiana (1565-1865). Washington, D.C.: Maranatha Press, 2000. ISBN 0994206714. 353p.

Tanya, an albino, has been mistaken for white on several occasions, but her identity is proven through her research revealing her West African heritage. While she is researching the family background, a doctoral student falls in love with Tanya, but she is in love with Caldwell, "a full black minister."

> *The principal was trying his best to explain his task. "This*
> *child should have been pre-registered. You will have to*
> *take her out to the elementary school near False River. I*
> *heard that none of the 'slots' reserved for white children*
> *have been filled. She can't come here."* (p. 63)

Keywords: family history • genealogy • Louisiana • men and women • West Africa

Morrison, Toni.

Beloved: A Novel. **New York: Alfred A. Knopf, 1987. ISBN 0-394-53597-9. 275p.**

Beloved is not easy to read, but the effort is worthwhile. The novel tells the story of Sethe, an escaped slave, who is literally haunted by the ghost of her baby daughter, Beloved. Sethe kills Beloved when her former owner comes after her in Cincinnati, because she would rather see her children dead than returned to slavery. The story unfolds in fragments via stream of consciousness. Dedicated to the "sixty million and more" blacks who died in the Middle Passage, the novel chronicles the unspeakable horrors of slavery and makes palpable the extent to which slavery survivors had to repress their memories of that horror to continue to live without going insane. (KA)

> [S]he worked hard to remember as close to noth-ing as was safe. Unfortunately her brain was devi-ous. . . . and suddenly there was Sweet Home rolling, rolling, rolling out before her eyes, and al-though there was not a leaf on that farm that did not make her want to scream, it rolled itself out before her in shameless beauty. It never looked as terrible as it was and it made her wonder if hell was a pretty place too. (p. 6)

Notes: American Book Award 1988 • Blackboard Bestseller List 1999 • Pulitzer Prize for Fiction 1988 • *Sacred Fire: The QBR 100 Essential Black Books*

Keywords: escaped slaves • parents and children • plantation life • slaves and owners • spirits

Pate, Alexs.

Amistad: A Novel. **New York: DreamWorks, 1997. ISBN 0451195167pa. 316p.**

This novel is based on the movie *Amistad*. In 1839, captive Africans, with Cinque as their leader, led a revolt on the slave ship *Amistad*. The Africans received no help from the then president, who was seeking re-election. Abolitionist Ted Joadson and former president John Quincy Adams helped the Africans fight for their freedom.

> Whenever trouble threatened, Sengbe, now called Cinque, always relied on two things to give him strength. A gris-gris charm his wife had given that he'd managed to hold on to and the memory of how he'd killed the lion. One was protection and hope; the other a true moment of bravery. (p.11)

Notes: Film by the same name, directed by Steven Spielberg and starring Morgan Freeman, Anthony Hopkins, and Djimon Hounsou (1997).

Keywords: court cases • movie novels • slave revolts • slave trade

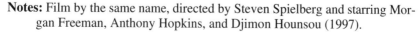

Rhodes, Jewell Parker.

🎗 *Douglass' Women: A Novel.* **New York: Atria Books, 2002. ISBN 0743410092. 358p.**

Another side of the great abolitionist is portrayed in this novel. Anna Murray Douglass, a free woman of color and Douglass's first wife, and Ottilie Assing, a beautiful and intellectual German heiress, find themselves in love with man who appears insensitive to their feelings. Surprisingly, the two women are revealed as complex individuals, while fiery and passionate Douglass comes across rather flat.

> *"He ain't here." "He ain't here." When the militia came. When curious neighbors came. When church gossips came. I said what I got used to saying the last twenty years: "he ain't here." (p. 309)*

Notes: BCALA Literary Award 2003; Black Issues Book Review Best Book 2002; Zora Neale Hurston/Richard Wright Fiction Award Finalist 2003

Keywords: abolition and abolitionists • husbands and wives • love affairs

Taylor, Mildred.

The Land. **New York: Phyllis Fogelman Books, 2001. ISBN: 0803719507. 375p.**

Paul-Edward Logan,the son of a white landowner and a slave woman of African and Native American descent, is acknowledged by his father and his brother, Robert (when it is convenient for Robert). Nevertheless, Paul-Edward's life in Mississippi during the late 1880s is a constant struggle as he comes to understand that most people will recognize him as black person. Paul-Edward's life as a white young man proves beneficial in some areas and a real struggle in others. With many unanswered questions, Paul-Edward becomes friends with Mitchell Thomas, whose identity is not questionable. Circumstances force the young men into their own world. This novel is the prequel to *Roll of Thunder, Hear My Cry.*

> *It was during the summer before Robert and I were supposed to go off to school that I came to the true realization that I had two families. (p 46)*

Keywords: family relationships • mixed-race children • prejudice

Trice, Dawn Turner.

An Eighth of August: A Novel. **New York: Crown, 2000. ISBN 0517707893. 298p.**

The celebration of the Emancipation Proclamation in the town of Halley's Landing has been a festive event since the late 1800s. Celebrants come to show off their best clothes and remember the good and bad times. In 1986, we hear the stories of Flossie Jo Penticott, and Aunt Cora and May Ruth, a white woman whose relationship with the black community is like that of another family member.

> *Everybody's getting ready. . . . The simple truth is you can't cram this many folk into one little town—get them eating*

*real good and laying back, talking 'bout who they
are, where they come from, the hard times behind
them and beyond—and expect things to remain
the same.* (p. 13)

Keywords: Emancipation Proclamation • race relations • women's friendships

Walker, Margaret.

Jubilee. **New York: Bantam, 1966. ISBN 0-55327-383-3. 416p.**

This highly researched book transforms the oral history that Walker
learned from her grandmother into a powerful work of historical fiction,
replete with authentic details. Vyry is the daughter of a slave owner and
his favored house slave. Orphaned as a child and shunned by the owner,
she is raised by other slave women. Smart and strong, Vyry is faced with
difficult choices throughout her life, which encompasses the antebellum
years, the Civil War, and Reconstruction. Presented with the opportunity
to escape to freedom with her husband, she chooses instead to stay with
her children. Remarried, Vyry later must make another decision when
her first husband reappears. (KA)

> *They thatched the roof with boughs of pine and oak
> complete with leaves and pine needles and they
> covered the open places left for windows with quilts
> until they could build shutters from saplings . . . And
> in their joy to be building a home of their own, ev-
> erything seemed possible.* (p. 267)

Notes: Houghton Mifflin Literary Fellowship 1966 • *Sacred Fire: The QBR 100
Essential Black Books*

Keywords: Civil War • escaped slaves • family relationships • interracial relationships • mixed-race children • orphans • Reconstruction

Williams, Sherley Anne.

Dessa Rose. **New York: Berkley Books, 1987. ISBN 0-425-10337-4. 260p.**

Two true events lie at the heart of this novel. In 1829, a pregnant black
woman in Kentucky instigated a slave revolt but was caught and hanged.
In 1830, a white North Carolina woman sheltered runaway slaves on her
remote farm. The premise of *Dessa Rose* is the fictional meeting of these
two women. Both outsiders, both strong and courageous, Dessa Rose and
Miss Rufel slowly learn to trust each other enough to join forces in the
cause of freedom. Along the way, they also forge an unlikely sisterhood.
(KA)

> *Runaways. Ada, Harker, how many others? And
> the white woman let them stay, nursed—Dessa
> knew the white woman nursed her baby; she had
> seen her do it. It went against everything she had
> been taught to think about white women but to in-
> spect that fact too closely was almost to deny her*

> *own existence. The white woman had let them stay—Even*
> *that was almost too big to think about. (p. 123)*

Keywords: 1800s • escaped slaves • race relations • slave revolts • Virginia • women's
friendships

Wilson, P. B. (P. Bunny).

Night Come Swiftly. **Eugene, Ore.: Harvest House, 1997. ISBN 1565077180. 220p.**

Meredith, the daughter of a slave owner, takes upon herself the burden of saving
her friend Tilly, a slave in their North Carolina home. Defying both her father and
the ways of the South, Meredith helps Tilly find freedom.

> *"Meredith Douglas Hunter was my friend and, I might add,*
> *a friend to all colored people. . . . There is a song that say,*
> *'Jesus love the little children all the children of the world, . . .*
> *they are precious in His sight' . . . Meredith Hunter believed*
> *the words of that song." (p. 273)*

Keywords: friendships • slaves and owners

Civil War and Reconstruction: 1861–1900

Bradley, David.

The Chaneysville Incident: A Novel. **New York: Harper & Row, 1981. ISBN 0-06-
010491-0. 432p.**

John Washington is a history professor in Philadelphia whose life is interrupted
when he finds out that Jack, the man who raised him in rural Pennsylvania, is dying. When he goes to visit Jack, the dying man tells him about a legendary incident in which 13 slaves were killed while trying to escape from the South. The
historian in John is intrigued and begins researching the incident to uncover the
truth, but the obsession becomes personal when John discovers his own family
history is tied to the event. In establishing the truth about the incident, John also
reveals a great deal about his father and his grandfather and ultimately comes to
understand himself. (KA)

> *We still believe that, by whatever haphazard means, the*
> *past is created, fixed; that it's understanding depends on*
> *finding out exactly when whoever did whatever to whom-*
> *ever. . . . And we believe that if we have been good little his-*
> *torians, just before they do whatever it is that they finally do*
> *with us, they'll take us in there and show us what was really*
> *going on. (p. 264)*

Notes: PEN/Faulkner Award 1982; *Sacred Fire: The QBR 100 Essential Black Books*
Keywords: family chronicles • historians • slavery • Underground Railroad

Brown, Linda Beatrice.

Crossing Over Jordan: A Novel. **New York: Ballantine Books, 1995. ISBN 0345378571. 290p.**

Four women living in Georgia tell their stories about slavery. One of the women lives long enough to see slavery come to an end; another recognizes the lack of power she faced after freedom. Another searches for the good life, while the last one breaks the cycle of oppression in the family.

> *We have found the covenant again. And the name of the covenant is "rebellion," and the name of the covenant is "yessuh" and the name of the covenant is "education," and the name of the covenant is "death," and the name of the covenant is "revolution," and the name of the holy, holy covenant is "survival".* (pp. 4–5)

Notes: Blackboard Bestseller List 1995

Keywords: mothers and daughters

Brown, Wesley.

Darktown Strutters: A Novel. **New York: Cane Hill Press, 1994. ISBN 0943433118pa. 224p.**

Jim Crow can dance better and faster than anybody, white or black. He begins his dancing career before the Civil War when he's leased out to white actor Tom Rice's minstrel show and later changes troupes. The dual nature of personality and the ambiguity of racial identity are explored through the acting and black face tropes that recur throughout the story.

> *He heard a stomping sound coming from inside a livery stable and decided to find out what it was. Rice stepped inside and picked up a foul smell . . . Feed was scattered . . . Then he saw a black man whose whole body looked like it wad having a fit of the hiccups. . . . At first Rice thought the man was crippled. Then he realized he wasn't . . . he was dancing.* (p.1)

Keywords: dancers • entertainers • minstrel shows • race relations • racism

Cooper, J. California.

The Wake of the Wind. **New York: Doubleday, 1998. ISBN 0385487045. 373p.**

The lives of two former slaves, Mordecai, known as Mor, and Lifee, are chronicled from marriage, through freedom from slavery, through the births of their children, to their deaths. Mor and Lifee lived the life of many slaves: enduring their master's harshness, comforting other slaves and being comforted by them.

> *Mor was always concerned about the house. He longed for the days of good, warm weather to come. He was aching to get started on "his" land. Every day he thought of himself, as his eyes roved over the land, "My land. I gots my own land." He imagined and pictured all things he would do.* (p. 148)

Notes: J. California Cooper is also listed in the "Slavery: 1619–1860" section of this chapter.
Blackboard Bestseller List 1999, 2000

Keywords: freed slaves • slavery • slaves and owners • Texas

Jenkins, Beverly.

Night Song. **New York: Avon Books, 1994. ISBN: 0380776588. 374p.**

Cora Lee Henson had witnessed the lynching of her grandfather. This act of cruelty produced an enduring hatred for Yankees and the military that Cora thought she would never let go. When Sergeant Chase Jefferson of the famous Tenth Colored Cavalry comes to town, his hot pursuit of Cora Lee, now a teacher, brings about a change in her feelings.

> *She'd tried to rid herself of memories of Chase Jefferson. . . . He was a soldier, a drifter, an adventurous man with no roots.* (p. 24).

Keywords: educators • Kansas • love stories • military officers

Jones, Winston A.

For God, Country and the Confederacy: Completing the Circle of Acceptance. **Portland, Ore.: Franklin Street Books, 2002. ISBN 0971941483. 328p.**

This novel portrays free African Americans during the Civil War. Not all blacks were slaves, and Andrew St. Claire's life story proves it. To show his loyalty, Andrew joins the Confederate Army and fights alongside his white counterparts. The peculiar institution of slavery is as profitable for Andrew St. Clair as it is for whites.

> *Andrew owns 640 acres of prime land and has 20 slaves working on it. He is a family man with two sons . . . a daughter . . . and his wife of twenty-five years. . . . Living in the South has not been easy, but Andrew knows, from his own experiences, it's not much different anywhere else in America, for a person of color whether he is free or not.* (p. 29)

Keywords: black slaveholders • Civil War • freemen • slavery

McEachin, James.

Tell Me a Tale: A Novel of the Old South. **New York: Berkley Books, 1996. ISBN 0425156893pa. 281p.**

The offspring of white plantation owner Archie McBride and a young, young Moses returns to his North Carolina birthplace in disguise. Posing as a reporter, he hears the stories of four men who wanted slavery to continue and now want it to return.

> *He was not the simpleton the men had thought. This was a master storyteller at work, and he spoke of many things, his voice aging with the telling. Trancelike, he sent their minds back, way back. He touched on the history of Red Springs, the early days of slavery.* (p. 51)

Keywords: freed slaves • mixed-race people • plantation life

Meriwether, Louise.

Fragments of the Ark. **New York: Pocket Books, 1994. ISBN 0671799479. 342p.**

Fragments is based on the true story of a real slave. Peter Mango stole a boat to gain freedom for himself and his family. After achieving their freedom, Peter, his family, and other runaway slaves unite in their efforts to fight for the families who remained behind.

> *One A.M. Peter and July broke into the captain's cabin. The curtain was pulled across a berth . . . shutting out the sun when the captain wanted to sleep. . . . The berth was empty . . . In the locker he found what they were looking for — the wide-brimmed black hat, a pistol and a smooth-bore gun.* (pp. 70–71)

Keywords: Civil War • escaped slaves • South Carolina

Rhodes, Jewell Parker.

Voodoo Dreams. **New York: St. Martin's Press, 1995. ISBN 0-312-09869-3. 436p.**

This novel is a fictional account of the life of Marie Laveau, the legendary nineteenth-century New Orleans voodoo queen. On her tenth birthday, Marie begins having visions. One of her first visions is of John, the man she meets when she moves to New Orleans as a teenager. John, the New Orleans conjure man, turns Marie's powers into a sordid voodoo business, taking advantage of her as well as the vast audiences who come seeking "money, love, vengeance, health, always something" (p. 415). But Marie finally uses her powers to break free of John's hold over her and becomes a famous healer in her own right, using her gift for good, not exploitation. (KA)

> *The second day, Grandmere would only utter omens and warnings. Marie exclaimed over a wounded crow that nonetheless managed to fly. Grandmere promptly replied, "A bird with a crooked wing means sorrow." When they by-passed a dirt path, Grandmere pointed: "A cracked gate means you'll leave and never come back." . . . . By nightfall, Marie thought she'd go crazy if she heard another saying.* (p. 39)

Keywords: con artists and con games • 1800s • men and women • supernatural • voodoo

Tademy, Lalita.

🎗 *Cane River.* **New York: Warner Books, 2001. ISBN 0446527327. 418p.**

Drawn from family memoirs, this is the fictional account of a Creole family living in Central Louisiana along the Cane River. The lives of Suzette, Philomene, and Emily, whose lives begin in slavery, are reconstructed. They are women who could have passed for white. Each woman has played a part in securing freedom for her family and forging her own success. Includes Cane family photos and documents.

> *I hope you can put some of these things together better than I did, you may have heard that my Brother or I did not finish School or no one thought me one thing about Typen but I know I know it, Smile. My God have blessed me to be here my three scores and ten.* (p. xii)

Notes: *Essence* Bestseller List 2002; Go On Girl Book Club New Author 2002; Oprah's Book Club 2001

Keywords: Creoles • family chronicles • family history • mothers and daughters • passing • skin color • slaves and owners

World War I and World War II: 1900–1949

Baker, Calvin.

Once Two Heroes. **New York: Viking, 2003. ISBN 067003164. 275p.**

The story opens with a prologue describing Nathan Hampton's death. Mather Rose, denied his Medal of Honor because he is black, is on the way to Washington, D.C., in an attempt to collect his medal. On his return to Los Angeles, he has a confrontation with racist Nathan Hampton that results in the white man's death. Hampton's brother Lewis, another veteran, vows revenge. Each half of the book is dedicated to a full exploration of each of the two war heroes' lives, leading up to the horrible point of intersection.

> *Other than . . . children's pranks, he had never done anything against the Negroes in the town. But neither had they done anything against him. Now is different. Something*

had broken this year, and they cannot just sit back and overlook it, at least Nathan cannot. (p. 218–19)

Keywords: race relations • vengeance • war stories

Bunkley, Anita Richmond.

Black Gold. **New York: Dutton, 1994. ISBN 0525937528. 404p.**

Life for an orphaned girl named Leela Brannon is full of prejudice and hard work. Then she meets Thomas Jacob Wilder (T. J.), who has been on his own since he was 11 years old. They marry, but the hard work of maintaining a farm in Texas leads to T. J.'s early death. When Leela finds "black gold" on their place, many people come into her life, but she is determined to keep the land and raise her family.

> *"You worked yourself into this sickness." She knew he could hear her. "You gave yourself away for this land . . . for me and Kenny." . . . She smiled and took T. J.'s hand in hers. "I learned my lesson years ago. Nothing will keep me from doing what I can to hold on to our land, our home." (p. 168)*

Notes: Anita Richmond Bunkley is also listed in the "Civil Rights and Politics: 1950–Present" section of this chapter.
  Blackboard Bestseller List 1994, 1995

Keywords: love stories • orphans • petroleum industry • Texas

Dash, Julie.

Daughters of the Dust. **New York: Dutton, 1997. ISBN 0525941096. 310p.**

The lives of the Gullah people, who are descendants of intermarried blacks and Native Americans, are chronicled. From the coast of the Carolinas, their roots and lifestyles are described by an anthropologist who is a black woman.

> *By the time the African captives arrived, the land would be known as the Sea Islands. . . . They would trade, share, and learn from the ancient people who still walked the islands. And from this blending of old and new came the unique culture and tongue known as Gullah or Geeche. (pp. 3–4)*

Notes: Film by the same name, directed by Julie Dash and starring Cora Lee Day and Alva Rodgers (1991).

Keywords: family chronicles • Gullahs • movie novels • Sea Islands

Due, Tananarive.

The Black Rose. **New York: Ballantine/Random House, 2001. ISBN 0345439600. 375p.**

This fictional "biography" of the first African American female millionaire, Madam C. J. Walker, begins with a visit to Delta, Louisiana, and chronicles other special events in her life, including her death.

> *So when a long, sleek black convertible touring car glided its way into Delta that day, driven by a somber-faced colored chauffeur in black cap and uniform, the entire street took notice. . . . And who was the primly dressed colored woman in a black suit and white shirtwaist who sat in the backseat with a smile fixed on her face, waving to people as she passed?* (p. 93)

Keywords: biographies • business people • cosmetics industry

Hatch, John W.

Mississippi Swamp. **New Africa Chronicles Series. Berkeley, Calif.: 2ndsightbooks.com, 2001. ISBN 0970685408. 354p.**

Rose and Cicero's political views lead them to refuse to accept the so-called freedom granted to slaves after the Civil War. This novel is the story of two people who live and survive in the swamps.

> *Together Cicero and Rose slept, ate, Cicero followed Rose around as she did cabin chores, she sat and listened to more of how his thinking had changed. In those first days they became one person again. Neither gave a thought to differences that might still exist. It was enough to be children at play.* (p. 252)

Keywords: freed slaves • Mississippi

Johnson, Guy.

Echoes of a Distant Summer: A Novel. **New York: Random House, 2001. ISBN 0375505679. 661p.**

This novel is the sequel to *Standing at the Scratch Line*. The protagonist, Jackson St. Clair Tremain, comes from a family where violence and bloodshed are a part of life. He distances himself from his family to live a quiet life. The young Tremain, living in California and working as a city employee, learns that even distance and time are not enough put the legacy of his ruthless grandfather in the past forever. Although they haven't spoken for over 20 years, Jackson is called to his grandfather's. Now grandfather's enemies are plotting to exact revenge from any and all of the family.

> *"I did what I knew to do at that time. Didn't have no words to explain to a child that his daddy was dead. You wouldn't have understood the why of it. And no words gon' make you feel any better with both yo' parents gone" . . . . "I wanted you with me, but I was a man on the run for a while."* (pp. 238–39)

Keywords: criminals • grandfathers and grandsons • Mexico • Oakland, California

Standing at the Scratch Line: A Novel. **New York: Random House, 1998. ISBN 0375501584. 548p.**

The life of LeRoi "King" Tremain, the main character, is chronicled from 1916 to 1946. Whether hunting for one of the family rivals in the swamps of Louisiana or fighting in World War I, "King" is known for his fight against racism, bigotry, and discrimination. While serving in the war, killing becomes easy for "King," and his life afterward is filled with violence and bloodshed. The novel is divided into three books: "LeRoi Bordeaux Tremain"; the "Saga of Serena and King Tremain"; and "The Family Loss".

> *"I'm King Tremain! You missed me the night you shot at me outside the Beau Geste. Try yo' luck now."* . . . . *I know about you, how you's supposed to be so tough! Yo' name's LeRoi Tremain. You ain't no king!* (p.186)

Keywords: family relationships • Oklahoma • World War I

Lacey, Earnest Edward.

FreeJoe. **Memphis, Tenn.: FreeJoe Enterprise, 1996. ISBN 1886371385. 545p.**

This novel chronicles the life of a young man whose father is a white plantation owner and mother is a slave. After becoming free, Joseph "FreeJoe" Harris, a man of faith and love, becomes a success. In addition to being an entrepreneur, he is a minister and productive in getting other slaves free.

> *"What was that all about?"* . . . *" Mister Adcock thought I was a slave.* . . . . *"I can't help what he thought"* . . . . *"I am the way God made me and if people don't understand that, then they don't understand God."* (p. 253)

Keywords: business people • church men • freed slaves • Memphis, Tenn. • mixed-race children

Major, Clarence.

Dirty Bird Blues: A Novel. **San Francisco: Mercury House, 1996. ISBN 1562790838. 279p.**

Old Crow Whisky, better known as Dirty Bird, has kept Manfred Bank moving from one place to another. Manfred, a musician with a blue-collar job, has wandered from Chicago to Omaha seeking solace in his relationships with a male buddy, a wife, and a child, but it is Dirty Bird that is his constant companion. After a nightmarish descent, Manfred takes hold of new possibilities.

> *And he suddenly now knew—even with death bells ringing in his ears—what he must do, had it come*

> *as a clear thought: I want to live . . . Yeah. Got to start acting*
> *my age and not my shoe size.* (p. 237)

Keywords: alcohol abuse and alcoholics • American Midwest • blues music and musicians • race relations

McBride, James.

Miracle at St. Anna. **New York: Riverhead Books/Penguin Putnam, 2002. ISBN 157322127. 271p.**

Four black soldiers from different regions of the United States are serving their country in Italy. They are a part of the African American 92nd Division fighting the Germans and are aware that the military division they are serving with discriminates against them. The soldiers' interactions with Italian civilians help them to see the common threads that exist in all humans.

> *The army was a confusing place. They gave him pictures,*
> *and training manuals to read. They pointed at things for him*
> *to shoot at. They put him on a boat. They told him Hitler was*
> *a bad man. But nothing they gave him was his. . . . The only*
> *person who had given him anything was Bishop. . . . He had*
> *given him knowledge. He had told him it was a white man's*
> *war.* (p. 141)

Notes: Black Issues Book Review Best Book 2002

Keywords: Italy • race relations • war stories

McEachin, James.

Farewell to the Mockingbirds: A Novel. **Encino, Calif.: rhari publishing group. ISBN 096566190. 512p.**

Based on a true account of African American soldiers in World War I, this novel recounts one of the most disgraceful chapters in America's military history. While many U.S. troops were being shipped out to fight a war in France, these men—the "Mockingbirds"—were fighting a war against their fellow soldiers in America. When they revolted against the racist and inhumane treatment to which they were subjected, they were tried, and many were subsequently executed.

> *"Listen to me careful: The soldier said our sergeant always*
> *told us 'the word nigger is only used by a nigger.' So guess*
> *what you is? A fat, slop-eatin', pig-faced nigger. You white,*
> *but you ain't nothin' but a pig-faced nigger all the same. . . .*
> *When I get outta here, I'm gonna find out just how much*
> *sports you like."* (pp. 268–69)

Keywords: courts martial • Houston, Texas • "the Mockingbirds" • race relations • race riots • war stories • World War I

Rhodes, Jewell Parker.

Magic City. **New York: HarperCollins, 1997. ISBN 0060187328. 270p.**

Joe Samuel, a shoe shiner and son of a Tulsa black banker, is falsely accused of raping a white woman. Mary Keane, a young white woman and rape victim, can help exonerate him. As the chain of events moves toward the devastating riot that destroyed the "Black Wall Street" in Tulsa, each of the two must examine his or her own heart.

> *A small crowd of men, arguing heatedly, blocked the path to Mary's elevator. For a second . . . her hand [was] on the release bar, ready to shut the interior gilded doors. "Wait." She had a passenger. The Negro boy who'd brushed past [Allen] earlier was in the elevator. . . . Negroes took the stairs. . . . "A nigger. Riding the elevator." "I'll be damned." (p. 66)*

Keywords: race relations • race riots • Tulsa Riot of 1921

Tarpley, Natasha.

Girl in the Mirror: Three Generations of Black Women in Motion. **Boston: Beacon Press, 1998. ISBN 0807072028. 181p.**

This is the story of three generations of Tarpley women, who frequently find it necessary to "to gather ourselves up and move." Grandmother, mother, and daughter tell stories about the lives they lived, the losses they endured, and the world they encountered in different regions of the United States and Africa.

> *Nana taught me that my hands could heal, that my heart could reach out and embrace another, that I had something to give that she, and others who had given me so much, really needed; that history's greatest secret. (p. 181)*

Keywords: family chronicles • mothers and daughters

Taylor, Mel.

The Mitt Man: A Novel. **New York: Morrow, 1999. ISBN 0688160948. 372p.**

In the 1920s, with connections to New Orleans and Harlem, Malcolm Cage and King Fish team up in a religious con game. Cage is a wealthy, white racist and so-called minister of the gospel whose background goes against everything the Bible advocates. King Fish is a black man, skilled at picking pockets and using the Bible to get himself out of trouble or to justify his actions.

> *A bright Saturday morning greeted King Fish when they stepped outside, a strange quiet with no one in sight. Malcolm led the way . . . They reached the barn together and Malcolm . . . insisted King Fish open the door. King Fish saw them everywhere . . .*

> *"You want me to preach—just like that? . . . It ain't even Sunday."* (pp. 72–73)

Keywords: con artists and con games

Wideman, John Edgar.

John Edgar Wideman is a 1992 MacArthur Fellow.

The Cattle Killing. **New York: Houghton Mifflin, 1996. ISBN 0395785901. 212p.**

When Philadelphia is hit with the yellow fever epidemic, the blame is placed on the blacks in the city. The deaths are compared to the Xhosa practice of killing cattle to drive the whites from their land in Africa.

> *We are being blamed in the newspapers. They say we are immune to the fever and require no assistance. They say black slaves, refugees from the troubles in Haiti, brought the fever to these shores.* (p. 34)

Keywords: church men • epidemics • race relations • racism

Civil Rights and Politics: 1950–Present

Bunkley, Anita Richmond.

Starlight Passage. **New York: Dutton, 1996. ISBN 052594009X. 364p.**

Kiana Sheridan's doctoral dissertation will be research into her family history. However, there are family secrets that many would like to never have uncovered. There are questions to be answered about great-great grandfather and his escape from slavery in Tennessee, where he had worked as an artisan.

> *Kiana's eyes gripped the brittle page in shock. Stunned, she blinked, turning the book over to see if there were more pages to read. . . . There was an ugly scrawl extending from the last word, down the page in a scraggly blue line. . . . Suddenly, her mouth felt as dry as sandpaper. What was Louise Sheridan about to write?* (p. 171)

Notes: Anita Richmond Bunkley is also listed in the "World War I and World War II: 1901–1949" section of this chapter.

Keywords: family history • genealogy • graduate students

Clair, Maxine.

Rattlebone. **New York: Farrar, Straus & Giroux, 1994. ISBN 0-374-24716-1. 213p.**

Set in the 1950s in Rattlebone, a fictional black town near Kansas City, this collection of intertwined stories explores the character and the community of the pre-civil rights Midwest. Told from multiple points of view, from adolescent Irene's to schoolteacher October Brown's, the stories tell how Rattlebone is shaped by its ordinary and eccentric people, but also how Rattlebone shapes its residents. (KA)

> *It was two summers before I would put my thin-penny bus token in the slot and ride the Fifth Street trolley all the way to the end of the line to junior high. Life was measured in summers then, and the expression "I am in this world, but not of it" appealed to me. I wasn't sure what it meant, but it had just the right ring for a lofty statement I should adopt.* (p. 55)

Notes: BCALA Literary Award for Fiction 1995

Keywords: American Midwest • black towns • children's point of view • coming of age • small-town life and culture

Davis, Thulani.

1959: A Novel. **New York: Grove Weidenfeld, 1992. ISBN 0802112307. 297p.**

Willie Tarrant is a 12-year-old motherless child who spends her time imitating Audrey Hepburn and reading Nancy Drew books. With the arrival of college students who are staging a sit-in at the local Woolworth's lunch counter, things change for Willie, and growing up takes on a different meaning.

> *When eight students went into our local Woolworth's that Monday morning, February 8, 1960, and sat down at the counter, I didn't know anything about it.* (p. 197)

Keywords: Civil Rights Movement • race relations • sit-ins • Virginia

Ellison, Ralph.

Juneteenth: A Novel. New York: Random House, 1999. ISBN 0394464575. 368p.

Reverend A. Z. Hickmanand and 14 women had come to give the senator a message. Hickman and the women were black, and the senator was "passing." Two days later, Senator Sunraiderson is shot on the Senate floor. While he is in the hospital following his shooting, the senator's colleagues learn his true identity.

> *"You just tell the Senator that Hickman has arrived. When he hears who's out here he'll know that it's important and want to see us" . . . "Are you his constituents?" "Constituents?" . . . "No, miss, . . . the Senator doesn't even have nobody like us in his state. We're from down where we're among the counted but not among the heard."* (p. 4)

Keywords: church men • legislators • passing • race relations

French, Albert.

I Can't Wait on God. **New York: Anchor Books/Doubleday, 1998. ISBN 0385483633.
246p.**

Over a five-day span, Jeremiah Henderson and his companion, Wilet Mercer,
leave a trail of blood and speculation as they flee Pittsburgh en route to New
York. Knowing that they will be sought after, the criminals try correcting some
past mistakes before leaving for a life on the run.

> *"You didn't have to leave . . . ." I know, Mama. I know,
> mama, but you didn't understand. . . . I wanted to go places,
> that why I went up to Wilmington . . . But you keep Mason
> now, Mama . . . You keep him."* (pp. 242)

Keywords: criminals • fugitives • Homewood (Pittsburgh, Pennsylvania)

Golden, Marita.

And Do Remember Me. **New York: Doubleday. ISBN 0385415060. 192p.**

Jessie Foster needs to find her identity, her true worth. A young girl fleeing from a
sexually abusive relationship with a family member, Jessie goes into the world to
fight for freedom—freedom slightly different from what she needs, but still freedom. Jessie becomes involved in the Civil Rights Movement and makes friends
with Lincoln, her lover, and Macon, a college professor.

> *Dear Mae Ann:*
>
> *I don't know when I'll be able to send for you like you asked.
> But I am safe and have met a nice man who really likes me
> and treats me good. We are someplace nearby doing im-
> portant work that's gonna help us all live the way we was
> meant to. . . . I am afraid but not really scared, like I used to
> be. I am helping to fight for freedom.*
>
> *Love, Jessie* (p. 27)

Keywords: child molestation • Civil Rights Movement • Mississippi • personal identity •
political activism and activists • sexual abuse

Grooms, Anthony.

Bombingham: A Novel. **New York: Free Press, 2001. ISBN 0743205588. 304p.**

Walter Burke, latter called Tibbs, grew up in a middle-class family in a Birmingham suburb. Following the death of his mother and at the suggestion of his father,
Burke volunteers for the military. The memory of Birmingham and duty in Vietnam are much alike; they are both battlefields. Burke wonders why he is there.

> *After my mother died, my father promised my sister and me
> a dog. He never got it for us. He promised us a trip . . . he
> never took us. At times he and I went months without say-
> ing a word to each other. One day my father came to me
> and said, "You might as well join the military. You'll be*

drafted . . . That was ten o'clock in the morning.
When I came back that afternoon, I was in the
army. (pp. 298–99)

Notes: Black Issues Book Review Best Book 2002; Lillian Smith Award for
Fiction 2002; Zora Neale Hurston/Richard Wright Fiction Award Finalist
2002

Keywords: Civil Rights Movement • war stories

Hill, Ernest.

Satisfied with Nothin': A Novel. **New York: Simon & Schuster, 1996. ISBN**
0684822598. 316p.

The setting is rural Louisiana in the 1970s, where whites' beliefs about
blacks and where they should and should not tread are quite clear. Jamie
Ray Griffin has set out to be different, disregarding those around him,
both black and white. Jamie Ray finishes high school and goes to college
in New Orleans, where his own desires differ from those of his advisor
and others in academia.

> *His [Jamie Ray] thoughts shifted to the few black*
> *teachers who were working in the desegregated*
> *schools in town. He thought about how invisible*
> *they were. They could have pushed the black kids*
> *more. . . . He couldn't understand why they sat*
> *back and watched kids like him fail.* (p. 311)

Keywords: black men and society • college • football • interracial relationships •
Ku Klux Klan

Hunt, Marsha.

Free. **New York: Dutton, 1993. ISBN 0525935754. 277p.**

Teenotchy Smith, a young black man working as a servant in a Quaker
household in Germantown, Pennsylvania, in 1913, is demoralized by
racism and haunted by his mother's brutal rape and murder. When emotionally crippled Teenotchy becomes a young English aristocrat's object
of affection, a complex and potentially disastrous relationship develops.

> *They agreed they'd have another cup of tea and*
> *Teenotchy went to the well for water while Alexan-*
> *der knelt for fifteen minutes. . . . That's when*
> *Teenotchy knew for sure he was a friend.* (p. 152)

Keywords: gay men • race relations • sexual abuse • slaves and owners

Johnson, Charles Richard.

Charles Richard Johnson is a 1998 MacArthur Fellow.

Dreamer: A Novel. **New York: Scribner, 1998. ISBN 068481224X. 236p.**

Reverend Martin Luther King Jr. and Chaym Smith, physical twins, intellectual equals, and moral opposites, are thrown together when King's

aides recognize the usefulness of a body double for the famous (and overworked) man. But the FBI, seeking to discredit the civil rights leader, also recognizes the value of having a King look-alike on the payroll.

> *He sensed how close he was to the end, this Christian boy from Atlanta, this product of three generations of black preachers . . . sometimes he wished he were two people, or perhaps three.* (p. 18)

Notes: Charles Johnson is also listed in the "Slavery: 1619–1860" section of this chapter.

Keywords: Civil Rights Movement • impersonation • race relations

Jones, Edward P.

Edward P. Jones is a 2004 MacArthur Fellow.

Lost in the City: Stories. **New York: Morrow, 1992. ISBN 0688115268 (acid free paper). 250p.**

In 14 short stories, Johnson evokes the 1950s and 1960s in Washington, D.C. As the stories move from street to street, the reader meets a variety of characters, each with a unique story and a personal strategy for surviving and keeping dreams alive in the violent and soul-crushing city.

> *"So thas what all yall hens here for?" Mrs. Garrett said and turned to Carmena at the other end of the table. Carmena nodded with a smile. "Oh, but I hope yall ain't gonna have that Reverend Sawyer again. He ain't nothing but jackleg, Bonne. 'As jackleg as they come.' "* (A Dark Night, p. 225)

Notes: National Book Award Finalist 1992

Keywords: short stories • urban life and culture

Lester, Julius.

And All Our Wounds Forgiven. **New York: Arcade/Little, Brown, 1994. ISBN 1559702583. 228p.**

John Calvin Marshall (a fictionalized Martin Luther King Jr.) was a spokesman and leader for the Civil Rights Movement in the 1960s whose life was cut short by an assassin. Through flashbacks and conversations, Marshall's life is remembered by his long-suffering wife, Andrea; his white and privileged mistress, Lisa Adams; his devoted chief lieutenant, Bobby Card; and Marshall himself, who speaks to us from beyond the grave.

> *She had understood that John Calvin's effort to ride history bareback made him shine like hope fulfilled. Someone had to kill him, not from racial hatred but for the erotic fulfillment. From the moment she knew, she had thought of herself as the younger woman married to a man twenty years her senior who will die before her.* (p. 133)

Keywords: adultery • Civil Rights Movement • Freedom Riders • husbands and wives • Ku Klux Klan • men's friendships • sit-ins

McFadden, Bernice L.

This Bitter Earth. **New York: Dutton, 2002. ISBN 0525946365. 276p.**

In this sequel to McFadden's earlier novel *Sugar*, Sugar's life is continually marred by disastrous events. Born out of wedlock and abandoned by her parents, Sugar was reared by three women who ran a house of ill repute and became a prostitute herself. Emotionally and physically battered, Sugar returns home and is nursed back to health by the three. Following the death of the women, who name her as heir, Sugar lives a comfortable material existence but is haunted by ghosts from her past and eventually leaves home again to rescue a friend.

> *The scars, all five of them, ran horizontal, from hip bone to hip bone. The flesh had been stitched badly and the thread had torn in places, pulling the flesh apart and allowing it to smile, open mouthed, up at them.* (p. 20)

Notes: *Essence* Bestseller List 2002; Gold Pen Award Best Mainstream Fiction Nominee 2002

Keywords: Arkansas • drug addiction • friendships • prostitutes and prostitution • teenagers • Saint Louis, Missouri

Mitchell, Kathryn.

Proud and Angry Dust. **Boulder: University Press of Colorado, 2001. ISBN 087081608X. 233p.**

This is the story of Theodore Roosevelt "Moose" O'Malley, a young man of Irish and African American heritage who comes of age during the 1920s in Knox Plain, Texas. Moose helps his mother with a small general store in the community, but his dream is to become a scientist. Life changes dramatically—and not necessarily for the better—on the black side of town when oil is discovered on their "worthless" farmland.

> *One Sunday as we were walking home from the Wilson's, I said to Barnett, "Miss Cora's a pretty good cook, and I like the food she gives us, but I wish we could have some chicken. I don't understand why there's always gravy, but never any chicken. If she's serving us chicken gravy, there's got to be some chicken in that house someplace."* (p. 27)

Keywords: coming of age • mixed-race children • petroleum industry

Muhanji, Cherry.

Her: A Novel. **San Francisco, Calif.: Aunt Lute Books, 1990. ISBN 0933216661. 179p.**

This novel tells the story of men and women who travel to Detroit looking for work in the 1950s and 1960s. Ford Motor Company is where they congregate during the day. At night they come together to forget the day, to hold each other up, and sometimes, to let each other down.

> *"I loved ya from the first time I seen ya . . . pretendin' ya didn't care that ya had to leave New York. I knew that place held somethin' special for ya, Charlotte. Never knowed it was a woman though."* (p. 163)

Keywords: autoworkers • gay men • lesbian relationships

Perry, Phyllis Alesia.

Stigmata. New York: Hyperion, 1998. ISBN 0786864087. 235p.

Elizabeth Lizzie DuBose's torment begins when she inherits a trunk filled with documents, a quilt, and other treasures that belonged to her enslaved great-great grandmother, Ayo. Unable to convince her loved ones that the physical stigmata and emotional horrors are, in fact, genuine manifestations of the ancestors who occupy her body, she is institutionalized as mentally ill. Only when Lizzie is able to make new quilts from the pieces of lives that came before can she truly understand the pain of those who came before and finally find peace.

> *I was sitting up in bed and then I was not there. I looked from the eyes of another person. A person now dead. . . . I was there. I was Grace.* (p. 73)

Keywords: family history • family relationships • mental illness • quilts and quilters • slavery • stigmata

Reynolds, April.

Knee Deep in Wonder: A Novel. New York: Metropolitan Books, 2003. ISBN 0805073469. 301p.

Helene Strickland doesn't understand why she was abandoned as a child, but when she returns to Arkansas for her aunt's funeral, she decides to confront her estranged mother, Queen Ester, about it. Much is revealed about the family history, but Queen Ester provides only half-truths and oblique responses, leaving Helene with more questions than answers.

> *Helene had seen Queen Ester vanish in her rearview mirror but she had hoped . . . Perhaps Queen Ester had secretly left the porch without Helene noticing and was trotting behind the car, saying, "You didn't hear what you heard, and even if you did I'm sorry about it."* (p. 254)

Keywords: absentee parents • family history • illegitimate children

Ridley, John.

A Conversation with the Mann: A Novel. New York: Warner Books, 2002. ISBN 0446528366. 433p.

Jackie Mann wants to escape from life in Harlem with his abusive father by one day becoming a well-known comedian. In 1950, his desperation to make his dream come true means ignoring his identity as a black man and being a "yes man" to whites. Getting in the spotlight is Mann's greatest desire, a dream achieved, ironically, at the price of being invisible.

> *I didn't see much waiting for me, and what I did see wasn't much good. The prospects for a black man in the fifties were limited to being famous or to being nothing.* (p. 69)

Keywords: Civil Rights Movement • comedians • personal identity • racial identity

Riley, Len.

Harlem. **New York: Doubleday, 1997. ISBN 0385485085. 366p.**

A poor preacher's daughter, Geneva leaves the South for the exciting Harlem of the New Negro Movement and Harlem Renaissance. She reinvents herself and fulfills her ambition of marrying into Harlem's black aristocracy, but her comfortable life and persona are threatened when her past appears in the person of her penniless Cousin Virginia.

> *She [Geneva] was . . . delighted now . . . No more lectures from Uncle Tom idiots who accused her of acting so high falutin'. . . . She . . . thought of how she'd surprise the folks back in Jacksonville one day and flaunt her diamonds and fur coats. . . . She'd make that sneaky little bitch, Cousin Virginia, wish she'd never been born.* (p. 45)

Keywords: class relations • Harlem Renaissance • intraracial relations • upper class

Chapter 7

Inspirational Literature

Melanie Sims

> *As long as there are people hurting and healing, struggling and surviving, there will be an audience for spiritual book.*—Kelly Starling (1998, 98)

Religion has played an essential role in the lives of African Americans from slavery to the present day. In times of torment and sorrow, the faith of African Americans has been a source of strength that has allowed them to weather the storms of life and to triumph over adversity. In times of prosperity and temptation, faith has provided guidance and meaning. Inspirational literature by black authors reflects primarily Protestant Christianity, although other religions and philosophies have played a significant role in shaping African American beliefs. Today, African Americans who are seeking inspiration have a growing body of literature, both fiction and nonfiction, from which to choose.

Definition

This chapter includes the types of inspirational literature that are most popular with today's African American readers. Christian fiction comprises a preponderance of African American inspirational fiction, and only titles reflecting biblical values are included in the fiction section. Inspirational literature that is spiritual, though not necessarily Christian, is included in the nonfiction section of this chapter and reflects the current diverse approaches to spirituality in the African American community.

Christian Fiction

Christian fiction applies biblical ethics and morality to life issues. These are stories of complex problems and of the trials of the Christian individual whose faith is tested by the challenges and promises of the real world. These authors do not provide allusions or metaphors grounded in the Christian religion; the Christian doctrine is overt and specific.

In one of the first works about Christian fiction written for librarians, Walker (1998) examines policies of various Christian publishing houses. She lists Tyndale's policy, which appears to epitomize the criteria for Christian fiction. To be considered for publication by the Christian publishing house, a manuscript must include one or more of the following:

- *Characters professing faith in Jesus Christ.*

- *Significant references to biblical stories, verses, and characters.*

- *Dialogue or narrative that communicates Christian truths.*

- *Stories that express moral values, lifestyles, and choices based on Christian faith and truth.* (Walker 1998, 4)

Much Christian fiction by African American authors is evangelical in nature. Mort's (2002) distinction between Christian fiction and the narrower subgenre of evangelical fiction is largely a matter of degree. That is, beyond reflecting the moral values of Christianity and making references to biblical stories, evangelical fiction overtly and very specifically draws on biblical authority. It is the driving force behind the characters' actions and the central issue in plot development. Characters do not simply profess a belief in a distant Christ; there is an emotional commitment to Jesus as a personal savior.

Inspirational Nonfiction

Although virtually all inspirational fiction by African American authors is properly characterized as Christian fiction, inspirational nonfiction includes influences from many belief systems.

The term "inspirational literature" has been used to describe almost every type of nonfiction that gives people hope or in some way shapes their lives. Pamela Aue suggests that "many people associate religion with an institutional expression of faith," while "spirituality, on the other hand, encourages personal experience and encounters with the transcendent" (Aue and Carrigan 2000, xi). Genres as varied as popular psychology and personal finance, poetry and biography, religion and politics have been joined under the rubric "inspirational."

In this chapter, inspirational literature is defined rather narrowly. It is nonfiction that is based in some way on the individual's attempt to find meaning beyond him or herself. It is a search characterized by reflection on the sacred or divine. The inspirational nonfiction in this text, then, is confined to the individual's relationship with a higher being, however that being is defined. It includes works by authors such as Reverend T. D. Jakes, pastor of the nondenominational Potter's House Church, whose message is grounded in Christianity, as well as that of Yoruba priestess Ilyana Vanzant, who asserts, "You can put God in every aspect of your life whether you read the Bible, the Koran, or . . . sit by a tree" (Starling 1998, 98).

Appeal

Publishers Weekly reports that "70% of African Americans identify themselves as Christians and attend church at least monthly" (Riess 2000, S8). Is it any wonder, then, that Christian fiction is growing in popularity within the African American community? Christian fiction by black authors captures the religious and spiritual experience in a way that is relevant to African American readers. The plots are based in familiar situations; readers are or have been confronted with the same decisions. The characters are their peers. They are fallible, everyday people who are struggling to lead Christian lives at every level, every day.

Without being pedantic, these novels give Christian readers the opportunity to think about their faith, their lives, and their destinies. Christian fiction also provides affirmation and a sense of belonging to believers. In addition, it gives nonbelievers a stance from which to observe and understand the faith of others.

Inspirational nonfiction is written to provide the opportunity to reflect and to learn, to affirm personal values, to offer direction in the search for something greater, to answer spiritual questions, and to motivate and inspire. The popularity of African American inspirational literature reflects the broader trend of growing interest in spirituality and a return to religion by many Americans. People need solace and security. They need to try to find meaning in a world that is no longer meaningful—or even understandable—to them. "People seek hope as they confront the weighty problems of AIDS, domestic violence, drugs, child abuse, and everyday disappointments that come with living and loving" (Starling 1998, 98).

Evolution

African American authors have been influenced by religion since America's colonial period. The earliest works were written primarily to convert or inspire, to praise God or to demonstrate the power of the Christian faith; they were essentially didactic. Over time, the nature of inspirational literature has changed, and the use of religious allusions and themes has become more complex and varied. With the emergence of a Christian fiction genre identifiable apart from mainstream literature, we see a return to the earlier clear purpose of demonstrating the value of faith. Religious nonfiction, including advice books and daily devotionals, now reflects the influence of belief systems other than Christianity.

As Christianity has spread to different nations and different peoples, it has often taken on their character and melded local religious practice into the faith. Hubbard observes that the sermon, which he characterizes as "black people's first poetry in the United States," represents a "synthesis of European and African cultures" (1997, 648). Earliest recorded slave folklore combines Christian beliefs quite comfortably with traditions of magic such as spells and curses. Imagery of transfiguration is common in folk myths; for instance, freedom is achieved as a spell turns a person into a bird who may fly away. Such a marriage recurs in the twentieth century with "hoodoo" and "Santaria" elements (Jackson 1997, 628).

Literacy and religion are inextricably linked in the evolution of African American literature, and until the twentieth century African American literature presented a positive faith-based approach. Most slaves and free blacks, as well as many other Americans, were taught to read using the Bible. The Bible was the first, and in some minds, the only acceptable text, representing a compromise between salvation through God's word (the Bible) and empowerment through the key to radical and independent thought (literacy). Early oral and written accounts refer to the Bible as a primer, and many suggest that the text itself was responsible for the miracle of literacy (Foster 1997a, 59).

Citing Briton Hamon's autobiography, *A Narrative of the Uncommon Sufferings, and Surprizing Deliverance* (1760) and Phillis Wheatley's *Poems on Various Subjects, Religious and Moral* (1773) as examples of the pervasiveness of biblical influence, Foster notes that, "The earliest extant published literature by African Americans was inspired by Christian theology, structured after Biblical models, and punctuated with Biblical references and quotes" (1997a, 59).

Sunday schools were (and are) another example of the close link between literacy and religion in America, and the literature again provides a positive message. Early Sunday schools were not conceived solely as an adjunct to church services. They were at one time a primary educational institution in America for those children and adults whose weekdays were filled with labor. Various materials in addition to the Bible were made available, although these were generally didactic in nature regardless of genre. In 1796, one of the earliest Sunday schools was established at the Bethel African Methodist Episcopal (AME) Church expressly to teach parishioners to read, and in 1817 the AME Book Concern began publishing materials including the *A.M.E. Review,* which published serialized novels and short stories in addition to official church announcements (Foster 1997b, 708).

Although today's Sunday schools do not typically teach basic reading skills, the tradition of lessons and discussion groups persists. Through the years, Sunday school groups have discussed titles from various genres, from Griggs's *Imperium in Imperio* (1899), a speculative fiction story (see Chapter 11), to autobiographies by Briton Hamon (1790) and Andrew Young (*A Way Out of No Way,* 1994). Theological works created specifically for African Americans, such as *The Original African Heritage Study Bible* (1993), have also found an eager audience.

In much earlier work by African Americans, Christianity is viewed as a source of strength and salvation, and the images and allegories are essentially positive However, some authors explore the flaws in its practitioners or reject the religion itself. There are African American characters who wonder why a just God would create such an unjust world or why their white Christian brothers and sisters do not treat them as God's children.

While earlier authors, including Langston Hughes ("On the Road," 1934), might question the religious implications of the relationship of black and white believers, the most overt repudiation of Christianity came with the Black Arts Movement in the late 1960s. Growing from a swelling black nationalism, religion and its components took on increasingly political meaning.

The movement denounced Christianity as a slave religion and labeled almost all African American literature published before 1960 "Old Spirituality," neither relevant nor appropriate to the modern-day African American experience (Jackson 1997, 12). The need for what was termed a "New Spirituality" opened the door for different ways to fulfill spiritual needs. Rastafarianism and the Black Muslim faith offered alternatives to traditional religion and placed African Americans squarely at the center of religious practice and power. Hoodoo (belief in magic and relationships among spiritual forces) and Santeria (a transfigured worship of Catholic saints) both have strong ties to African traditions (Jackson 1997, 628). These influences are most evident in current nonfiction works, which tend to reflect a more diverse approach to spirituality and may draw from many sources for inspiration and guidance.

Although the belief systems in which inspirational nonfiction is grounded have expanded, spiritual or inspirational fiction grounded in religious traditions other than Protestant Christianity is rare. There are a few exceptions, however, such as Margaret Blair Young and Darius Alden Gray's *One More River to Cross* (Deseret Books, 2000), about early black members of the Latter-Day Saints. Publishers may be more receptive to diversity should such titles prove profitable.

Christian allegories and images, both positive and negative, are plentiful in modern African American mainstream literature quite apart from the more narrowly defined and overtly inspirational genre works. Jackson attributes "Religion's prevalence in the literature . . . to the fact that millions of African Americans know spirituals and the Biblical literature they echo" (1997, 626). In mainstream African American literature, primarily literary fiction, treatment of religious themes has become more complex, use of images and allusions is more diverse, and the message is more often political (Foster 1997a, 60).

Themes and Trends

African American inspirational literature is a robust and growing genre that is garnering increased attention from publishers as it has proven its profitability. Inspirational fiction remains a largely female arena composed primarily of contemporary Christian romance. Inspirational nonfiction, with its more diverse spiritual approach, draws from many philosophies, although Christian works are the most popular. Women comprise the greatest audience for inspirational nonfiction as well, although choices are increasing for men (Starling 1998).

Publishing

Inspirational fiction is produced by denominational, Christian, and secular presses and by small independent African American publishing houses (such as Nia Publishing), under special imprints of major houses (Walk Worthy Press, an imprint of Warner Books), or in partnership between the two. Some denominational publishing houses, such as Pilgrim Press (United Church of Christ) and Judson Press (American Baptist Church), have a tradition of serving African American Christians, while others such as the Evangelical Lutheran Church in America's Augsburg Press have only recently begun trying to address their needs (Labbé 2000).

African American inspirational fiction is increasingly available in national book chain stores, but Christian bookstores and African American independent bookstores still are the best sources. Most recently, inspirational literature has been given a very real boost by major discount chains. Wal-Mart, which prefers to stock material of a conservative nature, has been given credit for playing "a pivotal role" in the success of *Armageddon*, an evangelical thriller (not African American) published by Tyndale House (Kirkpatrick 2003, A1). Kirkpatrick (2003, A21) further reports that an AOL Time Warner executive established a religious imprint at

Warner because a book buyer for Wal-Mart told him that more than half of the chain's book sales were Christian fiction titles.

Christian Fiction

Tone

Perhaps in reaction to complex, equivocal, and sometimes dark mainstream fiction, inspirational or visionary fiction by and for African Americans is developing into a distinct genre. Paralleling the enormous growth in Christian fiction in the general marketplace, African American Christian fiction is growing steadily in popularity. It is most reflective of the biblical tradition of black literature, in which Christianity is seen as salvation and Jesus as a close acquaintance.

Although Christian fiction is growing in complexity and may describe difficult situations, it is never brutal or graphic. It generally gives a somewhat more innocent view of life (even with the struggles) than much mainstream fiction and, as does most genre literature, provides readers with expected (and hoped for) conclusions.

The religion that is portrayed is one of justice, forgiveness, love, and salvation. African American Christian fiction does not invoke the graphic imagery of the New Testament book of Revelations so frequently the foundation of evangelical thrillers. Ultimately, the tone is one of comfort and redemption.

Character

Characters in Christian fiction are accessible and fallible. We know them. They look and sound like us or our friends and families. Even good and moral Christians may be tempted; some may even succumb. Frequently, the characters who present the greatest problems for the protagonist are charming and engaging, rather than evil. They thus more realistically represent the real-life temptations facing those for whom faith is the most important aspect of life. This allows the reader to identify more readily with the protagonists' failings and to receive reassurance that weakness may be overcome and that a fall from grace is not permanent. There are few saints in Christian fiction. In a world fraught with danger, materialistic attitudes, and attractive diversions, the characters search for—and find—meaning. Their faith is revealed through literal translation of the scripture.

Romance

Christian fiction is reflected in a variety of genres, and romance is particularly popular. It isn't surprising, then, that romantic love continues to be a prevalent theme in African American Christian fiction. Christian fiction for black audiences is almost exclusively romance. This may be an indication of the relative newness of the field; mainstream Christian romances were well established before Christian authors branched into other genres.

A Christian approach to romantic love is grounded in the Bible. The thirteenth chapter of I Corinthians describes love as one of God's greatest gifts. True love never fails. The beginning of a new relationship is often the catalyst that requires a character to look within and examine personal self-concept and religious principles. Before a lifetime commitment to another individual can be made, a commitment to God must be defined and affirmed. Recognizing and accepting God's love helps the character develop self-respect and high self-esteem and recognize that he or she is worthy of being loved. Placing God at the center of the love relationship gives it meaning and elevates it beyond simple romance or physical attraction.

Redemption

The stories of Christian fiction revolve around common, everyday problems. Christian fiction novels may present stories about adultery, fornication, greed, lust, and backsliding. Characters are generally faced with temptation and are tested, but they ultimately find redemption. In many of the romances, a woman must decide between secular love and her faith. The battles in these stories are ultimately won through the characters' continuous hope, trust, and faith in God. Although temptation and sorrow may have external causes, the resolution of the problem depends on the protagonist's faith and internal resolve.

Forgiveness

The theme of forgiveness extends beyond the redemption that an individual may receive through God's forgiveness. Many of the characters have difficulty emulating this divine characteristic, although they are called upon by their faith to do so. The stories may revolve around the importance of extending forgiveness and love to another human being who has in some way hurt or wronged the protagonist. The protagonist can only achieve grace by absolving another, and this may be the hardest challenge he or she faces.

Submission

The third chapter of Proverbs offers another important theme for Christian fiction: "Trust in the Lord with all your heart and lean not on your own understanding; in all your ways acknowledge him, and he will make your paths straight." The storylines in African American Christian fiction focus on the need for trust and faith in God in accordance with biblical principles. Some characters become too independent and self-sufficient, seeing their successes as the result of personal ability or endeavor, rather than as a gift from God. As the stories unfold, the successes are seen as empty, lives are revealed as meaningless, and self-sufficiency proves to be merely an illusion. To achieve redemption, the characters must humble themselves as they come back to Christ. They learn once again the importance of willing submission.

Inspirational Nonfiction

Popularity

The production of inspirational nonfiction for African Americans has seen extraordinary growth since 1990, and black authors "are making spirituality the hottest ticket in literature" (Starling 1998, 96). *Woman Thou Art Loosed* (1993), by Reverend T. D. Jakes, sold over one million copies; Iyanla Vanzant's books of meditations regularly debut at the top of best-seller lists.

Gospel and Girl Talk

Labbé notes the success of a "gospel and girl talk" (2000, 32) genre, some of which have sold 65,000 or more hardcover copies. Titles such as *What to Do Until Love Finds You: Preparing for Your Perfect Mate* by Michelle McKinney Hammond (Harvest House, 1996); *Girl, Have I Got Good News For You: Heart to Heart Encouragement for Hurting Women* by Thelma Wells (Thomas Nelson, 1999); and *Girlfriend to Girlfriend: Everyday Wisdom and Affirmations from the Sister Circle* by Julia A. Boyd (Plume, 1999) are examples of this popular type. Although they echo the approach of the "girlfriend" novels of popular African American fiction, these advice and conversation books are firmly grounded in biblical teachings.

Male Audience

Traditionally, the biggest market for inspirational nonfiction, indeed, for all segments of the African American publishing audience, has been women. But Starling notes that "Fans of the inspirational texts can increasingly be found among men. At a recent Chicago book signing for Jakes, Brothers of all ages could be seen among the rows of seated women nodding their heads or calling out "Amen" to the minister's words" (1998, 96). Ilyana Vanzant, noted for the popularity of her meditations among women, published *The Spirit of a Man*, which targets a male audiences, as does *40 Days in the Wilderness: Meditations for African-American Men* by Kwasi Issa Kena (Abingdon Press, 1998). *One Brother to Another: Voices of African American Men,* edited by William J. Key and Robert Johnson-Smith II (Judson Press, 1996); *Manhood, God's Style* by Wilbur Conway (Destiny Image, 1999); and *Ten Principles of Black Self-Esteem: Lessons of Heritage, Lessons of Hope* by Hammond Oglesby (Pilgrim 1999) are further examples of the growing popularity of inspirational nonfiction written with men in mind.

Religious Diversity

Although Christian releases continue to dominate African American inspirational work, there is a continuing and slowly growing audience for books about Islam and African religions. In addition, African Americans are increasingly demanding additions to the relatively rare titles published expressly for some Christian denominations, especially Catholics and Mormons. A few breakthrough authors, such as Vanzant, are open to any path to spirituality, and their works are accepted by Christians as well as those of different faiths. There is evidence that religious diversity is growing within inspirational literature, but demand outstrips supply for interdenominational or alternative titles (Labbé 2000).

Selection Criteria and Scope

African American Christian fiction is an evolving genre, still in its beginning stages. There is not an abundance of Christian fiction titles produced specifically for black audiences, nor can inspirational nonfiction meet the demand. The approach here therefore is inclusive, rather than selective, within the general scope of this book. That is, this chapter includes Christian fiction and inspirational nonfiction titles written by African American authors and published between 1990 and 2003. The primary goal of this chapter is to identify and categorize appropriate titles.

Relevant collection development tools that focus on inspirational literature, such as those by Walker, Mort, and Aue, have been consulted, as well as those that concentrate on multicultural literature. Mort (2002) includes a section comprising six titles by four African American authors. African American titles are typically not included in bibliographies of Christian fiction written for more general audiences. The Blackboard list and Black Caucus of the American Library Association (BCALA) Literary Award lists were consulted.

There are few reviews of African American Christian fiction and inspirational nonfiction; there are fewer genre and audience-specific lists available. Articles about both African American Christian fiction and inspirational nonfiction were identified by searching journal indexes, with the most useful being the monthly "Faith Reviews" column in *Black Issues Book Review* and articles in *Publishers Weekly* and *Ebony*, and by examining publisher specialty catalogs such as those from Walk Worthy Press (Warner), Lift Every Voice, and HeartQuest (Tyndale House). A search for Web sources led to several bibliographies. Some books were already known to the author; others were identified by consulting with other readers. The most useful sources are included in Chapter 12.

Once identified, titles were assessed firsthand for relevance. Two main criteria were used for Christian fiction:

- **The plot reflects biblical ethics and morality**. Many of the storylines quote biblical scriptures, while others may only allude to them. A few of the stories may be considered secular, but they have been included because the storylines represent strong biblical principles of unconditional love and forgiveness.

- **The storyline presents a realistic Christian who may at one point or another falter in his or her judgment.** This allows the character as well as the reader to reexamine life choices. Christian fiction has a growing appeal because it now extends beyond the emotional appeal for salvation to include the day-to-day victories and struggles confronted by Christian readers.

Criteria for inclusion of inspirational nonfiction are reflected in the definition above. Only literature that in some way addresses an individual's attempt to live life guided by some sacred or divine principle is included. Biographies and autobiographies that might easily be considered inspirational are not included in this chapter; they may be found in Chapter 8.

Advising the Reader

The most obvious and frequent point of decision is whether the reader prefers inspirational fiction or nonfiction. Thus, this chapter organizes annotations into two major categories: Christian fiction and inspirational nonfiction.

- **Christian Fiction**. African American Christian fiction depicts Christians who have fun, make mistakes, and suffer the consequences. The characters strive to live their lives in accordance with their faith, but they sometimes fail. Christian fiction includes a biblical message that will leave readers with hope and the inspiration to make changes in their lives. The Christian novel can be described as refreshing, and it appeals to many readers because it lacks explicit violence, sex, and language that is present in many secular novels and may be offensive to some readers. The annotations included in this chapter have been organized into four categories:

- "Christian Life" includes plots that examine the various struggles that Christians face in their everyday lives that do not easily fit in the other categories or are a combination of the other categories. This category touches on the difficulties faced in relationships, in the church, and with forces of evil.

- The "Family" category focuses on issues that affect the family as a whole. In their Christian walk, the family must learn to cope with difficult situations that attack their very being, such as adultery and death. The family is forced to trust and lean on the Lord as they seek his guidance to help them survive.

- "Inspirational Romance" is a combination of romantic and spiritual growth between individuals. Each character must resolve a spiritual issue with God before a new love relationship can blossom.

- The "Young Adult" category focuses on the lives of teens who are struggling to live a Christian life as they encounter problems with sex, drugs, and alcohol, as well as coping with peer pressure, racism, and other prejudices.

- **Inspirational Nonfiction**. The categorization of inspirational nonfiction reflects the material's purpose and the manner in which it is likely to be read.

  - "Bibles, Bible Study, and Religious Texts" include guides for both men and women that reflect an African American perspective on Bible study.

  - "Devotional Calendars" are collections of short devotionals or meditations. Readers are expected to read one each day to focus their thoughts and activities or to inspire their actions.

  - "Essays and Reflections" are collections of medium-length pieces by a single or multiple authors that provide personal thoughts and observations. Readers are expected to read others' views, to think about the ideas, and to develop a personal view of their own.

  - "Guidance and Self-Help" books are written as cohesive guides or manuals, typically organized into chapters. These are instructive in nature. Readers are expected to read the entire text as a unit, to learn, and to adopt an overall approach to life based on religious or philosophical belief systems.

Christian Fiction

Christian Life

Bell, Derrick A.

Gospel Choirs: Psalms of Survival for an Alien Land Called Home. **New York: Basic Books, 1996. ISBN 0-465-02412-2. 228p.**

Legal scholar Derrick Bell uses himself and his fictional civil rights lawyer, Geneva Crenshaw, to tell allegorical stories about racial disparity and injustices in America. Gospel music is referenced throughout the essays, which discuss such topics as the Bell Curve and affirmative action, to suggest solutions to current problems. Although many of the resolutions are not practicable, the music has the potential to touch and unite us across barriers of race and class.

> Humph! Heaven don't seem to be in the retaliation
> business, either– seein' as how the rich get richer,
> the poor get poorer, the good people die young,
> while the bastards live on year after year. (p. 144)

Keywords: class relations • gospel music and musicians • prejudice • race relations • race riots • racism • sexism

Berry, Bertice.

The Haunting of Hip Hop: A Novel. **New York: Doubleday, 2001. ISBN 0-385-49845-4. 210p.**

Harry "Freedom" Hudson is a hot hip-hop producer and songwriter in New York City who wants to buy a seemingly haunted brownstone in Harlem. He directs his lawyer, Ava Vercher, and her childhood friend and real estate attorney, Charles Campbell III, to check on the property. When Ava and Charles visit the house they are met by a gathering of spirits, including Ngozi, an African slave drummer; Bella, a singer murdered by her white gangster lover; and Johnny, a boy killed by his father. All of the spirits have stories that they want to pass on to the living, particularly Ngozi, who wants to pass along his beat, which is not found in rap music. Charles's grandmother can speak with the spirits, and she tries to guide and protect her grandson.

> I know the feeling of emptiness. It comes from our
> inability to connect to one another in spirit and in
> life, from past to present. Freedom will tie the pres-
> ent to the past. He is the son who has called for a
> father. We have been listening and now we have
> answered. (p. 166)

Notes: *Essence* Bestseller List 2001

Keywords: hip hop • rap music and musicians • slavery • spirits

Bowen, Michele Andrea.

 Church Folk: A Novel. **West Bloomfield, Mich.: Walk Worthy Press/Warner Books, 2001. ISBN 0-446-52799-8. 352p.**

The handsome young Reverend Theophilus Simmons of Greater Hope Gospel United Church is smitten with "jook-joint" cook Essie Lee Lane. After a long distance courtship, Theophilus and Essie marry. They have a short honeymoon as they begin to deal with the challenges of the local church. In particular, Theophilus's ex-girlfriend has vowed revenge against the pastor for ending their relationship. But the biggest problem arises when they attend the national Triennial Conference in Virginia and discover that the church leadership is running a call-girl service out of the local funeral home. It is up to Reverend Theophilus Simmons to reveal this corruption to the congregation at the conference.

> *You know something, Saphronia, decent women aren't dick-teasers. I know you understand that word, because I do, and I'm a preacher. And I understand exactly what you're trying to start here. If I weren't so tired, I'd call up all the good sisters of Mount Nebo's prayer circle and get them over here, so we could loose some of that mess out of your stuck-up butt.* (p. 82)

Notes: *Essence* Bestseller List 2001, 2002; Go On Girl Book Club New Author 2002

Keywords: church life • church men • love stories • prostitutes and prostitution • scandal

Coburn Whack, Rita.

Meant to Be: A Novel. **New York: Strivers Row/Villard, 2002. ISBN 0-375-75809-7. 307p.**

Patience Jan Campbell is an ambitious young black woman who comes of age in Chicago. Jan enjoys listening to stories told by her Aunt Ada, who urges her to reach out in prayer to the spirits of the dead for advice and comfort: "Our spirits are not confined to these bodies." Jan summons the spirit of her grandmother, who becomes an omniscient narrator of Jan's life story, telling of her college experiences, her career as a radio disc jockey, and her relationship with two lovers. Jan's spiritual awakening leads her to maturity and self-fulfillment.

> *Life is like that, Jan. Most people don't stop and draw the poison out. Most of us run, living with poison in our veins. And some of us just learn to live with a snake.* (p. 117)

Keywords: ancestors • coming of age • family relationships • radio personalities • spirits

Foster, Sharon Ewell.

 Ain't No River. **Sisters, Ore.: Multnomah Publishers, 2001. ISBN 1-57673-628-8. 359p.**

Garvin Daniels is a rising young attorney at Winkle and Straub, the only black in the Washington, D.C., law firm, when everything begins to go wrong. She is placed on administrative leave pending an investigation of alleged bias in a lawsuit, and her supervisor has assigned her a discrimination case that's surely meant to ruin her career. However, Garvin is really distressed when she receives a mysterious phone call about a young ex-football player, GoGo Walker, who is womanizing her grandmother. Garvin decides it is time to visit her grandmother in North Carolina and rescue her from GoGo. As Garvin strives to get her life back on track, she learns she must trust God rather than trying to control her life herself.

> *You're going to remember that a lot of good people paid a big price—some blood, some beatings, some prison—for you to be able to get to this place, and you not going to give up because of this little price you might have to pay. You going to walk out of here with dignity and make me even prouder than I was the day you first walked in here. And you going to keep hope in your heart.* (p. 63)

Notes: Gold Pen Award Best Christian Fiction 2001

Keywords: attorneys • family relationships • racism • trust

Passing by Samaria: A Novel. **Sisters, Ore.: Alabaster Books, 2000. ISBN 1-57673-615-6. 382p.**

At age 18, Alena's dreams are shattered when she discovers her best friend's lynched body. To keep her safe and quiet, her parents send Alena to Chicago to live with her aunt, a decision that leaves Alena feeling bitter and angry. In the aftermath of several race riots, Alena returns to Mississippi to make peace with her parents. While she is home, the white sheriff who is responsible for her friend's death is killed in a "hunting accident," and Alena realizes the meaning of forgiveness and mercy.

> *The Lord sent me to tell you that I. . . . I can't forgive for no one else, but I forgive him for what he has done. For what he tried to do. I can't tell you that I'm sorry that he's gone instead of my baby. But I do, Lord help me, I forgive him.* (p. 350)

Notes: Christy Award First Novel 2001; Gold Pen Award Best Christian Fiction Nominee 2001; RITA Award Best First Book Finalist 2001; RITA Award Best Inspirational Finalist 2001

Keywords: betrayal • family relationships • forgiveness • grief • love • prejudice • race riots

Riding Through Shadows. **Sisters, Ore.: Multnomah Publishers, 2001. ISBN 1-576-73807-8. 333p.**

Eight-year-old Shirley, growing up in East St. Louis during the Vietnam War and the Civil Rights Movement, is sent to live with a distant relative in Tyler, Texas, when her father is killed in Vietnam and her mother is committed to a mental institution. Shirley is not prepared for the overt racism and ostracism that she experiences in the South and withdraws into silence. The narrative shifts between the 1960s and 1980s, as Shirley battles with demonic forces and her caretaker helps her fight the dark angels.

> *But there also have to be storms. Places with no storms dry up and die. Let the storms come, Deacon. You don't have to be afraid. God is with you in the storm. I think maybe your son is trying to tell you that you've been trying so hard to keep him and the rest of your family in order, to keep peace, that you're making dry, dead places. (p. 253)*

Keywords: coming of age • racism • segregation • self-esteem • spirits

G'orge-Walker, Pat.

Sister Betty! God's Calling You! **2d ed. Elmont, N.Y./Brooklyn, N.Y.: A & E Sivells Publications/Done Deal Entertainment, 1998. ISBN 1-889732-25-7. 33p.**

Lil Bit and June Bug have an argument about whether or not Sister Betty, a member of "Ain't Nobody Right But Us—All Others Goin' to Hell Church," really received a telephone call from the Lawd. When MaCile, the children's grandmother, prepares to whip them for getting into grown folks' business, Sister Betty asks MaCile to wait as she decides to tell the three of them about her phone call from God.

> *Sister Betty felt the room spin around, and as she put her hand to her head for balance, her good wig fell to one side, exposing tiny braids that resembled a long ago forgotten cornfield. (p. 29)*

Keywords: children's point of view • faith • gossip • South Carolina

Gray, Maurice M.

 To Whom Much Is Given: A Novel. **Wilmington, Del.: Write The Vision, 2000. ISBN 0-9700514-0-9. 356p.**

Max Carson and Donna Randall are drawn to each other through separate dreams and are captivated when they unexpectedly meet at church. Their budding romance is filled with adventure as they both realize that God has given them special abilities, which they must use to save hundreds of innocent people from dying.

> *Donna took a deep breath. "Max, what I want to know is how did you—do what you did? You—you ordered them to drop their weapons and they just did it. And your voice even sounded different, like thunder or something." (p. 100)*

Notes: Gold Pen Award Best Christian Fiction Nominee 2001

Keywords: blackmail • Delaware • faith • love stories • trust

Jackson, Derek A.

Destiny's Cry: A Novel. **Bloomington, Ind.: 1st Books, 2002. ISBN 1-4033-1190-0. 225p.**

Terrell Robinson is a young, former campus chaplain who is doubting his call to the ministry. As Terrell struggles with doubts about his future, he meets a popular sorority girl whose boyfriend has cheated on her. Terrell witnesses to Lauren about what real love is, and he once again begins to feel that fire for the Word stir inside him. But it isn't until he has the opportunity to witness to a praying mother's son that he truly realizes his calling.

> *Every person in the Bible had weaknesses, issues, sin. Everyone except Jesus. All those people were just like you and me, with problems in their life. But they had one thing in common—they heard from God and knew what they were called to do.* (p. 181)

Keywords: church men • love • men and women • singers

Jarrett, Norma L.

Sunday Brunch: A Novel. **Houston, Tex.: E-Page Publishing, 1998. ISBN 0-9671923-5-8. 223p.**

Every Sunday after church all of the who's who in society meet at Etiennes Café for brunch to discuss their lives, loves, and spiritual problems. *Sunday Brunch* focuses on the lives of five African American female attorneys, all at different points both professionally and spiritually. Alexis (Lexi) has a private law firm and is the common thread that keeps the women together as she struggles to find the perfect mate. The story follows the changes in the lives of the women as they mature and grow.

> *"Well, Lexi, I just don't feel comfortable with all that right now. If you want to pray for me later that's fine. Right now, I am not too happy with God. If He has the ability to heal me, then He never should have allowed this to happen to me in the first place. If He loves me, He sure has a funny way of showing it," she said.* (p. 162)

Keywords: attorneys • greed • men and women • religion • sexuality • women's friendships

Kee, John P.

Not Guilty! The Script. **Chicago: Lift Every Voice/Moody Press, 2002. ISBN 0-8024-1517-2. 139p.**

Ministering to the lost is not an easy task. When Pastor John P. Kee stops on "the Hill" in his old neighborhood to minister to drug dealers, he convinces them to pray. But when they join hands, they are immediately arrested for drug possession. Kee unsuccessfully argues with the police and is forced to spend the night in jail. He refuses to pay the $250,000 bond and chooses instead to remain in jail to spread God's word. When Kee goes to trial, he is forced to admit illegal activities in his past.

> *I go to court tomorrow, some would say not knowing my fate. But by faith I believe God that I'll be at home in a few days . . . And when you have been exonerated, don't forget the God who delivered you. I can't judge your sin, but I say to all of you right now, in Jesus Christ you are NOT GUILTY.* (p. 60)

Keywords: church men • drug dealers and dealing • faith • prison life

Mason, Felicia.

Testimony: A Novel. **New York: Dafina Books/Kinsington Publishing, 2002. ISBN 0-7582-0059-5. 231p.**

Roger McKenzie, leader of the gospel group Triumphant Voices of Praise, is having nightmares about an incident that occurred in his past that affects the choir's unity and causes dissension among the members. When family difficulties cause more conflicts among choir members, they realize they must settle their disputes and bring harmony and a focus on God back to the group.

> *"But when that kind of sh–" He caught himself. "When that kind of stuff is going on in the church and with the so-called people of God, doesn't that mean that there are a whole bunch of church people going straight to hell?"* (p. 171)

Keywords: gospel music and musicians • guilt • husbands and wives • singers

Turney, Denise.

Love Has Many Faces: When You Find a Friend You Find a Circle of Love. **Bensalem, Penn.: Chistell Publishing, 2000. ISBN 0-9663539-1-9. 373p.**

Roommates Robin, a black writer, and Leslie, a white actress, are up and coming stars who, despite their differences, develop a strong friendship that endures through many hardships. Each character tells a unique story involving drugs, alcohol, death, and fame. The reader is able to see how the characters' lives are affected by the choices they make and the friends they keep.

> *Christianity is about being there when someone needs you. It's about being a friend. A lot of people don't know what it is to truly, really love another person. Most people don't have a clue. When you love someone, you'll stay even when the chips are down. Don't be a fair weather friend. Be a good Christian. Be a true friend.* (p. 11)

Keywords: alcohol abuse and alcoholics • drug addiction • interracial relationships • love • self-esteem • women's friendships

Family

Benson, Angela.

Abiding Hope. **Wheaton, Ill.: Tyndale, 2001. ISBN 0-8423-1940-9pa. 235p.**

Shay and Marvin Taylor, founders of Genesis House in Atlanta, leave to start a second house in Odessa, Mississippi, in the aftermath of their six-year-old son's death and the subsequent near breakdown of their marriage. Rededicating themselves to God's work does not remove Shay's desperate wish for another child nor Marvin's reluctance to experience another potentially painful situation. As they pray at cross-purposes, a young teen comes into their lives and between them.

> *"How?" she asked, tears falling from her eyes. "Love is love. You either give it or you don't. How can you give it to Bo and not to our child?"* (p. 126)

Notes: Angela Benson is also listed in the "Suggestive" section of Chapter 10. Emma Award 2002; Gold Pen Award Best Christian Fiction Nominee 2002; Romance in Color Reviewers' Choice Award 2002

Keywords: death of a child • faith • friendships • husbands and wives • mourning • trust

Brown, Parry.

 7

Sittin' in the Front Pew: A Novel. **New York: Strivers Row/Villard, 2002. ISBN 0-375-75705-8. 237p.**

It's never easy to lose a loved one, and it's even more difficult when skeletons come out of the closet. The Naylor family must deal with the sudden death of the patriarch of the family, a beloved daddy, fiancé, and friend. Edward Naylor raised his four daughters after the death of his wife, and each of the women deal with his death in a different way. Their disagreements about funeral plans intensify when a woman, claiming to be Edward's first child whom he had planned to introduce at the next family reunion, appears on the scene.

> *"I may be the only Jesus anyone ever sees, and I need to be as much like Him as I can be. Understand that has nothing to do with sittin' in the front pew, but everything to do with what I do for my brother." Those were the words Edward Zachary Naylor said to me consistently.* (p. 229)

Notes: Parry Brown is also listed in the "Stories of Contemporary Life" section of Chapter 9.
Essence Bestseller List 2001, 2002, 2003, 2004

Keywords: Baltimore, Maryland • family relationships • fathers and daughters • mourning

Ellis, Jamellah.

🏵 *That Faith, That Trust, That Love*. Bowie, Md.: All the While Reconcile Publishing, 2001. ISBN 0-9709150-0-4. 318p.

Successful lawyer Marley Shepherd has second thoughts about her engagement to Gerrard Shore, one of Atlanta's black elite, when he is seen with another woman. Marley turns to her mother and grandmother for guidance and support, but instead encounters their anger with each other. Even with counseling, Marley and Gerrard are unable to reconcile. Marley returns to church and discovers what trust and faith in God can do. She extends her new-found faith to her mother and grandmother, who also rededicate themselves to God, and the three of them develop a new relationship.

> *Of course I loved my children. I got up and went to work every day, came home and cooked every night, and got up every weekend morning to cart them around town to where they needed to be so they could have opportunities in life. If that's not love, then I don't know what is.* (p. 138)

Notes: Gold Pen Award Best Christian Fiction (tie) 2001

Keywords: faith • family relationships • Georgia • love • trust

Files, Lolita.

Child of God: A Novel. New York: Simon & Schuster, 2001. ISBN 0-684-84143-6. 316p.

Child of God is the saga of three generations of the Boten family of Downtown, Tennessee, who deal with the curse of incest and voodoo. Ophelia Boten, herself the result of an incestuous relationship between her mother and her uncle, becomes pregnant by her older brother, a heroin dealer. The death of their child, Hamlet, in a mysterious fire changes the lives of the Boten family as the family's secret history of betrayal, violence, and confusion is revealed. Ophelia must confront the family curse so she can embrace a new life and a family of her own.

> *"Ya'll going to hell," she said. "Both of you. Evil sinners. That's why they took her baby, and that's why we can't have no chillun now."* (p. 160)

Notes: *Black Issues Book Review* Best Book 2002

Keywords: death of a child • drug dealers and dealing • family chronicles • homosexuality • incest • Tennessee • voodoo

Griggs, Vanessa Davis.

The Rose of Jericho. Birmingham, Ala.: Free To Soar, 2000. ISBN 0-9673003-1-2. 303p.

The relationships of J. M. Taylor, her husband, her mother, and her friends are explored through their private journals. Many stories emerge as the innermost thoughts of the characters are revealed. One of the main plots centers around who has plagiarized J. M.'s story, "The Moroccan Rose," and had it published in a magazine.

> *"Jericho's a good name for that old tumbleweed looking thing," he said. "Looks can be deceiving. Like that J.M. you go by . . . how many folks mistake you for a man?" He stopped and smiled at me. "Ain't no mistaking when they hear Johnnie Mae though. You're a rose, Baby Girl. The rose of Jericho."* (p. 167)

Notes: Vanessa Davis Griggs is also listed in the "Christian Fiction—Inspirational Romance" section of this chapter.

Keywords: family relationships • journals and diaries • men and women • trust • women's friendships • writers

Haley, Patricia.

No Regrets: A Novel. **Washington, D.C.: New Spirit Books/BET Publications, 2002. ISBN 1-58314-299-1. 227p.**

High school sweethearts Johnny and Karen Clark have the perfect marriage, with three beautiful children and a lifestyle to be envied. But after 18 years of marriage, their lives begin to crumble as Karen struggles with a serious illness and Johnny yields to infidelity. It is not until Karen faces death that Johnny realizes how much he loves her, and he finally comes to grip with his weaknesses and fears to turn his life over to God and put his family back together.

> *I'm not into that touchy-feely crap. Leave that religious stuff for the poor slobs who don't have anything else going for them. I prefer to put my faith in my hard work and a few lucky breaks.* (p. 174)

Keywords: adultery • cancer patients • faith • husbands and wives • love

Jackson, Sheneska.

Blessings: A Novel. **New York: Simon & Schuster, 1998. ISBN 0-684-85035-4. 395p.**

Blessings is the story of four women who work in a Los Angeles beauty shop, all facing challenges with motherhood. Pat, the owner of Blessings, desperately wants a child, but she is infertile and she and her husband have problems finding a child to adopt. Zuma struggles with the grief of aborting her child as a teen and plans on artificial insemination because she can't find a suitable father. Faye is a single mother raising two children after the death of her husband. Sandy, the white manicurist, has two children that she neglects and never wanted in the first place. When tragedy strikes Sandy's life, she leaves the greatest gift of all.

> *"They took her and her baby to the hospital," Pat said. "Sandy is a basket case." "I know," Zuma*

said, and looked at Pat baffled. "It's like she didn't give a damn about the kids. The only person she called for was Surgeon or Circus, or whatever his name is—was." (p. 382)

Notes: Blackboard Bestseller List 1997, 1998, 1999

Keywords: hair stylists • infertility • motherhood • single parents • women's friendships

Murray, Victoria Christopher.

🎗 *Temptation*. **West Bloomfield, Mich.: Walk Worthy Press/Warner Books, 2000. ISBN 0-446-52792-0. 353p.**

Kyla and Jefferson Blake and their adorable daughter are the perfect family. Jefferson's Los Angeles medical clinic is flourishing, and life could not be better. But Kyla's unhappy and lonely friend, Jasmine, sets out to destroy the Blakes' relationship. Kyla is crushed by her husband's unfaithfulness and her friend's betrayal. Kyla's best friend Alexis provides support to the family, even while facing her own challenges in keeping her commitments to God.

That woman, that person that you call a friend . . . is . . . a . . . snake. And, I pray that one day you don't find her slithering around on her belly eating everything in your backyard. (p. 75)

Notes: Blackboard Bestseller List 2000; NAACP Image Award Nominee 2001

Keywords: adultery • forgiveness • husbands and wives • jealousy • love • religion

Ray, Francis.

🎗 *I Know Who Holds Tomorrow*. **New York: St. Martin's Press, 2002. ISBN 0-312-30050-6. 310p.**

Well-known Dallas talk show host Madison Reed and TV correspondent Wes Reed are the picture perfect couple until the death of their child, when they become strangers to one another. When Wes stops to change a flat tire for Bridget, with whom he is having an affair, the two of them are hit by a drunk driver. On his deathbed, Wes tells Madison about the affair and asks her to raise Manda, his and Bridget's baby. Madison is angry and bitter, but Wes's best friend Zachary convinces her to accept Manda. Madison and Zachary become closer, but when Madison discovers that Zachary knew of Wes's infidelity, she once again feels betrayed.

You and I both know that life isn't promised. Don't waste time denying what is right in front of you or wondering about what other people think. If love comes along, snatch it with both hands. You deserve happiness without conditions. (p. 199)

Notes: *Essence* Bestseller List 2002

Francis Ray is also listed in the "Suggestive" section of Chapter 10.

Keywords: adultery • betrayal • death of a child • forgiveness • grief • love • television talk show hosts

Roby, Kimberla Lawson.

 Casting the First Stone. **New York: Kensington Publishing, 2000. ISBN 0-7582-0179-6. 384p.**

Tanya Black has everything a woman could want until she suspects her husband, Pastor Curtis Black, is having an affair with one of the church members. Curtis denies the accusations, refuses to go to counseling, and vows that their relationship will be better. But then Tanya finds proof that Curtis has been having not just one affair, but others as well. Scandal erupts in the church when Pastor Black's secrets are exposed at the second annual Pastor Appreciation Day.

> *Ridin' around in their fine cars and expensive suits and then looking like some drug dealer with all those gold rings lined up on every finger. It's a crying-out-loud shame how low-down some of these ministers are. And that Negro you're married to, Tanya, is no different. (p. 89)*

Notes: Blackboard Bestseller List 2000; Gold Pen Award Best Christian Fiction Nominee 2001

Keywords: adultery • church men • forgiveness • men and women • scandal

Thomas, Jacquelin.

The Prodigal Husband. **Washington, D.C.: New Spirit Books/BET Publications, 2002. ISBN 1-58314-254-1. 277p.**

Prodigal Husband begins with Jake Madison in the hospital with injuries from a car accident that killed his 15-month-old daughter. Unable to face his estranged wife Tori, he sneaks out of the hospital and out of town with Shelia, his business partner. Jake returns a year later to find that Tori is moving on with her life; she has opened a bookstore and has become re-acquainted with her old friend Nicholas. Jake continues to have strong feelings for his wife, but Shelia has other plans. Tori, however, never falters in her trust in God nor her love for Jake.

> *Don't try to shush me, girl! I'm gonna have my say. Jake Madison is not gonna do right by you, Tori. Mark my words, I don't blame him much, though. It's that Shelia Moore. She got roots on him. And if you look at her good– she's got these two spots on her face, right above her eyebrows. It looks like there used to be horns there. (p. 216)*

Notes: Jacquelin Thomas is also listed in the "Christian Fiction—Inspirational Romance" section of this chapter and the "Sensual" section of Chapter 10.

Keywords: adultery • death of a child • faith • forgiveness • love • mourning • reconciliation

Inspirational Romance

Benson, Angela.

Awakening Mercy. Wheaton, Ill.: Tyndale House Publishers, , 2000. ISBN 0-8423-1939-5. 265p.

CeCe Williams isn't looking for romance when she meets Nate Richardson while doing community service after forgetting to pay parking tickets. A young, successful Atlanta real estate agent, CeCe has dedicated her life to her son and to her relationship with God. Although CeCe and Nate both believe that God has brought them together, CeCe must learn to forgive past hurts before she can embrace a future with Nate.

> Thank you so much for sending her to me, Lord. Teach me
> to love her as you want her to be loved. More than anything,
> I want her to be confident in my love for you and my love for
> her and David. (p. 125)

Notes: Angela Benson is also listed in the "Suggestive" section of Chapter 10.
Gold Pen Award Best Christian Fiction Nominee 2001

Keywords: forgiveness • single parents • teen pregnancy • vengeance • working mothers

Berry, Bertice.

Redemption Song: A Novel. New York: Doubleday, 2000. ISBN 0-385-49844-6. 181p.

Ross Buchanan and Josephine "Fina" Chambers meet when they simultaneously reach for a slave woman's memory book on the shelf at Black Images bookstore. But the store's owner, Miss Cozy, refuses to sell the book to either customer. Sensing something special, Miss Cozy convinces them to read the book aloud in her small African American bookshop. The memory book tells the love story of a couple enslaved on the same plantation and concludes with a spiritual affirmation of love and what Miss Cozy calls a "Recipe for Life."

> "The point I'm trying to make," Fina continued, "is that all of
> the things that I've collected throughout my life are not my
> life. They have no value, but what I've ascribed to them. I
> wanted to believe that I had a piece of the South African
> struggle, and that's what the man sold me." (p. 96)

Keywords: forgiveness • journals and diaries • professionals • slavery

Ford, Aisha.

Pride and Pumpernickel. Uhrichsville, Ohio: Barbour Publishing/Heartsong Presents, 2001. ISBN 1-58660-472-4. 170p.

Dana Edwards, general manager of Grady's Bakery, is hurt when her boss hires gourmet chef Ethan Miles to revitalize the bakery's failing popularity. Dana is further devastated when she discovers that she will be Ethan's assistant. Despite the tension between them, Dana and Ethan immediately feel a strong attraction to one another. As the two develop a working relationship, they also begin to fall in love. However, Ethan and Dana are unable to separate their work from their romance, and pride threatens the growth of their relationship.

> *"My point? God doesn't make mistakes. If He planned something, we're the only ones who can mess up His plan by not doing what He wants us to. So, if He wants us to be together, do you think He's looking down here saying, 'Oops, they live in different cities. Better scratch that one'."* (p. 101)

Keywords: pride • restaurant business

Stacy's Wedding. Uhrichsville, Ohio: Barbour Publishing/Heartsong Presents, 1999. ISBN 1-57748-748-6. 170p.

Max Edwards's pursuit of wedding coordinator Stacy Thompson results in a whirlwind courtship. But the couple's relationship is jeopardized as they struggle with personal fears and interference from friends and family. Max is about to propose when he discovers that they belong to the same online book discussion group and is devastated to learn that Stacy is Ms. Drew, the newest member of the group. Online, Ms. Drew and Sherlock (Max) are constantly bickering, their behavior far from Christlike. Can their relationship withstand this discovery?

> *Max laughed. "No, I'm not getting married . . . at least not this summer. Unless you and I decide we're extremely in love with each other over lunch. Then how soon could you fit our wedding in?"* (p. 19)

Keywords: book discussion groups • Kansas City • trust • wedding coordinators

The Wife Degree. Urichsville, Ohio: Barbour Publishing/Heartsong Presents, 2000. ISBN 1-58660-069-9. 170p.

When Madison "Maddy" Thompson arrives home for the summer after graduating from college she finds a dog on her porch, only to be accused of being a dognapper by former high school classmate Jordan Sanders. After a brief confrontation, Maddy realizes that Jordan has changed; he asks her to forgive him and says he wants to be her friend. When Maddy confides that she wants to change herself to please her new boyfriend, Jordan agrees to help. As Maddy and Jordan let go of past hurts and explore their worth as individuals, they become more than friends.

> *It says in the Bible that the truth will set me free. And I'm telling you this because I need to be free. I started out trying to get your attention by learning how to cook. I thought that if I knew how to cook, it would make you take notice of me . . . A good friend of mine kept telling me that a man should love me for who I am, not who I can make myself be, but I didn't believe him.* (p. 167)

Keywords: educators • graduate students • reunions • self-esteem

Griggs, Vanessa Davis.

🏵 *Promises Beyond Jordan: A Novel.* **Birmingham, Ala: Free To Soar, 2002. ISBN 0-9673003-2-0. 260p.**

"Have you ever loved someone that you never had?" Minister George Landris asks his fiancée Theresa nine days before their wedding as he departs to visit his first love, recently injured in a car accident with her husband and daughter. Theresa's insecurities are compounded when she discovers that her father and his wife have kept a secret from her that could destroy their family. As the wedding draws near, a scandal erupts in the church, with George and Theresa at the center of it.

> *It's not doing the right thing sometimes. It's doing it without hurting other people in the process. You know, Mom? Most people, even Christians, have a hard time with telling or hearing the truth.* (p. 153)

Notes: Vanessa Davis Griggs is also listed in the "Christian Fiction—Family" section of this chapter.
Gold Pen Award Best Christian Fiction Nominee 2002

Keywords: church life • church men • scandal • trust

Haley-Brown, Patricia.

Nobody's Perfect. **Valley Forge, Pa.: Anointed Vision, 1998. ISBN 0-9663174-1-6. 324p.**

Rachel's fiancé Ken meets all of the criteria on her 12-point perfect husband checklist, but when she becomes pregnant with his child, his response forces her to recognize that he isn't perfect after all. In fact, as Rachel confronts the changes in her life, she realizes that nobody's perfect, including herself. She discovers that a checklist won't work—she must first develop a relationship with God before she can find the perfect love.

> *She yelled through the door, "You sure didn't mind giving me your undivided attention when we were laying up in New York. Now that the dust has settled, and I'm pregnant, all of a sudden you're confused and don't have any time. You are a pathetic excuse for a man, let alone a father."* (p. 247)

Keywords: pregnancy • premarital sex • self-examination

Hudson-Smith, Linda.

Ladies in Waiting: A Novel. **Washington, D.C.: New Spirit/BET Publications, 2002. ISBN 1-58314-295-9. 308p.**

Four women from completely different walks of life meet at a correctional facility in the California desert and form an unlikely support group. Marlene is the devout wife of a preacher who has been convicted of a crime he didn't commit; Keisha continues to support her faithless boyfriend, the father of her children; Rosalinda works two jobs to pay the legal fees of her career-criminal lover; and the beautiful, sophisticated, and snobbish Alexis visits her husband, imprisoned for embezzlement. As the women evaluate themselves and their lives, they form a support group, "Ladies in Waiting," for people who love someone in prison. The women help each other through hard times and discover truths about themselves and their men.

> *Don't you old coots dare try to patronize me. I'm a darn good Christian, but I can whip a little Satan out of me whenever I find it necessary to do so. Don't underestimate me because of my good nature and the fact that I'm a woman. That would be a big mistake.* (p. 163)

Keywords: forgiveness • guilt • prison life • self-esteem • women's friendships

Moore, Stephanie Perry.

Flame. **Chicago: Lift Every Voice/Moody Press, 2001. ISBN 0-8024-4197-1. 200p.**

Bacall Lee's future is bright: She has earned her college degree, is dating a handsome new boyfriend, and has an exciting music career with Yotown Records. However, Bacall didn't realize how all of these things would interfere with her relationship with God. Bacall must choose between her boyfriend Rory and living the Christian life she has been taught. Even though their desire for one another remains strong, Rory and Bacall decide to quit dating. When the pressures of the music industry nearly destroy Rory, he seeks help from Bacall to get his life back on the right track.

> *I had to admit, last night did feel good. But today, I felt terrible. Doubts rose within me. Rory had no obligation to me in the eyes of God.* (p. 117)

Notes: Stephanie Perry Moore is also listed in the "Christian Fiction—Young Adult" section of this chapter.

Keywords: California • friendships • music business • premarital sex • trust

Murray, Victoria Christopher.

Joy. **West Bloomfield, Mich.: Walk Worthy Press/Warner Books, 2001. ISBN 0-446-52875-7. 373p.**

Anya Mitchell appears to have her life together: She is the owner of a successful financial management firm, is engaged to the handsome Braxton Vance, and is deeply committed to God. But Anya begins to have doubts about her marriage and convinces Braxton to see their pastor for counseling. Anya's concerns are complicated by her attraction to one of her employees. When Anya is brutally attacked, she finds that her friends are absorbed by their own personal struggles, leaving her to depend on the guidance and protection of God to pull her life together and regain peace within herself.

> *Anya, you were raped two days ago and you're acting as if you were suppose to walk around like nothing happened. Yes, you love the Lord, but that doesn't stop you from being human.* (p. 229)

Notes: Gold Pen Award Best Christian Fiction Nominee 2001

Keywords: faith • financial consultants and managers • rape

Nunez, Elizabeth.

Discretion. New York: Ballantine Books, 2002. ISBN 0-345-44731-X. 276p.

When Oufoula Sindede, an African diplomat, falls in love with Marguerite, a New York artist, he discovers a passion that is lacking with his African wife. Oufoula is comfortable having an African family and an American lover, but Marguerite ends the affair when she discovers that he is married. Years later, the two meet again and Oufoula must once more choose between being a faithful husband or surrendering to the desires of his heart and flesh.

> *I think back now and I realize that in those days when I thought wife, I thought of them both, for each of them was an aspect of wife that was essential to me. I could not think of one as my wife without thinking of the other. I could not imagine living with one without being able to be with the other.* (p. 97)

Keywords: adultery • Africa and Africans • polygamy

Thomas, Jacquelin.

Singsation: A Novel. West Bloomfield, Mich.: Walk Worthy Press/Warner Books, 2001. ISBN 0-446-52798-X. 338p.

Each Sunday as she sang in church, police dispatcher Deborah Anne Peterson dreamed of becoming a professional singer. Her dream becomes reality when she is discovered by superstar rapper Triage Blue. Triage arranges for an audition for Deborah Anne with a popular rhythm and blues singer, who likes her and offers her a contract. When Deborah moves to Hollywood, she learns the difficulties of maintaining her devout Christian lifestyle in this environment. While Triage helps her adjust to life as a superstar, the murder of a friend forces Deborah to question what God wants her to do with her gift of singing.

> *"I didn't do right by God," Phoebe whispered. "Please ask Him to forgive me." Deborah's lips trembled with grief, but she took Phoebe's hand in both of hers. "I don't have to do that for you, Phoebe. You can do it."* (p. 261)

Notes: Jacquelin Thomas is also listed in the "Christian Fiction—Family" section of this chapter and the "Sensual" section of Chapter 10.

Keywords: faith • friendships • murder • music business

Young Adult

Moore, Stephanie Perry.

The Payton Skky Series.

Living a Christian life can be difficult, especially for teenagers, who often feel an enormous amount of peer pressure. The <u>Payton Skky</u> series, named for the main character, presents the lives of high school and college age teens who are struggling to live a Christian life while confronting the many issues facing young adults: drugs, alcohol, love, sexuality, discrimination, friendship, racism, and other prejudices. The characters learn you can be a Christian and still be cool, that you can even be respected for your beliefs and convictions.

> *Lord, I'm struggling bad in the area of fornication. But You know me. Even when I let You down, I still plead for Your help. Father, only You know that I'm trying really hard to stay pure. After all, I did finally say, "no!" even if it was after I almost had my clothes off.* (Staying Pure, p. 14)

Notes: Stephanie Perry Moore is also listed in the "Christian Fiction—Inspirational Romance" section of this chapter.

Keywords: Christian life • friendships • interpersonal relations • peer pressure

Staying Pure. Chicago: Lift Every Voice/Moody Press, 1997. ISBN 0-8024-4236-6. 195p.

It's Payton Skky's senior year at Lucy Laney High School, and she has it all—popularity, excellent grades, and the most sought-after guy on campus, Dakari Graham. However, she meets a bump in the road when Dakari wants to take their two-year relationship to another level.

Keywords: celibacy • dating • premarital sex • trust

7

Sober Faith. Chicago: Lift Every Voice/Moody Press, 2000. ISBN 0-8024-4237-4. 139p.

Payton, a senior in high school, is on top of the world as she celebrates her introduction to society as a Links' debutante. The evening was perfect, but Payton's friends wanted to celebrate with more than punch after the ball.

Keywords: alcohol abuse and alcoholics

Saved Race. Chicago: Lift Every Voice/Moody Press, 2001. ISBN 0-8024-4238-2. 159p.

Payton is excited about going to college after graduating from high school with honors. She continues to struggle with her feelings for her first love, Dakari Graham, and her present boyfriend, Tad Taylor, who is a gentle, caring Christian. The summer proves to be interesting for Payton and her friends as they deal with racism and date rape.

Keywords: interracial relationships • jealousy • racism

Sweetest Gift. Chicago: Lift Every Voice/ Moody Press, 2001.ISBN 0-8024-4239-0. 205p.

Payton Skky quickly discovers that college isn't everything that she had imagined—she must learn to deal with fast-paced classes, racism, and discrimination as she meets new friends and challenges. Payton continues to wrestle with her feelings for her old boyfriends, Dakari and Tad, although she is no longer dating either one. Payton's life is full as she meets challenges with new and old friends.

Keywords: interracial relationships • jealousy • racism

Surrendered Heart. Chicago: Lift Every Voice/Moody Press, 2002. ISBN 0-8024-4240-4. 179p.

After the death of her grandfather, Payton Skky has a new determination to lead her life for Christ. She realizes the importance of witnessing to others even if they reject the message of salvation. After reconciling their relationship, Payton and Tad help Dakari to survive after the death of his brother, and they introduce him to Christ.

Keywords: faith • missionaries • mourning

Inspirational Nonfiction

Bibles, Bible Study, and Religious Texts—General

The African American Devotional Bible: King James Version **(Congress of National Black Churches). Grand Rapids, Mich.: Zondervan Publishing House, 1997. ISBN 0-310-91826-X. 1474p.**

The *African American Devotional Bible* features the complete text of the King James Version of the Bible, coupled with a thematic introduction to each book and daily devotions.

> Brothers and sisters: We must not stop the struggle. "Quitters don't win and winners don't quit!" Persistence pays off!
> (p. 43)

Keywords: devotional calendars • inspirational sayings

The Original African Heritage Study Bible. **Nashville, Tenn.: James C. Winston Publishing, 1993. ISBN 1-55523-674-X. 1893p.**

The *Original African Heritage Study Bible* interprets the Bible as it relates specifically to people of African descent. The Old and New Testaments of the Bible are presented in conjunction with several articles that provide a guide to African presence in the Bible.

Keywords: biblical characters

Bibles, Bible Study, and Religious Texts—Men

Banks, Mel.

Men of Color Study Bible. **Iowa Falls, Iowa: World Bible Publishing, 2001. ISBN 052-911-4941. (various paging)**

Specifically designed for men of African descent, this study guide is a counterpart to *Women of Color Study Bible*. It follows the same layout, with the King James version of the Bible accompanied by commentaries from well-known African American men, including John P. Kee, Dr. Jawanza Kunjufu, and Derrick C. Moore.

> When we are placed upon this planet, God has a mission—an assignment—for each of us to complete. To get us there, He will often lead us down the most unexpected routes. (p. 726, 14)

Keywords: Christian life • Christian men

Bibles, Bible Study, and Religious Texts—Women

Gill, LaVerne McCain.

Daughters of Dignity: African Women in the Bible and the Virtues of Black Womanhood. **Cleveland, Ohio: The Pilgrim Press, 2000. ISBN 0-8298-1373-X. 140p.**

Daughters of Dignity explores the link between African women in the Bible and African American women in terms of their reliance on the Christian virtues of justice, love, faith, wisdom, and perseverance. Gill profiles biblical women such as Hagar, Zipporah, Rahab, the Queen of Sheba, and the Canaanite woman, as well as African American women such as Rosa Parks, Osceola McCarty, Sojourner Truth, Mary McLeod Bethune, and Fannie Lou Hamer.

> For Jesus, love is the one act that overcomes adversity and brings about a change in the condition of the oppressed, freeing their spirits so that they might participate in the reign of God. (unpaged)

Keywords: biblical characters • Christian life • Christian women

Lawson, Marjorie, ed.

Women of Color Study Bible. **Iowa Falls, Iowa: World Bible Publishing, 1999. ISBN 052-911-0962. (various paging)**

This study Bible, created by and for contemporary women of African descent, includes the complete books of the Old and New Testaments along with analysis of scriptures and commentaries on "Life Lessons."

> Joy Giver, let me always rejoice in Your ability to bring me through difficult situations. Keep me focused on You. (p. 822)

Keywords: Christian life • Christian women • essays and reflections • meditations

Devotional Calendars

Copage, Eric V.

🏵 *Black Pearls for Parents: Meditations, Affirmations, and Inspirations for African-American Parents.* **New York: Quill William Morrow, 1995. ISBN 0-688-13098-4. Unpaged.**

This collection of daily quotes provides inspiration and actions to guide and comfort African American parents as they strive to deal with and understand their children in today's society, a much different world than the one they knew.

> *On this day, I will pledge to encourage my child's interests and talents and expose him to all he can do and be. I will do my best to foster a positive attitude, a desire to excel, a commitment to proper work/study habits, and the ability to persevere despite obstacles and setbacks.* (March 29)

Notes: Blackboard Bestseller List 1995

Keywords: meditations • parents and children

🏵 *Black Pearls: Daily Meditations, Affirmations, and Inspirations for African-Americans.* **New York: Quill William Morrow, 1993. ISBN 0-688-12291-4. 400p.**

African proverbs and words of wisdom from Sojourner Truth, Malcolm X, Oprah Winfrey, Quincy Jones, and Terry McMillan are offered each day, accompanied by a specific daily action. The meditations help prepare for the day's events by covering such topics as self-determination, love, power, success, dieting, stress, and jealousy.

> *I have learned to take "no" as a vitamin.—Suzanne de Passe* (May 24)

Notes: Blackboard Bestseller List 1994, 1995, 1996, 1997

Keywords: African proverbs • inspirational sayings • meditations • self-actualization

Stewart, Julia.

African Proverbs and Wisdom: A Collection for Every Day of the Year, from More Than Forty Nations. **New York: Dafina Books/Kensington Publishing, 1997. ISBN 0-7582-0298-9. 192p.**

Many African proverbs, fables, and songs have been passed down orally from generation to generation. *African Proverbs and Wisdom* provides a collection of some of these sayings and tales for every day of the year. A reflection of thoughts from over 40 African nations, the book is illustrated and includes indexes of holidays by country and ethnic group.

> *People are like plants in the wind: they bow down and rise up again.—Malagasy proverb on resilience.* (p. 150)

Keywords: African proverbs

Vanzant, Iyanla.

 Acts of Faith: Daily Meditations for People of Color. **New York: Fireside, 1993. ISBN 0-671-86416-5. Unpaged.**

> A daily inspirational book for people of color, *Acts of Faith* is divided into four sections—self, world, others, and money—to help people of color learn to live a stress-free and peace-filled life.

> *I am the only one who can limit me.* (April 21)

> **Notes:** Iyanla Vanzant is also listed in "Essays and Reflections—General and Women" and in "Guidance and Self -Help—General, Men, and Women," all in the "Inspirational Nonfiction" section of this chapter.
> Blackboard Bestseller List 1994, 1995, 1996, 1997, 1998, 1999, 2000

> **Keywords:** meditations • spirituality and spiritual life

One Day My Soul Just Opened Up. **New York: Fireside, 1998. ISBN 0-684-84134-7. 316p.**

> Vanzant provides a 40-day program to pursue spiritual and personal growth. Inspirational thoughts are given along with exercises to help work through problems.

> *Honor Your Self with . . . CONSERVATION.* (p. 107)

> **Notes:** Iyanla Vanzant is also listed in "Essays and Reflections—General and Women" and in "Guidance and Self-Help—General, Men, and Women," all in the "Inspirational Nonfiction" section of this chapter.

> **Keywords:** meditations • self-actualization • spirituality and spiritual life

 Until Today! Daily Devotions for Spiritual Growth and Peace of Mind. **New York: Simon & Schuster, 2000. ISBN 0-684-84137-1. Unpaged.**

> This collection of affirmations encourages self-examination for personal growth. Each month focuses on a spiritual principle such as love, acknowledgment, forgiveness, faith, worth, and peace. At the end of each day's passage, an old way of thinking is presented, followed by a new approach to practice throughout the day.

> *I am now receptive to the idea that . . . if I don't ask for what I need, the need will keep getting bigger!*
> (May 12)

> **Notes:** Iyanla Vanzant is also listed in "Essays and Reflections—General and Women" and in "Guidance and Self-Help—General, Men, and Women," all in the "Inspirational Nonfiction" section of this chapter.
> *Essence* Bestseller List 2001, 2002

> **Keywords:** meditations • self-actualization • self-examination

Essays and Reflections—General

Copage, Eric V.

Soul Food: Inspirational Stories for African Americans. New York: Hyperion, 2000. ISBN 0-7868-8499-1. 269p.

Soul Food is a collection of stories for African Americans written by Eric Copage, with excerpts from other famous African Americans such as Ruby Dee, Patti LaBelle, Arthur Ashe, Colin Powell, Nikki Giovanni, and Henry Louis Gates Jr. This collection, which is filled with hope, joy, humor, and love, is divided into seven sections: Love, Self-esteem, Family, Creativity, Tenacity, Wisdom, and Faith.

> *A taste of disappointment is good, because you'll work that much harder so that you never have to have that feeling again.—Michael Jordan* (p. 181)

Keywords: spirituality and spiritual life

LaBelle, Patti, and Laura Randolph Lancaster.

Patti's Pearls: Lessons in Living Genuinely, Joyfully, Generously. New York: Warner Books, 2001. ISBN 0-446-52794-7. 145p.

Grammy Award winning singer Patti LaBelle shares pearls of wisdom learned from her grandmother, Ellen, as well as from family and friends. Patti enhances each with a personal anecdote about experiences in her life.

> *Accept everything you are and nothing you are not.* (p. 47)

Notes: *Essence* Bestseller List 2002

Keywords: inspirational sayings • singers

Taylor, Susan L.

In the Spirit: The Inspirational Writings of Susan L. Taylor. New York: Amistad, 1993. ISBN 1-56743-032-5. 121p.

Editor-in-chief of *Essence* magazine, Susan L. Taylor inspires readers with a collection of essays from her popular column as well as new essays. Personal anecdotes encourage looking inside for strength.

> *All that humankind has created down through the ages shows that human beings are capable of doing wondrous things. Your great challenge is to believe this about yourself.* (p. 53)

Keywords: journalists and journalism • self-actualization • spirituality and spiritual life

Lessons in Living. New York: 1st Anchor Books/Doubleday, 1995. ISBN 0-385-47868-2. 163p.

This collection of inspirational writings offers personal strategies for finding inner peace as one faces life's challenges. As Taylor explores themes of self-empowerment, love, self-worth, faith, and commitment, she makes it clear that we are given the opportunity to grow from the challenges presented in life.

No one makes you angry. Anger, like love, is something you choose. (p. 92)

Notes: Blackboard Bestseller List 1996

Keywords: journalists and journalism • self-actualization • spirituality and spiritual life

Vanzant, Iyanla.

 Every Day I Pray: Prayers for Awakening to the Grace of Inner Communion. **New York: Simon & Schuster, 2001. ISBN 0-684-86000-7. 158p.**

This collection of prayers written by Vanzant over the years in her journals addresses a variety of topics such as guidance, anxiety, debt, and relationships. Vanzant says "your every thought, every word, every action is a prayer. If we can remain mindful of that, focusing our attention on honoring God's presence in everything and everyone, prayer will become as natural as breathing." (p. 20)

The Freedom of Forgiveness

Today, I ask for and claim forgiveness from everyone for all ills I have created in

thought, word or deed.

Today, all is forgiven. I am free to pursue my highest good.

Today, I know no harm, no hurt, no condition, situation or person is more

powerful than the power of God or God's love.

God's love protects me, provides for me and guides me.

All is well in my soul.

Today, I open my heart to the power of God's love. I forgive. I am forgiving. I

am forgiven.

Thank you God.

And So It Is! (p. 83)

Notes: Iyanla Vanzant is also listed in "Devotional Calendars," "Essays and Reflections—Women" and "Guidance and Self-Help—General, Men, and Women," all in the "Inspirational Nonfiction" section of this chapter. *Essence* Bestseller List 2002, 2003

Keywords: meditations • spirituality and spiritual life

Essays and Reflections—Men

Key, William J., and Robert Johnson-Smith.

From One Brother to Another: Voices of African American Men. **Valley Forge, Pa.: Judson Press, 1996. ISBN 0-8170-1250-8. 242p.**

This is a collection of devotions that reflects how African American men from various disciplines have been able to triumph over the many struggles presented by modern society through their faith in God. Personal stories provide strength and encouragement for men struggling to overcome the crises presented in life.

> *Cherish your relationships, not your possessions. Make the time now to enjoy your life.* (p. 90)

Keywords: black men and society • meditations • spirituality and spiritual life

Wright, Jeremiah A., Jr.

From One Brother to Another: Voices of African American Men. **Valley Forge, Penn.: Judson Press, 2003. Volume 2. ISBN 0-8170-1362-8. 223p.**

Pastor Jeremiah A. Wright Jr. has compiled a follow-up volume to *From One Brother to Another* with more devotions and prayers by men who have a strong African American Christian faith. The authors are clergy, officers in the church, and just plain "pew members" who represent a variety of professions including business, law, education, and religion. These men give their perspectives on such topics as family, perseverance, redemption, love, and responsibility.

> *Our loving Heavenly Father, break the barriers that stand between us and our vulnerability. Teach us to cry again. Amen.* (p. 145)

Keywords: black men and society • meditations • spirituality and spiritual life

Essays and Reflections—Women

Boyd, Julia A.

Girlfriend to Girlfriend: Everyday Wisdom and Affirmations from the Sister Circle. **New York: Plume Book, 1999. ISBN 0-452-27392-7. 131p.**

These humorous and thought-provoking words of wisdom from sister circle meetings across the country offer hope, empowerment, and encouragement to weather the many obstacles that women face in their daily lives. The book is divided into four major themes: Self-Care; Family, Friends, and Lovers; Health Issues; and Daily Struggles.

> *My tears are part of my strength.* (p. 89)

Notes: Blackboard Bestseller List 1995, 1996

Keywords: inspirational sayings • self-actualization

Jakes, Jacqueline.

Sister Wit Devotions for Women. New York: Warner Books, 2002. ISBN 0-446-52972-9. 250p.

Jacqueline Jakes shares her touching story of surviving a brain tumor and encourages women with the wisdom she has gained on her journey through life. She offers advice grounded in scripture and laced with humor that will help to overcome any challenge life presents.

> *In the midst of coping with the pressures of daily living, stop and consider that you have the substance, the stuff, to live and to live well.* (p. 169)

Keywords: Christian life • Christian women

Jakes, T. D.

God's Leading Lady: Out of the Shadows and into the Light. New York: Putnam, 2002. ISBN 0-339-14883-3. 290p.

Bishop T. D. Jakes encourages women to step out of the shadows and onto center stage as "God's Leading Ladies." Using personal stories and profiling several women of the Bible as well as contemporary women, he provides inspiration and strategies for overcoming the adversities of life and achieving the success God has promised.

Notes: *Essence* Bestseller List 2002, 2003

Keywords: Christian life • Christian women

The Lady, Her Lover, and Her Lord. New York: Putnam, 1998. ISBN 0-399-144144-5. 208p.

To have balanced relationships, women are encouraged to nurture themselves and become more receptive and understanding of others. However, Jakes reminds women that they must always keep the Lord as the focal point of life.

> *When a wise woman seeks a husband, she chooses on the basis of his character and not his financial portfolio. She wants a man who is secure enough to feel comfortable with her success. But by no means does she need him to fulfill her financial dreams. She has her future wrapped up in her relationship with God.* (p. 178)

Keywords: Christian life • Christian women • husbands and wives

Woman, Thou Art Loosed: Healing the Wounds of the Past. Shippensburg, Pa.: Treasure House, 1993. ISBN 0-7684-3040-2. 180p.

Bishop T. D. Jakes touches the heart of women as he prescribes God as the cure for any crisis and points out scriptures that will help a woman become the person God created her to be.

> *For every struggle in your life, God accomplished something in your character and in your spirit.* (p. 74)

Keywords: Christian life • Christian women • self-actualization

Mckenzie, Vashti M.

Journey to the Well. **New York: Viking, 2002. ISBN 0-670-88484-7. 240p.**

The first female bishop of the African Methodist Episcopal Church, Vashti McKenzie, uses the Samaritan woman's meeting with Jesus at the well to show women how to transform their lives. McKenzie intermingles personal stories with 12 lessons that include biblical quotations, affirmations, and meditational activities.

> *Learned ignorance is a crutch that some people use; they deliberately appear ignorant or helpless when they are not. They think the same way they've always thought or think the same way the people around them think because it's easier than thinking for themselves.* (p. 113)

Notes: Black Issues Book Review Best Book 2002; *Essence* Bestseller List 2003

Keywords: biblical characters • Christian life • Christian women • meditations

Vanzant, Iyanla.

Yesterday, I Cried. **New York: Simon & Schuster, 1998. ISBN 0-684-86424-X. 304p.**

Yoruba priestess, Iyanla Vanzant, tells how she overcame a childhood of physical, emotional, and sexual abuse and met the challenge of raising three children alone on welfare, to obtain an undergraduate degree, a law degree, and personal success.

> *Prayer can do things that you can't do. It can fix things that you didn't even realize were broken.* (p.156)

Notes: Iyanla Vanzant is also listed in "Devotional Calendars," "Essays and Reflections —General," and "Guidance and Essays—General, Men, and Women," all in the "Inspirational Nonfiction" section of this chapter.
Blackboard Bestseller List 1999, 2000; *Essence* Bestseller List 2001

Keywords: autobiographies • life stories • self-actualization • single women • spirituality and spiritual life

Wells, Thelma.

Girl, Have I Got Good News for You. **Nashville, Tenn.: Thomas Nelson Publishing, 2000. ISBN 0-7852-7547-9. 160p.**

Using humor and the Holy Scriptures, Wells provides wisdom and power to help women triumph over some of their most common trials including depression, abortion, debt, addiction, and sexuality.

> *My parents might have had an illegitimate relationship, but I'm not illegitimate. I did nothing to get here.* (p. 22)

Keywords: Christian life • Christian women • humor

Guidance and Self-Help—General

Vanzant, Iyanla.

In the Meantime: Finding Yourself and the Love That You Want. **New York: Simon & Schuster, 1998. ISBN 0-684-84806-6. 326p.**

Vanzant uses the metaphor of house cleaning to describe how to find the perfect love. Cleaning begins in the basement, by acknowledging there is a problem, and ends in the attic with unconditional love.

> *The majority of challenges in our relationships come about when we forget our goal, when we forget the lessons we have learned in the past, when we live in fear, which in effect creates the very thing we fear, and when we do things we subconsciously know do not work.* (p. 142)

Notes: Iyanla Vanzant is also listed in "Devotional Calendars," "Essays and Reflections—General and Women," and "Guidance and Self-Help—Men and Women," all in the "Inspirational Nonfiction" section of this chapter.

Keywords: men and women • self-esteem • single women

Living Through the Meantime. **New York: Fireside, 2001. ISBN 0-7432-2710-7. 221p.**

This "meantime" workbook is designed to help both men and women deal with past experiences, motivations, and desires. Unless they are grounded in love, men and women will find themselves in one "meantime" experience after another.

> *You've got to—COORDINATE!*
>
> *Clean*
>
> *Out*
>
> *Old*
>
> *Rigid*
>
> *Destructive*
>
> *Ideas*
>
> *Now*
>
> *And*
>
> *Truthfully*
>
> *Evaluate your beliefs about life and love.* (p. 33)

Notes: Iyanla Vanzant is also listed in "Devotional Calendars," "Essays and Reflections —General and Women," and "Guidance and Self-Help—Men and Women," all in the "Inspirational Nonfiction" section of this chapter.

Keywords: love • self-actualization • self-examination

Guidance and Self-Help—Men

Kena, Kwasi Issa.

40 Days in the Wilderness: Meditations for African American Men. **Nashville: Abingdon Press, 1998. ISBN 0-687-071801. 144p.**

Society constantly attacks and challenges the African American male. To succeed, Africans and African Americans must return to their roots of spirituality. The "wilderness" provides a place of transformation, and the number 40 represents an important time span throughout the Bible. "In the wilderness, God provokes us to greatness, toughens us to withstand temptation, and calls forth our hidden potential." This book provides scriptures, stories, and prayers, along with a section "For Further Meditation," in a 40-day journal format that will spark permanent changes in life.

> *Dear Lord, help me to see that my real self-worth comes from things that money cannot provide. Show me those godly qualities that really define manhood and personal value. Amen.* (p. 70)

Keywords: black men and society • devotional calendars • meditations • spirituality and spiritual life

Munroe, Myles.

The Principle of Fatherhood: Priority, Position and the Role of the Male. **Lanham, Md.: Pneuma Life Publishing, 2000. ISBN 1-56229-160-2. 135p.**

Dr. Myles Munroe believes the purpose of all men is fatherhood and discusses the roles of a true father: progenitor, source, sustainer and nourisher, protector, teacher, disciplinarian, leader, head, caring one, and developer. Tips are given to the father for strengthening himself and his ties with family, community, and society as a whole.

> *A father doesn't dominate or control his house. He develops the potential of everyone in his house through his leadership.* (p. 111)

Keywords: black men and society • fatherhood • spirituality and spiritual life

Vanzant, Iyanla.

 The Spirit of a Man: A Vision of Transformation for Black Men and the Women Who Love Them. **San Francisco: HarperSanFrancisco, 1996. ISBN 0-06251236-6. 277p.**

Vanzant dissects many of the problems and challenges that black men face in society and provides a guide for spiritual awareness as a source of self-improvement, as well as of other benefits in life and relationships.

> We can stop what is going on in the world when we really believe that we have the power of God within us and stop waiting for it to show up via federally funded programs. (p. 107)

Notes: Iyanla Vanzant is also listed in "Devotional Calendars," "Essays and Reflections—General and Women," and "Guidance and Self-Help—General and Women," all in the "Inspirational Nonfiction" section of this chapter. Blackboard Bestseller List 1996, 1997, 1999

Keywords: black men and society • men and women • spirituality and spiritual life

***Up from Here: Reclaiming the Male Spirit: A Guide to Transforming Emotions into Power and Freedom.* San Francisco: HarperSanFrancisco, 2002. ISBN 0-06-251759-7. 228p.**

Iyanla Vanzant describes seven African American men who are dealing with various challenges and presents a "transformation plan." The men must use "power tools" of awareness, acceptance, acknowledgment, responsibility, forgiveness, stillness, commitment, and understanding to combat their struggles and grow emotionally and spiritually.

> Remember that responsibility is synonymous with power. Taking responsibility is the only way to have power psychologically, emotionally and spiritually. (p. 168)

Notes: Iyanla Vanzant is also listed in "Devotional Calendars," "Essays and Reflections—General and Women," and "Guidance and Self-Help—General and Women," all in the "Inspirational Nonfiction" section of this chapter.

Keywords: black men and society • self-actualization • self-examination

Guidance and Self-Help—Women

Cook, Suzan D. Johnson.

***Sister to Sister Devotions for and from African American Women.* Valley Forge, Penn.: Judson Press, 1995. ISBN 0-8170-1221-4. 235p.**

This collection of meditations from African American women provides nurturing, healing, and restoration. Readers are given real-life testimonies from mothers and daughters that deal with love, grief, strength, failure, and success.

> My mother taught me that "difference" is a positive, a strength, rather than something strange or exotic. (p. 65)

Notes: Blackboard Bestseller List 1996, 1998

Keywords: meditations • mothers and daughters

Hammond, Michelle McKinney.

How to Be Blessed and Highly Favored. **Colorado Springs, Colo.: Waterbrook Press, 2001. ISBN 1-57856-449-2. 197p.**

Many people use the popular phrase, "Blessed and highly favored!" However, do we really know the meaning and responsibility behind the phrase? Michelle McKinney Hammond uses Mary, the mother of Jesus, to show how you can truly be blessed when you live your life solely for God.

> *A good name cannot be spent, it will not tarnish, and, like perfume, it lingers long after you've left the room.* (p. 120)

Keywords: biblical characters • Christian life • self-actualization

If Men Are Like Buses Then How Do I Catch One? **Sisters, Ore.: Multnomah Publishers, 2000. ISBN 1-57673-691-1. 185p.**

In a humorous and scriptural manner, Michelle McKinney Hammond explains how women can find happiness and fulfillment while waiting for that "godly" man to enter into their lives. Extending the bus metaphor, she asserts that God has written the bus route and schedule, so there's no need for women to map out the journey to the altar.

> *I suggest that you pull that cord, stand up, and run for the nearest exit. Leave behind all tokens, transfers, and passes. Get off that bus, girl. Run! Do not walk, do not pass go, do not collect two hundred dollars! Head straight back into the arms of your Father until you find your strength renewed.* (pp. 114-115)

Keywords: Christian women • men and women • single women

Vanzant, Iyanla.

The Value in the Valley: A Black Woman's Guide Through Life's Dilemmas. **New York: Simon & Schuster, 1995. ISBN 0-684-80287-2. 318p.**

Inspirational speaker Iyanla Vanzant discusses light, understanding, courage, knowledge and wisdom, other people's problems, come-uppance, purpose and intent, nonresistance, success, and love. Using personal experiences, Vanzant describes how black women can approach each of these issues for a fuller life.

> *If you think you cannot take it, make it, stand it any longer, it is a guarantee that your life will be plagued by situations and people who will reinforce those thoughts.* (p. 195)

Notes: Iyanla Vanzant is also listed in "Devotional Calendars," "Essays and Reflections—General and Women," and "Guidance and Self-Help—General and Men," all in the "Inspirational Nonfiction" section of this chapter
Blackboard Bestseller List 1995, 1996, 1997, 1998, 1999

Keywords: self-actualization • self-esteem

Weems, Renita J.

Showing Mary: How Women Can Share Prayers, Wisdom, and the Blessings of God. **West Bloomfield, Mich.: Walk Worthy Press/Warner Books, 2002. ISBN 0-446-53066-2. 194p.**

Using the Gospel according to Luke as a foundation, Weems details the relationship between Mary, the mother of Jesus, and her pregnant cousin, Elizabeth. As women go through "spiritual" pregnancy they are able to grow in all aspects of life and live the fullness that God has intended for them. Prayers are included at the end of each chapter.

> *Teach me, O God, how not to apologize for what's taking place within me.*
>
> *Teach me how not to rush to protect others from the work they too must do.*
>
> *It hurts. But I will survive the hurt. We all will survive the hurt.*
>
> *These are only labor pains,*
>
> *They are not forever.*
>
> *I can't wait to be born. (p. 78)*

Keywords: biblical characters • Chrisitan life • Christian women • meditations

Wilson, P. B.

Seven Secrets Women Want to Know. **Eugene, Ore.: Harvest House, 2000. ISBN 0-7369-0165-5. 223p.**

According to P. B. Wilson, all women should learn about "The 'S' Factor" in order to have all that God desires for us in life. The "S" factor is described as seven secret principles: submission, servanthood, seasons, success, sacrificial love, suffering (long-suffering), and steadfastness. Wilson explains how these biblical principles can enable women to reach new heights of understanding. She also includes a workbook after each chapter.

> *When the devil attacks us, his intention is destruction. When God prunes us, His intent is distinction—bigger growth and sweeter fruit. It's important to know the difference. (p. 153)*

Keywords: Christian life • Christian women • self-actualization

Chapter 8

Life Stories

Connie Van Fleet

The self belongs to the people, and the people find a voice in the self.—Stephen Butterfield in *Black Autobiography in America*

Definition

Life stories include three forms: biographies, autobiographies, and memoirs. A biography in its most specific sense is a factual narrative account of the life history of a real person by another person. An autobiography or memoir is a life history told by the person whose life is the subject of the book; use of the term *memoir* connotes a more personal and idiosyncratic account of events. In reality, it appears that the terms *memoir* and *autobiography* are used interchangeably.

Many of the autobiographical works included here are coauthored. Because they tell an individual's story from that person's viewpoint, they are considered to be autobiographies and are identified as such. Some biographies written by family members are included. These essentially tell the story of shared lives and are considered autobiographies of the family, although the more famous family member is usually the dominant character. This chapter includes only autobiographies, memoirs, and biographies by family members. Biographies by third parties are not included because they may not reflect the shared experience or perspective of the subject. Biographers are expected to offer objective reality rather than the personal truth that draws people to autobiography.

Although all forms of biography are expected to be factual, they are in actuality interpretive. The author includes some details and omits others, thus shaping the life and his or her personal story as the reader perceives it. Most authors attempt to give a holistic view of themselves, although some autobiographies are limited to a specific area of a person's life. Private lives are the focus of some books, while other narratives juxtapose public and personal life and offer a description of society as well as the individual. Autobiographies are likely to include philosophical reflection and political commentary from the individual's perspective.

Appeal

The appeal of African American autobiography is multilayered. Many life stories contain elements of genre fiction—adventure, mystery, romance. For some readers, this adds to the story's appeal. Autobiography invites the reader to identify with the subject to recapture heritage and history, to gain a sense of community and belonging, and to share the lives of individuals. To an extent, all African American autobiography appeals on all three levels, although the emphasis may vary.

The African American life story plays an important role in documenting the history of people of African descent in America. The stories are written to reclaim history from the participant's perspective. Many of these stories help shape public understanding of African American history and culture, while recounting the life of an individual. The perspective is historical; the appeal is in understanding and appreciating African American heritage.

Other readers are drawn to the political and social aspects of biography. "The appeal of black autobiographies is in their political awareness, their empathy for suffering, their ability to break down the division of 'I' and 'you', their knowledge of oppression and discovery of ways to cope with that experience, and their sense of shared life, shared triumph, and communal responsibility" (Butterfield 1974, 3). Identification with the author is important to readers who prefer this type of autobiography. The emphasis is on the individual as representative of other members of the community.

Ultimately, it is the personal story that draws readers—the intimacy of shared humanity, the individual spirit, the special characteristics and thoughts of unique individuals. The authors rise above pain, deprivation, and loss, and their stories provide inspiration, hope, and joy. The appeal is in recognizing oneself in the experiences of others or simply learning about the way others approach life. The emphasis is on the uniqueness of each human being. To put it in terms of Saricks and Brown's appeal features, it is the character of the character that draws readers in (1997, 45).

Autobiography was among the most popular forms of expression among African Americans in colonial America. Its value and appeal persist in the twenty-first century. Life stories, learned from personal struggle, are instruments for the expression of political, cultural, and educational lessons learned from the past. They inform the present and shape the future. They offer readers entertaining stories, cautionary tales, or inspirational models.

Evolution

Early African American autobiographies were built on biblical themes of conversion, piety, and salvation and often combined spiritual autobiography with other forms, particularly travel writing, captivity narrative, or slave narrative (Bassard 1997). (Please see Chapter 7 for a related discussion.) Although more secular than many later such works, *A Narrative of the Uncommon Sufferings and Surprising Deliverance of Briton Hammon* (1760) adheres to the religious themes representative of the genre in eighteenth-century America, with its story of trials, suffering, and ultimate salvation. Even the later two-volume autobiography, *Interesting Narrative of the Life of Olaudah Equiano, or Gustavus Vassa, the African* (1789), which was decidedly political with its analysis of slavery, economics, and culture, is argued in terms of Christian morality (Andrews 1997). Although

Equiano spent very little time in North America, he is generally viewed as an African American writer, and this work served as the model for slave narratives in the nineteenth century (Nelson 2002). The growth of a black, Christian, and literate population resulting from favorable conditions, both secular and religious, in the North led to the production of a number of African American autobiographies (Bassard 1997). These eighteenth-century works were written for a religious purpose: to give glory to God and to convert others to Christianity.

A shift in the nature and purpose of African American autobiography came about in the early nineteenth century as a result of the abolitionist movement. Escaped slaves were encouraged to write about their experiences as slaves and the miracle of freedom. Their accounts, many published in pamphlet form under the sponsorship of abolitionists, were very popular and overtly political. *Narrative of the Life of Frederick Douglass, an American Slave* (1845), for example, sold tens of thousands of copies in several languages (Andrews 1997). In just two years, William Wells Brown, an escaped slave, doctor, and professional writer, sold 10,000 copies of *Narrative of William W. Brown, a Fugitive Slave. Written by Himself.* Published in 1847, *Narrative* was one of several autobiographies by Brown, whose notable publications include *Clotel, or the President's Daughter: A Narrative of Slave Life in the United States* (1853), considered the first African American novel, and *The Escape, or a Leap for Freedom* (1858), regarded as the first African American drama (Carter 2002). Although such works were still often grounded in faith and religious in tone, the very act of writing an autobiography was in itself an act of rebellion and the subtitle, *Written by Himself,* on a fugitive slave narrative was a significant political statement (Andrews 1997, 35).

Nor was race the only issue to be addressed. African American women looked at religious institutions and denounced the sexism of the black religious hierarchy. Zilpha Elaw, who traveled to England in the course of her ministry, "raised issues of nationality as well as gender, race, and class differences" in her 1846 autobiography (Bassard 1997, 39).

Between the end of the Civil War and the beginning of the Great Depression, autobiographies by former slaves revealed a new tone. As exemplified by Booker T. Washington's best-selling autobiography, *Up from Slavery,* the purpose was to celebrate having survived slavery, to espouse middle-class ideals, and to gain the respect of both blacks and whites (Dudley 2002). Although a celebration of individual achievement, the autobiographies of this era included a subtext that was a call for racial solidarity through support of African American institutions (Andrews 1997).

In contrast, autobiographies by Ida B. Wells-Barnett and William Pickens Andrews published during the New Negro era of the 1920s were militant in their call for civil rights activism and the need for dramatic action to ensure a rightful place for African Americans individually and as a race (Andrews 1997; Domina 2002). The Depression era created a climate in which these themes were incorporated in a growing number of African American bibliographies.

African American autobiography for the next two decades was marked by the work of literary figures and social activists who recognized institutional repression and the difficulty of representing an entire group of people. Zora Neal Hurston

(*Dust Tracks on a Road,* 1942) celebrated her individuality. While she strove to authenticate her experience as an African American, she eschewed the efforts of those "race men/women" who would require her to use her work to foster race awareness (Sample 2002). Similarly, in Richard Wright's *Black Boy* (1945) the themes of individuality and authentic selfhood are central. Wright's theme of personal authenticity was adopted by political autobiographers in the 1960s, but these civil rights activists asserted that individual identity was formed by and inseparable from the black experience (Andrews 1997). Works such as *The Autobiography of Malcolm X* combined the political activism and denunciations of oppressive social systems typical of the fugitive slave narrative with the calls for African American solidarity and institutional control of the late nineteenth century. Further, these political autobiographies were written as much to inform and confront white audiences as to communicate with black ones.

In the 1970s black women emerged to tell their own stories and to shape literary forms in new and meaningful ways. Mostern (1999) suggests that the Black Power movement, in creating a black mass identity built on ideals of manhood and manliness, provoked a response from women. It required African American women to examine their identities in terms of both race and gender. As a result, women have taken different approaches to defining themselves.

Nikki Giovanni's *Gemini* (1971) is a return to the individual and self-authenticated perspective; Angela Davis's *Autobiography* (1974) is overtly public and political. Maya Angelou's *I Know Why the Caged Bird Sings* (1970) is personal, intimate, and emotional. Angelou's story deals with devastating themes but is told with warmth, love, and humor and marks the beginning of the trend in publication of women's personal texts.

Although African American autobiography remained preeminent in the succeeding decades, biographies of historical and contemporary figures by third parties were published with increasing frequency. Scholars examined primary source material and analyzed the impact of eminent African American figures in carefully documented works. In addition, popular biographies written for the adult general audience were increasingly profitable and available.

The growth of these forms of biography has probably resulted from three cultural trends. First, the establishment and maturity of African American studies programs in colleges and universities has created a group of scholars dedicated to preserving and reclaiming African American heritage. Honoring individuals who made contributions is a natural outgrowth of that goal. Second, as educational and economic opportunity has improved for African Americans, contemporary noteworthy figures and their accomplishments have become more visible, and there is an increased readership for these stories. Third has been the growth of the culture of celebrity, a sociological phenomenon discussed in Schickel's study, *Intimate Strangers* (1985).

According to Schickel, our current notion of celebrity is a recent phenomenon, differing from the past in two ways. First, fame is quickly achieved and sometimes as quickly lost, with a lower level of sustained accomplishment necessary for status. In addition, the traditional distance between the average person and the person of note has disappeared, and readers want to know the personal details of a celebrity's life. For publishers of autobiographies, this means a greater pool of authors from whom to draw and an audience that ensures profitability. African American autobiography has followed this broader trend.

Since 1980, African America biography has increased in numbers and diversity. Literary autobiographies are plentiful, with contributions from writers as diverse as poet Nikki Giovanni and journalist Brent Staples. Political, spiritual, entertainment, and sports figures tell their stories. Although there is great diversity among the authors, style, and approach of current autobiographies, there are common themes, some of which are continuations and some of which have emerged over the previous decade.

Themes and Trends

Returning to Religion

Religion, primarily but not exclusively Christianity, has returned to play a significant role in the literature, much as it did in the earliest African American autobiographies. The power of religion is the defining theme for some authors. Neurosurgeon Ben Carson's autobiography, *Gifted Hands*, was published by Christian publishing house Zondervan and received a Gold Medallion Award, which is given for outstanding Christian publications. Mason Betha tells how he gave up a lucrative career as successful rapper Ma$e to become a pastor. Patti LaBelle's autobiography is rich with the role that religion has played in her life, and another of her books appears in Chapter 7. Other authors, from poet/performance artist Estella Conwill Màjozo to civil rights activist Al Sharpton, simply make known the power of religion in their lives, weaving a spiritual perspective into their stories.

Being Black

Nearly all African American autobiographies in some way address the question of race. Many autobiographies relate personal experiences with racial discrimination and its impact on emotional and material well-being. Lorene Cary, in *Black Ice*, takes an interior look at the way in which her experiences in a predominantly white prep school affected her self-image. Professional athletes Doug Williams, Earl Woods, and Arthur Ashe talk about racial discrimination in sports, but while Ashe is reflective, Williams is angry. In *Makes Me Want to Holler*, Nathan McCall, product of a middle-class, two-parent family, attributes his adolescent violence, imprisonment, and subsequent difficulty in achieving success as a journalist to society's pervasive racism. In contrast, Shelby Stewart, broadcaster, millionaire, and entrepreneur, was subjected to racism, but he places it in the context of a childhood of abuse relieved only by the kindness of white strangers.

The impact of racism is personal, but the focus broadens beyond the individual in some autobiographies. Many family histories provide an historical perspective. Some authors describe what it was like for their parents to live during a time of lynchings and Jim Crow laws; others trace their lineage back through pre-Emancipation days. The focus of authors Johnny Cochran and Bruce Wright is more current, and they offer an engaged but less personal societal and political perspective.

Some autobiographies are calls to political activism and change; others recount what was; others just tell it the way it is. Although the centrality of racism to African Americans' life stories may vary, it is rare to find an autobiography in which the question of what it means to be black in America is not addressed in some manner.

Staying Alive

Themes of violence and survival pervade many of these autobiographies. Brent Staples begins and ends his autobiography with the violent death of his brother. Nathan McCall and Carl Upchurch describe the seeming inevitability of despair, violence, and imprisonment among young black men born in the inner city. Children are subjected to the emotional abuse of growing up surrounded by violence or are themselves victims of physical neglect or overt abuse. Death surrounds poor black people. Some are active combatants; others are innocent bystanders too often in the wrong place at the wrong time. Tragically, that place is home.

The violence born of despair is turned inward, but it can also emerge as abuse of others. Young black men join gangs, deal drugs, and kill each other. Black women are used and abused. Family violence is not uncommon. Mothers are beaten or injured by fathers; Stuart Shelly witnessed his mother falling to her death trying to escape his brutal father. Even in light and uplifting stories such as Yolanda Young's *On Our Way to Beautiful*, there is domestic violence. Her mother, shot by her enraged father, carries a bullet above her heart for years.

Family

In contrast to the themes of violence, warm and supportive family relationships are central to many other life stories. Some authors such as Buck Colbert Franklin and the Delany sisters begin their stories with descriptions of parents and grandparents. Charles Blockson explains his genealogical research as evidence of the necessity and value of preserving African American literature. Yolanda Young and Faith Ringgold share the role their mothers played in their lives. Men, from athletes (Bo Jackson) to surgeons (Ben Carson), praise their mothers and give them credit for their life successes. Others, including Berry Gordy, acknowledge and appreciate the role of a strong and loving father.

Making a Difference

Civil rights activism and social reform have been dominant themes since the earliest African American autobiographies. Civil rights activists Charles Evers, Vernon Jordan, and John Lewis tell the story of their lives in terms of their involvement in the movement. Women civil rights activists such as Dorothy Height, Myrlie Evers-Williams, and Ada Lois Sipuel Fisher are beginning to make the role and perspective of women more visible. Wilson Goode, Bruce Wright, and others who have served in public office focus on racial equality and talk about trying to change the system from within. Authors Carl Upchurch, Faye Wattleton, Joycelyn Elders, and Salome Thomas-El address race more indirectly by focusing on social issues such as educational opportunities and reproductive choice.

Achieving Success

Horatio Alger stories, in which the protagonist overcomes childhood poverty to achieve financial success, have always been popular with biographers and readers. Stories of the journey from slavery to freedom are particularly important to African American readers.

In the case of African American success stories, the two combine to reflect the Civil Rights Movement's concept of economic freedom. Entrepreneurs Shelby Stewart and Anthony Mark Haskins tell the stories of their very different career paths and financial achievements. Professional athletes and entertainers share their stories of earning and sometimes losing fortunes, while former rapper Mason Betha tells the story of divesting himself of all his hard-earned worldly goods to be born again in faith.

Setting the Record Straight

Public figures often write autobiographies to set the record straight by revealing insider details or explaining their actions. Wilson Goode tells us about the political maneuverings and vendettas during his term as mayor of Philadelphia; Reverend Al Sharpton explains that his aim and responsibility are protecting the weak and calling attention to social injustice; defense attorney Johnny Cochran asserts his commitment to the Constitution and equal justice before the law while revealing the facts and strategies behind his famous cases. Joycelyn Elders lets us know what she really said and how political realities affected both her confirmation as Surgeon General of the U.S. and her forced resignation. John Lewis gives a vivid, detailed account of the pragmatic concerns as well as the political maneuverings involved in the Civil Rights Movement.

Revisiting

People change over time, adding experiences, shifting perspectives, evaluating and reflecting on what they've seen and what they've become. Some authors, like Maya Angelou, write multipart or serial autobiographies in which each volume recounts a different time in their lives. Others write several autobiographical works that are independent of one another. Sidney Poitier's second work is a spiritual autobiography that reflects on the events detailed in his first book; Sarah Delany reflects on "life without Bessie," her follow-up to *The Delany Sisters' First Hundred Years*. Classic autobiographies by Sojourner Truth, Frederick Douglass, and Booker T. Washington are reissued with new introductions that offer contemporary perspectives.

Cowriting

Most of the autobiographies in this chapter, other than those by writers and literary figures, are coauthored. Some coauthors are actively sought based on previous work in African American autobiography. For instance, Cecil Murphey, coauthor of Gold Medallion-winning Gifted Hands (neurosurgeon Ben Carson), was asked to work on another inspirational autobiography, educator Salome Thomas-El's *I Chose to Stay*.

Sports figures often produce their autobiographies with the assistance of knowledgeable sports writers. Sonja Steptoe, senior editor of *Sports Illustrated,* worked with Jackie Joyner-Kersee, and Coach Eddie Robinson's coauthor Richard Lapchick is founder of the Center for the Study of Sport in Society and one of *Sporting News*' "100 most powerful people in Sport." Similarly, singer DMX worked with Smokey D. Fontaine, former music editor of *The Source*.

Involving Family

Autobiographies written by family members may be categorized in two ways: individual biography and family autobiography. An individual biography often purports to be a biography by a family member about a single notable individual. In reality, such biographies are usually autobiographical accounts about the shared lives of the family members (as in the case of Rachel Robinson's *Intimate Portrait* of husband Jackie) or about the relationship between the author and the dominant family member (as in Tracey Davis's *Sammy Davis, Jr., My Father*). *The Color of Water* is actually a dual biography of McBride and his mother.

Family autobiographies focus on the family as a whole and the interaction of all of the members. Stories such as Yolanda Young's *On Our Way to Beautiful* and Yvonne Thornton's *The Ditchdigger's Daughters* truly are about the wonders and trials of family life.

Making Their Stories Known

These autobiographies by family members may be part of a larger trend of third-person "autobiographies," in which a person other than the subject writes the life story, sometimes in the first person and often using the individual's exact words. Entrepreneur Reginald Lewis's "autobiography" is actually a biography written by Blair Walker, which includes extended direct quotations from an autobiography Lewis left incomplete, and so it is not included. Clayborne Carson's excellent *The Autobiography of Martin Luther King Jr.* was commissioned by King's family after his death and is based on Reverend King's personal papers and public record. The book resonates with King's wisdom, determination, and hope, and Carson's role is virtually transparent in this meticulously researched and carefully documented work. This work, while highly recommended, is not within the scope of this chapter, which is limited to autobiographies. Conversely, Buck Colbert Franklin left a substantially complete manuscript of *My Life and an Era*. Because his sons acted as editors and not authors, Franklin's autobiography is included.

Selection Criteria and Scope

This chapter includes autobiographies published between 1990 and 2003. Biographies written by family members that reflect the perspective of the family member are considered to be autobiographies, as they generally revolve around shared lives. "Autobiographies" written by third parties are excluded because they are actually biographies. Earlier autobiographies, such as those by Sojourner Truth, Booker T. Washington, and Zora Neale Hurston, that are considered especially significant and have been reprinted since 1990 (and so are more likely to be available), have been included.

The preliminary list of titles was drawn from *African American Autobiographers: A Sourcebook* (Nelson 2002). A list of biographies was compiled by Gladys Smiley Bell, Assistant Director of Public Services, William R. and Norma B. Harvey Library, Hampton University. This list was edited to remove any works that were not autobiographies or were generally unavailable. Searches of WorldCat and Books In Print (online) were conducted, using "African-American biography" and field of endeavor (women social reformers, poets, lawyers, entertainers, etc.). WorldCat has no separate format for autobiography, so lists were then examined to eliminate those titles that were biographies rather than autobiographies. Current periodicals and publisher lists were reviewed for new releases of interest.

Advising the Reader

This chapter profiles the lives of African Americans who contributed to America in many different ways and in different eras. There are writers, educators, physicians, politicians, civil rights workers, artists, entertainers, and others. Some led visible and public lives, while others are important but overlooked figures. Still others are everyday people who represent the experience of the majority of people. Because most people look for autobiographies by name of the subject and field of endeavor, the stories are organized into four broad categories:

- **Athletes**. Sports figures were among the earliest and most visible figures to integrate previously all-white institutions. They still are often cast as role models, and many are admired for their achievements off the field as well as for their athletic prowess. This chapter includes autobiographies by athletes and coaches from all sports.

- **Entertainers**. Gifted performers touch the lives of many, bringing us together in times of celebration and sorrow. Autobiographies of actors, musicians and composers, dancers and choreographers, and singers are included.

- **Professionals**. Men and women of color have achieved prominence in a number of fields, including education, business, law, medicine, and military service. The struggle to achieve and the joy of service are detailed in their autobiographies.

- **Politicians and Activists**. Those who have made significant contributions in reforming society and its laws offer valuable insights and provide more detailed and critical accounts than those that are sometimes provided in history books. This chapter includes autobiographies of social and political activists and public officials, in all levels of government service.

- **Writers**. Some people observe and record, preserving a history, a moment, a perspective. Some compel reflection, some invite escape. Writers, including historians, journalists, and novelists, tell their own stories.

Within each of the occupational categories, the books are listed in alphabetical order by the last name of the person whose life story is being told. Keywords are included to group occupations within the category in the index. For instance, in the professional category, the term "educators" is included among the terms describing autobiographies by teachers; similarly, the terms "entrepreneurs," "attorneys," and "physicians" appear in the keyword lists for relevant titles.

If a person is noted for work in more than one area, the work has been classified in the dominant area, determined either by the author's own self-definition or by firsthand analysis of the work. For instance, Star Jones might easily be grouped with entertainers because she is known to many people through *The View* television show. In her autobiography, however, she asserts that she defines herself as a lawyer, so her work may be found in the professional section with both "television talk show hosts" and "attorneys" in the keyword list. On the other hand, Ada Sipuel Fisher gained fame when she became a test case for a civil rights suit, completed law school, and taught at the university level. While she might easily have been classified in the social activists section, her career focus on teaching has led to her inclusion in the professional section, with "educators," "physicians," and "social activism and activists" as descriptive terms. Keywords that acknowledge specific and secondary areas of endeavor accompany each annotation. In the index, therefore, both Jones and Fisher will be found under the "attorneys—nonfiction" heading.

Athletes

Aaron, Hank, with Lonnie Wheeler.

I Had a Hammer: The Hank Aaron Story. **New York: HarperCollins, 1991. ISBN 0-06-016321-6. 333p.**

Aaron describes his anger and the frustration of being endlessly compared to other players, black and white; of being overshadowed by the more charismatic Willie Mays and Babe Ruth; of being slighted by baseball management and Atlanta fans during his record-breaking career with the Braves; and of trying to find a meaningful position when his playing days were over. But while this book is about discrimination, perseverance, and success, it is first and foremost about baseball. It includes an historical overview by Wheeler to introduce each chapter, 20 pages of black-and-white photos, quotes from players and colleagues, and transcripts of hate mail received during the race to break Ruth's home run record.

> *The way I saw it, the only thing Atlanta was too busy for was baseball. It didn't seem to give a damn about the Braves, and it seemed like the only thing that mattered about the home run record was that a nigger was about to step out of line and break it. (p. 231)*

Keywords: baseball players • major league baseball • professional sports • racial discrimination

Allen, Marcus, with Carlton Stowers.

Marcus: The Autobiography of Marcus Allen with Carlton Stowers. **New York: A Thomas Dunne Book/St. Martin's Press, 1997. ISBN 0-312-16924-8. 313p.**

Allen offers a sports memoir rich in intelligent observation and insider detail. He not only recounts his memorable moments on the field (of which there are many) and off (the O. J. Simpson trial) but addresses such issues as the business of football; player compensation, performance-enhancing drugs, personal responsibility, and the cult of celebrity. The book includes eight pages of photographs (most in color) and an appendix of Allen's college records and professional rushing statistics. (Allen was inducted into the Pro Football Hall of Fame in 2003.)

> *I am what I am, believe in what I believe, and can cause only a small effect on the course of human events. Yet I feel a responsibility to do what I can, always bearing in mind that my actions are not only being watched but constantly judged. (p. 140)*

Keywords: football players • Heisman Trophy winners • National Football League • professional sports

Ashe, Arthur, and Arnold Rampersad.

🎗 *Days of Grace: A Memoir.* **New York: Alfred A. Knopf, 1993. ISBN 0-679-42396-6. 317p.**

Intelligent, warm, and wise, Ashe's far-ranging memoir is an emotional family story, a philosophical exploration of life, and a piercing commentary on personalities in sports, politics, and the media. It includes 16 pages of black-and-white photographs and an index.

> *Although Sharpton and others like him in the African American world gain the headlines, I am grateful for those other blacks who quietly prepare themselves to occupy positions of authority and to represent all of us in a morally responsible way.* (p. 173)

Notes: ALA Best Book for Young Adults 1994; *New York Times* Notable Book 1993

Keywords: Christian biography • HIV/AIDS • professional sports • tennis players

Jackson, Bo, and Dick Schaap.

Bo Knows Bo: The Autobiography of a Ballplayer. **New York: Doubleday, 1990. ISBN 0-385-41620-2. 218p.**

Bo Jackson parlayed his athletic talent into the opportunity to attend college, earn a Heisman Trophy, and play two professional sports. Tracing his story from juvenile hell raiser to devoted family man, Bo is honest, entertaining, and, endearingly, still surprised by his great good fortune and natural talent. Brief third-person commentaries by Schaap precede each of Bo's chapters. The book includes "Appreciations" by George Brett and Howie Long, "Bo—as others see him" chapter, and 14 pages of black-and-white photographs.

> *My mom. When I was growing up, she cleaned people's houses during the day and cleaned a motel at night. She also raised ten children. And people try to tell me that playing two sports is hard.* (Dedication)

Keywords: baseball players • football players • Heisman Trophy winners • professional sports

Joyner-Kersee, Jackie, with Sonja Steptoe.

A Kind of Grace: The Autobiography of the World's Greatest Female Athlete. **New York: Warner Books, 1997. ISBN 0-446-52248-1. 336p.**

Olympic heptathlon champion Joyner-Kersee's successful career, marriage to coach Bobby Kersee, family relationships with brother Al and sister Flo-Jo, and drive to excel are all revealed in this candid look at life as an African American, a woman, and an extraordinary athlete. Included are eight pages of black-and-white photographs and Joyner-Kersee's athletic record.

> *When I'm competing, I'm engaged in a battle. And when you're in a battle, things sometimes get untidy . . . I've got bigger concerns than whether every strand of my hair is in place.* (p. 220)

Keywords: family relationships • husbands and wives • Olympic champions • track and field athletes

O'Neil, Buck, with Steve Wulf and David Conrads.

I Was Right on Time: My Journey from the Negro Leagues to the Majors. **New York: A Fireside Book/Simon & Schuster, 1996. ISBN 0-684-83247-Xpa. 254p.**

Filled with buoyant good humor, astute observations on baseball and its personalities, and great storytelling, Buck O'Neil's story of himself, the Negro Leagues, and major league baseball is an engaging slice of history. Warm, uplifting, and informative.

> *There is nothing greater for a human being than to get his body to react to all the things one does on a ballfield. It's as good as sex; it's as good as music. It fills you up. Waste no tears for me. I didn't come along too early—I was right on time.* (pp. 2–3)

Keywords: baseball players • major league baseball • Negro Baseball Leagues • professional sports

Payton, Walter, with Don Yaeger.

The Autobiography of Walter Payton: Never Die Easy. **New York: Villard, 2000. ISBN 0-679-46331-3. 268p.**

Walter "Sweetness" Payton, who never went out of bounds to avoid a hit, faced liver disease and death with the same determination he brought to his game. This poignant story, told alternately by Payton and his family and colleagues, reveals a man who transcended accomplishments on the football field to be remembered for his grace and strength of character. Included are eight pages of black-and-white photographs, a foreword by teammate Matt Shuey, and a cast of characters. (Payton was inducted into the Pro Football Hall of Fame in 1993.)

> *If all I'm remembered for is a bunch of yards and a lot of touchdowns, I've failed. That was just my work. I want to be remembered as a guy who raised two pretty special kids and who taught them to be great people. Please have them write that about me.* (p. 249)

Keywords: football players • National Football League • organ donation • professional sports

Robinson, Eddie, with Richard Lapchick.

Never Before, Never Again: The Stirring Autobiography of Eddie Robinson, the Winningest Coach in the History of College Football. **New York: St. Martin's Press, 1999. ISBN 0-312-24224-7. 268p.**

Eddie Robinson, coach of traditionally black Grambling State University's football team for 57 years and a national icon, talks about his experiences growing up in segregated Louisiana; challenges and opportunities on and off the field and his philosophy for dealing with them; and his love for his wife Doris, his children, and each of the young men who played for him. The story of his life is told with simplicity, pride, and an eye to the future. Included are eight pages of black-and-white photographs, a foreword by George M. Steinbrenner III, and an afterword by Reverend Jesse Jackson.

> *If you don't have success, don't look for an excuse.*
> *Look for a way to get the success.* (p. 142)

Keywords: football coaches • Grambling College • husbands and wives • race relations

Robinson, Rachel, with Lee Daniels.

Jackie Robinson: An Intimate Portrait. **New York: Abrams, 1996. ISBN 0-8109-3792-1. 240p.**

Jackie Robinson's widow, Rachel, allows the reader the privilege of sharing a family album and her memories of an American icon and her beloved husband. Warm, honest, and full of justifiable pride, this is the story of a family and an enduring love affair. Includes a foreword by Roger Wilkins, epilogues by Sharon Robinson and David Robinson, a selected readings list, a list of photo credits, and an index.

> *On the personal side, Jack and I began to realize*
> *how important we were to black America, and how*
> *much we symbolized its hunger for opportunity*
> *and its determination to make dreams long de-*
> *ferred possible.* (p. 66)

Keywords: baseball players • civil rights activists • major league baseball • professional sports • racial discrimination

Sifford, Charlie, with Jim Gullo.

Just Let Me Play: The Story of Charlie Sifford, the First Black PGA Golfer. **Latham, N.Y.: British American Publishing, 1992. ISBN 0-945167-44-X. 237p.**

An insider's story of racism and ageism in professional golf, Sifford's account is told with anger at wrongs, a sense of satisfaction in overcoming them, and the style of a natural storyteller. Includes a foreword by Arthur Ashe and 16 pages of black-and-white photographs.

> *I would be proud to be compared to Jackie [Robinson] in al-*
> *most anything, but not in a lie that says I'm the same sym-*
> *bol of freedom and racial equality in my sport that he was in*
> *his.* (p. 109)

Keywords: age discrimination • golfers • National Negro Open (golf) • professional sports • racial discrimination

Williams, Doug, with Bruce Hunter.

Quarterblack: Shattering the NFL Myth. **Chicago: Bonus Books, 1990. ISBN 0-929387-47-3. 209p.**

The first African American quarterback to play in the Super Bowl, Williams re-veals the personalities and organizational racism that conspired to keep him underappreciated and underpaid. Bitter insights into his second marriage distract from the story. Included are a chapter of statistics, eight pages of black-and-white photographs, and an index.

> *A lot of people with closed minds in the NFL don't want to*
> *give black quarterbacks a fair shot, and nothing is going to*
> *change their attitude. I know I didn't. And whatever Randall*
> *and Warren and Andre Ware do isn't going to change their*
> *way of thinking.* (p. 188)

Keywords: football players • Heisman Trophy winners • husbands and wives • National Football League • professional sports

Woods, Earl, with Fred Mitchell.

Playing Through: Straight Talk on Hard Work, Big Dreams, and Adventures with Tiger. **New York: HarperCollins, 1998. ISBN 0-062-70222-X. 269p.**

Green Beret Vietnam veteran and divorced father of three, Earl Woods's life reached a turning point with a second marriage and the birth of son Tiger. This story of a father's devotion and a son's achievements may take place in the world of golf, but it is universal in its message of love and respect for family. It includes black-and-white photographs throughout, a foreword by Tiger Woods, Tiger Woods's career statistics, an index, and the mission statement of the Tiger Woods Foundation.

> *When I learned that Vietnam had fallen, and that Tiger*
> *Phong was likely still there, I vowed that if I ever had another*
> *son, I would nickname him Tiger, in the hope that my son*
> *would be as strong and courageous as my friend.* (p. 39)

Keywords: fathers and sons • golfers • professional sports • racial discrimination

Entertainers

Ailey, Alvin, with A. Peter Bailey.

Revelations: The Autobiography of Alvin Ailey. **New York: Carol Publishing, 1995. ISBN 1-559-72255-X. 183p.**

From his poor Texas childhood, thrashing "through the terrain looking for a place to call home" to the world stage, Ailey invites us to share the struggles, soaring successes, inner turmoil, and even the most prosaic details of his life and career. Recognized for his strong and athletic dance and the brilliant originality of his choreography, Ailey is quick to give credit to those who influenced his development and supported him through his triumphant years. The book includes 16 pages of black-and-white photographs, a foreword by Lena Horne, an introduction by A. Peter Bailey, a chapter titles "Remembrances of Alvin," and an index.

> He [Lester Horton] came to me after he had completed "Cumbia" and said, 'It's time for you to get started, Alvin, so I'm going to make this a dance for you and Carmen.' I was scared to death because she was such a goddess to me. Here Carmen was his lead dancer, and I was this country bumpkin who was athletic and could wiggle a little. (p. 63)

Keywords: Alvin Ailey American Dance Theater • choreographers • dancers

Betha, Mason, with Karen Hunter.

Revelations: There's a Light After the Lime. **New York: Pocket Books, 2001. ISBN 0-7434-3418-8. 201p.**

Mason Betha recounts his journey through childhood, life as successful rapper Ma$e, and his miraculous redemption. Told with sincerity and zest, Pastor Betha's story (and the sermon woven throughout the book) will inspire many readers.

> I've turned state's evidence on the devil and I'm now testifying against him. . . . I'm sold out for Jesus. (p. 181)

Keywords: Christian biography • clergy • rap music and musicians • singers

Davis, Tracey, with Dolores A. Barclay.

Sammy Davis, Jr., My Father. **Los Angeles: General Publishing, 1996. ISBN 1-881649-84-9. 272p.**

This is the story of Tracey and her famous father, from their loving but distant relationship in her childhood to their finally forging a deeply loving and close bond. On the way, we get an insider's look at both the good (room service and famous people) and bad (racism and secondhand celebrity) aspects of growing up as the daughter of a famous entertainer. The book includes 16 pages of black-and-white photographs.

> *I couldn't be "normal" if he showed himself, if he flashed his celebrity. Why couldn't he drive himself in an ordinary car? Why did he have to be so Sammy Davis Jr.?* (p. 65)

Keywords: actors and actresses • children of celebrities • dancers • fathers and daughters • husbands and wives • singers

Guillaume, Robert, with David Ritz.

Guillaume: A Life. **Columbia: University of Missouri Press, 2002. ISBN 0-8262-1426-6. 220p.**

Guillaume's autobiography is an odyssey that seems driven as much by the need for self-knowledge as a desire to record the facts. This is the candid and searching story of his life, from a "little black bastard" to a respected and popular actor. It includes 22 pages of black-and-white photographs, a combined filmography and discography, and an index.

> *We're all looking for breakthroughs. I know I was—not a personal, but a professional, breakthrough. Actors survive on hopes and dreams, and the biggest dream is that one role will catapult you to fortune and fame.* (p. 123)

Keywords: actors and actresses • singers

Jamison, Judith, with Howard Kaplan.

Dancing Spirit: An Autobiography. **New York: Doubleday, 1993. ISBN 0-385-42557-0. 273p.**

Judith Jamison shares her uniquely individual no-nonsense perceptions of events, characters, and the (sometimes) glamorous life of a professional dancer. The design and form of the more than 60 photographs interspersed throughout this book convey the presence and elegance of this extraordinarily talented dancer, accomplished artistic director, and inspiring woman. Included are excerpts of interviews, a complete list of interviewees, a list of the people involved in the Alvin Ailey American Dance Theater, and a brief select bibliography.

> *There's more to life than what is thought of as stereotypical beauty. When you're looking at yourself in the mirror you have to remember that that image is only a part of you. The you is inside. If you have any kind of brain at all, any kind of sense of self, you realize how unique that is.* (p. 251)

Keywords: Alvin Ailey American Dance Theater • choreographers • dancers

Jones, Bill T., with Peggy Gillespie.

Last Night on Earth. **New York: Pantheon Books, 1995. ISBN 0-679-43926-9. 286p.**

In a work that is alternately lyrical and straightforward, Bill T. Jones tells the story of his love affair with romantic and artistic partner Arnie Zane, his passion for dance, and the creation of his various works. The book includes black-and-white photographs throughout, many by Arnie Zane, and a list of choreographic works by Bill Jones.

> *Together, Arnie and I formed some mythical beast.*
> *We flew. . . . We had no reason to be together, no*
> *validation from anyone, no children, nothing but his*
> *vision, my arms, his legs, my wings, our loving.*
> (pp. 152–53)

Keywords: Bill T. Jones/Arnie Zane Dance Company • choreographers • dancers • gay men • HIV/AIDS • interracial relationships

Jones, Quincy.

Q: The Autobiography of Quincy Jones. **New York: Doubleday: 2001. ISBN 0-385-48896-3. 412p.**

Sometimes you eat rats because that's all there is to eat. And sometimes—if you're lucky—you find the one thing in life that lets you overcome the pain and loneliness of growing up after mental illness turns your once-beloved mother into a stranger. For young Quincy, music was his salvation. The story of this musical genius and gentle soul is alternately poignant, uplifting, and humorous as Q recounts his life with help from those who know him best. Included are chapters by family, childhood friends, and musicians; 38 pages of black-and-white photographs, a discography, a filmography, a list of awards and honors, and an index.

> *We were stuffing ourselves with pie when I broke*
> *into a small room next door. There was a tiny stage*
> *in the room and on it was an old upright piano. . . .*
> *That's where I began to find peace. I was eleven. I*
> *knew this was it for me. Forever.* (p. 26)

Notes: *Essence* Bestseller List 2002

Keywords: brothers • composers • family relationships • jazz music and musicians

King, B. B., with David Ritz.

Blues All Around Me: The Autobiography of B. B. King. **New York: Avon Books, 1996. ISBN 0-380-97318-9. 336p.**

Blues great B. B. King's indomitable spirit and joi de vivre shine through as the story of his life unfolds through provocatively and humorously titled chapters such as "Why I Love Arthur Godfrey" and "Someone Asked Me about Oral Sex." The book includes 16 pages of black-and-white photographs, including Mark Norberg's classic portrait of B. B. and his guitar Lucille, an afterword by David Ritz, a selected discography arranged by decade, a list of awards, an index, and a list of song permissions.

> *I liked seeing my guitar as a lady. I liked seeing her as someone worth fighting or even dying for. I liked giving her a name and attitude all her own. . . . With the possible exception of real-life sex with a real-life woman, no one gives me peace of mind like Lucille.* (p. 130)

Keywords: blues music and musicians • men and women • music business

Knight, Gladys.

Between Each Line of Pain and Glory: My Life Story. **Thorndike, Maine: G. K. Hall, 1998. ISBN 0-7838-8394-3 (large print hardcover). 353p. (Originally published New York: Hyperion, 1997.)**

Gladys Knight traces her successful professional life from her first public performance, a church benefit at age four, through her time with the Pips and her solo career. Her personal life, a roller-coaster ride full of romantic disappointments and debilitating setbacks, is revealed in this honest and sometimes humorous autobiography of a woman who refused to give up. Included are 16 pages of black-and-white photographs.

> *I sang through love affairs and abusive relationships, through addiction and recovery (both mine and others'), through bare-floored poverty and marble-tiled affluence. . . . On March 30, 1989, I sang purely for myself.* (p. 12)

Notes: Blackboard Bestseller List 1998, 1999

Keywords: gambling and gamblers • men and women • music business • rhythm and blues music and musicians

LaBelle, Patti, with Laura B. Randolph.

Don't Block The Blessings: Revelations of a Lifetime. **New York: Riverhead Books, 1996. ISBN 1-57322-039-6. 305p.**

Patti LaBelle tells the story of a private life riddled with tragedy, guilt, and grief hidden behind the outrageous façade of a successful entertainer. The only one of four sisters to survive beyond the age of 44, she overcame her fear and insecurities to find serenity. Twenty-four pages of personal and professional black-and-white photographs trace fashion trends and hairdos. Included are a discography and an index.

> *When I'm singing, I'm not trying to outshine or upstage anyone. I'm just doing what I can't help doing. Singing what I feel with all the pain and passion that powers it. My voice is a gift from God and I must use it as God intended.* (p. 107)

Notes: Patti LaBelle is also listed in the "Essays and Reflections—General" section of Chapter 7.
Blackboard Bestseller List 1997, 1998, 1999

Keywords: cancer patients • Christian biography • rhythm and blues music and musicians • singers

Marsalis, Wynton, and Carl Vigeland.

Jazz in the Bittersweet Blues of Life. Cambridge, Mass.: De Capo Press/Perseus Books, 2001. ISBN 0306810336. 249p.

Jazz is less a narrative than an immersion into the life of a band's road tour and Marsalis's reflections on life, music, and the world. By turns analytical, thoughtful, wistful, and boisterous, this sensitive and engaging memoir is like the music, ever changing but always real.

> *This music heals people because music is vibration and proper vibration heals . . . . I can't begin to imagine all the people Louis Armstrong's music heals. All the people Bach's music has healed. Beethoven. Coltrane. Not made them feel good—healed. (p. 31)*

Keywords: composers • jazz music and musicians

Pendergrass, Teddy, and Patricia Romanowski.

Truly Blessed. New York: Putnam, 1998. ISBN 0-399-14420-X. 319p.

Soul singer Teddy Pendergrass, famous for his sensual style and women-only concerts, was at the height of his career when an automobile accident left him a quadriplegic. His fight back through depression, physical pain, and spiritual doubt to reclaim his career and his life is an inspiring story told with candor and dignity. Included are 16 pages of black-and-white photographs and a discography.

> *God, how I missed it: the audience's love, the sense of transcendence, the joy—even the panties. . . . I missed the immediacy, the intimacy. I felt as if part of me would always be on stage somewhere, and if I couldn't make it there, I never would be whole. (p. 270)*

Keywords: blues music and musicians • Christian biography • people with disabilities • singers

Poitier, Sidney.

The Measure of a Man: A Spiritual Autobiography. San Francisco: HarperSanFrancisco/HarperCollins, 2001. ISBN 0-06-251608-6pa. 255p.

In this, his second autobiography, Poitier attempts to explore the meaning behind the events and chronology of his life. The tone is very conversational, and he frequently stops ("You know?" "You follow?") to create a dialogue with the reader.

> *Many years ago I wrote a book about my life . . . More recently I decided that I wanted to write a book about life. Just life itself. (p. xi)*

Notes: *Essence* Bestseller List 2001

Keywords: actors and actresses

Pryor, Richard, with Todd Gold.

Pryor Convictions and Other Life Sentences. **New York: Pantheon Books, 1995. ISBN 0-679-43250-7. 257p.**

The story of Pryor's life is like one of his comedy routines: funny, sad, profane, perceptive, and unapologetic. His gift for characterization transfers effectively from the stage to the printed word. Interspersed in italics are comedy routines that spring from the true circumstances.

> *Family is a mixed blessing. You're glad to have one, but it's also like receiving a life sentence for a crime you didn't commit.* (p. 21)

Notes: Blackboard Bestseller List 1996

Keywords: actors and actresses • comedians • drug addiction • family relationships • men and women

Quivers, Robin.

Quivers: A Life. **New York: ReganBooks, 1995. ISBN 0-06039-153-7. 341p.**

In this honest, sometimes brutal, autobiography from the co-host of *The Howard Stern Show*, strong-willed fighter and overachiever Robin Quivers traces her battles, from averting rape as a child through depression and alienation back to recovery. Each chapter begins with a brief paragraph—an observation, a journal entry, or a dream—that sets the tone for what follows. Included are 14 pages of black-and-white photographs.

> *As I turn onto the street where I grew up, I realize for the first time that forgiving is an ongoing process, something I'm going to have to work on every day. I'm pleased, though, that I'm strong enough to try.* (p. 341)

Keywords: *Howard Stern Show* • radio personalities

Simmons, Earl.

E.A.R.L: The Autobiography of DMX as Told to Smokey D. Fontaine. **New York: HarperCollins, 2002. ISBN 0-06-018826-X. 346p.**

Abused and neglected as a child, Earl Simmons was smart but bad. Often jailed and violent, he nevertheless found a voice through his music, companionship with his dogs, love with his beloved Tashera and their children, and meaning through faith. Life is a battle to keep the real Earl from being taking over by the violent, angry X persona. Included are 16 pages of full-page photos, most in full color (some disturbing images), black-and-white photos throughout, an epilogue, notes, and an appendix of song lyrics. Street language is authentic but may overwhelm some readers.

> *Luck lasts for a few hours sometimes a day or two,*
> *but not a lifetime. I'm not alive because I'm lucky*
> *—with as much dirt as I've done and pain that I've*
> *caused—I'm alive because I'm blessed.* (p. 290)

Keywords: child abuse • inner-city life and culture • men and women • parents and children • rap music and musicians • singers

Simone, Nina, with Stephen Cleary.

I Put a Spell on You: The Autobiography. **New York: Da Capo Press, 1993. ISBN 0-679-41068-6. 181p.**

Eunice Waymon, who took the name Nina Simone so her mother wouldn't find out she was singing in nightclubs, gives a straightforward account of her life, with all its challenges and triumphs. She interweaves the stories of her career, failed marriages and love affairs, and disastrous business mistakes with her civil rights activism and world travels. Included are 16 pages of black-and-white photos, a discography, and an index.

> *So I felt part of the struggle, yet separated from it. I*
> *was lonely in the movement like I had been lonely*
> *everywhere else. Sometimes I think the whole of*
> *my life has been a search to find the one place I*
> *truly belong.* (p. 113)

Keywords: civil rights activists • expatriates • men and women • rhythm and blues music and musicians • singers

Professionals

Baker, Vernon J., with Ken Olsen.

Lasting Valor. **Columbus, Miss.: Genesis Press, 1997. ISBN 1-885478-30-5. 294p.**

Vernon Baker shares his childhood years during the Depression, his heroic campaign in World War II, and the White House ceremony at which he received the first Congressional Medal of Honor awarded to an African American, an honor that was 50 years overdue. Included are eight pages of black-and-white photographs, a foreword by General Colin L. Powell, USA (Ret.), an appendix comprising descriptions of the actions of the six black soldiers who received the medal posthumously, a select bibliography, and an index.

> *I longed for impossible companionship—for my*
> *men, for the other Medal of Honor recipients. I was*
> *the only man among the black Medal of Honor re-*
> *cipients to survive to see this day.* (p. 275)

Notes: *Black Issues Book Review* Best Book 2002

Keywords: Congressional Medal of Honor • family relationships • military officers • segregation • war-time romances • World War II

Bragg, Janet Harmon, as told to Marjorie M. Kriz.

Soaring Above Setbacks. **Smithsonian History of Aviation Series. Washington, D.C.: Smithsonian Institute Press, 1996. ISBN 1-56098-458-9. 120p.**

Supported by a loving family, Bragg overcame every obstacle placed in her way to become the first African American woman to earn a full commercial pilot's license, but that was just one of this resourceful and giving woman's accomplishments. Includes a foreword by Johnetta B. Cole, eight pages of black-and-white photographs, and an index.

> *I suppose that, in the back of my mind, I had been interested in flying since my childhood reveries of a long-legged Jesus walking on the clouds.* (p. 25)

Keywords: air pilots • entrepreneurs • National Airman's Association of America • racial discrimination • sexism

Carson, Ben, with Cecil Murphey.

Gifted Hands: The Ben Carson Story. **Grand Rapids, Mich.: Zondervan Publishing, 1990. ISBN 0-310-54650-8. 232p.**

Ben Carson, a gifted neurosurgeon who accepts any challenge to save a child's life, tells his story with humility and honesty, constantly giving credit for his remarkable achievements to his mother, brother, and God. This is an inspiring story of determination, love, and faith from a man who rose from material poverty to become Johns Hopkins's head of pediatric neurosurgery.

> *For whatever reason, the God of the universe, the God who holds galaxies in his hands, had seen a reason to reach down to a campus room on Planet Earth and send a dream to a discouraged ghetto kid who wanted to become a doctor.* (p. 78)

Notes: Gold Medallion Finalist 1990

Keywords: Christian biography • family relationships • inner-city life and culture • physicians

Cary, Lorene.

Black Ice. **New York: Alfred A. Knopf, 1991. ISBN 0-394-57465-6. 238p.**

Lorene Cary's scholarship to attend the traditionally all-white, all-male St. Paul's School was a mixed blessing that included the benefits of a superior education and the anxiety of self-doubt. An adult Cary returned to teach as a way of supporting black students and confronting her own memories.

> *Was it true that these teachers expected less of me than of my white peers? Or had I mistaken kindness for condescension? Were we black kids a social experiment? . . . Did it make any difference if we were?* (p. 5)

Notes: Lorene Cary is also listed in the "Slavery, 1619–1860" section of Chapter 6.

Keywords: coming of age • educators • family relationships • race relations • self-esteem

Cochran, Johnnie L., with Tim Rutten.

Journey to Justice. **New York: Ballantine Books, 1996. ISBN 0-345-40583-8. 383p.**

Cochran tells the story of a life based on ambition and advocacy, with dual lodestars of Jesus and the Constitution. A number of famous celebrity defendants are mentioned, with over 150 pages devoted to the workings of the defense in the O. J. trial. Included are 32 pages of black-and-white photographs.

> But constitutionalism is as close to an established church as we Americans have. The courts are, in that sense, a kind of civic temple and our lawyers and judges a sort of priesthood. (p. 367)

Notes: Blackboard Bestseller List 1997

Keywords: attorneys • Christian biography • court cases • criminal justice system • O. J. Simpson murder trial

Davis, Benjamin O., Jr.

Benjamin O. Davis, Jr., American: An Autobiography. **Washington, D.C.: Smithsonian Institution Press, 1991. ISBN 0-87474-742-2. 442p.**

Son of a brigadier general, Benjamin O. Davis Jr. confronted individual and institutionalized racism with perseverance, stoicism, and the unwavering support of wife Agatha. From his appointment as commander of the first black U.S. flying squadron through his 35-year military career, his clash with Cleveland Mayor Carl Stokes, and service in several high-level government posts, Davis tells the personal story behind the public record with dignity and honesty. Included are 20 pages of black-and-white photos, a foreword by Virginia Governor L. Douglas Wilder, and an index.

> In 1941 the Army still regarded all blacks as totally inferior to whites—somewhat less than human, and certainly incapable of contributing positively to its combat mission. But . . . events in the approaching conflict would prove once and for all the fallacy of that position. (p. 69)

Keywords: air pilots • military life • military officers • racial discrimination • Tuskegee Airmen • West Point • World War II

Davis, Sampson, George Jenkins, and Rameck Hunt, with Lisa Frazier Page.

🎗 *The Pact: Three Young Men Make a Promise and Fulfill a Dream.* **New York: Riverhead Books/ Penguin Putnam, 2002. ISBN 1-57322-216-X. 248p.**

> Three young black men—typical except for their amazing friendship, the people who believed in them, and the will to succeed—overcome low expectations, economic hardship, street temptations, and their own poor judgment to become doctors. Determined to help other young men like themselves, all three returned to practice in the old neighborhood to serve as role models and to establish the Three Doctors Foundation to provide financial support for students aspiring to a college education. By describing their failures and temptations as well as their strengths and successes, the authors help us to see the possibilities inherent in other young men.
>
> > *We know firsthand that the wrong friends can lead you to trouble. But even more, they can tear down hopes, dreams, and possibilities. We know, too, that the right friends inspire you, pull you through, rise with you.* (p. 3)
>
> **Notes:** *Essence* Bestseller List 2002, 2003, 2004
>
> **Keywords:** black men and society • inner-city life and culture • medical school • men's friendships • Newark, New Jersey • physicians • Seton Hall University

Delany, Sarah Louise, and A. Elizabeth Delany, with Amy Hill Hearth.

🎗 *Having Our Say: The Delany Sisters' First 100 Years.* **New York: Kodansha International, 1993. ISBN 1-56836-010-X. 210p.**

> The distinct personalities of Misses Sadie and Bessie Delany, two delightful centenarians, emerge as they tell the story of their lives in alternating chapters. The sisters combine down to earth wisdom, sly humor, and trenchant observations on both the past and current state of affairs in America. Included are 16 pages of black-and-white photographs and a family tree.
>
> > *Truth is, I never thought I'd see the day when people would be interested in hearing what two old Negro women have to say. Life still surprises me. So maybe the last laugh's on me.* (p. 209)
>
> **Notes:** Sarah Delany wrote a second book (with Amy Hill Hearth, illustrated by Brian M. Kotzky) after the death of her sister: *On My Own at 107: Life Without Bessie* (New York: HarperSanFrancisco, 1997. ISBN 0-062-51485-7. 149p.). Blackboard Bestseller List 1994, 1995
>
> **Keywords:** aging • centenarians • dentists • educators • family relationships • race relations • segregation • skin color

Elders, Joycelyn, and David Chanoff.

Joycelyn Elders, M.D.: From Sharecropper's Daughter to Surgeon General of the United States of America. **New York: Morrow, 1996. ISBN 0-688-14722-4. 355p.**

> Jocelyn Elders, successful, compassionate, pragmatic, and outspoken, shares her personal life story, from growing up in poverty to becoming the most visible

doctor in America, and the love and support she received along the way. In her typical straightforward and logical manner, she exposes the political machinations and religious right moralizing that led to her forced resignation and explains her views on political issues from affirmative action to health care. Included are 16 pages of black-and-white photographs and an index.

> *What was right and made sense had no racial or gender color. Most of all, it had no political color. For a scientist that approach was as noncontroversial as you could get. For a public servant it had drawbacks.* (p. 198)

Keywords: Arkansas • family relationships • health care • physicians • politics and politicians • race relations • segregation

Fisher, Ada Lois Sipuel, with Danney Goble.

A Matter of Black and White: The Autobiography of Ada Lois Sipuel Fisher. **Norman: University of Oklahoma Press, 1996. ISBN 0-8061-2819-4. 294p.**

Ada Lois Sipuel Fisher, the first African American to be admitted to the University of Oklahoma Law School, recounts the joy of growing up educated, middle-class, and loved; the challenges of being a civil rights test case; and the satisfaction of teaching. The book includes 20 black-and-white illustrations, a foreword by Robert Henry, a chronology that details both family history and key events in civil rights history, a list of contributors, and an index.

> *The faculty was always fair, and my fellow students were generally friendly. Still, I felt that I was being observed across campus and by much of the nation, watching to see if I succeeded as a student.* (p. 147)

Keywords: attorneys • civil rights activists • court cases • educators • family relationships • Oklahoma • race relations • segregation

My Life and an Era: The Autobiography of Buck Colbert Franklin. **Edited by John Hope Franklin and John Whittington Franklin. Baton Rouge: Louisiana State University Press, 1997. ISBN 0-8071-2213-0. 288p.**

Franklin gives an articulate firsthand account of societal changes and their impact on personal lives during an era of sweeping change in the United States. From early days in Indian Territory through the Tulsa Race Riot of 1921 to the civil rights legal victories in the 1950s, readers benefit from Franklin's observations and reasoned opinion. The text is carefully and minimally edited by Franklin's two sons, scholars in their own right. It icludes an editors' preface, an appreciation of Buck Colbert Franklin, 15 pages of black-and-white photographs, a frontispiece, a map, and an index.

> *I learned . . . that most great issues are moral, not political;*
> *are human, not racial; that the statesman can never be dis-*
> *placed by the politician without harmful dislocations of nat-*
> *ural evolutionary processes; and the entire world is both*
> *mentally and spiritually ill today because of this derange-*
> *ment.* (p. 133)

Keywords: attorneys • court cases • Oklahoma • race relations • Tulsa Race Riot of 1921

Gordy, Berry.

To Be Loved: The Music, the Magic, the Memories of Motown. **New York: Warner Books, 1994. ISBN 0-446-51523-X. 432p.**

From the time he was eight, Berry Gordy had "a burning desire to be special, to win, to be somebody." Deciding that the work was too hard, the payoff too small, and celibacy too big a price to pay, he abandoned a boxing career for the music business. This story is full of details about the family, the music, the business, and the celebrities that coalesced around Gordy to create the Motown legend. The book includes 32 pages of star-studded black-and-white photographs, a list of Gordy's released compositions, and an index.

> *[O]ur music's popularity started overcoming the prejudices.*
> *But there were so many other color barriers to overcome. I*
> *remember one day . . . when I noticed I was the only black*
> *person in the room. My own company!* (p. 245)

Keywords: celebrities • composers • entrepreneurs • Motown • music business

Hankins, Anthony Mark, with Debbie Markley.

Fabric of Dreams: Designing My Own Success. **New York: Dutton, 1998. ISBN 0-525-94329-3. 288p.**

Hankins reveals his buoyant personality, determination, and undying love and admiration for his mother as he tells his rags-to-riches story. From his first creation (a suit with crooked seams made at age seven) through apprenticeship at major fashion houses to his own multi-million-dollar business, he keeps us laughing and hoping.

> *Child, I was determined to go even further than that in my*
> *career plans. I knew I was going to be a designer, with my*
> *own clothing labels in stores all around the world. When it*
> *came to my dreams, honey, I wouldn't take no for an an-*
> *swer. You shouldn't either.* (p. 287)

Keywords: costume design • entrepreneurs • fashion designers • retail clothing business

Hill, Anita.

 Speaking Truth to Power. **New York: Doubleday, 1997. ISBN: 0385476256. 374p.**

Six years after the famous confirmation hearings, Anita Hill finally breaks down and publishes a book that completely and forthrightly chronicles the events

leading to her testimony in Clarence Thomas's Supreme Court confirmation hearings. Why a private woman dropped a sexual bombshell into the proceedings, what her honesty cost her, and how she found the strength of character to maintain her dignity and sense of self-worth are the focus of her story. Although a tale of adversity, it is also a story in praise of family, friends, and faith. It includes an index.

> *I did not choose the issue of sexual harassment;*
> *rather, it chose me. Having been chosen, I have*
> *come to believe that it is up to me to try to give*
> *meaning to it all. (p. 6)*

Notes: Bruce K. Gould Book Award 1998

Keywords: attorneys • civil rights • confirmation hearings • family relationships • hostile work environment • judges • sexual harassment

Jones, Star, with Daniel Paisner.

You Have to Stand for Something or You'll Fall for Anything. **New York: Bantam Books, 1998. ISBN 0-553-10864-9. 235p.**

Star Jones, known best as legal correspondent to *Today* and outspoken cohost on *The View*, provides not so much a chronology as a series of anecdotes that reveal her beliefs and illustrate her life lessons. Told in the engaging and sometimes outrageous style that has made Jones a popular television personality, Star's book is humorous and perceptive.

> *It's only white women who obsess about their weight.*
> *Black women obsess about their hair. (p. 168)*

Keywords: attorneys • Christian biography • criminal justice system • fathers and daughters • friendships • television talk show hosts

McCray, Carrie Allen.

Freedom's Child: The Life of a Confederate General's Black Daughter. **Chapel Hill, N.C.: Algonquin Books of Chapel Hill/ Workman Publishing, 1998. ISBN 1-56512-186-4. 270p.**

Through conversations with her dead mother's best friend, Aun' Tannie (poet Anne Spencer) and extensive research, Carrie learns about the people and forces who shaped her mother's loving nature and aggressive commitment to "full freedom". As she does, she confronts complex truths about the white grandfather she had never accepted. The characters in this family chronicle are richly drawn and unforgettable. It includes a selected bibliography and a detailed table of contents.

> *Perhaps poetry is the thread that connects me*
> *most truly back to Mama's father, the white man*
> *who rode down dirt roads reciting poetry to his*
> *young black daughter. (p. 211)*

> **Keywords:** civil rights activists • educators • Gregory Willis Hayes • John Robert Jones • Mary Rice Hayes Allen • mixed-race children • segregation • race relations • Virginia Seminary

Petersen, Frank E., Lt. Gen., with J. Alfred Phelps.

Into the Tiger's Jaw: America's First Black Marine Aviator. **Novato, Calif.: Presidio Press, 1998. ISBN 0-89141-675-7. 334p.**

Petersen, first African American Marine Corps pilot and three-star general, tells a story full of military action and behind the scenes political maneuvering. He reveals the power of determination and dignity in the face of the military's pervasive racial discrimination. "Mutual voices" sections throughout give other perspectives. Included are 16 pages of black-and-white photographs and a frontispiece.

> *I didn't want to be held up as a role model for blacks, or deal with the racial issue at all. I did want to prove myself an effective commander and pilot rather than a black commander or black pilot.* (p. 317)

> **Keywords:** air pilots • Korean Conflict • military life • military officers • racial discrimination • United States Marine Corps • Vietnam War

Smith, Charlene E. McGee.

Tuskegee Airman: The Biography of Charles E. McGee, Air Force Fighter Combat Record Holder. **Boston: Branden Publishing, 1999. ISBN 0-8283-2046-2. 204p.**

Smith's father is Colonel Charles E. McGee, a highly decorated soldier and holder of the three-war record for combat missions. Although his military contributions are detailed in full, it is McGee the family man, patriot, and leader who shines through. An excellent chronology of events precedes each chapter, providing a context for McGee's accomplishments. Included are three maps, 14 pages of black-and-white photos, tributes, a resource list, and an index. The text would have benefited from careful proofreading.

> *Too often African American men are not portrayed in mainstream America as loving husband, fathers, patriots or role models. In order to dispel ill-conceived notions and share a greater understanding, I commit my father's biography to paper.* (p. 11)

> **Keywords:** air pilots • Korean Conflict • military life • military officers • Tuskegee Airmen • Vietnam War • World War II

Stewart, Shelley, with Nathan Hale Turner Jr.

The Road South: A Memoir. **New York: Warner Books, 2002. ISBN 0-446-53027-1. 316p.**

As a child, he was stripped, hung upside down, and whipped, had salt rubbed into the wounds, and was left overnight—by family. Blessed with an indomitable spirit, love of learning, and will to survive, Stewart overcame physical, sexual, and emotional abuse, poverty, racial discrimination, and depression to find professional and financial success—and peace. Included are four pages of black-and-white photographs.

> *The station bosses crafted a 12 noon to 1 p.m. daily show, and I poured my energy into the flippant, bombastic character that served as a disguise for the tortured, grief-stricken individual who wept every night in the seclusion of his room.* (p. 181)

Keywords: child abuse • entrepreneurs • family relationships • men and women • poverty • racial discrimination • radio personalities

Thomas-El, Salome, with Cecil Murphey.

I Choose to Stay: A Black Teacher Refuses to Desert the Inner City. **New York: Dafina Books/Kensington Publishing, 2003. ISBN 0-7582-0186-9. 304p.**

Salome Thomas-El's story is one of dedication and commitment in the face of almost impossible odds. Declining higher paying and more prestigious jobs, this teacher refused to leave an inner-city school and the students who desperately needed a positive black male role model and an adult who believed in them. Throughout he acknowledges the support of his mother, mentors, and beloved wife. Included are a foreword by Arnold Schwarzenegger and a note dedicating a portion of the royalties to support the college education of featured students.

> *I kept thinking about inner-city kids. As long as they're alive, they have a chance to turn their lives around. As long as there are teachers and leaders out there giving of ourselves, we can make changes. Sadness filled my heart when I remembered those we hadn't been able to snatch from destruction.* (p. 300)

Keywords: at-risk children • educators • family relationships • inner-city life and culture

Thornton, Yvonne S., as told to Jo Coudert.

The Ditchdigger's Daughters: A Black Family's Astonishing Success Story. **New York: Carol Publishing, 1996. ISBN 1-559-72271-1. 261p.**

When Donald and Tass Thornton, a remarkable hardworking couple who hold menial jobs, decide that their six daughters are going to be independent, successful women, nothing can stop them. Sacrifice, love, and the ability to dream help them realize their goals. Readers will love this uplifting family biography rich in humor and folk wisdom.

> *I love you better than I love life. . . . But I'm not always gonna be around to look after you, and no man's gonna come along and offer to take care of you because you ain't light-skinned. That's why*

you gotta be able to look after yourselves. And for that you
gotta be smart. (p. 3)

Notes: Made for television movie by the same name, directed by Johnny E. Jensen and starring Monica Calhoun, Carl Lumbly, Victoria Dillard, and Kimberly Elise (1997).

Keywords: family relationships • physicians • sisters • Thornton family

Washington, Booker T.

Up From Slavery. **With a new introduction by Ishmael Reed. New York: Signet Classic/New American Library, Penguin Putnam, 2000. ISBN 0-451-52754-2pa. 228p. (Text from first book edition New York: Doubleday, Page, 1901.)**

Washington's emphasis on the importance of economic independence as a prerequisite to full and responsible citizenship for former slaves was criticized by contemporary black intellectuals, yet his approach served as a cornerstone of the 1960s Civil Rights Movement. His surprisingly readable autobiography describes his boyhood days and development of the Tuskegee Institute, revealing a man of vision, integrity, and commitment. Included are an introduction by Ishmael Reed, notes, and a bibliography.

In order to be successful in any kind of undertaking, I think
the main thing is for one to grow to the point where he com-
pletely forgets himself; that is, to lose himself in a great
cause. In proportion as one loses himself in this way, in the
same degree does he get the highest happiness out of his
work. (p. 126)

Notes: *Sacred Fire: The QBR 100 Essential Black Books*

Keywords: educators • race relations • Reconstruction • Tuskegee Institute

Politicians and Activists

Brown, Elaine.

A Taste of Power: A Black Woman's Story. **New York: Pantheon Books, 1992. ISBN 0-679-41944-6. 452p.**

Replete with the rhetoric and paranoia of the 1970s, Brown's memoir is a reminder of the political activism and violence of the times. A pampered child who eschewed her piano lessons and education as "too white," she moved from cocktail waitress and mistress to chairman of the Black Panther Party. Brown reveals the brutal inner workings of the party; warfare among factions; her love for many of the people involved; and the fear, sexism, and devotion to her daughter that led her to break ties with the movement that had been her life. Included are 16 pages of black-and-white photographs.

"We don't have ambulance service," the hospital's emer-
gency registration clerk said casually. I drew the Browning
from Joan's purse. I aimed it at the clerk's face and cocked

*it. There was a round in the chamber. "Well, you're
going to need one, bitch!"* (p. 166)

Keywords: Black Panther Party • Black Power Movement • Bobby Seale •
Eldridge Cleaver • Huey Newton • political radicals

Brown, Tracey L.

The Life and Times of Ron Brown: A Memoir by His Daughter. **New York:
Morrow, 1998. ISBN 0-688-15320-8. 318p.**

It's nearly impossible not to share Tracey's anguish and tears as she describes her father's death in a plane crash over Croatia. In an intimate
portrait brimming with love, Ron Brown is remembered as the central
figure in a warm and loving family as well as the dedicated and visionary
politician who returned the Democratic Party to the White House and
revolutionized the moribund Commerce Department with a commitment
to a global economy and economic independence for people of color. Included are 22 pages of black-and-white photographs, an introduction by
President Bill Clinton, "Afterword: Why the Plane Crashed," "Epilogue:
My Father's Legacy," the Welborn family tree, a diagram of the actual
flight path, and an index.

> *When dinner was over, we did one of our routines:
> Dad reminded me that I was "the most brilliant and
> beautiful daughter in the world" and I responded
> that he had "made me that way." We hugged and
> kissed, and went our separate ways. I would never
> see him again.* (p. 20)

Keywords: Cabinet officers • conspiracy theorists • Democratic Party • fathers
and daughters • politics and politicians

Evers-Williams, Myrlie, with Melinda Blau.

*Watch Me Fly: What I Learned on the Way to Becoming the Woman I Was
Meant to Be.* **New York: Little, Brown, 1999. ISBN 0-316-25520-3. 324p.**

Myrlie Evers-Williams grows from being defined in terms of others—
"nothing more than Mrs. Beasley's granddaughter, Mrs. Polk's niece, the
unfortunate widow of Medgar Evers"—to an independent woman of accomplishment. She shares her journey from naïve schoolgirl to successful business executive and civil rights leader to provide life lessons for
other women.

> *Each of us has to accept and take responsibility for
> the fact that too often we still classify and judge
> one another in terms of race, ethnicity, faith, sexual
> orientation, class, even age. Take a hard look at
> your own attitudes toward different groups, and be
> mindful of the overt and covert ways you express
> them.* (p. 271)

Keywords: business people • Civil Rights Movement • court cases • husbands and wives • National Association for the Advancement of Colored People (NAACP) • public officials • race relations • social activism and activists • widows

Goode, W. Wilson, with Joann Stevens.

In Goode Faith. **Valley Forge, Pa.: Judson Press, 1992. ISBN 0-8170-1186-2. 316p.**

W. Wilson Goode, Philadelphia's first black mayor, sets the public record straight with his insider story of corrupt and incompetent city officials, of racism and brutality, and of the deadly police assault on MOVE headquarters. This is also a deeply personal account of a mother's faith and love and a man's unwavering spiritual commitment. It includes an epilogue in the form of an open letter to his children, 14 pages of black-and-white photographs, notes, and an index.

> *The MOVE incident was the darkest hour of my Christian experience. The ghosts of the MOVE tragedy haunt me daily. The deaths of those children, of those people, continue to haunt me. My God, how I wish I could bring them back!* (p. 301)

Keywords: mayors • MOVE bombing 1975 • politics and politicians

Guinier, Lani.

Lift Every Voice: Turning a Civil Rights Setback into a New Vision of Social Justice. **New York: Simon & Schuster, 1998. ISBN 0-684-81145-5. 336p.**

Guinier dissects her nomination to Assistant Attorney General for Civil Rights, attributing the failure to confirm her to an incompetent White House and a vindictive Republican power structure. She builds from the negative, reclaiming her voice as she briefly outlines the Civil Rights Movement, recounts her triumphs and failures in the pursuit of equal representation, and offers a model for making sure that every voice is heard. This narrowly focused political biography reveals little of events in her personal life, but the impact of her upbringing is evident throughout. Included are an extensive listing of sources and an index.

> *I had been humbled by the president. I felt humiliated by the president, my friend, not just because he had buckled in the face of pressure but because he justified his action by mischaracterizing who I was and what I stood for.* (p. 165)

Keywords: Civil Rights Movement • civil rights activists • confirmation hearings • politics and politicians • race relations

Height, Dorothy.

 *Open Wide the Freedom Gates: A Memoir.* **New York: PublicAffairs/Perseus Books, 2003. 322p.**

Dorothy Height's memoirs span a lifetime of political involvement and service, from her work with the YWCA and the National Council of Negro Women in 1939 to her involvement with every significant group and event of the Civil

Rights Movement to the 2003 dedication of the NCNW's Dorothy I. Height Building in Washington, D.C. A coalition builder, behind the scenes leader, and "shock absorber," this woman of courage expanded the Civil Rights Movement to include women and a global perspective. Included are eight pages of black-and-white photographs, a foreword by Maya Angelou, and an index.

> *Women of color everywhere are often the back-bones of their families. They have to work—often alongside their men in the fields or factories—and they also have to provide the emotional, intellec-tual, social, and spiritual support their men and their children need.* (p. 233)

Notes: *Essence* Bestseller List 2003, 2004

Keywords: Civil Rights Movement • Great Mississippi Project • National Council of Negro Women (NCNW) • social activism and activists • Young Women's Christian Association (YWCA)

Jordan, E. Vernon, Jr., with Annette Gordon-Reed.

🎗 *Vernon Can Read!: A Memoir.* New York: PublicAffairs, 2001. ISBN 1-891620-69-X . 344p.

Even as Jordan recounts the impact of hearing the surprised exclamation "Vernon can read!" he acknowledges that the employer who made the re-mark was already a relic of an earlier time. This is the goal of this straightforward recounting of events and political observations: to trace the rise and accomplishments of the Civil Rights Movement and to re-mind a new generation of the battles and sacrifices required to attain the rights they now enjoy. Included are 16 pages of black-and-white photo-graphs and an index.

> *I have never been one for indiscriminately sharing my innermost thoughts and feelings. I have always had the feeling people wanted me to do that—that they wanted to hear me complain about the prob-lems I faced on my job or talk (or cry) openly about Shirley's illness. But that is not my way.* (p. 267)

Notes: BCALA Literary Award Nonfiction 2002; Bruce K. Gould Book Award 2002; *Essence* Bestseller List 2002

Keywords: attorneys • Civil Rights Movement • National Urban League • polit-ical activism and activists

King, Dexter Scott, with Ralph Wiley.

Growing Up King: An Intimate Memoir. New York: IPM Intellectual Properties Management, Inc./Warner Books, 2003. ISBN 0-446-52942-7. 312p.

King's story is his own, and he tells it with surprising candor. He describes the conflict of preserving his father's legacy and carrying his cause forward while finding the freedom to be his own man. Alternately reflective in discussing race relations today, angry in recounting the betrayals and criticism the family has endured, and perceptive in describing the political workings of the King Center and civil rights leadership, this is a complex and compelling narrative. It includes eight pages of black-and-white photos, a prologue, and an index.

> *Freedom never comes easy. Neither does life; maybe that's part of my contribution. Maybe to show how easy it isn't, is my contribution. I don't know. I've learned that not knowing is permissible—it carries no shame. . . . You still must give yourself permission to live. Would he approve? Would he disapprove? I let it go.* (p. 307)

Keywords: children of celebrities • Civil Rights Movement • coming of age • court cases • King Center • Loyd Jowers • Martin Luther King Jr. • political activism and activists

Lewis, John, with Michael D'Orso.

Walking with the Wind: A Memoir of the Movement. **New York: Simon & Schuster, 1998. ISBN 0-684-81065-4. 496p.**

Vivid detail and rich texture characterize Lewis's account of his life and times. The reader is transported to another, more peaceful time and place by his lovingly drawn pictures of his childhood. Lewis pulls the reader inside a church being attacked by an angry mob; aboard a bus of freedom riders; into the midst of a riot—creating a sense of immediacy and anguish, as well as respect for those who faced hatred with strength and courage. One-time chair and an organizer of SNCC, Lewis explains the political maneuvering within the Civil Rights Movement and his commitment to "aggressive nonviolence" and the Beloved Community.

> *Then a brick came crashing through one of the stained-glass windows, and now there was some alarm. Women and children screamed as broken glass flew through the air. Tear gas began drifting in, and people started coughing, covering their faces. But no one lost control.* (p. 163)

Keywords: Civil Rights Movement • Freedom Riders • legislators • politics and politicians • Student Nonviolent Coordinating Committee (SNCC)

Malcolm X.

The Autobiography of Malcolm X. with the assistance of Alex Haley. **New York: Ballantine Books, 1964 (1973). ISBN 0-345-35068-5pa. 466p.**

Malcolm X's famous autobiography reveals the man behind the one-sided stereotypical black revolutionary. This is a portrait of a criminal who sees the light; an intelligent man who constantly learns, questions, assesses, and acts; a loving husband and father, frustrated with political, religious, economic, and social systems that combine to keep his people weak and fragmented. Malcolm X had the courage to hold a mirror to American society and the strength of character to grow and change. More than a political diatribe, this is the compelling story of a man of vision. Includes a foreword by Attallah Shabazz, an introduction by M. S. Handler, an epilogue by Alex Haley, and an afterword by Ossie Davis.

> *I had never dreamed of anything like that atmosphere among black people who had learned to be proud they were black, who had learned to love other black people instead of being jealous and suspicious. I thrilled to how we Muslim men used both hands to grasp a black brother's hands . . . . The Muslim sisters . . . were given an honor and respect that I'd never seen black men give to their women, and it felt wonderful to me.* (p. 199)

Notes: *Sacred Fire: QBR 100 Essential Black Books*

Keywords: Black Muslims • Civil Rights Movement • Elijah Muhammad • political radicals

Mfume, Kweisi, with Ron Stodghill II.

No Free Ride: From the Mean Streets to the Mainstream. **New York: One World, 1996. ISBN 0-345-39220-5. 373p.**

Filled with vivid description and thoughtful commentary, this is the compelling story of how Frizzel Gray, a promiscuous, angry, inner-city dropout, hustler, and father of five illegitimate children, defied odds to be reborn as Mfume Kweisi, political activist, U.S. congressman, and leader of the NAACP. Incuded are 16 pages of black-and-white photographs.

> *God had given me a second chance that night. He'd ripped my insides out and shaken me to the core. I knew I'd never, ever, go back to the life I'd been leading.* (p. 176)

Notes: Blackboard Bestseller List 1997

Keywords: Congressional Black Caucus • inner-city life and culture • legislators • National Association for the Advancement of Colored People (NAACP) • political activism and activists

Parks, Rosa, with Jim Haskins.

Rosa Parks: My Story. **New York: Dial Books, 1992. ISBN 0-8037-0673-1. 192p.**

Ms. Parks describes the influence of her ancestors in making her historic refusal inevitable and gives an insider view of the tumultuous civil rights era and the critical incident that became a symbol and energized a movement. Published in larger print and written in a simple, straightforward manner, this book is suitable for some younger audiences. It includes 32 black-and-white photographs throughout, a chronology, and an index.

> *I could be the test case the NAACP had been looking for. I did not think about that at all. In fact if I had let myself think too deeply about what might happen to me, I would have gotten off the bus. But I chose to remain.* (p. 116)

Keywords: bus boycott • Civil Rights Movement • Montgomery, Alabama • National Association for the Advancement of Colored People (NAACP) • political activism and activists • race relations • segregation

Ringgold, Faith.

We Flew Over the Bridge: The Memoirs of Faith Ringgold. **Boston: Bullfinch Press Book/Little, Brown,1995. ISBN 0-8212-2071-3. 288p.**

Ringgold's identities as artist, civil rights activist, and feminist come together in her life and in this vibrant recounting. Equal detail is given to her personal life, protests on behalf of black artists, and her growth and technique as an artist. Included are black-and-white family photos and illustrations of Ringgold's work throughout; 16 color plates of art; an appendix, "Matisse's Chapel" (the text for the quilt); a Faith Ringgold chronology; a list of public and private collections holding Ringgold's work, and an index.

> *In the 1970's, being black and a feminist was equivalent to being a traitor to the cause of black people. . . . But the brothers' rap that was the most double-dealing was the cry that "the black woman's place is behind her man," when frequently white women occupied that position.* (p. 175)

Keywords: art and artists • family relationships • men and women • mothers and daughters • multimedia art • performance artists • social activism and activists

Shabazz, Ilyasah, with Kim McLarin.

Growing Up X. **New York: One World, 2002. ISBN 0-345-44495-7. 235p.**

Through her candid and very personal account of her family's struggles and trials, triumphs and successes, Shabazz gives a sense of what it feels like to grow up "X." Shabazz's pointed political observations are included throughout, but the book never loses its intimate perspective. She describes a life that was shaped by the philosophy and notoriety of her famous father, but this memoir is a tribute to the strength and courage of her loving and protective mother. Included are 16 pages of of black-and-white family photographs.

> *What I knew about my father at this point in my life came not from what I'd read but from what was shared by Mommy and family friends. I knew about Malcolm the husband, Malcolm the father, Malcolm the friend, not Malcolm X the spokesman, the revolutionary, the icon.* (p. 165)

Notes: *Essence* Bestseller List 2002, 2003

Keywords: Betty Shabazz • children of celebrities • Civil Rights Movement • coming of age • family relationships • Malcolm X • political activism and activists

Sharpton, Al.

 Go and Tell Pharaoh: The Autobiography of the Reverend Al Sharpton. New York: Doubleday, 1996. ISBN 0-385-47583-7. 276p.

Sharpton, an ordained Pentecostal minister at age 10, reflects on the pervasiveness of his religious calling throughout his political and civil rights endeavors and defends his reputation and motives. Included are 14 pages of black-and-white photos.

> [S]ometimes events that seem to involve heavy theoretical, philosophical and ideological argument really boil down to personal animosity based on something that happened somewhere and that has nothing to do with all those heavy things. (p. 62)

Notes: Blackboard Bestseller List 1996

Keywords: Christian biography • Civil Rights Movement • clergy • politics and politicians

Truth, Sojourner.

The Narrative of Sojourner Truth. **Edited and with an introduction by Margaret Washington. New York: Vintage Classics/Vintage Books, Random House. ISBN 0-679-74035-Xpa. 141p.**

Sickened by the cruelties of slave owners who treated her people with deliberate cruelty or unthinking neglect, tired of broken promises, and fearful for her children, Isabella rescues her son, frees herself, is filled with the Holy Spirit, and begins her life as Sojourner Truth, an ardent abolitionist and women's rights advocate. Washington's lengthy introduction and appendix with notes on the original 1850 text recorded by Olive Gilbert are valuable in helping the reader to more fully understand the narrative. Included are William Lloyd Garrison's stirring preface to the 1850 edition, Truth's "Ar'n't I a Woman" speech, a bibliography, and an index.

> She says that God revealed himself to her, with all the suddenness of a flash of lightning, showing her, "in the twinkling of an eye, that he was all over"—that he pervaded the universe—"and that there was no place where God was not." (p. 49)

Keywords: abolition and abolitionists • antebellum North • Christian biography • slavery • social activism and activists

Upchurch, Carl.

Convicted in the Womb: One Man's Journey from Prisoner to Peacemaker. **New York: Bantam Books/ Bantam Doubleday Dell, 1996. ISBN 0-553-09726-1. 236p.**

In three major sections, Upchurch uses his life to illustrate the principles of niggerization, the process by which societal conditions and low expectations lead

poor black men to despair; deniggerization, the process of developing an awareness of self and soul through education, religion, and self-examination; and finally, antiniggerization, the process of challenging niggerization in all its forms.
Upchurch closes with scathing observations about current civil rights "leaders"
and a call for action.

> We cannot generalize forever about how "they" see us,
> treat us, and feel about us. Such grumbling may satisfy
> some conditioned reaction in us to be victims and therefore
> not responsible, but it does nothing to change our circum-
> stances or improve our children's lives. (p. 198)

Keywords: Civil Rights Movement • Council for Urban Peace and Justice • gang sum-
mits • prison life • Progressive Prisoner's Movement • social activism and activists

Wattleton, Faye.

Life on the Line. **New York: Ballantine Books/Random House, 1996. ISBN 0-345-
39265-5. 489p.**

At age 34, Faye Wattleton, nurse, midwife, and mother, became the youngest person, the first African American, and the first woman since founder Margaret
Sanger to lead the Planned Parenthood Federation. In her richly detailed and
well-documented story, she shares her personal life, values, political views, and
keen social commentary. Included are notes and an afterword in the form of a letter to her daughter, Felicia.

> As an African American, I'm secure in the belief that our
> Constitution protects you from discrimination because of
> your skin color and that the state cannot officially control
> your destiny because of your race. . . . It pains me to say
> that, as a woman, you are not equally secure from govern-
> ment oppression because of the unique reproductive char-
> acteristics of your gender. (p. 469)

Keywords: Planned Parenthood Federation of America • pro-choice movement • sexual
discrimination • social activism and activists • women's rights

Watts, J. C. (Julius Caesar), with Chriss Winston.

What Color Is a Conservative?: My Life and My Politics. **New York:
HarperCollins, 2002. ISBN 0-06-019436-7. 294p.**

Chapter titles such as "Opportunity Is Just Hard Work in Disguise" and "God
Gives You What You Need, You Have to Work for What You Want" encapsulate
Watt's conservative philosophy. Readers will enjoy the former Oklahoma congressman's stories of family and everyday life, which are lively and affectionate,
but may find the insertion of superfluous political opinions distracting.

> Football is as popular in Oklahoma as spending money is in
> Washington. (p. 81)

Keywords: football players • legislators • Oklahoma • politics and politicians

Wright, Bruce.

Black Justice in a White World: A Memoir. New York: Barricade Books, 1996. ISBN 1-56980-076-6. 239p.

Judge Wright describes his confrontations with racial discrimination from his childhood and college days through his military career and AWOL adventures in Paris to his eventual election to the New York Supreme Court. Original poetry, judiciary analysis, and social commentary are woven with biography. Included are 16 pages of black-and-white photographs.

> For many years I have ridiculed formal religion and especially Christianity. Often, I have wondered about and been baffled by the passionate allegiance of blacks to Christianity, the religion of the slave owners. (p. 207)

Notes: American Book Award 1991

Keywords: criminal justice system • judges • military life • mixed-race children • New York • poets

Writers

Angelou, Maya.

Autobiographical Series.

Noted poet and playwright Angelou's autobiographies have been challenged for their descriptions of sex and sexual violence and criticized for the use of fictional techniques. More often, they are cherished for their honest and sensitive portrayals of the lives of black women and praised for development of relevant themes such as motherhood, personal and racial identity, and freedom and imprisonment. A captivating storyteller whose prose is alternately evocative and compelling, Angelou is recognized as one of the first modern authors to give voice to African American women. To date, there are six entries in Angelou's serial biography. Original publication information is provided for each, although most are now currently available in paperback editions.

> The African-American leaves the womb with the burden of her color and a race memory chockablock with horrific folk tales. Frequently there are songs, toe-tapping, finger-popping, hand-slapping, dancing songs the say, in effect, "I'm laughing to keep from crying." (A Song Flung Up to Heaven, p. 46)

Keywords: men and women • playwrights • poets

I Know Why the Caged Bird Sings. New York: Random House, 1969. ISBN 0-394-42986-9. 281p.

Angelou tells the story of her childhood as Marguerite Johnson, devoid of affection except from her brother Bailey and marred by rape but later enriched by a love of reading and the kind attention of a strong and well-educated woman. This first entry ends with Angelou's foray into sexual activity and her resulting pregnancy at age 16.

Notes: National Book Award Nominee 1970; *Sacred Fire: The QBR 100 Essential Black Books*

Keywords: brothers and sisters • child molestation • children's point of view

Gather Together in My Name. New York: Random House, 1974. ISBN 0-394-48692-7. 214p.

Angelou's life follows a typical pattern of unwed teenage mothers, as she is exposed to violence, drugs, and tragedy while attempting to remain independent by working at low-skill jobs, performing as a dancer, and working for a short while as a prostitute. She takes a lover, finds generous friends, and never loses her love of the written word.

Keywords: dancers • drug addiction • single parents

Singin' and Swingin' and Gettin' Merry Like Christmas. New York: Random House, 1976. ISBN 0-394-40545-5. 269p.

Growing awareness of the importance of her black heritage to herself and her son creates conflict in her marriage to a white man, which eventually leads to its failure. Marguerite emerges as Maya Angelou, dancer at the Purple Onion. A part in the touring company of *Porgy and Bess* takes her from the cabaret in San Francisco to a European tour in the company of people whom she enjoys and respects and broadens her horizons, but her love for her son and guilt over leaving him compel her to return home.

Keywords: motherhood • racial identity

The Heart of a Woman. New York: Random House, 1981. ISBN 0-394-51273-1. 272p.

Still engaged in show business, Angelou discovers her calling as a writer. She engages the reader in her discovery and the way in which she learned her craft. Concerned about race relations, she uses her talents to support the Civil Rights Movement. Through her political involvement, she meets the South African freedom fighter who will be her second husband.

Notes: Blackboard Bestseller List 1997, 1998; Oprah's Book Club 1997

Keywords: civil rights activists

All God's Children Need Traveling Shoes. New York: Random House, 1986. ISBN 0-394-52143-9. 210p.

Angelou, husband Make, and son Guy move to Egypt, where Make's unfaithfulness leads to divorce. Angelou remains in Africa, experiencing the joy of immersion in her African heritage and entering into a stormy relationship with the great love of her life. She decides to return to America, her true home, hoping to help it realize its potential for equality.

Keywords: Africa and Africans • expatriates • Ghana

A Song Flung Up to Heaven. New York: Random House, 2002. ISBN 0-375-50747-7. 212p.

Song is about reunions, relationships, and growth. Angelou returns from Ghana and explores her place and ideas about America; her changing relationship with her family and maturing son; and reconciliation with her African lover. She grows in stature as a writer and poet, with this entry in the series ending with a call from Random House inviting her to write an autobiography.

Notes: *Black Issues Book Review* Best Book 2002; *Essence* Bestseller List 2002

Keywords: civil rights activists • family relationships • James Baldwin • Malcolm X • Martin Luther King, Jr. • 1960s

Baraka, Amira.

***The Autobiography of LeRoi Jones.* Revised edition. Chicago: Lawrence Hill Books, 1997. ISBN 1556522312. 465 p. (Originally published New York: Freundlich Books, 1984. ISBN 0-88191-000-7. p. 329)**

Vividly written, compellingly honest, and disarmingly self-assessing, Baraka's autobiography is a study of one man's constant struggle and growth. Leroy Jones, "a little brown big-eyed boy" grew into Beat poet LeRoi Jones, who then transformed himself into political activist Imamu Amira Baraka, moving force behind the Black Arts Movement and the global Diaspora concept.. This is the story not only of an individual's metamorphosis but of a movement's creation and coming of age. The 1997 edition contains the entire original manuscript revised by Baraka, as well as material originally excised (for length) from the earlier version.

> Where I was comin from, the brown side, we just wanted to keep stepping. The black had shaped us, the yellow had taunted us, the white had terrified and alienated us. And cool meant, to us, to be silent in the face of all that, silent yet knowing. It meant knowledge. It meant being smart, intelligent too. So we hooked up the weirdness and the intelligence. (p. 62, 1984 text)

Keywords: Black Arts Movement • essayists • playwrights • poets • political radicals • social activism and activists

Blockson, Charles L.

"Damn Rare": The Memoirs of an African-American Bibliophile. Tracy, Calif.: Quantum Leap Publisher, 1998. ISBN 1-892697-00-9. 334p.

Part history, part reflection, part autobiography, part who's who of the African American community, Charles Blockson's literate work invites the reader to share his passion for his book collecting and his mission: preserving his people's past, building pride, and shaping the future. The book includes nine pages of black-and-white photographs, a list of rare books and pamphlets mentioned or quoted in *"Damn Rare,"* and an index.

> *The final challenge for all of us [African American biblio-philes] is to ensure that our work and through our work the work of the many thousands and millions of African people whose stories we have so jealously preserved and de-fended speaks to eternity.* (p. 257)

Keywords: bibliophiles • book collectors • historians • writers

Datcher, Michael.

Raising Fences: A Black Man's Love Story. New York: Riverhead Books, 2001. ISBN 1-57322-330-1pa. 280p.

As a boy, Datcher longed to grow up to be the father in an ideal family, to have a wife and children he could love and protect, to become the idealized father he never had. In this evocative, often poignant coming-of-age story, he tells how he nearly became the very person he most despised but instead redeemed himself and his dreams. Includes Datcher's poetry.

> *I've been obsessed with being a husband and father since I was seven years old. Quiet as it's kept, many young black men have the same obsession. Picket-fence dreams.* (p. 3)

Keywords: fatherhood • inner-city life and culture • Los Angeles, California • men and women • poets

Dickerson, Debra Gladys.

An American Story. New York: Pantheon Books, 2000. ISBN 0-375-42069-X. 285p.

An intelligent little girl strives to be different from—and better than—her family and the rest of the poor black working class but succeeds in isolating herself in the process. As she becomes stronger and more successful through the rigors of the air force, officer candidate school, and Harvard Law School, Dickerson grows in self-awareness and understanding. This intelligent, engaging, and surprisingly humorous story is filled with complex individuals and pointed political observations.

> *I was used to the intellectual dishonesty of the left and black apologists—they pushed me right. But then, the intellectual shamelessness and moral clay feet of conservatives pushed*

me left. The left annoys me, but the right insults my intelligence. (p. 139)

Keywords: family relationships • Harvard • intraracial relations • journalism and journalists • men and women • military life

Duke, Lynne.

Mandela, Mobutu, and Me: A Newswoman's African Journey. **New York: Doubleday, 2003. ISBN 0-385-50398-9. 294p.**

In this evocative, thoughtful, and ultimately personal memoir, Duke, former *Washington Post* bureau chief in Johannesburg, describes the political turmoil of Africa in the 1990s, a decade that changed the political map of that country. Surrounded by terrible cruelty and triumphant humanity, Duke offers both broad level political observation and intimate glimpses into the everyday life and thoughts of the people with whom she lived for years, savoring "a life between fear and freedom." Included is an index of names and places.

> *Somehow I felt responsible. I felt journalism had failed. Late at night sometimes, I'd reread my dispatches. If I'd written more searingly, more elegantly, perhaps more angrily, could I have made a difference? Could I have roused Americans to demand more from their government.* (p. 173)

Keywords: Africa and Africans • Congo-Zaire (Democratic Republic of Congo) • intraracial relations • Mobutu Sese Seko • Nelson Mandela • news correspondents • Rwanda • South Africa

Fisher, Antwone Quenton, with Mim Eichler Rivas.

Finding Fish: A Memoir. **New York: Morrow/HarperCollins, 2001. ISBN 0-688-17699-2340. 342p.**

Born in prison to a single teenage mother two months after his charismatic but reckless young father is killed by another woman, Antwone is left in the hands of a cruel, greedy, and cunning foster mother. Why do some people break and others survive to achieve a full life? Fish has no answers for anyone but himself, and he shares his journey with the reader, mingling his memories and reflections with case file reports of the 13 social workers and two psychological examiners who were charged with his well-being.

> *To me, these children my own age seem new somehow . . . I don't feel new. My body feels old, weathered before its time, like tires on a car that's been driven too much in too short a period of time.* (p. 143)

Keywords: child abuse • coming of age • foster children • homeless people • military life • screenwriters

Hurston, Zora Neale.

Dust Tracks on a Road. **The restored text established by the Library of America. With a foreword by Maya Angelou. New York: Harper Perennial/HarperCollins, 1996. ISBN 0-06-092168pa. 308p. (Text originally published J.B. Lippincott, 1942.)**

An imaginative and truthful telling of her life or a reconstructed story designed for commercial success with white audiences? Either way, Hurston's sprightly prose, sense of self, and wry humor create an entertaining and thought-provoking read. Part life story, part folk tale, part personal observation, and part political philosophy, *Dust Tracks* describes the evolution of the feisty, intelligent child of an unhappy home to an accomplished woman of warmth and determination. The book includes a foreword by Maya Angelou, an afterword by Henry Louis Gates Jr., a selected bibliography, and a chronology.

> *It seems to me that trying to live without friends, is like milking a bear to get cream for your morning coffee. It is a whole lot of trouble, and then not worth much after you get it.* (p. 202)

Notes: Zora Neale Hurston is also listed in the "Classic Stories" section of Chapter 9.

Keywords: anthropology and anthropologists • folklore • personal identity • racial identity

Màjozo, Estella Conwill.

Come Out the Wilderness: Memoir of a Black Woman Artist. **The Cross-Cultural Memoir Series. New York: Feminist Press at the City University of New York, 1999. ISBN 1-55861-206-8. 241p.**

Màjozo spends her life looking for meaning. What does it mean to be Catholic, black, divorced, a woman, a wife, a mother, a poet, a teacher? In this spiritual autobiography, she traces her search with all of its physical and emotional pitfalls, from the physical agony of childbirth and the anguish of an indifferent church to eventual triumph. Included are 10 pages of black-and-white photographs.

> *I was that part of the Catholic Church that will not go away, the woman of it, and the Black of it, and the divorced of it, and the human of it, that stands open-eyed, signifying and waiting at the jump-rope railings.* (p. 192)

Keywords: Catholicism • educators • feminism and feminists • Harlem • husbands and wives • men and women • performance artists • poets

McBride, James.

The Color of Water: A Black Man's Tribute to His White Mother. **New York: Riverhead Books. 1996. ISBN 1-57322-022-1. 233p.**

Ruth Shilsky, rabbi's daughter, teenage runaway, and twice-widowed mother of 12 children survives incest, ghetto neighborhoods, racism, poverty, and sorrow to instill in her children a sense of pride, love of life, and need for accomplishment.

In this dual coming-of-age story, McBride lets his wonderfully fallible, feisty, exasperating, vulnerable, and indomitable mother come vividly to life in her own words.

> *The nuts and bolts of raising us was left to Mommy, who acted as chief surgeon for bruises ("Put iodine on it"), war secretary ("If somebody hits you, take your fist and crack 'em"), religious consultant ("Put God first"), chief psychologist ("Don't think about it"), and financial adviser ("What's money if your mind is empty?"). (p. 6)*

Notes: James McBride is also listed in the "World War I and World War II, 1900–1949" section of Chapter 6.
ALA Notable Book 1997

Keywords: family relationships • interracial relationships • mixed-race children

McCall, Nathan.

Makes Me Wanna Holler: A Young Black Man in America. **New York: Random House, 1994. ISBN 0-679-74070-8pa. 416p.**

After an adolescence filled with violence, rape, robbery, and drugs, McCall is sentenced to prison, where he decides to take control of his life. Although he becomes a respected journalist, his life is plagued by hostile working environments and a failed marriage. This novel is graphic in descriptions of violence and uses authentic but obscene street language.

> *I didn't even know him and I hated the hell out of him. Instinctively, I sensed he was an Uncle Tom, one of those head-scratching niggers, willing to put his devalued life on the line to protect the white man's property. (p.139)*

Notes: Blackboard Bestseller List 1994, 1995, 1996, 1997.

Keywords: *Atlanta Journal-Constitution* • black men and society • hostile work environment • journalism and journalists • prison life • racial discrimination • *Washington Post*

Miller, E. Ethelbert.

Fathering Words: The Making of an African American Writer. **New York: St. Martin's Press, 2000. ISBN 0-312-24136-4. 178p.**

As much a series of brief essays as an autobiography, *Fathering* tells the life stories that are "too deep and heavy for poems." In his attempt to know his father, his brother, and himself, poet Ethelbert ponders the paradox of the power and inadequacy of words. In a work full of vivid imagery and emotion, he gives a picture of life and love that words sometimes cannot express.

> *It doesn't matter how old I am, his words will find a place in*
> *the cuff of my pants, in the corner of my coat pocket, or as I*
> *turn a corner on a cold winter afternoon and turn my collar*
> *up. My father is blowing down my neck.* (p. 31)

Keywords: brothers • family relationships • fathers and sons • men and women • personal identity • poets

Nelson, Jill.

 Volunteer Slavery: My Authentic Negro Experience. **New York: Penguin Books, 1993. ISBN 0-1402-3716-X pa. 244p.**

Nelson, the first black woman to write for *The Washington Post,* is sometimes angry, sometimes wry, sometimes bemused, but always entertaining in recounting the story of her life and professional career and the compromises it takes to succeed.

> *There is a thin line between Uncle Tomming and*
> *Mau-Mauing. To fall off that line can mean disaster.* (p. 10)

Notes: American Book Award 1994

Keywords: hostile work environment • journalism and journalists • racial discrimination • Washington, D.C. • *Washington Post*

Staples, Brent.

 Parallel Time: Growing Up in Black and White. **New York: Pantheon Books, 1994. ISBN 0-679-42154-8. 274p.**

This highly personal, often angry, life story of a man who is not at home in either the black or white worlds begins and ends with the violent death of Staples's brother. We learn that the power of education and perseverance leads to professional success, but sometimes at the cost of close family relationships.

> *These were what I'd come to call The Real Negro ques-*
> *tions. He wanted to know if I was a Faux, Chevy Chase,*
> *Maryland, Negro or an authentic nigger who grew up poor*
> *in the ghetto besieged by crime and violence. White people*
> *preferred the latter.* (p. 259)

Notes: Anisfield-Wolff Book Award 1995

Keywords: black men and society • black on black crime • criminal justice system • family relationships • journalism and journalists • race relations

Walker, Rebecca.

Black, White, and Jewish: Autobiography of a Shifting Self. **New York: Riverhead Books/Penguin Putnam, 2001. ISBN 1-57322-169-4. 320p.**

What happens to a "movement child" when her white Jewish father and her black feminist mother go their separate ways? This is the simple and evocative story of a child who grows to womanhood searching for a place to belong.

Now as I move from place to place, from Jewish to black, from D.C. to San Francisco, from status quo middle class to radical artist bohemia, it is less like jumping from station to station on the same radio dial and more like moving from planet to planet be-tween universes that never overlap. (p. 115)

Keywords: coming of age • interracial relationships • mixed-race children • self-awareness

Watkins, Mel.

Dancing with Strangers: A Memoir. **New York: Simon & Schuster, 1998. ISBN 0-684-80864-1. 320p.**

Mel Watkins describes his development in the 1950s and 1960s from an innocent boy with an idyllic childhood to a young man forced to ac-knowledge the polite but thoroughly ingrained racism of Ohio. Sustained even after her death by his grandmother's special love, sage advice, and folklore, he learns the importance of independence and personal respon-sibility while developing a growing respect for his African American culture and heritage.

Unlike the South, there were no signs indicating COLORED ONLY or WHITE ONLY. It wasn't nec-essary. As if by some silent edict, everyone knew his place, knew also that he was expected to stay in it. (p. 143)

Keywords: coming of age • editors • family relationships • race relations • writ-ers • Youngstown, Ohio

Young, Yolanda.

On Our Way to Beautiful: A Family Memoir. **New York: Villard/Random House, 2002. ISBN 0-375-50493-1. 213p.**

From frying her hair to (unsuccessfully) becoming a preppy, columnist Yolanda Young shares a delightful coming-of-age story in which she learns that being beautiful on the outside means growing in grace and beauty on the inside. Sustained by her mother, "Honeymoon," and grandmother, "Big Momma," she begins to see the real meaning of faith.

Momma had only flesh wounds, so like her spirit, they quickly healed. Instead of letting my father's rage rise in her with bitterness and fear, Momma packed up those old memories like last summer's straw hats. (p. 29)

Keywords: adolescence • Christian biography • coming of age • family relation-ships • journalism and journalists • Shreveport, Louisiana • writers

Chapter 9

Mainstream Fiction

Karen Antell

Yes, the books in our canon must work as literature, but they must also reach the heart. And they must speak to communal truths.—Rodriguez, Rasbury, and Taylor (1999, 3)

Definition

At first glance, it might seem incongruous to use the term "mainstream" with regard to African American literature. After all, much African American literature is a celebration of difference—of nonconformity to mainstream white ideals of value.

But in the readers' advisory tradition, we use "mainstream" here to refer to fiction that cannot be classified into a genre, such as romance, crime, science fiction, historical, or inspirational. Any given work of mainstream fiction might employ elements of one or more genres, but mainstream fiction ultimately resists pigeonholing into such categories, which usually follow some kind of predictable formula. Mainstream fiction is popular contemporary fiction with literary aspirations—in which the voice of the storyteller becomes central to the story. In fact, "literary" and "mainstream" are terms often used interchangeably.

Pearl defines contemporary mainstream fiction as "novels set in the twentieth century that realistically explore aspects of human experience (e.g., love, hate, friendship, aging, illness, death, coming-of-age), as well as the moral and ethical decisions and choices made throughout a lifetime. Some mainstream fiction can easily be categorized in genres, but more often the book's appeal lies in such features as language, setting, character, and story or in the themes it explores" (1999, xiii).

Appeal

One of the appeals of genre fiction for many people is that although the story might be suspenseful or the plot tortuous, the reader's worldview is usually affirmed in the end. In romance fiction, for example, there is always a happy ending. In traditional mysteries, readers know the crime will be solved. It is this mixture of the expected and the unexpected that makes genre fiction so popular for entertainment or escapist reading. Mainstream fiction, on the other hand, generally challenges the reader's beliefs. "Mainstream novels aren't written strictly for escapism, nor to they exist to deliver happy endings or pat solutions" (Morrell 2002). Instead, mainstream fiction is "a piece of reality brought into sharper focus; it is life made larger than life. It asks questions, causes introspection, shakes up rules and makes them unruly" (Robyn Carr, cited by Morrell 2002).

In African American mainstream fiction, an excellent example of this is Richard Wright's *Native Son* (1940). Its protagonist, Bigger Thomas, is not exactly a sympathetic character. A small-time thief with an attitude, 20-year-old Bigger grudgingly agrees to work as driver for a wealthy family to help support his struggling mother and younger siblings. But after a series of events both in and out of his control, Bigger unwittingly smothers his employer's daughter—and then tries, ultimately unsuccessfully, to cover up his crime. Like most good mainstream fiction, *Native Son* introduces a strong element of ambiguity into Bigger's tragedy. One could argue that society is responsible for the forces of racism and poverty that both create and destroy Bigger Thomas. Or one could assert that Bigger himself is responsible for his situation; in responding to the events that happen to him, he makes poor choices almost every time—and yet it is hard not to feel some sympathy for him. This moral ambiguity is a key element of mainstream writing. It leaves readers with more questions than answers.

Native Son also epitomizes another facet of mainstream fiction. This particular novel contains many elements of the crime novel: page-turning suspense, tragedy, and insight into the mind of the criminal. But it clearly transcends the crime category; for instance, good does not triumph over evil (or perhaps even more to the point, it is impossible to pinpoint exactly who or what is good or evil in this novel). Readers looking for an escape will not find it here. Indeed, the book is likely to leave them feeling more troubled than before.

So what's the appeal of mainstream fiction? One way to articulate it is that mainstream fiction makes readers think. It stays with them long after they've put the book aside. It challenges their assumptions about the world, leaving them different somehow, either with renewed faith in their beliefs, with stronger reasons for holding them, or with their worldview changed in some subtle or dramatic way.

In comparison to genre fiction, mainstream novels' themes are far more varied, but they share a common element of grappling with universal problems. Their characters are more complex, often combining traits of good, evil, and ambivalence in one persona. And mainstream fiction's language is deeper and richer, often skillfully evoking a strong sense of personality, place, or time. It is this quality that readers refer to when they say things like, "it made me feel like I was *there*" or "I felt like I *knew* that character."

Evolution

Like all mainstream fiction, African American mainstream fiction resists easy classification. But because of African Americans' uniquely troubled history in this country, oppression and freedom are themes that emerge repeatedly in a variety of contexts and over several centuries of African American mainstream writing (Plant 1999).

Not surprisingly, much early African American writing dealt with slavery and its aftermath. But even in recent fiction, written after the Civil Rights Movement ameliorated many forms of institutionalized oppression, African American writers continually reexamine what freedom means, what obstacles to it remain, and how to achieve it—not only politically but also personally. Deborah Plant (1999) notes that in many African American novels, it is as though the shackles of slavery have not so much been removed as transformed into other physical and nonphysical barriers to freedom: stereotypes of black inferiority, inner-city life, the prison system, and de facto segregation along socioeconomic fault lines. For example, the seven women of Gloria Naylor's *The Women of Brewster Place* (1980) confront obstacles as diverse as homophobia, poverty, racism, sexism, crime, and drug addiction. These obstacles are not unique to the African American experience, but they are complicated by it in ways not always apparent to white Americans.

Even in the very act of writing, African American novelists have had to struggle for freedom from preconceived notions of what the African American novel should or should not be. The earliest African American writers conformed to prevailing literary forms and white standards of literary merit; in other words, they wrote for a mainly white reading audience. Not to do so would have meant literary death, because all aspects of the publishing world were controlled by the white elite. In fact, the first African American novel, *Clotel: Or, the President's Daughter, A Narrative of Slave Life in the United States* (1853), by William Wells Brown, was not published in its complete form until more than 100 years after its first appearance, because the publishing establishment deemed too controversial Brown's assertion that Thomas Jefferson had children with his enslaved mistresses (Rodriguez, Rasbury, and Taylor 1999, 18).

African American writers have had to contend with not only the white establishment's expectations for African American writing but also with the black community's prescriptions. During the Harlem Renaissance of the 1920s, leading African American writers began the process of forming an alternative canon, calling for "Negro" art and writing to portray "Negro folk life true in both letter and spirit to the idiom of the folk's own way of feeling and thinking" (Locke in Harris 1997, 68). The Harlem Renaissance "rightly deconstructed the idea of black people as monolithic" (Plant 1999, xvii), embracing instead the many voices, themes, and complexities of black life. On the one hand, this movement freed many writers to abandon the shackles of white literary forms. On the other hand, some excellent African American writers experienced neglect among the black literati during this time because their writing did not promote the "cause" of the "new Negro." Zora Neale Hurston, for example, chafed under the pressure to tell a story about the "race problem" rather than the story she wanted to tell (Plant 1999, xvii). (Hurston's autobiography is included in Chapter 8.)

During the 1930s and early 1940s, Marxism became fashionable among American writers of all colors, and African American novels of this time were not alone in delivering large doses of Marxist propaganda. Indeed, Wright's *Native Son* has been denounced for its "cardboard portrayal of black pathology and heavy-handed Marxist message" (Rodriguez, Rasbury, and Taylor 1999, 201). In the late 1940s and early 1950s, a younger generation of African American novelists emerged who "rejected the idea that political issues should play a role in literary expression" (Andrews, Foster, and Harris 1997, 456). During this time, two of Wright's admirers and protégés, Ralph Ellison and James Baldwin, openly distanced themselves from him and his politics. Ellison and Baldwin are often grouped together with Wright and Ann Petry, another leading novelist of this time, because their work shares Wright's and Petry's sense of bleakness and despair. However, both Wright in *Native Son* and Petry in *The Street* (1946) focus on economic barriers to black people's freedom, whereas Ellison in *Invisible Man* (1952) and Baldwin in *Go Tell It on the Mountain* (1953) operate on a more metaphysical level, describing the "alienation and the pain of existing in a world that would deny one's existence" (Plant 1999, xviii).

In the highly charged 1960s, African American writing again turned political with the rise of the Black Arts Movement. Like the contemporaneous Civil Rights and Black Power Movement, the Black Arts Movement "sought to redress the imbalance of power on all levels of American society" (Plant 1999, xviii), leading Larry Neal to assert that, "the artist and the political activist are one" (Harris 1997, 68). No one author epitomizes this approach more dramatically than LeRoi Jones/Amiri Baraka, a moving force behind the Black Arts Movement. Baraka was among the leaders when the Black Arts Movement took a global view with its presupposition of "cultural, political and spiritual unity among peoples of African descent throughout the African Diaspora" (Smith 1997, 458). (Baraka's autobiography is included in Chapter 8.) In one sense, this movement broadened the scope of African American writing, enabling it to transcend the black experience in America alone. However, some writers felt that the Black Arts Movement limited them to "a narrowly defined political and aesthetic agenda . . . . [O]nly certain styles, topics, and positions were considered authentically black" (Smith 1997, 458).

Current Themes and Trends

The reaction against the Black Arts Movement's constraints has led African American fiction since the 1970s to grow more inclusive and less political once again. In particular, the canon has expanded to accept many more women writers; works by gay, lesbian, and bisexual authors and about gay, lesbian, and bisexual themes; and novels that explore the interplay between African and non-African people and cultures. Much recent writing "challenge[s] notions of the authentic black subject" (Smith 1997, 459), leaving writers freer to create and develop their own unique literary identities and subjects.

Relationships between Men and Women

Alice Walker's *The Color Purple* is perhaps the clearest example of how a novel by a woman writer changed the African American literary landscape. Its unflinching treatment of incest and domestic abuse as forms of oppression from within the African American community made it a highly controversial book when it was first published in 1982. In particular, many readers criticized Walker's portrayal of black men—and yet this novel not only remains highly regarded 20 years after its publication, it also has paved the way for other novelists, both male and female, to examine issues of intraracial oppression. Although they do not deal with issues as harsh or profound as those explored in *The Color Purple*, Terry McMillan's *Waiting to Exhale* and Connie Briscoe's *Sisters and Lovers* follow Walker's lead in their treatment of the conflicted relations between black men and black women.

Homosexual Relationships

The Color Purple also is a pioneering work in its exploration of homosexual love. In the decades since its publication, gay, lesbian, and bisexual fiction has "come out" into the mainstream with the proliferation of novels by E. Lynn Harris, April Sinclair, Stephen Corbin, and others. In addition, many recent novels that are not explicitly "about" non-hetero themes nonetheless include gay, lesbian, and bisexual characters and issues and portray them in a sensitive and realistic manner.

Diversity

Recent African American fiction also tends to be fairly inclusive in scope, unlike some periods of literary history—particularly the Harlem Renaissance and the Black Arts Movement—during which African American writing was almost exclusively about black characters and black issues. Danzy Senna's *Caucausia* is perhaps the most striking example of this. The protagonist of this coming-of-age story, the daughter of a black man and a white woman who have divorced, navigates her identity and her emerging adulthood by defining herself in terms of both of her parents. Yet this book avoids the stereotype of the "tragic mulatto" caught between two worlds. Blackness and whiteness are part of this novel, but they are just one part among many; they are not the main poles according to which the protagonist chooses her alliances.

Selection Criteria and Scope

The titles included in this chapter are by no means a comprehensive listing of all mainstream African American novels. A number of selective bibliographies were used in choosing titles. *Sacred Fire: The QBR 100 Essential Black Books* (Rodriguez et al. 1999) provides an excellent bibliography of outstanding works. Among other useful resources are *Best Literature By and About Blacks* (Richards and Schlager 2000); *The Schomburg Center Guide to Black Literature: From the Eighteenth Century to the Present* (Valade 1996); *Contemporary African American Novelists: A Bio-Bibliographical Critical Sourcebook* (Nelson 1999). Special attention was paid to award-winning books and to works frequently included in college classes on African American literature. Although the scope of this book covers the most recent decade, this chapter includes many out-of-scope novels that have been seminal in canon formation (e.g., *The Color Purple*, *Invisible Man*, *The Bluest Eye*, *Go Tell It on the Mountain*, and *The Ways of White Folks*).

Advising the Reader

It has already been mentioned that mainstream fiction is difficult to categorize, and many of the novels included in this chapter could fit quite well into two or more of the following categories. However, the following arrangement attempts to group together stories that have similarities in terms of appeal or "feel." For works that have particularly strong ties to more than one category, a secondary appeal is listed. The following categories are used in organizing this chapter:

- **Classic Stories**. These are some of the most important works of fiction by African Americans published before 1960. These include significant "firsts": the first novel written by an African American man (*Clotel, or, The President's Daughter* by William Wells Brown) and the first written by an African American woman (*Our Nig, or, Sketches from the Life of a Free Black* by Harriet E. Wilson). Even people who usually read only current fiction are likely to enjoy some of these novels, which were chosen for their appeal as well as their relevance to today's readers.

- **Coming-of-Age Stories**. Growing up is difficult—and being black can be a blessing, a curse, or even a nonissue when it comes to carving out one's own identity and finding one's place in the world.

- **Community Stories**. Some places just have more, well, "placeness" about them than others. In these stories, a place or a community serves as an extended family or even almost as a character in its own right—sometimes nurturing, sometimes stifling, but always an important component in its inhabitants' lives.

- **Stories of Contemporary Life**. These novels have a hip, up-to-the minute feel about them. Their characters, who often speak in a breezy vernacular, are familiar people dealing with life in today's world.

- **Family Stories**. Tender, complex, or dysfunctional, "family" means different things to different people, sometimes all at once. These stories place family—for better or for worse—at the center of their characters' lives.

- **Racial and Political Issues**. These novels delve deep into questions about racism and justice and the role that these issues play in people's lives. In most of these stories, racism contributes to the destruction of a person or a community, but these works are about more than their characters or their communities. In a sense, their philosophical issues are the main characters of these books.

Classic Stories

Baldwin, James.

🎗 *Go Tell It on the Mountain*. New York: Modern Library, 1995 (1953). ISBN 0-679-60154-6. 291p.

> John Grimes, age 14, is marginalized in just about every way possible. A black boy in Harlem in the 1930s, he is ostracized for being unmanly and intellectual. Even within his own family, he is an outsider. Quiet and obedient, but almost overlooked, he is the only stepchild in a family of four children. His hypocritical

stepfather dominates the family with a mixture of religion and brutality. All the "action" of the novel takes place in one day—the day when John embraces religion in an ecstasy at an evening church service, after struggling with his many sinful urges, including (by implication) his feelings for an older teenage boy. But the novel also encompasses John's family history and, indeed, the Great Migration itself, in its account of John's parents' youth and their own secret sins.

> [H]e was able, as his teachers said, to think. But this brought him little in the way of consolation, for today he was terrified of his thoughts. He wanted to be with these boys in the street, heedless and thoughtless, wearing out his treacherous and bewildering body. (p. 30)

Notes: *Sacred Fire: The QBR 100 Essential Black Books*

Keywords: coming of age • dysfunctional families • family life • Great Migration • homosexuality • 1930s • religion • religious conversion

Brown, William Wells.

 Clotel, or, The President's Daughter. **Boston and New York: Bedford/St. Martin's Press, 2000 (1853). ISBN 0-312-22758-2. 527p.**

Originally published in 1853, *Clotel* is widely acknowledged to be the first novel by an African American author. An escaped slave himself, Brown tells the story of Currer, a concubine of Thomas Jefferson, and her daughters Clotel and Althesa, who attempt to escape slavery after being sold at auction. Along the way, readers witness many of the horrors of the slave trade: ruthless separation of families, gambling in which the stakes are human beings, and the brutal treatment of old or sick slaves. Although the style suffers somewhat from Brown's reliance on abolitionist sermons and pamphlets, the novel is valuable as a firsthand account of slavery and its effects.

> We can but blush for our country's shame when we recall to mind the fact, that while George and Mary Green, and numbers of other fugitives from American slavery, can receive protection from any of the governments of Europe, they cannot return to their native land without becoming slaves. (p. 225)

Notes: *Sacred Fire: The QBR 100 Essential Black Books*

Keywords: abolition and abolitionists • 1800s • family chronicles • slavery

Ellison, Ralph.

 Invisible Man. **New York: Quality Paperback Book Club, 1994 (1952). ISBN: none. 439p.**

At the beginning of *Invisible Man*, the nameless narrator is a favored student at a college for blacks in the South. Eager to please, he hopes that he might someday become one of the leaders of his race. He understands some of the "rules" he must follow to be a "good" black in the eyes of whites; for example, he knows he must flatter the rich white college trustee visiting from the North. However, he makes the mistake of driving the trustee through a squalid black settlement near the college, and he is expelled for this error: "The only way to please a white man is to tell him a lie! What kind of education are you getting around here?" (107). This is the beginning of his true education, in which he gradually realizes the extent of his "invisibility" in American culture. He moves to New York and becomes involved in a radical black political organization, the Brotherhood, believing that they will help bring about greater racial equality. But ultimately he realizes that he, as an individual, is invisible even to the Brotherhood, which values only conformance to the group's ideals. His descent into invisibility is accompanied by greater self-knowledge, and in the end, he lives a reclusive, "invisible" life, writing his memoirs in a secret basement room, but possessed of much more truth about the world and his station in it.

> *Whence all this passion toward conformity anyway?—diversity is the word. Let man keep his many parts and you'll have no tyrant states. Why, if they follow this conformity business they'll end up by forcing me, an invisible man, to become white, which is not a color but the lack of one. Must I strive toward colorlessness? But seriously, and without snobbery, think of what the world should lose if that should happen. America is woven of many strands; I would recognize them and let it so remain.* (p. 435)

Notes: National Book Award 1953; Russwurm Award 1953; *Sacred Fire: The QBR 100 Essential Black Books*

Keywords: coming of age • political activism and activists • race relations • racism • self-awareness

Harper, Frances Ellen Watkins.

Iola Leroy; or Shadows Uplifted. **College Park, Md.: McGrath Publishing, 1969 (1892). ISBN: None. 282p.**

Originally published in 1892, this novel (one of the first by a black American woman) personifies class and racial contradictions in the character of one woman, Iola Leroy. Although white-skinned and wealthy, Iola Leroy is discovered to have partly black parentage, and she is subsequently enslaved. However, Iola Leroy maintains her grace and charm throughout her ordeal, and after slavery is abolished, she becomes an articulate activist for the rights of women and blacks. Not appearing to be black, she has advantages that other black women do not enjoy, but the secret of her black "blood" must be negotiated when white suitors become interested in marrying her.

> *"Yes," she said to herself, "I do like him; but I can never marry him. To the man I marry my heart must be as open as the flowers to the sun. I could not accept his hand and hide from him the secret of my birth. . . . Perhaps some day I may have the courage to tell him my sad story."* (p. 111)

Keywords: abolition and abolitionists • class relations • 1800s • passing • racism • skin color • slavery

Hughes, Langston.

The Ways of White Folks **(short stories). New York: Vintage Classics, 1990 (1933). ISBN 0-679-72817-1. 255p.**

Each of these perfectly crafted stories looks at the black–white divide from a slightly different angle: sometimes tragic, sometimes funny, and always right on target. In "Cora Unashamed," a black household servant puts up with her white employers' pretensions until tragedy forces her to speak her mind—loudly and publicly. "Slave on the Block" tells the story of two ridiculous white "artists" who enjoy "Negroes" for their supposedly fresh and naïve spirit—and then are bewildered when their "Negro" household workers become fed up and quit. "Passing," short but haunting, is a letter from a mulatto man to his mother, apologizing for pretending not to know her when he sees her in public. All of the stories represent a different point of view, but all together, the picture that emerges is remarkable in its three-dimensionality and coherence.

> *"Where you been, boy?" the white fellow asked. "Paris," said Roy. "What'd yuh come back for?" a half-southern voice drawled from the edge of a baggage truck. . . . The eyes of the white men about the station were not kind. He heard some one mutter, "Nigger." His skin burned. For the first time in half a dozen years he felt his color. He was home.* (pp. 36–37)

Notes: *Sacred Fire: The QBR 100 Essential Black Books*

Keywords: passing • race relations • racism • short stories

Hurston, Zora Neale.

Jonah's Gourd Vine. **Philadelphia: J. B. Lippincott, 1971 (1934). ISBN: none. 316p.**

John Buddy Pearson is the irrepressible protagonist of this novel, set in early twentieth-century Florida. Although a successful and charismatic Baptist minister, John Buddy also maintains close ties to folkloric, non-Christian ways of behaving and knowing. His folk wisdom makes him highly appealing, but it also leads him to act in ways that offend his flock. To him, sexual exploits are just another manifestation of his vast spirit, but he almost loses his pastorate due to adultery. His wife, Lucy, helps him change his ways, but he never entirely reconciles his role as a preacher, supposedly above reproach, with his natural inclinations.

> *One little girl with bright black eyes came and stood before him, arms akimbo. She must have been a leader, for several more came and stood back of her. She looked him over boldly from his*

> *tousled brown head to his bare white feet. Then she said, "Well, folks! Where you reckon dis big yaller bee-stung nigger come from?" Everybody laughed. He felt ashamed of his bare feet for the first time in his life. How was he to know that there were colored folks that went around with their feet cramped up like white folks?* (pp. 30–31)

Notes: Zora Neal Hurston is also listed in the "Writers" section of Chapter 8.

Keywords: adultery • clergy • folklore • husbands and wives

🎗 *Their Eyes Were Watching God.* **New York: Negro Universities Press, 1965 (1937). ISBN 0-8371-1885-9. 286p.**

Their Eyes Were Watching God is one of the first African American feminist novels, and its protagonist, Janie Crawford, possesses a strength and an independence unusual for a woman of her time. Through three marriages, Janie develops her sense of self and refuses to live according to anyone's rules but her own. Married first to a property-owning farmer, Janie becomes bored and divorces him to marry a wealthy storekeeper, but this marriage is not much more fulfilling. After her second husband's death, Janie is not in a hurry to marry again—but then she meets Tea Cake and discovers a passion and fulfillment that sustain her through the challenges to come.

> *"Uh woman by herself is uh pitiful thing," she was told over and over again. "Dey needs aid and assistance. . . ." Janie laughed at these well-wishers because she knew that they knew plenty of women alone. . . . Besides she liked being lonesome for a change. This freedom was feeling fine. These men didn't represent a thing she wanted to know about.* (p. 139)

Notes: Zora Neal Hurston is also listed in the "Writers" section of Chapter 8.
Sacred Fire: The QBR 100 Essential Black Books

Keywords: black towns • divorce • Eaton, Florida • feminism and feminists • widows

Johnson, James Weldon.

Autobiography of an Ex-Colored Man. **New York: Alfred A. Knopf, 1966 (1912). ISBN: none. 211p.**

Originally published in 1912, this novel tells the fictional life story of a nameless mulatto boy who, due to his coloring, moves easily between the white world and the black world but belongs to neither. Not being of either world, he moves in and out of both worlds, eventually marrying a white woman and choosing to live as a white person. However, even having made his choice, he still feels uneasy: "I cannot repress the thought that, after all, I have chosen the lesser part, that I have sold my birthright for a mess of pottage" (p. 211)

> *And this is the dwarfing, warping, distorting influence which operates upon each and every coloured man in the United States. He is forced to take his outlook on all things, not from the view-point of a citizen, or a man, or even a human*

being, but from the view-point of a coloured man. It is wonderful to me that the race has progressed so broadly as it has, since most of its thought and all of its activity must run through the narrow neck of this one funnel. (p. 21)

Keywords: cultural identity • mulattoes • 1900s • passing • racial identity • racism

McKay, Claude.

***Home to Harlem*. Boston: Northeastern University, 1987 (1928). ISBN 1-55553-024-0. 340p.**

Home to Harlem was the first African American novel to become a true best seller, a distinction achieved mostly due to its controversial nature at the time of its publication in 1928. Jake Brown, the novel's protagonist, deserts the army during World War I and returns to Harlem, where he enjoys black culture to the fullest, including its less savory aspects: drinking, gambling, and "loose" women. In contrast to Jake, his coworker Ray is educated and has aspirations beyond working as a waiter. However, with all his ambition, Ray is miserable, whereas Jake, soaking up all the delights of Harlem, is happy. At the time of the novel's publication, many prominent black reformers were uneasy with the perception that *Home to Harlem* merely reinforced stereotypes of black laziness and primitivism, but the novel remains important for its questioning of the adoption of white middle-class ideals.

> *Going away from Harlem. . . . Harlem! How terribly Ray could hate it sometimes. Its brutality, gang rowdyism, promiscuous thickness. Its hot desires. But, oh, the rich blood-red color of it! The warm accept of its composite voice, the fruitiness of its laughter, the trailing rhythm of its "blues" and the improvised surprises of its jazz.* (p. 267)

Keywords: cultural identity • Harlem Renaissance • inner-city life and culture • racial identity

Petry, Ann.

★ ***The Street*. Boston: Beacon Press, 1974 (1946). ISBN 0-8070-6357-6. 435p.**

Lutie Johnson is a single mother of an eight-year-old son in 1940s Harlem. What she wants most is financial security—at least, the means to raise her son in a safe neighborhood, in a little house somewhere with a white picket fence. With Benjamin Franklin as her role model, she hopes that hard work will pay off and she will be able to move away from the "Street"—the ghetto that is the only home she can afford. But events conspire against her dreams, and in the end Lutie realizes that she faces the same impossible choices that have always confronted poor black women.

> *So it was a circle . . . because if you were black and you lived in New York and you could only pay so much rent, why, you had to live in a house like this one. And while you were out working to pay the rent on this stinking, rotten place, why, the street outside played nursemaid to your kid. The street did more than that. It became both mother and father and trained your kid for you, and it was an evil father and a vicious mother. (pp. 406–7)*

Notes: *Sacred Fire: The QBR 100 Essential Black Books*

Keywords: childrearing • inner-city life and culture • 1940s • poverty • single parents

Thurman, Wallace.

🎗 ***The Blacker the Berry*. Salem, N.H.: Ayer, 1987 (1929). ISBN 0-4050-1897-5. 262p.**

Originally published in 1929, this novel is one of the first to focus on intraracial prejudice, particularly with regard to color differences. Unlike most of her family, Emma Lou is "cursed" with very dark skin. However, rather than becoming more open-minded as a result of her "affliction," Emma Lou turns into more of a snob. When she goes to college, she is one of very few black students, and yet she shuns those who speak in black dialect or who dress differently from the white students. Meanwhile, those who speak mainstream English and dress "appropriately" shun Emma Lou because of her skin color. Moving to Harlem, Emma Lou hopes that she will find acceptance, but discovers that the change she needs to make is in herself.

> *Negroes always bedecked themselves and their belongings in ridiculously unbecoming colors and ornaments. It seemed to be a part of their primitive heritage which they did not seem to have sense enough to forget and deny. Black girl—white hat—red and white striped sport suit— white shoes and stockings—red roadster. The picture was complete. All Hazel needed to complete her circus-like appearance, thought Emma Lou, was to have some purple feathers stuck in her hat. (pp. 38–39)*

Notes: *Sacred Fire: The QBR 100 Essential Black Books*

Keywords: Boise, Idaho • class relations • Harlem • Harlem Renaissance • intraracial relations • Los Angeles, California • 1920s • skin color

Toomer, Jean.

🎗 ***Cane*. New York: Boni and Liveright, 1923. ISBN: none. 239p.**

Cane is not exactly a novel but rather a collection of stories or vignettes interspersed with poems. Each story introduces a different character or a different voice, but the element holding all the parts together is Toomer's poetic evocation of African American folklore, particularly from the South. *Cane* is experimental not only in its unusual format but also in its explicit treatment of controversial topics such as sexuality, interracial relationships, and slavery. Although critics still debate about *Cane*'s identity as poetry, drama, or prose, the work remains a Harlem Renaissance classic that is widely read for its lyrical treatment of its wide-ranging subject.

> *Becky had one Negro son. Who gave it to her? Damn buck nigger, said the white folks' mouths. She wouldn't tell. Common, God-forsaken, insane white shameless wench, said the white folks' mouths. . . . Who gave it to her? Low-down nigger with no self-respect, said the black folks' mouths. She wouldn't tell. Poor Catholic poor-white crazy woman, said the black folks' mouths. White folks and black folks built her cabin, fed her and her growing baby, prayed secretly to God who'd put His cross upon her and cast her out.* (p. 8)

Notes: *Sacred Fire: The QBR 100 Essential Black Books*

Keywords: drama • folklore • Harlem Renaissance • interracial relationships • 1900s • poetry • sexuality • slavery

Wilson, Harriet E.

🎗 *Our Nig, or, Sketches from the Life of a Free Black*. **New York: Random House, 1983 (1859). ISBN 0-394-53210-4. 140p.**

The full title of this novel, the first published by an African American woman, is *Our Nig, or Sketches from the Life of a Free Black, in a Two-Story White House, North. Showing That Slavery's Shadows Fall Even There*. Frado is a mulatto girl whose mother abandons her after her father's death. Taken in by a white family in the supposedly free North, Frado is nevertheless treated like a slave, educated only minimally, and grudgingly allowed to become a Christian. Although Frado grows up and leaves the household, she marries a con man who leaves her pregnant and impoverished. However, the novel ends on a positive (and autobiographical) note, as Frado decides to write her life story and hopes that its sales will support her and her child.

> *"Did the same God that made her make me?" "Yes." "Well, then, I don't like him." "Why not?" "Because he made her white, and me black. Why didn't he make us both white?" "I don't know; try to go to sleep, and you will feel better in the morning," was all the reply he could make to her knotty queries.* (p. 51)

Notes: *Sacred Fire: The QBR 100 Essential Black Books*

Keywords: antebellum North • con artists and con games • domestic workers • 1800s • mulattoes • poverty • race relations • writers

Wright, Richard.

🏅 *Native Son*. **New York: HarperPerennial, 1993 (1940). ISBN 0-06-081249-4. 594 p.**

Bigger Thomas is not a likeable character. Yet it is testimony to Wright's skill that readers may find themselves sympathetic to him as he attempts to flee an impossible situation. A sullen young man and petty thief, Bigger grudgingly accepts a job as chauffer for the Dalton family to help out his struggling family. When young Mary Dalton becomes too drunk to walk one night, Bigger carries her to her bedroom—then accidentally smothers her while trying to keep her quiet so he won't be detected in her room. His attempts to hide the body and escape suspicion lead him to yet another murder and lend elements of a crime thriller to this best-selling novel. More than this, though, *Native Son* is the story of one man's spiritual and social awakening. Ironically, it is only after killing Mary and facing death himself that Bigger realizes, for the first time in his life, that he is connected to the rest of humanity.

> *During the last two days and nights he had lived so fast and hard that it was an effort to keep it all real in his mind. So close had danger and death come that he could not feel that it was he who had undergone it all. And yet, out of it all, there remained to him a queer sense of power. He had done this. He had brought all this about.* (p. 277)

Notes: *Sacred Fire: The QBR 100 Essential Black Books*
Film by the same name, directed by Pierre Chenal and starring Richard Wright, Jean Wallace, and Gloria Madison (1950). Remake, directed by Jerome Freedman and starring Victor Love, Matt Dillon, and Elizabeth McGovern (1986).

Keywords: attorneys • Communism • criminal justice system • domestic workers • movie novels • murder • poverty • racism

Coming-of-Age Stories

Bailey-Williams, Nicole.

A Little Piece of Sky. **New York: Harlem Moon, 2002. ISBN 0-7679-1216-0. 161p.**

Song Byrd is growing up in a dysfunctional family in a blighted north Philadelphia Hispanic neighborhood. Her mother is a prostitute, her sister a drug addict, her brother a rapist. Yet her voice, which tells her own story in a series of short, lyrical chapters, somehow rises above the chaos of her surroundings and reveals her hope for a better life. With the support of a caring neighbor, Miss Olga, Song remains resilient and, in the end, triumphant.

> *The truth, or suspected truth as was the case, was too much for Oedipus to face. So he consulted the oracle for answers, just like my mother consulted the Ninth-Street fortune-teller and Sojourn asked some chick on the Psychic*

Phone Line. . . . We can never outrun our fate.
Does that mean that we never try? (pp. 81–82)

Keywords: drug addiction • family relationships • inner-city life and culture • mothers and daughters • murder

Clarke, Breena.

🏅 *River, Cross My Heart*. Boston: Little, Brown, 1999. ISBN 0-316-89998-4. 245p.

In the 1920s, when Johnnie Mae is 12 years old, she is in charge of her little sister Clara on summer days. The girls and their friends swim in the Potomac River, even though there is a sparkling new neighborhood swimming pool, because as black children they are not allowed to use it. When Johnnie Mae witnesses Clara's drowning in the Potomac River, she is racked by guilt and confusion. Everyone agrees that Johnnie Mae's efforts to rescue Clara were heroic, but she knows she should not have taken Clara to that part of the river. As Johnnie Mae and her family attempt to cope with Clara's death, Johnnie Mae must renegotiate her role in the family while growing up in racially segregated Georgetown.

> *This pool, so small in reality, but so much a symbol*
> *of the line drawn round her life by prejudice, had*
> *become an obsession. Throughout the stagnant*
> *July days, a clear but fanciful image of herself*
> *stroking lap after lap the length of the pool domi-*
> *nated Johnnie Mae's thoughts. She imagined the*
> *pale girls of the periphery gaping in surprise, not at*
> *the audacity of this colored girl using their play-*
> *ground and their pool, but at her absolute, con-*
> *summate skill.* (p. 41)

Notes: Alex Award

Keywords: death of a child • family life • Potomac River • segregation • sisters

Jackson, Brian Keith.

🏅 *The Queen of Harlem*. New York: Doubleday, 2002. ISBN 0-385-50295-8. 239p.

Coming from a life of privilege in a wealthy family, Mason feels the need to find his true identity via an "authentic" black experience. Pretending to be poor, he moves to Harlem, changes his name to "Malik," and rents a room from Carmen England, a Harlem socialite whose façade is almost as false as Mason's. But then he meets a woman who forces him to confront himself honestly and come to terms with the life he has tried to abandon.

> *I'd finally made my mark: the best-dressed bum in*
> *New York City. I stopped midstride and threw my*
> *arms up in the air, embracing my self-proclaimed*

> *title, not at all caring what another living soul thought. Free-*
> *dom.* (p. 189)

Notes: *Black Issues Book Review* Best Book 2002

Keywords: class relations • family relationships • men and women • personal identity •
upper class

Jones, Tayari.

Leaving Atlanta. **New York: Warner Books, 2002. ISBN 0-446-52830-7. 255p.**

Set during the Atlanta child murders of 1979–1980, *Leaving Atlanta* witnesses
this frightening time through the eyes of three preteen children. For Tasha,
Rodney, and Octavia, the typical schoolyard romances and politics play out
against a backdrop of mounting terror as their classmates begin to disappear and
they realize that even the strongest adults cannot protect them.

> *Jashante was missing. Somebody had snatched him. Then*
> *the next thought, that Tasha herself had brought it upon*
> *him with her hateful words. I hope the man snatches you.*
> *Asphyxiated. Decomposed. And she had meant it when*
> *she said it. Mad about ruining her coat, stinging from the*
> *laughter of her classmates, she had meant it.* (p. 72)

Keywords: Atlanta child murders of 1979–1980 • children's point of view • family life •
serial killers

Meriwether, Louise.

Daddy Was a Number Runner. **New York: Feminist Press at The City University**
of New York, 1970. ISBN 0-935312-57-9. 234p.

Twelve-year-old Francie lives in Harlem during the Depression. Like everyone
else, her family is coping with unemployment, poverty, and neighborhood crime.
But everyone "plays the numbers," gambling a nickel or a dime on lucky numbers
for a chance to win thirty dollars or more, and Francie's life is complicated by the
fact that her father is a "number runner"—the person who collects the bets and delivers the winnings. Trying to keep his illegal earnings a secret from the social
worker who delivers the relief check, facing the wrath of the local grocer when the
credit runs out, and avoiding the perverts lurking on the streets and in the movie
houses are all part of Francie's coming of age in this realistic but tender tale.

> *Almost every time I came to the show by myself he would*
> *sit next to me, hand me a dime, and start feeling me under*
> *my skirt. We never said a word to each other, he would just*
> *hand me the money and start feeling. I never let him get his*
> *hands too far inside my bloomers, though. By the time he*
> *worked his way up inside the elastic leg and got too close, I*
> *would shift my butt and he would have to start all over*
> *again, or I would change seats.* (p. 89)

Keywords: family life • gambling and gamblers • Great Depression • poverty • urban life
and culture

Pate, Alexs.

West of Rehoboth. New York: Morrow, 2001. ISBN 0-380-97679-X. 241p.

In the summer of 1962, Edward Massey and his family vacation in Rehoboth, Delaware, to escape Philadelphia's heat and gang violence. An avid reader and a fan of Agatha Christie's detective Hercule Poirot, Edward decides to solve a mystery in his own family—figuring out the real identity of the strange, secretive man known as "uncle" Rufus, whom his mother warns him to stay away from. Edward disobeys his mother and places himself in danger, but he succeeds in finding out the reticent Rufus's story—and takes a step toward maturity himself.

> *Edward thought back to a case of his mentor, Poirot. It was a situation where a woman had participated in the murder of her brutal husband. . . . But of course Poirot caught them. And yet, because he sympathized with the woman . . . he looked the other way. He determined justice. . . . Edward felt the same way about Rufus.* (p. 237)

Notes: BCALA Fiction Honor Book 2002

Keywords: alcohol abuse and alcoholics • gangs and gangsters • middle class

Sinclair, April.

Coffee Will Make You Black. New York: Hyperion, 1994. ISBN 1-56282-796-0. 239p.

Growing up on Chicago's South Side in the 1960s, Stevie's dream is to be cool and popular—but her first boyfriend's contemptible behavior makes her question whether being popular is worth the price. Chafing under her mother's rules, exploring her sexual identity, and questioning the racial roles of her day, Stevie negotiates her own coming of age against the backdrop of the 1960s cultural upheavals.

> *Now I just sat in the swing and let it rock me gently back and forth. . . . I felt somebody's hands pushing up against my back. I started moving forward and I grabbed onto the swing's chains. I turned around. I couldn't believe it: Yusef Brown was pushing me! I liked the way his hands felt against my back. And the rubber swing felt good up under my butt.* (p. 83)

Notes: Blackboard Bestseller List 1994, 1995, 1996, 1997

Keywords: Civil Rights Movement • racial identity • racism • sexuality

Smith, Mary Burnett.

Miss Ophelia. New York: Morrow, 1997. ISBN 0-688-15234-1. 277p.

Told from the point of view of Belly Anderson, an 11-year-old girl living in rural Virginia in 1948, this novel captures perfectly the perspective of an adolescent. Sent to another town for the summer to take care of an unpleasant aunt, Belly meets Miss Ophelia, a piano teacher from whom Belly learns a great deal about getting along—happily—in the world. Belly learns from other people as well, and some of the lessons involve adult matters such as teen pregnancy and adultery, but Miss Ophelia's example serves to guide Belly through this trying time, and she emerges older and more centered, ready for the next phase of growing up.

> *There are moments in our lives that never pass from our memory. They reside in the recesses of our minds to be brought to life by a song, a word, or a quiet moment in a sunlit garden; we pause and close our eyes and see ourselves in a dream grown hazy with the passage of time, forever residing in our hearts. So is my memory of that afternoon in Miss Ophelia's garden.* (p. 209)

Keywords: abortion • adultery • children's point of view • teen pregnancy

Trice, Dawn Turner.

Only Twice I've Wished for Heaven. **New York: Crown, 1996. ISBN 0-517-70428-5. 304p.**

When Tempestt Rose Saville is 11 years old, her family moves from its working-class Chicago neighborhood to Lakeland, a gated oasis for wealthy black people. Tempestt hates Lakeland immediately and escapes as often as possible to 35th Street, the ghetto just outside Lakeland's tall fences, where she is mesmerized by the street life: sidewalk preachers, liquor stores, night life. Tempestt meets Miss Jonetta, a liquor store owner who is the living history of the neighborhood, and befriends Valerie, a troubled girl who lives in Lakeland with her janitor brother but whose roots are in 35th Street. By the end of this coming-of-age tale, Tempestt gets what she wanted all along—her family leaves Lakeland—but only after witnessing unspeakable tragedy.

> *I thought about . . . how sometimes when his father would come home from work, yelling and screaming at him, we would meet in the middle and wait for a train to rumble through. Then we would scream out swear words at his father. We'd curse him until the train passed and fragments of bad words shook loose from the steel beams and concrete supports, echoing off broken glass and the leaning back porches of old people too poor to move away from the tracks.* (p. 26)

Notes: Alex Award 1998; BCALA Fiction Honor Book 1998

Keywords: class relations • family relationships • inner-city life and culture • intraracial relations

Verdelle, A. J.

The Good Negress. **Chapel Hill, N.C.: Algonquin Books, 1995. ISBN 1-56512-085-X. 298p.**

In the 1960s, at age 12, Neesey Palms is uprooted from her life with her grandmother in Virginia to Detroit, where her pregnant mother, stepfather, and two older brothers need help around the house. Neesey attends school for a while in Detroit, where a teacher recognizes her talent and tries to mentor her, particularly by improving her mastery of English. But after the baby arrives, Neesey is needed at home so her mother can work. However, Neesey keeps up with her school work even while absent, writing and looking up words while the baby naps. As her grammar improves, so does her sense of self—so that in the end, Neesey finds a way to enter the "bigger world" that her teacher has told her about.

> *I filled a composition book a month studying on my own. The thick pages with my handwriting gave me something to show myself for my days. Missus Pearson said that it was my not knowing the English language that cut me off from a bigger world. But it was Margarete's baby that kept me in the house, that cut me off from outdoors, even.* (p. 192)

Notes: BCALA Fiction Honor Book 1996; Blackboard Bestseller List 1995, 1996

Keywords: domestic workers • educators • family relationships • mothers and daughters

Community Stories

Bambara, Toni Cade.

The Salt Eaters. **New York: Random House, 1980. ISBN 0-394-50712-6. 295p.**

This multilayered novel is not light reading, but that's not surprising for a book this ambitious. Weaving together social activism, history, community, and mental and physical health, *The Salt Eaters* tells the concentric stories of an individual and of a town. Velma Henry is attempting to recover from a suicide attempt, and the faith healers of Claybourne are attempting to discover the healing properties of salt. But it is not clear that Velma—or Claybourne—is ready for the responsibility of being well.

> *Are you sure, sweetheart, that you want to be well? . . . I'm just asking is all," Minnie Ransom was saying, playfully pulling at her lower lip till three difference shades of purple showed. Take away the*

> *miseries and you take away some folks' reason for living."*
> (p. 15-16)

Notes: American Book Award 1981; Medallion Award 1986; Zora Neale Hurston Society Award 1986

Keywords: healers and healing • people with mental illness • small-town life and culture • social activists and activism

Kenan, Randall.

🎗 *Let the Dead Bury Their Dead*. **New York: Harcourt Brace Jovanovich, 1992. ISBN 0-15-149886-5. 334p.**

This collection of stories deals with an assortment of characters—funny and tragic, black and white, rich and poor, simple and sophisticated—but the setting of Tims Creek, North Carolina, unites them all. Drawing on folk tradition, several of the stories involve the supernatural; communications with ghosts and angels do not particularly surprise some of Kenan's characters. But superstition resides comfortably alongside modern themes in these stories. One rural woman tries hard to come to terms with her grandson's homosexuality; another slowly loses her mind and commits infanticide. Richly drawn characters and a strong sense of place make these stories highly memorable.

> *As for Francis, oddly enough Wilma Jones stopped proclaiming the hog's oracular powers and eventually butchered him. But at the last minute, with the poor thing roasting over a pit, Wilma had a crisis of conscience and couldn't eat it; so she gave it a semi-Christian burial with a graveside choir and a minister and pallbearers, all made hungry by the scent of barbecue. (p. 23)*

Notes: Whiting Award 1994

Keywords: family relationships • short stories • small-town life and culture • supernatural

McFadden, Bernice.

🎗 *Sugar*. **New York: Dutton, 2000. ISBN 0-525-94531-8. 229p.**

Sugar is the story of two women from very different worlds who meet in a small black town in the 1950s. Pearl embodies all the stereotypes of the "good wife"—she is quiet, unassuming, dependable, involved in the local church. Since the brutal murder of her daughter years ago, Pearl is also sexually dysfunctional. When Sugar arrives in town, the preacher asks Pearl to "bring her into the fold." But Sugar is everything that the other local women are not—brazen, single, sexually provocative. Even before they realize she is a prostitute, the local women shun Sugar—all except Pearl, that is. Something about Sugar reminds Pearl of her dead daughter, and as the two women become friends, the truth about Sugar's past emerges.

> *"Why you gotta dress like that for?" Pearl continued, her tone becoming more spiteful. "Why you dress like that?" Sugar was mocking her now. Pearl let out a heavy sigh.*

> *She stared at Sugar's neck, at the thick scar that*
> *healed ugly and crooked like a dead tree branch.*
> *She stared at the false hair that adorned her head,*
> *at the skimpy T-shirt and tiny shorts that molded to*
> *her body like second skin instead of cloth. Who else*
> *other than a whore would dress this way?* (p. 89)

Notes: BCALA Fiction Honor Book 2000; Blackboard Bestseller List 2000; Go On Girl Book Club Award 2000

Keywords: Bigelow, Arkansas • black towns • death of a child • murder • prostitutes and prostitution • sexual dysfunction • small-town life and culture

Naylor, Gloria.

 The Women of Brewster Place. **New York: Penguin Books, 1980, 1982. ISBN 0-14-006690-X. 192p.**

Subtitled "a novel in seven stories," this book traces the lives of seven women—Cora Lee, Etta Mae Johnson, Kiswana Browne, Lorraine, Lucielia Louise Turner (Ciel), Mattie Michael, Theresa—who find themselves living at Brewster Place, a group of run-down buildings on a street walled off from the rest of the city. Although they follow different paths to Brewster Place, they transcend their separate sorrows and develop the courage born of community—finally emerging triumphant over fate.

> *"It broke my heart when you changed your name. I*
> *gave you my grandmother's name, a woman who*
> *bore nine children and educated them all, who held*
> *off six white men with a shotgun when they tried to*
> *drag one of her sons to jail for 'not knowing his*
> *place.' Yet you needed to reach into an African dic-*
> *tionary to find a name to make you proud."* (p. 86)

Notes: American Book Award for Best First Novel 1983; *Sacred Fire: The QBR 100 Essential Black Books*
Television movie by the same name, directed by Donna Dietch and starring Oprah Winfrey (1989).

Keywords: housing projects • inner-city life and culture • movie novels • political activism and activists • poverty • women's friendships

Rainey, John Calvin.

 The Thang That Ate My Grandaddy's Dog. **Sarasota, Fla: Pineapple Press, 1997. ISBN 1-56164-130-8. 360p.**

This novel is really a series of intertwined stories with a strong sense of place and an even stronger sense of family. Set in the swampland of Florida, most of the tales are narrated by Johnny Woodside, a boy transplanted from New York City to live with his extended family. Johnny and his many cousins grow up exploring the secrets of the swamp and the even deeper secrets of kinship, ultimately learning that nothing—and no one—is completely good or completely evil.

> *What I learned about my mother is that I would never quite be a man to her. I would never quite outgrow the child. I would always feel her presence and she would always be watching. No matter where I was, Manasha would be watching. . . . Not God—Manasha! God could not be everywhere at once, so he sent Manasha.* (p. 352)

Notes: BCALA Fiction Honor Book 1998

Keywords: family chronicles • family relationships • folklore • humor • interracial relationships • short stories

Wideman, John Edgar.

John Edgar Wideman is a 1992 MacArthur Fellow.

Damballah **(in** *The Homewood Books***, collection of three novels). Pittsburgh: University of Pittsburgh Press, 1992. ISBN 0-8050-1184-6. 520p.**

This series of interrelated tales tells the story of one vast extended family in the Homewood neighborhood of Pittsburgh. Former slaves Sybela Owens and Charlie Bell are founders of the neighborhood in the 1860s when they arrive from the South, and they soon populate the neighborhood by having 20 children. The stories of their descendants, both tragic and triumphant, evoke a strong sense of place and an even stronger sense of family history.

> *Yes, she wants to scream. Of course he's dead. . . . She had heard him fall all the way from the kitchen and flew up the steps two and three at a time getting to him. . . . It was Fred Clark who came first. Who helped her drag John French from between the toilet and the tub that was always bumping his knees. . . . Someone always comes . . . Homewood people are good about coming. And they're best about coming around when there's nothing they can do.* (p. 69)

Notes: John Edgar Wideman is also listed in the "Stories of Contemporary Life" section of this chapter and the "World War I and World War II: 1901–1949" section of Chapter 6.
Sacred Fire: The QBR 100 Essential Black Books

Keywords: family chronicles • family relationships • short stories • slavery

Stories of Contemporary Life

Adams, Jenoyne.

Selah's Bed. **New York: Free Press, 2003. ISBN 0-684-87353-2. 239p.**

Raped at age 13, impregnated and abandoned at age 19, Selah learns that sex is powerful. Selah aborts her baby and marries, learning to wield sex with other men as a means of gaining power over them—and over her husband. But when she meets a man with whom she can be honest, she realizes that she will not heal completely until she comes to terms with her abortion and the baby she never had.

> I killed you in my womb for reasons I thought were strong enough to take another's life. I thought you were going to take mine. I thought that with you I would have been destined to relive the lives of my mother and my grandmother. I thought you would bury me under the smell of your bottled milk and diaper changes. I convinced myself of this, and I missed you every moment afterward. (p. 231)

Keywords: abortion • adultery • grandmothers and granddaughters • husbands and wives • photographers • rape • sexuality

Briscoe, Connie.

Big Girls Don't Cry. New York: HarperCollins, 1996. ISBN 0-06-017277-0. 375p.

Growing up in the 1960s in Washington, D.C., Naomi Jefferson is a quiet child who likes to read and sew, preferring to leave the "showing off" to her talented older brother, Joshua. But when Joshua is killed in a suspicious accident on his way to a civil rights demonstration, Naomi discovers in herself a passion for activism that defies her former self-image. Although this passion leads her down the wayward paths of drug use and disappointing relationships, Naomi eventually finds her own way to honor her dead brother and fulfill her own ambitions.

> No matter how well she did, Joshua always did better. She had long ago decided never to try to compete with him or anybody else if she could help it, unless she was pretty sure she would come out on top. That meant keeping to herself a lot, but it worked for her. (p. 6)

Notes: Blackboard Bestseller List 1996, 1997

Keywords: brothers and sisters • Civil Rights Movement • drug addiction • family relationships • love affairs • men and women • politics and politicians • race relations • sexism

Sisters and Lovers. New York: HarperCollins, 1994. ISBN 0-06-017116-2. 339p.

Sisters Beverly, Charmaine, and Evelyn lead very different lives. Beverly is single and disappointed by a string of boyfriends. Charmaine is struggling to work, raise a son, and support her good-for-nothing husband. Evelyn is a therapist with two children and a successful husband—but even her seemingly perfect world is starting to fall apart. Repeatedly betrayed by the men in their lives, the three women find that even with their differences, sisterhood gives them more of what they need than men do.

> *Clarence was wearing her out. While she worked her tail off trying to get ahead, he seemed to put in double time trying to knock her back. Well, she wasn't putting up with this shit one more day. This time she meant it. Wherever he was now, she hoped he was having the time of his life, 'cause it was the last time he was getting over on her. Tomorrow— no, tonight—his ass was going to be out on the street.* (p. 282)

Notes: Blackboard Bestseller List 1994, 1995, 1996, 1997; Go On Girl Book Club New Author of the Year 1995

Keywords: husbands and wives • men and women • sisters

Brown, Parry.

 The Shirt Off His Back. New York: Striver's Row/Villard, 2001. ISBN 0-375-75659-0. 237p.

Terry Winston is the single father of 10-year-old twins Alisa and Ariana, whose wealthy mother has had little contact with them since their birth. A man of character and a doting father, Terry is fortunate to have good friends and a devoted extended family, not to mention a tender and stable relationship with a woman he hopes to marry, herself a single mother of twins. But the secure world Terry has carefully created for himself and his daughters threatens to crumble when the girls' mother suddenly sues for custody. The legal battle that ensues pits love and devotion against wealth and deceit, but throughout it all, Terry remains steadfast in his love for his children and his dedication to doing the right thing.

> *She had asked the dreaded Do-I-look-like-I-have-gained-weight-to-you? question—the question to which any man will tell you there is no correct answer. But Terry simply replied, "Baby, if you have, I love every ounce of it, and damn, you wear it well."* (p. 95)

Notes: Blackboard Bestseller List 1999, 2000; *Essence* Bestseller List 2003, 2004

Keywords: child custody • childrearing • fathers and daughters • men and women • single parents

Campbell, Bebe Moore.

 Singing in the Comeback Choir. New York: Putnam, 1998. ISBN 0-399-14298-3. 372p.

This is a novel about second chances. Maxine McCoy, a successful television producer in Los Angeles, is pregnant again after a miscarriage. She is also trying hard to trust her husband, Satchel, who is truly repentant after having once gone astray. And she is helping her grandmother, a former singer who raised Maxine after her mother's death, become independent again after a mild stroke. Even the Philadelphia neighborhood where Maxine grew up is undergoing a renewal of sorts. But perhaps the most important second chance in this novel is Maxine's need to trust again—and it looks as though she might make it this time around.

> *"You looked at me the way your mother did once. . . .*
> *I was playing at a little club in South Philly. It wasn't*
> *very nice, didn't even have a dressing room. I was*
> *changing in the ladies' room, which was sticking,*
> *and she came in. She looked at me and then*
> *looked around and then back at me. Never opened*
> *her mouth, but her eyes were saying that I was*
> *wasting my life."* (p. 234)

Notes: Bebe Campbell Moore is also listed in the "Racial and Political Issues" section of this chapter.
Blackboard Bestseller List 1998, 1999

Keywords: adultery • alcohol abuse and alcoholics • family relationships • grandmothers and granddaughters • men and women • pregnancy

Cleage, Pearl.

I Wish I Had a Red Dress. **New York: Morrow, 2001. ISBN 0-380-97733-8. 323p.**

Joyce Mitchell, a forty-something social worker in the black community of Idlewild, Michigan, runs a program called The Sewing Circus that, in her own words, helps young women (mostly single mothers) develop into "free women." Despite numerous tragedies in her life, including the death of her beloved husband, Joyce remains a shining example of positive living, and her very full life is missing only one thing—someone to share it with. But when she meets Nate, a newcomer in town, things change in a way she never counted on.

> *I wanted to look sexy without being obvious;*
> *age-appropriate but not dowdy; sensual but not*
> *slutty. . . . I was rewarded with the sight of myself*
> *looking exactly like who I was: a free woman with a*
> *gentleman caller.* (p. 267)

Notes: BCALA Literary Award for Fiction 2002; *Essence* Bestseller List 2002

Keywords: rape • small-town life and culture • social workers • teen mothers • widows

What Looks Like Crazy on an Ordinary Day. **New York: Avon, 1997. ISBN 0-380-97584-X. 244p.**

Cleage takes the raw materials of tragedy—illness, widowhood, addiction, violence—and forms from them a story that somehow is funny without making light of its subjects. Ava Johnson doesn't intend to stay long when she returns from Atlanta to her tiny hometown of Idlewild, Michigan. Newly HIV-positive, Ava has sold her beauty shop and come home to visit her widowed sister Joyce before moving on to San Francisco. But home looks different this time around. Joyce is the kind of person everyone turns to in a crisis, and Idlewild is no longer the sleepy little town Ava remembered. Big-city problems have arrived, and before long, Ava is helping Joyce raise a crack addict's baby and run an outreach group for teen mothers. And, surprising even herself, she is falling in love.

> *I knew there was going to be trouble when Joyce came home with four packages of juicy jumbo hot dogs and six boxes of latex condoms, but I don't think any of us had any idea how much trouble until Gerry walked into the fellowship hall and saw Aretha unrolling a very slippery lubricated condom over a jumbo juicy that, to facilitate matters, had been mounted straight up on a chopstick like a hard-on from hell.* (p. 158)

Notes: Go On Girl Book Club Award 1999

Keywords: drug addiction • HIV/AIDS • sisters • small-town life and culture • teen mothers

Some Things I Thought I'd Never Do. **New York: One World, 2003. ISBN 0-345-45606-8. 274p.**

Regina never thought she would work for Beth Davis again, not after Beth broke up Regina's planned marriage to Beth's son. But after months of rehab, near-bankruptcy, and the son's death in New York on September 11, Regina takes on the job of donating the son's papers to Morehouse College in Atlanta. Besides providing some much-needed income, the move to Atlanta changes Regina's life in ways she never thought possible.

> *I felt like I had fallen through the rabbit hole and come out into a peaceful place filled with thriving black businesses, industrious black men, a twenty-four-hour beauty shop, and a blue-eyed gangster with a house painter who likes Bob Marley.* (p. 32)

Keywords: blues music and musicians • drug addiction • men and women • September 11, 2001 • women's friendships

Corbin, Stephen.

Fragments That Remain. **Boston: Alyson Publications, 1993. ISBN 1-55583-218-0. 317p.**

This novel is about racism, homophobia, family dysfunction, and the skin color prejudices within the black community. For all that, it is also a novel about Skylar, a gay black actor involved with white lover. Told in turns from multiple points of view—Skylar's, his parents', his brother's, his lover's—the narrative brings to the foreground the many biases and tensions that underlie the characters' multifaceted relationships with one another. On one hand, the novel highlights the difficulty of achieving true intimacy when burdened with so much emotional baggage. Yet in the words of Charles Harmon in *Booklist*, *Fragments*

That Remain also "strips away layer after layer of unconscious yet learned predisposition so that his characters can find both peace and understanding."

> The most liberal, least homophobic people didn't place a gay relationship on the same level as a straight one. Aside from the obvious differences, many of the dynamics were incredibly similar, far more than straights were willing to admit. But somehow one was legitimate, the other wasn't. Some part of his relationship with Evan was forever being denied and discredited and attacked by someone. And they weren't always straight people. . . . he and Evan had gotten the most disparaging stares and challenges from the gay community. (p. 102)

Keywords: actors and actresses • dysfunctional families • family relationships • gay men • homophobia • interracial relationships • skin color

Dickey, Eric Jerome.

Liar's Game. **New York: Dutton, 2000. ISBN 0-525-94483-4. 327p.**

Vince Browne and Dana Ann Smith are both starting over in Los Angeles in their late twenties—Vince after his marriage has gone sour and his ex has taken his daughter out of the country, Dana after a disastrous relationship and a move from New York. Although they are both ready to make a fresh start when they meet, they each hold back part of their pasts from each other. One lie leads to another and before long, they have fallen in love not with each other, but with the façades each has created for the other's benefit. But when their former lovers turn up in L.A., the truth about the past starts to emerge, and Vince and Dana must try to build a new relationship rooted in reality. Told from both points of view, this novel portrays characters who are not always likeable but seem refreshingly real.

> An anxious dick, misplaced romance, and some misguided sperm have changed many a man's plans. Made him wake up every day wishing he could turn back the hands of time. Which proved that there's no such thing as free sex, only delayed payments. (p. 61)

Notes: Blackboard Bestseller List 2000; *Essence* Bestseller List 2001

Keywords: absentee parents • divorce • love affairs • men and women

Harris, E. Lynn.

A Love of My Own. **New York: Doubleday, 2002. ISBN 0-385-49270-7. 386p.**

When Raymond Tyler and Zola meet, they are both fresh from recent breakups. Living the fast-paced lifestyle of hip, successful African Americans in the publishing business in New York, they have to negotiate their pasts and their schedules to find a way to connect. But the September 11 attacks and the reappearance of Raymond's ex-lover cause them both to reflect on their priorities, bringing about a beneficial change of perspective.

> *After I got off the phone, I checked my e-mails. The first one was from the corporate office, about how Davis and Veronica had given five million dollars to the 9/11 relief fund. I was impressed, but I thought both Davis and Veronica probably spent just as large a sum of money on a stylist to pick out the right outfit when they posed for the cameras.* (p. 170)

Notes: *Black Issues Book Review* Best Book 2002; *Essence* Bestseller List 2002, 2003; NAACP Image Award Nominee 2003

Keywords: bisexuality • men and women • September 11, 2001

Invisible Life: A Novel. New York: Anchor Books, 1994. ISBN 0-385-46968-3. 268p.

Raymond Tyler is a buppie lawyer: smart, successful, attractive—and secretly bisexual. Torn between shame and desire, he divides his time between his mainstream life and his "invisible life." But when his ex-lover infects a young woman with HIV, Raymond can no longer live with his secret. Like earlier generations of African Americans who confronted the issue of passing for white, Raymond confronts and ultimately rejects the option of passing for straight.

> *I was overcome with a tremendous amount of guilt regarding Candace's death. I was part of a secret society that was endangering black women like Candance to protect our secret desires.* (pp. 253–54)

Notes: Blackboard Bestseller List 1994, 1995, 1996, 1997, 1999

Keywords: attorneys • bisexuality • buppies • family relationships • HIV/AIDS • sexual identity

Hill, Donna.

If I Could. New York: Kensington Books, 2000. 1-575-66597-2. 245p.

Everyone agrees that Regina got lucky with Russell, her wealthy, handsome, caring husband—everyone except Regina, that is. Despite Regina's talent in her professional life as a journalist, Russell believes her main job should be taking care of the children and the house. When she can no longer pretend she is happy, Regina divorces Russell and even quits her beloved job. Although at first she can't articulate what is driving her to shed the relics of her predictable life, Regina gradually realizes that it is time for her to work on herself. Nearing middle age, and regardless of her friends' and family's reservations, she embarks on a new career and finds a different kind of love—this time, according to her own rules.

She plopped down spread-eagled on the bed, a smile beaming across her face. What to do first? she mused. Well, she had time, that was for sure, and she certainly had some money. Then it dawned on her, clear as crystal. . . . She'd work on herself, inside and out. And when she was ready for the next step, whatever that might be, she'd take it. (p. 78)

Keywords: family life • men and women • midlife crisis • professionals • women's friendships

Jackson, Sheneska.

★ *Li'l Mama's Rules.* **New York: Simon & Schuster, 1997. ISBN 0-684-81842-6. 269p.**

Madison McGuire, a.k.a. "Li'l Mama," is a successful 30-year-old teacher at a fancy private school for black children. Abandoned as a child by her father, she remains unable to develop trusting relationships with men, as evidenced by her ever-growing list of "rules for dating." Both funny and sad, the rules serve to protect Madison from entering into a committed relationship. But when she learns she is HIV-positive, Madison is forced to reexamine and ultimately change some of her rules, confront her father, and ultimately make room in her life for the relationships that really matter.

But like I said before, men have always been my weakness, and here is my dilemma: Terrence is fine. This is a fact. But Terrence is an asshole. This too is a fact. Then again, I haven't had sex in, oh, two, three weeks. Major fact. So, what do I do? Stick to my dating rules or get my freak on? Decisions, decisions. (p. 36)

Notes: Blackboard Bestseller List 1997, 1998

Keywords: educators • fathers and daughters • HIV/AIDS • men and women

Joe, Yolanda.

★ *He Say, She Say.* **New York: Doubleday, 1996. ISBN 0-385-48507-7. 262p.**

Breezy and contemporary, this novel is told alternately in the four voices of its main characters: Sandra Mae "Sandy" Atkins, 25 years old and worried about finding a good man, given the publicized "shortage" of African American men; Beatrice Mae "Bebe" Thomas, Sandy's somewhat older and wiser confidante; Timothy James "T. J." Willet Jr., a talented jazz musician and the object of Sandy's affections; and Speed, T. J.'s father and mentor. T. J. seems the answer to Sandy's quest for a good man, but when betrayal, revenge, and well-intentioned friends enter the mix, the results are both touching and funny.

> *I asked her what she was feeling. I knew, but saying your pain is like throwing up—it's uncomfortable but it gets the bad stuff out. Sandy said, "I feel like a fool and I feel mad and stupid and silly and I want to knock his block off." She was taking this therapy well. She sipped on her coffee and I could smell that she had spiked it. Heavy.* (p.189)

Notes: Yolanda Joe is also listed in the "Psychological Suspense" section of Chapter 4 and under the name Ardella Garland in the "Amateur Detectives—Women" section in Chapter 4.
Blackboard Bestseller List 1997, 1998, 1999

Keywords: fathers and sons • friendships • love affairs • men and women

Jones, Gayl.

🎗 *The Healing.* **Boston: Beacon Press, 1998. ISBN 0-8070-6314-2. 283p.**

Faith healer Harlan Jane Eagleton narrates her story backward, starting on the bus that takes her from town to town in the South. Her tale encompasses her travels in Africa with her former husband, an anthropologist; her coming of age in her grandmother's beauty shop; and her stint as business manager for a visionary but abusive rock star. Jones manages to weave together a story that resonates with the trials and triumphs of modern life.

> *And the minute we got to the tourist hotel, before I could rest up from the previous expedition to meet some new African medicine man or woman, he'd rent a Jeep or a Land-Rover or a van and head toward the next wilderness. I used to wonder what the women did when they got trapped in the wilds without their tampons or SNs. Did they use leaves?* (p. 212)

Notes: BCALA Literary Award for Fiction 1999; National Book Award for Fiction Finalist 1998

Keywords: Africa and Africans • healers and healing • stream of consciousness

Mosquito. **Boston: Beacon Press, 1999. ISBN 0-8070-8346-1. 616p.**

Sojourner Jane Nadine Johnson, a.k.a. "Mosquito," is an irrepressible, independent trucker whose dialectal, stream-of-consciousness narration of this novel flies from ethno botany to "hooch" to McDonald's architecture in the space of a few sentences like some impossible tangle of hyperlinks. When Mosquito discovers a pregnant Mexican woman in the back of her truck in Texas, Sojourner becomes involved in a new Underground Railroad, which provides even more fodder for her over-associative—and highly witty—ruminations on contemporary life and culture.

> *What I got me back there is a pregnant Mexican woman. . . . She wearing them ragged baggy blue jeans—not them ragged baggy stylish designer rags them college girls wear looking like beggar's holiday, the kind that shows they knees and even they ass, they buttocks, I mean—and one*

*of them horse-blanket ponchos, but you can still
tell that belly big.* (pp. 26–27)

Keywords: American Southwest • stream of consciousness • truck drivers • undocumented workers • women's friendships

LaValle, Victor D.

🏆 *Slapboxing with Jesus*. **New York: Vintage Contemporaries, 1999. ISBN
0-375-70590-2. 213p.**

In this collection of stories, Lavalle provides unflinching glimpses into
contemporary urban male life in all its grittiness as well as its occasional
tenderness. From the college student on the prowl for a woman to satisfy
his urges in "Raw Daddy," to the father who, with his sons, witnesses a
brutal beating in "Chuckie," to the delusional young man who goes off
his medications and starts collecting his urine in bottles in the closet in
"Ghost Story," the unique and eccentric voices in these stories are
provocative and compelling.

> *I took the phone down to my room to call Keisha.
> While it rang I folded the clothes I'd washed yester-
> day. Some of them were still a little wet and this
> pissed me off because I'd spent a whole hour with
> them in the dryers. Instead of hanging them out to
> dehydrate I creased them up and put them in their
> drawers. I saw this as some kind of punishment . . .
> I shoved them in like they were headstrong chil-
> dren determined to do their own thing. I slammed
> the drawers closed like I was locking the clothes in
> a room. Keisha's mother answered.* (pp. 12–13)

Notes: Victor D. LaValle is also listed in the "Family Stories" section of this
chapter.
PEN/Open Book Beyond Margins Award 2002

Keywords: black men and society • New York City • people with mental illness
• short stories • urban life and culture

Little, Benilde.

🏆 *Good Hair: A Novel*. **New York: Simon & Schuster, 1996. ISBN
0-684-80176-0. 237p.**

Both a romance and a tale of class prejudice, *Good Hair* tells the story of
Alice Andrews, a middle-class journalist, and Jack, a young doctor from
an "old" Boston family. Jack seems to be everything Alice is looking
for—but can their attraction survive their differences when Jack's family
enters the picture? Although Alice is firmly opposed to judging people
by whether or not they have "good" (straight) hair, it turns out that she
does hold some prejudices herself that must be overcome before her relationship with Jack can succeed.

> *It seemed insane to me that a people, twelve generations from one of the most inhumane systems of slavery in history, could actually be so cruel to one another. Maybe I was just too crazy for Jack. He probably needed somebody like that Stephanie woman, who seemed perfectly nice and had probably never had a bad mood or original thought in her entire life.* (pp. 99–100)

Notes: Blackboard Bestseller List 1997, 1998; Go On Girl Book Club Award 1996-97

Keywords: class relations • intraracial relations • journalism and journalists • love affairs • men and women • physicians • racism

Major, Marcus.

Good Peoples. New York: Dutton, 2000. ISBN 0-525-94535-0. 260p.

Myles Moore is a "nice guy," a Philadelphia middle school teacher who takes his twin nieces to the zoo on weekends and cooks homemade meals for a date. Unlike his brother and friends, he takes his time with women, waiting for the right one to come along. When he meets Marisa Marrero, she seems to be the one—but their differences threaten to overshadow their apparent rightness for each other. Marisa is successful, ambitious, and wealthy, and when she is promoted to an even better position in Washington, D.C., Myles finds himself resentful and disappointed in ways that surprise the "nice guy" in him.

> *Could he really be that simple? His woman, whom he professes to "love," tells him about a golden opportunity in her career and he sulks like a selfish eight-year-old? Was that his brand of love he prattled on so effusively about? He couldn't for one instant be thrilled for her without thinking about the impact it would have on him? Why, because his source of chocha would not be so readily available as it was now? What a big fucking baby, she thought.* (p. 210)

Notes: Blackboard Bestseller List 2000

Keywords: educators • journalism and journalists • love affairs • men and women

McLarin, Kim.

Meeting of the Waters. New York: Morrow, 2001. ISBN 0-688-16905-8. 338p.

Lenora "Lee" Page and Porter Stockman, both journalists, meet for the first time during the Los Angeles riots of 1992. Porter, who is white, is assailed by rioters; Lee, who is black, comes to his rescue. Thus begins a tumultuous love affair in which racial issues threaten to overshadow the couple's underlying affection. Lee is unsure whether loving a white man is a betrayal of her people; Porter grows weary of convincing Lee that he loves her as a woman, not merely as a black woman. As they come to terms with their own insecurities, they must also grapple with societal issues and, in the end, with what they really want from love.

> *If he had dated other black women, if he had slept with them, he was a chocolate lover, a white boy with a fever for the flavor, and his attraction to her had more to do with that*

than with her. . . . On the other hand, if he really had reached such an advanced bachelor age without sleeping with a black woman, why now? (pp. 167–68)

Keywords: interracial relationships • journalism and journalists • love affairs • men and women • Philadelphia, Pennsylvania

McMillan, Terry.

Waiting to Exhale. **New York: Viking, 1992. ISBN 0-670-83980-9. 409p.**

Coming from very different walks of life, Savannah, Bernadine, Gloria, and Robin have little in common—except their solid friendship and their disastrous relationships with men, who repeatedly betray and exploit them. Although the message seems to be that black men cannot be trusted, there is more to this novel than mere "brother bashing." The four protagonists are portrayed with humor, sensuality, and realism—far from perfect themselves, they bear some of the blame for their disappointment with the men in their lives. As their friendship develops, so does the women's sense of self, which ultimately leads them to discover that there are decent men out there after all.

> *"I'm serious. The ones that are good for us we find dull and boring, like Michael, for instance, and then we pick the assholes, like Russell, the ones who won't cooperate, the ones who offer us the most challenge and get our blood flowing and shit. Those are the motherfuckers we fall in love with."* *"Thank you, Mrs. Nietzsche," Savannah said.* (p. 328)

Notes: Terry McMillan is also listed in the "Family Stories" section of this chapter.
Blackboard Bestseller List 1994, 1995, 1996; *Sacred Fire: The QBR 100 Essential Black Books*
Film of the same name, directed by Forest Whitaker and starring Whitney Houston, Angela Bassett, Loretta Devine, and Lela Rochon (1995).

Keywords: adultery • infidelity • love affairs • men and women • movie novels • women's friendships

Pinckney, Darryl.

High Cotton. **New York: Farrar Straus & Giroux, 1992. ISBN 0-374-16998-5. 309p.**

This novel explores racial identity—in particular, black middle-class identity—through the eyes of its unnamed narrator. This young man, raised in an upper-middle-class black neighborhood, grows up to question some of his class's hypocrisies, such as its obsession with "good"

hair and light skin. His coming of age involves a tour, so to speak, of different conceptions of blackness: radical activism, Harlem culture, working-class life, even the expatriate lifestyle. Yet despite—or perhaps because of—these various experiences, his grandfather's reminiscences about the old South play an increasingly important role in his conceptions of modern blackness.

> *Some days when the streets were filled, I wondered where all the people were going. I picked out the blacks in the fancy restaurant windows, the way my elderly relatives used to examine the television screen and count the number of black faces in the chorus. It was as though I went around the city conducting my own informal survey, "Blacks I Have Seen." (p. 292)*

Notes: *Los Angeles Times* Book Award 1992

Keywords: intraracial relations • racial identity • skin color • upper class

Porter, Connie.

Imani All Mine. **Boston: Houghton Mifflin, 1999. ISBN 0-395-83808-8. 212p.**

After being raped, 15-year-old Tasha finds she is pregnant. Without much support from her own mother, Tasha struggles to raise her baby, attend high school, and create a more loving life than the one she has always known. Told in first-person black vernacular, this novel indulges in neither sentimentality nor social criticism; it simply and poignantly expresses the reality of Tasha's situation.

> *Last night is when I got to thinking it'd be so much easier if I can lie to her like Mama been lying to me. To tell Imani he dead. I can have a story about him with a end instead of beginnings and middles in my dreams. . . . I can say, Imani, me and your daddy was young. We was just children when we had you, but we loved each other very much. I called your daddy Honey and he called me Sugar and he called you his Little Cupcake. Now, ain't that sweet? (p. 171)*

Notes: ALA Best Book for Young Adults 2000; Alex Award 2000; BCALA Fiction Honor Book 2000

Keywords: Buffalo, New York • death of a child • inner-city life and culture • mothers and daughters • rape • teen mothers

Rice, Patty.

Somethin' Extra. **New York: Simon & Schuster, 2000. ISBN 0-684-85340-X. 366p.**

"Tina Turner said, 'What's love got to do with it,' and damn if she wasn't right," says twenty-something Genie as this novel opens. Genie is out to get what she wants from men—and love and commitment aren't on her list. Dating married men seems the perfect strategy—the risk of commitment is low. This approach works for Genie until she meets David, a married professor in his fifties. By the time Genie realizes that she's in love, it's too late to back out. But their tumultuous affair teaches Genie the one lesson she never wanted to learn—that love and commitment might mean something to her after all.

> *"Uhm, I don't fall in love. I've never fallen in love. Usually when I meet a man and we're going to start something, I just tell him that I know he wants my pussy and I want him to know that he can have it without playing games as long as he's willing to treat me with respect and isn't cheap." . . . "Let me get this straight," he said. "You exchange sex for money?"* (p. 179)

Keywords: adultery • love affairs • men and women

Roby, Kimberla Lawson.

 A Taste of Reality. **New York: Morrow, 2003. ISBN 0-06-050565-6. 287p.**

Anise has an MBA, a Lexus, and a seemingly stable marriage. But when she applies for a promotion at work, she is turned down for the second time in favor of a less-qualified white man. And as if that weren't bad enough, she learns that her husband is cheating on her, and her best friend may be betraying her at work. But Anise is not the kind of person who can accept injustice lying down. She has a plan—and when she follows through on it, she realizes that she is strong enough to face whatever comes her way.

> *All I wanted was for them to do what Martin Luther King had asked. I wanted them to judge me by the content of my character and not the color of my skin. But I knew now that this was impossible. I knew Jim, Lyle and Tom would never rid themselves of that racist mentality they'd been taught by their parents and grandparents. I learned the hard way that I could never change that. This was my taste of reality.* (p. 282)

Notes: *Essence* Bestseller List 2003

Keywords: husbands and wives • infidelity • racial discrimination • sexual discrimination • workplace politics

Smith, Faye McDonald.

 Flight of the Blackbird. **New York: Scribner, 1996. ISBN 0-684-82971-1. 352p.**

Mel Burke and her husband Builder seem to have the perfect middle-class life in Atlanta. Mel is a successful executive; Builder owns his own business; their daughter Sasha is smart and popular. But when Mel loses her job in a downsizing, the fragility of their perfect life is revealed. On the verge of bankruptcy, Mel and Builder's marriage falls apart, as does Mel's relationship with her mother and brother. Mel escapes to stay with a friend in Seattle for a few months, hoping to find some solace there. But tragic events in Atlanta force her home to rebuild whatever can be salvaged of her life and her marriage.

> *She spoke with resentment, angry that he had found her and was forcing her to face her real identity. As Raven, she could hide behind the façade of a floppy waitress; but Ron's presence was an instant reminder that she was Mel Burke, former successful Chamber of Commerce executive, reduced to waiting tables in a place of questionable repute.* (p. 179)

Notes: BCALA Fiction Honor Book 1997

Keywords: bankruptcy • family life • husbands and wives • middle class • Seattle, Washington

Whitehead, Colson.

Colson Whitehead is a 2002 MacArthur Fellow.

John Henry Days. New York: Doubleday, 2001. ISBN 0-385-49819-5. 389p.

John Henry is the legendary figure, immortalized in story and ballad, who triumphed over the steam drill (and subsequently dropped dead). J. Sutter, on the other hand, is an utterly unlikable freelance writer who lives on padded expense accounts and the free meals provided at publicity events. When J. goes to Talcott, West Virginia, to cover its John Henry Days in celebration of a postage stamp release, his only aim is to track down his next free meal and continue his "streak" of attending at least one publicity event a day. But in Talcott, John Henry's history unfolds and provides a foil for the soul-killing bleakness of J.'s life.

> *J. deposits his trash and the trash from the middle tray into the bag. He returns his tray to the upright position. He almost shuts the middle tray too but then realizes that he may have trespassed by disposing of her trash. She has extended her zone to cover the empty seat fair and square. At least his armrests are uncontested. Just to make sure he grips them tightly.* (p. 14)

Notes: BCALA Fiction Honor Book 2002

Keywords: antiheroes • journalism and journalists

Wideman, John Edgar.

John Edgar Wideman is a 1992 MacArthur Fellow.

Philadelphia Fire. New York: Henry Holt, 1990. ISBN 0-8050-1266-4. 199p.

Based loosely on a real event, the bombing of a militant black group's headquarters in Philadelphia in 1985, this novel explores the loss of a generation of African American young people to the urban streets and to prison. Cudjoe, a black writer living on a Greek island, feels compelled to return to Philadelphia when he hears about the bombing. He attempts to find Simba Muntu, the boy who was the only survivor of the bombing. However, this quest is not his only reason for returning to the United States; he also becomes aware of his need to recapture some of the passion he once had for his work, his ideals, and his children. By witnessing the city's deterioration, he comes to form new beliefs about his own mission in life.

> *"You see, my friend, when you think about it, when you go beneath the skin, we're very much alike. Brothers of sorts. Don't you agree? We're victims, aren't we, both of us? Stuck playing roles we have been programmed to play. You never had a chance; neither did I. . . . Brothers after all in this City of Brotherly Love. . . . Two coffees, please. And a couple of those delectable double-Dutch chocolate-fudge goo-goo doughnuts for my amigo here. What did you say your name is?"* (p. 175)

Notes: John Edgar Wideman is also listed in the "Community Stories" section of this chapter and the "World War I and World War II: 1901–1949" section of Chapter 6.
American Book Award 1991; PEN/Faulkner Award 1991

Keywords: expatriates • MOVE bombing 1985 • urban life and culture • writers

Youngblood, Shay.

Black Girl in Paris. New York: Riverhead Books, 2000. 1-57322-151-1. 238p.

Eden, a 26-year-old American "girl," arrives in Paris in 1986, hoping to meet James Baldwin, hoping to become a writer. Without working papers, Eden must take a series of low-paying jobs—artist's model, au pair, "poet's helper" (maid/personal care attendant)—but her adventures in making her own way in Paris constitute her apprenticeship as an artist, and she never loses sight of what she came for. Written in the style of a personal journal, this novel is fun, but it is not fluffy or lightweight. Eden is strong, smart, savvy, and utterly likeable.

> *I don't want to be anybody's girl. My mother worked for white people all her life so I wouldn't have to, she constantly reminds me. I don't want to disappoint her, but I have not met James Baldwin, written a novel, or fallen in love. I want to stay a little longer in this place, and for that I am willing to do many things.* (p. 124)

Keywords: art and artists • coming of age • domestic workers • expatriates • writers

Family Stories

Adams, Jenoyne.

Resurrecting Mingus. New York: Free Press, 2001. ISBN 0-684-87352-4. 244p.

A young, successful, biracial lawyer, Mingus Browning is struggling to deal with the breakup of her most recent relationship when her family's problems overwhelm her. Her father has been having an extramarital affair, and her parents' ensuing divorce forces her to reconsider her loyalties to both parents. Meanwhile, her envious sister seems determined to achieve some kind of victory over Mingus, even if she has to resort to betrayal. As the novel opens, Mingus is in the throes of painful contractions. The reader suspects she is giving birth, but it turns out she is having severe menstrual cramps that echo the pain of her personal life. However, by the end of the novel, it is clear that the pain of this seeming labor is not futile, for Mingus is indeed giving birth to a new person—herself.

> *I never would have thought I'd call my father out of his name. But that's what he was to me at that moment. A Punk Ass Nigga. The words were like a plug in my throat. I couldn't breathe unless I said it. All he said back was I'm sorry you feel that way. He wouldn't even argue with me. He called to wish me a Merry Christmas anyway. I wonder if he knows I got a Christmas card with a picture of his new family on it. The handwriting wasn't his.* (pp. 233–34)

Keywords: adultery • attorneys • family relationships • interracial relationships • men and women • mixed-race people

Allen, Jeffery Renard.

Rails Under My Back. New York: Farrar Straus & Giroux, 2000. ISBN 0-374-24626-2. 563p.

This complex novel tells the story of a family: sisters Gracie and Sheila McShan marry brothers John and Lucifer Jones, so their sons, Jesus and Hatch, are double first cousins. But despite this closeness in blood, and despite having grown up together, Jesus and Hatch are quite different from one another. Jesus is deeply involved in the urban drug culture, whereas Hatch is an aspiring blues musician. The family's story is revealed only gradually through multiple points of view and shifting place and time settings, and the vernacular dialogue is often abrupt and staccato-like. But the tale remains vivid and coherent, in the end yielding an overarching picture of the family and its history, its tragedies, and its triumphs.

> *He was crying not for Lula Mae but for himself. Not her death but what he had lost, what was forever beyond him now because she was gone. Summer. Her house. Her yard. Her kerosene lamps. Her lil house. Her trees. Her red gravel road. Her railroad plank that covered the grass-choked drainage ditch. . . . This bridge. West Mem-*

phis. The South. His tears were private, selfish, for him only. He would never cry again. (p. 481)

Notes: *New York Times* Notable Book of the Year 2000; Whiting Award 2002

Keywords: blues music and musicians • drug dealers and dealing • family chronicles • family relationships • men and women • musicians • urban life and culture

Ansa, Tina McElroy.

Baby of the Family. **San Diego: Harvest/Harcourt, 1989. ISBN 0-15-610150-5. 265p.**

When Lena is born with a caul over her head, one of the attending nurses knows she is destined to be a special person who can communicate with ghosts. Although Lena grows into young adulthood bathed in her family's love, she becomes increasingly different from her peers—more fearful and even, at times, seemingly crazy. When her grandmother's ghost tells her the truth about her special birth, she is able to come to terms with her difference and start finding her way in the world.

> *"Nurse Bloom is a sweet woman, going to all this trouble for my baby, yes, she is, for my sweet little Lena." Nellie looked down at the baby at her breast, who seemed to stop sucking and listen. "But if she thinks I'm gonna give my baby girl any of this old-fashioned potion shit—God only knows what's in it—she better think again."* (p. 33)

Notes: ALA Best Book for Young Adults 1990; Blackboard Bestseller List 1994, 1995; *New York Times* Notable Book of the Year 1989

Keywords: family life • folklore • small-town life and culture • spirits • supernatural

You Know Better. **New York: Morrow, 2002. ISBN 0-06-019779-X. 322p.**

In the course of one day, three generations of women confront their family's past mistakes and triumphs as they come together to help the youngest, a wayward 18-year-old, who has run away. As they face up to the painful components of their relationships, they are aided by spirits who help them find a place for forgiveness and healing.

> *"Mama Mama say black men and black women finally all-out hate each other. She say, 'Just listen to what the young men say about you in their music! . . . I say that all those years of Sandra and her friends calling men dogs their whole life right in front of their little boys and little girls is enough to turn 'em all into dogs. Then she got the nerve to be mad at something as everyday normal as Snoop Dogg's Dog Pound."* (p. 280)

Notes: BCALA Literary Award Fiction Honor Book 2003

Keywords: family relationships • folklore • Mulberry, Georgia • small-town life and culture • spirits

Haynes, David.

🎗 *Somebody Else's Mama*. Minneapolis, Minn.: Milkweed Editions, 1995. ISBN 1-57131-003-7. 340p.

Paula and Al Johnson are living the perfect middle-class life in a small black town in Missouri. Successful in their careers, with well-adjusted twin sons, they are not prepared for the upheaval that arrives in the form of Al's elderly mother. Angry about being back in the home where she lived with her first husband, who treated her like "a piece of furniture," (p. 259), Miss Kezee is hateful in her relations with her son's family. Told from alternating points of view, the novel chronicles the family's gradual adjustment to change and understanding of each other.

> *"Listen: here is what my life was like. In the morning I'd do A.B.'s books. Count his money. Then I'd clean his big old house and fix his supper. And at night I'd listen to the radio or watch TV. Sometimes if I was lucky I'd go sit in someone else's house for a while." "That's horrible." "No, no, no." She shook her head violently. "That ain't a bad life at all. Some people'd be happy to have what I had. It just wasn't for me." (p. 259)*

Notes: GRANTA Best Young Novelist Award 1996

Keywords: family relationships • men and women • middle class • small-town life and culture

Jackson, Brian Keith.

🎗 *The View from Here*. New York: Pocket Books, 1997. ISBN 0-671-56895-7. 229p.

In an unusual and refreshing twist, this novel is narrated by an unborn child. Anna Anderson Thomas and her husband J. T. already have five beloved boys, but Anna knows that number six will be the girl she has always wanted. However, J. T. says five children to feed are enough, and decides that they will give the sixth baby to his spiteful, infertile sister Clariece. Anna does not argue with him, but she talks to unborn "li'l Lisa" constantly and secretly hopes that something will change J. T.'s mind.

> *"This used to be my swing. Your gram used to come out here and push me, and I would scream like a crazy person. . . . . Then one day when we were in the kitchen, I didn't have anythin' to do, so I asked her to come push me. She said that she wouldn't because I had to learn how to do it myself . . . . Before long, I was swingin' myself, and I got up real high . . . And you know what, l'il Lisa? I was much higher than your gram had ever pushed me, but I didn't scream. Not once did I scream." (pp. 161–62)*

Notes: BCALA Literary Award for First Novelist 1998

Keywords: childrearing • family life • family relationships • husbands and wives • pregnancy

Jones, Gayl.

Corregidora. **Boston: Beacon Press, 1975. ISBN 0-8070-6315-0. 185p.**

Ursa's last name, Corregidora, comes from her brutal grandfather and great-grandfather, an incestuous "Portuguese slave breeder and whoremonger" (pp. 8–9). And yet, through several marriages, Ursa keeps this last name as her own. Stories of Corregidora's abuses—passed down from generation to generation through the female line—are the only evidence keeping this violent legacy alive. Ursa's mother and grandmother implore her to "make generations"—to have children and to bear witness to their ancestors' brutality. But when her husband pushes her down a flight of stairs, Ursa miscarries and is left incapable of having children. Unable to pass along the family legacy to future generations, Ursa must find a way to live in the present without being destroyed by her forebears' nightmares.

> *"When I'm telling you something don't you ever ask if I'm lying. Because they didn't want to leave no evidence of what they done—so it couldn't be held against them. And I'm leaving evidence. And you got to leave evidence too. And your children got to leave evidence."* . . . *I was five years old then.* (p. 14)

Keywords: domestic violence • family chronicles • infertility • men and women • slavery

LaValle, Victor D.

🎗 *The Ecstatic, or, Homunculus*. **New York: Crown, 2003. ISBN 0-609-61014-7. 272p.**

By the time 23-year-old Anthony's sister, mother, and grandmother arrive in Ithaca, New York, to "rescue" him, schizophrenia has caused him to flunk out of Cornell, reach the weight of 315 pounds, and retreat naked to his apartment. The women are not surprised, because mental illness runs in the family. But nor do they seek psychiatric help; instead, they accept Anthony's sometimes unusual behaviors and reintegrate him into their dysfunctional family life in Queens. Anthony's return adds an element of adventure to everyday life: He incites a riot at his sister's beauty pageant, takes in a teenager set on poisoning himself to lose weight, and compulsively writes out the plot of every horror movie he's ever seen. Told from Anthony's point of view, *The Ecstatic* reveals many sides of life with mental illness, from the vulnerable to the hilarious to the wise.

> *I didn't want to stand there carrying Grandma's handbag while people watched me so I patted my suit jacket and pants as if I'd bought cigarettes, but couldn't find them. I tapped myself harder. I almost*

> *hurt myself because the more I acted this way the more people inside the clinic looked at me. That only made me more frantic to seem normal as I slapped myself around looking for a cigarette I never even had in the first place.* (p. 219)

Notes: Victor D. Lavelle is also listed in the "Stories of Contemporary Life" section of this chapter.
PEN/Faulkner Award Finalist 2003; Zora Neale Hurston/Richard Wright Fiction Award Finalist 2003

Keywords: family relationships • immigrants • people with mental illness • women-headed families

Lee, Helen Elaine.

The Serpent's Gift. **New York: Atheneum, 1994. ISBN 0-689-12193-8. 374p.**

Two families, brought together by violence and death, grow together and bring each other serenity in this tender family saga. The families first meet when Eula Small, brutally beaten by her husband Ontario, flees with her two children and finds refuge with Ruby Staples—the only neighbor willing to open her door. Although Eula returns to her husband, she turns to Ruby once more when Ontario dies in a window-washing accident. Unable to pay the bill for the broken window, Eula moves her family into Ruby's basement, where the two families function as one and the children grow up as siblings. The power of this created family sustains all of them throughout their lives, despite many trials over the years.

> *When LaRue and Olive were in their early forties and had just about given up on having children, they had a daughter, whom they named Selena, child of the moon. . . . As he stood next to Selena's crib or held her smallness in his arms, he couldn't believe the fragility of the skull that precisely fit within his palm and the tiny limbs that shuddered when she cried. He felt the smooth, unlined feet that wouldn't touch ground for a long time yet. There were no limits on what she required of him, nor, he realized, on his love.* (p. 279)

Notes: BCALA Literary Award for First Novelist 1995

Keywords: domestic violence • family chronicles • family life • friendships

major, devorah.

An Open Weave. **New York: Berkley Books, 1995. ISBN 0-425-15665-6. 243p.**

All the action in this novel takes place in the course of one day, but this day's events reveal a great deal about Imani, her epileptic mother Iree, and her blind grandmother Ernestine. Iree and Ernestine have planned a party for Imani's seventeenth birthday. A few relatives and family friends are gathered at their house, waiting for the birthday girl to arrive. But she is delayed, helping her friend Amanda decide what to do about an unplanned pregnancy. Their conversations alternate with the waiting family's reminiscences, combining to provide a tender portrait of this three-generational family of women.

> *Imani had always been able to see memories and worries and spirits hovering around people. She had never questioned the waves of color she saw surrounding everyone. It took her years before she realized that everyone didn't see that which was as obvious to her as obsidian-colored hair or red-tinted lips. . . . She often tried to push aside the shadows of colors that hovered around everyone she saw. Sometimes, she almost succeeded, but not that morning.* (pp. 223–25)

Notes: BCALA Literary Award for First Novelist 1996

Keywords: family relationships • teen pregnancy • women-headed families • women's friendships

Marshall, Paule.

Paule Marshall is a 1992 MacArthur Fellow.

✿ *The Fisher King*. New York: Scribner, 2000. ISBN 0-684-87283-8. 222p.

Jumping over decades, this novel is set both in 1949 and in 1984. In 1949, jazz musician Sonny-Rett Payne moves from New York to Paris, where he can escape his family's disappointment about his chosen profession and where he is freer to pursue his musical career. In 1984, his brother in New York arranges a concert on the occasion of the fifteenth anniversary of Sonny-Rett's death in Paris. The event brings together members of Sonny-Rett's family from both sides of the Atlantic, and the time and distance between them contribute to the complexity of family history, loyalty, and reunion.

> *"Who's the daddy? . . . African?" Hattie, who hadn't said a word as yet, simply nodded. Dismay for a moment, followed by a philosophical sigh, and then the woman was smiling at him. "You got some of all of us in you, dontcha? What you gonna do with all that Colored from all over creation you got in you? Better be somethin' good." He didn't understand, so he shrugged.* (p. 34)

Notes: BCALA Literary Award for Fiction 2000

Keywords: expatriates • family chronicles • family relationships • jazz music and musicians

McMillan, Terry.

✿ *Mama*. New York: Pocket Books, 1987. ISBN 0-671-74523-9. 260p.

Domestic violence, alcohol abuse, and desperate poverty are just part of everyday life for Mildred Peacock. She is 17 when her first child is born, and four more children "had fallen out every nine or ten months after that" (p. 12). After she divorces her husband, who routinely beats her simply for talking to other men, life becomes both better and worse. It is this ambiguity that makes *Mama* such a fascinating read. The sacrifices Mildred must make simply to raise her children threaten, at times, to alienate them from her. It is fair to say that they both love her and hate her; she does the best she can within the impossible bounds of poverty, and the result is both affection and dysfunction.

> *Seem to me like all these years I been telling y'all kids what's the right thing to do and how y'all can get over in this world, and I swear, y'all done it by yourselves. Shit. My period done dried up, did I tell you that? For the longest I worried about going through the change of life. Then I realized I already been through it! I said, good goddamn riddens when it didn't come.* (p. 258)

Notes: Terry McMillan is also listed in the "Stories of Contemporary Life" section of this chapter.
American Book Award 1987; Blackboard Bestseller List 1994

Keywords: absentee parents • alcohol abuse and alcoholics • childrearing • domestic violence • domestic workers • dysfunctional families • family chronicles • mothers and daughters • working poor

Morrison, Toni.

Song of Solomon. **New York: Alfred A. Knopf, 1977. ISBN 0-679-44504-8. 362p.**

Like all of Morrison's novels, *Song of Solomon* combines poetry, folklore, allegory, and magic into a reading experience that requires patience but, for those willing to invest the effort, yields a rare vision of meaning. Born in 1931, Macon Dead III, better known as "Milkman," explores a lineage full of racial violence and conflicting values. His grandfather, the first Macon Dead, was murdered for his property by a white man, and later his father and Aunt Pilate kill another white man in turn. This legacy of violence leads in two separate directions: Milkman's father becomes a greedy businessman, whereas Pilate turns away from material values to a more otherworldly existence. Milkman's destiny is to reconcile these two by setting off on a quest to reclaim his family's history, achieving self-knowledge along the way.

> *It was a good feeling to come into a strange town and find a stranger who knew your people. All his life he'd heard the tremor in the word: "I live here, but my people . . ." or: "She acts like she ain't got no people," or: "Do any of your people live there?" But he hadn't known what it meant: links.* (p. 250)

Notes: Tony Morrison is also listed in the "Racial and Political Issues" section of this chapter.
Blackboard Bestseller List 1997; Janet Heidinger Kafka Prize 1977; National Book Critics Circle Award 1977; Oprah's Book Club 1996; *Sacred Fire: The QBR 100 Essential Black Books*

Keywords: family chronicles • family relationships • folklore • murder • racial violence • self-awareness

Pate, Alexs.

Finding Makeba. **New York: Putnam, 1996. ISBN 0-399-14200-2. 244p.**

Writer Ben Crestfield, overwhelmed by the combined pressures of marriage, fatherhood, and his perceived failure as an artist, abandons his wife, Helen, and young daughter, Makeba, to dedicate his energy to writing. When Makeba turns up at his book signing, she gives Ben a rare gift: the journal of her thoughts and feelings on reading his novel. It is this gift that enables Ben and Makeba to have a second chance at becoming a family. The novel's unusual format is highly effective: Chapters about Ben's and Helen's courtship and marriage are interspersed with Makeba's journal responses. Although deeply wounded by Ben's abandonment, in the end, Makeba's courage and honesty make emotional room for healing and even forgiveness.

> *I'm an artist. I don't want to think about bills and buying houses. I don't want stocks and mutual funds. Sometimes I don't even want to be Makeba's father. She deserves better than me. . . . It's too hard.* (pp. 202–3)

Keywords: absentee parents • fathers and daughters • Philadelphia, Pennsylvania • writers

Losing Absalom. **Minneapolis, Minn.: Coffee House Press, 1994. ISBN 1-56689-017-9. 204p.**

Absalom Goodman is the loving patriarch of a black Philadelphia family that has worked hard to achieve a better life. But now he is dying, and as his family gathers, they are forced to confront unresolved issues of race, ambition, and family ties.

> *"I just don't understand how you can grow up around all these black people and go live somewhere where they ain't none."*
>
> *" 'Come on, Mom. . . . You know good and well that there are black people there."*
>
> *" 'I know, Sonny, I'm just messing with you. I know why you're living up there. . . . Because you can be a part of this family but not have to deal with any of the problems."* (pp. 178–79)

Notes: BCALA Literary Award for First Novelist, 1994

Keywords: family life • family relationships • fathers and sons • husbands and wives

Senna, Danzy.

Caucasia. **New York: Riverhead Books, 1998. ISBN 1-57322-091-4. 353p.**

Growing up in Boston in the 1970s, Birdie and Cole are as close as two sisters can be. They even have their own unique language, Elemeno, named after their favorite letters of the alphabet. But their parents—a white mother and a black father—are political activists whose differences drive them apart. Their father takes Cole, the darker-skinned girl, to Brazil; Birdie goes into hiding with her mother after a revolutionary scheme goes wrong. Coming of age without her father or sister is painful, and eventually Birdie sets off to find them—and to negotiate her own identity in the shifting racial landscape.

> *My mother liked to tell Cole and me that politics weren't complicated. They were simple. People, she said, deserved four basic things: food, love, shelter, and a good education. Everything else was extra. But for my father, politics were more complicated. He was obsessed with theories about race and white hypocrisy, and seemed to see my mother's activism as a distraction.* (p. 19)

Notes: Alex Award 1999

Keywords: brothers and sisters • fathers and daughters • mixed-race children • mothers and daughters • political activism and activists • racial identity

West, Dorothy.

The Wedding. **New York: Doubleday, 1995. ISBN 0-385-47143-2. 240p.**

In an exclusive black community on Martha's Vineyard, Shelby Cole's engagement to a white jazz musician causes family conflict. But conflict is second nature to this family, descended from slaves and aristocrats, afflicted by the secretive turmoil of adultery and resentment. Young Shelby, an innocent victim of the family's legacy, and Gram, her bitter great-grandmother, equally embody the family's mottled history. When a black furniture mogul sets his sights on Shelby in an attempt at social climbing, race, class, and color enter the mix as this family struggles to sort out its heritage and its current relationships.

> *"Gram, you say 'dark' as if it were a dirty word. . . . Look at Laurie's skin beside mine. Hers makes mine look washed out. Maybe past generations had color prejudice, but my generation has color appreciation." Liz held the baby out to Gram, who shrank against the wall for support, for succor, as the tiny hand reached out to her.* (p. 53)

Notes: Blackboard Bestseller List 1995, 1996, 1998

Keywords: class relations • cultural identity • family history • family relationships • intraracial relations • racial identity • skin color

Racial and Political Issues

Campbell, Bebe Moore.

Your Blues Ain't Like Mine. New York: Putnam, 1992. ISBN 0-399-13746-7. 332p.

Black Chicago teen Armstrong Todd is beaten to death by white men after speaking a few words of French to a white woman in a pool hall. Although fictional, the novel recollects the true story of Emmett Till, murdered in 1955 for whistling at a white woman. Campbell skillfully traces the murder's long-lasting aftereffects on those involved, both black and white, and shows the victimhood not only of the innocent but also of the guilty.

> Not that the Quarters didn't contain people of all complexions; the multicolored offspring of every conceivable race's union with blacks could be found there. . . . These rainbow children were testimony that if colored women hadn't been honored, they'd certainly been desired. Although in practical terms that meant only that they and their children had been abandoned by men of every race. (p. 35)

Notes: Bebe Moore Campbell is also listed in the "Stories of Contemporary Life" section of this chapter.
Blackboard Bestseller List 1994, 1995; Go On Girl Book Club Award 1993; NAACP Image Award 1994

Keywords: American South • criminal justice system • family chronicles • hate crimes • murder • racism

What You Owe Me. New York: Putnam, 2001. ISBN 0-399-14784-5. 533p.

Matriece is on a mission to collect a debt on behalf of her dead mother, Hosanna. In the 1940s, Hosanna befriended Gilda, a Jewish immigrant from Poland, and together the two women founded a cosmetics company. When Gilda disappeared with the company's assets, Hosanna was left betrayed, angry, and in debt. Years later, without revealing her identity, Matriece goes to work for Gilda's thriving cosmetics empire. Set on recovering what is rightfully hers, Matriece cannot foresee the surprising form that the reconciliation takes.

> "When I arrived in this country I was a Jew who had been hunted like a dog because I was different . . . . You can't imagine how seductive the thought of acceptance was . . . ." Her eyes met Matriece's. "Of course you can. . . . Black people in this country had to suffer, and if I chose to be with one I would suffer as well. And, my dear, I had suffered

enough. I could be white if I separated from your mother."
(p. 503)

Notes: Bebe Moore Campbell is also listed in the "Stories of Contemporary Life" section of this chapter.
Los Angeles Times Best Book of 2001

Keywords: betrayal • business people • corporate practice • family chronicles • immigrants • Los Angeles, California • race relations • restitution

French, Albert.

Billy. New York: Viking, 1993. ISBN 0670850136. 214p.

One Saturday in Mississippi in the 1930s, 10-year-old Billy and his friend Gumpy wander into the white part of town to cool off in a pond. But the pond belongs to a white family, and two white teenage girls sneak up and attack the boys. One of them pins Billy down in the mud until he is hurt, frightened, and enraged. When she lets go, he stabs her, and she dies a short time later. In the uproar that ensues, violence overtakes the town, and Billy and Gumpy end up being tried as adults in a process that begins and ends with injustice.

> *"I tell ya what, I don't care how young them niggers are, they go and do something like this, kill that poor girl, they need killin themselves. I don't want that kind all around me, killin folks like that. I think they ought to just take em out somewhere, get it done with. Havin em around just keeps remindin ya what they done."* (p. 161)

Keywords: criminal justice system • murder • racism • vengeance

Gaines, Ernest J.

Ernest J. Gaines is a 1993 MacArthur Fellow.

❧ *A Lesson Before Dying*. New York: Vintage Contemporaries, 1993. ISBN 0-375-70270-9. 256p.

In a small Louisiana town in the 1940s, young and mildly retarded Jefferson is sentenced to die by electrocution for a murder he did not commit. His grandmother, Miss Emma, is prepared to accept this injustice, but there is one thing she cannot accept: While defending him to the jury, Jefferson's lawyer pleads, "What justice would there be to take this life? Justice, gentlemen? Why, I would just as soon put a hog in the electric chair as this." So Miss Emma asks Grant Wiggins, a local teacher who is planning to leave the small town and its stifling environment, to stay just long enough to teach Jefferson how to die like a man, not a hog. The intersection of these two lives—one almost at its end, one just beginning—comprises the remainder of this well-crafted, moving novel.

> *"Do you know what a myth is, Jefferson?" I asked him. "A myth is an old lie that people believe in. White people believe that they're better than anyone else on earth—and that's a myth. . . . As long as none of us stand, they're safe. . . .*

*I want you to chip away at that myth by standing. I
want you—yes, you—to call them liars."* (p. 192)

Notes: Ernest J. Gaines is also listed in the "Slavery—1619–1860" section of
Chapter 6.
BCALA Literary Award for Fiction 1994; Blackboard Bestseller List
1994, 1998; National Book Critics Circle Award 1993; Oprah's Book Club
1997; ALA notable book 1994; *Sacred Fire: The QBR 100 Essential Black
Books*
Television movie by the same name, directed by Joseph Sargent and star-
ring Don Cheadle, Cicely Tyson, and Mekhi Phifer (1999).

Keywords: criminal justice system • death row • educators • movie novels •
prison life • racism

Ladd, Florence.

🎗 *Sarah's Psalm*. **New York: Scribner, 1996. ISBN 0-684-80410-7. 319p.**

It is the 1960s, and Sarah seems to have everything going for her. A graduate student of African literature at Harvard, Sarah and her husband both
come from prominent black families in Washington, D.C., and are apparently destined for highly successful academic careers. However, their
marriage starts to fall apart as Sarah becomes obsessed with meeting
Ibrahim Mangane, the Senegalese writer who is the subject of her dissertation. Lincoln cannot understand why Sarah wants to travel to Senegal
at a time when there is so much to be done for the civil rights cause in the
United States. But Sarah nonetheless goes to Senegal and becomes inti-
mately involved in Mangane's work and family life, fulfilling some of
her dreams, but only at the expense of other aspirations.

> *Ibrahim's niece, Fatou Kamara, a conscientious
> university student, came twice a week to type her
> uncle's French correspondence. We exchanged
> very few words. Once she asked what I was read-
> ing. I said I was reading Mangane. She was
> amused. I asked what she was reading. Rather
> smugly she said, "Ralph Ellison—in English."* (p. 74)

Notes: BCALA Literary Award for Fiction 1997

Keywords: Africa and Africans • Civil Rights Movement • feminism and feminists • graduate students • writers

Morrison, Toni.

🎗 *The Bluest Eye*. **New York: Plume, 1970, 1993. ISBN 0-452-27305-6.
215p.**

Eleven-year-old Pecola Breedlove comes from a family known as ugly,
but she believes that she would be beautiful if only she had blue eyes.
Told from multiple points of view, this novel chronicles Pecola's search
for blue eyes, her rape and impregnation by her father, and her descent

into madness. It is not only Pecola's family who are implicated in the destruction of this little girl, however. Also to blame is Pecola's community, who conspire with the white American beauty myth to convince Pecola that she is ugly and therefore unworthy. Madness, however, along with a fraudulent healer, finally allow Pecola to believe that her eyes have turned blue, possibly the best outcome for her, as it allows her an escape from the appalling reality of her situation in her family and community.

> *"My eyes." "What about your eyes?" "I want them blue."*
> *Soaphead pursed his lips, and let his tongue stroke a gold*
> *inlay. He thought it was at once the most fantastic and the*
> *most logical petition her had ever received. Here was an*
> *ugly little girl asking for beauty. . . . For the first time he hon-*
> *estly wished he could work miracles. Never before had he*
> *really wanted the true and holy power—only the power to*
> *make others believe he had it.* (p. 174)

Notes: Toni Morrison is also listed in the "Family Stories" section of this chapter. Nobel Prize in Literature 1993; Oprah's Book Club 2000

Keywords: coming of age • dysfunctional families • incest • people with mental illness • rape • self-esteem • small-town life and culture

Singleton, Elyse.

This Side of the Sky. New York: Bluehen Books, 2002. ISBN 0-399-14920-1. 326p.

Close friends Lilian and Myraleen leave the poverty and racism of 1940s Mississippi to seek their fortunes elsewhere, and the war provides opportunities for jobs, travel, and even love affairs. But wherever they go—Philadelphia, England, even Paris—the women find that they must negotiate racial and gender bias that ranges from subtle to pervasive.

> *"So what's your plan?"*
>
> *"Fly. . . . Make it through the war. . . . Get on as a pilot for*
> *one of the commercial airlines." . . .*
>
> *"Well, maybe it's just my evil mind, but when those white*
> *folks find out a Negro is flying the plane, they gonna para-*
> *chute out of there whether they got parachutes on or not." . . .*
>
> *"That's the crack in my plan."* (pp. 182–83)

Keywords: men and women • Nadir, Mississippi • racism • sexism • women's friendships • World War II

Walker, Alice.

The Color Purple. New York: Harcourt, 1982. ISBN 0-15-119154-9. 290p.

This groundbreaking novel is narrated in the form of letters—letters to God and letters between two sisters, one in the South, and one in Africa. Celie, repeatedly raped as a young teenager by her stepfather, gives birth to two children, but they are taken away. Celie is forced to marry a man she does not love, and when her beloved sister Nettie moves to Africa, Celie is left without love or support—until Shug, a blues singer, enters her life. She gives Celie the gift of sexual love and teaches her how to stand up for herself. This novel broke new ground in many areas: in its treatment of topics such as incest, domestic violence, and homosexual love and in its spectacularly effective use of black dialect.

> *But one day when I was sitting quiet and feeling like a motherless child, which I was, it come to me: that feeling of being part of everything, not separate at all. I knew that if I cut a tree, my arm would bleed. And I laughed and I cried and I run all round the house. I knew just what it was. In fact, when it happen, you can't miss it. It sort of like you know what, she say, grinning and rubbing high up on my thigh. Shug! I say. Oh, she say. God love all them feeling. That's some of the best stuff God did.* (p. 191)

Notes: Pulitzer Prize 1983; *Sacred Fire: The QBR 100 Essential Black Books* Film by the same name directed by Steven Spielberg and starring Danny Glover and Whoopi Goldberg (1985).

Keywords: Africa and Africans • dysfunctional families • family relationships • feminism and feminists • incest • lesbian relationships • missionaries • movie novels • rape

Chapter 10

Romance Fiction

Dana Watson

Romance is the glamour which turns the dust of everyday life into a golden haze.—Elinor Glyn (1864–1943), English novelist, short story writer

What do you do when the hero and heroine ride off into the sunset to live happily ever after? Find another romance novel, of course! For many, this is more difficult than it seems. Although there are many romance novels available, locating one with special appeal, one that speaks to the heart, and one that evokes a similar life experience can be frustrating. For those seeking romances with African American characters, this chapter can provide direction and, hopefully, a happy ending.

Definition

Everyone understands the romance novel to be a love story. But not all love stories are, by definition, romances. Many novels include romantic elements to support and provide secondary interest to a predominant mystery, science fiction, historical fiction, or other format. The focus of the genre romance is specifically on the love relationship. It has been defined as a "love story in which the central focus is the development of the love relationship between the two main characters, written in such a way as to provide the reader with some degree of vicarious emotional participation in the courtship process" (Ramsdell 1987, 5). The Romance Writers of America (RWA) Web site (www.rwanational.org) succinctly describes the romance as "a book whereby the love story is the main focus of the novel and the end of the book is emotionally satisfying." Thus the critical elements for the romance genre are concentration on the love relationship and a satisfactory ending. Other novels of family relationships (siblings, parent-child, etc.) often contain romantic elements, but these are generally considered "relationship novels" or "women's fiction" and are not included in the genre romances listed in this chapter.

Appeal

What do African American readers look for in their romance novels? One author of these novels, Gwynne Forster, knows her readers appreciate stories about black middle-class individuals and those portraying the black male "as a caring, loving man, who respects his woman, nurtures her and his children." She also reports "readers enjoy seeing themselves in stories and love being able to identify with the characters" (Osborne 1999, 40).

There is no doubt the romance genre has great appeal for many readers. Statistics compiled by RWA in 2002 indicate romance fiction comprised nearly 55 percent of all popular paperbacks sold and nearly 36 percent of all popular fiction sold. Romance readers numbered 51.1 million, an increase of 10 million over 1998 data. These readers, half of whom are married, are predominantly women, live in all parts of the country, and range in age and educational level. Most of them read between one and five romance novels each year. Of particular interest here is that 6.72 million (11 percent) of these readers are African American. (www.rwanational.org).

But what is it about the romance novel that generates such a response? When asked, romance readers suggest that these novels provide an escape from reality or the frustration of everyday life into an arena where life experiences are new, different, and exciting, and where everything turns out "right" (Chelton 1991, 44). Although readers are drawn to the triumph of true love above all odds, they also appreciate the knowledge of history and other cultures they gain from this fiction. The strong heroine who triumphs provides vicarious satisfaction whether the setting is historical, contemporary, or futuristic. Interestingly, Janice Radway, in her research with romance readers (1984), provided another insight into the appeal of romance fiction. She reported that busy readers knew they could read romances intermittently, a concern of women with multiple roles and little time.

Whatever the type of romance, the setting, or the ethnicity of the characters, the appeal comes from the love story and conflicts inherent in the story. Julie Tetel, romance author and associate professor of English at Duke University, indicates the power of the story and the written format: "[t]he appeal of romance novels comes from the intense intimacy of the portrayal of the love relationship . . . romances give the reader a kind of straight shot of emotion that is very wonderful and almost exclusive to the reading experience—since reading is such an intimate activity. On the whole, romance novels do a consistently better job of creating that 'interior intimacy' than most movies with a romance theme" (Osborne 1999, 40).

Although readers of romances written by African American authors and featuring African American characters may themselves share that culture, this does not mean readers from other cultures will not enjoy them as well. Readers seek out and enjoy favorite subgenres (contemporary, romantic suspense, etc.) and situations and characters with which they can identify.

Evolution of the Genre

The romance fiction genre, as initiated by Harlequin in the late 1940s, focused on the lives and loves of white Americans. As the genre became more established, black writers began to produce stories about relationships, both novels and short stories. Although not genre romances by definition, Frank Yerby had African Americans as main characters in

Speak Now: A Modern Novel (1969), *The Dahomean: An Historical Novel* (1971), and its sequel, *A Darkness in Ingraham's Crest* (1979).

McFadden/Sterling, publisher of *True Confessions* magazine, produced a number of pulp magazines for black consumers about this same time. Short stories by contemporary black romance novelists (e.g., Donna Hill, Francis Ray, Louré Bussey and Sinclair LeBeau) appeared in *Bronze Thrills, Black Romance*, and *True Confessions*. Elsie B. Washington (writing as Rosalind Welles) published *Entwined Destinies* in 1980. This is believed to be the first romance with African American characters written by an African American author (Osborne 2002). These efforts paved the way for the African American romances available today.

In the late 1980s, frustrated by her inability to locate a publisher for her romances, author Leticia Peoples founded Odyssey Books. Although short-lived, Odyssey romances were populated with African American characters who appealed to readers. In addition, the company contributed to the careers of many current African American romance authors, among them Donna Hill, Rochelle Alers, and Francis Ray (Osborne 1999, 40).

In 1994 Kensington Publishing became the first major publisher to concentrate on African American romances. The Pinnacle Arabesque imprint initially released two titles, *Serenade* by Sandra Kitt and *Forever Yours* by Francis Ray. This line emphasized characters with African characteristics—various eye and skin colors and hairstyles—and depicted typical middle-class black people grappling with everyday problems. yet set in romantic situations. Now owned by Black Entertainment Television (BET), Pinnacle has become a dominant publisher in this arena, producing more than 250 titles by more than 50 African American authors (Osborne 2002). In 2000, Pinnacle released nearly 70 novels. In 1994 another major publisher, Avon, entered the field with Beverly Jenkins's first novel, *Night Song,* set in the nineteenth century with all-black characters. The success of this romance clearly indicated the appeal of romances by black authors (Israel and Drew 1995).

In recent years, a major influence on publishers' decisions to develop lines geared to the African American romance reader was the success of black mainstream novelists Terry McMillan, Toni Morrison, and Alice Walker. Francis Ray commented, "I truly believe that if these three outstanding authors had not shown publishers that African Americans can write, that they have disposable income, and that they do read and buy books, publishers would never have looked seriously at African American romances" (Osborne 1999, 40).

In 1995 Genesis Press published two African American romance novels under its Indigo imprint. Many of these early publications were reprints of novels by then well-known authors such as Donna Hill and Rochelle Alers, along with Washington's trailblazer, *Entwined Destinies*. The company has since expanded and introduced new authors to their readers.

The first romance by and about African Americans produced by Harlequin was Sandra Kitt's *Adam and Eva* (1997). Kitt also wrote novels for Harlequin that featured white characters. She also is notable for being the first author published under Kensington's Arabesque line and for her interracial titles for Signet. Harlequin currently includes few African American authors among its contributors. Best known are Eva Rutland, Maggie Ferguson, and Gwen Pemberton.

Other publishers producing African American romance titles include Ballantine (whose One World's <u>Indigo Love Stories</u> emerged from a partnership with Genesis), Signet, Pocket Books, St. Martin's Press, Windsor, and HarperCollins. Sepia, BET's follow-up to Arabesque, produces contemporary African American stories by more than 20 authors. Combining Christian beliefs with African American romance is a developing aspect of such publishers as Harvest House and Tyndale.

Dedicated publishing houses such as Genesis have been instrumental in providing African American romances to readers. Interesting to note is how major publishers, realizing the need and the opportunity, have responded to the demand by developing separate lines and encouraging beginning authors. The transition from paperback to hardcover initial publications among established African American romance authors is another indicator of the firm establishment of the subgenre.

Recent efforts among the African American romance community—authors, booksellers, and fans—has led to the establishment of the Emma Awards. These awards, presented at the now annual Romance Slam Jam conference (sponsored by authors, booksellers, and book clubs around the country), honor excellence in the romantic fiction of new and established African American authors. Information about the development of the conference and award winners is available at www.romanceslamjam.com.

Current Themes and Trends

African American romance fiction reflects much of what is happening in the genre as a whole. Settings may be contemporary or historical, but most African American romances focus on the contemporary, representing the joys and stresses of modern times (post-world wars) and typically take place in big cities with large African American populations, such as Atlanta, New York, or New Orleans. Others are set in such historical contexts as the Civil War or the American West of the mid- to late 1800s. The recent surge in fiction containing Christian ethics and spiritual themes is also represented in African American romance fiction by such authors as Angela Benson, Debra White Smith, and Jacquelin Thomas.

Independent Heroines

What is evident in most African American romance fiction available today is the independent nature of the heroines. These are career women, forging a place for themselves and, in many cases, their families in a complex environment. They are generally strong, yet with vulnerabilities, and their inner strength (sometimes surprising even to them) comes through. Although most heroines are young women of an age for that abiding love, older women are also featured in the heroine role.

Sensitive Heroes

The men our heroines love represent a wide variety of professions. These men have qualities heroines seek: compassion, courage, humor, resourcefulness, intelligence, and sex appeal. Of course there are always the scoundrels, but at some point their real nature is revealed.

Home and Family

The settings are generally domestic, presenting surroundings familiar to most of us. If some of the action occurs abroad, it is usually of a temporary nature: a vacation, a visit to family, or a career opportunity. The importance of friends and family in supporting the main characters is a recurring theme among the novels.

Sex

Today's African American love stories also demonstrate society's relaxation of social mores. Most heroines are likely to engage in sexual relations before marriage. There are, of course, exceptions, most notably those African American romance novels with strong inspirational content.

Romance novels differ in the amount of sexual activity described, ranging from the discreetly closed door or suggested intimacy to very specifically described sexual activity. This may be one of the most problematic areas for readers' advisors because they must not only determine the reader's preferences but also have a working knowledge of which titles and publisher's lines represent which degree of "spiciness." For example, Genesis Press developed its <u>Indigo Sensual Love Stories</u> line for those preferring more detailed descriptions.

Challenges

Subject matter reflects cares and problems from everyday life, including homelessness, single parenthood, rape, incest, medical problems, and employment issues. Several recent novels have characters representing a mixed racial heritage. This family background has a defining influence on subsequent events.

Race

The aspect of race is certainly present in these novels but usually not a major component. Some of the romances could have an entirely different set of characters with little impact. Others include aspects of African American life that set the novel firmly within the black community—for example, by the activities described, holidays celebrated, allusions to family connections and history, or dialect. Racial difficulties, especially in terms of family reaction to interracial marriages, emerge as part of some story lines.

Readers who enjoy a specific type of African American romance novel may also appreciate other romances not reflective of a particular ethnic culture. For example, those who enjoy contemporary, fast-paced, sexy romances such as Arabesque provides may also enjoy those of a Silhouette Desire. Or those that like to combine romance with mystery or romance within a Christian context could find other enjoyable titles within the general romance collection.

Suspense

A popular subcategory of romance novels is suspense. Romantic suspense novels combine the love interest with some ongoing mystery or element of intrigue. Those that truly belong in the romance genre are those in which the predominant thread is the romance or that have at least an equal balance of the romance and suspense components.

African American romance as a category often includes novels by Canadian authors Kayla Perrin and LaFlorya Gauthier and British author Sonia Icilyn. These romances from blacks of various countries explore the experiences and cultures of their characters (Osborne 1999). Because these authors are not African American, their work is outside the scope of this book and is not included in this chapter.

Series

Romances, by their nature, do not lend themselves to a series format as do other genres. (Once the hero and heroine "live happily ever after," what else is there to say?) However, an alternative in these romances are related series, more like family sagas, in which different characters in an extended family are the focus of the story. Several African American authors use this approach. Examples include Rochelle Alers in her romantic suspense Hideaway series and Eboni Snoe's *The Ties That Bind*, the third volume in the trilogy of the Johnson family, following Geri Guillaume's *Hearts of Steel* and Shirley Hailstock's *A Family Affair*.

Sequels, while not common, do exist in African American romances. For example, Leslie Esdaile's *Still Waters Run Deep* follows her earlier *Rivers of the Soul*, and Margaret Johnson-Hodge's *Some Sunday* shares with readers developments in the life of the heroine introduced in *Butterscotch Blues*.

Many romance readers rely on specific imprints when selecting books, much in the same way readers in other genres look to a specific series. Genesis Press, for example, has several imprints: Indigo, for traditional romance stories featuring African American characters; Indigo Love Spectrum, focusing on cross-cultural relationships; and Indigo After Dark, for those seeking more erotic fare. Those seeking contemporary romances often look to BET's Arabesque line, which includes stories by new and veteran African American authors.

Format

Romance fiction has been predominantly available in paperback format, and that trend holds true for African American romances. As authors become more established their novels are typically released in hardback editions. African American romance novels are increasingly becoming available in this format. In addition to print versions, many titles are now available in audiotape and compact disc formats. Griot Audio, an imprint of Recorded Books, has produced a number of titles written by African American romance authors included in this chapter.

Selection Scope and Criteria

Romance titles listed in this chapter represent the recent growth in African American fiction, with most published since 1997. Authors were identified from a variety of print and online sources. These include bibliographies from databases (*NoveList* and *What Do I Read Next?*), readers' advisory sources (*Genreflecting, The Romance Readers' Advisory,* and *Romance Fiction*), public libraries, the *Romantic Times* Web site, and publishers' Web sites. Efforts were made to include as many identified authors as possible, with emphasis on those authors appearing in multiple sources and those receiving Emma Awards from within the community. No books were included that were not personally examined. All titles are listed in WorldCat, a searchable database of bibliographic records. This ensures access through local libraries or via interlibrary loan.

Listed titles are written by African American authors, are designed for adults, and include African American characters. No collections of stories are included. The listed titles cover a range of quality, complexity, and described sexual content. These are books read for personal pleasure or escape. Although a few titles may be considered mainstream, these are not books described as "literary" or complex. They are designed to by enjoyed, not studied.

Not all titles by the authors listed are included. The intent is to provide a base of authors and titles to help readers find African American romance novels to enjoy. From this beginning, readers can identify authors, publishers, and imprints likely to provide the reading enjoyment they seek.

Advising the Reader

Although all romances have the love relationship as a predominant theme, many readers prefer those reflecting contemporary lives and issues. These are romances set in the post-World War II era and that reflect current lifestyles and issues. The majority of African American romances currently available fit this category. Other readers may look for an historical setting for additional content or an exotic feel. Another distinct and popular combination is that of romance and suspense. Since these major categories help readers select preferred titles, the annotations in this chapter include descriptors which, through use of the indexes, will lead to appropriate choices.

A major decision point for romance readers is the degree of sexual content in the story. Readers' comfort levels with described sensuality in novels vary widely. Some readers prefer a chaste romance, with little or no implied sexual content. Others accept, or embrace, much more descriptive sexual content. Knowledge of what to expect is often difficult to determine. Publishers' guidelines for series, actual markings on covers that indicate sensuality level, and independent sources (www.likesbooks.com/kissburn.html; www.theromancereader.com) may be accessed for additional clarification. To address this concern, the following annotations are broadly grouped according to degree of sexual content or description into three sections:

- **Suggestive**. These romances have suggestions of sexual activity but nothing explicit or highly descriptive.

- **Sensual**. These have more descriptive accountings of lovemaking but are not graphic or explicit.

- **Erotic.** Titles in this category include more explicit descriptions and more emphasis on sexual feelings.

Those looking for little or no sensual content are referred to the "Inspirational Literature" chapter (Chapter 7).

Suggestive

Alers, Rochelle.

Careless Whispers. Columbus, Miss.: Genesis, 1996. ISBN 1885478003pa. 189p.

After being stood up at the altar, Dyana Randolph rebuilds her life and rises to a prestigious editorial position at a magazine publishing company. Though aware of gossip about her involvement with a much older boss, Dyana chooses silence as a way to prevent any man from getting too close. After her older mentor retires, Nicholas Bradshaw, a younger, award-winning journalist, is appointed to run the magazine. Surprisingly, Dyana finds herself attracted to this man, and their relationship follows. When Nicholas hears the "careless whispers," he must make an important decision. The extensive dialogue contributes to the fast pace.

> *It's time you faced reality, Dyana. You're a beautiful and talented woman and the time for hiding is over. You must learn to accept the accolades as well as the deprecation.* (p. 122)

Notes: Rochelle Alers is also listed in the "Sensual" and "Erotic" sections of this chapter.

Keywords: journalism and journalists • New York City

Gentle Yearning. Columbus, Miss.: Genesis, 1998. ISBN 1-885478-24-0pa. 213p.

Daniel Clinton's best friend is killed, and the beautiful widow, Rebecca, depends on him to survive without her husband. Although both are torn by guilt and deceit, their passion for each other grows.

> *A tense silence enveloped the room as Daniel and Rebecca stared at each other. She had just verbalized what both of them had wanted for months; what both of them needed from the first time they'd shared a bed—each other.* (p. 168)

Notes: Rochelle Alers is also listed in the "Sensual" and "Erotic" sections of this chapter.

Keywords: widows

Reckless Surrender. Columbus, Miss.: Genesis Press, 1997. ISBN 1-885478-17-8pa. 174p.

Accountant Rina Matthews has her life in order—a successful Atlanta business and a love relationship with her business partner, Jason. When she agrees to work on Abigail Whitney's financial affairs, she finds immediate tension with Abigail's son, District Attorney Cleveland Whitney. Living in the Whitney's Savannah home, Rina finds this handsome and sensual man a powerful force to resist.

> *His gaze and the timbre of his voice sent shivers of fire and ice throughout her body. Her whole being was trembling, poised and waiting, and Rina could feel the force of the sexual magnetism that made Cleveland Whitney the confident man he was.* (p. 49)

Notes: Rochelle Alers is also listed in the "Sensual" and "Erotic" sections of this chapter.

Keywords: accountants and accounting • district attorneys

Anderson, Bridget.

All Because of You. Washington, D.C.: BET, 2002. ISBN 1-58314-332-7pa. 254p.

Vanessa Benton is shocked to learn her coworker Christopher Harris is dead, an apparent suicide. The two had often worked together on accounting projects for Brightline. Atlanta Detective Eric Daniels is assigned to the case and finds Vanessa a challenge. Not only does her desire to help solve the case complicate their undeniable attraction, but Eric also worries she may find herself the next victim. This fast-paced story unfolds through extensive dialogue, with minimal description.

> *Eric walked out of Brightline not sure if John Eagan was responsible for that list or not. With a little luck, maybe this meeting would shake things up. The death of three suspected thieves in two years sounded like this company was involved. He prayed Vanessa wasn't caught in the middle of something.* (p. 131)

Keywords: accountants and accounting • police detectives—men • romantic suspense

Reunited. Washington, D.C.: BET, 2001. ISBN 1-58314-208-8pa. 253p.

Rosie Wright has moved on since ending her marriage two years ago. When LeMar Reed, her college sweetheart, returns to Atlanta 12 years after leaving town, Rosie is surprised at the depth of feelings that resurface. Rosie's design firm is contracted to decorate LeMar's new house, and the constant interaction opens old wounds and forces them to reexamine their relationship and come to terms with what happened years before.

> *This meeting wasn't going the way LeMar had hoped. He wanted to discuss their past and get that out of the way. Instead, he was talking to the only woman he'd ever truly loved as if they'd just met.* (p. 61)

Keywords: interior designers • reunions

Benson, Angela.

The Nicest Guy in America. Thorndike, Maine: Thorndike, 1998 (1997). ISBN 0-7862-1461-9 (large print). 384p.

Kimberla Washington, writer for *Urban Style Magazine*, is assigned to find the perfect man through a magazine-sponsored contest. Nominations for the "Nicest Guy in America" contest are to come from the women who have dumped them. Based on personal experience, Kim knows the perfect man doesn't exist but goes forward with the search.

Through the contest contacts, she meets Reggie Stevens, not only handsome and intelligent but also single. The two face off and explore their own feelings.

> *The only way you're going to know for sure how I feel about*
> *women, how I treat women, is to be the woman in my life.*
> *For a short while, anyway. (p. 160)*

Notes: Angela Benson is also listed in the "Christian Fiction—Family" and "Christian Fiction—Inspirational Romance" sections of Chapter 7.

Keywords: contests • journalism and journalists

Berry, Charlene A.

Cajun Heat. **Columbus, Miss.: Genesis, 1999. ISBN 1-885478-59-3pa. 165p.**

Sent to New Orleans to track down a serial killer, Detective Symone Rawlings is teamed with FBI agent Josiah La'Mon. Before long the two feel a strong attraction. When he is arrested as a suspect, she is devastated but determined to clear his name and find the real killer. This fast-paced, suspenseful novel builds suspense through extensive use of dialogue.

> *With her arms tightly secured around his neck, and his*
> *strong, muscular arms. wrapped around her waist,*
> *Symone and Josiah were as close as two strangers could*
> *get. His attractiveness was enticing. She realized how dan-*
> *gerous it was being this close to him. Their faces were so*
> *near that their noses touched. (p. 55)*

Keywords: FBI agents • police detectives—women • romantic suspense • serial killers

Love's Deceptions. **Columbus, Miss.: Genesis, 1996. ISBN 1-885478-11-9; 1885478100pa. 245p.**

Four women and their relationships with the men in their lives are portrayed within the corporate setting of a major medical insurance company's San Diego office. Rachel, with both beauty and brains, finds herself trapped. Lesa, good looking and with a taste for the high life, fears commitment. Struggling single mother Stacy must choose a path when her ex-husband returns. Mattie, now widowed, transfers her energy to her job. Through mutual support they find their own way to deal with love's deception. Berry's first novel.

> *"Let me run it down for you, Stace. There are only three*
> *ways to get anything in life. One, you can work for it; two,*
> *you can wish for it; and three, you can get it by any means*
> *necessary." Stacy laughed as Lesa worked her neck back*
> *and forth like the true sistah she was. "I'm afraid to ask you*
> *which way you're going," Stacy said. (p. 11)*

Keywords: women's friendships

Bunkley, Anita Richmond.

Wild Embers. **New York: Dutton, 1995. ISBN 0-525-93753-6. 386p.**

Shortly after the military ban on racial barriers is lifted during World War II, Janelle Taylor enlists in the army as a military nurse stationed at Tuskegee, Alabama. She hopes a fresh start away from a lingering scandal will provide new direction. The men in her life—especially Perry, her brother, and Lance, her lover—provide elements of danger, romance, and loss. The story is recounted from the three perspectives and provides insight into a charged period in American history.

> *And Alabama? Thank God Booker T. Washington had created an intellectual oasis in the middle of the state. She'd heard enough horror stories and read enough in the newspapers about Jim Crowism in the South not to hold any illusions that colored military personnel would be warmly welcomed down there.* (p. 125)

Notes: Anita Richmond Bunkley is also listed in Chapter 6.
  Blackboard Bestseller List 1995, 1996

Keywords: nurses • war stories • World War II

Bussey, Louré.

Just the Thought of You. **Washington, D.C.: BET, 2002. ISBN 1-58314-387-Xpa. 286p.**

Novelist Diamond Tate has given up on true love and instead pours all of her energy and passion into her writing. On a Caribbean cruise she meets entertainment attorney Jake Dupree, a man whose failed marriage convinced him he could never love again. Together both begin to feel new love is possible. When Diamond's past encroaches on their relationship, Jake is determined to protect her.

> *Diamond simply turned around, looking intensely in his eyes, sending him a message in the way they lingered. She wanted him. She wanted him just as much as he wanted her. He knew it just as he knew they would be lovers. Burning hot lovers.* (p. 58)

Keywords: Caribbean nations • cruises • writers

Carmichael, Giselle.

Magnolia Sunset. **Columbus, Miss.: Genesis, 2002. ISBN 1-58571-067-9pa. 370p.**

Nicole Edwards, a 25-year-old schoolteacher, meets 35-year-old U.S. Air Force Major Xavier Ramon at a dinner given by their engaged best friends. Nicole, of Vietnamese and African American heritage, still feels the effect of being abandoned as an infant and raised by foster parents. A recent rejection due to her heritage has made her wary of all men. Xavier is a single parent from a wealthy family and his own issues make relationships difficult. Yet they feel an undeniable attraction to each other.

> *Reluctantly, Nicole admitted that there was something developing between them. And if she had any common sense at all, she would be just as upset as Xavier was. She of all people knew first hand that military men were wanderers. Sure they spoke of love, marriage, and had families, but they also cheated and abandoned those families. She couldn't allow herself to be fooled by a pair of magnet gray eyes or a titillating smile.* (p. 36)

Keywords: Biloxi, Mississippi • educators • foster children • military officers • mixed-race people

Copeland, Sheila.

A Chocolate Affair. Washington, D.C.: BET, 2001. ISBN 1-58314-234-7pa. 232p.

Four women friends, beautiful and talented, find themselves and their relationships with men revealing. Keisha Johnson worries about her Laker husband's move to Los Angeles but feels there is a divine purpose behind it. Jade Ross, now pregnant, feels caught between career demands as an artist and her basketball star husband. Singing star Topaz feels her lifelong friend Keisha may be the key to locating her former lover Germain. Nina, Topaz's cousin, dreams of being a writer but finds herself involved with a record producer.

> *"I have a name for the foundation." She was so excited she was about to explode. "A Chocolate Affair. Chocolate because this is about black people and an affair is a concern, not some kind of forbidden love relationship."* (p. 134)

Keywords: art and artists • men and women • singers • women's friendships

Chocolate Star. New York: St. Martin's, 1997. ISBN 0-312-96729-2pa. 422p.

Three young "chocolate stars" find their lives intersecting as they strive for fame. Topaz, a model turned singer, Gunther, a film director, and Sean, college basketball star, discover they must come to terms with themselves as they embrace the ranks of the rich and famous. Undemanding prose, considerable dialogue, and contemporary descriptive terms accelerate the pace of the story, but very small print may be difficult for some.

> *She slowly exhaled and opened the door. Standing there in faded jeans and a heavy teal sweater, Germain was finer than she had remembered. She couldn't keep herself from looking into his hazel eyes, and she felt her stomach turn flip-flops as their souls knowingly rejoined because they were together once again.* (p. 300)

Keywords: basketball players • celebrities • fame • film and filmmakers • singers

Esdaile, Leslie.

Rivers of the Soul. **Columbus, Miss.: Genesis, 2001. ISBN 1-58571-059-8pa. 516p.**

Antoinette has lost her job, is separated from her husband, and finds herself moving into her stepmother's Philadelphia condominium. At 37, she needs to rebuild her life and care for her young daughter. Luckily she has family and friends as a support group. Her old friend Jerome, aware that he married Karen on the rebound from Antoinette, finds himself stuck in a loveless marriage with children to support and bills to pay. When he finds Antoinette once again he feels a more positive future could be his.

> *"Look at me, boy," she said with tenderness in her voice. It had the kind of balm in it that he hadn't heard since his own grandmother had died. "You got the face of a young man, but the eyes of an old one. Don't you lose your faith, jus' do right by the chirren. Stay in they life, love 'em, an' let 'em know they's got a Daddy."* (p. 245)

Notes: Gold Pen Award Best Romantic Fiction Nominee 2002

Keywords: reunions • single parents

Still Waters Run Deep. **Columbus, Miss.: Genesis, 2002. ISBN 1-58571-068-7pa. 433p.**

High school sweethearts Antoinette and Jerome (Toni and Jay) meet again 20 years later. Now Antoinette is a well-established business-woman and both have married and had families. Their renewed passion is set among family dynamics and responsibilities and resonates with depth, maturity, and sensuality. Sequel to *Rivers of the Soul.*

> *"Listen," he said after a long while, "I can't promise you a lifetime without problems. That's the way of the world. All I can do is try my best, Toni. Will you take my best, for now, as long as it improves as we go along?"* (p. 396)

Keywords: business people • family relationships • reunions • single parents

Ford, Bette.

When a Man Loves a Woman. **Washington, D.C.: BET, 2002. ISBN 1-58314-237-1pa. 345p.**

Successful interior designer Amanda Daniels, shaken by her parents' failed relationship, is convinced her hasty marriage to Colorado rancher Zachary McFadden was a tragic mistake, one that will only lead to heartbreak for both of them. Zachary insists they give their marriage a one-year trial. Despite Amanda's reluctance and her relocation to the city, Zachary's attention and sensuality contribute to a growing bond between them.

> *The last thing she wanted to hear about was her husband's virtues. Besides, she knew what a giving and wonderful man she had married. It was one more reason why it was so important for her to give him back his freedom. He deserved that much and so much more.* (p. 20)

Keywords: husbands and wives • interior designers • ranchers and ranching

Forster, Gwynne.

Scarlet Woman. Washington, D.C.: BET, 2001. ISBN 1-58314-192-8pa. 329p.

Melinda Rodgers, recently widowed at 29, is shocked to learn her husband's will requires her to set up a charitable foundation and remarry within one year or she will lose her inheritance. Executor of the will, handsome lawyer Blake Hunter is adamant she follow the will's dictates and he must approve her decisions. Melinda would prefer to lose the inheritance rather than marry other than for love again. She and Blake are strongly attracted to each other, yet misperceptions keep them apart. This fast-paced story includes elements of suspense and intrigue revolving around the willed fortune.

> *By the time she reached her car, her breath came in short gasps, but that didn't explain her inability to steady her fingers enough to get the key in the ignition and start the vehicle. After a few minutes, she gave up. Why had everything become so difficult? She wanted to lay her head on the steering wheel and wake up in Italy, Switzerland, Kenya, or anywhere but Ellicott City.* (p. 47)

Keywords: attorneys • educators • heirs • widows

When Twilight Comes. New York: Kensington, 2002. ISBN 1-57566-919-6. 260p.

When Marge Hairston falls ill and must name a successor to run her influential African American newspaper, she insists one of her children assume the responsibility. Neither of her two self-centered older children, Drogan and Cassie, want the job, so quiet Sharon gives up her dreams to stay in North Carolina and take it on. Not only does she make a success of it, she also finds love in her life. But the once close relationship with her siblings is now threatened, and she must confront rivalry and mistrust.

> *He shook his head. "I don't want coffee or anything else in your kitchen. We've been fencing long enough, Sharon. You told me that if I wanted sweetness, I should provide the sugar. I want sweetness, and I want it from you. Come here, sweetheart."* (p.131)

Notes: Romance in Color Award of Excellence May 2002

Keywords: journalism and journalists • sibling rivalry

Green, Carmen.

Doctor, Doctor. Washington, D.C.: BET, 2002. ISBN 1-58314-327-0pa. 254p.

Shayla Crawford may have just graduated from Emory University medical school in Atlanta, but she must convince her family she is now independent and mature by working for a year in an impoverished area of Alberta, Mississippi. Once there she finds fellow doctor Jake Parker questioning her commitment to the clinic. Despite her attitude and his fiery temper, Shayla finds herself falling in love with Jake.

> *Who was he to judge her? She didn't need attitude from a doctor who probably got his degree through the mail. When he finally looked at her again, her first reaction was to get into her car, turn around, and go home. She could always be a pharmacist.* (p. 19)

Keywords: physicians • small town life and culture

Greene, Gloria.

Love Unveiled. **Columbus, Miss. Genesis, 1996. ISBN 1-885478-08-9pa. 178p.**

World-renowned fashion model Sammi Hart introduces her fiancé to her sister Julia, photographer and fashion magazine art director. Julia and Brad Coleman feel an immediate attraction. Julia is torn between her love for her sister and her desire for Brad but must also deal with some painful memories. Brad also finds himself caught between a painful past and an obsession for Julia.

> *Brad stood gazing at Julia, his dark eyes full of naked admiration as they boldly traveled from her tawny shoulders down her slender body to her slim, sandled feet and upward again to blazing dark eyes. She's more lovely than I imagined, he thought.* (p. 7)

Keywords: fashion models • photographers • sisters

Griffin, Bettye.

Closer Than Close. **Washington, D.C.: BET, 2003. ISBN 1-58314-276-2pa. 254p.**

Successful businesswoman Ivy Smith wants to attend her twentieth class reunion and invites Ray Jones to go with her. Ray is her local post office worker and a single father of two daughters. Though mismatched in income levels, they develop a true friendship, helping each other. Ray is hard working and dedicated to his family. Ivy's friends and family are puzzled by the relationship and favor her relationship with prominent, handsome Mitch, also a single father.

> *In his heart he knew he had no right to complain. He was the one who used his own children as buffers to prevent them from getting too close too fast.*

> *How could he object to her following his lead and pulling back as well? But he didn't like it. His gut instinct told him he'd been terribly wrong. He'd hurt himself by not being with her, and more important, he'd hurt Ivy.* (p. 224)

Keywords: business people • friendships • high school reunions • reunions • single parents

Gunn, Gay G.

Everlastin' Love. **Thorndike, Maine: Thorndike, 1996. ISBN 0-7862-1262-4(large print). 362p.**

Jaz Chandler had the perfect life—a wonderful marriage to her high school sweetheart, a growing career, and a supportive and loving family. Tragically, her life was shattered when her brother, T.C., and her beloved husband, Qwayz, went overseas and never came back. Jaz is so besieged by memories that all attempts to move on with her life fail, at least until Kyle Jagger comes into her life.

> *"No one's asking you to. He was a very important part of your life, and the love you shared will always be. You can't trade one love for another. Everyone has a special place that no one else can occupy."* (pp. 318–319)

Notes: Gay G. Gunn is also listed in the "Sensual" section of this chapter.

Keywords: architects • grief • Vietnam War impact

Nowhere to Run. **Columbus, Miss.: Genesis, 1997. ISBN 1-885478-13-5pa. 261p.**

Cassie Lee, a beautiful 20-year-old slave in the antebellum South, is purchased by a stranger and heads west. Though her life has been difficult, she dreams of being rich and free and thinks her future in California has to be better than her past. Little did she know this stranger and the man who sent him would have such an impact on her life.

> *Husband. The word hung in the mid-air of her mind. Would she ever have one? Mate. A lifetime mate would suffice. Slaves seldom had either, and when they did, it was subject to the whim and feelings of the master. She'd met her lifetime mate even if they would never be together again.* (p. 136)

Notes: Gay G. Gunn is also listed in the "Sensual" section of this chapter.

Keywords: American West • 1800s • pioneers • slavery

Hill, Donna.

Interlude. **Columbus, Miss. Genesis, 1999. ISBN 1-885478-58-5pa. 178p.**

As a personal shopper in New Orleans, Michelene Tyner has intimate knowledge of the Louisiana elite—politicians, law officers, art dealers, and restaurateurs—and charms them all. One special client, criminal defense attorney Chase Alexander, has stolen her heart. When Michelene's childhood friend is murdered and Chase defends the accused, she is truly torn between her love for him and her loyalty to her friend's memory. Complicating matters is her discovery of evidence that can both convict the murderer and ruin Chase's career.

> *He found joy in her laughter, the mischievous twin-kle in her eyes. He marveled at her business skills, her eye for the tiniest detail and her precision with every item, price, color, size. But what was most amazing and kept him in a state of incredulity was her effortless ability to get whatever she wanted, when she wanted it and how she wanted it.* (p. 54)

Notes: Donna Hill is also listed in the "Sensual" and "Erotic" sections of this chapter and in the "Contemporary Life" section of Chapter 9.

Keywords: attorneys • personal shoppers

Jackson, Brenda.

Perfect Timing. **New York: Kensington, 2002. ISBN 1-57566-921-8. 291p.**

Mya Rivers and Maxine Chandler, close friends in their early Savannah school days, went their separate ways after high school graduation. A 10-year school reunion cruise reunites them and brings Christopher Chandler, class outcast turned handsome, successful businessman, into Maxi's life. Beautiful and with a job she loves, Maxine still mourns a lost fiancé and her dashed hopes. Mya and Garrett, the seemingly perfect couple, begin to experience difficulties in their marriage. At a time when both Mya and Maxie are experiencing emotional upheavals, they rekindle their friendship.

> *She and Mya made a point to talk at least two or three times a week. A lot had happened in both their lives and they needed each other more than ever.* (p. 260)

Notes: Brenda Jackson is also listed in the "Sensual" section of this chapter.

Keywords: Caribbean nations • cruises • high school reunions • infidelity • women's friendships

Johnson, Doris.

Just One Kiss. **Washington, D.C.: BET, 2000. ISBN 1-58314-125-1pa. 316p.**

Novelist Dory Jones travels to Chicago from New York by train to research her next book, in which her character discovers a murder on board. She looks forward to a personal visit with Alma Manning, the elderly woman who raised her. While traveling she encounters Reid Robinson, a former coworker who disappeared years ago shortly after they met at an office party and shared one kiss. Reid is on holiday to try and sort out what he believes is a family sexual problem. Their on again, off again relationship befuddles Dory until she confronts him about his concern.

> *Now she couldn't help but think about her sister's words.*
> *Had Reid Robinson, with just one kiss, shackled her heart?*
> (p. 19)

Keywords: Albuquerque, New Mexico • family relationships • reunions • sexual dysfunction • writers

Johnson-Hodge, Margaret.

Butterscotch Blues. **New York: St. Martin's Press, 2000. ISBN 0-312-26484-4. 294p.**

Sandy Hutchinson, age 34, has finally found a man to light up her life. Adrian Burton is a butterscotch-complexioned Trinidadian who wants to marry her. When Sandy learns his ex-wife is dying of AIDS, she must seriously consider her commitment to their relationship, as she must again later when Adrian becomes ill. Sandy and her three girlfriends continue the close bond formed in college and are there to listen and support each other's lives. These interlocking relationships are also explored.

> *Sandy opened her door, expecting nothing, anticipating*
> *nothing, not knowing why Adrian had come, only that he*
> *had. She stood there, her eyes searching his face, trying to*
> *decipher the look she was seeing in his eyes, her heart*
> *thumping hard when the message was received.* (p. 89)

Notes: Blackboard Bestseller List 2000

Keywords: HIV/AIDS • Trinidadians • women's friendships

Some Sunday. **New York: Kensington, 2001. ISBN 1-57566-916-1. 305p.**

Sandy Hutchinson grieves over the death of her young Trinidadian husband from AIDS but is comforted by her brother-in-law, Winston, who recognizes his deep feelings for her are not reciprocated in the same way. She falls for a handsome carpenter, Randall, and is forced to choose between the comfortable love of Winston and the compelling attraction of Randall. Her close friends from college continue to affect her life, experience life-altering events, and provide mutual support in this sequel to *Butterscotch Blues*. Includes Reading Group Guide.

> *Cornered like a mouse. Cornered and nailed to the wall, all*
> *Sandy could offer was her truth and hoped it was enough.*
> *Even though she was found out, even though her betrayal*
> *was clear, she still was not ready to leave Winston. Still felt*
> *a strong alliance with him. Was not willing to give Randall*
> *that second chance.* (p. 253)

Keywords: HIV/AIDS • men and women • Queens, New York • Trinidadians • widows • women's friendships

True Lies. **New York: Kensington, 2002. ISBN 1-57566-917-X. 357p.**

Dajah Moore, a street-wise accountant, meets corrections officer Rick Timmons and the attraction is instant and mutual. Unfortunately, Gina Alexander, the mother of Rick's cherished young daughter Kanisha, schemes to prevent their relationship and budding happiness. Some clichéd dialogue and uneven treatment of characters, but these are real people to whom readers will relate. Includes Reading Group Guide.

> *You're right. Love doesn't go away. But it's not just about who you love, it's about who loves you back. Gina hasn't loved me in a while. You do. I haven't felt anything for her since I met you, nothing. And I know it's just words, but damn, Dajah, I waited so long for someone like you, there's no way I'm going to do anything to risk it. (p. 329)*

Keywords: accountants and accounting • police officers • Queens, New York • women's friendships

Kitt, Sandra.

Between Friends. **Thorndike, Maine: Thorndike, 1998. ISBN 0-7862-1710-3 (large print). 590p.**

Two lifelong friends, one African American and one white, attend the funeral of a mutual friend, where they meet the deceased's brother and both fall in love with him. This tests both their friendship and their relationship and places Alex Marco, ex-Navy SEAL, in a difficult situation. This compelling story with a biracial heroine and illegitimate hero raises compelling, sometimes uncomfortable, questions but also offers realistic, hopeful, solutions.

> *When Dallas opened the door and saw Alex standing there, she felt an odd displacement of time. She was suddenly sixteen again. When she'd needed someone to turn to, Alex had been there. Like now. She didn't even question his presence, but seeing him brought her perilously close to tears. Only this time there wasn't anything he could do to rescue her. (p. 464)*

Notes: Sandra Kitt is also listed in the "Sensual" section of this chapter.

Keywords: interracial relationships • women's friendships

Color of Love. **Thorndike, Maine: Thorndike, 1995. ISBN 0-7862-0919-4 (large print). 561p.**

Leah Downey is more than surprised when Jason Horn reveals he is a cop working with troubled teenaged boys in New York. She had enjoyed his company all afternoon but reacted to what she knew about white cops and black teenaged boys. Yet her attraction to him persists, despite objections from family and friends. Together they focus on their relationship and ignore the disapproval of others, a process only heightened by Leah's near death.

> *Leah guessed she should have known better. She had,*
> *back at the beginning. At the moment, however, she was*
> *perilously close to caring for a New York City cop named*
> *Jason Horn far more than could possibly be good for her.*
> *She was, all at once, both miserable and happy. Happy*
> *with the time spent with him. Incredulous with how good*
> *they seemed together. Miserable because it had no place*
> *to go. And everyone was telling her so.* (p. 321)

Notes: Sandra Kitt is also listed in the "Sensual" section of this chapter.
Blackboard Bestseller List 1996

Keywords: interracial relationships • police officers • prejudice

Significant Others. **Thorndike, Maine: Thorndike, 1996. ISBN 0-7862-0920-8**
(large print). 664p.

Of racially mixed heritage herself, guidance counselor Patricia Gilbert feels she
can reach Kent Baxter, a troubled biracial teenager. Kent has recently arrived in
Brooklyn, leaving his mother's wealthy family in Colorado, to live with his black
father. Patricia finally confronts Morgan Baxter in his office; he acknowledges
there is a problem. As they work together to deal with Kent's problems, Morgan
overcomes Patricia's reluctance to become involved in a relationship.

> *Morgan stood next to his son, and Patricia's gaze traveled*
> *back and forth between them. The early evening light hit*
> *both male faces in the same way, ads she was struck with*
> *the startling similarities. Even their expressions were the*
> *same. Patricia felt a funny kinship between the three of*
> *them, a mutual attraction that for a second pulled them all*
> *together. It was quickly gone.* (p. 276)

Notes: Sandra Kitt is also listed in the "Sensual" section of this chapter.
Blackboard Bestseller List 1996, 1997

Keywords: coming of age • fathers and sons • guidance counselors • interracial relationships • mixed-race people • racial identity

Major, Marcus.

4 Guys and Trouble. **New York: Dutton, 2001. ISBN 0-525-94568-7. 309p.**

Four young men promise their dying fraternity brother they will take care of his
little sister, Bunches. Each conscientiously takes on the role of brother—being
there for advice and counseling as well as support. When Bunches becomes less a
friend's little sister and more an attractive young woman, the "brothers" find it
difficult to accept her newfound independence and their changing feelings. They
also reevaluate their own relationships with women.

> *She sure would be happy when her workload lightened a*
> *bit. Bunches missed spending time with the fellas. Hell, she*
> *missed being pampered. The boys had spoiled her rotten,*
> *to be sure. She scratched through the purple satin scarf*
> *tied around her head. She was badly in need of a perm, not*

that it mattered much. Her social life teetered be-
tween nonexistence and parody. (p. 16)

Keywords: brothers and sisters • men and women • men's friendships • Philadelphia, Pennsylvania

Mañees, Raynetta.

Heart of the Matter. **Washington, D.C.: BET, 2002. ISBN 1-58314-262-
2pa. 285p.**

Affrica Bryant, newly elected mayor of Passion, Michigan, has among
her supporters her predecessor. The former mayor, involved in illegal activities with her two-timing boyfriend, Delroy, plans to control Affrica's
actions. Affrica intends to fulfill her campaign promise to clean up a run-
down housing project and improve the lives of her constituents. Chief of
Police Alex Bartholomew has his doubts about her but changes his mind
when he sees her determination. When Affrica starts making her own decisions, trouble begins. Affrica and Alex are drawn into a dangerous investigation and are increasingly attracted to each other.

> *Affrica was so upset she could barely see. "Listen,*
> *Mr. Bartholomew, let's just drop this mess that we*
> *do. You just take care of what you need to take*
> *care of on your end. And I'll do my job as mayor."*
> (p. 48)

Keywords: mayors • police officers • politics and politicians • romantic suspense

Moore, Chinelu.

Dark Storm Rising. **Columbus, Miss.: Genesis, 1996. ISBN 1-885478-05-
4pa. 190p.**

As fitness coordinator with a popular health club chain, Starmaine
Lassiter knows both success and independence. Star is convinced Nige-
rian oil trader Daran Ajero is too arrogant and sexist for her and their cultural backgrounds too diverse. Yet Star is surprised by the effect he has
on her. Daran is wealthy, mysterious, and charming and is determined to
convince Star they have more in common than she thinks.

> *"Well, no man can ever say that you didn't warn*
> *him. I like that. And I like your ideas about things.*
> *They're challenging. I prefer a woman who says*
> *what's on her mind, and you certainly don't have a*
> *problem with that—at least sometimes."* (p. 110)

Keywords: adultery • Africa and Africans • health and fitness clubs • Nigerians

Palfrey, Evelyn.

Everything in Its Place. **New York: Simon & Schuster, 2002. ISBN
0-671-04224-6pa. 241p.**

Bobbie Strickland has more going on in her life than she wants to handle. Her daughter is so troubled that Bobbie is raising a granddaughter. An elderly neighbor is beaten and robbed. She is principal of an elementary school with questionable test scores. When a handsome divorced man introduces himself into her life, she is reluctant. Yet he makes her feel desirable and she finds herself attracted to him.

> *Ray pulled her hands down, put his arms around her shoulders, and pressed her head against his chest. He leaned back, his weight against the counter, and held her to him. That seemed to make her cry harder, but he knew she needed the release, so he didn't try to stop her.* (p. 154)

Notes: Evelyn Palfrey is also listed in the "Sensual" and "Erotic" sections of this chapter.

Keywords: child rearing • educators

Poarch, Candice.

Lighthouse Magic. Washington, D.C.: BET, 2003. ISBN 1-58314-349-1pa. 254p.

Cecily Edmonds learns at her mother's deathbed that her beloved departed father was not her birth father and that her original home was on Coree Island, off the coast of North Carolina. Cecily is determined to find out more about her origins and claim family property on the island. She meets Ryan Anderson, who is originally interested in a business partnership with Cecily, and mutual attraction follows. Her parents' legacy, however, includes an enemy whose efforts threaten their relationship.

> *The waves rushed against the shore, singing a musical tune. Cecily was an independent woman, but right now she was pleased Ryan was here to share this moment. She wanted him here. She willed him not to move.* (p. 48)

Keywords: heirs • restaurant business

Ray, Francis.

Forever Yours. New York: Windsor, 1994. ISBN 0-7860-0025-2pa. 224p.

Victoria Chandler, successful Fort Worth businesswoman, likes her life until her grandmother demands she marry or lose financial support for her stores. Victoria feels she has no choice—she must find a husband—but plans to make it a business arrangement only. Kane Taggert has loved her since they were young and, refusing the business arrangement, jumps at the chance to win her love. He knows there is a warm, sexy woman under the wary surface. This fast-moving, at times humorous, story was one of the two romances to introduce the Arabesque line.

> *Warmth Victoria didn't want to feel, shouldn't feel, spread through her. Kane always said the right words. Why couldn't she do the same without getting restless? She pulled away and this time he let her go.* (p. 120)

Notes: Francis Ray is also listed in the "Christian Fiction—Family" section of the Chapter 7.
Blackboard Bestseller List 1994, 1995

Keywords: business people • grandmothers and granddaughters • ranchers and ranching

Riley, Mildred E.

No Regrets. **Columbus, Miss.: Genesis, 1998. ISBN 1-885478-33-X pa. 304p.**

At the time of the Harlem Renaissance, Maddie and Roy share both a love of music and an attraction to each other. Maddie, a gifted soprano, wants to become a classical singer. Roy, a talented musician, wants her to sing with his band. As they pursue their careers, Maddie goes to Paris, and Roy finds work in a Harlem nightclub. Yet their paths continue to cross and diverge amid exciting musical developments and venues.

> *As Maddie walked out of the record producer's office, she wondered what she would say to Roy if and when they met. And how would it feel to sing her blues numbers with Roy and his band?* (p. 209)

Notes: Mildred Riley is also listed in the "Erotic" section of this chapter

Keywords: Harlem Renaissance • musicians • singers

Snoe, Eboni.

Beguiled. **New York: Windsor, 1994. ISBN 0-7860-0046-5 pa. 395p.**

Soon after losing her job and her boyfriend, Raquel Mason somehow agrees to impersonate a missing heiress for one night, and the adventure begins. She is immediately kidnapped by fortune hunter Nate Bowman, who whirls her across the Caribbean and into remote parts of Central America. The exotic location and the tension between Nate and Raquel heighten the drama.

> *It rattled Raquel to realize despite her cautious nature, what she did not know about Nate was less important to her than her growing feelings for him. She feared their intensity more than his cloaked past.* (p. 291)

Keywords: Belize (Central America) • impersonation • kidnapping

The Ties That Bind. **Washington, D.C.: BET, 2002. ISBN 1-58314-338-6 pa. 252p.**

Massage therapist Essence Stuart learns from her dying mother that her biological father is politician Cedric Johnson, also uncle to her close friends Shiri and Brenda. When she contacts him, he denies paternity and hires Titan Valentine to investigate her claims. Cedric, concerned about the upcoming election, is shocked when Essence arrives at the Johnson family reunion in Florida. Essence finds herself caught between loyalty to her friends and the desire to expose a man who abandoned her and her mother. Complicating matters are her growing feelings for Titan. This third volume in a trilogy about the Johnson family follows Geri Guillaume's *Hearts of Steel* and Shirley Hailstock's *A Family Affair.*

> *It was Essence's turn to look away. She couldn't tell him the real reason: that he put her on edge, created a kind of bodily craving. Her instincts warned that it would only take one touch. . . . "Like I said, it's late." Essence looked back at him. Her eyes blinked over and over, attempting to veil the lie.* (p. 65)

Keywords: estranged parents • family chronicles • family relationships • politics and politicians

Starr, Pamela.

Fate. Columbus, Miss.: Genesis, 1999. ISBN 1-885478-74-7pa. 222p.

Vanessa Lewis loves to spend time with her sister's three fatherless children. She enjoys them and it gives her sister a break. Scott Halloway wishes he could spend more time with the two young daughters he is raising by himself. The two meet under unusual circumstances and are attracted to each other, although they recognize the difficulty this interracial relationship presents for their families.

> *Here was a man as crazy as she was. And he was winning her over with his charm. Scott made it easy to know him, tease him, touch him. What was it Monica said? "Let it happen!" Well, it was definitely happening, and a whole lot faster than Vanessa thought.* (p. 97)

Keywords: interracial relationships • single parents

Thomas, Wanda Y.

Truly Inseparable. Columbus, Miss.: Genesis, 1998. ISBN 1-885478-54-2pa. 330p.

Shelby is a successful wedding dress designer with a select Denver clientele who owns her own boutique. Nelson has risen to upper management level with the cable company he joined right out of college. Their careers are thriving, but their marriage came apart after their baby died suddenly from SIDS. Once a passionate and devoted couple, they could no longer tolerate each other and divorced. Even more miserable, both consider what it will take to go on with their lives, separately or perhaps together again.

> *She loved this man, this wonderful, handsome man who filled her heart with so much joy. She knew Nelson so well, as well as she knew herself. But her husband's unpredictability was something Shelby knew she'd never get a handle on.* (p. 290)

Notes: Wanda Y. Thomas is also listed in the "Sensual" section of this chapter.

Keywords: business people • death of a child • divorce • fashion designers • husbands and wives

Tillis, Tracey.

Final Act. **New York: Penguin Books, 1998. ISBN 0-451-40785-7. 298p.**

Shannon LaCrosse manages to survive over two years in prison after her conviction for killing her stepson. But the stepson who coveted his father's wife wasn't the stalker, and the motive for destroying Shannon's life may have been strictly business. Shannon's still a target, and only an ex-cop turned private investigator is willing to help solve the mystery of her old life and help her build a future.

> *She was dead. Shannon knew it the moment the door slammed two floors below her in the foyer of her brownstone. The edge of the curtain she held away from the study window slid from her fingers to flutter against the glass. Outside a storm raged. Inside, her stalker had come for her. (p. 1).*

Keywords: corporate intrigue • family relationships • husbands and wives • murder mysteries • prison life • romantic suspense • sibling rivalry

Final Hour. **New York: An Onyx Book /Penguin Books, 1999. ISBN 0-451-40879-9pa. 295p.**

Young, ambitious FBI special agent Jennifer Bennett and legendary Sean Alexander both have something to prove when they are teamed up on the kidnapping of Charlie Lattimore, son of a former U.S. senator. The original friction between the two is replaced by respect, then love, as they race against time to save a child's life.

> *His broad hands gripped the steering wheel now with competence and confidence. Involuntarily, Jennifer had a flashing image of them on the delicate skin of a woman's spine as they contoured their way down to more intimate contact. Jesus. She did not need to be thinking about Sean Alexander this way. (p. 70)*

Keywords: FBI agents • hostage negotiators • interracial relationships • kidnapping • romantic suspense

White, Monica.

Shades of Desire. **Columbus, Miss.: Genesis, 1996. ISBN 1-885478-06-2pa. 134p.**

Jasmine Smith knows journalist Jeremy Collins is something special. He's successful, passionate, clear about his feelings for her, attractive, and white. She is surprised at her feelings for him, especially since she has never believed in mixed relationships. While most friends and family members are supportive, some are strongly opposed, and Jasmine must examine her deepest feelings.

> *I watched them talking and laughing together and felt a kind of happiness I had never experienced. If only this could go on forever, I thought. I have love and friendship, and my lover and my friend like each other. Maybe it's possible, barely possible, that it won't change.* (p. 71)

Keywords: interracial relationships • journalism and journalists

Wiggins, Alicia.

Promises to Keep. **Columbus, Miss.: Genesis, 2002. ISBN 1-58571-073-3pa. 378p.**

Still reeling from her mother's death, Audrey Bryson is introduced to Omar, a coworker's brother. As the relationship develops, Omar's former girlfriend stirs up trouble. Extensive description of events overwhelms the developing character interaction.

> *Omar knew he was falling in love with Audrey and there was nothing he could do to change how he felt. This realization brought with it a mixture of joy and fear. Joy, because he found the capacity to live again, and fear, because the past reminded him that he was not totally free.* (p. 154)

Keywords: death of a parent • men and women • mourning

Unconditional Love. **Columbus, Miss.: Genesis, 1999. ISBN 1-885478-56-9pa. 283p.**

Olivia Ross had given up on men. The breakup with her first love was devastating, and subsequent relationships did not endure. When she meets computer whiz and businessman Alex Deveraux, she feels immediate attraction. His persistence in wooing her is persuasive, as are his positive contributions to the Cleveland community and the school system she works for. Just as she is ready to move forward, a ghost from the past steps back into her life and threatens her newly found emotional strength.

> *It wasn't as easy as she thought. Not only was Alex's gaze penetrating and seductive, he was causing a reaction in her that she hadn't expected. Her palms were damp, her throat was dry, and her heart raced with tremendous speed. She wanted to scold herself for the excitement she felt and for letting him wreak such havoc with her feelings, but she couldn't bring herself to do it.* (p. 166)

Keywords: business people • educators • men and women

Winters, Angela.

Love on the Run. **Washington, D.C.: BET, 2002. ISBN 1-58314-216-9pa. 316p.**

Bree Hart, setting out to prove her independence from her well-to-do Baltimore family, heads to New York City, where she befriends and rooms with Robin, an ex-con. A series of misadventures and a myriad of jobs seem to define her life. When Robin defrauds a loan shark, life-threatening episodes involve Bree. Graham Lane, college professor, is sent by her family to find her. Despite their personal differences, the two find themselves attracted to each other.

> *Against his better judgment, Graham sat down on the sofa. He could see her eyes light up. She was a magnet to danger and mystery. The exact opposite of himself. He had to remember that. "It's complicated, Bree."* (p. 107)

Keywords: educators • family relationships • men and women

Sensual

Alers, Rochelle.

Homecoming. Washington, D.C.: BET, 2002. ISBN 1-58314-271-1pa. 315 p.

Reporter Dana Nichols goes home to Mississippi to bury her last relative. She is also determined to find out the truth about her parents' deaths. Their reported murder/suicide does not ring true. While there she meets Dr. Tyler Cole, son of a prominent family and a dedicated physician set on lowering the infant mortality rate. He is attracted to her and determined to overcome her distrust of men. Their relationship and his career are threatened as Dana pursues the truth about her family. This ninth title in Alers's 10-book <u>Hideaway</u> series depicts experiences and interactions of the Cole family in succeeding generations.

> *She held her breath for several seconds, and then let it out slowly. If Tyler Cole was playing a game, then she wanted no part of it, because she had to keep reminding herself why she'd come back to Hillsboro. And it was not to become involved with a man.* (p. 65)

Notes: Rochelle Alers is also listed in the "Suggestive" and "Erotic" sections of this chapter.

Keywords: death of a parent • journalism and journalists • physicians • romantic suspense

No Compromise. Washington, D.C.: BET, 2002. ISBN 1-58314-270-3pa. 379p.

Jolene Walker, executive director of The Sanctuary in Washington, D.C., is dedicated to the women's shelter and its victimized women. Her own twin sister died at the hands of an abuser. She has no time or energy for a personal life but meets Michael Kirkland, a U.S. Army captain, on a blind date and finds the intelligence expert sexy and compelling. Michael, currently on leave, is immediately attracted to her and sets out to be part of her life. The happy new relationship is threatened when someone vandalizes The Sanctuary, makes an attempt on Jolene's life, and murders one of her clients. Michael vows to protect her. This first installment of the <u>Hideaway Sons and Brothers Trilogy</u> continues the saga of the <u>Hideaway Legacy</u> series with Joshua and Vanessa Kirkland's son.

> *He'd just revealed a lot about himself. He was used to being in control. She wanted to turn around and see the face that matched the deep baritone voice, but she was enjoying their subtle cat-and-mouse game. It had been a long time—too long—since she'd flirted with a man.* (p. 31)

Notes: Rochelle Alers is also listed in the "Suggestive" and "Erotic" sections of this chapter. Emma Award 2003; Gold Pen Award Best Romantic Fiction Nominee 2002

Keywords: military officers • romantic suspense • women's shelters

Amos, Robyn.

Bring Me a Dream. **New York: HarperCollins, 2001. ISBN 0-380-81542-7pa. 384p.**

Former policewoman Jasmine White, now a bodyguard (Close Protection Specialist) and fed up with her typical low-level assignments, insists on equitable treatment from her boss. She takes on a radio D.J., "The Sandman," Spencer Powell. He needs protection but doesn't want it and does all he can to thwart her efforts. His growing respect for her talent and her concerns with protecting him despite escalating threats and necessary public appearances are complicated by undeniable physical attraction.

> *"Sweetheart, just in case, I think this needs saying. You embody everything that's good in women. You're as strong and smart and capable as any man, and yet you're as beautiful and soft and sexy as woman should be . . . . Who you are speaks for itself."* (pp. 316–17)

Keywords: bodyguards • celebrities • family relationships • radio personalities • romantic suspense

Andrews, Vicki.

Midnight Peril. **Columbus, Miss.: Genesis, 1998. ISBN 1-8885478-27-5pa. 247p.**

Leslie Hughes, mother, widow, and successful corporate attorney, must choose between her longtime friend Robert, a man with whom she has a platonic relationship, and Bryan, a man who awakens her long dormant passions.

> *She does not know how much she means to me, Robert thought, as he listened to the beautiful sound of her voice or the sensuous tone in her laughter. He felt a kind of freedom with her—an unpretentiousness—that made his heart swell with pride just because he knew her.* (p. 75)

Keywords: attorneys • single parents • widows

Byrd, Adrianne.

My Destiny. Washington, D.C.: BET, 2003. ISBN 1-58314-292-4pa. 248p.

Destiny Brockman considers her easygoing next-door neighbor Miles Stafford just a good friend. This feeling has been constant for the 10 years they have lived across the hall from each other. She has been focused on her career as a lawyer and he on living life to the fullest. When she declares there are no good men to be found in Atlanta, Miles proposes a bet—that each set the other up with the perfect match. Complicating matters, however, is the long-simmering attraction between them.

> *Rooted by her door, she watched him cross over to his apartment, but managed, thankfully, to snap out of her reverie in time to close her door before he caught her gaping at him. But even then, she stood staring at the back of the door wondering what in hell had just happened.* (p. 94)

Keywords: attorneys • friendships

Clark, Beverly.

Bound by Love. Columbus, Miss.: Genesis, 2000. ISBN 1-58571-016-4pa. 291p.

Lesley Wells has moved to Los Angeles and is now a successful designer. Years earlier her fiancé, Darren Taylor, owner of Taylor Made Creations, accused her of stealing new spring designs from his firm. Stunned and betrayed, she fled and also gave birth to Darren's child. Darren has now tracked her down and plans his revenge. He insists she return to Philadelphia but, upon discovering the existence of his daughter, relents and wants to marry her. Lesley still loves him but worries his past lack of trust will again come between them unless she can identify the person who stole the designs.

> *After all these years she would have thought that she had gotten over Darren. But just the sight of him had resurrected feelings she'd thought were long since dead and buried.* (p. 25)

Keywords: fashion designers • reunions • single parents • vengeance

Cherish the Flame. Columbus, Miss.: Genesis, 2001. ISBN 1-58571-063-6pa. 348p.

Alexander Price has still neither forgiven nor forgotten Valarie Baker for leaving him despite the eight years that have passed since she left. Though their love affair was intense and promising, Valarie had to yield to Alex's father's objections. Her move to Quinneth Falls, Michigan, her marriage, and the birth of her son set the direction for a new life. When

Alex comes back into her life, determined to make her pay for his years of sleepless nights, her new world is no longer as stable as she thought.

> *When Valerie thought about the scene in Alex's suite, it sent a quiver of fear up her spine. If revenge was what he was after, she was sure he had more of the same in store for her.* (p. 93)

Keywords: reunions • romantic suspense • vengeance

Love to Cherish. Columbus, Miss.: Genesis, 1998. ISBN 1-885478-35-6pa. 287p.

Tracey Hamilton, soul food restaurant manager and mother of five-year-old twins, is shocked when pro football player Cornell Robertson walks into her Springfield, Illinois restaurant. The shock brings back the humiliating memories of their failed relationship, an experience she has no intention of repeating despite the feelings she realizes remain in her heart. Cornell is surprised how strongly he still feels about Tracey. Over the years he has wanted to find her and apologize for his actions. Now, after a failed marriage, he knows what is truly valuable in life and is determined to gain Tracey's forgiveness and love.

> *What it boiled down to was trust, and since it was lacking on both their parts, their relationship was doomed. How were they ever going to make their way back to each other if they ever did make it back to each other?* (p. 246)

Keywords: football players • restaurant managers • reunions

The Price of Love. Columbus, Miss.: Genesis, 1999. ISBN 1-885478-61-5pa. 239p.

As a young woman, Brenda Davis gave up a son for adoption. She felt her parents and lawyer had betrayed her and subsequently suffered a breakdown. She later decided to relocate and met Gil Jackson, who embodied all she didn't like in a man. What's worse, he was a lawyer.

> *Gil was everything she ever dreamed about in a man, though she hadn't dreamed about one for a long time. She didn't think such a man existed, at least not for her. She had promised herself she would never get involved again. Now look at her, she couldn't get more deeply involved if she tried.* (p. 125)

Keywords: adoption • attorneys

Emery, Lynn.

All I Want Is Forever. New York: HarperTorch, 2002. ISBN 0-06-008928-8pa. 374p.

Talia Marchand enjoys her life as a political consultant in Washington, D.C., and has no plans to ever return to the small Louisiana town of her roots. Then Derrick Guillory, now an investigator for the local district attorney, walks back into her life. Both realize that the passion and secrets they shared when young are still very much part of who they are and, if they are to go forward together, they must face the ghosts of the past.

> *At that moment the confident, bold woman dissolved. Talia closed her eyes briefly, then opened them and took another sip of wine. Her smooth skin seemed pale with dread as though a ghost had sat down next to her. In a way that was exactly what he represented, a haunting reminder of something she'd buried long ago.* (p. 30)

Keywords: police detectives—men • political analysts • reunions

Tell Me Something Good. **New York: HarperTorch, 2002. ISBN 0-380-81305-Xpa. 375p.**

Lyrissa Rideau has been hired to appraise the art collection of the powerful Creole St. Denis family. She has heard all her life how the St. Denis family stole an ancestor's painting and ruined her family. Now she is in a position to find out more about this lost legacy. Unfortunately, Noel St. Denis gets in the way. New Orleans's most eligible and seductive bachelor is used to getting what he wants, and this time it's Lyrissa. Family displeasure and the social stratification of modern Creole society present barriers to their relationship, despite the developing passion between them.

> *Something in her tone must have caught his attention. He looked at her with an intensity that could have started a fire. Lyrissa swam against a strong tide that threatened to pull her into those smoky amber eyes. Noel wore the ghost of a smile as though very much aware of this effect on her.* (p. 34)

Keywords: art appraisers • class relations • Creoles

Gilmore, Monique.

The Grass Ain't Greener. **Thorndike, Maine: G.K. Hall, 1996. ISBN 0-7838-8508-3 (large print). 360p.**

Ramona Snow takes time to rest and reevaluate her life. As the wife of a workaholic, a mother of two, and a graduate student, she finds herself pulled in so many directions she is stressed and above all, very tired. Although she loves her businessman husband, recent tensions between them compel her to visit her sister in Detroit. Surprising events there prompt her to follow her heart.

> *Madrid really didn't want to hear about how good Romana was, or how blessed he was to be married to her. Somewhere, deep down, he still harbored some ill feelings about how things had gone down between them a few days back. Somehow they would have to meet in the middle or call it*

> *quits—some way, somehow, something was going to have*
> *to change between them.* (p. 317)

Keywords: graduate students • husbands and wives • working mothers

Guillaume, Geri.

***Simply Irresistible*. New York: Kensington, 1998. ISBN 0-7860-0476-2pa. 270p.**

Editor Dara Lange is caught trying to steal her car back from her ex-boyfriend. She is surprised to meet executive Nick Bordeaux, the new owner. Reluctantly, Dara agrees to join him for four weekends of volunteer work. Based on her past relationships with men, Dara is wary and tries to deny the heat smoldering between them. Attracted from the start, Nick needs her in his life.

> *Dara experienced another attack of panic. She didn't want*
> *Nick to know anything about her. She didn't want him to*
> *know what had driven her to seek revenge against David.*
> *She didn't want him know about the desperation, and the*
> *anger, and the months of self-recrimination. She glanced*
> *up at her reflection once more, and bit her lip to cease its*
> *trembling. He image blurred before her eyes as tears*
> *welled up in them.* (p. 29)

Keywords: business people • editors

Gunn, Gay G.

***Pride and Joi*. Columbus, Miss.: Genesis, 1998. ISBN 1-885478-34-8pa. 232p.**

Joi Martin always knew she wanted a man who could fulfill her dreams of security and privilege. Now she is caught between Joe Pride, the dependable blue-collar factory worker whose love is real, and Claude Jeeter, who comes bearing gifts and a promise of a golden future. That choice will determine her future.

> *Joe Pride would have been a good way to pass the time in*
> *her younger days, but she needed to concentrate on*
> *heavyweights now, contenders for the championship wed-*
> *ding ring, men who had to be able to provide well for her in*
> *a manner she planned to grow accustomed to.* (p. 16)

Notes: Gay G. Gunn is also listed in the "Suggestive" section of this chapter.

Keywords: dating • Detroit, Michigan • men and women

Hailstock, Shirley.

***A Family Affair*. Washington, D.C.: BET, 2002. ISBN 0-7394-2883-7. 300p.**

Well respected in her field, Dr. Brenda Reid moves to Meyers University in California to become a professor of astronomy. She hopes to start over again, putting a bad relationship behind her. When she meets the sexy Dr. Wesley Cooper, she can't help feeling an attraction but is determined to limit their time together. Dr. Cooper, who bet his colleagues he could find a surrogate mother for his child within one year, feels a strong connection with Brenda.

She heard her name called. She knew it was Wes's voice, but she kept walking. She'd ignore him. She didn't want to admit how much she wanted to talk to him, to be in his company, to go to that party where she could see him, possible dance with him one more time. (p. 45)

Keywords: educators • family life • physicians

Hampton, Robin Lynette.

Breeze. **Columbus, Miss.: Genesis, 1994. ISBN 1-885478-07-0pa. 219p.**

R&B queen Breeze Blackwell seemingly has the world at her feet. But her heart still aches for her lost love, Alexander "Lex" Franklin, renowned guitarist and record producer. Now a decade after treachery tore them apart, he returns and wants her back.

> *Lex had changed from the picture she had planted in her mind. The teenager had become a man, an undeniably handsome man with confidence, even a bit of cockiness in his demeanor. Breeze sensed a seen-it-all, done-it-all air surrounding him, a wariness in his deep, dark brown eyes. His hair was combed back rippled with waves, and he sported a smooth beard.* (p. 137)

Notes: Robin Lynette Hampton also writes under the name Robin Hampton Allen, listed in the "Erotic" section of this chapter.

Keywords: reunions • rhythm and blues music and musicians • singers

Hill, Donna.

Quiet Storm. **Columbus, Miss.: Genesis, 1998. ISBN 1-88478-29-1pa. 185p.**

Concert pianist Deanna Winters finds her career and personal life in shambles after a riding accident leaves her without sight. Her adjustment to the changes in her life is difficult but made easier once she meets Clay McDaniels. Not only does she start to realize what she is missing by withdrawing from life, but she also falls in love. Although events from Clay's past surface and threaten their relationship, so does the presence of other suitors, especially the surgeon who is confident he can restore Deanna's sight.

> *"Because from the little I've seen and what I've heard from someone very close to you, you're worth caring about. The world misses your music, your playing. They miss the magic spells that you cast over their lives. I know I do."* (p. 67)

Notes: Donna Hill is also listed in the "Suggestive" and "Erotic" sections of this chapter and in the "Contemporary Life" section of Chapter 9.

Keywords: jazz music and musicians • New York City • people with disabilities

Soul to Soul. **Columbus, Miss.: Genesis, 2000. ISBN 1-58571-000-8pa. 179p.**

Leone Weathers, owner of the Soul to Soul nightclub and restaurant in Brooklyn, feels her life is finally together: She is over a divorce, her teenaged daughter is thriving, and business is good. When her bandleader, Cole Fleming, hires saxophonist Ray Taylor, Leone is immediately attracted to Ray despite his being younger and a reputed ladies' man. Ray is determined to convince Leone he is the man for her. Cole, however, teaches Leone much about love.

> *Guilt stabbed her with his last comment. She sat there for several minutes thinking about what Cole said, trying to search out what was in her heart, but the image wouldn't come clear.* (p. 24)

Notes: Donna Hill is also listed in the "Suggestive" and "Erotic" sections of this chapter and in the "Contemporary Life" section of Chapter 9.

Keywords: intergenerational love affairs • musicians • restaurant owners • single parents

Jackson, Brenda.

Ties That Bind. **New York, St. Martin's Press, 2002. ISBN 0-312-30611-3pa. 357p.**

Jenna and Randolph meet at college and feel their love will last forever. They do not foresee the difficulties—deceitfulness, his wealthy grandmother's disapproval and other family complications, even pregnancy. Divided into three sections and covering a span of more than 30 years, this character-driven novel highlights important and critical moments in their lives.

> *Randolph wished he could tell Trey the truth that he had never loved Angela. His heart had always belonged to Jenna, and if Angela hadn't been so deceitful, he would be married to Jenna today.* (p. 238)

Notes: Brenda Jackson is also listed in the "Suggestive" section of this chapter.

Keywords: Atlanta, Georgia • friendships • husbands and wives • men and women

Jenkins, Beverly.

A Chance at Love. **New York: Avon, 2002. ISBN 0-06-050229-0pa. 372p.**

On her way to California, Loreli Winters, a wealthy gambler, travels with several mail-order brides. In Kansas, charming twin orphan girls plead convincingly with her to become their new mother. Although their bachelor uncle, Jake Reed, desperately needs someone to care for his nieces, he is a farmer with strict morals and little experience with any woman, let alone one so knowledgeable about the ways of the world. These opposite personalities inevitably lead to dynamic conflicts and fiery attraction.

> *His honesty made Loreli wonder why he'd revealed such a truth to her, a woman he'd known only a few days. On the other hand, she'd revealed a truth about herself and could find no reason as to why. She did know that they'd just exchanged tiny parts of their souls. As a result, something*

touched her inside, but she wasn't sure what it was. (p. 52)

Notes: Romance in Color Award of Excellence September 2002

Keywords: gambling and gamblers • mail-order brides

Through the Storm. New York: Avon, 1998. ISBN 1-56865-852-4. 368p.

Sable, illegitimate daughter of a plantation owner raised and educated in the Big House, is about to become the property of Henry Morse, a local opportunist who had long had his eye on her. She escapes and finds refuge in a camp for former slaves run by the Union Army. The camp leader, Major Raimond LeVeq, is clearly enchanted by her. She earns her keep doing laundry, working tirelessly in the camp hospital, and assisting others by reading and writing for them. When Morse locates her, she feels threatened and escapes to the North. Despite their growing relationship, she did not tell LeVeq her plans and stole travel money from his tent. A few years later she finds herself in New Orleans and is introduced to LeVeq's family. They unwittingly choose her to be Raimond's wife—a wife Raimond wants only to fulfill inheritance requirements.

> *"I have no desire to be your mistress or anyone else's."*
>
> *"Why not?"*
>
> *Sable pretended to think deeply. "Well, let's see. I've been a slave for thirty years, subject to the whims of whoever owned me. Why in heaven would I trade my newly found freedom for a different kind of enslavement?"* (p. 139)

Keywords: Civil War • escaped slaves • mixed-race people • reunions • slavery

Joe, Yolanda.

Bebe's By Golly Wow. New York: Doubleday, 1998. ISBN 0-385-49255-3. 289p.

Fireman Isaac Sizemore spots Bebe, a middle-aged bank supervisor, at her graduation ceremony and makes a date with her. Isaac is divorced with a 13-year-old daughter, Dashay, who does all she can to thwart the budding romance. The story is told through the voices of these three characters and Bebe's best friend, Sandy. Young enough to be Bebe's daughter, Sandy has her own love and faces career roadblocks. Comedic elements and lively dialogue contribute to an entertaining, lightweight story.

> *I packed me a triumph kit. Forget survival. I wanted to triumph. I put in it several packs of ribbed condoms, a bottle of wine with one glass, two cassette tapes of love songs, and scented body oil. I took it with me in a little leather bag I could sling over my shoulder.* (p. 239)

Notes: Yolanda Joe is also listed in the "Psychological Suspense" and (as Ardella Garland) in the "Amateur Detectives—Women" sections of Chapter 4 and in the "Contemporary Life" section of Chapter 9.

Keywords: Chicago, Illinois • family life • firefighters • humor • interpersonal relations • single parents

Johnson, Doris.

Rhythms of Love. **Washington, D.C.: BET, 2002. ISBN 1-58314-214-2pa. 302p.**

Modern dancer Brynn Halstad focuses her life on her art until an injury forces her to take time off to heal both body and spirit. Simeon Story, musician and jazz club owner, feels she is much too much a diva for him but cannot deny the attraction between them. He challenges her to leave New York and use his Poconos retreat to recover from her injuries. Brynn knows her career and her future, perhaps even Simeon's love, are at stake.

> *Simeon's thick brows drew together in a thoughtful frown. If he'd held her in disdain all these years he'd been wrong and had to set things right within himself. He owned himself that much. And her. Only then he'd be able to finish his composition. In his heart he knew that it would never do another dancer justice. Dared he dream that one day she would dance for him?* (p. 29)

Notes: Doris Johnson is also listed in the "Suggestive" section of this chapter.

Keywords: dancers • musicians

Kitt, Sandra.

Close Encounters. **Thorndike, Maine: G. K. Hall, 2000. ISBN 0-7838-9271-3 (large print). 426p.**

Out walking her dog one night, Carol Taggert is caught in the crossfire of an undercover drug bust. Surprisingly, the bullet wound is revealed to be from Lt. Lee Grafton's gun rather than the criminal's. When the divorced, white police officer and Carol meet, there is an immediate connection and he becomes her companion as she recovers. Carol is reluctant to file a lawsuit, although urged to do so by her family and friends. Rather, she wants to focus on her new appreciation of life and the understanding of her changing views on race and identity as well as her relationship with Grafton.

> *Carol had her own regrets as she watched the car pull away. The thing is, was the shooting the kind of barrier that they could bridge? Afterward, crossing back to the world as they'd known it might not be possible. Perhaps it was even unwise to cultivate any kind of relationship under the circumstances, except that what stood between her and Lee was also the thing they both had in common.* (p. 235)

Notes: Sandra Kitt is also listed in the "Suggestive" section of this chapter.

Keywords: interracial relationships • police officers

Louise, Kim.

True Devotion. **Washington, D.C.: BET, 2002. ISBN 1-58314-284-3pa. 316p.**

Marti Allgood is an artist who paints for the healing potential rather than profit. When one of her paintings is mistakenly sold to art collector Kenyon Williams, she sets out to retrieve it, with unexpected results. Kenyon believes Marti may be the next great African American woman artist and wants to support her efforts. Though Kenyon feels unworthy of love because of a past family experience, romance blossoms—for a time.

> *He was dark and mysterious like a smoky night. His deep black eyes, long nose, and marvelous mouth were always set, always stern. She had yet to see him smile. Whenever she came to the mansion, he was always businesslike and treated their time together like one more item to check off his daily task list. And that fact was starting to work on Marti's nerves.* (p. 69)

Keywords: art and artists • Atlanta, Georgia

Palfrey, Evelyn.

Dangerous Dilemmas. **New York: Simon & Schuster, 2001. ISBN 0-671-04222-Xpa. 255p.**

Audrey Roberts's life is in turmoil. She is divorcing her lawyer husband after finding him in bed with another man. Her son Malcolm is accused of robbing and murdering a store clerk, a charge he denies. Just as she feels she has reached her limit, she meets Kirk Maxwell, a widower, and the two are attracted to each other. Once she learns Maxwell is the lieutenant in charge of her son's case, the situation changes for both of them.

> *Intense pain ripped through her foot and tears rushed to her eyes. She couldn't stop them—the tears she hadn't allowed to come for what Sam had done to her, the tears she hadn't allowed to come for her son. In this moment of weakness, they were stronger than she was. She couldn't hold them back now. They streamed down her face, melting the mask.* (p. 24)

Notes: Evelyn Palfrey is also listed in the "Suggestive" and the "Erotic" sections of this chapter.

Keywords: divorce • mothers and sons • police officers • romantic suspense • Texas

Thomas, Jacquelin.

Stolen Hearts. **Washington, D.C.: BET, 2002. ISBN 1-58314-347-5pa. 279p.**

Raven Christopher's child has been kidnapped. She knows Andre Simon can help her. Once lovers, Raven destroyed their relationship by participating in an art heist. Andre, a gifted artist, felt betrayed and refused to have any more contact with her. Now, two years later, Raven begs for his assistance. Andre's impulse is to refuse, but he recognizes a mother's anguish.

> *Resigned, Raven hung up, tears spilling down her face. She closed her eyes, feeling utterly miserable. Andre hated her and he had every right to feel that way, but it didn't lessen the pain.* (p. 10)

Notes: Jacquelin Thomas is also listed in the "Christian Fiction—Family" and "Christian Fiction—Inspirational Romance" sections of Chapter 7.

Keywords: art and artists • kidnapping • men and women • reconciliation

Thomas, Wanda Y.

Passion's Journey. **Columbus, Miss.: Genesis, 2002. ISBN 1-58751-076-8pa. 376p.**

Jacqueline Tyler, a woman of mixed race, meets Henrico Augustini while on a Caribbean vacation cruise. She is recovering from a broken relationship while he is taking a well-deserved vacation. He is also separating himself from his father's meddling efforts to choose his bride. Henrico realizes Jacqueline is the woman for him and relentlessly pursues her. She is reluctant to acknowledge his powerful attraction. Jacqueline has to come to terms with a love that does not recognize color.

> *He was right about one thing. This was definitely something she would have to work through for herself. But she couldn't shake the feeling that somehow an examination would not be necessary as in one little corner of her mind the conflict had already been resolved.* (p. 158)

Notes: Wanda Y. Thomas is also listed in the "Suggestive" section of this chapter.

Keywords: Caribbean nations • interracial relationships • mixed-race people

Walters, Linda.

On a Wing and a Prayer. **New York, BET, 2002. ISBN 1-58314-355-6pa. 297p.**

Lauren Traynor, senior flight attendant, meets wealthy entrepreneur Michael Townsend on one of her flights. Hesitant about developing any type of relationship, she is especially reluctant to date a passenger, however appealing. Michael's business connections with the family of Lauren's roommate provide further complications, as does his focus on work rather than personal matters. Yet neither can deny their passion.

> *They both laughed, realizing each would be a formidable opponent. She had to admit that he was at least quick on his feet, but then that too was part of the game. She smiled then, realizing it was going to be an interesting evening after all.* (p. 44)

Keywords: entrepreneurs • flight attendants • New York City

Weber, Carl.

★ *Lookin' for Luv.* **New York, Kensington, 2000. ISBN 1-57566-695-2pa. 342p.**

Four male coworkers at a Queens high school search for love through a dating service (1-900-Black-Luv). Despite having decidedly different backgrounds and motivations, each matures through his encounters with women. The drama of love, coupled with humorous episodes, treachery, competition, and revenge, all contribute to the progress of true connections.

> *Alicia knew she was revealing a lot of information for a first date, but she had decided that if she met a man who couldn't handle her past, she wanted to know right away. She wasn't about to waste time.*
> (p. 30)

Notes: Blackboard Bestseller List 2000

Keywords: dating • educators • men and women

★ *Married Men.* **New York, Kensington, 2001. ISBN 1-57566-696-0pa. 360p.**

Lifelong friends Kyle, Allen, Wil, and Jay all experience difficulties in their relationships with women, especially their wives. These stereotypical characters represent a variety of careers and situations. Kyle owns a beauty supply business but focuses on hiding his white wife from his customers. Jay married Kenya more out of duty than love and has difficulty with monogamy. Allen is a mama's boy who is ready to commit to Rose. Her controlling behavior, however, produces conflict between Allen and his mother. Wil shares everything with his wife, Diane, but then struggles to maintain a relationship with her. Through it all the friends are there for each other.

> *"I want you all to know I love you. We've been best friends since the fifth grade and better friends a man has never had. You three have always been there for me, and I wanna thank you for that. Lisa may have my heart, but it's you guys that built it. I love you."* (p. 4)

Notes: *Essence* Bestseller List 2002

Keywords: husbands and wives • men and women • men's friendships

Wright, Courtni.

Paradise. **Washington, D.C.: BET, 1999. ISBN 1-58314-006-9pa. 253p.**

History teacher Ashley Stephens chooses to join an archaeological dig in Egypt during her sabbatical. While working on the tomb of an ancient king, Ashley meets archaeologist Kasim Sadam, whose exotic looks and intensity fascinate her. Kasim is definitely attracted to her but focuses on the seriousness of his expedition, especially when evidence points to intended theft of artifacts. When Ashley is kidnapped the realities of their connection take precedence over all.

> *The click of the latch sounded like the closing of a prison door to Ashley's ears as she wondered if the manager would find her and if she would ever by free again. She listened as the retreating sound of Omar's sandals grew fainter and fainter. She doubted that any intercontinental police force regardless of its ability would find him either.* (p.171)

Keywords: archaeology and archaeologists • educators • kidnapping

Erotic

Alers, Rochelle.

Private Passions. Washington, D.C.: BET, 2001. ISBN 1-58314-151-0pa. 333p.

After Emily Kirkland, a successful and beautiful journalist, returns from a post-Christmas break in the Caribbean to cover the New Mexico gubernatorial race, she discovers her long-awaited promotion has gone to someone else. Moreover, she now must cover the campaign of the sleazy opponent of her close childhood friend, Christopher Delgado. Chris, spurred by media reports of Emily's engagement, determines to speak his mind. The two, both emotionally intense and fiercely independent, confront this new level of relationship. His race for governor, family scandal, and her professional responsibilities provide tension and conflict in their relationship.

> *The kiss lasted only seconds but everything that was Christopher Blackwell Delgado had lingered. Every boy and man she'd ever met or dated paled when she compared them to the young man who had captured her heart with a single kiss.* (p. 63)

Notes: Rochelle Alers is also listed in the "Suggestive" and the "Sensual" sections of this chapter.

Keywords: Caribbean nations • family relationships • Jamaica • journalism and journalists • Mexico • politics and politicians

Allen, Robin Hampton.

Hidden Memories. Columbus, Miss.: Genesis, 1997. ISBN 1-885478-16-Xpa. 288p.

Sage Kennedy was instrumental in ensuring the new Georgia governor's election. It had been a fiery campaign characterized by racial overtones. Now Sage is at a crucial decision point in both her career and her relationship with her fiancé, Ramion Sandidge. Sage is pulled to the forefront as Ramion begins his own campaign for the Senate against his unscrupulous former lover.

> *"I believe you," Sage said, knowing in the deepest corner of her heart that Ramion wouldn't betray her like that. But it was hard to trust. She was afraid of being made a fool. She didn't want to be betrayed the way Aaron had betrayed her mother.* (p. 161)

Notes: Robin Hampton Allen also writes under the name Robin Lynette Hampton, listed in the "Sensual" section of this chapter.

Keywords: political campaigns • politics and politicians

Hill, Donna.

A Scandalous Affair. Washington, D.C.: BET, 2000. ISBN 1-58314-118-9pa. 349p.

Activist Samantha Montgomery agrees to help handsome civil rights attorney Chad Rushmore with a police brutality case in Washington, D.C. What she doesn't expect is conflict with her attorney sister Simone and an overpowering attraction to Chad. Sequel to *Scandalous*.

> *She felt him behind her before he uttered a word. It was as if the air was suddenly cut off and a gentle warmth wrapped around her. The muscles in her stomach fluttered and she nearly sloshed the dark amber liquid on the sideboard as she added a stirrer to each drink.* (p. 105)

Notes: Donna Hill is also listed in the "Suggestive" and the "Sensual" sections of this chapter and in the "Contemporary Life" section of Chapter 9.

Keywords: attorneys • police brutality • sisters • social activists and activism

Palfrey, Evelyn.

The Price of Passion. New York: Simon & Schuster, 1997. ISBN 0-671-04220-3pa. 370p.

Vivian Carson's defining moment comes when Walter, her husband of nearly 20 years and a Texas state representative, brings home his illegitimate baby girl for her to look after. Long aware of his philandering, Vivian has considered leaving him, and this is the last straw. Childless herself, she decides to take the baby (supposedly a "homeless adoptee") with her. She struggles to keep her law-school schedule, spend time with the baby, Passion, and arrange childcare. She meets a local professor, Marc Kline, who offers her friendship and helps in many ways, including avoiding Walter who, for political reasons, wants her to come home.

> *Vivian felt like a lightning bolt had struck her. Although she recovered quickly, the smile froze on her face as her body went cold all over. What could she do? Cry? Fall out in a dead faint? She had the urge to throw the chair back, grab the mike and yell, "He's a liar! This is his yard-baby!"* (p. 35)

Notes: Evelyn Palfrey is also listed in the "Suggestive" and "Sensual" sections of this chapter.

Blackboard Bestseller List 1999; *Romantic Times Magazine* Best Multicultural Book of 2000

Keywords: educators • graduate students • husbands and wives • illegitimate children • politics and politicians

Riley, Mildred E.

Love Always. **Columbus, Miss.: Genesis, 1997. ISBN 1-885478-15-1pa. 191p.**

Simone Harper, a successful Boston financial consultant, meets and soon marries Dr. Anton (Tony) Housner. The combination of career stress, being newlyweds, and the clash of their strong personalities soon has Simone considering separation and divorce. Adding to the tension is the appearance of Simone's ex-husband claiming their annulment is not legal. Tony's love of Simone and determination for a successful marriage are thoroughly tested.

> *Despite everything, she did feel content when she was with her husband. He had a natural talent for making her feel that way. She only wanted him to understand her and appreciate her more. He always seemed happiest when he was in charge, as if he alone could make decisions. Why was she like that, she wondered, and why did she rail at authority when she enjoyed being cared for?* (p. 76)

Notes: Mildred Riley is also listed in the "Suggestive" section of this chapter.

Keywords: divorce • financial consultants and managers • husbands and wives • physicians

Zane.

The Heat Seekers. **New York: Atria Books, 2002. ISBN 0-7434-4289-X. 292p.**

This is the steamy story of two sets of best friends and their relationships. Tempest, tired of the sorry "mofos" she's been dating, and Geren, tired of desperate gold diggers, meet at a local bar where both are reluctantly accompanying their best friends, Janessa and Devonté, both of whom are looking for fast and easy sex. Tempest and Geren's relationship develops slowly, while Janessa and Devonté quickly become lovers. The relationships are threatened, however, by the secrets Tempest and Geren are afraid to reveal, Janessa's pregnancy, and Devonté's fear of commitment. Told with humor, sexual detail, and sympathy.

> *Tempest pushed the leather jacket off him and noticed his dick was hard. She rubbed her belly button up against it and licked a trail from his chest up to his chin. "So how can I make it up to you?"* (p. 179)

Keywords: adoption • husbands and wives • men and women • unwed mothers

Chapter 11

Speculative Fiction

Kari Moore

Through science fiction you can have a black president, a black world, or simply a say in the way things are. This power to imagine is the first step in changing the world. It is a step taken every day by young, and not so young, black readers who crave a vision that will shout down the realism imprisoning us behind a wall of alienating culture.—Mosley (2000, 406)

Definition

The term *speculative fiction* can be used to cover a broad array of current and past literature. Darko Suvin's definition, though intended to describe only science fiction, is useful in defining the speculative fiction genre as a whole. It is "a literary genre whose necessary and sufficient conditions are the presence and interaction of estrangement and cognition, and whose main formal device is an imaginative framework alternative to the author's empirical environment" (Suvin in Hartwell 1984, 122). In each of the genres of speculative fiction—science fiction, fantasy, and horror—readers are exposed to a reality that is to some degree distorted or alternative to the one in which we live.

The genres that comprise speculative fiction are so closely related that authors may disagree with the categorization of their works, may change genres from book to book, or may use elements of each in a single novel. Distinctions among these genres are important, however, for readers often evince a distinct preference for one and may even have a strong dislike for another.

Science fiction and fantasy have traditionally been closely linked. Science fiction is generally recognized as having some basis in accepted scientific principle. "What fantasy and science fiction share is a preoccupation with 'other' worlds—science fiction in a universe still full of mystery but potentially to be understood; fantasy in a universe boundlessly extended through the author's imagination" (Rosenberg 1982, 210). That is, the events and context of a science fiction story could occur, though in some cases it appears extremely unlikely. A science fiction universe is ordered according to laws of nature as we on Earth have discerned them. As Sam Moskowitz explains in his *Explorers of the Infinite*, "Science fiction is a branch of fantasy identifiable by the fact that it eases the 'willing suspension of disbelief' on the parts of its readers by utilizing an atmosphere of scientific credibility for its imaginative speculations in physical science, space, time, social science and philosophy" (1963, 11).

On the other hand, fantasy is not limited to the possible—simply to the imaginable. Fantasy worlds are governed only by a set of rules created by the author. Although the order must be consistent, it must only be consistent within itself and need have no relationship to reality as we know it. The workings of the fantastic universe are possible only in our imaginations.

These distinctions between genres are sometimes ambiguous, and rigid classification is inappropriate. A modern trend is the infusion of fantastic elements into traditional science fiction. This deliberate marriage of the two forms has led to the recognition of "science fantasy" as a subgenre of science fiction (Herald 2000).

Horror, the third genre included in speculative fiction, shares elements of both fantasy and science fiction but is distinguished by two elements. The key device of horror is its reliance on a personification of evil, whether that tangible form is an alien, a monster, or a haunted house. Indeed, Fonseca and Pulliam define the genre in terms of the presence of "a monster," whatever its form (1999, 4). In addition, horror focuses on the emotional reaction of the reader. The monster is menacing; the genre is intended to evoke feelings of dread and fear.

Appeal

Speculative fiction appeals "to those who are dissatisfied with the way things are: adolescents, post-adolescents, escapists, dreamers, and those who have been made to feel powerless" (Mosley 2000, 405). It allows readers to explore the unknown and the wonderful and terrible possibilities of the past, present, or future in the safety and security of their own homes. Fantasy and horror offer the liberating but sometimes eerie feeling of freedom, of a world without limits, but also without the familiarity of natural law. Fantasy and horror appeal to the emotions and share an imaginative and magical approach to the world, but whereas horror is menacing and lends a sense of dread, fantasy is optimistic and tends to be heroic in scale. Science fiction, on the other hand, appeals to the intellect and takes a rational outlook (Saricks 2001). It allows the freedom of "what if?" but makes the goals and ideas seem reachable. As Paul Levinson, president of Science Fiction and Fantasy Writers of America says, "It's the literature of hope and liberation, and this resonates with black Americans because it speaks positively to worlds that are different than the ones that sometimes have marginalized them" (Arnold 2000).

Speculative fiction, then, may appeal to different readers for different reasons. Some will read for the physical rush associated with fear, others because they enjoy liberating their imaginations, and still others because they find the format useful for exploring societal and psychological themes from a unique and unfamiliar vantage point. In each case, these thoughts and emotions allow the reader to explore the world from the safe and removed perspective of a reality that does not—and perhaps will never—exist.

Evolution

Samuel Delany (2000), a prolific writer of science fiction and critical commentary, refers to the beginnings of black authors in "proto-science fiction." The earliest African American authors used elements of speculative fiction in their writing to further their political message, and their stories focused almost entirely on alternative realities dealing with relationships between owners and slaves, whites and blacks. In *Blake, or the Huts of Africa* (1859), Martin R. Delany told the (fictional) story of a successful slave revolt in Cuba and several southern states, ending with the implication of further widespread and permanent changes in the social order (Govan 1997). Sutton E. Griggs provided an instantly recognizable Texas in his *Imperium in Imperio* (1899), but described an alternate reality in which a secret society plots the overthrow of the existing government and the substitution of a separate black state governed by black men. A ride in a blimp leads to suspended animation in Edward Johnson's *Light Ahead for the Negro* (1904). When the protagonist awakens, he is greeted by a socialist state in which the American South is leading a movement for social equality among races (Govan 1997). Pauline Hopkins, writer and editor-in-chief of *Colored American Magazine*, introduced a feminist matriarchal element in *Of One Blood* (originally serialized in *CAM* between 1902 and 1903). The descendants of the people of Meroe (Ethiopia/ ancient Kush) are found in the hidden African city of Telassar, where a female monarch and her council of sages plan to restore the nation of Kush (Grayson 2003, 10–11).

Other early African American authors enriched their novels with supernatural elements. In *The Conjure Woman* (1899), Charles Waddell Chesnutt mixed black folklore, fantasy, magic, and voodoo to tell moving stories of slave life in which escape and freedom imagery is presented in easily accessible and everyday terms. Pauline Hopkins allowed her villain to see into the future in *Contending Forces* (1900). To study the nature of evil, she reflected on whether the vision of his terrible death would affect his behavior or whether uncontrollable "bad blood" had preordained his evil actions (Govan 1997).

The most immediately recognizable forerunner of modern science fiction is perhaps George Schuyler. In his *Black No More: Being an Account of the Strange and Wonderful Workings of Science in the Land of the Free, A.D. 1933–1940* (1931), a three-day treatment allows black people to turn themselves white, resulting in tragic and unforeseen consequences. The mad scientist whose work has the potential for changing the world, a common device in speculative fiction, is often used to explore the relationship of man and nature. Schuyler returns to the political message of earlier black speculative authors with two long stories in which a black organization plots to take over the world (Delany 2000). Written under the pen name Samuel I. Brooks, *The Black International* and *Black Empire* were initially published as weekly serial installments in the *Pittsburgh Courier* between 1936 and 1938. They were not published as complete texts in book form until 1991 (under the title *Black Empire*) (Govan 1997).

Truly speculative texts are not seen again until nearly the1960s. As earlier work employed fantasy and alternative histories to call attention to the Negro's right to freedom and equality, the newer works used imaginative elements to popularize the social and political ideologies that created and sustained the modern Civil Rights Movement. William Melvin Kelley's *A Different Drummer* (1959) delves into the relationship of the races through a story line in which all of the African Americans in a community mysteriously and suddenly disappear. Other writers focus on more institutionalized racism, focusing on the relationship of African Americans to their government. John A. Williams's *The Man Who Cried I Am* (1967) explores the possibility of a government genocide policy directed against African Americans, presaging a common theme that persists to the present day in novels such as Arnold Xavier's *The Genocide Files* (1997, see Chapter 4). Williams's *Captain Blackman* (1972) involves a protagonist who travels through time to serve as a soldier in every American war from the Revolution and into the future. Conversely, it is an African American CIA agent who plots racial unrest and revolution in *The Spook Who Sat by the Door* (1969) by Sam Greenlee (Govan 1997).

This mixing of elements from different eras takes on a new look in the work of contemporary author Ishmael Reed. Although not generally considered a genre writer, Reed introduced many speculative aspects into his stylish and satirical work (Govan 1997). He combines cowboys and ray guns, taxicabs and cavalries, and playfully juxtaposes hoodoo and technology.

The African American authors most often associated with science fiction and fantasy in the current context are Delany, Butler, Barnes, and juvenile author Virginia Hamilton (Castro et al. 1997; Govan 1997). Each has a unique style and is responsible for the growing richness and diversity of the field. Samuel R. Delany, generally recognized as the first African American science fiction writer of note, emerged in the early 1960s with the publication of *The Jewels of Aptor* (1962). A prolific as well as literate and eloquent writer, his significant contributions to the field have been recognized with several Nebula awards, the Hugo award, and an American Book Award Nomination. He has employed a number of devices and styles, incorporating variously elements of physics, geology, anthropology, sociology, psychology, and linguistics to address issues of race and sexuality. His pioneering work and sensitive treatment of these important themes led to a Bill Whitehead Memorial Award for Lifetime Excellence in Gay and Lesbian Literature. His fascination with language and literature, so apparent in his fiction, has in more recent years led him to concentrate on literary criticism (for which he has also been honored) and commentary on the publishing industry.

Octavia Butler, an imaginative and creative writer and one-time student of Delany's, published her first science fiction story, "Crossover," in 1971 and her first novel, *Patternmaster*, in 1976. The winner of both Hugo and Nebula Awards, she is noted for her success in appealing to both traditional and nontraditional audiences with elegantly written stories that combine racial and feminist themes. An author of great skill and insight, she is noted for her deft handling of complex and often paradoxical facets of a diverse culture: power and powerlessness, intelligence and self-destruction, creativity and conformity. She has been recognized for her extraordinary work with a MacArthur Prize Fellowship Award (the "genius" award).

Virginia Hamilton introduced science fiction to the African American juvenile audience. Her <u>Justice Trilogy</u> (*Justice and Her Brothers*, 1978; *Dustland*, 1980; and *The Gathering*, 1981) features an 11-year-old black girl (Justice), who becomes The Watcher, a being with extraordinary powers who visits the future to find that ecology is an issue that current generations cannot afford to overlook.

Steven Barnes brings a different focus to speculative fiction and actually prefers the term science fiction, placing his work squarely in the context of genre fiction. Unpretentious in his efforts, he brings elements of action adventure, mystery, and martial arts to his work. His first novel, *Dream Park* (1981), was coauthored with Larry Niven and has been followed by several other collaborative efforts. His work has a very contemporary feel, with its emphasis on martial arts, virtual reality, the human-machine interaction as exemplified in interactive computer games, and the nature of humanity in a culture that values science and technology. His first solo novel, *Street Lethal* (1983), marked the beginning of the series featuring Aubrey Knight, an African American martial arts expert who lives in a violent near-future.

Traditionally, horror fiction per se has not seemed to resonate with African American readers, although certainly elements of voodoo and magic abound in all forms of black literature. Black authors have only recently entered into the horror genre, but their numbers are growing as middle-class black audiences are creating larger markets for all types of fiction. Modern authors in the genre often use the supernatural being as a vehicle to explore alienation and the life of those who are marginalized by society. Themes of family and community, immortality and morality are often explored in speculative fiction, echoing a trend in other forms used by African American authors.

A racially and culturally diverse community of vampires is portrayed by Jewell Gomez in *The Gilda Stories: A Novel* (1991), which received Lambda Awards for Lesbian Science Fiction/Fantasy and Lesbian Fiction. Tananarive Due, author of *The Between* (1996) and *My Soul to Keep* (1997), has been recognized in the horror community with nominations for the International Horror Guild Award, Locus Poll Award, and the Bram Stoker Award. Her first two novels contain elements of the supernatural and evoke the visceral response typical of horror fiction while exploring themes of family, immortality, and morality.

Current Themes and Trends

Although it appears that speculative fiction is growing in popularity among African American authors, a debate over the nature—the very existence—of a unique category composed solely of black writers is apparent. Delany (2000) asserts that such a categorization is inherently racist: "But as long as racism functions *as* a system, it is still fueled by aspects of the perfectly laudable desires of interested whites to observe this thing, however dubious its reality, that exists largely by means of its having been named: African American science fiction." Mosley outlines limitations traditionally placed on African American authors and argues for the importance of a black perspective in speculative fiction as a means of envisioning and ultimately creating a new society: "We make up, then make real" (2000, 405).

Charles Saunders, an African Canadian writer in the genre, both anticipates and reinforces Mosley. He writes that in the 1970s, "[a] literature that offered mainstream readers an escape route into the imagination and, at its best, a window to the future, could not bestow a similar experience for black and other minority readers." (Saunders 2000, 398). He notes advances, but still urges African Americans to enter the field that "serves as the mythology of our technological culture." He concludes: "The onus is on us. We have to bring some to get some in outer space and otherspace, as we have done here on Earth. Just as our ancestors sang their songs in a strange land when they were kidnapped and sold from Africa, we must, now and in the future, continue to sing our songs under strange stars" (Saunders 2000, 404).

Given this debate within the field and the limited number of books and authors to analyze, it is somewhat difficult to define a set of unified characteristics that suggest trends common to African American speculative fiction. Elements such as race, sexuality, culture, and power, recur with growing frequency. The mere growth in demand for and production of speculative genre fiction by African American authors, however, is in itself the most remarkable aspect of the field.

Heritage

African heritage, traditions, and history play an important role in many of the novels as authors use them at different levels within the story and for varying effects. Octavia Butler interweaves Yoruba, Igbo, and ancient Kush traditional beliefs into her Patternist and Earthseed series (Grayson 2003, 5). Charlotte Watson Sherman uses traditions brought with the slaves as a healing influence in her stories. Steven Barnes's alternate history Bilalian Series relies heavily on the culture and religions of ancient African nations.

Just as important are the heritage, traditions, and culture African Americans inherited from their enslaved ancestors. One of the devices used by authors to show this is the "modern slave narrative." In Octavia Butler's *Kindred* she sends her character back to experience slavery firsthand. The experience of the main characters' ancestress under slavery is one of Steven Barnes's story lines in *Blood Brothers*.

Difference and Diversity

The exploration of the issues, feelings, and historical truths arising out of the African American experience suggest an emerging perspective. The stories explore issues of cultural perception and structure arising from sexual, racial, political, economic, or psychological difference.

Many of the books are set in multicultural communities. Works may feature black characters in prominent roles and people of color from varying ethnic backgrounds. Jewelle Gomez's *The Gilda Stories* covers all parts of the United States at different times, bringing in Native Americans, Mexicans, African Americans and other diverse characters from the local community. Interracial couples are not uncommon; Dee Williams's Trent Calloway series, in which the main characters' ex-wife is Mexican American, is just one example. Other stories, such as Octavia Butler's Xenogenesis Trilogy, in which humans and non-humanoid aliens marry, may feature the interrelationships of different species as a means of metaphorically exploring the interactions of characters who are alien to one another.

Sexuality

Sexuality is a common theme, either as a means of exploring power relationships or the ambiguity and arbitrariness of sexual labels. There is frankness about sexuality. No punches are pulled in describing even rape and incest; the language may be harsh and the images graphic, as in Percival Everett's *Zulus*. The writers see sexuality as a part of life, part of the story, and portray that part, as the character would feel it, not from the absolute and distant stance of an observer who may subscribe to a different moral code. Sexual mores and practices that differ from the generally accepted two-party heterosexual romantic relationship are frequently a part of the social landscape. If a character is homosexual or bisexual, that character's sexuality is usually portrayed accurately but matter-of-factly. The main character in Octavia Butler's *Patternmaster* readily accepts another's bisexuality; sexual practices other than the typical two-party adult heterosexual romantic relationship are frequently a central element in Samuel Delany's social landscapes.

Family

Themes of family relationships and cultural structures that support them are frequently, though not always, interwoven with racial and sexual ones. Such relationships play a pivotal role in Octavia Butler's work. Families are redefined in a surprising variety of ways, yet these seem not illogical based on current structures. Authors stretch the limits, bend the rules, and yet still keep the new families within the realm of the possible in the distant future. A fine example of this is Samuel Delany's *Nova,* in which crab-like aliens adopt human children and blend them into their own family structure.

Power

Not surprisingly, power and powerlessness are common themes. Many of the tales are of people who lack power, suffer abuse, and are committed to claiming power over their own lives and to exercising that power harshly when necessary. In some works, stupidity, ineptness, and lack of confidence are the results of deliberate programming, or they naturally fall out of a corrupt system perpetuated by class structures. In many novels, inspiration is drawn from the growing self-awareness and empowerment of the previously downtrodden. Nobility, self-sacrifice, and unexpected heroism serve to reinforce the human connections among all of us and bring hope to the least of us. The character Justice Douglass in Virginia Hamilton's Justice exemplifies these qualities.

Along with power comes the ability to change. Novels may feature a sub-theme of teaching, healing, and activism or the message that change is essential for a healthy future. Nalo Hopkinson, a Caribbean/Canadian author outside the scope of this chapter, features black female characters as active agents of change who fight for and claim their freedom in many of her novels, such as *Brown Girl in the Ring* and *Midnight Robber*, as does LeVar Burton in *Aftermath* (Grayson 2003, 81).

Publication Format

A word about form is important in appreciating the evolution of African American speculative fiction. Historically, the short story has served as an important format for speculative fiction authors, and this continues to be the case, as evidenced by the number of stories published in magazines and later collected, or that originally appeared in anthologies and collections. Sheree Thomas's *Dark Matter: A Century of Speculative Fiction from the African Diaspora,* is perhaps the best known anthology of short stories by African American authors. Anthologies by editors of the African Diaspora, such as *Mojo: Conjure Stories* (2003) by Nalo Hopkinson, may not contain African American authors exclusively. A reader may be unaware that authors are African American because their stories are not confined to collections based on author ethnicity. Instead, they are peppered throughout speculative fiction mainstays or specialty anthologies such as *Swords of the Rainbow: Gay and Lesbian Science Fiction* (1995).

To some extent, Web publishing appears to be the coming publication venue for beginning authors who need to make their work known. In some cases, entire books as well as short stories are available online at individual author sites. Further, several of the books in this chapter started as online or CD-ROM versions produced by their publishing houses as a means of determining demand, with paper copies subsequently produced in response. This can be seen with Brandon Massey's *Thunderland,* which was twice published as an on-demand book and a third time self-published before finally being picked up by Dafina Books.

Authors

Readers may be surprised to see familiar names included as speculative fiction authors. Better known as actors, LeVar Burton and Billie Dee Willams have tried their hands at science fiction, as has crime and mystery writer Walter Mosley. There appears to be something about the speculative form that encourages exploring talent and transcending boundaries.

Mood

Many of these stories occur in very dark and disturbing worlds, with horrible things happening to people. This doesn't mean, however, that all of the books are filled with weighty prose and deep thoughts. The books run the gamut from reflective to action packed, complex to simple, purposefully depressive to lively and visionary. Eric James Fullilove writes about a world that is dark as night in his Jenny Sixa Series, but his tone is such that the reader doesn't feel oppressed by it. In contrast ,Colson Whitehead's *The Intuitionist* takes place under an overcast sky, which is reflected in the story line to give the reader a palpable feeling of foreboding. Even though they may present a dark and grim picture, the stories usually carry a message of hope: No matter how grisly life gets there is a light at the end of the tunnel. Ultimately, this is the literature of survivors.

Advising the Reader

Typically, readers of speculative fiction will prefer one of the three genres and may even refuse to read another. Thus, this chapter is organized into sections based on the three genres of speculative fiction: science fiction, fantasy, and horror. Within each genre, annotations are organized by dominant themes:

- **Science Fiction**. Science fiction answers the question "what if?" (Herald 2000). With science fiction a reader must be willing to suspend disbelief but is given a plausible scientific context to make this suspension somewhat easier. Science fiction deals with such topics as space, time, aliens, and alternate dimensions.

  - **Alternate Realities**: a different, but possible, history

  - **Commentaries**: social, environmental, and political issues

  - **Post-civilization**: a ruined society in which people must find a new way to survive

  - **Psionic powers**: precognition, telepathy, clairvoyance, telekinesis, or teleportation

  - **Science fantasy**: an intermingling of fantasy settings with science and technology

  - **Space opera**: action, adventure, political intrigue, and sociological relationships

- **Fantasy**. Fantasy can take place in the mythical past, the present, or the distant future, but the story is one in which the worlds of the mundane and the magical intertwine. Fantasy involves powers or beings outside the realm of what our civilization considers real. Settings may look like our world or may be lavishly fantastic or primitively austere.

- **Horror.** Our nightmares are the raw material of horror. Filled with monsters, ghouls, vampires, and psychotic killers, horror is a journey into the unknown, the forbidden and the dangerous.

  - **Immortality:** the search for and implications of eternal life

  - **Supernatural**: all things existing or occurring outside humanity's normal experience

- **Short Fiction Collections**. Short stories, novellas, novelettes, and serials of science fiction, fantasy, horror, or all three brought together in an anthology.

Science Fiction

Alternate Realities

Barnes, Steven.

Bilalian Series.

> The series takes place in an alternate world where Africa is the center of power and Europe is a primitive place. Black Africans have colonized the New World, and Northmen sell abducted Irish and Germans into slavery. Barnes focuses on the coming of age of his two young protagonists, the effects of slavery, and the universal search for freedom by both master

Kai and slave Aidan. His subtle style leads the reader into an understanding of the different cultures involved.

> *Kai looked at Aidan for a long moment, and then pulled his knife. Aidan watched, more puzzled than fearful as Kai pressed the blade against his own left thumb. Kai flinched, and then a red drop of blood welled up. Kai stared at it, fascinated, then remembered his purpose and passed the knife to Aidan.* (p.151)

Keywords: Bilalistan • 1870s • family relationships • interracial relationships • slavery

Lion's Blood. New York: Warner Books, 2002. ISBN 0-44652-668-1. 461p.

Eleven-year-old Aidan O'Dere is captured and sold into slavery to a vast Southern plantation where he begins a turbulent 10-year friendship with his equally young master, Kai. The years see them through death, love, war, and eventually freedom.

Notes: Gold Pen Award Best Mainstream Fiction Nomination 2002

Keywords: coming of age • 1860s • honor

Zulu Heart. New York: Warner Books, 2003. ISBN 0-44653-122-7. 463p.

Four years have passed since Kai and Aidan have seen each other. Kai is entangled in intrigue surrounding a coming war • Aidan is on the frontier building a settlement of ex-slaves. But to save their families and the world from an apocalyptic civil war, they must join forces, and Aidan must once again become a slave.

Keywords*:* martial arts • mysticism • national identity • polygamy

Whitehead, Colson.

Colson Whitehead is a 2002 MacArthur Fellow.

The Intuitionist. **New York: Anchor Books, 1999. ISBN 0-38549-299-5. 255p.**

Lila Mae, the first female "colored" elevator inspector, is an Intuitionist in an Empiricist world. An inspector who feels and sees in her mind the health of the elevator, Lila Mae thinks she has been framed for an elevator freefall and must find the plans for the first Intuitionist elevator to clear herself. But finding the plans won't be easy with an Empiricist in power and the current Guild chair coming up for election. The language and detailed descriptions focus on Lila Mae's bleak surrounding and her struggles with racism and politics. The operation of elevators is used as a subtle and clever metaphor for life.

> *So complete is Number Eleven's ruin that there's nothing left but the sound of the crash, rising in the shaft, a fall in opposite: a soul.* (p. 65)

Keywords: New York City • politics and politicians • race relations • racial identity

Commentaries

Delany, Samuel R.

Dhalgren. New York: Bantam Books, 1982 (1974). ISBN 0-55325-391-3pa. 879p. New edition published by Vintage Books, 2001. ISBN: 0375706682.

A mysterious disaster has stricken the Midwestern city of Bellona, and its aftereffects are disturbing. Although most of the inhabitants have fled, others are drawn to the devastated city, among them the Kid, a biracial (Native American/white), bisexual drifter apparently suffering from amnesia. He becomes an acclaimed poet, the leader of a teenaged gang, and in the end is ejected from the city by a mysterious natural disaster. His reflections upon leaving cast doubt on the reality of the city. Delany creates a feeling of alienation and unreality through use of a nontraditional structure and unfamiliar use of language.

> The language that happened on other muscles than the tongue was better for grasping these. Things he could not say wobbled in his mouth, and brought back, vividly in the black, how at age four he had sat in the cellar, putting into his mouth, one after the other, blue, orange, and pink marbles, to see if he could taste the colors. (p. 543)

Notes: Locus Poll Award All Time Best SF Novel Nomination 1987; Locus Poll Award All Time Best SF Novel before 1990 Nomination 1998; Locus Poll Award Best SF Novel Nomination 1976; Nebula Award Nomination Novel 1975

Keywords: art and artists • Bellona • class relations • fictional religions • outcasts • race relations • sexual identity

Stars in My Pocket Like Grains of Sand. New York: Bantam Books, 1985 (1984). ISBN 0-55325-149-Xpa. 375p.

Rat Korga, programmed from birth to believe he is stupid and worthless, agrees to a Radical Anxiety Termination operation and becomes an industrial slave on his home world of Rhyonon. The sole survivor of the destruction of his planet, he is sent to live on Velm with Marq Dyeth, the industrial diplomat who is his erotic ideal. He lives with Marq's "nurture stream," a nongenetic, multigenerational, multi-species "family" grouping. After only one day, Rat's presence threatens Velm's stability and he is taken away from Marq, who may never recover. Delany uses creative and ambiguous language—for instance in the way that the pronouns "he" and "she" are imbued with different meanings in different cultures or the different connotations of "father" and "mother"—to explore issues of family and gender. Although sexual themes woven throughout the work reflect different moralities and intense feelings, the descriptions of physical acts are not graphic.

> *. . . wondering what I should say if I spoke first. . . . I thought of: Among the thousands of males I've bedded, at least a dozen times somebody has said to me, "You'll have to meet so-and-so. You'll just love him!" But this has got to be the strangest route I've ever traveled to end up sleeping with someone. And didn't say it. I glanced at him instead; he shifted mountains, planes, -wr.* (p. 213)

Notes: Locus Poll Award Best SF Novel Nominee 1985; Prometheus Award Best Libertarian SF Novel Preliminary Nominee 1985; Arthur C. Clarke Award Nominee 1987

Keywords: cultural conflict • family relationships • future civilizations • loneliness • sex roles • slavery

Trouble on Triton: An Ambiguous Heterotopia (also published as *Triton*). **Hanover, N.H.: University Press of New England, 1996 (1976). ISBN 0-81956-298-Xpa. 312p.**

Delany wrote this book without an ending so as to engage the reader in a conversation with him. Bron Helstrom is looking for love as well as self-discovery on the psychological utopia of Triton, where he finds true equality of the sexes, a welfare system that really works, and accommodation for any sexual or personal philosophy. He soon realizes that this utopia unsettles him, so he changes himself and the search begins all over again. Though there is no graphic sex or violence, some people may find the sexual possibilities unsettling. "On Delany the Magician," a foreword by Kathy Acker, discusses the intent of this novel and two appendixes by Delany, "From the *Triton* Journal" and "Ashima Slade and the Harbin-Y Lectures," explain why he wrote *Trouble*.

> *Bron lay her head back on the pillow. "I had to Lawrence. There are certain things that have to be done. And when you come to them, if you're a man . . . ." The drugs were making her laugh—"you just have to do them."* (p. 231)

Notes: James Tiptree Jr. Award Classics 1995; Locus Poll Award Best SF Novel Nomination 1977;
Nebula Award Novel Nomination 1976

Keywords: personal identity • sexual identity • Triton • 2100s • utopian communities

Lee, Mona.

Alien Child. **Seattle: Open Hand Publishing, 1999. ISBN 0-94088-062-8pa. 283p.**

Unbeknownst to Dana Krandel and her adoptive Earth family, she is half alien, mothered by a native of the peaceful planet Gallata. Dana gradually comes to recognize and understand the unusual psychic abilities that enable her to facilitate the transformation of a warring Earth into a just and peaceful society. The novel's antiwar message is served by the use of aliens to question our societal norms, taboos, and politics.

> *Wella shivered at the references they made to their institutionalized killing games.* (p. 10)

Keywords: aliens (humanoid) • family relationships • San Juan Islands, Washington • social activists and activism • telepathy

Lewis, Elbert, Jr.

The Dawn of MAN. **Lincoln, Neb.: Writers Club Press; iUniverse.com, 2001. ISBN 0-595-18587-8pa. 383p.**

The Dawn of MAN is an intriguing mix of military/political terrorist thriller with alternate history and alien invasions thrown in, based on the premise that humans are the result of alien DNA tampering in an attempt to breed the ultimate warrior. The aliens succeeded in producing their MAN (Mutation Accelerated Nemesis) with Logan, who seeks revenge on white supremacists for the death of one of his protégés. He foils their plot to kill off African Americans, then goes on to battle hostile aliens who plan on subjecting Earth.

> *In his hyper-percipient state, Driscoll's reactions and movements appeared pitifully slow and predictable. At the last possible moment Logan turned his torso and watched the bullet pass within an inch of his chest, seemingly to float by at less than a tenth of its actual velocity.* (p. 103)

Keywords: aliens (humanoid) • eugenics • FBI agents • hate crimes • journalism and journalists • 2000s • war stories

Lofton, Saab.

A.D. **Gualala, Calif.: III Pub, 1995. ISSN 0-96229-378-4pa. 306p.**

In the year 2030 AD, the White Aryan Resistance runs most of America, with several Midwestern states given to the Nation of Islam to run as they see fit. Elijah Isiah is arrested by the Fruit of Islam for the act of sedition and put into suspended animation as a medical experiment for 380 years. When he awakens, America has become a Libertarian Socialist Democracy, where blacks and whites live together in harmony. But all is not well in utopia. The hatreds and fears of the past have not totally departed. This intellectually humorous political commentary requires the reader to have some knowledge about 1960s and 1970s politics along with the political and philosophical differences between the Black Panthers and Black Muslims.

> *Since the general population was never taught in school or anywhere else what corporations were capable of, or even had the political will to fund fascists or overturn governments, no one thought it was unusual that by the summer of 2005, the Black Muslims no longer had to hawk their newspapers on street corners.* (p. 28)

Keywords: Chicago, Illinois • intraracial relations • politics and politicians • racism • religious persecution • 2030s • 2410s • utopian communities

Robinson, John C.

Secret of the Snow Leopard. Fort Bragg, Calif.: Lost Coast Press, 1999. ISBN 1-88289-729-3pa. 284p.

As colony ships desert a deteriorating Earth, Paul Torrden manages to continue the family's project to save Earth's snow leopards by relocating them to planet Refander. It is up to Paul's grandson Ian to fulfill his destiny and uncover the secret role of the creatures in saving humanity. The strong environmental message is complemented by detailed descriptions of nature, both terrain and alien.

> *Through the portal's technologically attuned speakers, he could hear Colonel purring, a quiet puffing sound typical of snow leopards. It were as if the leopard seemed to understand the thoughts that were going on inside his head.* (p. 21).

Keywords: environmentalists • space colonies • 2100s

Simms, William A.

Zuro!: A Tale of Alien Avengers. Glenside, Pa.: Waverly House, 1996 (1995). ISBN 0-96509-700-5pa. 340p.

Blacks and whites are descendants of people who came to Earth long ago from two different planets, Zuro and Cyripiton. Zurons, led by Captain Salumbai Eumgwa, revisit the Earth. Finding that the majority of blacks are poverty-stricken, powerless, and dominated by the descendants of the white Cyriptions, the Zurons seek parity for the dark peoples of the Earth. When negotiation and persuasion fail, they find they must resort to force in response to massive white resistance. Simms's story is a fun and lively read, though somewhat flawed by one-dimensional, stereotypical characters.

> *"No, General, I'm not going to annihilate the white man, as you call him; I'm going to educate the black man."* (p. 57)

Keywords: aliens (humanoid) • racism

Post-Civilization

Barnes, Steven.

Aubry Knight Series.

In a Los Angeles of the future devastated by earthquakes and fires, Aubry Knight is a virtual superman, raised and trained as an assassin for organized crime. At first he uses his awesome fighting skills for revenge, but once he begins to fight alongside his beautiful mate Promise, he takes on a corrupt world. Barnes pits his characters against their environment, making their growth all the more realistic and poignant in this rough and tumble series.

> *Death. Death was not the ultimate indignity. He had to die, as so many good men had died, had gone into the muck so that Aubry Knight might live. It was merely what was right,*

what was appropriate. And it felt good to be dying now, in this place, in this way. (Gorgon Child, p. 335).

Keywords: bioengineering • family relationships • martial arts

Street Lethal. New York: Ace, 1983. ISBN 0-44179-068-2pa. 310p.

Disgusted with his life as enforcer for the Ortegas and their bloody empire of drugs, prostitution, and black market body parts, Aubry realizes that he will have to become a hero if he is to walk away and still survive.

Keywords: organized crime • telepathy • 2020s

Gorgon Child. New York: Tor, 1989. ISBN 0-81253-152-3pa. 345p.

Aubry must save America from enslavement at the hands of a fanatical religious leader who plots to use genetically enhanced super-soldiers to overthrow the government. He must also confront the terrors of his past while Promise tries to discover the fate of their child. Neither is prepared to face the link between their separate missions.

Keywords: church men • communes • homophobia • 2020s

Firedance. New York: Tor,1995 (1994). ISBN 0-81251-024-0pa. 376p.

When his wife Promise and their unique child Leslie are threatened, Aubry travels to Africa to kill the dictator of United Africa. Exploring his mysterious past, he must face his own clones to save himself and his family.

Keywords: Africa and Africans • clones • hermaphrodites • 2030s

Burton, LeVar.

Aftermath: A Novel about the Future. **New York: Aspect, 1997. ISBN 0-44651-993-6. 274p.**

After several disasters befall the country, culminating in an all-out race war, Americans have very little formalized government and live in shantytowns plagued by cancer and other diseases. Dr. Rene Reynolds has developed a device that allows people to cure themselves. When those who don't want the populace cured kidnap her, she discovers a side effect of her invention: She can send her thoughts to some people. Unknown to her and to each other, three unlikely individuals have answered her call: a derelict, an orphaned child, and an elderly medicine man. Well-developed minor characters lighten this stark post-apocalyptic tale.

> *Leon's mother had tried to teach him how to share her love for God, but even as a child, Leon found it impossible to respect a God who could allow the world to be so full of pain. Science had become his religion. Now, he had nothing.* (p. 11).

Keywords: medicine men • orphans • race relations • telepathy • 2010s

Butler, Octavia E.

Octavia Butler is a 1995 MacArthur Fellow.

Earthseed Series.

Hyper-empath Lauren Olamina is crippled by the pain of others and, if she is lucky, she gets to revel in their pleasure. Development of Earthseed, her personal philosophy, and a community based on its principles, eventually puts her at odds with an extremist Christian element, as well as her own daughter and brother. In this dark and gripping series, Butler examines all the meanings of family and our need for it.

> *All that you touch you change. All that you change changes you. The only lasting truth is change. God is change.* (Parable of the Sower, p. 3).

Keywords: California • empathy • fictional religions • mothers and daughters

 Parable of the Sower. New York: Warner Books, 1993. ISBN 0-44660-197-7pa. 295p.

Lauren lives a sheltered life until violence explodes and the walls of her neighborhood are smashed, annihilating Lauren's family and friends. As she walks up the California coast seeking a new beginning, Lauren gathers a tiny band of other lost souls who are drawn to the promises of new life and a new faith in the form of Earthseed.

Notes: Arthur C. Clarke Award Early Submission 1996; Best Books for Young Adults 1995; Locus Poll Award Best SF Novel Nomination 1995; Nebula Award Novel Nomination 1994; YALSA Outstanding Books for the College Bound

Keywords: coming of age • 2020s

 Parable of the Talents. New York: Seven Stories Press, 1998. ISBN 1-88836-381-9. 365p.

The story of Acorn's establishment, destruction, and spiritual resurrection is told through a narrative written 50 years later by Lauren's daughter and the writings of her mother, father, and uncle.

Notes: Arthur C. Clarke Award Nomination 2001; Locus Poll Award Nomination Best SF Novel 1999; Locus Poll Award Best SF Novel 1999; James Tiptree Jr. Award Gender-bending SF Nomination 1998

Keywords: Portland, Oregon • religious persecution • 2030s

Butler, Octavia E.

Octavia Butler is a 1995 MacArthur Fellow.

Patternist Series.

Each novel in the <u>Patternist</u> series stands alone, and unlike many series, they may be read in any order. Regardless of whether the setting is the seventeenth century or the distant future, all are stories of the age-old quest for immortality and power. Whether the protagonists are vampires or shapeshifters, telepaths, aliens, or even mutated humans, alienation is the underlying theme as each "superior" race comes up against fear, discrimination, and segregation.

> *A telepath. One with more control of her ability than any I've produced so far, I hope. And from the body I used to father her, I hope she'll have inherited a few other abilities.* (Mind of My Mind, p. 16)

Notes: Books are listed in order of publication, not chronologically by story line.

Keywords: eugenics • immortality • psionic powers

Patternmaster. New York: Warner Books, 1995 (1976). ISBN 0-44636-281-6pa. 202p.

The Earth of the far future is ruled by the Pattern, the mind-force of a human telepathic race. Coexisting are the Clayarks, humans infected by an alien virus. The Patternists and the Clayarks wage war for control of Earth as brothers Coransee and Teray vie for control of the Pattern.

Notes: Blackboard Bestseller List 1995

Keywords: bisexuality • future civilizations • sibling rivalry • telepathy

Mind of My Mind. New York: Avon Books, 1978 (1977). ISBN 0-38040-972-0. 221p.

For 4,000 years, Doro has spread the seeds of an evolutionary master race, using the downtrodden underclass as his private breeding stock, hoping always to father an empire. But now his daughter Mary has found the way to awaken—and rule—her superhuman kind with the Pattern, and Doro is the only thing that stands between Mary and the infinite prospect of her empire.

Keywords: fathers and daughters • Forsyth, California • telepathy

Survivor. New York: Doubleday, 1978. ISBN 0-38513-385-5. 185p.

Missionaries devoted to spreading the sacred God-image of humankind adopt Alanna Verrick, a wild human. They carry Alanna to Canaan, a distant planet inhabited by two warring tribes, where they promptly form an alliance with the wrong (but more physically attractive) side. The humans are saved by Alanna's alien husband, Duit, one of the color-changing, hair-covered humanoid Kohns whom they found repulsive and rejected.

Notes: Butler over time has become dissatisfied with this book and it probably will never be re-released.

Keywords: aliens (humanoid) • interspecies marriage • prejudice

Wild Seed. New York: Warner Books, 1999 (1980). ISBN 0-44660-672-3pa. 279p.

In deep Africa, Doro finds the perfect mother to birth his nation, the centuries-old Anyanwu, who can heal with a touch and transform into anything she wills herself to be. When she doesn't wish to go to America to carry out his plan, Doro forces her to go. Now begins the centuries-long battle for her freedom.

Notes: James Tiptree Jr. Award Classics 1995; Locus Poll Award Nomination Best SF Novel 1981

Keywords: Africa and Africans • Avoyelles Parish, Louisiana • 1800s • healers and healing • mutants • 1900s • shapeshifting • 2000s

Clay's Ark. New York: St. Martin's Press, 1984. ISBN n/a. 186p.

Asa Elias Doyle, the sole survivor of the ill-fated starship *Clay's Ark*, is the leader of desperate people who have become innocent victims of a "close encounter" with an alien life form. The deadly entity attacks like a virus, but survivors of the disease genetically bond with it, developing amazing powers, near-immortality, and unnatural desires. They exile themselves to the desert to avoid contaminating others and create a secret colony of the transformed and the inhuman babies born within it. Their compulsion to infect others becomes overwhelming and, in a desperate plea for help, they kidnap Dr. Blake Maslin and his two daughters, Keira and Rane.

Notes: Locus Poll Award Best SF Novel Nomination 1985

Keywords: California desert • mutants • plague • 2020s

Butler, Octavia E.

Octavia Butler is a 1995 MacArthur Fellow.

Xenogenesis Trilogy.

A cataclysmic war on Earth has left most of the people dead and the rest dying when nonhumanoid aliens rescue some survivors. After 250 years of healing the Earth and studying humans, they are ready to reseed the Earth—but with a new combined race. Will the humans be willing to pay the price and accept their plan? The series examines humanity, both the good and the bad, through human and alien eyes, and gives us some hope for our survival.

> *Human beings fear difference . . . Oankali crave difference. Humans persecute their different ones, yet they need them to give themselves definition and status. Oankali seek difference and collect it. They need it to keep themselves from stagnation and overspecialization.* (Xenogenesis: Adulthood Rites, p. 321).

Notes: The trilogy is collected in *Xenogenesis* (New York: Warner Books, n.d.. ISBN 1-56865-033-7. 726p.)
Original copyright dates are included for each book in the trilogy.

Keywords: aliens (nonhumanoid) • eugenics • prejudice • mutants • self-esteem

Dawn. New York: Warner Books, 1987.

Lilith Iyapo is "awakened" to find that she has been chosen to revive her fellow humans. She must first prepare them to meet the utterly terrifying aliens and then train them to survive in the wilderness that the planet has become. Bonded to the aliens in ways no human has ever known, Lilith tries to fight them even as her own species comes to fear and loathe her.

Notes: Ditmar Award Best International Long Fiction Nomination 1989; Locus Poll Award Best SF Novel Nomination 1988

Keywords: love • outcasts • survival

Adulthood Rites. New York: Warner Books, 1988.

Akin, the son of Lilith, is part human, part Oankali. Kidnapped by the last generation of the savage and self-destructive humans, it is up to Akin to save the future of humanity.

Notes: Locus Poll Award Best SF Novel Nomination 1989

Keywords: decay of civilization • mixed-species children

Imago. New York: Warner Books, 1989.

Jodahs, another of Lilith's children, was thought to be a male but is actually maturing into the first ooloi from a human/Oankali union. He finds a pair of resisters who prove that some pure humans are still fertile. These humans may be his only hope to find successful mates, but they have been raised to revile and despise his species above all else.

Notes: Locus Poll Award Best SF Novel Nomination 1990

Keywords: mixed-species children • prejudice

Delany, Samuel R.

The Fall of the Towers.

In the distant past, Earth suffered an apocalyptic war, and only the small empire of Toromon is now free of radiation. The radiation has led to the formation of three separate races: what we think of as humans, the superior Forest People who are developing telepathy, and the inferior neo-Neanderthals. They are now in danger from an alien entity, The Lord of the Flames. Representatives of Earth, with the help of a second alien, the Triple Being, must try to save Earth from him and themselves. Characters recur throughout the series, assuming sometimes central, sometimes peripheral roles. You can only find the series as a collection now, which is fine as it is still a manageable length.

> *Jerk someone from one location; fling him in another. The elements in one location define the other. But sometimes the shock of transition is so great that definition does not begin.* (The Fall of the Towers: Out of the Dead City, p. 91).

Notes: The trilogy is collected in *The Fall of the Towers* (New York: Bantam Books, 1986. ISBN 0-55325-648-3pa. 401p.)

Original copyright dates are included for each book in the trilogy.

Keywords: aliens (humanoid and nonhumanoid) • computers • cultural conflict • Telphar • Toron • war stories

Out of the Dead City. New York: Ace Books, 1965 revised edition. (Previously published unrevised as *Captives of the Flame*.)

The men of Toromon have declared war on whatever is on the other side of the radiation barrier. What they don't know is that their enemy is The Lord of the Flames, an alien entity residing in one of them.

Keywords: conspiracies • prejudice

The Towers of Toron. New York: Ace Books, 1965 revised edition.

It's three years later and the war is in full swing, but there is no physical war. It is all run by a supercomputer and is the plot of The Lord of the Flames.

Keywords: propaganda • psychology

City of a Thousand Suns. New York: Ace Books, 1965 revised edition.

The computer that ran the war uses what it has learned to protect itself from being dismantled, and The Lord of the Flames is still hovering near.

Keywords: civil unrest • economics • vengeance

Everett, Percival.

Zulus. Sag Harbor, N.Y.: Permanent Press, 1990. ISBN 0-93296-697-7. 245p.

No one cares when fat and unattractive Alice Achtiophel doesn't comply with the government's postwar edict requiring sterilization of all women. When she is raped and becomes pregnant, rebels sneak her out of the city to protect her and wait for the birth, but no one expects the outcome of this pregnancy. Language is very harsh and graphic, giving the story a gritty, angry tone.

> *Alice Achitophel watched him make a face, watched him look at her with wide eyes and knew, she knew that she would be pregnant, pregnant by this tall man with a little boy's penis, by this malodorous beast who said he only wanted to watch the snow.* (p. 11)

Keywords: future civilizations • political radicals

Psionic Powers

Fullilove, Eric James.

Jenny Sixa Series.

Jenny Sixa's telepathic talent nearly made her a high-priced prostitute in the mind-sex centers of Los Angeles. Now it earns her a morbid living as a police consultant, catching a glimpse of killers from the last thoughts of their victims.

Though the series deals with dark subjects it still manages to be a fast-paced read. The frank language and Jenny's sardonic sense of humor establish the tone without being crude or graphic.

> *The legacy of her capabilities, the filthy residue they left behind in her, indelible stains of dark fantasy and wild emotion that couldn't be washed away like semen from an unwanted lover.* (Circle of One, p. 12)

Keywords: murder • telepathy • 2050s

Circle of One. New York: Bantam Spectra, 1996. ISBN 0-55357-575-9pa. 247p.

A serial killer on the loose is leaving personal messages for Jenny in the minds of his victims, and Jenny must catch him before she succumbs to the brain disease that gifted her with her abilities.

Keywords: immortality • serial killer • stalkers

The Stranger. New York: Bantam Spectra, 1997. ISBN 0-55357-576-7pa. 249p.

Jenny has her hands full with Zombies from South Central chasing her, dead boys without IDs turning up all over Los Angeles, and a serial rapist who has a private channel into her head.

Keywords: drug dealers and dealing • resurrection • serial rapists

Hamilton, Virginia.

Virginia Hamilton is a 1995 MacArthur Fellow.

The Justice Cycle.

Siblings who have extrasensory abilities are locked in a deadly rivalry in both the present and the future. In the far future, several alien-seeming species of extraordinary beings—human, cyborg, and machine—search for a solution to desperate conditions and survival against hopelessly severe odds. Hamilton may have initially written this series for the juvenile audience, making for a quick read, but adults shouldn't shy away from this surprisingly well-written and deeply thoughtful story.

> *The unit hummed. It had the power of four. It was Thomas, the magician. It was Dorian, the healer. It was Justice, who was the Watcher and the balance for the unit's strength. And it was Levi, brother of Justice and identical brother of Thomas. Levi suffered for them all.* (Dustland, p. 1)

Keywords: brothers and sisters • sibling rivalry • twins

Justice and Her Brothers. San Diego: Harcourt Brace Jovanovich, 1989 (1978). ISBN 0-15241-640-4pa. 282p.

Left on their own during the day this summer, Justice comes into more and more conflict with her brother Thomas, who is the mirror image of her favorite, Levi. The lines between her two brothers seem to be blurring as Thomas's extrasensory powers grow. It all comes to a head when Justice finally realizes, with the help of their friend Dorian Jefferson and his mother Leona, that she too has powers.

Keywords: personal identity

Dustland. San Diego: Harcourt Brace Jovanovich, 1989 (1980). ISBN 0-15224-315-1pa. 214p.

The unit journeys to a dry, barren land of the future, where three-legged, humanlike Slakers desperately search for water and a way out of their world of endless dust. Thomas's jealousy of Justice's supreme power proves too much for him, and taking Levi with him, he breaks the unit on which survival depends. Justice and Dorian, with the help of the beast Miacis, must find the two boys if they are ever to return to the present.

Keywords*:* mutants • teleportation • time travel

The Gathering. San Diego: Harcourt Brace Jovanovich, 1989 (1981). ISBN 0-15230-592-0pa. 214p.

The unit returns to Dustland to lead the thirsty life forms from the desert into a high-tech city of domes. It is here, while battling an evil force known as Mal, that the unit learns the ultimate fate of Earth and discovers the purpose of its journey.

Keywords: mutants • teleportation • time travel

Ridley, John.

Those Who Walk in Darkness. **New York: Aspect/Warner Books, 2003. ISBN 0-446-53093-X. 310p.**

After May Day. After half of San Francisco is destroyed by a battle between two metanormals. The citizens of the United States realize that they've relied too much on superheroes and react with hatred and paranoia, stripping the "freaks" of their civil rights and authorizing special police units to kill them on sight. Officer Soledad "Bullet" O'Roark performs her duty with a vengeance, using technology to stop the metanormals where others have failed, but she finds herself facing formidable enemies—both within the department and on the streets.

> *Maybe, we got to thinking, it was all their fault: the metanormals, good and bad. Running around like demigods in their rainbow wear. Who asked them to fight for us? Who asked them to save us? Who needed them?* (p. 56)

Notes: John Ridley is also listed in the "Crime Novels" section of Chapter 4.

Keywords: mutants • police corruption • police officers • prejudice

Williams, Billy Dee, and Rob MacGregor.

Trent Calloway Series.

Trent Calloway is a retired veteran of the Air Force's Eagle's Nest, a remote viewing intelligence organization. He tries to escape his past by moving out to the Colorado desert and becoming a rafting guide, but his former life keeps finding him. Now taking jobs for hire, he works with his former monitor Miriam "Doc" Boyle to aid him in his viewing. To his delight, it has also brought back into his life his ex-wife Camila Hidalgo, a White House spokesperson. The series combines a blend of spy thriller, mystery, romance and the supernatural.

> *Am I a demon or a god? Whichever, you answer, you are right and you are wrong. The light and the dark are all part of the same thing. I am all things to all people. I bring you awareness.* (Just/in Time, p. 313)

Keywords: reconciliation • remote viewing

PSI/Net. New York: Tom Doherty Associates, 1999. ISBN 0-31286-766-2. 254p.

Gordon Maxwell, the former leader of Eagle's Nest, has gotten together as many members of the former team as possible to work on projects for hire. Currently they are working for a fanatical former general and his separatist group, who plan to blow up Washington, D.C., and kill the president.

Keywords: psychic warfare

Just/in time. New York: Forge, 2000. ISBN 0-31287-271-2. 317p.

Camila wants a reluctant Calloway to investigate charismatic Justin Logos, a man proclaimed by some to be the reincarnation of Jesus Christ and called the Antichrist by others. When a lethal virus is released in Washington, D.C., Calloway pinpoints its source as followers of Logos. Exposed to the virus and facing his own death, Calloway attempts to return to the near past to create an alternate reality in which the virus has not been released and Camila is still his.

Keywords: bioterrorism • Christianity • New Mexico • supernatural • time travel

Science Fantasy

Delany, Samuel R.

🏵 ***The Einstein Intersection*** (also published as *A Fabulous, Formless Darkness*). New York: Bantam Books, 1981 (1967). ISBN 0-55320-310-Xpa. 147p. New edition by Wesleyan University Press, 1998. ISBN: 0819563366.

Before aliens who colonize an abandoned Earth can continue their own development, they must first cope with the lingering human psychic presence by living out our myths and constantly mutating to try to become more human. Lobey lived the simple life of a shepherd until he lost his first true love. Now he must go on a quest to discover what is killing those who are different and stop it. The reenacted legends, sorcery, and quests explore the meaning of myth in society, while the aliens are a metaphor for how we look at differences in identity.

> *"Oh, we're not human, Spider. Life and death, the real and the irrational aren't the same as they were for the poor race who willed us this world. . . . But we have taken a new home, and we have to exhaust the past before we can finish with the present. We have to live out the human if we are to move on to our own future."* (p. 78)

Notes: Nebula Award Novel 1967; Hugo Award Best Novel Nomination 1968

Keywords: aliens (humanoid and nonhumanoid) • evolution • future civilizations • mutants • mythology • personal identity • prejudice

The Jewels of Aptor. New York: Bantam Books, 1982 (1962). ISBN 0-55320-311-8pa. 165p.

Two students, a thief and a sailor, join forces to steal the last of the powerful jewels and save the current incarnation of the Goddess Argo from the sacred island of Leptar. But first Geo, Iimmi, Snake, and Urson must survive the mutated inhabitants of the isle and discover the secret of the Goddesses and their ancient religion. Delany's first published novel contains many of the elements that will later become his trademarks: a quest, a marginal young protagonist, and mythology. This novel also foreshadows the characteristic science fiction bent of his fantasy fiction.

> *The movement stopped in front of a tier of three berths; on the bottom one lay—Geo! But Geo with a starved, pallid face. His mop of hair was bleached white. On his chest was a pulsing darkness, a flame, a heart, shimmering with the indistinctness of absolute black.* (p. 39)

Keywords: fictional religions • mutants • mythology • quests

Delany, Samuel R.

Return to Nevèrÿon Series.

This collection of short stories, long narrations, novelettes, and novels share, the same setting and recurring characters. Delany's Nevèrÿon is a land of the mythic past in the midst of sweeping change. The varying emphasis on the different characters allows the reader to see the change through the eyes of many people. Gorgik becomes a slave, then a freer of slaves, and finally a minister of the high court. Norema invents a more usable writing system and becomes a traveling storyteller. Pryn witnesses the changes in power that are overtaking the land, and many others have their tales to tell. The characters don't grow in the ordinary sense but expand their horizons to make Delany's point. Delany plays with structure and character, with tales reflecting back on themselves and offering viewpoints not so much opposite as slightly twisted, sometimes giving the reader the feeling of having fallen through the looking glass. His sense of irony and imaginative style engage the reader, but the message is never obscured. This series is highly readable, literate, and thought-provoking.

> *You came to court with the favor of the Vizerine. Everyone knows— or thinks they know— that such favor from Myrgot is only favor of the flesh, which they can gossip about, find amusing, and therefore tolerate. Most do not realize that Myrogt decides when to let such news of her favor enter the circuit of gossip—and that, in your case, such decision was made well after your flesh ceased to interest her; and in such ways the rumor can be, and has been, put to use.* (Tales of Nevèrÿon, p. 59)

Keywords: sexual identity • slavery • storytelling

Tales of Nevèrÿon. Hanover, N.H.: University Press of New England, 1993 (1979). ISBN 0-81956-270-Xpa. 260p.

Five interwoven tales of people and places within NevPrlon are gathered in this volume. The nature of slavery and power are reflected in three of the stories, with Gorgik and Small Sarg experiencing different reflections of the institution. *The Tale of Gorgik* traces Gorgik's life from carefree son of an importer through slavery in the mines, servitude in the High Court, military service, and ultimate freedom, while Small Sarg, once a barbarian prince, becomes Gorgik's slave and lover in *The Tale of Small*. Gorgik and Small Sarg are on a mission to free slaves in *The Tale of Dragons and Dreamers*. Norema learns about life with the help of old Venn's stories in *The Tale of Old Venn*. In *The Tale of Potters and Dragons*, three travelers—Norema, Bayle, and Raven—are sailing to Garth and Lord Aldamir on separate missions. When Norema is almost killed, she and Raven go adventuring to learn the secret of Lord Aldamir.

Keywords: coming of age • economics • short stories

🌹 *Neveryóna, or: The Tales of Signs and Cities, Some Informal Remarks toward the Modular Calculus, Part Four*. Hanover, N.H.: University Press of New England, 1993 (1983). ISBN 0-81956-271-8pa. 399p.

Pryn, an almost literate girl in a largely preliterate land, journeys from her mountain home looking for a new life. She has many adventures and meets several interesting people, including Gorgik "the Liberator," Madame Keyne, and the Earl Jue-Grutn family. Along the way she encounters jealousy and carnality and learns just how dangerous real power can be.

Notes: Locus Poll Award Best Fantasy Novel Nominee 1984; Prometheus Award Best Libertarian SF Novel Preliminary Nominee 1984

Keywords: language • personal identity • stereotypes

 Flight from Nevèrÿon. New York: Bantam, 1985. ISBN 0-553-24856-1pa. 385p.

Three novellas containing tales of NevPrlon are included in *Flight*. In the *Tale of Frog and Granite*, a young smuggler searches for his hero Gorgik and is thwarted until he meets Raven. In *The Mummer's Tale*, an actor tells an old friend about the young smuggler's early life. *The Tale of Plagues and Carnivals, or, Some Informal Remarks toward the Modular Calculus, Part Five* is a mixture of autobiographical thoughts on the early days of AIDS and plague on the Bridge of Lost Desire.

Notes: Locus Poll Award Best Collection Nomination 1986

Keywords: friendships • hero worship • HIV/AIDS • New York City • novellas

The Bridge of Lost Desire (also published as *Return to NevPrlon*). New York: St. Martin's Press, 1988 (1987). ISBN 0-312-91138-6pa. 310p.

Two more novellas and a story tell more tales of Nevèrÿon. In *The Game of Time and Pain*, Gorgik, now a minister of the High Court, reflects on his life to a barbarian boy, and retired Vizerine Myrgot hallucinates having a conversation with Gorgik. *The Tale of Rumor and Desire* explores the way in which lust and desire affect the whole life of a man. The first tale of the first book of NevPrlon is repeated in *The Tale of Gorgik*, concluding the series with its beginning, a neat and very Delanyan touch.

Notes: Locus Poll Award Best Collection Nomination 1988

Keywords: novellas

Space Opera

Delany, Samuel R.

Babel-17. New York: Bantam Books, 1982 (1966). ISBN 0-55320-156-5pa. 193p. New edition by Vintage Books, 2002. ISBN: 0375706690.

The Alliance is plagued by sabotage that is always accompanied by the Invaders' mysterious battle code. Rydra Wong is The Linguist, who has retired to write poetry. Now she has been called back to service to solve the mystery of Babel-17. The poetic writing adds to Wong's story of language, love, and isolation.

> *Flung through loops of blue and wrung with indigo, drifted the complex of stations and planetoids making up the War Yards. A musical hum punctured with burst of static sound over the earphones. The olfactory emitters gave a confused odor of perfumes and hot oil charred with the bitter smell of burning citrus peel.* (p. 62)

Notes: Hugo Award Best Novel Nomination 1967; James Tiptree Jr. Award Classics 1995; Locus Poll Award All Time Best Novel Nomination, 1975; Nebula Award Novel 1966

Keywords: language • mathematics • personal identity • poets • war stories

The Ballad of Beta-2. **New York: Bantam Books, 1982 (1975). ISBN 0-55320-312-6pa. 115p.**

The Star Folk left Earth in generation ships heading for the stars, but before they could reach their destination new technology had allowed others to get there first. When they finally arrive, missing a few ships, their culture degenerates into superstition and fear, the people there are perfectly happy to just make them go away. Now Joneny has been assigned to research the story behind their Ballad of Beta-2. What he discovers is an amazing story of survival and alien encounter that has the ability to affect the whole of society. Delany explores the origins of mythology and its potential for developing an understanding of the past. The lyrical writing lends a feeling of myth to this novel.

> *Then came one to the city, over sand with her bright hair wild. With her eyes coal black and her feet sole sore, And under her arms a green-eyed child.* (p. 6)

Notes: Nebula Award Novella Nomination 1965

Keywords: aliens (nonhumanoid) • anthropology and anthropologists • prejudice • space colonies • 2400s

Empire Star. **New York: Bantam Books, 1983 (1966). ISBN 0-55323-425-0pa. 132p.**

This fast-paced read is unique in that it is based on a cycloid caused by a star system that can warp time so that characters meet themselves coming and going without knowing it. Comet Jo becomes involved when a dying alien whose ship crashed on the backwater world of Rhys gives him a strange living Jewel and begs him to take it to the fabled Empire Star.

> *Then I want you to take a complex statement with you that is further in need of multiplex evaluation: The only important elements in any society are the artistic and the criminal, because they alone, by questioning the society's values, can force it to change.* (p. 103)

Keywords: political intrigue • quests • slavery • time travel

Nova. **New York: Bantam Books, 1975 (1968). ISBN n/apa. 215p.**

The economics of the thirty-second century hinge on the ability to obtain and use the element Illyrion. Lorq von Ray, in an attempt to save his family's empire, is willing to fly through the core of a recently imploded sun to obtain seven tons of Illyrion, but to be successful he must get there before the Reds. The settings are well developed, adding depth to this action adventure, but are so complex—seven planets and three stellar empires—that the location and year are stated at the top of each page.

> *The Mouse watched the thick features, the pale hair: famil-*
> *iarity? You adjust it like you would a mist-mask, the Mouse*
> *thought; then fit it on the face that must wear it. Leo has*
> *changed so much. The Mouse, who had had so little child-*
> *hood, lost some more of it now.* (p. 148)

Notes: Hugo Award Best Novel Nomination 1969

Keywords: Ark • coming of age • creative process • cyborgs • economics • quests • 3100s • vengeance

Nichols, Nichelle, and Margaret Wander Bonanno.

Saturn's Child. New York: Putnam, 1995. ISBN 0-39914-113-8. 340p.

Tetrok, the ambitious young leader of the Fazisians, falls in love with Nyota, the human commanding officer of the starship Dragon's Egg. Thanks to DNA ma-nipulation they conceive Saturna. However, such conception violates the wishes and laws of both races, and it throws Saturna into a key role in the succession cri-sis of the Fazisians. The plot is an interesting spin on "Romeo and Juliet give birth to Cinderella in space," although it does not read as a fairy tale.

> *"Watching" her in his mind, standing but a half-klick distant,*
> *the WiseOne Krecis marveled as he always did at the*
> *young woman's clarity of soul. On the cusp of adulthood,*
> *she was becoming more than even he had dared to dream.*
> *(p. 3)*

Keywords: aliens (humanoid) • family relationships • genetic engineering • telepathy • Titan • 2000s • 2100s

Fantasy

Butler, Octavia E.

Octavia Butler is a 1995 MacArthur Fellow.

Kindred. Boston: Beacon Press, 1988 (1979). ISBN 0-80708-305-4pa. 264p.

In an attempt to write a new slave memoir, Butler has combined elements of fan-tasy travelogue and slave narrative to create a gripping story in which Dana Franklin, a black woman from 1976, is snatched by unseen forces from her home in southern California and transported to the antebellum South to save Rufus Weylin, the white son of a plantation owner. She must return again and again to the plantation to protect Rufus and ensure that he will grow to manhood and be-come her ancestor. This edition is introduced with a critical analysis by Robert Crossley.

And I lost about a year of my life and much of the comfort and security I had not valued until it was gone. (p. 9)

Notes: Locus Poll Award Best Fantasy Novel Nomination 1980

Keywords: interracial relationships • plantation life • 1600s • slavery • time travel • Weylin Plantation, Maryland

Delany, Samuel R.

They Fly at Çiron. **Seattle: Incunabula, 1993. ISBN 0-96336-370-0. 222p.**

Çiron is a village in which true violence is unknown until the inhabitants face conquest and domination by the technologically superior army of Myetra. In spite of Lieutenant Kire's rejection of the violence of his fellow Mytreans, the Cironians are subdued with great cruelty. Resistance is led on one front by a village garbage collector and an itinerant singer. On the other, a village youth, Rahm, escapes and forms an alliance with the mysterious and surprisingly friendly Winged Ones, who have long hovered above the village, and together they drive off the Myetrans. Delany offers two themes: that war, hatred, and dishonesty have to be taught and that trust and friendship can overcome the odds. This edition includes a publication history of *They Fly at Çiron* and two short stories in the same "world": *Ruins* and *Return to Çiron*.

But soon you will see, in a band from water to water, is the growth of a rich, intelligent, and wonderfully hardworking and resourceful people, taking land, making food, imparting their ways and wonders on these myriad backwards folk who have no notion of their own histories for more than five or six generations into the past—the length of time a burial scroll will last before it simply rots away. (p. 136)

Keywords: friendships • international relations • war stories

Myers, Walter Dean.

Legend of Tarik. **New York: Viking Press, 1981. ISBN 0-59033-775-0pa. 180p.**

Tarik was just a boy when El Muerte massacred his family. Now he thinks of nothing but taking his revenge, but first he must seek the advice of a wise man and capture three magical things. Only then will he be able to face his enemy and defeat him or perish. Although written as a juvenile book, this slightly dark and suspenseful novel makes a nice light read for adults.

Before you face your enemy you must rid yourself of all hatred and anger. For hatred will make your eyes as blind as mine. It will make your limbs move when they should be still. It will make you cry out when you should be silent. (pp. 17–18)

Keywords: mythology • quests • vengeance

Sherman, Charlotte Watson.

One Dark Body. New York: HarperCollins, 1993. ISBN 0-06016-924-9. 209p.

Twelve-year-old Raisin's father committed suicide before she was born and her mother, Nola Barnett, abandoned her—but not before disfiguring her in an unsuccessful abortion attempt. Her friend Sin-Sin has never known his father. Now Nola has returned to calm the restless spirits of her dead husband and her own violent mother. The quartet of intermingled lives is completed by old Blue, a shaman with his own tragic past. This novel is a fine example of Sherman's unique use of language.

> *See, we all got scars, boy. We all got em. Some sitting on the outside, others way down, deep down. Ain't no sin in having em. Scars learn us what this life-thing's about. Make us real. Not trying to heal a scar's the sin.* (p. 143)

Keywords: coming of age • heritage • 1960s • self-esteem • spirits • supernatural

Horror

Immortality

Barnes, Steven.

Blood Brothers. New York: TOR, 1996. ISBN 0-31285-707-1. 282p.

White supremacist Austin Tucker's family has been massacred; ex-computer hacker Derek Waites's family may be next. They must get past their racial differences to interpret their common ancestor's slave narrative and discover the truth behind the immortality ritual that requires human sacrifice. Barnes manages to juggle both the Tucker/Waites story line and the slave narrative with a twist of mystery that combines them admirably. The language can be harsh at times but is appropriate for the characters.

> *Soul and skin are linked: Soul can lead skin. Skin can call soul. Both soul and skin can be stolen or torn apart. Shun the man who would tear skin-for he is evil. But fear the man who steals the soul, for that man can steal stars from the sky.* (p. 9)

Keywords: California (southern) • 1800s • interracial relationships • occultism • reconciliation • ritual killings • 1700s • slavery

Charisma. New York: Tor, 2002. ISBN 0-31287-004-3. 380p.

Renny Sand is onto a dark secret about his former hero, African American Alexander Marcus, who raised himself from poverty to wealth and power. A young boy named Patrick Emory is trying to deal with the turmoil of his life in a trailer park. Children seem to be having mysterious accidents all over the nation. What do these events and the dark secret that the at-risk children invited to a summer camp have in common? The dark and ambiguous ethics of the story contrast with the positive feelings the reader has for the characters.

> *One car is cruising the jungle, like a lion stalking the Serengeti. In the car is a buyer. He is a white man, taller and heavier than average. He is in his late fifties, but the extra weight is muscle. His motions are very precise as he steers the wheel, searching for what he needs.* (p. 189)

Keywords: at-risk children • Claremont, Washington • psychosocial experimentation • serial killers

Due, Tananarive.

Life Brothers Series.

How do you deal with finding out that your husband is immortal and wants a family that is also immortal even if it means breaking his most sacred vow? That is what Jessica Jacobs-Wolde must ask herself. In this dark and foreboding series of love between a man and a woman and love of family, she must find a way to go on.

> *My name is DAH-weet. I was born in what is now called Ethiopia nearly five hundred years ago. I am an immortal. There are fifty-eight others like me. Our blood lives forever, and our bodies heal. We do not age. We were not born this way, and our condition is not genetic. We underwent a Ritual.* (My Soul to Keep, p. 198)

Keywords: family relationships • Lalibela, Ethiopia • occultism

My Soul to Keep. New York: HarperCollins, 1997. ISBN 0-06018-742-5. 346p.

Jessica Jacobs-Wolde is a Miami investigative reporter with a beautiful daughter, Kira, and a husband, David, so loving, brilliant, and attentive that she calls him Mr. Perfect. Suddenly, however, her life takes a terrifying turn when her best friend is brutally and mysteriously murdered and David reveals his secret. He is really Dawit and plans to break his vow and defy his brothers by making Jessica and Kira immortal.

Notes: Bram Stoker Award Superior Achievement in a Novel Nomination 1997; International Horror Guild Award Best Novel Nomination 1997; Locus Poll Award Best Fantasy Novel Nomination 1998

Keywords: husbands and wives • journalism and journalists

The Living Blood. New York: Pocket Books, 2001. ISBN 0-67104-083-9. 515p.

Four years later, Jessica is still coming to terms with the fact that David gave her and their second daughter, Fana, the gift of his healing blood.

Just three and a half years old, Fana is displaying signs of tremendous power. Unaware that they are being tracked by Lucas Shepard, a doctor from Florida who hopes to save his dying son, and by a group of fortune hunters who will stop at nothing to exploit the power coursing through her veins, Jessica journeys to Ethiopia in search of the Life Brothers. There, she will be reunited with David and the full force of Fana's powers will be revealed. Jessica, David, Fana, and Shepard will engage in an epic and transcontinental battle over the ultimate fate of humanity.

Keywords: healers and healing • mothers and daughters

Gomez, Jewelle.

The Gilda Stories. **Ithaca, N.Y.: Firebrand Books, 1991. ISBN 0-93237-994-Xpa. 252p.**

Girl is a runaway slave who is taken in and raised by a white vampire and her Lakota vampire lover. When Girl comes of age, she takes the name Gilda and is given the gift of living until she wishes to die. She spends her next 200 years exploring what it is to be African American, how to truly live life, and the many ways one can love. Though there are evil vampires in the story, it is the slow undercurrent of hate in the nation that makes it horror. Each chapter is written at a different point in Gilda's life, giving a journal-like feel. This very enjoyable and thoughtful work contains lesbianism but is much more interested in African Americans' history and future.

> *She described her first bath, the scent of her mother's sweat, the feel of Bird's arm around her waist, the sound of laughter from the women at Woodard's, the thrill of moving beside the wind and how the smell of the wind had changed in the years since she'd taken to the road.* (p. 128)

Notes: Lambda Award Lesbian Science Fiction/Fantasy 1991; Lambda Award Lesbian Fiction 1991

Keywords: lesbian relationships • racial identity • vampires

Supernatural

Aczon, Kimile.

BJ. **Pakland, Fla.: Universal Pub., 1998 [Upublish.com, 1998]. ISBN 1-58112-861-4pa. 252p.**

Denise and Wesley Johnson, an African American couple, become pregnant and their lives, as well as the lives of a priest in a small village in Africa, a homeless Vietnam veteran, an elderly widow, and a traumatized five-year-old boy, are forever changed. They find themselves beset by supernatural events and mysteriously drawn to the baby that Denise carries.

> *"You are like the Podo tree—no matter which way the wind blows, no matter how great the storm, you still stand tall—Negative influences can not change who you are, positive influences can only make you grow. You are planted in firm soil. You are like the Podo tree."* (p. 236)

Keywords: Catholicism • Pasadena, California

Barnes, Steven.

Iron Shadows. New York: Tor, 2000 (1998). ISBN 0-81254-808-6pa. 383p.

The Juvell Associates (sleuth Cat Juvell, her ex-husband Jax Carpenter, and Cat's paraplegic hacker brother Tyler) have been hired to rescue a member of the Golden Sun cult headed by Japanese African twins Joy and Tomo Oshita. In their investigation, Cat and Jax are forced to go undercover into one of the cult's "relationship seminars" where some sort of blood sharing seems to be going on. There they discover that the twins have genuine psi-abilities. Now they must decide if the twins are a force for good or evil, and what they should do about it. Barnes has taken the cynical detective novel and turned it on its ear by blending in some supernatural elements and adding a dash of romance, making a recipe for a fast-paced thriller that leaves you guessing until the end.

> *The moment of fierceness swept away the cobwebs. If this was the end. If this was death, if the creature coming to take their lives could not be stopped, then by heaven she would die fighting, rather than spend the rest of her life wondering if she could have saved him. Saved the man she loved. (p.391)*

Keywords: California (southern) • cults • private investigators—teams • psionic powers • reconciliation • twins

Kundalini Equation. New York: Tom Doherty Associates, 1986. ISBN 0-81253-150-7pa. 348p.

Adam Ludlum, in his search for a solution to his weight problem, discovers that the martial arts are mere fragments of a greater, more powerful killing art—an art that can produce in a man the power to manipulate matter and energy at will. Unfortunately, the effect on the mind is so deadly that, uncontrolled, the result is an inhuman killer. Barnes utilizes his vast knowledge of the martial arts to good advantage in this dark and mystical book.

> *It was here, in the dark and quiet of his father's home, his home, that he could see that dark fringe. The tears that filmed his eyes acted as a prism, a diffraction lens that somehow twisted the colors of the rainbow away from the bed, leaving behind that billowing black fringe. (p. 257)*

Keywords: cults • evolution • martial arts • mysticism

Due, Tananarive.

The Between. New York: HarperCollins, 1995. ISBN 0-06017-250-9. 274p.

Hilton James was saved from drowning as a child at the cost of his grandmother's life. Now 30 years later he is starting to think his borrowed time is running out. He's a dedicated social worker, married to the only elected African American judge in Dade County, Florida, and the father of two beautiful children. When his wife begins receiving racist hate mail from a man she once prosecuted, Hilton becomes obsessed with protecting his family. He begins having nightmares more horrible than any he has ever experienced. Hilton's sense of reality begins slipping away as he battles both the psychotic who stalks his family and the even more terrifying unseen enemy that plagues his sleep. In this gripping account of a man's descent into psychological and supernatural terror, Due places the reader squarely inside Hilton's mind so that, like him, the reader remains unsure of which reality to trust until the final chilling resolution.

> *No one is meant to live in the between. They thought the hearse would take care of it, but I fled again. Now it's nearly time for another birthday. I've stolen thirty birthdays from them. That's why they've sent him . . . . Charles Ray. He isn't a traveler, but they talk to him when he sleeps . . . . I already told you. They're not dreams. There's no such thing as dreams.* (p. 208)

Notes: Blackboard Bestseller List 1995; Bram Stoker Award Superior Achievement in a First Novel Nomination 1995

Keywords: hate mail • near-death experiences • racism • stalkers

Massey, Brandon.

Thunderland. New York: Dafina Books/Kensington Publishing, 2002. ISBN 0-7582-0246-6pa. 293p.

Jason Brooks thought that his world couldn't get any worse, between this alcoholic abusive mother Linda and cheating workaholic father Thomas, but shortly before his fourteenth birthday it did. Now that everything could be improving because his parents are trying to mend their ways, some forgotten *thing* from his past is out to destroy his friends and family. The last of four versions of the novel, this is a well-written and thought-out thriller, full of unexpected twists and turns, and with realistic and intriguing subplots.

> *Slowly Jason blinked. Mr. Magic was nuttier than they had expected. Jason understood, right now then, that reasoning with Mr. Magic was impossible. He was mad as any dictator who'd dreamed of world domination.* (p. 219)

Notes: Gold Pen Award for Best Thriller 2000

Keywords: alternate dimensions • self-esteem • spirits

Mosley, Walter.

Blue Light. Boston: Little, Brown, 1998. ISBN 0-31657-098-2. 296p.

In 1960s San Francisco, rays of extraterrestrial blue light enter the bodies of several people, giving them superhuman abilities. Chance is not himself a recipient of the light, but after a blood transfusion from the leader of the Blues, his consciousness expands. Still, he is powerless in the face of the Gray Man—a vicious incarnation of evil who seems intent on wiping out the entire Blue population. This work focuses not on the aliens but on the horrors perpetrated by the humans they touch.

> *There were other transformations on the night that Ordé, the prophet, saw blue light. These I have gleamed from conversations, newspaper articles, interviews, obituaries, and a peculiar facility that Ordé endowed upon me—the ability to read blood.*
> (p. 4)

Notes: Walter Mosley is also listed in the "Short Fiction" section of this chapter and in the "Crime Novels" and "Private Investigators—Men" sections of Chapter 4.

Keywords: aliens (nonhumanoid) • evolution • fictional religions • murder • mutants • 1960s • possession

Olden, Marc.

Frank DiPalma Series.

Frank DiPalma, a former New York police detective turned investigative reporter, is reunited with his young son, Todd Hansard, after the murder of the boy's mother. Todd is at times possessed by the spirit of a ruthless fourteenth-century samurai who has unfinished business and is using the boy to carry out his mission of honor. The series blends supernatural mystery with martial arts and explores the similarities and differences between traditional and modern oriental cultures.

> *Few men dared carry such a sword. It had been forged by the legendary Muramasa, a brilliant but unstable swordsmith. His blades, said to hunger after men's lives, were so bloodthirsty that they maddened their owners, compelling them to kill or commit suicide.* (Dai-sho, p. 3)

Keywords: honor • martial arts • New York City • oriental religion and philosophy • possession • reincarnation

Dai-sho. New York: Berkley, 1985 (1983). ISBN 0-42507-657-1pa. 407p.

Frank DiPalma must battle would-be samurai Kon Kenpachi to save his son and ex-fiancé. Kenpachi and his mentor, Zenzo Nosaka, have decided to return Japan to its former glory by reforming a WWII death squad, the Blood Oath League, to kill those they perceive as being enemies of Japan.

Keywords: Japanese culture

Sword of Vengeance. New York: Jove Books, 1990. ISBN 0-51510-370-5pa. 341p.

Frank must again try to protect the people he loves when Todd continues the mission of honor by going after Lin Pao, the mastermind behind the most feared gang in global history, who takes Frank's new wife prisoner.

Keywords: Chinese culture • organized crime • Taiwan

Short Fiction

Butler, Octavia E.
Octavia Butler is a 1995 MacArthur Fellow.

 ***Bloodchild: And Other Stories*. New York: Seven Stories Press, 1996 (1995). ISBN 1-88836-363-3pa. 145p.**

This book begins with a preface by Butler describing how she feels about writing short stories and ends with an autobiographical article, "Positive Obsession," and a brief essay on writing for publication, "Furor Scribendi." Each of the seven stories has been previously published and is followed by an afterword that includes Butler's inspiration for the story and her thoughts and comments about the work. United by the theme of the necessity of leaving something behind as a prelude to moving on in life, the stories share a sad, almost wistful, tone. In the poignant coming of age love story "Bloodchild," a boy must give up his naiveté about bearing an alien's child. A woman discovers there is no cure for her deadly diseases, but she can ease the suffering in the sad but hopeful story "The Evening and the Morning and the Night." In "Near of Kin," a sympathetic story of incest, a daughter must accept that her dead mother really did love her. When a virus destroys most people's ability to communicate in "Speech Sounds," they still find a way to interact. "Crossover" is a dark story of a woman's hopelessness and her inability to move on.

Notes: Blackboard Bestseller List 1996; Locus Poll Award Best Collection Nomination 1996

Keywords: aliens • interpersonal relationships • short stories • writers

Delany, Samuel R.

 ***The Complete Nebula Award Winning Fiction*. New York: Bantam Spectra, 1986. ISBN 0-55325-610-6. 425p.**

This collection gathers in one place all of Delany's Nebula Award winners:*Babel-17* (Best Novel, 1966); *A Fabulous, Formless Darkness* (Best Novel, 1967; also published as *The Einstein Interaction*); "Aye, and Gomorrah . . ." (Best Short

Story, 1967); and *Time Considered as a Helix of Semi-Precious Stones* (Best Novelette, 1969).

Notes: Locus Poll Award Best Collection Nomination 1987

Keywords: novellas • sex roles • sexual identity • short stories

Distant Stars. **New York: Bantam, 1981. ISBN 0-53301-336-Xpa. 352p.**

The stories in this volume are augmented by Delany's introduction, "Of Doubts and Dreams," and illustrations by a variety of young artists (Jeanette Adams, John Coffey, John Collier, John Jude Palencar, John Pierard, John Pound, and Michel Sorkin). Of particular note is the variation in writing style among the stories in this anthology. *Prismatica's* theme is complemented by the enchanting fairy tale quality of the writing. This contrasts with the sparse but vivid prose in "Corona," the story of a scared man and a little girl who find an unusual bond. In *Time Considered as a Helix of Semi-Precious Stones*, an ironic and cynical tone permeates the story of a small-time thief who learns the perils of becoming a big time thief. "Omegahelm," a prequel story to *Stars in My Pocket Like Grains of Sand,* uses the complex and ambiguous language of that novel to look at the different meanings of family. In "Ruins," a thief has a terrible scare in a haunted temple. Different philosophies on how to live come into conflict, in *We, in Some Strange Power's Employ, Move on a Rigorous Line.* Rounding out the collection is the independent short novel *Empire Star*, which focuses on life as a cycle.

Keywords: family relationships • prejudice • sex roles • sexual identity • short stories • slavery

Driftglass: Ten Tales of Speculative Fiction. **New York: NAL/Signet, 1986 (1971). ISBN 0-45112-092-2pa. 278p.**

The stories in this collection are about people who come to realize how precious life is. A man goes to the end of the galaxy in *The Star Pit* to escape his family, only to realize its importance. In the sad tale, "Dog in a Fisherman's Net," a fisherman learns his life is the most important thing in the world. "Aye, and Gomorrah . . ." is a melancholy story of being isolated but also of being admired for being different. A disabled amphiman worries about the younger generation above and below the sea in *Driftglass.* In the oddly pleasant "Cage of Brass," a man refuses to leave prison. The mind is a fragile thing as seen in *High Weir,* in which a linguist loses his mind on Mars. In the shadowy story "Night and the Loves of Joe Dicostanzo," one of two men is hallucinating that the other exists. Also included are "Corona"; *We, in Some Strange Power's Employ, Move on a Rigorous Line;* and *Time Considered as a Helix of Semi-Precious Stones* which were also collected in *Distant Stars* (1981).

Notes: Locus Poll Award Best Reprint Anthology/Collection (Old) Nomination 1972

Keywords: family relationships • prejudice • sex roles • sexual identity • short stories

Johnson, Charles Richard.

Charles Richard Johnson is a 1998 MacArthur Fellow.

> ### *The Sorcerer's Apprentice: Tales and Conjurations*. New York: Plume, 1994 (1986). ISBN 0-45227-237-8pa. 169p.
>
> These eight stories examine the human experience of transformation through a surreal lens, giving them a kaleidoscopic nature and a spooky, darkish tone. In the dialect-rich story "The Education of Mingo," a farmer learns that when you make someone over into your own image you need to be careful what you teach. "Exchange Value" is a sad tale of how money can posses a person. "Menagerie, a Child's Fable," is a surprising story of war in a pet shop. In "China," a story of inspiration and jealousy, a man improves himself and leaves his wife wanting the old him back. A student, "Alēthia," teaches a professor about the frenzied, swirling world outside of academia. The story of a poet selling out in "Moving Pictures" resembles the flapping end of film on a reel. A UFO teaches a doctor about himself in "Popper's Disease." "The Sorcerer's Apprentice" is a boy who becomes a man when he learns it takes more than knowledge to make him so.
>
> **Keywords:** short stories • supernatural

Mosley, Walter.

> ### *Futureland: Nine Stories of an Imminent World*. New York: Warner, 2001. ISBN 0-44652-954-0. 356p.
>
> These nine stories have in common a grim, cyberpunkish, near-future world setting, a dark but humorous tone, and a theme of hope out of tragedy. Ptolemy Bent is a boy genius who goes to prison for setting his uncle and grandmother free from their pain in "Whispers in the Dark." Fera Jones wins major boxing matches against males in "The Greatest" but goes on to more important fights. Fayes Akwande tries to run a con against the all-powerful "Doctor Kismet" to save a country but discovers it can't be done. Bits gets himself into and out of a high-tech prison, "Angel's Island," by using his high-tech mind. In "The Electronic Eye," Folio Johnson is the last private detective in New York, and he may have to save the world. Leon Jones got a partial brain transplant and now has "Voices" living with him. In "Little Brother," Frendon Blythe tries to beat the system and ends up joining it. Neil Hawthorne is taught to live by a computer in "En Masse." "The Nig in Me" saves Harold Bottoms while a plague kills all those with less than 12.5 percent African blood.
>
> **Notes:** Walter Mosley is also listed in the "Horror" section of this chapter and in the "Crime Novels" and "Private Investigators—Men" sections of Chapter 4.
> *Essence* Bestseller List 2002
>
> **Keywords:** short stories • survival

Sherman, Charlotte Watson.

> ### *Killing Color*. Corvallis, Ore.: Calyx Books, 1992. ISBN 0-93497-118-8. 107p.
>
> Only six of the eleven stories in this volume are by definition speculative. A little girl in "Swimming Lessons" takes a walk of faith. "Cateye" is a boy given a gift

he can't handle. In "Killing Color," a mysterious woman gets her revenge. "The Pink Dolphin" gives a woman the will to live. In "Spirit Talk," a woman finds what she is. "Negril" discovers how to heal his pain. Although five of the entries do not contain overtly speculative elements, Sherman's writing has a lyrical quality that blends poetry with dialect, giving all of the stories a supernatural, otherworldly feel. Her work conveys a great deal of emotion in very few words. The remaining five pieces are highly recommended. "Floating" is an excerpt from the novel *One Dark Body*. "BigWater" transforms a girl into a woman. "Emerald City: Third & Pike" is about never giving up your dreams. "Talking Mountain" shows the price of freedom for one woman. "A Season" is a poem about healing. This anthology contains an introduction by Colleen J. McElroy.

Keywords: personal identity • self-esteem • short stories • supernatural

Thomas, Sheree R.

Dark Matter: A Century of Speculative Fiction from the African Diaspora. New York: Warner Books, 2000. ISBN 0-44652-583-9. 427p.

> This first anthology of speculative fiction by authors of the African Diaspora contains 29 stories written in the last century, ranging in length from 2 to 30 pages. The collection includes stories from the early pioneers Charles W. Chestnutt ("The Goophered Grapevine," 1887), W. E. B. Du Bois ("The Comet," 1920), and George S. Schuyler ("Black No More," 1931). Established modern authors are represented as well, with works including Samuel R. Delany's "Aye, and Gomorrah . . ." (1967), Octavia E. Butler's "The Evening and the Morning and the Night" (1987), and Steven Barnes's "The Woman in the Wall" (2000). The collection also includes stories from mainstream author Ishmael Reed and trailblazing horror authors Tananarive Due ("Like Daughter," 2000) and Jewelle Gomez ("Chicago 1927," 2000).

> **Notes:** Locus Poll Award Best Anthology Nomination 2001; Gold Pen Award Best Anthology 2001; World Fantasy Award Best Anthology Nomination 2001

> **Keywords:** classic stories • short stories • supernatural

Toure.

The Portable Promised Land: Stories. Boston: Little, Brown, 2002. ISBN 0-31666-643-2. 256p.

> This collection of stories and vignettes filled with surreal but familiar characters that use racial stereotypes as their basis provide a comic look at the ups and downs of urban African American culture. "The Steviewondermobile" is about Huggy Bear Jackson, who so loves Stevie Wonder that he installs in his Cadillac a sound system that will play only Wonder's songs. "Attack of the Love Dogma" portrays a center at which black men are treated for their "Blonde Obsession." In "A Hot Time at

the Church of Kentucky Fried Souls . . ." Daddy Love, a minister who loves some of his congregation more than others, sets up a chapel in an abandoned KFC. A young boy has been possessed by every imaginable black stereotype in "The Sambomorphosis." A trilogy of stories are about the Black Widow, a female hip-hopper/ghetto guerrilla out to turn the world of the whites upside down but who deep down thinks of herself as an "Oreo." The book also contains commentaries on black language along with lists of pop culture references and words and phrases in the black lexicon.

Keywords: magical realism • social satire • supernatural • urban life and culture

Chapter 12

Resources

This chapter represents the combined work of both contributors and editors. It is provided to assist librarians who have responsibility for development of readers' advisory services, particularly to African American populations. It also provides specific tools for those selecting titles written by African American authors and for those developing collections of African American literature. Part 1, "Award Winners and Nominees" includes titles of works and authors who have received awards for excellence in specific genres and for outstanding literary accomplishments. Part 2, "Readers Advisory Resources." is divided into two major sections, "General Resources" and "Genre Resources." Materials listed in the "General Resources" section were identified independently by the editors or listed as useful by contributors in more than one genre. General Resources include readers' advisory services, core readers' advisory tools, background sources for African American literature, review sources, best-seller lists, bookstores, book clubs, and other online resources. Genre sources were provided by contributors and augmented with additional material by the editors. For all genre resources, print, electronic, and Web-based resources are represented where available. All URLs were active as of March 4, 2004.

Part 1: Awards—Winners and Nominees

Additional information about these awards can be found on cited Web pages and in *Awards, Honors, and Prizes*, volume 13, parts 1 and 2 (Detroit: Gale, 1997). **Award-winning books are noted in boldface type.** Award nominees are not boldface. Award lists are not comprehensive; only titles included in this book are listed.

Agatha Awards (1992–present)
www.malicedomestic.org

Agatha Awards are given by Malice Domestic, Ltd., a nonprofit corporation established in 1992. Named in honor of Agatha Christie, the awards recognize mysteries written in the traditional style of "mysteries of manners," with an amateur detective, characters who know one another, and a "cozy" style. Recognizing "materials first published in the United States by a living author during the calendar year, either in hardcover or as paperback originals. Agathas are awarded in four categories: Best Novel, Best First Mystery, Best Short Story, and Best Non-Fiction."

1993   **Neely, Barbara.** *Blanche on the Lam.* Detective and Crime Fiction. *Best First Novel.*

ALA Best Book for Young Adults (1996–present)
www.ala.org

The American Library Association's Young Adult Library Services Association compiles an annual list of fiction and nonfiction titles selected for their proven or potential appeal to the personal reading tastes of the young adult and for their literary quality.

1990   **Ansa, Tina McElroy.** *Baby of the Family.* Mainstream Fiction.

1994   **Ashe, Arthur and Arnold Rampersad.** *Days Of Grace: A Memoir.* *Life Stories.*

1995   **Butler, Octavia E.** *Parable of the Sower.* Speculative Fiction.

2000   **Porter, Connie.** *Imani All Mine.* Mainstream Fiction.

ALA Notable Books List (1994–present)
www.ala.org/rusa/notable.html

Since 1994, the Reference and User Services Association of the American Library Association has selected more than 2,200 books for its Notable Books List. The titles are selected annually by a 12-member committee that meets at regular American Library Association conferences.

1994   **Gaines, Ernest.** *A Lesson Before Dying.* Mainstream Fiction.

1997   **McBride, James.** *The Color of Water: A Black Man's Tribute to His White Mother.* Life Stories.

2004   **Jones, Edward P.** *The Known World.* Historical Fiction.

Alex Award (1998–present)
www.ala.org/yalsa/booklists/alex

Alex Awards are presented to recognize adult books that have a strong appeal for young adult readers. The American Library Association's Young Adult Library Services Association has given Alex Awards to 10 authors each year since 1998.

1998   **Trice, Dawn Turner.** *Only Twice I've Wished for Heaven.* Mainstream Fiction.

1999   **Senna, Danzy.** *Caucasia.* Mainstream Fiction.

2000   **Clarke, Breena.** *River, Cross My Heart.* Mainstream Fiction.

Porter, Connie. *Imani All Mine*. Mainstream Fiction.

2002   Durham, David Anthony. *Gabriel's Story*. Frontier Literature.

American Book Award (1978–present)
www.stanford.edu/~rickford/award.html

Established in 1978 by the Before Columbus Foundation, American Book Awards recognize outstanding contributions to contemporary American literature. Winners are selected by a panel of authors, editors, and publishers representing the broad spectrum of the American multicultural literary tradition.

1981   Bambara, Toni Cade. *The Salt Eaters*. Mainstream Fiction.

1983   Naylor, Gloria. *The Women of Brewster Place*. Mainstream Fiction. *Best First Novel.*

1987   McMillan, Terry. *Mama*. Mainstream Fiction.

1988   Morrison, Toni. *Beloved*. Historical Fiction.

1991   Wideman, John Edgar. *Philadelphia Fire*. Mainstream Fiction.

Wright, Bruce. *Black Justice in a White World: a Memoir.* Life Stories.

1994   Nelson, Jill. *Volunteer Slavery: My Authentic Negro Experience.* Life Stories.

Anisfield-Wolf Book Awards (1934–present)
64.29.213.171/about_awards.htm

The Anisfield-Wolf Book Awards, created in 1934 by poet-philanthropist Edith Ansfield-Wolf, honor books that "expose racism or explore the richness of human diversity."

1995   Staples, Brent. *Parallel Time: Growing Up in Black and White.* Life Stories.

Anthony Awards. (1986–present)
www.mysterynet.com/awards/anthony/

Anthony Awards are presented by Bouchercon, the world mystery convention, and selected by Bouchercon attendees. The award is named for Anthony Boucher (pseudonym of William Anthony Parker), mystery writer and critic. Awards are given for Best Novel, First Novel, Paperback Original, Short Story, and Criticism/Biography. Awards are presented annually.

1993   Neely, Barbara. *Blanche on the Lam*. Crime and Detective Fiction. *Best First Novel.*

2000   West, Chassie. *Killing Kin*. Detective and Crime Fiction. *Best Paperback Original.*

Woods, Paula. *Inner City Blues.* Detective and Crime Fiction. *Best First Novel.*

Arthur C. Clarke Award (1987–present)

www.appomattox.demon.co.uk/acca/index.htm

Given each year for the best science fiction novel published in the United Kingdom the previous year. The award is chosen by jury. The British Science Fiction Association and the Science Fiction Foundation, each of which provides two judges each year, administer the award jointly. Most recently, the Science Museum has joined the award and provides one judge each year.

1987   Delany, Samuel R. *Stars in My Pocket Like Grains of Sand*. Speculative Fiction.

1996   **Butler, Octavia E. *Parable of the Sower*. Earthseed Series.** Speculative Fiction. *Early submission*.

2001   Butler, Octavia E. *Parable of the Talents*. Earthseed Series. Speculative Fiction.

BCALA Literary Awards (1994–present)

www.bcala.org

The Black Caucus of the American Library Association (BCALA) presents annual literary awards to recognize outstanding works of fiction and nonfiction by African American authors for adult audiences. A cash prize of $500 is given to the author of the winning book in each of three categories: fiction, nonfiction, and first novelist. The fiction awards recognize books of exceptional merit relating to the African American experience. The nonfiction award recognizes achievements that significantly add to the body of knowledge within the African American experience. In addition, an annual citation is given for the year's outstanding contribution to publishing.

BCALA Literary Award for Fiction

1994   **Gaines, Ernest J. *A Lesson Before Dying*.** Mainstream Fiction.

1995   **Clair, Maxine. *Rattlebone*.** Mainstream Fiction.

1996   Verdelle, A. J. *The Good Negress*. Mainstream Fiction.

1997   **Ladd, Florence. *Sarah's Psalm*.** Mainstream Fiction.

Smith, Faye McDonald. *Flight of the Blackbird*. Mainstream Fiction.

1998   **Jackson-Opoku, Sandra. *The River Where Blood is Born*.** Historical Fiction.

Rainey, John Calvin. *The Thang That Ate My Grandaddy's Dog*. Mainstream Fiction.

Trice, Dawn Turner. *Only Twice I've Wished for Heaven*. Mainstream Fiction.

1999   **Jones, Gayl. *The Healing*.** Mainstream Fiction.
Bland, Eleanor Taylor. *See No Evil*. Crime and Detective Fiction.

Edwards, Grace. *A Toast Before Dying*. Crime and Detective Fiction.

2000 **Marshall, Paule**. *The Fisher King*. Mainstream Fiction.

Olden, Mark. *The Ghost*. Detective and Crime Fiction.

Porter, Connie. *Imani All Mine*. Mainstream Fiction.

2001 **McFadden, Bernice.** *Sugar*. Mainstream Fiction.

2002 **Cleage, Pearl.** *I Wish I Had a Red Dress*. Mainstream Fiction.

Bates, Karen Grigsby. *Plain Brown Wrapper*. Crime and Detective Fiction.

Whitehead, Colson. *John Henry Days*. Mainstream Fiction.

2003 **Rhodes, Jewell Parker.** *Douglass' Women*. Historical Fiction

Ansa, Tina McElroy. *You Know Better*. Mainstream Fiction.

BCALA Literary Award for Nonfiction

2002 **Jordan, E. Vernon, Jr. with Annette Gordon-Reed.** *Vernon Can Read! A Memoir*. Life Stories.

BCALA Literary Award for First Novelist

1994 **Pate, Alexs.** *Losing Absalom*. Mainstream Fiction.

1995 **Lee, Helen Elaine.** *The Serpent's Gift*. Mainstream Fiction.

1996 **major, devorah.** *An Open Weave*. Mainstream Fiction.

1998 **Jackson, Brian Keith.** *The View From Here*. Mainstream Fiction. 1998

2000 **Woods, Paula L.** *Inner City Blues*. Detective and Crime Fiction.

2001 **Ballard, Allen B.** *Where I'm Bound*. Frontier Literature.

2002 **Durham, David Anthony.** *Gabriel's Story*. Frontier Literature.

2003 **Carter, Stephen L.** *The Emperor of Ocean Park*. Crime and Detective Fiction.

2004 **Jones, Edward P.** *The Known World*. Historical Fiction.

Black Issues Book Review Best Books (2002–present)
www.bibookreview.com

The editors of *Black Issues Book Review* select their favorite books at the end of the year.

2002 **Angelou, Maya.** *A Song Flung Up to Heaven*. Life Stories.

Barnes, Steven. *Lion's Blood*. Speculative Fiction.

Carter, Stephen. *The Emperor of Ocean Park*. Crime and Detective Fiction.

Durham, David Anthony. *Walk Through Darkness.* Historical Fiction.

Files, Lolita. *Child of God: A Novel.* Inspirational Literature.

Grooms, Anthony. *Bombingham.* Historical Fiction.

Harris, E. Lynn. *A Love of My Own.* Mainstream Fiction.

Jackson, Brian Keith. *The Queen of Harlem.* Mainstream Fiction.

Jones, Tayari. *Leaving Atlanta.* Historical Fiction.

Jordan, Vernon E. with Annette Gordon-Reed. *Vernon Can Read! A Memoir.* Life Stories.

Mason, Felicia. *Testimony: A Novel.* Romance Literature.

McBride, James. *Miracle at St. Anna.* Historical Fiction.

McKenzie, Vashti M. *Journey to the Well.* Inspirational Literature.

Mosley, Walter. *Bad Boy Brawly Brown.* Detective and Crime Fiction.

Rhodes, Jewell Parker. *Douglass' Women.* Historical Fiction.

Toure. *The Portable Promised Land.* Speculative Fiction.

2003   **Jones, Edward P.** *This Known World.* Historical Fiction.

Blackboard Bestseller (1990–2000) usinfo.state.gov/usa/blackhis/best01.htm

The Blackboard Bestseller list, the first national black best-seller list, was a monthly list featured in *Essence* magazine for seven years, until it was displaced by the *Essence* Bestseller List in January 2001. Five fiction and five nonfiction titles were compiled from monthly sales from United States independent booksellers.

1994   **Ansa, Tina McElroy.** *Baby of the Family.* Mainstream Fiction. (May, June, August, September, December)

Briscoe, Connie. *Sisters and Lovers.* Mainstream Fiction. (August, September, October, November, December)

Bunkley, Anita Richmond. *Black Gold.* Historical Fiction. (July, August)

Campbell, Bebe Moore. *Your Blues Ain't Like Mine.* Mainstream Fiction. (May, June, July, August, September, October, November, December)

Copage, Eric V. *Black Pearls: Daily Meditations, Affirmations, and Inspirations for African-Americans.* Inspirational Literature. (May, June, July, August, September, October, November, December)

Delany, Sarah Louise and A. Elizabeth Delany with Amy Hill Hearth. *Having Our Say: The Delany Sisters' First 100 Years.* Life Stories. (May, June)

Gaines, Ernest. *A Lesson Before Dying.* Mainstream Fiction. (May)

Harris, E. Lynn. *Invisible Life.* Mainstream Fiction. (July, August, September, October, November, December)

McCall, Nathan. *Makes Me Wanna Holler: A Young Black Man in America.* Life Stories. June, July, August, September, October, November, December)

McMillan, Terry. *Mama.* Mainstream Fiction. (May, June, July, August)

McMillan, Terry. *Waiting to Exhale.* Mainstream Fiction. (May, June, July, August, September, October)

Mosley, Walter. *Black Betty.* Detective and Crime Fiction. (September, October, November, December)

Mosley, Walter. *Devil in a Blue Dress.* Crime and Detective Fiction. (September, October, November, December)

Ray, Francis. *Forever Yours.* Romance Literature. (October, November, December)

Sinclair, April. *Coffee Will Make You Black.* Mainstream Fiction. (June, July, October, November)

Vanzant, Iyanla. *Acts of Faith: Daily Devotions for People of Color.* Inspirational Literature. (May, June, July, August, September, October, November, December)

1995   **Ansa, Tina McElroy.** *Baby of the Family.* Mainstream Fiction. (March)

Boyd, Julia A. *Girlfriend to Girlfriend: Everyday Wisdom and Affirmations from the Sister Circle.* Inspirational Literature. (October, November, December)

Briscoe, Connie. *Sisters and Lovers.* Mainstream Fiction. (January, February, March, April, June, July, August, September, October, November, December)

Brown, Linda Beatrice. *Crossing Over Jordan.* Historical Fiction. (March, October, November)

Bunkley, Anita Richmond. *Black Gold.* Historical Fiction. (October)

Bunkley, Anita Richmond. *Wild Embers.* Romance Literature. (August, September)

Butler, Octavia E. *Patternmaster.* Speculative Fiction. (November)

Campbell, Bebe Moore. *Your Blues Ain't Like Mine.* Mainstream Fiction. (January, February, March, April, June)

Copage, Eric V. *Black Pearls: Daily Meditations, Affirmations, and Inspirations for African-Americans.* Inspirational Literature. (January, February, March, April, June, August, October)

Copage, Eric V. *Black Pearls for Parents: Meditations, Affirmations, and Inspirations for African-American Parents.* Inspirational Literature. (August)

Delany, Sarah Louise and A. Elizabeth Delany with Amy Hill Hearth. *Having Our Say: The Delany Sisters' First 100 Years.* Life Stories. (February, July)

Due, Tananarive. *The Between.* Speculative Fiction. (December)

Harris, E. Lynn. *Invisible Life.* Mainstream Fiction. (January, February, March, April, June, July, August, September, October, November, December)

McCall, Nathan. *Makes Me Wanna Holler: A Young Black Man in America.* Life Stories. (January, February, March, April, June, July, August, September, October, November, December)

McMillan, Terry. *Waiting to Exhale.* Mainstream Fiction. (February, March)

Mosley, Walter. *Black Betty.* Detective and Crime Fiction. (January, February, March, April, June, September)

Mosley, Walter. *Devil in a Blue Dress.* Detective and Crime Fiction. (January, February, March, April, June)

Pryor, Richard. *Pryor Convictions and Other Life Sentences.* Life Stories. (November, December)

Ray, Francis. *Forever Yours.* Romance Literature. (January, April)

Sinclair, April. *Coffee Will Make You Black.* Mainstream Fiction. (June, July, September, November)

Vanzant, Iyanla. *Acts of Faith: Daily Devotions for People of Color.* Inspirational Literature. (January, February, March, April, June, July, August, September, October, November, December)

Vanzant, Iyanla. *The Value in the Valley: A Black Woman's Guide Through Life's Dilemmas.* Inspirational Literature. (July, October, November, December)

Verdelle, A.J. *The Good Negress.* Mainstream Fiction. (October, November, December)

Wesley, Valerie Wilson. *Devil's Gonna Get Him.* Crime and Detective Fiction. (December)

Wesley, Valerie Wilson. *When Death Comes Stealing.* Crime and Detective Fiction. (December)

West, Dorothy. *The Wedding.* Mainstream Fiction. (July, August, September, October, November, December)

1996   **Boyd, Julia A.** *Girlfriend to Girlfriend: Everyday Wisdom and Affirmations from the Sister Circle.* Inspirational Literature. (January, February, April, May, June)

Briscoe, Connie. *Big Girls Don't Cry.* Mainstream Fiction. (September, November)

Briscoe, Connie. *Sisters and Lovers.* Mainstream Fiction. (January, February, May, October, November)

Bunkley, Anita Richmond. *Wild Embers.* Romance Literature. (July, August)

Butler, Octavia E. *Bloodchild: And Other Stories.* Speculative Fiction. (March, April, June)

Cook, Suzan D. Johnson. *Sister to Sister Devotions For and From African American Women.* Inspirational Literature. (September, October)

Copage, Eric V. *Black Pearls: Daily Meditations, Affirmations, and Inspirations for African-Americans.* Inspirational Literature. (April, May, June)

Harris, E. Lynn. *Invisible Life.* Mainstream Fiction. (January, August, September, October)

Kitt, Sandra. *Color of Love.* Romance Literature. (March)

Kitt, Sandra. *Significant Others.* Romance Literature. (November)

McCall, Nathan. *Makes Me Wanna Holler: A Young Black Man in America.* Life Stories. (February, March, April, June, November).

McMillan, Terry. *Waiting to Exhale*. Mainstream Fiction. (April, May, June, July)

Mosley, Walter. *Black Betty.* Detective and Crime Fiction. (January)

Neely, Barbara. *Blanche Among the Talented Tenth.* Crime and Detective Fiction. (February)

Pryor, Richard. *Pryor Convictions and Other Life Sentences.* Life Stories. (January, February)

Sharpton, Al. *Go Tell Pharaoh: The Autobiography of the Reverend Al Sharpton.* Life Stories. (October)

Sinclair, April. *Coffee Will Make You Black.* Mainstream Fiction. (January, February, March, April, May, June, July, November)

Taylor, Susan L. *Lessons in Living.* Inspirational Literature. (March, April, May, June, July)

Vanzant, Iyanla. *Acts of Faith: Daily Devotions for People of Color.* Inspirational Literature. (January, February, March, April, May, June, July, August, October)

Vanzant, Iyanla. *The Spirit of a Man: A Vision of Transformation for Black Men and the Women Who Love Them.* Inspirational Literature. (November)

Vanzant, Iyanla. *The Value in the Valley: A Black Woman's Guide Through Life's Dilemmas.* Inspirational Literature. (January, February, March, April, May, June, July, August, November)

Verdelle, A.J. *The Good Negress.* Mainstream Fiction. (January, February, September, October)

Wesley, Valerie Wilson. *Devil's Gonna Get Him.* Crime and Detective Fiction. (January, February, March, April, May, June, July)

Wesley, Valerie Wilson. *When Death Comes Stealing.* Crime and Detective Fiction. (January, February, March, April, June, July, August)

West, Dorothy. *The Wedding.* Mainstream Fiction. (January, February, March, April, May, June, September)

1997 Angelou, Maya. *The Heart of a Woman.* Life Stories. (October, November, December)

Briscoe, Connie. *Big Girls Don't Cry.* Mainstream Fiction. (December)

Briscoe, Connie. *Sisters and Lovers.* Mainstream Fiction. (January)

Cochran, Johnnie L. with Tim Rutten. *Journey to Justice.* Life Stories. (February, April)

Copage, Eric V. *Black Pearls: Daily Meditations, Affirmations, and Inspirations for African-Americans.* Inspirational Literature. (May, June)

Harris, E. Lynn. *Invisible Life.* Mainstream Fiction. (April, May, June, July)

Jackson, Sheneska. *Blessings.* Inspirational Literature. (October, November, December)

Jackson, Sheneska. *Li'l Mama's Rules.* Mainstream Fiction. (October, November, December)

Joe, Yolanda. *He Say, She Say.* Mainstream Fiction. (July, September)

Kitt, Sandra. *Significant Others.* Romance Literature. (January)

LaBelle, Patti. *Don't Block the Blessings: Revelations of a Lifetime.* Life Stories. (February, April, May, June, July, August, September, October, November, December)

Little, Benilde. *Good Hair.* Mainstream Fiction. (January, February, April, May, June, July, August, November)

McCall, Nathan. *Makes Me Wanna Holler: A Young Black Man in America.* Life Stories. (January, February, April, May, June, July)

Mfume, Kweisi with Ron Stodghill. *No Free Ride: From the Mean Streets to the Mainstream Fiction.* Life Stories. (January, February, April)

Morrison, Toni. *Song of Solomon.* Mainstream Fiction. (February, April, May, June, August)

Sinclair, April. *Coffee Will Make You Black.* Mainstream Fiction. (January, February)

Vanzant, Iyanla. *Acts of Faith: Daily Devotions for People of Color.* Inspirational Literature. (January, February, March, April, May, June, July, August, October, November, December)

Vanzant, Iyanla. *The Spirit of a Man: A Vision of Transformation for Black Men and the Women Who Love Them.* Inspirational Literature. (January, February, July)

Vanzant, Iyanla. *The Value in the Valley: A Black Woman's Guide Through Life's Dilemmas.* Inspirational Literature. (January, February, April, May, June, July, September, October, November, December)

Wesley, Valerie Wilson. *Where Evil Sleeps.* Crime and Detective Fiction. (January)

1998 **Angelou, Maya.** *The Heart of a Woman.* Life Stories. (January, February, June)

Campbell, Bebe Moore. *Singing in the Comeback Choir.* Mainstream Fiction. (July, August, September)

Cook, Suzan D. Johnson. *Sister to Sister Devotions For and From African American Women.* Inspirational Literature. (May)

Gaines, Ernest. *A Lesson Before Dying.* Mainstream Fiction. (April)

Jackson, Sheneska. *Blessings.* Inspirational Literature. (October, November)

Jackson, Sheneska. *Li'l Mama's Rules.* Mainstream Fiction. (January, February, March, May, October, November)

Joe, Yolanda. *He Say, She Say.* Mainstream Fiction. (August)

Knight, Gladys. *Between Each Line of Pain and Glory: My Life Story.* Life Stories. (February, March, April)

LaBelle, Patti. *Don't Block the Blessings: Revelations of a Lifetime.* Life Stories. (June, August)

Little, Benilde. *Good Hair.* Mainstream Fiction. (February, March, April, May, July)

Neely, Barbara. *Blanche Cleans Up.* Detective and Crime Fiction. (September)

Vanzant, Iyanla. *Acts of Faith: Daily Devotions for People of Color.* Inspirational Literature. (January, February, March, April, May, June, July, August, September, October, November)

Vanzant, Iyanla. *The Value in the Valley: A Black Woman's Guide Through Life's Dilemmas.* Inspirational Literature. (January, July, September)

Wesley, Valerie Wilson. *No Hiding Place.* Crime and Detective Fiction. (February)

West, Dorothy. *The Wedding.* Mainstream Fiction. (July)

1999   **Brown, Parry.** *The Shirt Off His Back.* Mainstream Fiction. (November, December)

Campbell, Bebe Moore. *Singing in the Comeback Choir.* Mainstream Fiction. (November, December)

Cooper, J. California. *The Wake of the Wind.* Historical Fiction. (February, March, May)

Harris, E. Lynn. *Invisible Life.* Mainstream Fiction. (October, November)

Jackson, Sheneska. *Blessings.* Inspirational Literature. (January, February, October, November, December)

Joe, Yolanda. *He Say, She Say.* Mainstream Fiction. (January)

Knight, Gladys. *Between Each Line of Pain and Glory: My Life Story.* Life Stories. (May)

LaBelle, Patti. *Don't Block the Blessings: Revelations of a Lifetime.* Life Stories. (February, March)

Palfrey, Evelyn. *The Price of Passion.* Romance Literature. (May, June)

Vanzant, Iyanla. *Acts of Faith: Daily Devotions for People of Color.* Inspirational Literature. (January, February, March, April, May, June, August, September, October, November, December)

Vanzant, Iyanla. *The Spirit of a Man: A Vision of Transformation for Black Men and the Women Who Love Them.* Inspirational Literature. (March, June)

Vanzant, Iyanla. *The Value in the Valley: A Black Woman's Guide Through Life's Dilemmas.* Inspirational Literature. (April, October)

Vanzant, Iyanla. *Yesterday, I Cried.* Inspirational Literature. (August, September, October, November, December)

Wesley, Valerie Wilson. *Easier to Kill.* Crime and Detective Fiction. (February, March, October)

Wesley, Valerie Wilson. *No Hiding Place.* Crime and Detective Fiction. (February)

2000   Brown, Parry. *The Shirt Off His Back.* Mainstream Fiction. (April)

Clarke, Breena. *River, Cross My Heart.* Mainstream Fiction. (April)

Cooper, J. California. *The Wake of the Wind.* Historical Fiction. (May, June, July, August)

Dickey, Eric Jerome. *Liar's Game.* Mainstream Fiction. (October, November, December)

Johnson-Hodge, Margaret. *Butterscotch Blues.* Romance Literature. (November)

Major, Marcus. *Good Peoples.* Mainstream Fiction. (June)

McFadden, Bernice. *Sugar.* Mainstream Fiction. (June)

Murray, Victoria Christopher. *Temptation.* Inspirational Literature. (December)

Roby, Kimberla Lawson. *Casting the First Stone.* Inspirational Literature. (April, May, June, July, August)

Vanzant, Iyanla. *Acts of Faith: Daily Devotions for People of Color.* Inspirational Literature. (April, October)

Vanzant, Iyanla. *Yesterday, I Cried.* Inspirational Literature. (April, May, June, July, August, October, November)

Weber, Carl. *Lookin' for Luv.* Romance Literature. (December)

Wesley, Valerie Wilson. *The Devil Riding.* Crime and Detective Fiction. (October, November, December)

Bram Stoker Award (1983–present)
www.horror.org/stokers.htm

Each year, the Horror Writer's Association presents the Bram Stoker Awards for Superior Achievement for horror published in English. The HWA membership recommends titles for consideration. Beginning in 2001, the awards are presented in 12 categories: Novel, First Novel, Short Fiction, Long Fiction, Fiction Collection, Poetry Collection, Anthology, Nonfiction, Illustrated Narrative, Screenplay, Work for Young Readers, and Alternative Forms.

1995   Due, Tananarive. *The Between.* Speculative Fiction. *Superior Achievement in a First Novel.*

1997   Due, Tananarive. *My Soul To Keep.* Life Brothers Series. Speculative Fiction. *Superior Achievement in a Novel.*

Bruce K. Gould Book Award (1990–present)

www.tourolaw.edu

Named for Bruce K. Gould, a principal in Gould Publications, one of the largest legal publishers in the United States, this award is presented annually to "the author of an outstanding publication related to the law, legal profession or legal system."

1998   **Hill, Anita. *Speaking Truth to Power.*** Life Stories.

2002   **Jordan, Vernon Jr. *Vernon Can Read! A Memoir.*** Life Stories.

Christy Awards (1999–present)

www.christyawards.com,

The Christy Awards are given to novelists in recognition of excellence in nine genres of Christian fiction. This award began in 1999 in honor of Catherine Marshall, one of America's most notable and best-selling Christian writers.

2001   **Foster, Sharon Ewell. *Passing By Samaria: A Novel.*** Inspirational
                  Literature. *First Novel*

Ditmar Award (1969–present)

home.vicnet.net.au/~sfoz/dityear.htm

The Ditmar is awarded each year by the Australian National Science Fiction Convention for the best SF published in Australia. Although nominations are open to fandom in general, to vote one must be a member of the national convention.

1989   Butler, Octavia E. *Dawn.* Xenogenesis Trilogy. Speculative Fiction.
                  Best International Long Fiction.

Edgar Awards (1945–present)

www.mysterynet.com/edgars/

Edgar Awards are presented by Mystery Writers of America, Inc., the self-proclaimed premier organization for mystery writers and other professionals in the mystery field. The Edgar is named for Edgar Allan Poe. Categories include Best First Novel, Best Paperback Original, Best Novel, Best Short Story, and Best Critical or Biographical Work as well as awards for juvenile and young adult fiction and various categories of media. Awards are presented annually.

1991   Mosley, Walter. *Devil in a Blue Dress.* Detective and Crime Fiction.
                  Best First Novel.

1995   West, Chassie. *Sunrise.* Detective and Crime Fiction. *Best Original
                  Paperback.*

2000   **West, Chassie. *Killing Kin.*** Detective and Crime Fiction. *Best
                  Original Paperback.*

Emma Awards

www.romanceslamjam.com/Nominations/index.html

The Emma Awards, named for the Romance Slam Jam cofounder Emma Rodgers, recognizes outstanding work in African American romance novels. The awards, which cover a number of categories, are announced at the yearly conference.

2002   **Benson, Angela.** *Abiding Hope.* Inspirational Literature.

2003   **Ayers, Rochelle.** *No Compromise.* Romance Literature.

Essence **Bestseller List** (2001–present)
www.essence.com

Essence magazine compiles a monthly list of best-selling books based on reports of retail sales from African American bookstores.

2001   **Berry, Bertice.** *The Haunting of Hip-Hop: A Novel.* Inspirational Literature. (July)

Bowen, Michelle Andrea. *Church Folk: A Novel.* Inspirational Literature. (October, December)

Brown, Parry. *Sittin' in the Front Row Pew.* Inspirational Literature. (October, December)

Dickey, Eric Jerome. *Liar's Game.* Mainstream Fiction. (January, March, April, November)

Mosely, Walter. *Fearless Jones.* Crime and Detective Fiction. (October)

Poitier, Sidney. *The Measure of a Man: A Spiritual Autobiography.* Life Stories. (January)

Randall, Alice. *The Wind Done Gone.* Historical Fiction. (October, November)

Vanzant, Iyanla. *In the Meantime: Finding Yourself and the Love That You Want.* Inspirational Literature. (January, March)

Vanzant, Iyanla. *Until Today! Daily Devotions.* Inspirational Literature. (January, May, June, July, August, September, October, November, December)

Vanzant, Iyanla. *Yesterday, I Cried.* Inspirational Literature. (January, February, March, April, May, July, August, September, October)

Weber, Carl. *Lookin' for Luv.* Romance Literature. (January)

2002   **Angelou, Maya A.** *A Song Flung Up to Heaven.* Life Stories. (June, August, September)

Bowen, Michelle Andrea. *Church Folk: A Novel.* Inspirational Literature. (February, March, April, May, June, July, August, September, October)

Brown, Parry. *Sittin' in the Front Row Pew.* Inspirational Literature. (April, August, September, October, December)

12

Carter, Stephen. *Emperor of Ocean Park.* Crime and Detective Fiction. (October)

Cleage, Pearl. *I Wish I Had a Red Dress.* Mainstream Fiction. (February)

Davis, Sampson, George Jenkins, and Rameck Hunt with Lisa Frazier Page. *The Pact: Three Young Men Make a Promise and Fulfill a Dream.* Life Stories. (October, December)

Harris, E. Lynn. *A Love of My Own.* Mainstream Fiction. (December)

Holmes, Shannon. *B-More Careful.* Detective and Crime Fiction. (June, July, August, October, December)

Jakes, T.D. *God's Leading Lady.* Inspirational Literature. (December)

Jones, Quincy. *Q: The Autobiography.* Life Stories. (March, April, May)

Jordan, Vernon E. with Annette Gordon-Reed. *Vernon Can Read!: A Memoir.* Life Stories. (April, May, June, November).

LaBelle, Patti. *Patti's Pearls.* Inspirational Literature. (March, April)

McFadden, Bernice. *Bitter Earth.* Historical Fiction. (May, June, July, August, October)

McKenzie, Vashti Murphy. *Journey to the Well.* Inspirational Literature. (November)

Mosley, Walter. *Futureland.* Speculative Fiction. (April)

Randall, Alice. *The Wind Done Gone.* Historical Fiction. (April)

Ray, Francis. *I Know Who Holds Tomorrow.* Inspirational Literature. (August, September, December)

Shabazz, Ilyasah. *Growing Up X.* Life Stories. (September, October)

Tademy, Lalita. *Cane River.* Historical Fiction. (February, May)

Vanzant, Iyanla. *Every Day I Pray.* Inspirational Literature. (February, March, April, May, July, August, September)

Vanzant, Iyanla. *Until Today! Daily Devotions.* Inspirational Literature. (January, February, March)

Weber, Carl. *Married Men.* Romance Literature. (January, March, April, June, July, September, October)

2003   Brown, Parry. *The Shirt Off His Back.* Mainstream Fiction. (July)

Brown, Parry. *Sittin' in the Front Row Pew.* Inspirational Literature. (February, March, May, August)

Davis, Sampson, George Jenkins, and Rameck Hunt with Lisa Frazier Page. *The Pact: Three Young Men Make a Promise and Fulfill a Dream.* Life Stories. (January, April, June, July, August, September)

Harris, E. Lynn. *A Love of My Own.* Mainstream Fiction. (January, March, April, July)

Height, Dorothy. *Open Wide the Freedom Gates: A Memoir by Dorothy Height.* Life Stories. (October, November)

Holmes, Shannon. *B-More Careful.* Crime and Detective Fiction. (February, March, April, June, August, October)

Jakes, T.D. *God's Leading Lady.* Inspirational Literature. (January)

McKenzie, Vashti Murphy. *Journey to the Well.* Inspirational Literature. (December)

Roby, Kimberla Lawson. *A Taste of Reality.* Mainstream Fiction. (May, June)

Shabazz, Ilyasah. *Growing Up X.* Life Stories. (January, February)

Vanzant, Iyanla. *Every Day I Pray.* Inspirational Literature. (March, April)

2004   **Brown, Parry.** *The Shirt Off His Back.* Mainstream Fiction. (March)

Brown, Parry. *Sittin' in the Front Row Pew.* Inspirational Literature. (March)

Davis, Sampson, George Jenkins, and Rameck Hunt with Lisa Frazier Page. *The Pact: Three Young Men Make a Promise and Fulfill a Dream.* Life Stories. (January, April, May, June, August)

Gurley-Gate, Hilda. *Sapphire's Grave.* Historical Fiction. (March)

Height, Dorothy. *Open Wide the Freedom Gates: A Memoir by Dorothy Height.* Life Stories. (January, March, June)

Jones, Edward P. *The Known World.* Historical Fiction. (February)

Sister Souljah. *Coldest Winter Ever.* Crime and Detective Fiction. (January)

Georgia Author of the Year (1965–present)

Established in 1965, this award recognizes outstanding contributions to literature by authors born in or residing in Georgia. Awards are presented in the categories of fiction, nonfiction, juvenile literature, poetry, and other categories when applicable. This award includes a plaque.

1999   **Perry, Phyllis Alesia.** *Stigmata.* Mainstream Fiction. *First Novel.*

Go On Girl! Book Club Author Awards (1992–present)

www.goongirl.org/awards.htm

The Go On Girl Book Club Author Awards were created in 1992 to recognize authors and publishers who have made significant contributions in the writing and publication of quality books for and about people of African descent. Each year, authors are selected based on book reviews from each Go On Girl! Book Club chapter.

1993   **Campbell, Bebe Moore**. *Your Blues Ain't Like Mine*. Mainstream Fiction.

1996–1997   **Little, Benilde**. *Good Hair: A Novel*. Mainstream Fiction.

1999   **Cleage, Pearl**. *What Looks Like Crazy on an Ordinary Day*. Mainstream Fiction.

2000   **McFadden, Bernice**. *Sugar*. Mainstream Fiction.

New Author of the Year

1995   **Briscoe, Connie**. *Sisters and Lovers*. Mainstream Fiction. *New Author of the Year*.

2002   **Bowen, Michelle Andrea**. *Church Folk: A Novel.* Inspirational Literature. *New Author of the Year*.

  Tademy, Lalita. *Cane River*. Historical Fiction. *New Author of the Year*.

Gold Medallion Book Awards (1978–present)

www.ecpa.org

The Gold Medallion Awards are one of the most prestigious awards in the Christian publishing industry. Since 1978, the Evangelical Christian Publishers Association has given this award to recipients in several different categories, including fiction.

1991   Carson, Ben with Cecil Murphey. *Gifted Hands: The Ben Carson Story*. Life Stories. *Finalist*.

Gold Pen Awards (2000–present)

www.blackwriters.org

The Gold Pen Awards, sponsored by the Black Writers Alliance, honor the best literature from the worldwide African community.

2000   **Massey, Brandon.** *Thunderland.* Speculative Fiction. *Best Thriller*.

  Mickelbury, Penny. *The Step Between*. Detective and Crime Fiction. *Best Mystery/Thriller*.

  Wesley, Valerie Wilson. *Easier to Kill*. Detective and Crime Fiction. *Best Mystery/Thriller*.

  Woods, Paula L. *Inner City Blues*. Detective and Crime Fiction. *Best Mystery/Thriller*.

2001   **Ellis, Jamellah.** *That Faith, That Trust, That Love.* Inspirational Literature. *Best Christian Fiction (tie).*

Foster, Sharon Ewell. *Ain't No River.* Inspirational Literature. *Best Christian Fiction (tie).*

Thomas, Sheree R. *Dark Matter: A Century of Speculative Fiction From the African Diaspora.* Speculative Fiction. *Best Anthology.*

Benson, Angela. *Awakening Mercy.* Inspirational Literature. *Best Christian Fiction.*

Bland, Eleanor Taylor. *Scream in Silence.* Crime and Detective Fiction. *Best Mystery/Thriller.*

DeLoach, Nora. *Mama Pursues Murderous Shadows.* Crime and Detective Fiction. *Best Mystery/Thriller.*

Edwards, Grace. *Do or Die.* Detective and Crime Fiction. *Best Mystery/Thriller.*

Foster, Sharon Ewell. *Passing By Samaria: A Novel.* Inspirational Literature. *Best Christian Fiction.*

Gray, Maurice M. *To Whom Much Is Given: A Novel.* Inspirational Literature. *Best Christian Fiction.*

Murray, Victoria Christopher. *Joy.* Inspirational Literature. *Best Christian Fiction.*

Phillips, Gary. *High Hand.* Detective and Crime Fiction. *Best Mystery/Thriller.*

Roby, Kimberla Lawson. *Casting The First Stone.* Inspirational Literature. *Best Christian Fiction.*

West, Chassie. *Killing Kin.* Detective and Crime Fiction. *Best Mystery/Thriller.*

2002   **Bland, Eleanor Taylor.** *Whispers in the Dark.* Crime and Detective Fiction. *Best Mystery/Thriller Award.*

Ayers, Rochelle. *No Compromise.* Romantic Literature. *Best Romantic Fiction.*

Barnes, Steven. *Lion's Blood.* Speculative Fiction. *Best Mainstream Fiction.*

Benson, Angela. *Abiding Hope.* Inspirational Literature. *Best Christian Fiction.*

Esdalie, Leslie. *Rivers of the Soul.* Romantic Literature. *Best Romantic Fiction.*

Griggs, Vanessa Davis. *Promises Beyond Jordan.* Inspirational Literature. *Best Christian Fiction.*

Hardwick, Gary. *The Color of Justice.* Crime and Detective Fiction. *Best Mystery/Thriller.*

McFadden, Bernice. *This Bitter Earth.* Historical Fiction. *Best Mainstream Fiction.*

Grand Prix. French Grand Prize for Mystery Stories (1948–present)

The Grand Prix de Littérature Policiére, originally awarded under the designation "Grand Prix du club des Detetives," is presented to the writers of the two best mystery stories published during the year—one written in French and one written in a language other than French and translated into French. (From Jane Clapp, *International Dictionary of Literary Awards* [New York: Scarecrow, 1963], p. 134.)

1957 **Himes, Chester.** *A Rage in Harlem*. Detective and Crime Fiction. *Best Detective Novel of the Year.*

Granta's Best of the Young American Novelists (1996–present)

In 1996, the British literary magazine *Granta,* which since 1983 has compiled lists of the best young British novelists, announced its first "20 Best American Novelists Under 40." Although this list is controversial, the authors on it have become some of the most critically acclaimed novelists of the new century.

1996 **Haynes, David.** *Somebody Else's Mama.* Mainstream Fiction.

Houghton Mifflin Literary Fellowship

Now discontinued, this monetary award was established in 1935 to recognize new American authors for works of outstanding literary merit in fiction and nonfiction.

1957 **Simmons, Herbert.** *Corner Boy.* Detective and Crime Fiction.

1966 **Walker, Margaret**. *Jubilee*. Historical Fiction.

Hugo Award (1954–present)

wsfs.org/hugos.htm

The Science Fiction Achievement Award, commonly called the Hugo (after Hugo Gernsback), is given annually by the World Science Fiction Society (WSFS). The award is sponsored by WSFS, administered by a committee of the World Science Fiction Convention (WorldCon) held that year, and determined by nominations from and a popular vote of the membership of WSFS. Current categories include Novel, Novella, Novelette, Short Story, Related Book, Dramatic Presentation, Professional Editor, Professional Artist, Semiprozine, Fanzine, Fan Writer, and Fan Artist.

1967 Delany, Samuel R. *Babel-17*. Speculative Fiction. *Best Novel.*

1968 Delany, Samuel R. *The Einstein Intersection* (also published as *A Fabulous, Formless Darkness*). Speculative Fiction.

1969 Delany, Samuel R. *Nova*. Speculative Fiction.

Hurston/Wright Legacy Award

www.hurston-wright.org/legacy_award.html

The Hurston/Wright Legacy Award is a national award for published writers of African American descent. The award is presented in partnership by the Hurston/Wright Foundation and Borders Books and Music. This award was designed to fill the unfortunate void in recognizing the highest quality fiction and nonfiction by contemporary black writers.

1992   **Durham, David Anthony.** *Gabriel's Story.* Frontier Literature. *Fiction Award.*

2002   Grooms, Anthony. *Bombingham.* Historical Fiction. *Finalist.*

2003   **Jones, Tayari.** *Leaving Atlanta.* Historical Fiction. *Debut Fiction Award.*

LaValle, Victor. *The Ecstatic.* Mainstream Fiction. *Finalist.*

Rodes, Jewell Parker. *Douglass' Women.* Historical Fiction. *Finalist.*

International Horror Guild Award (1995–present)

www.ihgonline.org/

Given by the Guild, the award recognizes outstanding achievements in the field of horror and dark fantasy. A jury of critics and reviewers selects the recipient based on public recommendations.

1997   Due, Tananarive. *My Soul To Keep.* Life Brothers Series. Speculative Fiction. *Best Novel Award.*

James Tiptree Jr. Award (1992–present)

www.tiptree.org/

The Tiptree Award is an annual literary prize for science fiction or fantasy that explores and expands the roles of women, but it is not limited to women authors. The award is named for Alice B. Sheldon, who wrote under the pseudonym James Tiptree Jr.

1995   **Butler, Octavia E.** *Wild Seed.* **Patternist Series.** Speculative Fiction. *Award classics.*

Delany, Samuel R. *Babel-17.* Speculative Fiction. *Award classics.*

Delany, Samuel R. *Trouble on Triton: An Ambiguous Heterotopia* (also published as *Triton*). Speculative Fiction. *Award classics.*

1998   Butler, Octavia E. *Parable of the Talents.* Earthseed Series. Speculative Fiction. *Award for Gender-bending SF.*

Janet Heidinger Kafka Prize (1975–present)

This biannual award was established in 1975 to memorialize a young editor who was killed in an automobile accident. It recognizes the American woman author who, in the opinion of the panel, has written the best recently published book-length work of prose fiction. The award includes a cash prize and a certificate.

1977   **Morrison, Toni.** *Song of Solomon.* Mainstream Fiction.

1979   **Chase-Riboud, Barbara.** *Sally Hemings.* Historical Fiction.

John Creasey Award (1973–present)

home.attbi.com/~dwtaylor1/creaseyaward.html

The John Creasey Award, sponsored by the Crime Writers' Association of Great Britain, is named after a British mystery/crime/suspense author. The award acknowledges the best crime novel by an author who has not previously published a full-length novel.

1991   **Mosley, Walter.** *Devil in a Blue Dress*. Detective and Crime Fiction.

Lambda Literary Award (1989–present)

www.lambdalit.org/lammy/index.htm

The Lambda Literary Awards have been given each year since 1989 by the Lambda Literary Foundation to superior achievement in works with themes dealing with alternative sexual lifestyles. Since 1994, science fiction and fantasy have had one category, combining both the gay men's and lesbian categories. Awards are presented for works from the previous year. Final nominees are announced by the Lambda Book Report staff, and the final voting is done by a small group of volunteer judges in each category.

1991   **Gomez, Jewelle.** *The Gilda Stories.* Speculative Fiction. *Lesbian Science Fiction/Fantasy; Lesbian Fiction.*

Lillian Smith Book Awards (1968–present)

www.southerncouncil.org/comm/smith.html

The Lillian Smith Book Awards have been presented each year since 1968 by the Southern Regional Council to recognize outstanding writing about the American South. The awards carry on Lillian Smith's legacy of promoting racial and social equality and proposing a vision of justice and human understanding.

2002   **Grooms, Anthony.** *Bombingham.* Historical Fiction. *Fiction.*

Locus Awards (1971–present)

www.locusmag.com/SFAwards/

Locus Magazine conducts an annual readership poll, with the results published in the August issue. Awards are given in the categories of SF Novel, Fantasy Novel, Horror/Dark Fantasy Novel, First Novel, Novella, Novelette, Short Story, Collection, Anthology, Nonfiction, Art Book, Editor, Magazine, Book Publisher, and Artist.

1972   Delany, Samuel R. *Driftglass: Ten Tales of Speculative Fiction.* Speculative Fiction. *Best Reprint Anthology/Collection (Old).*

1975   Delany, Samuel R. *Babel-17*. Speculative Fiction. *All Time Best Novel.*

Delany, Samuel R. *Dhalgren*. Speculative Fiction. *Best SF Novel.*

1977   Delany, Samuel R. *Trouble on Triton: An Ambiguous Heterotopia* (also published as *Triton*). Speculative Fiction. *Best SF Novel.*

1980   Butler, Octavia E. *Kindred*. Speculative Fiction. *Best Fantasy Novel.*

1981   Butler, Octavia E. *Wild Seed*. Patternist Series. Speculative Fiction. *Best SF Novel.*

1984   Delany, Samuel R. *Neveryóna, or: The Tales of Signs and Cities, Some Informal Remarks toward the Modular Calculus, Part Four.* Return to NevPrlon Series. Speculative Fiction. *Best Fantasy Novel.*

1985   Butler, Octavia E. *Clay's Ark*. Patternist Series. Speculative Fiction. *Best SF Novel.*

Delany, Samuel R. *Stars in My Pocket Like Grains of Sand.* Speculative Fiction. *Best SF Novel.*

1986   Delany, Samuel R. *Flight from NevPrlon*. Return to Nevèrÿon Series. Speculative Fiction. *Best Collection.*

1987   Delany, Samuel R. *The Complete Nebula Award Winning Fiction*. Speculative Fiction. *Best Collection.*

1987   Delany, Samuel R. *Dhalgren*. Speculative Fiction. *All Time Best SF Novel.*

1988   Butler, Octavia E. *Dawn*. Xenogenesis Trilogy. Speculative Fiction. *Best SF Novel.*

Delany, Samuel R. *The Bridge of Lost Desire*. Return to Nevèrÿon Series (also published as *Return to Nevèrÿon*). *Speculative Fiction.* Best Collection.

1989   Butler, Octavia E. *Adulthood Rites*. Xenogenesis Trilogy. Speculative Fiction. *Best SF Novel.*

1990   Butler, Octavia E. *Imago*. Xenogenesis Trilogy. Speculative Fiction. *Best SF Novel.*

1995   Butler, Octavia E. *Parable of the Sower*. Earthseed Series. Speculative Fiction. *Best SF Novel.*

1996   **Butler, Octavia. *Bloodchild: And Other Stories*.** Speculative Fiction. *Best Collection.*

1998   Due, Tananarive. *My Soul To Keep*. Life Brothers Series. Speculative Fiction. *Best Fantasy Novel.*

Delany, Samuel R. *Dhalgren*. Speculative Fiction. *All Time Best SF Novel before 1990.*

1999   **Butler, Octavia E. *Parable of the Talents*. Earthseed Series.** Speculative Fiction. *Best SF Novel.*

2001   **Thomas, Sheree R. *Dark Matter: A Century Of Speculative Fiction From The African Diaspora*.** Speculative Fiction. *Best Anthology.*

2002   Mosley, Walter. *Futureland: Nine Stories of an Imminent World*. Speculative Fiction. *Best Collection.*

Los Angeles Times **Book Prize** (1980–present)

The *Los Angeles Times* Book Prizes were established in 1980 to honor writers who have demonstrated outstanding craftsmanship and vision. A prize is awarded in each of six categories: fiction, poetry, history, biography, science and technology, and current interest. The prize includes a $1,000 cash award.

1992   **Pinckney, Darryl.** *High Cotton*. Mainstream Fiction.

Macavity Awards (1987–present)
www.mysteryreaders.org/macavity.html

Macavity Awards are presented annually by members of Mystery Readers International. The award is named for T. S. Eliot's "mystery cat" (*Old Possum's Book of Practical Cats*). Categories of Macavity Awards are Best Mystery Novel, Best First Mystery Novel, Best Nonfiction, and Best Mystery Short Story.

1993   **Neely, Barbara.** *Blanche on the Lam.* Detective and Crime Fiction. *Best First Mystery Novel.*

2000   **Woods, Paula.** *Inner City Blues.* Detective and Crime Fiction. *Best First Mystery Novel.*

Medallion Award

1986   **Bambara, Toni Cade.** *The Salt Eaters*. Mainstream Fiction.

NAACP Image Award (1962–present)
www.naacp.org

Established in 1962, the NAACP Image Awards recognize outstanding African American contributions to the arts. Awards are given in 41 categories encompassing music, film, television, visual arts, and literature.

1994   **Campbell, Bebe Moore.** *Your Blues Ain't Like Mine*. Mainstream Fiction.

2000   Briscoe, Connie. *A Long Way From Home.* Historical Fiction.

2001   Murray, Victoria Christopher. *Temptation.* Inspirational Literature.

National Book Award (1950–present)
www.nationalbook.org/

National Book Awards, established in 1950, are given annually by the National Book Foundation for outstanding literary achievement in fiction, nonfiction, poetry, and young people's literature. A five-member independent judging panel chooses the winner for each category. The prize includes a $10,000 cash award and a crystal sculpture.

1953   **Ellison, Ralph.** *Invisible Man.* Mainstream Fiction.

1977   **Haley, Alex.** *Roots.* Historical Fiction. *Special Award.*

1990   **Johnson, Charles.** *Middle Passage.* Historical fiction.

1992   Jones, Edward P. *Lost in the City.* Historical Fiction. *Finalist.*

1998   Jones, Gayl. *The Healing.* Mainstream Fiction. *Finalist.*

2003   Jones, Edward P. *The Known World*. Historical Fiction. *Finalist.*

National Book Critics Circle Award (1981–present)
www.bookcritics.org/

This award was established in 1981 for the best new book of the year in each of five categories: fiction, general nonfiction, biography/autobiography, poetry, and criticism.

1977   **Morrison, Toni.** *Song of Solomon*. Mainstream Fiction.

1993   **Gaines, Ernest.** *A Lesson Before Dying*. Mainstream Fiction.

2004   Jones, Edward P. *The Known World*. Historical Fiction.

Nebula Award (1965–present)
www.sfwa.org/awards/

The Nebula Awards are voted on and presented by active members of the Science Fiction and Fantasy Writers of America, Inc. Since 1965, the Nebula Awards have been given each year for the Best Novel, Novella, Novelette, and Short Story.

1965   Delaney, Samuel R. *The Ballad of Beta-2*. Speculative Fiction. *Novella.*

1966   **Delaney, Samuel R.** *Babel-17*. Speculative Fiction. *Novel.*

1967   **Delaney, Samuel R.** *The Einstein Intersection* (also published as *A Fabulous, Formless Darkness*). Speculative Fiction. *Novel.*

1975   Delaney, Samuel R. *Dhalgren*. Speculative Fiction. *Novel.*

1976   Delaney, Samuel R. *Trouble on Triton: An Ambiguous Heterotopia* (also published as *Triton*). Speculative Fiction. *Novel.*

1994   Butler, Octavia E. *Parable of the Sower*. Earthseed Series. Speculative Fiction. *Novel.*

1999   **Butler, Octavia E.** *Parable of the Talents*. **Earthseed Series.** Speculative Fiction. *Nebula Award Novel.*

New York Times Notable Book of the Year
www.nytimes.com

The *New York Times* recognizes an outstanding book every year.

1989   **Ansa, Tina McElroy.** *Baby of the Family*. Mainstream Fiction.

1993   **Ashe, Arthur and Arnold Rampersad.** *Days Of Grace: A Memoir.* Life Stories.

2000   **Allen, Jeffery Renard.** *Rails Under My Back.* Mainstream Fiction.

2001   **Durham, David Anthony.** *Gabriel's Story.* Frontier Literature.

2002   **Carter, Stephen L.** *The Emperor of Ocean Park.* Crime and Detective Fiction.

   Durham, David Anthony. *Walk Through Darkness.* Historical Fiction.

2003   **Mosley, Walter.** *Fear Itself.* Detective and Crime Fiction.

Nobel Prize in Literature (1901–present)
www.nobel.se/

In his will, which established the Nobel Prizes in 1901, Alfred Nobel indicated that the awards should be given to those who, during the preceding year, "shall have conferred the greatest benefit on mankind" and that one part is to be given to the person who "shall have produced in the field of literature the most outstanding work in an ideal direction."

1993   **Morrison, Toni.** *The Bluest Eye.* Mainstream Fiction.

Oprah's Book Club (1996–April, 2002; June 2003)
www.oprah.com

From 1996 to 2002, talk show host Oprah Winfrey hosted on-air book club discussions with fans and author-guests. Due to their exposure on the show, the books achieved best-seller success. In June 2003, Winfrey relaunched the book club, focusing on titles with lasting influence. Lists of back titles and study guides are available online.

1996   **Morrison, Toni.** *Song of Solomon.* Mainstream Fiction.

1997   **Angelou, Maya.** *The Heart of a Woman.* Life Stories.

   Gaines, Ernest. *A Lesson Before Dying.* Mainstream Fiction.

2000   **Morrison, Toni.** *The Bluest Eye.* Mainstream Fiction.

2001   **Tademy, Lalita.** *Cane River.* Historical Fiction.

PEN/Faulkner Award (1980–present)

Established in 1980 by the PEN/Faulkner Foundation, this award honors the best work of fiction published by an American writer in the preceding year. The award includes a $15,000 cash prize to the winner and $5,000 each to four runners-up.

1982   **Bradley, David.** *The Chaneysville Incident.* Historical Fiction.

1991   **Wideman, John Edgar.** *Philadelphia Fire.* Mainstream Fiction.

2003   LaValle, Victor D. *The Ecstatic.* Mainstream Fiction. *Finalist*

PEN/Open Book Beyond Margins Award (1991–present)
www.pen.org/openbook/opneindex.htm

Initiated in 1991, the PEN Open Book Program encourages racial and ethnic diversity within the literary and publishing communities. Its *Beyond Margins* is an ongoing series of public readings honoring outstanding writers of color.

2002   **LaValle, Victor D.** *Slapboxing with Jesus* (short stories). Mainstream Fiction.

Prometheus Award (1982–present)
www.lfs.org/awards.htm

Founded in 1982 to provide encouragement to science fiction writers whose books examine the meaning of freedom, the Libertarian Futurist Society presents the Prometheus Award for best libertarian science fiction novel of the year. A second annual award called the Hall of Fame Award is designed to honor a classic libertarian science fiction novel. The Hall of Fame Award is open to any work of fiction over five years old. Books for both awards are nominated and selected by all members of the LFS.

1984   Delany, Samuel R. *Neveryóna, or: The Tales of Signs and Cities, Some Informal Remarks toward the Modular Calculus, Part Four.* Return to Nevèrÿon Series. Speculative Fiction.

1985   Delany, Samuel R. *Stars in My Pocket Like Grains of Sand.* Speculative Fiction.

Publishers Weekly

www.publishersweekly.com

Publishers Weekly's annual Best Books list honors the best books of the year in various genres.

1994   **Mosley, Walter.** *Black Betty.* Detective and Crime Fiction.

1997   **Due, Tananarive.** *My Soul to Keep.* Speculative Fiction.

1998   **Butler, Octavia E.** *Parable of the Talents.* Speculative Fiction.

Pulitzer Prize (1917–present)
www.pulitzer.org/

The Pulitzer Prizes, established in 1917, recognize outstanding achievements by Americans in journalism, letters, music, and drama. The Pulitzer Prizes for writing include annual awards for fiction, history, biography, poetry, and general nonfiction. In addition, special citations are occasionally awarded for works that fall outside these categories; for example, Alex Haley's *Roots* was granted a special citation in 1977 for making an important contribution to literature on slavery.

1977   **Haley, Alex.** *Roots.* Historical Fiction. *Fiction.*

1988   **Morrison, Toni.** *Beloved.* Historical Fiction. *Fiction.*

1983   **Walker, Alice.** *The Color Purple.* Mainstream Fiction. *Fiction.*

2004   **Jones, Edward P.** *The Known World.* Historical Fiction. *Fiction.*

Romance in Color Award of Excellence

The Romance in Color Award of Excellence is awarded to romance novels that have received five-star ratings from at least two RIC reviewers (information from www.romanceincolor.com).

2002   **Benson, Angela. Abiding Hope.** Inspirational Literature. *Reviewers' Choice Award.*

Forster, Gwynne. *When Twilight Comes*. Romance Literature. *Award of Excellence.*

Jenkins, Beverly. *A Chance at Love*. Romance Literature. *Award of Excellence.*

Romance Writers of America's RITA Awards

www.rwanational.org

RITA Awards are presented in 12 different categories for excellence in the genre of romance fiction. "The Best Inspirational Romance" category recognizes the best romances that contain spiritual elements.

2001   Foster, Sharon Ewell. *Passing By Samaria: A Novel*. Inspirational Literature. *Finalist, Best First Book.*

Foster, Sharon Ewell. *Passing By Samaria: A Novel*. Inspirational Literature. *Finalist, Best Inspirational Literature.*

Russwurm Award (1971–present)

Awarded by the National Newspaper Publishers' Association, this award recognizes "outstanding contributions by African Americans and memorializes John B. Russwurm, founder of the Freedom Journal, the first Black-owned newspaper in America."

1953   **Ellison, Ralph.** *Invisible Man*. Mainstream Fiction.

Sacred Fire: The QBR 100 Essential Black Books

QBR: The Black Book Review is the leading critical review of contemporary African American books. In compiling *Sacred Fire*, the editors of QBR consulted prominent scholars, historians, authors, and booksellers to choose the 100 most important African American books. Inclusion in *Sacred Fire* thus constitutes a significant honor and is noted as an award in this volume.

Angelou, Maya. *I Know Why the Caged Bird Sings.* Life Stories.

Baldwin, James. *Go Tell It on the Mountain*. Mainstream Fiction.

Bradley, David. *The Chaneysville Incident.* Historical Fiction.

Brown, William Wells. *Clotel, or, The President's Daughter*. Mainstream Fiction.

Campbell, Bebe Moore. *Your Blues Ain't Like Mine.* Mainstream Fiction.

Chase-Riboud, Barbara. *Sally Hemings.* Historical Fiction.

Ellison, Ralph. *Invisible Man*. Mainstream Fiction.

Gaines, Ernest. *A LessonBefore Dying.* Mainstream Fiction.

Haley, Alex. *Roots.* Historical Fiction.

Hughes, Langston. *The Ways of White Folks* (short stories). Mainstream Fiction.

Hurston, Zora Neale. *Their Eyes Were Watching God*. Mainstream Fiction.

McMillan, Terry. *Waiting to Exhale*. Mainstream Fiction.

Morrison, Toni. *Beloved.* Historical Fiction

Morrison, Toni. *Song of Solomon*. Mainstream Fiction.

Mosley, Walter. *Black Betty.* Detective and Crime Fiction.

Naylor, Gloria. *The Women of Brewster Place.* Mainstream Fiction.

Petry, Ann. *The Street*. Mainstream Fiction.

Thurman, Wallace. *The Blacker the Berry*. Mainstream Fiction.

Toomer, Jean. *Cane*. Mainstream Fiction.

Walker, Alice. *The Color Purple.* Mainstream Fiction.

Walker, Margaret. *Jubilee.* Historical Fiction.

Washington, Booker T. *Up From Slavery.* Life Stories.

Wideman, John Edgar. *Damballah* (in *The Homewood Books*, collection of three novels). Mainstream Fiction.

Wideman, John Edgar. *Damballah* (in *The Homewood Books*, collection of three novels). Mainstream Fiction.

Wilson, Harriet E. *Our Nig, or, Sketches from the Life of a Free Black*. Mainstream Fiction.

Wright, Richard. *Native Son*. Mainstream Fiction.

Shamus Awards (1982–present)

www.thrillingdetective.com/trivia/triv72.html

Shamus Awards are presented by The Private Eye Writers of America (PWA), an organization devoted to private eye detective fiction, and open to fans, writers, and publishing professionals. A "private eye" is a professional investigator not employed by a police department or government. Winners are selected by committee, and categories include Best Hardcover P.I. Novel, Best P.I. Paperback Original, Best P.I. First Novel, and Best P.I. Short Story. Awards are presented annually.

| 1987 | **Haywood, Gar Anthony.** *Fear of the Dark*.Crime and Detective Fiction. *Best First Private-Eye Novel.* |

| 1991 | **Mosley, Walter.** *Devil in a Blue Dress*. Crime and Detective Fiction. *Best First Novel.* |

1995   Wesley, Valerie Wilson. *When Death Comes Stealing.* Crime and Detective Fiction. *Best First Private-Eye Novel.*

Spur Award (1953–present)

www.westernwriters.org/spur_awards.htm

The Spur Awards, established in 1953 by the Western Writers of America, recognize outstanding work in fiction and nonfiction Western titles, as well as television and film productions (information from Web site).

1999   **King, Hiram.** *Dark Trail.* Frontier Literature. *Spur Award for Original Western Paperback.*

St. Martin's Press/PWA Best First Mystery Novel Contest Award (1986–present)

www.thrillingdetective.com/trivia/triv72.html

The first mystery novel contest award is presented to an unpublished private eye novel by The Private Eye Writers of America and sponsored by St. Martin's Press.

1987   **Haywood, Gar Anthony.** *Fear of the Dark.* Detective and Crime Fiction.

Whiting Award (1985–present)

Established in 1985 by the Mrs. Giles Whiting Foundation, the Whiting Award is granted annually to 10 writers of exceptional promise. The award consists of a $30,000 cash prize and encompasses fiction, nonfiction, and poetry. Selections are based on the quality of writing and the likelihood of outstanding future work.

1994   **Kenan, Randall.** *Let the Dead Bury Their Dead.* Mainstream Fiction.

2002   **Allen, Jeffery Renard.** *Rails Under My Back.* Mainstream Fiction.

World Fantasy Award (1975–present)

www.worldfantasy.org/awards/

World Fantasy Award titles are nominated by members of the World Fantasy Convention and selected by a panel of judges to acknowledge excellence in fantasy writing and art. The panel also awards the World Fantasy Life Achievement Award to an individual.

2001   **Thomas, Sheree R.** *Dark Matter: A Century Of Speculative Fiction From The African Diaspora.* Speculative Fiction. *Best Anthology.*

Zora Neale Hurston Society Award

The Zora Neale Hurston Award, named in honor of the famous African American author, recognizes superior work in cultural scholarship.

1986   **Bambara, Toni Cade.** *The Salt Eaters.* Mainstream Fiction.

MacArthur Fellows Program (1981–present)

www.macfdn.org/programs/fel/fel_overview.htm

MacArthur fellowships are awarded by the MacArthur Foundation to writers, scientists, artists, social scientists, teachers, humanists, and entrepreneurs "who have shown extraordinary originality and dedication in their creative pursuits and a marked capacity for self-direction." Fellows receive a $500,000 stipend and are selected on the basis of three criteria: creativity, promise for important future advances, and the potential for the fellowship to encourage future work. Writers with works in *African American Literature: A Guide to Reading Interests* who have received the MacArthur fellowship are listed below.

Butler, Octavia. MacArthur Fellow, 1995.

Adulthood Rites. Speculative Fiction.

Bloodchild: And Other Stories. Speculative Fiction.

Clay's Ark. Speculative Fiction.

Dawn. Speculative Fiction.

Imago. Speculative Fiction.

Kindred. Speculative Fiction.

Mind of My Mind. Speculative Fiction.

Parable of the Sower. Speculative Fiction.

Parable of the Talents. Speculative Fiction.

Patternmaster. Speculative Fiction.

Survivor. Speculative Fiction.

Wild Seed. Speculative Fiction.

Gaines, Ernest L. MacArthur Fellow, 1993.

A Lesson Before Dying. Mainstream Fiction.

Hamilton, Virginia. MacArthur Fellow, 1995.

Dustland. Speculative Fiction.

Justice and Her Brothers. Speculative Fiction.

The Gathering. Speculative Fiction.

Johnson, Charles Richard. MacArthur Fellow, 1998.

Dreamer: A Novel. Historical Fiction.

Middle Passage. Historical Fiction.

The Sorcerer's Apprentice. Speculative Fiction.

Jones, Edward P. MacArthur Fellow, 2004.

Lost in the City. Historical Fiction.

The Known World. Historical Fiction.

Marshall, Paule. MacArthur Fellow, 1992.

The Fisher King. Mainstream Fiction.

Whitehead, Colson. MacArthur Fellow, 2002.

John Henry Days. Mainstream Fiction.

The Institutionist. Speculative Fiction.

Wideman, John Edgar. MacArthur Fellow, 1992.

Damballah. Mainstream Fiction.

Philadelphia Fire. Mainstream Fiction.

The Cattle Killing. Historical Fiction.

Part 2: Readers Advisory Resources

This section is divided into two major sections: General Resources and Genre Resources. All URLs were accurate as of March 4, 2004.

General Resources

Readers' Advisory Services

Burgin, Robert, and Kenneth D. Shearer, eds. *The Reader's Advisor's Companion.* Englewood, Colo.: Libraries Unlimited, 2001.
   The *Companion* is highly recommended for its in-depth essays on various aspects of readers' advisory services, including nonfiction for recreational readers, the readers' advisory interview, and the importance of leisure reading. Chapter 15, "The Future of Reader's Advisory in a Multicultural Society" (Dawson and Van Fleet), traces the history of multicultural genre literature, explores issues, and poses scenarios for the future.

Saricks, Joyce, and Nancy Brown. *Readers' Advisory Services in the Public Library.* 2d ed. Chicago: ALA, 1997.
   This is the classic guide to readers' advisory service and a must-have for librarians beginning to work in readers' advisory. Saricks and Brown use their substantial experience to outline key areas in educating readers' advisors, including basic "Reference Sources" (Chapter 2), "Articulating a Book's Appeal" (Chapter 3), and "The Background Readers' Advisors Need in Popular Fiction " (Chapter 5). Although some specifics are getting a bit dated, the concepts are sound.

Core Readers' Advisory Tools

Castro, Rafaelo G., Edith Maureen Fisher, Terry Hong, and David Williams. *What Do I Read Next? Multicultural Literature.* Detroit: Gale, 1997.
   WDIRN? offers a fine introduction to African American, Hispanic American, Asian American, and Native American authors. It is divided into chapters by ethnicity, rather than genre. The individual annotations are structured for easy browsing. The author, title, subject, geographic location, time period, character name, and character description indexes are invaluable for locating speculative fiction titles. If there is one weakness, it is that suggestions for further reading are based very broadly on similar ethnicity and genre.

Herald, Diana Tixier. *Genreflecting: A Guide to Reading Interests in Genre Fiction*. 5th ed. Englewood, Colo.: Libraries Unlimited, 2000.

> For many librarians and readers, the venerable (if one may use such a ponderous word for such a lively work) *Genreflecting* is THE general purpose guide to genre fiction. The crime chapter includes a list of African American detectives (from Bailey), but the real importance of this book is the structure and organization it imposes on each of the genres. In addition to classification schemes are bibliographies of anthologies, bibliographies, historical sources, criticism, writers' manuals, and works on film detectives.

Morton Grove (Illinois) Public Library Webrary. *Reader Services Page*. www.webrary.org/rs/rsmenu.html

> The Morton Grove Public Library's *Reader Services Page* is a portal to a range of valuable readers' advisory services. It provides links to a selected list of Web sites for readers, the library's MatchBook service, schedules for book discussion groups (including a low vision group) that meet at the library, best-seller previews, excellent bibliographies and pathfinders for fiction readers, and the wonderful Fiction_L list. Clearly and effectively designed, informative and entertaining, and supported by excellent services, this page is a model in both philosophy and design.

NoveList.

> *NoveList* is a subscription database offered by EBSCO. Originally conceived by Duncan Smith, it is the best of subscription online resources for genre fiction. The comprehensive database features title, author, subject, and keyword searches; annotations written by librarians; essays; and lists. Access to *NoveList* is available free of charge through many public libraries.

Overbooked. www.overbooked.org/genres/mystery/index.html

> Ann Chambers Theis maintains this site as "a non profit volunteer project and a by-product of the work of the Chesterfield County (VA) Public Library's Collection Management Department." The site is not an official service of the public library; it is a nonprofit service hosted by CVCO (Central Virginia's Community Online). This is a good general page that is useful for searching for specific genres as well. It contains a wealth of information and links to relevant resources, including awards, bookstores, authors, magazines, organizations, publishers, reviews, and reading lists.

Pearl, Nancy, Martha Knappe, and Chris Higashi. *Now Read This: A Guide to Mainstream Fiction, 1978–1998*. Englewood, Colo.: Libraries Unlimited, 1999.

> This resource provides an annotated list of 1,000 novels. Titles are arranged alphabetically by author within one of four categories: "Setting," "Story," "Characters," and "Language." Indexes for African American authors and characters are provided.

Pearl, Nancy. *Now Read This II: A Guide to Mainstream Fiction, 1990–2001.* Englewood, Colo.: Libraries Unlimited. 2002.

Similar in format to the first edition, this source lists 500 novels published between 1990 and 2001.

Saricks, Joyce G. *The Readers' Advisory Guide to Genre Fiction.* Chicago: American Library Association, 2001.

Saricks, whose *Readers' Advisory Service in the Public Library* (Chicago: American Library Association, 1997) is the primer for librarians interested in better service for recreational readers, takes a new approach in this book. Organized by genre rather than by functional area as in the previous work, this new title is more comparable to *Genreflecting*, providing definitions of various genres, sure bets, reference sources, and the added feature of suggestions for cross-genre readers.

Background Sources for African American Literature

Andrews, William L., Frances Smith Foster, and Trudier Harris, eds. *The Oxford Companion to African American Literature.* New York: Oxford University Press, 1997.

This one-volume reference work covers African American literary history from colonial times to the present day with encyclopedia-type entries that are informative, interesting, and readable. Topics range from the very broad ("crime and detective fiction") to the very specific (*"African American Review"*) . This is a well-researched and clearly written reference book and it's fun to browse as well as to use in looking up specific topics.

Contemporary Black Biography. Detroit: Gale Research, 1992– .

Each volume contains biographies of at least 65 persons of African heritage and includes information such as date and place of birth, education, address, career data, memberships, awards, and an in-depth essay. Biographies cover writers and are accessible through author and occupation indexes.

Gates, Henry Louis, and Nellie Y. McKay. *The Norton Anthology of African American Literature.* New York: W. W. Norton, 1997.

This anthology includes the works of 120 African American writers and features essays, poetry, novels, journals, novels, spirituals, gospels, sermons, and jazz.

Hatch, Shari Dorantes, and Michael R. Strickland, eds. *African-American Writers: A Dictionary.* Santa Barbara, Calif.: ABC-CLIO, 1992.

This volume examines a multitude of African American cultural leaders from the eighteenth century to the present, focusing on novelists, essayists, scholars, writers, teachers, playwrights, poets, and songwriters.

Josey, E. J., and Marva L. DeLoach. *Handbook of Black Librarianship.* 2d ed. Lanham, Md.: Scarecrow, 2000.

In eight sections and 50 chapters, this important reference work chronicles the history and achievements of black librarians and their work in libraries. Part V, "African American Resources" includes Lorrita Ford's chapter, "African American Literature, 1977–1997."

Nelson, Emmanuel S., ed. *Contemporary African American Novelists: A Bibliographical Critical SourceBook*. Westport, Conn.: Greenwood Press, 1999.

This biographical dictionary surveys the lives and works of 79 contemporary African American novelists, with each entry providing a biography, a discussion of issues, a summary of the critical reception, and a bibliography of primary and secondary sources.

Richards, Phillip M., and Neil Schlager. *Best Literature By and About Blacks*. Farmington Hills, Mich.: Gale Group, 2000.

This volume places the literature of and by African Americans in the following historical periods: 1750–1860, 1860–1900, 1900–1940, and 1940–present. An introduction is provided for each period. A range of genres is covered: fiction, nonfiction, poetry, drama, and literary criticism.

Rodriguez, Max, Angeli R. Rasbury, and Carol Taylor. *Sacred Fire: The QBR 100 Essential Black Books*. New York: Wiley, 1999.

This volume presents the 100 most influential books in African American history, chosen by a blue-ribbon panel of scholars, writers, and booksellers. The titles range from nineteenth-century poetry to current best sellers.

Smith, Valerie, ed. *African American Writers*. 2d ed. New York: Scribner, 2001.

This two-volume reference work includes 34 articles updated from the previous edition along with 20 new writers who have come to prominence since the 1980s. The focus is on authors.

Valade, Rodger M., ed. *The Schomburg Center Guide to Black Literature: From the Eighteenth Century to the Present*. New York: Gale Research, 1996.

The Schomburg Center of the New York Public Library offers a guide to authors, works, characters, themes, and topics related to black literature, including both fiction and nonfiction writings from African American and international authors.

Review Sources

Black Issues Book Review. Matthews and Associates, 1999– . Bimonthly. www.bibookreview.com

This magazine is essential reading for those interested in readers' advisory services.

It features articles by and about African American authors, offers fiction and nonfiction reviews, and reviews of inspirational literature (faith reviews) and other formats. It features many articles on self-publishing. The online version complements the print version with tables of contents and some full text articles. An online index for previous years is provided.

Booklist. American Library Association, 1905– . Semimonthly (monthly in July and August). www.ala.org/ala/booklist/booklist.htm
> Includes reviews of African American authors in all genres on a regular basis and publishes a regular theme issue on African American authors in February.

Ebony. Johnson Publishing Company, 1945– . Monthly. www.ebony.com
> Features articles and departments on black life and culture and regularly includes short reviews of books by African American authors.

Essence. Essence Communications, 1970– . Monthly. www.essence.online.com
> Although targeted toward the African American woman, *Essence* covers topics of broad interest: male/female relationships, fashion, books, health, fitness, financial management, and other topics. Sponsors the *Essence* Awards. Since 2001, features a best-sellers list.

Multicultural Review: Dedicated to a Better Understanding of Ethnic, Racial, and Religious Diversity. Greenwood Publishing Group, Inc., 1992– . Quarterly. www.mcreview.com
> This title includes articles on some aspects of diversity and librarianship and includes signed reviews of both fiction and nonfiction works.

Publishers Weekly. Cahners Business Information, 1872– . 51x yearly. www.publishersweekly.com
> The trade journal of the publishing industry, *Publishers Weekly* offers reviews of African American authors on a regular basis and provides special theme articles on trends in AA publishing.

QBR: The Black Book Review. QBR, 1995– . Quarterly. www.qbr.com
> Formerly *Quarterly Review of Black Books*, *QBR* reviews the latest works by African American and Caribbean writers. These include reviews of fiction, nonfiction, poetry, children's books, and other publications of interest to the black community. *QBR* frequently includes book excerpts of and interviews with authors. *QBR* has an online version of the journal that features its best-seller list, interviews with authors, and *QBR's 100 Essential Black Books.*

Bestseller Lists

Blackboard Bestseller List
> The Blackboard Bestseller list, endorsed by the American Booksellers Association, was the first national black best-seller list. A monthly list featured in *Essence* magazine for seven years, it was displaced by the *Essence* Bestseller List in January 2001. Each month, five fiction and five nonfiction titles were compiled from monthly sales reports from U.S. independent booksellers.

Black Issues Book Review (BIBR) Lists
> In addition to annual year-end reviews and listing of best titles, *Black Issues Book Review* features the column "Flying off the Shelves," which is a listing of best-selling authors in each bimonthly issue.

Essence Bestseller List
> Created in January 2001, the *Essence* Bestseller list now features the top 10 fiction and top 10 nonfiction titles by format, based on monthly sales at 20 African

American owned book stores across the United States; reporting stores change quarterly. Published monthly in the magazine and also online at Essence.com.

QBR Africana Top Ten. www.qbr.com

QBR: The Black Book Review launched this list, updated monthly, in 1996. It features top 10 fiction and nonfiction titles compiled from aggregate sales at 25 independent stores in all regions of the United States and at selected online booksellers. Now called "Books in Demand."

Bookstores, Book Clubs, and Other Online Resources

African American Literature Book Club. aalbc.com

This is an ambitious site, whose goal is "to increase everyone's knowledge of the diversity of African American literature, facilitate the exchange of opinions, satisfy your on-line book buying needs and serve as a resource and vehicle of expression for aspiring and professional writers." A regular newsletter contains full-length articles and book reviews. Reviews, written by regular reviewers, are straightforward and often offer very divergent opinions.

African American Web Connection/African American Publications. www.aawc. com/Zaap.html

Provides links to Web sites of more than 50 publishers of magazines, journals, etc., that specialize in works by and about African American authors.

African American Publications. www.africanpubs.com/

"African American Publications is committed to providing students and adult researchers with accurate, authoritative, and accessible information on a wide variety of ethnic and ethno-religious groups in the United States and Canada. In addition to Americans of African heritage, African American Publications also offers a variety of print reference sets and complementary biographical online resources covering Hispanics, Asian Americans, Native Americans, Middle Eastern Americans, Americans of European descent, and notable American men and women."

AllBlackBooks.com. www.allblackbooks.com

An online community with chat rooms, e-newsletters, and book reviews of African American authors.

Black Expression. www.blackexpressions.com

This site lists relevant books from the black publishing market that come from a variety of presses. Black Expressions Club is a member of Booksonline.com and has a membership of over 500,000.

Black Literature. www.BlackLiterature.com

This site provides information and links to books by, for, and about black people. Featured links includes excerpts, reviews, book events, book clubs, and author links.

Cushcity.com. Cushcity.com
>   A Web site of an African American bookstore in Houston, Texas. It features a list
>   of its top five fiction and nonfiction titles by format.

Mosaic Books. Mosaicbooks.com
>   Mosaicbooks.com, launched in 1998, is dedicated to showcasing African and
>   Hispanic literature. It is also a clearinghouse for African American book clubs
>   and maintains listings by geographic areas. An affiliate of amazon.com, it lists
>   top-selling titles on the site. The *Mosaic* magazine is currently on hiatus as the
>   magazine is reorganized as the Literary Freedom Project, a 501(c) 3 not-for-profit
>   organization.

Voices from the Gaps: Women Writers of Color. voices.cla.umn.edu/newsite/index.
htm
>   Created and maintained at the University of Minnesota, this site is devoted to
>   women writers of color and general sites where one may find information about
>   women writers of color.

Black Literary Conferences

Harlem Book Fair. www.harlemlive.org/community/events/harlembookfair/
harlembkfair.html
>   In 1999, Max Rodriquez founded the Harlem Book Fair to celebrate books by and
>   about African American authors. From a one-day event in 1999, the Harlem Book
>   Fair has grown to a weeklong cultural affair featuring panels of authors discuss-
>   ing their works and publishers providing insights about the industry and awards.
>   The book festival is held on 125th Street in New York, with panels featured at the
>   Schomburg Center for Research in Black Culture. The Harlem Book fair is
>   broadcast on C-Span's *Book TV*.

Black Caucus of American Library Association Conferences. www.bcala.org
>   The Black Caucus of the American Library Association sponsors the annual
>   BCALA Literary Awards. In addition, at the Black Caucus conferences, gener-
>   ally held every two years in different cities around the nation, African American
>   authors and booksellers are featured and celebrated in panel discussions,
>   booktalks, and presentations.

National Black Writers Conference. www.mec.cuny.edu/nbwc
>   The National Black Writers Conferences have been held at Medgar Evers Col-
>   lege since 1986 and attract a national and international audience. The conference
>   is convened over a period of four days to bring together writers, critics, booksell-
>   ers, book reviewers, and the general public to establish a dialogue on the social
>   responsibility of the black writer. Recent conferences have included discussions
>   on stereotypes in black literature, the direction of black literature, the renaissance
>   in black literature, and the impact of black literature on society.

Genre Resources

Crime and Detective Fiction

African American Mystery Writers. 2000. www.pratt.lib.md.us/booklists/
The Fiction and Young Adult Department, Enoch Pratt Free Library, created these booklists of African American mystery titles. Each entry contains author, title, and a very brief plot summary.

Bailey, Frankie Y. *Out of the Woodpile: Black Characters in Crime and Detective Fiction*. Westport, Conn.: Greenwood Press, 1991.
Bailey's exploration of the depiction of African American characters is not limited to African American authors and so provides a more complete picture of popular images in both print and film. Included in this volume are a very useful directory of "black characters in crime and detective fiction, film, and television," as well as a "symposium" presenting writers' views on creating black characters, and a chapter summarizing responses from members of the Mystery Writers of America to a survey about black characters. This title is scholarly but accessible to the intelligent reader.

DeAndrea, William L. *Encyclopedia Mysteriosa: A Comprehensive Guide to the Art of Detection in Print, Film, Radio, and Television*. New York: Prentice Hall General Reference, 1994.
DeAndrea's expertise in and enthusiasm for detective fiction translates into a lively compendium. The encyclopedia-type arrangement makes it easy for readers to find specific topics, but most will enjoy simply browsing the entries. This is a reference book that's as hard to put down as the detective works it describes.

Gorman, Michael B. *Blood, Bedlam, Bullets, and Badguys: A Reader's Guide to Adventure/Suspense Fiction*. Westport, Conn.: Libraries Unlimited, 2004.
This source deals with intrigue, thrillers, and other action and suspense fiction, and includes subgenres such as espionage, legal and medical thrillers, sea adventures, and the paranormal. Each chapter begins with introductory material on the subgenre and includes a selected listing of authors and titles. African American characters are designated within genres with the multicultural icon.

Klein, Kathleen Gregory, ed. *Diversity and Detective Fiction*. Bowling Green, Ohio: Bowling Green State University Press, 1999.
Klein has assembled a group of essays that explore many forms of diversity from many perspectives. Readers of African American detective fiction will be particularly interested in well-written essays by Macdonald and Macdonald ("Ethnic Detectives in Popular Fiction: New Directions for an American Genre") and Décuré ("In Search of Our Sisters' Mean Streets: The Politics of Sex, Race and Class in Black Women's Crime Fiction"). These interesting essays are scholarly in content but very readable.

Landrum, Larry. *American Mystery and Detective Novels: A Reference Guide.* Westport, Conn.: Greenwood Press, 1999.

Landrum's work is particularly useful for placing the work of African American detective and crime fiction in context, both intellectually and chronologically. Readers will find the "related formulas" and "authors" chapters particularly useful.

Niebuhr, Gary Warren. *Make Mine a Mystery: A Reader's Guide to Mystery and Detective Fiction.* Westport, Conn.: Libraries Unlimited, 2003.

This resource provides annotations of more than 2,500 titles by over 200 authors. Three types of detectives are covered: public, private, and amateur. It also includes considerable background material relating to readers' advisory services, the appeal of mystery fiction, how to build a mystery collection, and a history of the genre.

Soitos, Stephen F. *The Blues Detective: A Study of African American Detective Fiction.* Amherst: University of Massachusetts Press, 1996.

Soitos traces the evolution of African American detective fiction, including examination of "tropes," adaptations of detective conventions, and in-depth analysis of two seminal writers, Rudolph Fisher and Chester Himes. This work is most useful for critics and scholars.

Woods, Paula L. *Spooks, Spies, and Private Eyes: Black Mystery, Crime, and Suspense Fiction of the 20th Century.* New York: Doubleday, 1995.

Woods's introduction and carefully selected works are inspiring. She shares the personal impact of finding out about earlier authors, traces the evolution of African American mystery and crime fiction, and provides representative work from the most influential authors. Everyone interested in black mystery fiction, whether scholar or recreational reader, should read this book.

Frontier Literature

Adams, Ramon F. *Western Words: A Dictionary of the American West.* Norman, Okla.: University of Oklahoma, 1968.

From abajador (the workman in charge of the tools furnished to miners underground) to zorillas (cattle of the longhorn breed), Adam's classic dictionary of western terms and slang keeps the reader informed and amused. Some entries are quite brief (two or three words), while others may extend over several paragraphs to fully explain or to suggest related terms. Each section of the alphabet begins with a quote (not necessarily related to the letter). And remember, "Polishin' your pants on saddle leather don't make you a rider" (brought to you by the letter G).

African-American Pioneers in San Diego and California-Museum & Bookstore: Casa Del Moro Museum. 2471 Congress St., San Diego, CA. www.ambers.com

Professor Chuck Ambers, the Museum Educational Curator, provides an overview of the museum's collections, noting available multimedia exhibits on a broad array of topics. The museum's special focus s on the African American, African Spanish, and African Mexican heritage evident in San Diego and the rest of California.

Black American West Museum and Heritage Center. 3091 California Street, Denver, CO. www.blackamericanwest.org

The Black American West Museum and Heritage Center is a small museum that tells the story of the African American pioneers who helped shape the West. An interesting note is the museum's location in the former home of Justina Ford, Colorado's first African American female doctor. Readers will find the online bookstore is of particular value.

Black Cowboys: The Premiere Black Cowboys Site on the Internet. www. blackcowboys.com

This interesting and (somewhat) amusing Web site is valuable for its links, which include a description of the book *Black Cowboys of Texas* and its contributors, Cowboy Mike's Web site, cowboy jokes, and links to other Web sites about black cowboys. Bobby-approved for accessibility to people with disabilities.

Black Cowboys and Pioneers. www.madison.k12.wi.us/elib/elib.cgi?cat=178 ;o=alpha

This site includes a text-only overview of an article written by Kenneth Porter, an excerpt from the book *Negro on the American Frontier*. There are links for Cowboys, Part II and The Forgotten Cowboys. Contains historical information on the subject of black cowboys.

Cyberrodeo.com. cyberrodeo.com/guysgals/blkcowboys.htm

Sponsored by the Rodeo Steakhouse and Billy Miners Saloon (both in Fort Worth, Texas), this surprisingly informative site contains a number of links to sites of interest to those interested in African Americans on the frontier (and elsewhere). Look under Riding the Range and Cowboys and Cowgirls to find links such as Black Cowboys, Black Cowboys—Old Cowtown, Black Pioneers, Africans in the Diaspora, etc.

People of Color on America's Western Frontier. www.coax.net/people/LWF/ western.htm

"People Of Color On America's Western Frontier: Lest We Forget" by Bennie J. McRae Jr. is the featured article on this site. The site provides plentiful links to more interesting books and information about black cowboys; however, many links were obsolete when tested in March 2004.

Smithsonian National Museum of American History. americanhistory.si.edu/ paac/aquest/bibliography.htm

Smithsonian National Museum of American History: Behring Center is associated with the creation of this home page. This site provides a plethora of links to literature on the subject of black westerners, pioneers, and cowboys. Included are comprehensive bibliographies, picture profiles, and articles by noted authors on the subject of black cowboys.

Weston, Jack. *The Real Cowboy*. New York: Schocken Books, 1985. Reprint edition. New York: New Amsterdam Books, 1990.

Photographs, song lyrics, and personal memoirs support Weston's well-researched text and bring the cowboy era alive.

Inspirational Literature

Mort, John. *Christian Fiction: A Guide to the Genre.* Englewood, Colo.: Libraries Unlimited, 2002.
Mort's *Christian Fiction* is an excellent update to Walker (see below), providing a much more inclusive and current list of titles. His summaries of Christian classics are very useful, and he provides coverage of Catholic, Amish, Mennonite, Quaker, and Mormon fiction, areas often overlooked because of the rapid growth of novels that fit the Christian evangelical pattern. Although this is a fine general source, it contains only six annotations of African American works.

Romance in Color. www.romanceincolor.com/
Wayne Jordan maintains this site devoted exclusively to African American romance, including inspirational romance. It features author profiles, booklists, awards, and reviews.

Walker, Barbara J. *Developing Christian Fiction Collections for Children and Adults: Selection Criteria and a Core Collection.* New York: Neal-Schuman, 1998.
Walker's introduction to Christian fiction is invaluable for librarians not familiar with the area. She provides an excellent overview that includes definitions, publishers, selection criteria, sources, and ideas for promoting Christian fiction collections. In addition, she recommends core titles classified by genre for children, young adults, and adults. This is a good background source but of limited use in identifying black authors, as it lacks even an index heading for African Americans.

Life Stories

Nelson, Emmanuel S., ed. *African American Autobiographers: A Sourcebook.* Westport, Conn.: Greenwood Press, 2002. ISBN 0–313–31409–8. 416p.
This excellent source book contains well-written and researched essays examining the lives and work of 67 African American autobiographers. Each chapter has four sections: a brief biography, an analysis of autobiographical works and themes, a discussion of the critical reception of those works, and a bibliography divided into two sections: autobiographical works and studies of autobiographical works. Invaluable.

Romance

Ramsdell, Kristin. *Romance Fiction: A Guide to the Genre.* Englewood, Colo.: Libraries Unlimited, 1999.
Romance Fiction updates *Happily Ever After* with significant revisions. It includes four new chapters: "Ethnic and Multicultural Romance," "Alternative Reality Romance," "Regency Period Romance," and, especially for librarians, "Building the Collection." "Plantation Romance" and "Medical Romance" chapters have been deleted, and "Young Adult Romance" has been relegated to an appendix, so you should hold on to the earlier works that cover them.

Romance in Color. www.romanceincolor.com/
Wayne Jordan maintains this site devoted exclusively to African American romance, including inspirational romance. It features author profiles, booklists, awards, and reviews.

Romance Slam Jam. www.romanceslamjam.com
In 1995, Emma Rodgers, Ashire Tosihwe, and Frances Ray organized Romance SLAM JAM in Dallas, Texas. Their purpose was to take their love for romance to a new level by bringing writers and readers together. The conference has met in Dallas, Texas; Nassau, Bahamas, Orlando, Florida, and in 2004, in New York City. "It has grown from just a few to several hundred, and has welcomed writers and fans from more than twenty-five cities and four countries."

Romance Writers of America. www.rwanational.com
This site is great for lists of award winners and other topics of interest to romance writers and readers. There's even a special section for librarians, and RWA gives an award for Librarian of the Year. Do not neglect to visit this site if you (or your patrons) are interested in romance fiction.

Romantic Times. www.romantictimes.com
Both Chelton and Ramsdell mention this monthly magazine, the fanzine of romance addicts and those who love them.

Speculative Fiction

Afrofuturism list. *Afrofuturist Literature.* www.afrofuturism.net/text/lit.html
The *Afrofuturist Literature* page is maintained by Kalí Tal on the Afrofuturism Web site, which is affiliated with the listserv of the same name. The content of this page is broken down into Fiction, Poetry, and Speculative Fiction Influences. According to the page, "Most of the text on this site is drawn from the Afrofuturism listserv archives and is written by Afrofuturism subscribers."

The Carl Brandon Society. www.carlbrandon.org
The Carl Brandon Society is dedicated to addressing the representation of people of color in the fantastical genres such as science fiction, fantasy, and horror.

Clute, John, and Peter Nicholls, eds. *The Encyclopedia of Science Fiction.* New York: St. Martin's Press, 1993.
This encyclopedia focuses on mainstream and classic science fiction authors, subgenres, movements, and the history of the genre.

Fonseca, Anthony J., and June Michele Pulliam. *Hooked on Horror: A Guide to Reading Interests in Horror Fiction.* Englewood, Colo.: Libraries Unlimited, 1999.
This guide looks at horror films and in-print horror fiction from 1994 to 1998. The authors use the subject heading "African-American" to designate those items that contain African American characters or are by African Americans.

Fonseca, Anthony J., and June Michele Pulliam. *Hooked on Horror: A Guide to Reading Interests in Horror Fiction.* 2d ed. Englewood, Colo.: Libraries Unlimited, 2003.

> The second edition of this source includes horror films, anthologies, and collections, and is organized by topics such as "Vampires and werewolves" and "Small town horror." Separate indexes by subject, author/title, and short story title are provided.

Frequently Asked Questions. www.landfield.com/faqs/sf/written-faq/

> This is a newsgroup devoted to discussions of written SF. "SF" as used here means "speculative fiction" and includes science fiction, fantasy, horror (a.k.a. dark fantasy), etc. See section 16A: Black SF authors.

Quilter, Laura. *Index to Women SF Writers of Color.* www.feministsf.org/femsf/authors/wofcolor.html

> This page is maintained on the Feminist Science Fiction, Fantasy, & Utopia Web site.

Sci Fi Noir. *Black Science Fiction/Fantasy/Horror Writers.* www.geocities.com/celestial1555/scifinoir.html

> A source for potential leads to find Afrocentric SF/F writing or SF/F from black authors.

Thomas, Sheree R., ed. *Dark Matter: A Century of Speculative Fiction from the African Diaspora.* New York: Warner Books, 2000.

> *Dark Matter* consists of 29 short stories written in the last century by authors of African descent and five critical essays on speculative fiction. A fuller description of the included fiction can be found in the "Short Fiction" section of Chapter 11.

von Ruff, Al. *Internet Speculative Fiction DataBase.* www.sfsite.com/

> The stated purpose of the ISFDB is "to catalog works of Science Fiction, Fantasy, and Horror. It links together various types of bibliographic data: author bibliographies, publication bibliographies, award listings, magazine content listings, anthology and collection content listings, yearly fiction indexes, and forthcoming books." This site is highly recommended.

Reference Lists

Introduction

Barboza, Craigh. 2003. The next chapter. *USA Weekend*, February 7–9.

Johnson, Charles. 1999. Foreword to *Sacred fire: The QBR 100 essential black books,* ed. Max Rodriguez, Angeli R. Rasbury, and Carol Taylor. New York: Wiley.

Potts, Christian. 2003. Rewards of artistry. *The Norman Transcript*, December 14.

Saricks, Joyce G. 2001. *The readers' advisory guide to genre fiction*. Chicago: American Library Association.

Chapter 1

Castro, Rafaelo G., Edith Maureen Fisher, Terry Hong, and David Williams. 1997. *What do I read next? Multicultural literature*. Detroit: Gale.

Jacques, Geoffrey. 1995. A mix of feast and famine for African Americans. *Publishers Weekly* 242, no. 50 (December 11): 36–40.

Johnson, Charles. 1999. Foreword to *Sacred fire: The QBR 100 essential black books,* ed. Max Rodriguez, Angeli R. Rasbury, and Carol Taylor. New York, Wiley.

McClellan, A. W. 1977. Reading: The other side of the equation. *Journal of Librarianship* 9, no. 1 (January): 38–48.

Nell, Victor. 1988. *Lost in a book: The psychology of reading for pleasure*. New Haven, Conn.: Yale University Press.

Pearl, Nancy. 1999. *Now read this: A guide to mainstream fiction, 1978–1998*. Englewood, Colo.: Libraries Unlimited.

———. 2002. *Now read this II: A guide to mainstream fiction, 1990–2001*. Englewood, Colo.: Libraries Unlimited.

Readers' advisory 101: *Instructor/participant guide*. 2001. Developed by Novelist and EBSCO Publishing and St. Louis Public Library. n.p.: EBSCO Publishing.

Rodriguez, Max, Angeli R. Rasbury, and Carol Taylor, eds. 1999. *Sacred fire: The QBR 100 essential black books*. New York: Wiley.

Rosenberg, Betty. 1982. *Genreflecting*. Littleton, Colo.: Libraries Unlimited.

Ross, Catherine Sheldrick. 1991. Readers' advisory service: New directions. *RQ* 30, no. 4 (summer): 503–18.

————. 2001. What we know from readers about the experience of reading. In *The readers' advisor's companion*, ed. Kenneth D. Shearer and Robert Burgin, 77–96. Englewood, Colo.: Libraries Unlimited.

RUSA Guidelines for behavioral performance of reference and information professionals. 1996. Prepared by the RASD Ad Hoc Committee on Behavioral Guidelines for Reference and Information Services. Approved by the RASD Board of Directors, January 1996. *RQ* 36, no. 2 (winter): 200–3.

Saricks, Joyce G. 2001. *The readers' advisory guide to genre fiction*. Chicago: American Library Association.

Saricks, Joyce G., and Nancy Brown. 1997. *Readers' advisory service in the public library*. 2d ed. Chicago: American Library Association.

Smith, Duncan. 1993. Reconstructing the reader: Educating readers' advisors. *Collection Building* 12, nos. 3–4: 21–30.

Sturm, Brian. 2001. The reader's altered state of consciousness. In *The readers' advisor's companion*, ed. Kenneth D. Shearer and Robert Burgin, 98–117. Englewood, Colo.: Libraries Unlimited.

Wiegand, Wayne. 1997. Out of sight and out of mind: Why don't we have any schools of library and reading studies? *Journal of Education for Library and Information Science* 38, no. 4 (fall): 314–26.

Chapter 2

Abbott, Charlotte. 2001. The black market. *Publishers Weekly* 248, no. 50 (December 10): 19–20.

Africa World Press and Red Sea Press. 2003. "About us." http://www.africanworld.com/about_us.htm (accessed January 29, 2004).

Brown, Carolyn M. 1995. Writing a new chapter in book publishing. *Black Enterprise* 25, no. 7 (February): 108–10.

Brown, Vandella. 1997. African American fiction: A slamming genre. *American Libraries* 28, no. 10 (November): 48–50.

Davis, Bernadette Adams. 2004. To each, his or her own genre: Five hot African American writers who are creating novels for every kind of popular taste. *Black Issues Book Review* 6, no. 1 (January–February): 40–41.

Doubleday-Broadway Publishing Group. 2004. http://www.randomhouse.com/publishers/pub_double_broad.html (accessed May 23, 2003).

Fleming, Robert. 1999. Why commercial success won't spoil black fiction. *Black Issues Book Review* 1, no. 4 (July–August): 16–21.

————. 2001. Black book bounty: Despite recession and war, the black book market to keep growing. *Publishers Weekly* 248, no. 50 (December 10): 25–30.

Hoke, Zlatica. 2001. African American book clubs gain influence. *VOA News.com,* February 8. http://www.sistersbrothers.com/MEDIA/VOANEWS/VOANEWS.HTML (accessed June 2003).

Hunt, Sharita. 2001. God's reading rainbow. *Black Issues Book Review* 3, no. 3 (May–June): 50–51.

Jackson, David Earl. 2000. More venues for more black voices. *Publishers Weekly* 247, no. 49 (December 4): 24–25.

Jacques, Geoffrey. 1997. More than a niche. *Publishers Weekly* 244, no. 50 (December 8): 38–41.

Jacques, Geoffrey. 1998. More books, more readers, more sales. *Publishers Weekly* 245, no. 50 (December 14): 34–39.

Jones, Mondella S. 2002. Between the lines: The inside scoop on what's happening in the publishing industry. *Black Issues Book Review* 4, no. 2 (March–April): 8.

Joyce, Donald Franklin. 1997. Publishing. In *The Oxford companion to African American literature*, ed. William L. Andrews, Frances Smith Foster, and Trudier Harris, 604–10. New York: Oxford University Press.

———. 1983. *Gatekeepers of black culture: Black-owned book publishing in the United States, 1817–1981.* Westport, Conn.: Greenwood Press.

———. 1991. *Gatekeepers of black culture: Black book publishers in the United States: A historical dictionary of the presses, 1817–1990.* Westport, Conn: Greenwood Press.

Labbé, Theola S. 1999. Created in their image. *Publishers Weekly* 246, no. 50 (December 13): 3–35.

———. 2000a. Time to "maximize the moment." *Publishers Weekly* 247, no. 50 (December 11): 32–34.

———. 2000b. Black books in the house. *Publishers Weekly* 247, no. 50 (December 11) 36–42.

Mullen, Leah. 2000. A few good men. *Black Issues Book Review* 2, no. 5 (September–October): 44–46.

Murray, Victoria Christopher. 2002. Boom in Christian fiction. *Black Issues Book Review* 4, no. 6 (November–December): 60–61.

Osborne, Gwendolyn. 2003. Emma awards. *Black Issues Book Review* 5, no. 3 (May–June): 11.

Patrick, Diane. 2001. Community diversity: Black booksellers reveal what their customers want and how to give it to them. *Publishers Weekly* 248, no. 50 (December 10): 21.

———. 2003. Urban fiction. *Publishers Weekly* 250, no. 20 (May 19): 31.

Phillip, Mary-Christine. 1996. Black literature in the 90s. *Black Issues In Higher Education* 13, no. 6 (May 16): 18–22.

Random House Adult Trade Group. 2004. About us. http://www.randomhouse.com/randomhouse/about (accessed May, 23 2003).

Reid, Calvin. 2000. Black Christian fiction for Warner, Walk Worthy press. *Publishers Weekly* 247, no. 21 (May 22): 22.

Rosen, Judith. 1999. Love is all around you. *Publishers Weekly* 246, no. 45 (November 8): 37–43.

———. 2002a. African-American distributors. *Publishers Weekly* 249, no. 49 (December 9): 18.

———. 2002b. Black titles just keep growing. *Publishers Weekly* 249, no. 49 (December 9): 40–46.

Talkin' about black books. 2003. *Publishers Weekly* 250, no. 49 (December 8): 24–26, 28–30.

Target Market News. 2001. *The African American book buyers study 2000: The preferences and purchases of black consumers.* Matawan, N.J.: Book Industry Study Group.

Target Market News. 2004. *The buying power of black America—2003.* http://www.targetmarketnews.com/buyingpowerstats.htm (accessed May 10, 2004).

Taylor, Carol. 1999. A diverse market for African-American books keeps growing. *Publishers Weekly* 246, no. 50 (December 13): 37–40.

Chapter 3

Abdullahi, Ismail. 1993. Multicultural issues for readers' advisory services. *Collection Building* 12, nos. 3–4: 85–88.

Anderson, Joanne S., ed. 1996. *Guide for written collection policy statements.* 2d ed. Collection Management and Development Guides, no. 7. Chicago: American Library Association.

Andrews, William L., Frances Smith Foster, and Trudier Harris, eds. 1997. *Oxford companion to African American literature.* New York: Oxford University Press.

Baker, Sharon L. 1994. Quality and demand: The basis for fiction collection assessment. *Collection Building* 13, nos. 2–3: 65–84

Baker, Sharon, and Patricia J. Boze. 1992. *Fiction collection assessment manual.* Champaign, Ill.: Lincoln Trail Libraries System.

Baker, Sharon, and Karen L. Wallace. 2002. *The responsive public library: How to develop and market a winning collection.* 2d ed. Englewood, Colo.: Libraries Unlimited.

Brown, Vandella. 1997. African American fiction: A slamming genre. *American Libraries* 28, no. 10 (November): 48–50.

Davis, Burns. 1994. Designing a fiction assessment tool: The custom service approach. *Collection Building* 13, nos. 2–3: 65–84.

Dawson, Alma, and Connie Van Fleet. 2001. The future of readers' advisory in a multicultural society. In *The readers' advisor companion*, ed. Kenneth D. Shearer and Robert Burgin, 249–68. Englewood, Colo.: Libraries Unlimited.

Diaz, Joseph R. 1994. Collection development in multicultural studies. In *Cultural diversity in libraries,* ed. Donald E. Riggs and Patricia A. Tarin, 185–98. New York and London: Neal-Schuman.

Dietzel, Susanne B. 1997. Pulp fiction. In *The Oxford companion to African American literature*, ed. William L. Andrews, Frances Smith Foster, and Trudier Harris, 610–12. New York: Oxford University Press.

Evans, G. Edward. 1992. Needs analysis and collection development policies for culturally diverse populations. *Collection Building* 11, nos. 3–4: 16–27.

Ford, Lorrita E. 2000. African American literature 1977–1997. In *Handbook of black librarianship*, 2d ed., ed. E.J. Josey and Marva L. DeLoach, 277–95. Lanham, Md.: Scarecrow.

Futas, Elizabeth. 1993. Collection development of genre literature. *Collection Building* 12, nos. 3–4: 39–44.

Graham, Maryemma. 1997. Novel. In *The Oxford companion to African American literature*, ed. William L. Andrews, Frances Smith Foster, and Trudier Harris, 541–48. New York: Oxford University Press.

Holt, Karen. 2003. Fiction's fresh beat. *Publishers Weekly* 250, no. 36 (September 8): 19.

Hunter, Clarence W. 1991. African American collection development seminar: Academic and Mississippi public libraries. *Mississippi Libraries* 55 (summer): 51–52.

Johnson-Cooper, Glendora. 1994. Building racially diverse collections: An Afrocentric approach. *Reference Librarian*, nos. 45/46: 153–70.

Katz, William A. 1980. *Collection development: The selection of materials for libraries.* New York: Holt, Rinehart & Winston.

Kravitz, Rhonda, Adelia Lines, and Vivian M. Sykes. 1991. Serving the emerging majority: Documenting their voices. *Library Administration and Management* 5, no. 4 (fall): 184–88.

Marquis, Solina Kasten. 2003. Collections and services for the Spanish-speaking. *Public Libraries* 42, no. 2 (March/April): 106–12.

McCook de la Peña, Kathleen. 1993. Considerations of theoretical bases for readers' advisory services. *Collection Building* 12, nos. 3–4: 7–11.

O'Brien, Sue. 1999. Leading a genre study. *Public Libraries* 38, no. 6 (November/December): 384–86.

Olson, Georgine N. 1997. Managing fiction collections. In *Serving Readers*, ed. Ted Balcom for the Illinois Library Association, 9–20. Fort Atkinson, Wis.: Highsmith Press.

Osborne, Gwendolyn. 2001. The legacy of ghetto pulp fiction. *Black Issues Book Review* 3, no. 5 (September–October): 50–52.

Patrick, Diane. 2003. Urban fiction. *Publishers Weekly* 250, no. 20 (May 19): 31.

Ramsdell, Kirsten. 1999. *Romance Fiction.* Englewood, Colo.: Libraries Unlimited.

Randal, Dudley. 1976. Blacks as readers: Heritage, values, reading interests. In *Reading and the Adult New Reader,* ed. Helen Lyman, 93–97. Chicago: American Library Association.

Roy, Loriene. 1993. Recovering Native identity: Readers' advisory services for non-reservation Native Americans. *Collection Building* 12, nos. 3–4: 73–77.

Saricks, Joyce G. 1998. Providing your patrons the fiction they want: Managing fiction in a medium-sized public library. In *Fiction acquisition/fiction management,* ed. Georgine N. Olson, 11–28. New York: Haworth Press.

———. 2001. *The readers' advisory guide to genre fiction.* Chicago: American Library Association.

Saricks, Joyce, and Nancy Brown. 1997. *Readers' advisory service in the public library.* 2d ed. Chicago: American Library Association.

Scarborough, Katharine. 1991. Collections for the emerging majority. *Library Journal* 116, no. 11 (15 June): 44–47.

Serving Readers. 1997. Edited by Ted Balcom for the Illinois Library Association. Fort Atkinson, Wis.: Highsmith Press.

Talkin' about black books. 2003. *Publishers Weekly* 250, no. 49 (December 8): 24–26, 28–30.

Van Fleet, Connie. 2003. Popular fiction collections in academic and public libraries. *Acquisitions Librarian* 15, no. 29: 63–86.

Van Fleet, Connie, and Alma Dawson. In press. Books that inspire: Nonfiction for a multicultural society. In *Readers' advisory for nonfiction,* ed. Robert Burgin. Englewood, Colo.: Libraries Unlimited.

Wagers, Robert. 1981. Popular fiction selection in public libraries: Implications for public libraries: Implications of popular studies culture. *Journal of Library History* 16, no. 2 (spring): 342–51.

Chapter 4

BCALA (Black Caucus of the American Library Association) listserv. 2003. Message thread February 16–18.

DeAndrea, William L. 1994. *Encyclopedia mysteriosa: A comprehensive guide to the art of detection in print, film, radio, and television.* New York: Prentice Hall General Reference.

Décuré, Nicole. 1999. In search of our sisters' mean streets: The politics of sex, race and class in black women's crime fiction. In *Diversity and Detective Fiction*, ed. Kathleen Gregory Klein, 158–85. Bowling Green, Ohio: Bowling Green State University Popular Press.

Dietzel, Susanne B. 1997. Pulp fiction. In *The Oxford companion to African American literature*, ed. William L. Andrews, Frances Smith Foster, and Trudier Harris, 610–12. New York: Oxford University Press.

Gerald, Marc, and Samuel Blumenfeld, eds. 1996. Welcome to the old school. Introduction to *The scene* by Clarence Cooper Jr. New York: W.W. Norton.

Jones, Malcolm. 2003. It's black, white—And noir: Crime writers are taking a hard-boiled look at race. *Newsweek*, June 24. http://www.woodsontheweb.com/Bio/newsweek.htm (accessed July 23, 2003).

Macdonald, Gina, and Andrew Macdonald. 1999. Ethnic detectives in popular fiction; New directions for an American genre. In *Diversity and detective fiction*, ed. Kathleen Gregory Klein, 60–113. Bowling Green, Ohio: Bowling Green State University Popular Press.

NPR (National Public Radio). 2004. Readers embrace "ghetto lit" genre. *Morning Edition* broadcast, January 20. http://www.npr.org/features/feature.php?wfId=1606270 (accessed February 25, 2004).

Patrick, Diane. 2003. Urban fiction. *Publishers Weekly* 250, no. 20 (May 19): 31.

Soitos, Stephen F. 1997. Crime and mystery writing. In *The Oxford companion to African American literature*, ed. William L. Andrews, Frances Smith Foster, and Trudier Harris, 182–84. New York: Oxford University Press.

Woods, Paula L. 1995. *Spooks, spies, and private eyes: Black mystery, crime, and suspense fiction of the 20th century*. New York: Doubleday.

Chapter 5

Burt, Olive W. 1969. *Negroes in the early west*. New York: Julian Messner/ Simon & Schuster.

Cawelti, John G. 1976. *Adventure, mystery, and romance: Formula stories as art and popular culture*. Chicago: University of Chicago Press.

Clark, Arthur A. c1976, 2001. *Black pioneers in Colorado: A history 1528–1921*. Baton Rouge, La.

Cyberrodeo.com. 1995–2000. Black cowboys. http://cyberrodeo.com/guysgals/blkcowboys.htm (accessed December 1, 2003).

De Angelis, Gina. 1998. *The black cowboys*. Philadelphia: Chelsea House Publishers.

DeGraaf, Lawrence. 1995. Recognition, racism, and reflections on the writing of Western black history. *Pacific Historical Review* 44: 22–51.

Drew, Bernard A. 1993. *Western series and sequels.* 2d ed. New York: Garland Publishing.

Durham, Philip, and Everett L. Jones. 1965. *The Negro cowboys.* New York: Dodd, Mead.

Foster, Frances S. 1997. Detter, Thomas P. In *The Oxford companion to African American literature,* ed. William L. Andrews, Frances Smith Foster, and Trudier Harris, 211–12. New York: Oxford University Press.

Hardaway, Roger D. 2001. African American cowboys on the western frontier. *Negro History Bulletin* 64: 27–32.

Herald, Diana Tixier. 1995. *Genreflecting: A guide to reading interests in genre fiction.* 4th ed. Englewood, Colo.: Libraries Unlimited.

Herald, Diana Tixier. 2000. *Genreflecting: A guide to reading interests in genre fiction.* 5th ed. Englewood, Colo.: Libraries Unlimited.

Sadler, Geoff. 1991. *Twentieth-century western writers.* Chicago: St. James Press.

Searles, Michael N. 2004. *The Cowboy Mike page.* http://www.cowboymike.com (accessed July 9, 2003).

Tompkins, Jane. 1992. *West of everything: The inner life of westerns.* New York: Oxford University Press.

University of California San Diego. 1999. *The black West: Reinventing history, reinterpreting media.* http://ucsdnews.ucsd.edu/newsrel/soc/jblackwest.htm (accessed May 27, 2003).

Wellman, Jeffrey M. 1996. The western. In *Genre and ethnic collections: Collected essays,* ed. Milton T. Wolf and Murray S. Martin, 153–77. Greenwich, Conn.: JAI Press.

Chapter 6

Burt, Daniel S. 1997. *What historical novel do I read next?* Detroit: Gale Research.

Christian, Barbara. 1990. "Somebody forgot to tell somebody something": African American women's historical novels. In *Wild women in the whirlwind: Afra-American culture and the contemporary literary renaissance,* ed. Joanne M. Braxton and Andrée Nicola McLaughlin, 327–41. New Brunswick, N.J.: Rutgers University Press.

———. 2000. "The past is infinite": History and myth in Toni Morrison's trilogy. *Social Identities* 6, no. 4 (December): 411–23.

Donahue, Dick, and Judith Rosen. 2001. Love and history—A perfect match. *Publishers Weekly* 248, no. 46 (November 12): 24–30.

Hawking, James. 1999. Sources and trends in historical fiction. *Booklist* 95, no. 15 (April 1): 1394–95.

Labbé, Theola. 2000. Black books in the house. *Publishers Weekly* 247, no. 50 (December 11): 36–42.

Mitchell, Angelyn. 1998. "Sth, I know that woman": History, gender, and the South in Toni Morrison's *Jazz*. *Studies in the Literary Imagination* 31, no. 2 (fall): 49–60.

Morrison, Toni. 1974. Behind the making of the black book. *Black World* 24 (February 23): 36–90.

———. 1992. The mind of the masters. *New Statesman & Society* 5, no. 199 (April 24): 33–34.

Sale, Maggie. 1997. Historical novel. In *The Oxford companion to African American literature*, ed. William L. Andrews, Frances Smith Foster, and Trudier Harris, 358–59. New York: Oxford University Press.

Taylor, Carol. 1999. A diverse market for African-American books keeps growing. *Publishers Weekly* 246, no. 50 (December 13): 37–42.

Whitaker, Charles. 2000. What's behind the big boom in black women writers? *Ebony* 55, no. 5 (March): 34–36.

Chapter 7

Aue, Pamela Wilwerth, and Henry L. Carrigan Jr. 2000. *What inspirational literature do I read next?* Detroit: Gale Group.

Foster, Francis Smith. 1997a. Biblical tradition. In *The Oxford companion to African American literature*, ed. William L. Andrews, Frances Smith Foster, and Trudier Harris, 58–62. New York: Oxford University Press.

———. 1997b. Sunday school literature. In *The Oxford companion to African American literature*, ed. William L. Andrews, Frances Smith Foster, and Trudier Harris, 707–8. New York: Oxford University Press.

Hubbard, Dolan. 1997. Sermons and preaching. In *The Oxford companion to African American literature*, ed. William L. Andrews, Frances Smith Foster, and Trudier Harris, 648–52. New York: Oxford University Press.

Hughes, Langston. 1935. On the road. *Esquire* 3, no.1, entire issue no. 14 (January): 92.

Jackson, Agnes Moreland. 1997. Religion. In *The Oxford companion to African American literature*, ed. William L. Andrews, Frances Smith Foster, and Trudier Harris, 626–31. New York: Oxford University Press.

Kirkpatrick, David D. 2003. Shaping cultural tastes at big retail chains. *New York Times*, May 18, national edition, sec. 1.

Labbé, Theola S. 1999. Created in their image. *Publishers Weekly* 246, no. 50 (December 13): 33–35.

———. 2000. Time to "maximize the moment." *Publishers Weekly* 247, no. 50 (December 11): 32–34.

Mort, John. 2002. *Christian fiction: A guide to the genre.* Greenwood Village, Colo.: Libraries Unlimited.

Riess, Jana K. 2000. New genres, emerging audiences. *Publishers Weekly* 247, no. 34 (August 21): S4.

Starling, Kelly. 1998. New directions in black spirituality. *Ebony* 53, no. 12 (October): 92, 94, 96, 98.

Walker, Barbara J. 1998. *Developing Christian fiction collections for children and adults: Selection criteria and a core collection.* New York: Neal-Schuman.

Chapter 8

Andrews, William L. 1993. *African American autobiography: A collection of critical essays.* Englewood Cliffs, N.J.: Prentice Hall.

———. 1997. Autobiography—Overview. In *The Oxford companion to African American literature*, ed. William L. Andrews, Frances Smith Foster, and Trudier Harris, 34. New York: Oxford University Press.

Bassard, Katherine Clay. 1997. Autobiography—Spiritual biography. In *The Oxford companion to African American literature*, ed. William L. Andrews, Frances Smith Foster, and Trudier Harris, 37–39. New York: Oxford University Press.

Butterfield, Stephen. 1974. *Black autobiography in America.* Amherst: University of Massachusetts Press, 3. Quoted in Kenneth Mostern, *Autobiography and black identity politics: Racialization in twentieth-century America.* Cambridge: Cambridge University Press, 1999, 51.

Carter, Linda M. 2002. William Wells Brown. In *African American autobiographers: A sourcebook*, ed. Nelson S. Emmanuel, 56–60. Westport, Conn.: Greenwood Press.

Domina, Lynn. 2002. Ida B. Wells-Barnett. In *African American autobiographers: A sourcebook*, ed. Nelson S. Emmanuel, 373–78. Westport, Conn.: Greenwood Press.

Dudley, David L. 2002. Booker T. Washington. In *African American autobiographers: A sourcebook*, ed. Nelson S. Emmanuel, 365–72. Westport, Conn.: Greenwood Press.

Mostern, Kenneth. 1999. *Autobiography and black identity politics: Racialization in twentieth-century America.* Cambridge: Cambridge University Press.

Nelson, Emmanuel S.. 2002. Olaudah Equiano. In *African American autobiographers: a sourcebook*, ed. Nelson S. Emmanuel, 132–37. Westport, Conn.: Greenwood Press.

Nelson, Emmanuel S., ed. 2002. *African American autobiographers: A sourcebook.* Westport, Conn.: Greenwood Press.

Sample, Maxine 2002. Zora Neal Hurston. In *African American autobiographers: A sourcebook*, ed. Nelson S. Emmanuel, 208–19. Westport, Conn.: Greenwood Press.

Saricks, Joyce, and Nancy Brown. 1997. *Readers' advisory services in the public library*. 2d ed. Chicago: American Library Association.

Schickel, Richard. 1985. *Intimate strangers: The culture of celebrity*. Garden City, N.Y.: Doubleday.

Chapter 9

Andrews, William L., Frances Smith Foster, and Trudier Harris, eds. 1997. *The Oxford companion to African American literature*. New York: Oxford University Press.

Harris, William J. 1997. Black aesthetic. In *The Oxford companion to African American literature*, ed. William L. Andrews, Frances Smith Foster, and Trudier Harris, 67–70. New York: Oxford University Press.

Locke, Alain. 1968. *The new Negro: An interpretation*. New York: Johnson Reprint.

Morrell, Jessica Page. 2002. Writing within the genre. *ivillage*. Reviewed January 30. http://www.ivillage.com/books/expert/writecoach/articles/0,11872,200930_97447,00.html?arrivalSA=1&arrival_freqCap=1&pba=adid=5724408 (accessed June 19, 2003).

Nelson, Emmanuel S., ed. 1999. *Contemporary African American novelists: A bibliographical critical sourcebook*. Westport, Conn.: Greenwood Press.

Pearl, Nancy. 1999. *Now read this: A guide to mainstream fiction, 1978–1998*. Englewood, Colo.: Libraries Unlimited.

Plant, Deborah G. 1999. Introduction. In *Contemporary African American novelists: A bio-bibliographical critical sourcebook,* ed. Emmanuel S. Nelson, xv–xx. Westport, Conn.: Greenwood Press.

Rodriguez, Max, Angeli R. Rasbury, and Carol Taylor. 1999. *Sacred fire: The QBR 100 essential black books*. New York: Wiley.

Smith, Valerie. 1997. Literary history—Late twentieth century. In *The Oxford companion to African American literature*, ed. William L. Andrews, Frances Smith Foster, and Trudier Harris, 456–59. New York: Oxford University Press.

Valade, Rodger M., ed. 1996. *The Schomburg Center guide to black literature: From the eighteenth century to the present*. New York: Gale Research.

Chapter 10

Bouricius, Ann. 2000. *The romance readers' advisory: The librarian's guide to love in the stacks.* Chicago: American library Association.

Chelton, Mary K. 1991. Unrestricted body parts *and* predictable bliss: The audience appeal of formula romances. *Library Journal* 116, no. 12 (July): 44–49.

Israel, Betsy, and Nancy Drew. 1995. Heat in another color. *People Weekly* 43, no. 6 (February 13): 153–56.

Osborne, Gwendolyn. 1999. Our love affair with romance. *Black Issues Book Review* 1, no. 4 (July/August): 40-44.

———. 2002. Romance. *Black Issues Book Review* 4, no. 1 (January/February): 50.

Radway, Janice. 1984. *Reading the romance: Women, patriarchy, and popular literature.* Chapel Hill: University of North Carolina Press.

Ramsdell, Kristin. 1987. *Happily ever after: A guide to the reading interests of romance fiction.* Littleton, Colo.: Libraries Unlimited.

———. 1999. *Romance fiction: A guide to the genre.* Englewood, Colo.: Libraries Unlimited.

Chapter 11

Arnold, Martin. 2000. Science fiction, a black natural. *New York Times*, June 12, sect. E.

Castro, Rafaelo G., Edith Maureen Fisher, Terry Hong, and David Williams. 1997. *What do I read next? Multicultural Literature.* Detroit: Gale.

Crossley, Robert. 1998. Introduction. In *Kindred*, ed. Octavia E. Butler, ix–xxvii. Boston: Beacon Press.

Delany, Samuel R. 2000. Racism and science fiction. In *Dark matter: A century of speculative fiction from the African diaspora,* ed. Sheree R. Thomas, 382–97. New York: Warner Books.

Fonseca, Anthony J., and June Michele Pulliam. 1999. *Hooked on horror: A guide to reading interests in horror fiction.* Englewood, Colo.: Libraries Unlimited.

Govan, Sandra Y. 1997. Speculative fiction. In *The Oxford companion to African American literature,* ed. William L. Andrews, Frances Smith Foster, and Trudier Harris, 683–87. New York: Oxford University Press.

Grayson, Sandra M. 2003. *Visions of the third millennium: Black science fiction novelists write the future.* Trenton, N.J.: Africa World Press/The Red Sea Press.

Hartwell, David. 1984. *Age of wonders: Exploring the world of science fiction.* New York: Walker.

Herald, Diana Tixier. 2000. *Genreflecting: A guide to reading interests in genre fiction.* 5th ed. Englewood, Colo.: Libraries Unlimited.

Moskowitz, Sam. 1963. *Explorers of the infinite*. Cleveland: Meridian.

Mosley, Walter. 2000. Back to the future. In *Dark matter: A century of speculative fiction from the African diaspora,* ed. Sheree R. Thomas, 405–7. New York: Warner Books.

Nicholls, Peter, and Brian Stableford. 1993. Politics. In *The encyclopedia of science fiction*, ed. John Clute and Peter Nicholls, 945–47. New York: St. Martin's Press.

Rosenberg, Betty. 1982. *Genreflecting: A guide to reading interests in genre fiction*. Littleton, Colo.: Libraries Unlimited.

Saricks, Joyce G. 2001. *The readers' advisory guide to genre fiction*. Chicago: American Library Association.

Saunders, Charles R. 2000. Why blacks should read (and write) science fiction. In *Dark matter: A century of speculative fiction from the African diaspora*, ed. Sheree R. Thomas, 398–404. New York: Warner Books.

Author-Title Index

Subject Index

About the Editors and Contributors

Karen Antell, M.A., MLIS began her library career at the Norman Public Library in Oklahoma, where she served as a reference assistant, led a book discussion group, and taught public computer classes. In 2003 she was appointed to the position of Assistant Professor of Bibliography/Engineering Librarian at the University of Oklahoma. She holds a master's degree in English with an emphasis in twentith-century American literature and has published several articles on various aspects of library public services.

Alma Dawson, MLIS, Ph.D. is an associate professor in the School of Library and Information Science at Louisiana State University, where she teaches courses in collection development, academic libraries, information literacy instruction, and foundations of library and information science. A graduate of Grambling State University, she received her MLIS degree from the University of Michigan and her Ph.D. from Texas Woman's University. Dawson's published works include numerous articles and book chapters on collection development, distance education, and the contributions of African Americans to librarianship. Her edited works include *A History of the Louisiana Library Association, 1925–2000* (LLA, 2003). In 2003, she was named the Russell B. Long Professor in Library and Information Science at Louisiana State University.

Jacqueline L. Jones, MLIS is Head of Reference and Information Services at the Baton Rouge Community College. She is an active member of the American Library Association, the Association of College and Research Libraries, and the Louisiana Library Association. She is a community volunteer and frequent presenter for African American youth. She is coordinator of the Odell S. William Museum of American History in Baton Rouge, Louisiana.

Kari Moore, MLIS is a graduate of the Library and Information Studies program at the University of Oklahoma. A lifelong reader of speculative fiction and a freelance writer, she has contributed to Oklahoma Library Association's *Oklahoma Libraries*, but this is her first book chapter.

JoAnn Palmeri, M.A., Ph.D. is pursuing a master's degree at the School of Library and Information Studies at the University of Oklahoma, where she serves as an editorial assistant for *Reference & User Services Quarterly*. Her academic degrees are in the history of science and her research is focused on the intersections of astronomy, popular culture, and religion in the twentieth century. Since returning to graduate school her research interests have expanded to include communication in the sciences and information seeking in the humanities. Previously, she held the position of visiting professor in the history of science at the University of Oklahoma and worked as a mechanical engineer in the aerospace industry.

Ola Carter Riley, MLIS is Assistant Professor in Library and Information Science at Houston Baptist University, where she is the coordinator of bibliographic instruction. Riley's work in library services began in Badersfeld, Germany; she has served as a reference librarian and a public library branch manager in both Louisiana and Texas. She writes reviews for *Choice* magazine and has authored "Environmental Health: Sites That Focus on Protecting Natural Resources." Riley is active in the American Library Association and has served on several committees.

Jennifer Schultz, MLIS is a recent graduate of Louisiana State University. Her major focus is public librarianship.

Blinn Sheffield is a graduate student in the Louisiana State University School of Library and Information Science. His focus is youth services in public libraries.

Melanie Sims, MLIS is Reference Assistant Coordinator at Louisiana State University Libraries in Baton Rouge. Sims has been in reference services for several years and currently publishes in the area of virtual reference services. Sims also serves as editor for the Louisiana Library Association Minority Recruitment and Professional Concerns Interest Group newsletter. Sims is very active in the profession and has served on various national and state committees.

Linda Temple, MLIS entered the School of Library and Information Studies at the University of Oklahoma in 2002 after more than 25 years as a nonprofit administrator. Her experiences include writing and editing publications for local, national, and international organizations, and she is currently an editorial assistant for *Reference & User Services Quarterly*. Linda is a member of the American Library Association and the Intellectual Freedom Committee of the Oklahoma Library Association.

Connie Van Fleet, MLIS, Ph.D. is Professor in the School of Library and Information Studies at the University of Oklahoma, where she teaches courses in reference, readers' advisory services, research, and public librarianship. Her work focuses on services to multicultural populations, older adults, and people with disabilities. She is the author of numerous publications, a frequent presenter at conferences and coeditor of *Reference & User Services Quarterly*. Dr. Van Fleet is the recipient of the ALA/RUSA Margaret E. Monroe Library Adult Services Award (1996), the Louisiana State University School of Library and Information Science Outstanding Alumna award (2001), and the Association for Library and Information Science Excellence in Teaching Award (2004).

Dana Watson, MLIS, Ph.D currently teaches graduate-level classes on readers' advisory sources and services and reference as a visiting professor at Louisiana State University and the University of Alabama. She previously served on the faculty at the LSU School of Library and Information Services. Dr. Watson's publications include readers' advisory, collection development, and multicultural literature topics.